MW00777201

LONE WOLF
WOLF
2100

子連水狼

LONE WOLF 2100

OMNIBUS

WRITTEN BY
MIKE KENNEDY

ART BY
FRANCISCO RUIZ VELASCO
WITH ADDITIONAL COLORING BY STUDIO F

LETTERING BY
DIGITAL CHAMELEON, SNO CONE STUDIOS, AND JASON HVAM

RED FILE DESIGN
DARIN FABRICK AND DAVE NESTELLE

INSPIRED BY THE MANGA SERIES
LONE WOLF AND CUB
BY KAZUO KOIKE AND GOSEKI KOJIMA

DARK HORSE BOOKS

CONTENTS

PUBLISHER
MIKE RICHARDSON

SERIES EDITOR
RANDY STRADLEY WITH JEREMY BARLOW

COLLECTION EDITOR
CHRIS WARNER

ASSISTANT EDITOR
SHANTEL LaROCQUE

DESIGNER
ADAM GRANO

LONE WOLF 2100™ OMNIBUS

This volume collects material previously published in the Dark Horse graphic novels *Lone Wolf 2100: Shadows on Saplings*, *Lone Wolf 2100: The Language of Chaos*, and *Lone Wolf 2100: Pattern Storm*.

Dark Horse Books
A division of Dark Horse Comics, Inc.
10956 SE Main Street
Milwaukie, OR 97222

DarkHorse.com

To find a comics shop in your area, call the Comic Shop Locator Service toll-free at
1-888-266-4226

First edition: June 2013
ISBN 978-1-61655-141-4

10 9 8 7 6 5 4 3 2 1

Printed in China

LONE WOLF 2100™

子連れ狼

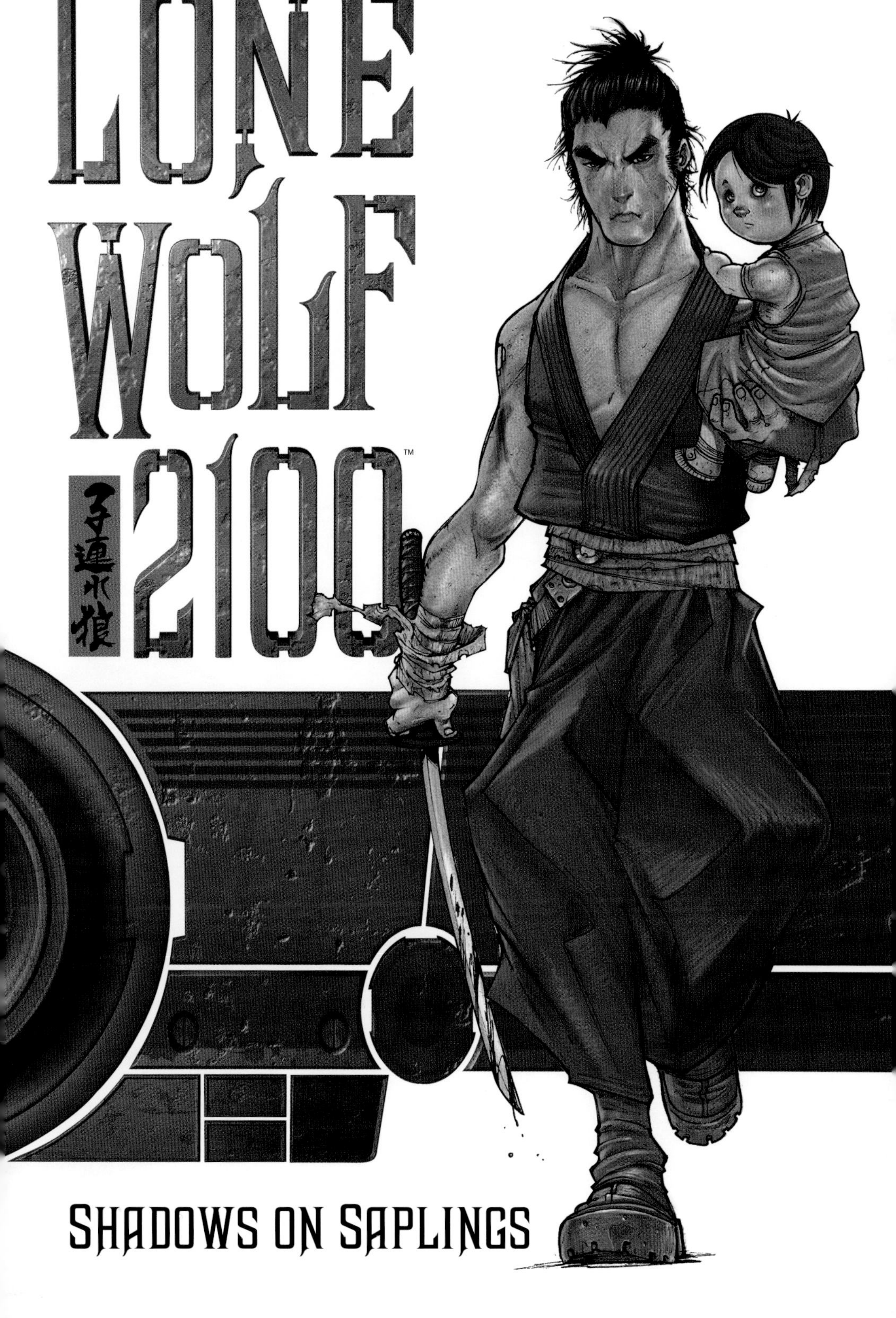

SHADOWS ON SAPLINGS

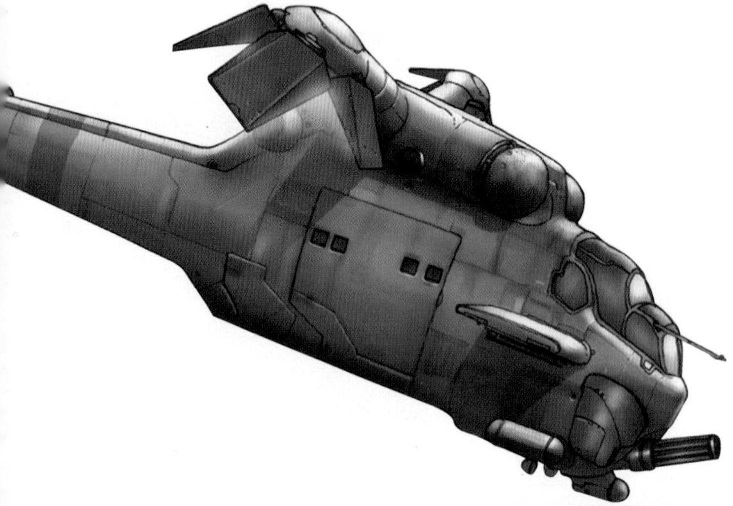

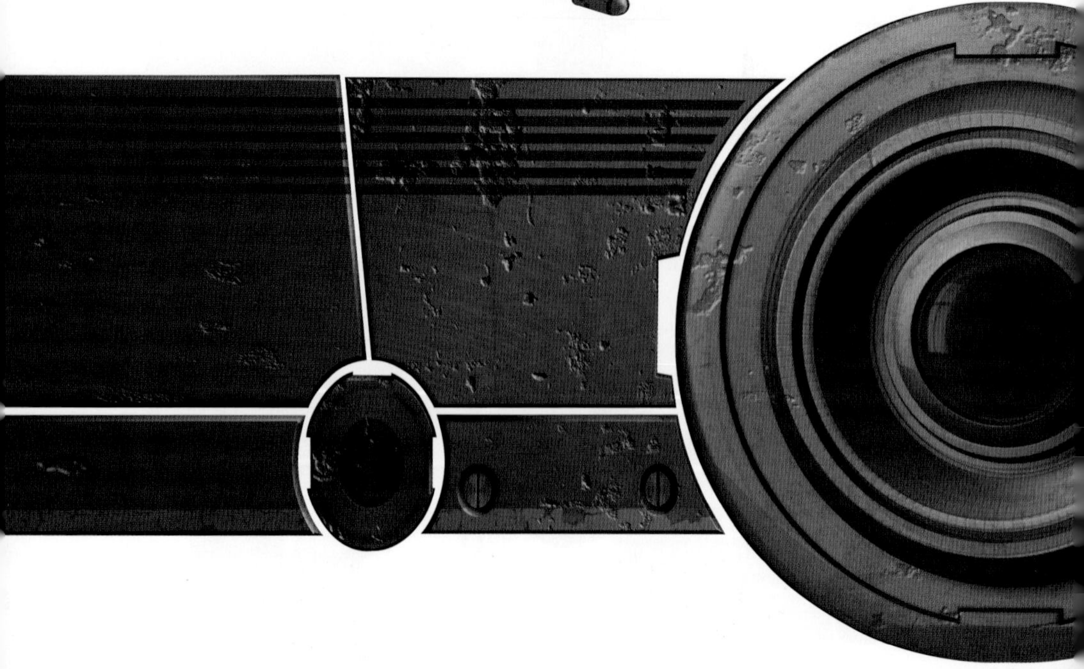

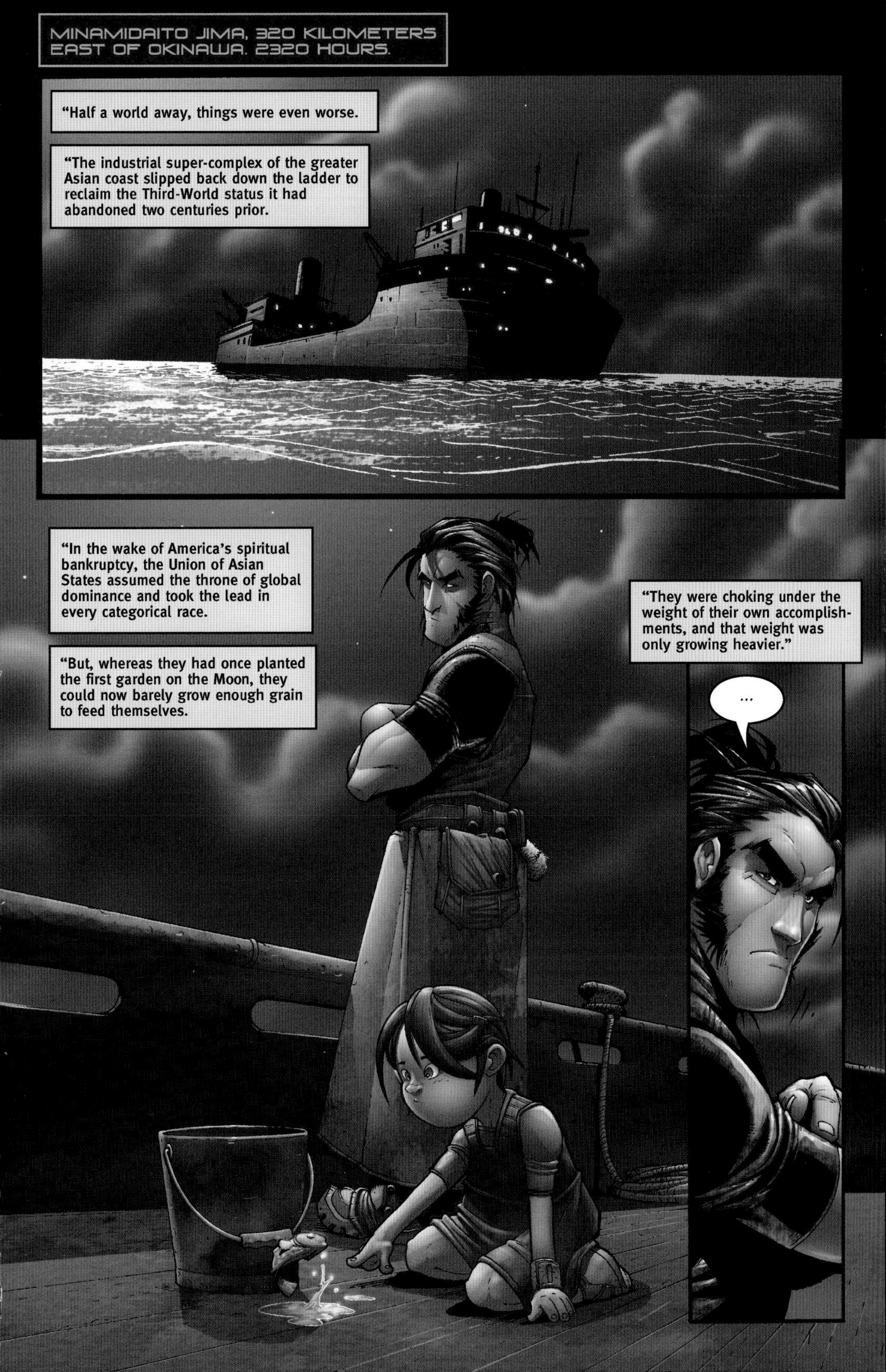
MINAMIDAITO JIMA, 320 KILOMETERS EAST OF OKINAWA. 2320 HOURS.
"Half a world away, things were even worse.
"The industrial super-complex of the greater Asian coast slipped back down the ladder to reclaim the Third-World status it had abandoned two centuries prior.
"In the wake of America's spiritual bankruptcy, the Union of Asian States assumed the throne of global dominance and took the lead in every categorical race.
"But, whereas they had once planted the first garden on the Moon, they could now barely grow enough grain to feed themselves.
"They were choking under the weight of their own accomplishments, and that weight was only growing heavier."
...

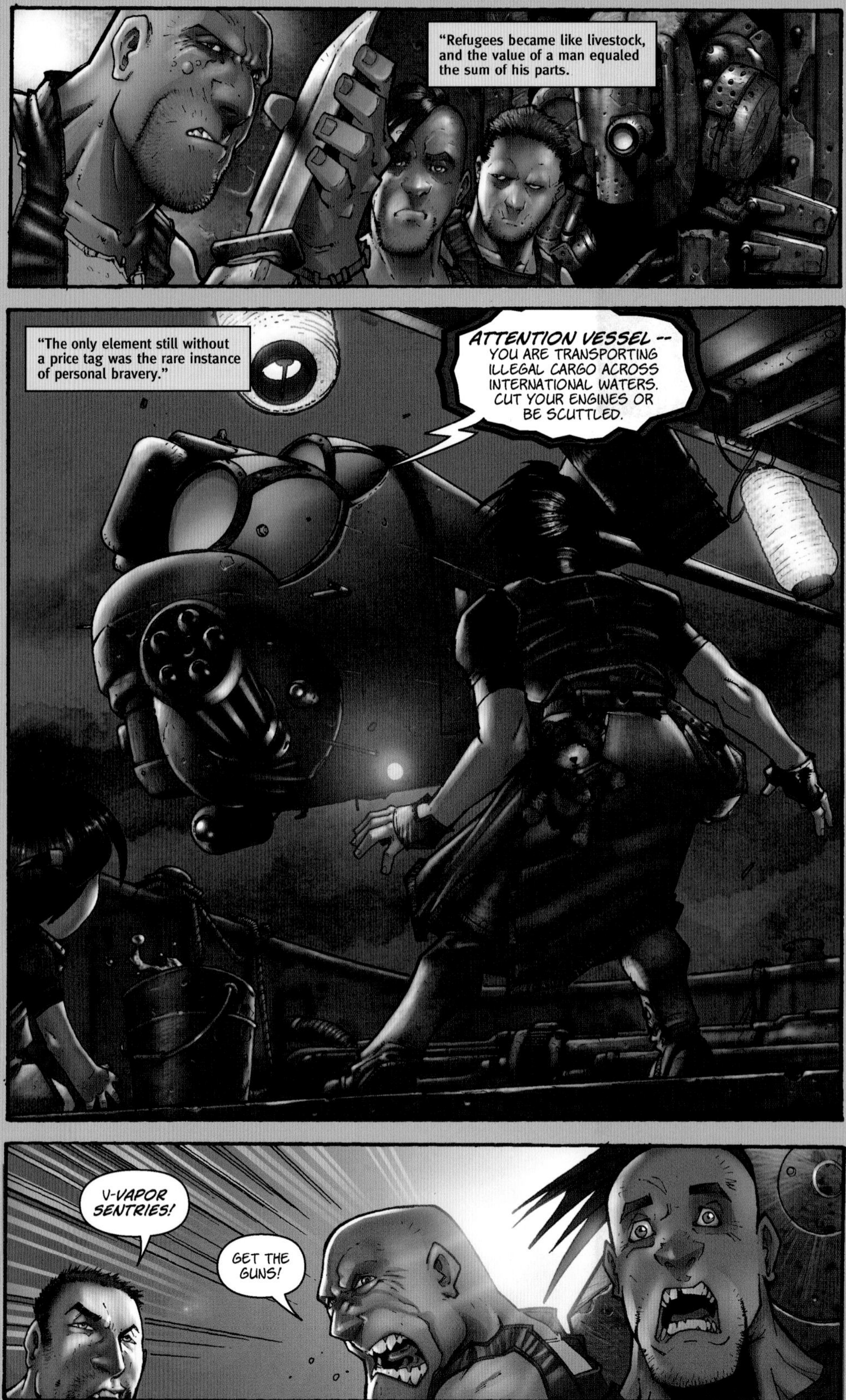
"Refugees became like livestock, and the value of a man equaled the sum of his parts.
"The only element still without a price tag was the rare instance of personal bravery."
ATTENTION VESSEL -- YOU ARE TRANSPORTING ILLEGAL CARGO ACROSS INTERNATIONAL WATERS. CUT YOUR ENGINES OR BE SCUTTLED.
V-VAPOR SENTRIES!
GET THE GUNS!

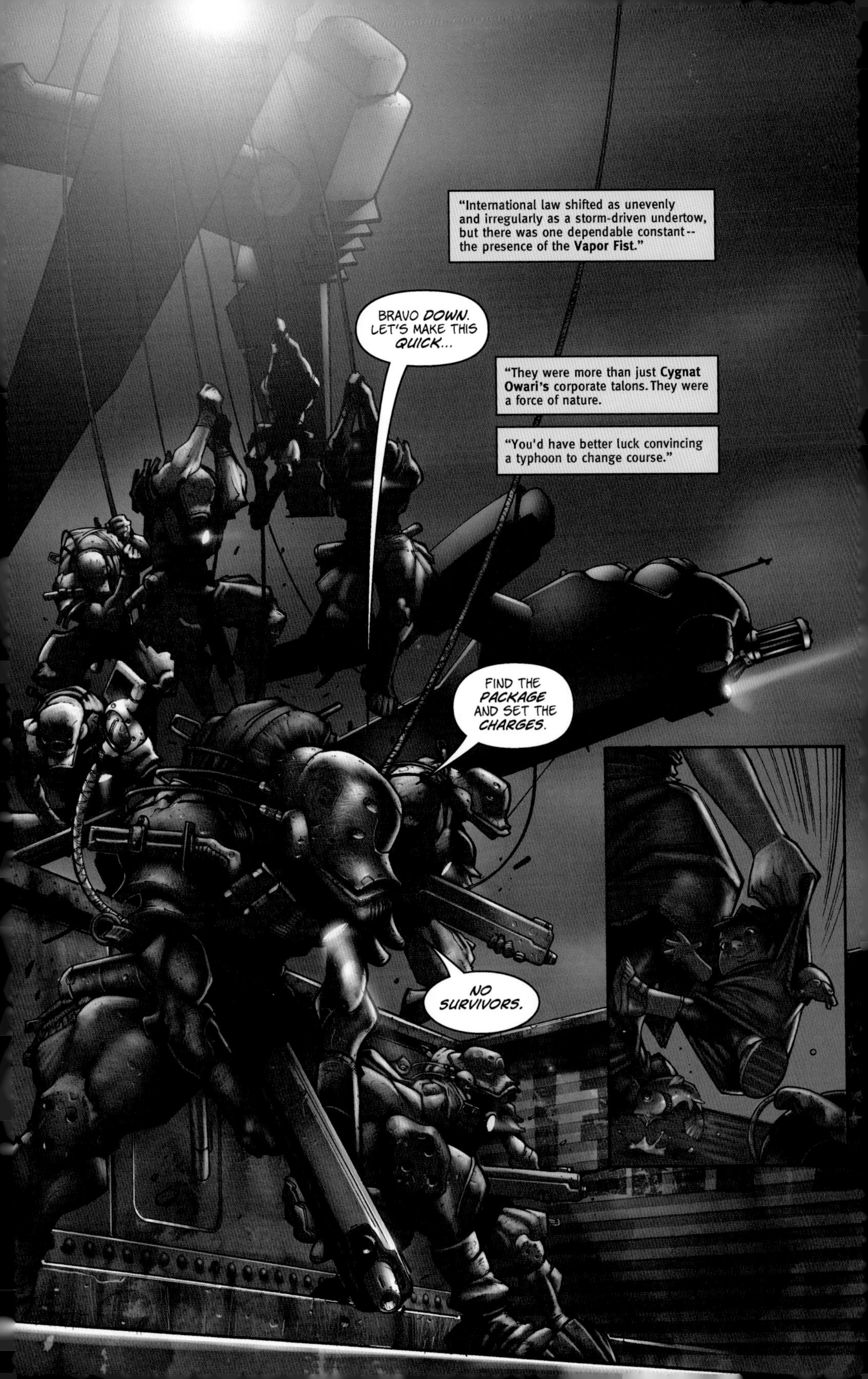

"International law shifted as unevenly and irregularly as a storm-driven undertow, but there was one dependable constant -- the presence of the **Vapor Fist**."
BRAVO *DOWN*. LET'S MAKE THIS *QUICK*...
"They were more than just **Cygnat Owari's** corporate talons. They were a force of nature.
"You'd have better luck convincing a typhoon to change course."
FIND THE *PACKAGE* AND SET THE *CHARGES*.
NO SURVIVORS.

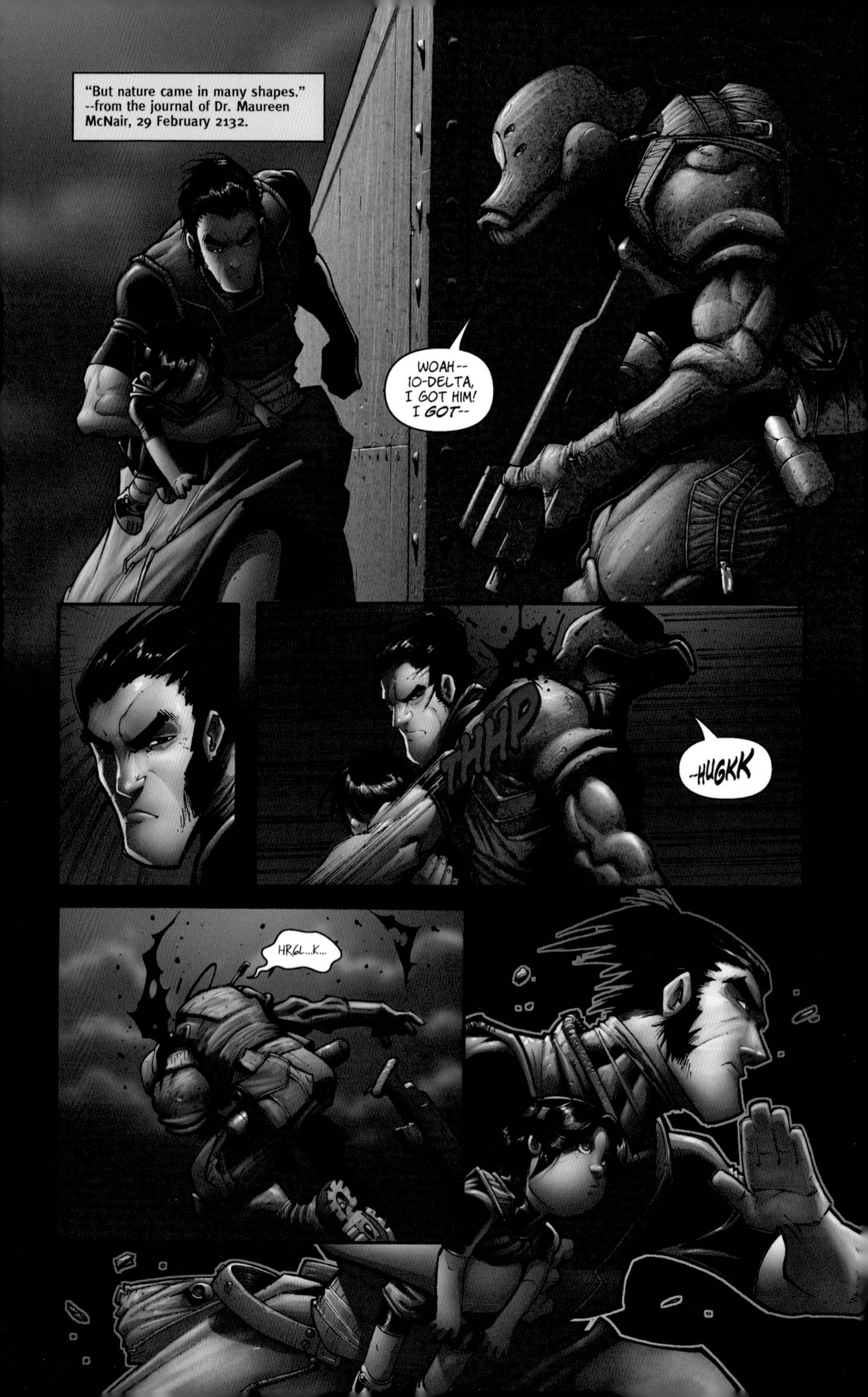
"But nature came in many shapes."
--from the journal of Dr. Maureen McNair, 29 February 2132.
WOAH-- 10-DELTA, I GOT HIM! I GOT--
THHP
--HUGKK
HRGL...K...

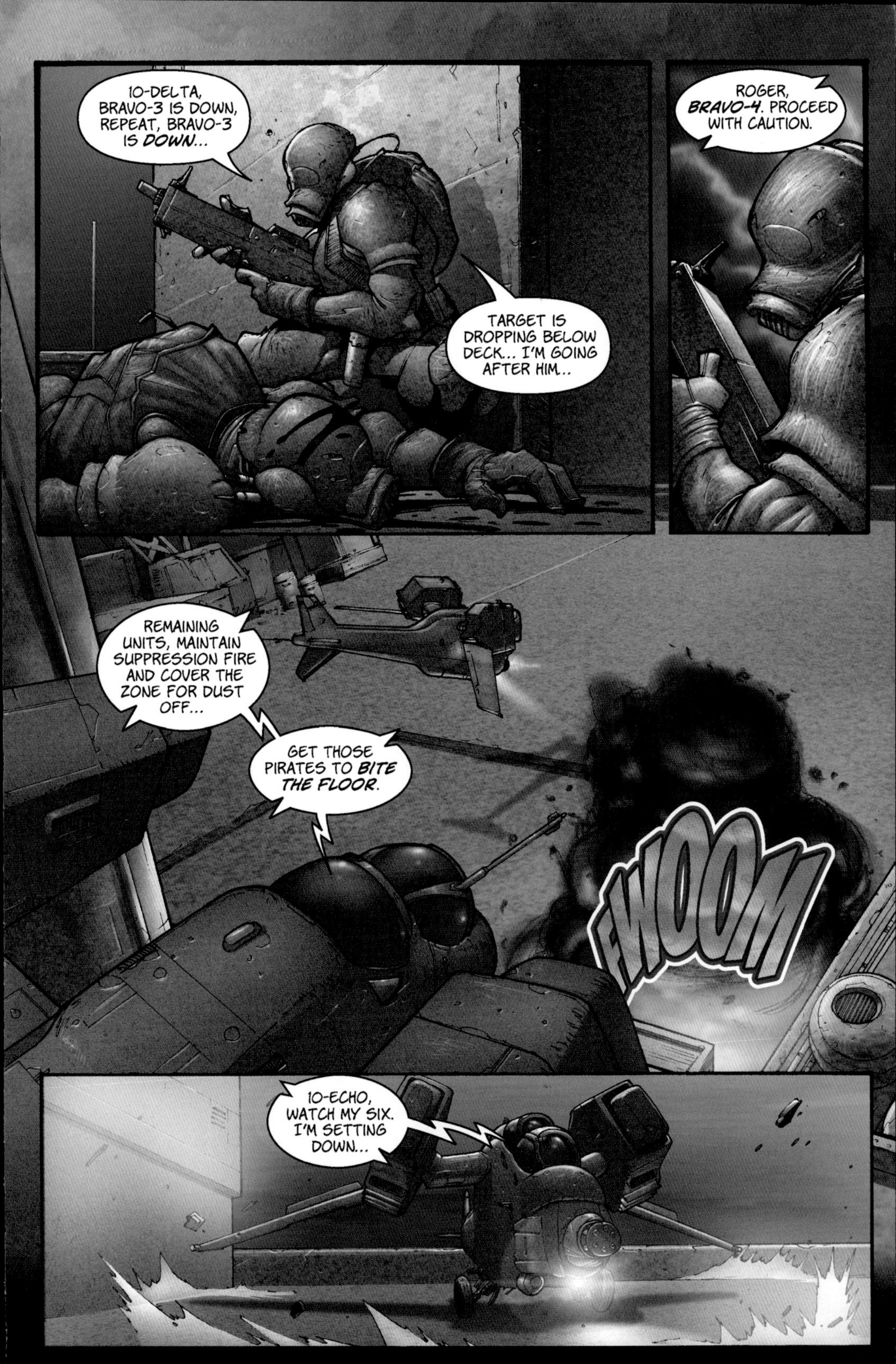
10-DELTA, BRAVO-3 IS DOWN, REPEAT, BRAVO-3 IS *DOWN*...
TARGET IS DROPPING BELOW DECK... I'M GOING AFTER HIM...
ROGER, *BRAVO-4*. PROCEED WITH CAUTION.
REMAINING UNITS, MAINTAIN SUPPRESSION FIRE AND COVER THE ZONE FOR DUST OFF...
GET THOSE PIRATES TO *BITE THE FLOOR*.
FWOOM
10-ECHO, WATCH MY SIX. I'M SETTING DOWN...

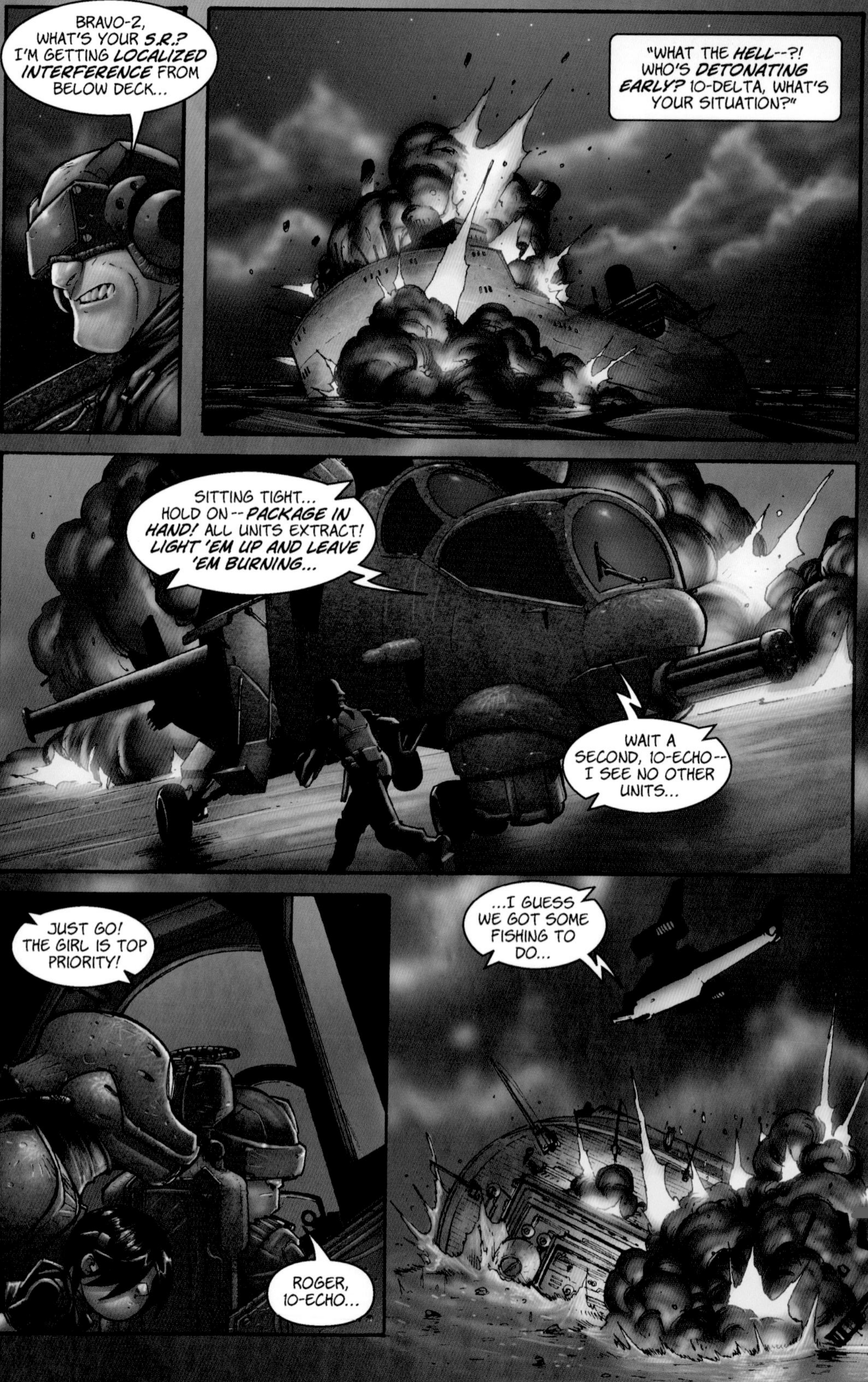
BRAVO-2, WHAT'S YOUR S.R.? I'M GETTING LOCALIZED INTERFERENCE FROM BELOW DECK...
"WHAT THE HELL--?! WHO'S DETONATING EARLY? 10-DELTA, WHAT'S YOUR SITUATION?"
SITTING TIGHT... HOLD ON--PACKAGE IN HAND! ALL UNITS EXTRACT! LIGHT 'EM UP AND LEAVE 'EM BURNING...
WAIT A SECOND, 10-ECHO--I SEE NO OTHER UNITS...
JUST GO! THE GIRL IS TOP PRIORITY!
ROGER, 10-ECHO...
...I GUESS WE GOT SOME FISHING TO DO...

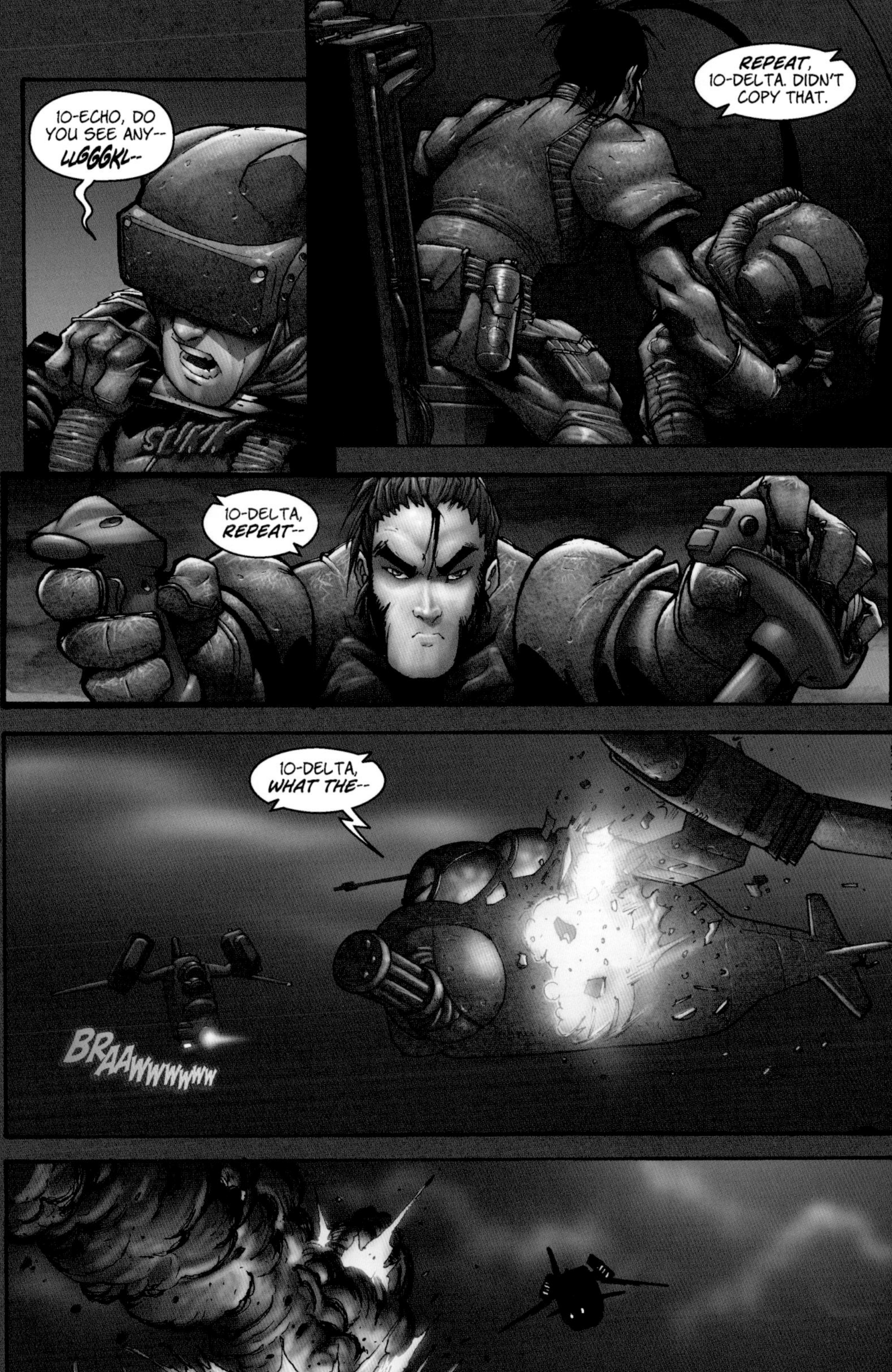
10-ECHO, DO YOU SEE ANY-- LLGGGKL--
REPEAT, 10-DELTA. DIDN'T COPY THAT.
10-DELTA, REPEAT--
10-DELTA, WHAT THE--
BRAAWWWWWW

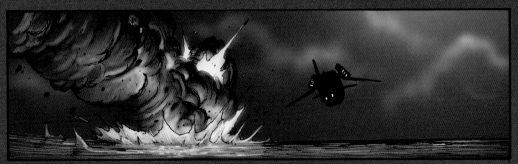

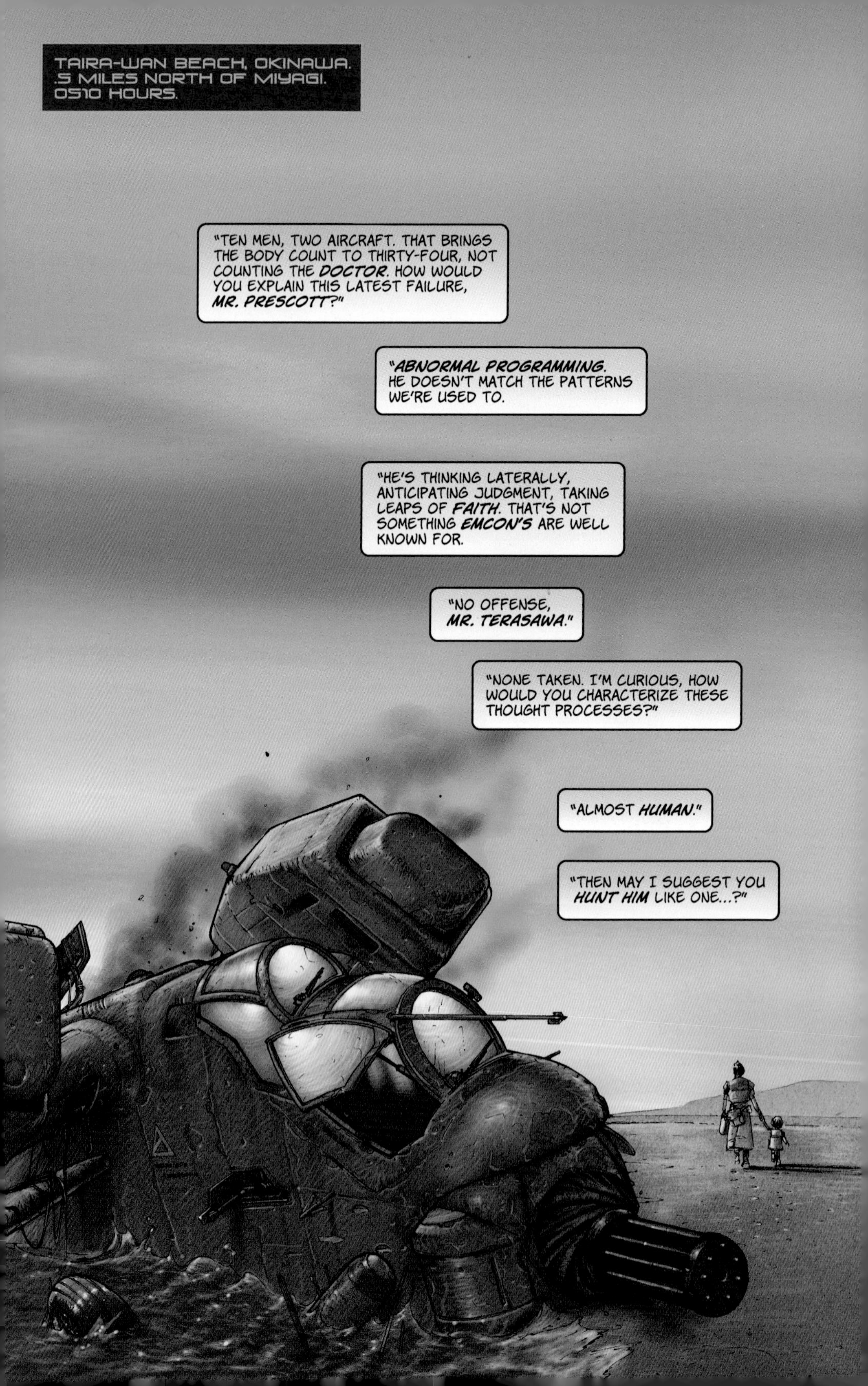
TAIRA-WAN BEACH, OKINAWA. .5 MILES NORTH OF MIYAGI. 0510 HOURS.
"TEN MEN, TWO AIRCRAFT. THAT BRINGS THE BODY COUNT TO THIRTY-FOUR, NOT COUNTING THE DOCTOR. HOW WOULD YOU EXPLAIN THIS LATEST FAILURE, MR. PRESCOTT?"
"ABNORMAL PROGRAMMING. HE DOESN'T MATCH THE PATTERNS WE'RE USED TO.
"HE'S THINKING LATERALLY, ANTICIPATING JUDGMENT, TAKING LEAPS OF FAITH. THAT'S NOT SOMETHING EMCON'S ARE WELL KNOWN FOR.
"NO OFFENSE, MR. TERASAWA."
"NONE TAKEN. I'M CURIOUS, HOW WOULD YOU CHARACTERIZE THESE THOUGHT PROCESSES?"
"ALMOST HUMAN."
"THEN MAY I SUGGEST YOU HUNT HIM LIKE ONE...?"

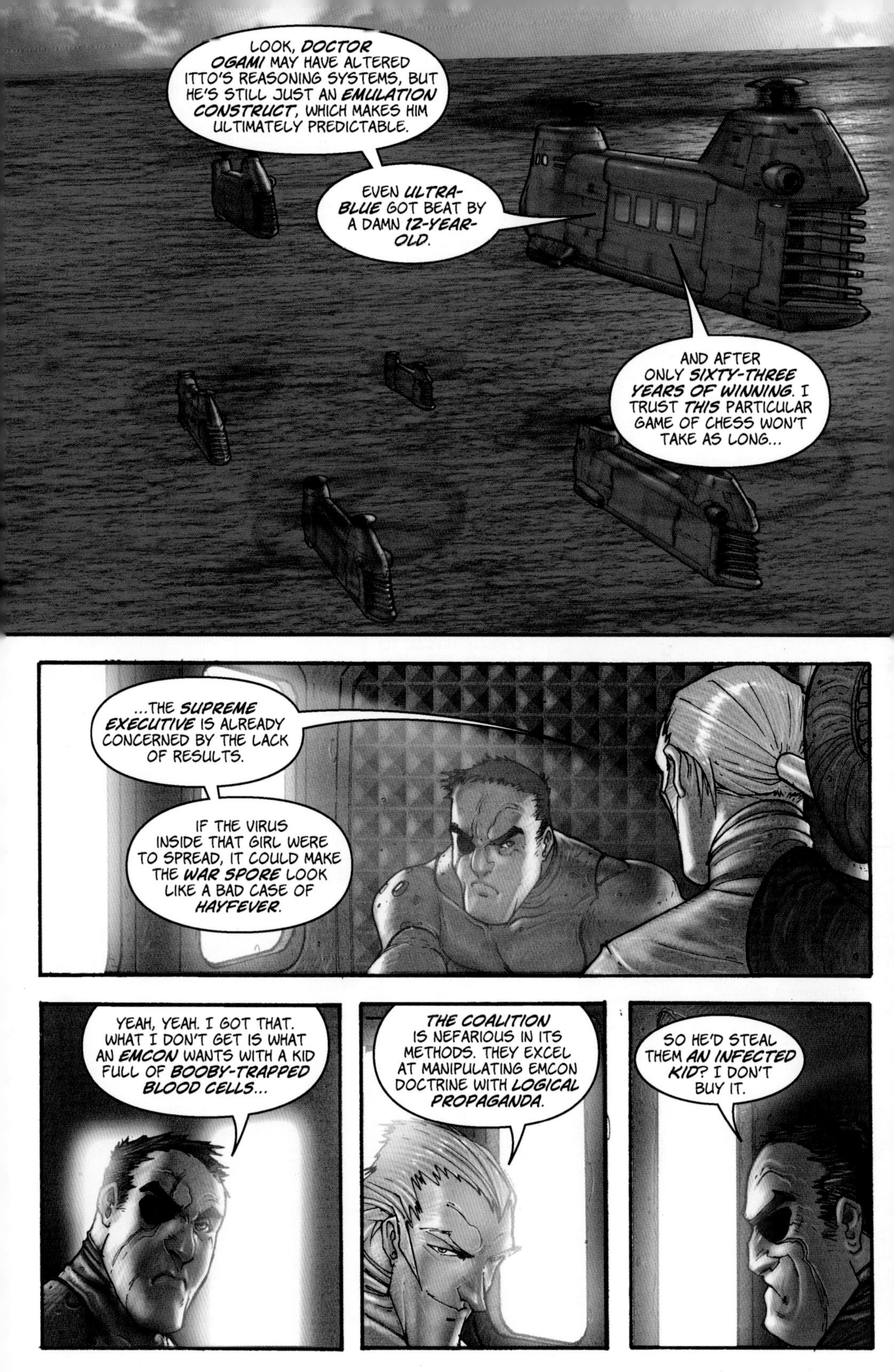
LOOK, DOCTOR OGAMI MAY HAVE ALTERED ITTO'S REASONING SYSTEMS, BUT HE'S STILL JUST AN EMULATION CONSTRUCT, WHICH MAKES HIM ULTIMATELY PREDICTABLE.
EVEN ULTRA-BLUE GOT BEAT BY A DAMN 12-YEAR-OLD.
AND AFTER ONLY SIXTY-THREE YEARS OF WINNING. I TRUST THIS PARTICULAR GAME OF CHESS WON'T TAKE AS LONG...
...THE SUPREME EXECUTIVE IS ALREADY CONCERNED BY THE LACK OF RESULTS.
IF THE VIRUS INSIDE THAT GIRL WERE TO SPREAD, IT COULD MAKE THE WAR SPORE LOOK LIKE A BAD CASE OF HAYFEVER.
YEAH, YEAH. I GOT THAT. WHAT I DON'T GET IS WHAT AN EMCON WANTS WITH A KID FULL OF BOOBY-TRAPPED BLOOD CELLS...
THE COALITION IS NEFARIOUS IN ITS METHODS. THEY EXCEL AT MANIPULATING EMCON DOCTRINE WITH LOGICAL PROPAGANDA.
SO HE'D STEAL THEM AN INFECTED KID? I DON'T BUY IT.

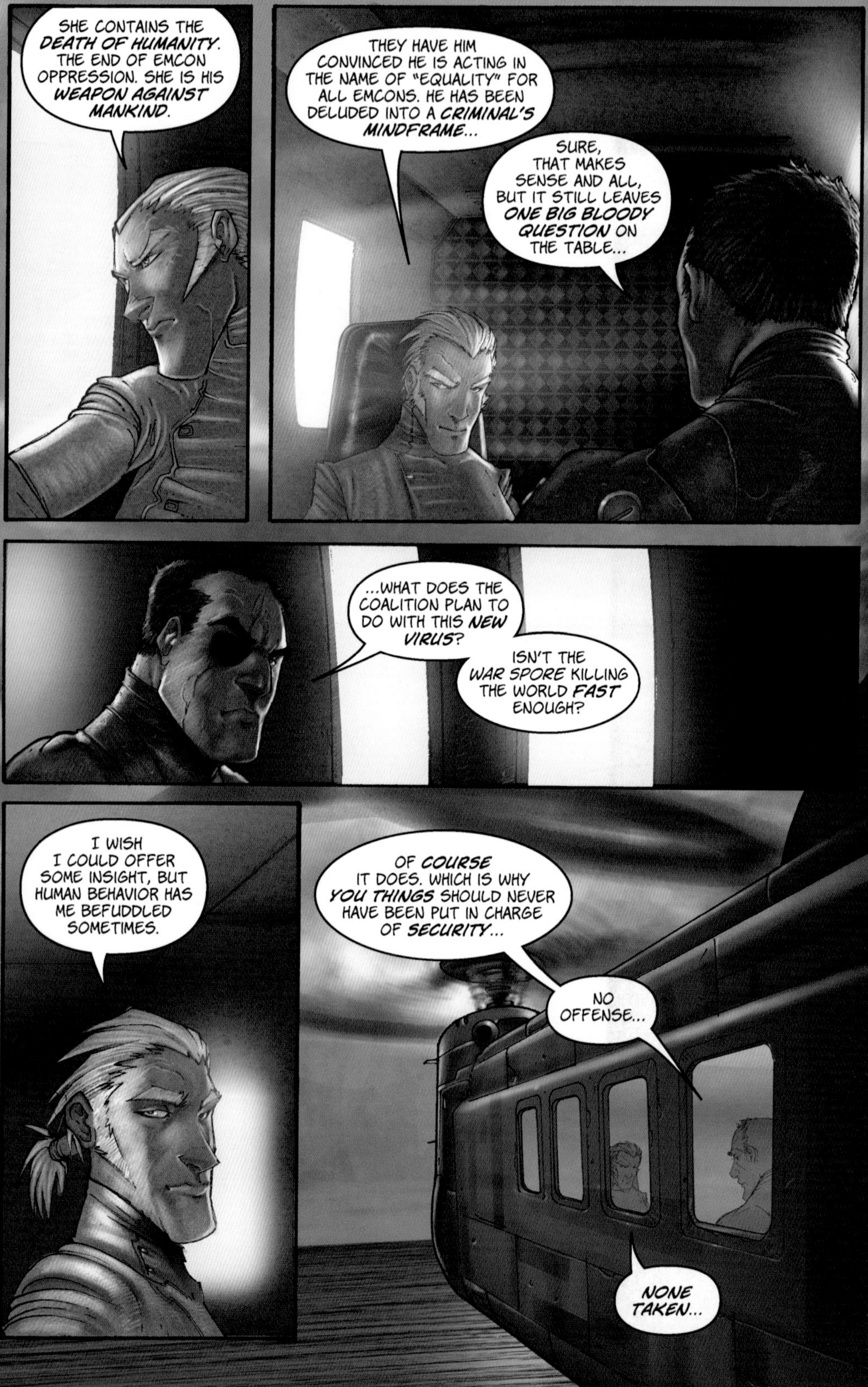
SHE CONTAINS THE DEATH OF HUMANITY. THE END OF EMCON OPPRESSION. SHE IS HIS WEAPON AGAINST MANKIND.
THEY HAVE HIM CONVINCED HE IS ACTING IN THE NAME OF "EQUALITY" FOR ALL EMCONS. HE HAS BEEN DELUDED INTO A CRIMINAL'S MINDFRAME...
SURE, THAT MAKES SENSE AND ALL, BUT IT STILL LEAVES ONE BIG BLOODY QUESTION ON THE TABLE...
...WHAT DOES THE COALITION PLAN TO DO WITH THIS NEW VIRUS?
ISN'T THE WAR SPORE KILLING THE WORLD FAST ENOUGH?
I WISH I COULD OFFER SOME INSIGHT, BUT HUMAN BEHAVIOR HAS ME BEFUDDLED SOMETIMES.
OF COURSE IT DOES. WHICH IS WHY YOU THINGS SHOULD NEVER HAVE BEEN PUT IN CHARGE OF SECURITY...
NO OFFENSE...
NONE TAKEN...

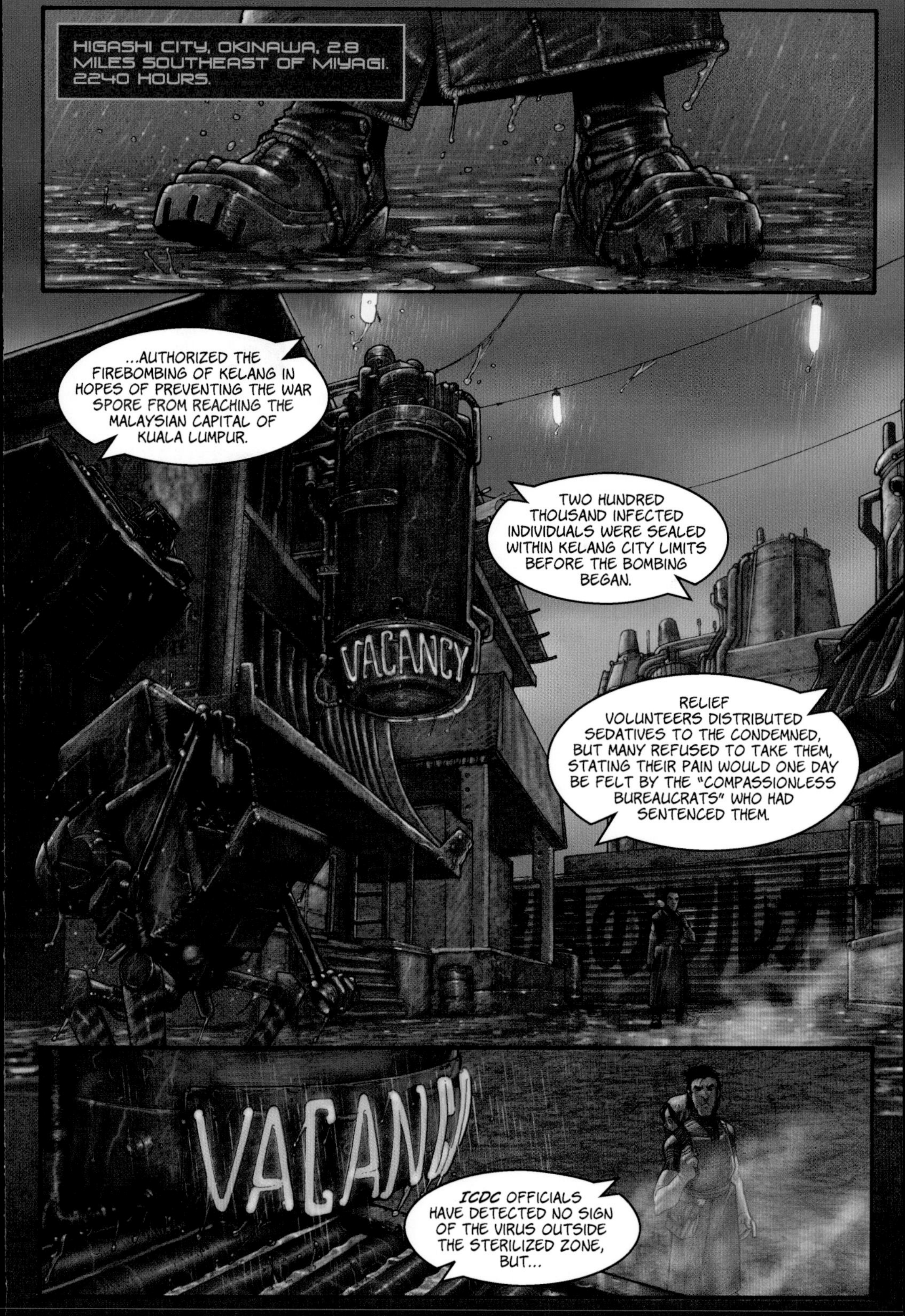
HIGASHI CITY, OKINAWA, 2.8 MILES SOUTHEAST OF MIYAGI. 2240 HOURS.
...AUTHORIZED THE FIREBOMBING OF KELANG IN HOPES OF PREVENTING THE WAR SPORE FROM REACHING THE MALAYSIAN CAPITAL OF KUALA LUMPUR.
TWO HUNDRED THOUSAND INFECTED INDIVIDUALS WERE SEALED WITHIN KELANG CITY LIMITS BEFORE THE BOMBING BEGAN.
VACANCY
RELIEF VOLUNTEERS DISTRIBUTED SEDATIVES TO THE CONDEMNED, BUT MANY REFUSED TO TAKE THEM, STATING THEIR PAIN WOULD ONE DAY BE FELT BY THE "COMPASSIONLESS BUREAUCRATS" WHO HAD SENTENCED THEM.
VACANC
ICDC OFFICIALS HAVE DETECTED NO SIGN OF THE VIRUS OUTSIDE THE STERILIZED ZONE, BUT...

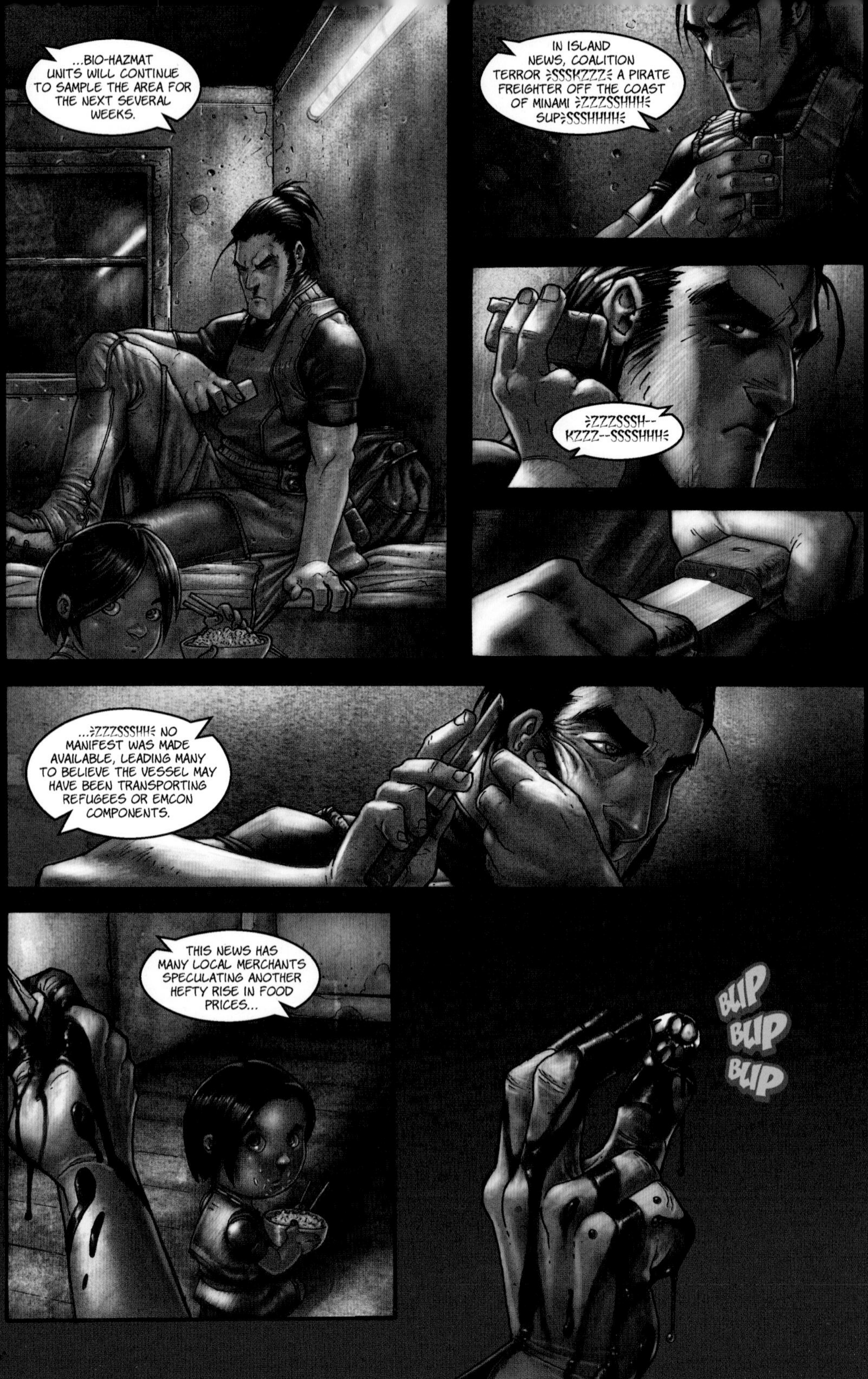

...BIO-HAZMAT UNITS WILL CONTINUE TO SAMPLE THE AREA FOR THE NEXT SEVERAL WEEKS.
IN ISLAND NEWS, COALITION TERROR ⋛SSSKZZZ⋚ A PIRATE FREIGHTER OFF THE COAST OF MINAMI ⋛ZZZSSHHH⋚ SUP⋛SSSHHHH⋚
⋛ZZZSSSH-- KZZZ--SSSSHHH⋚
...⋛ZZZSSSHH⋚ NO MANIFEST WAS MADE AVAILABLE, LEADING MANY TO BELIEVE THE VESSEL MAY HAVE BEEN TRANSPORTING REFUGEES OR EMCON COMPONENTS.
THIS NEWS HAS MANY LOCAL MERCHANTS SPECULATING ANOTHER HEFTY RISE IN FOOD PRICES...
BLIP
BLIP
BLIP

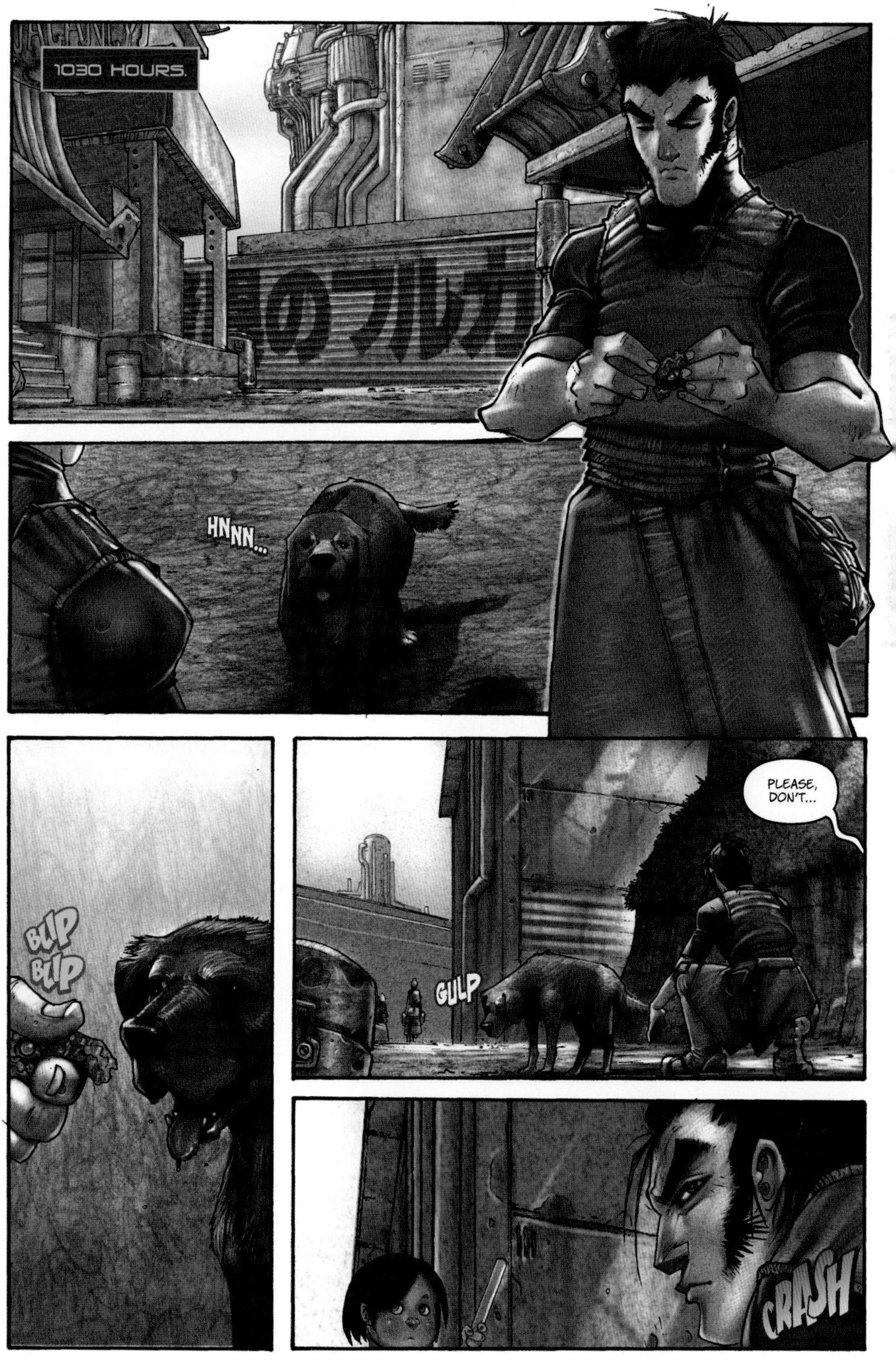
1030 HOURS.
HNNN...
BLIP
BLIP
PLEASE, DON'T...
GULP
CRASH

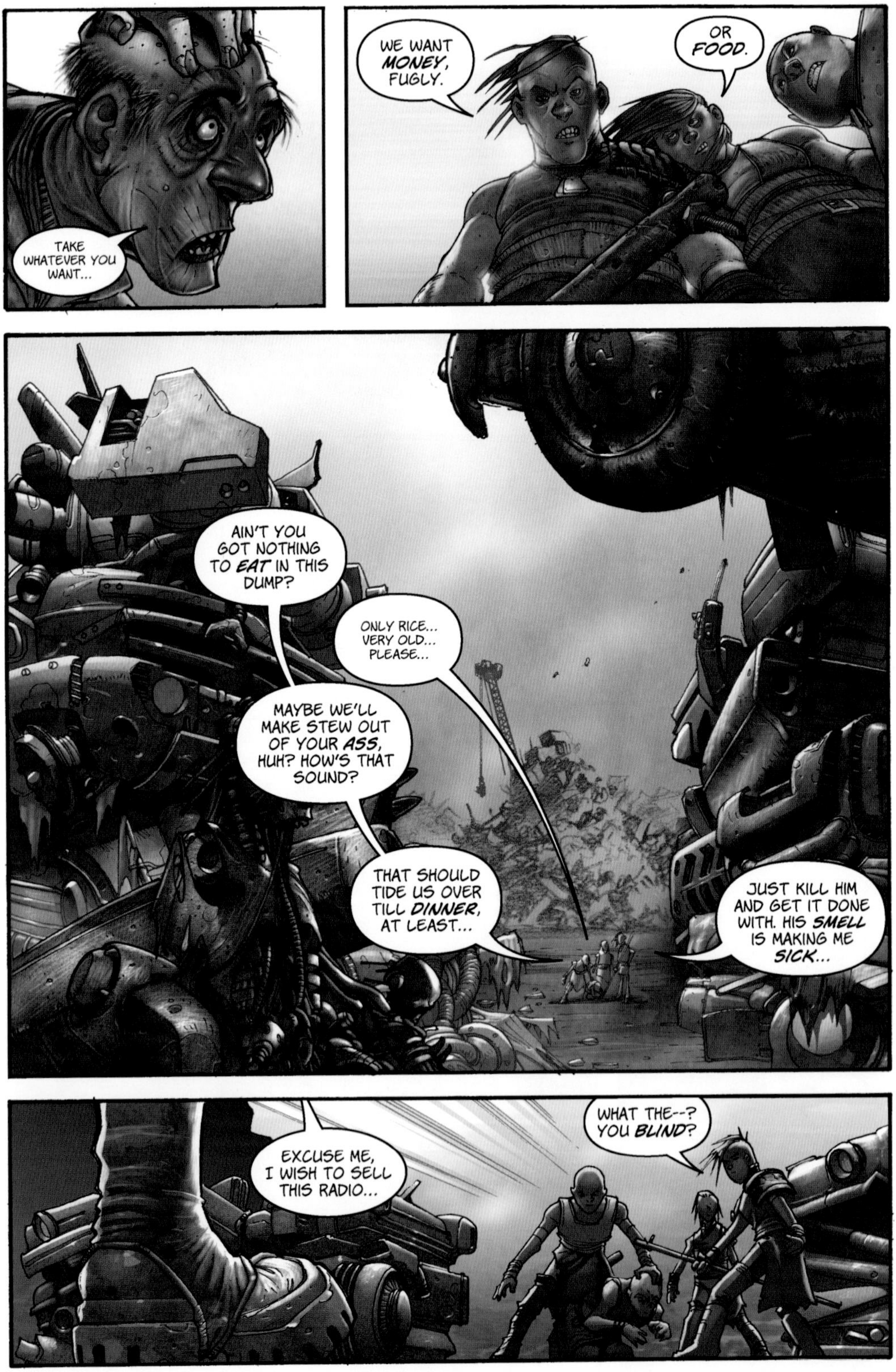
TAKE WHATEVER YOU WANT...
WE WANT MONEY, FUGLY.
OR FOOD.
AIN'T YOU GOT NOTHING TO EAT IN THIS DUMP?
ONLY RICE... VERY OLD... PLEASE...
MAYBE WE'LL MAKE STEW OUT OF YOUR ASS, HUH? HOW'S THAT SOUND?
THAT SHOULD TIDE US OVER TILL DINNER, AT LEAST...
JUST KILL HIM AND GET IT DONE WITH. HIS SMELL IS MAKING ME SICK...
EXCUSE ME, I WISH TO SELL THIS RADIO...
WHAT THE--? YOU BLIND?

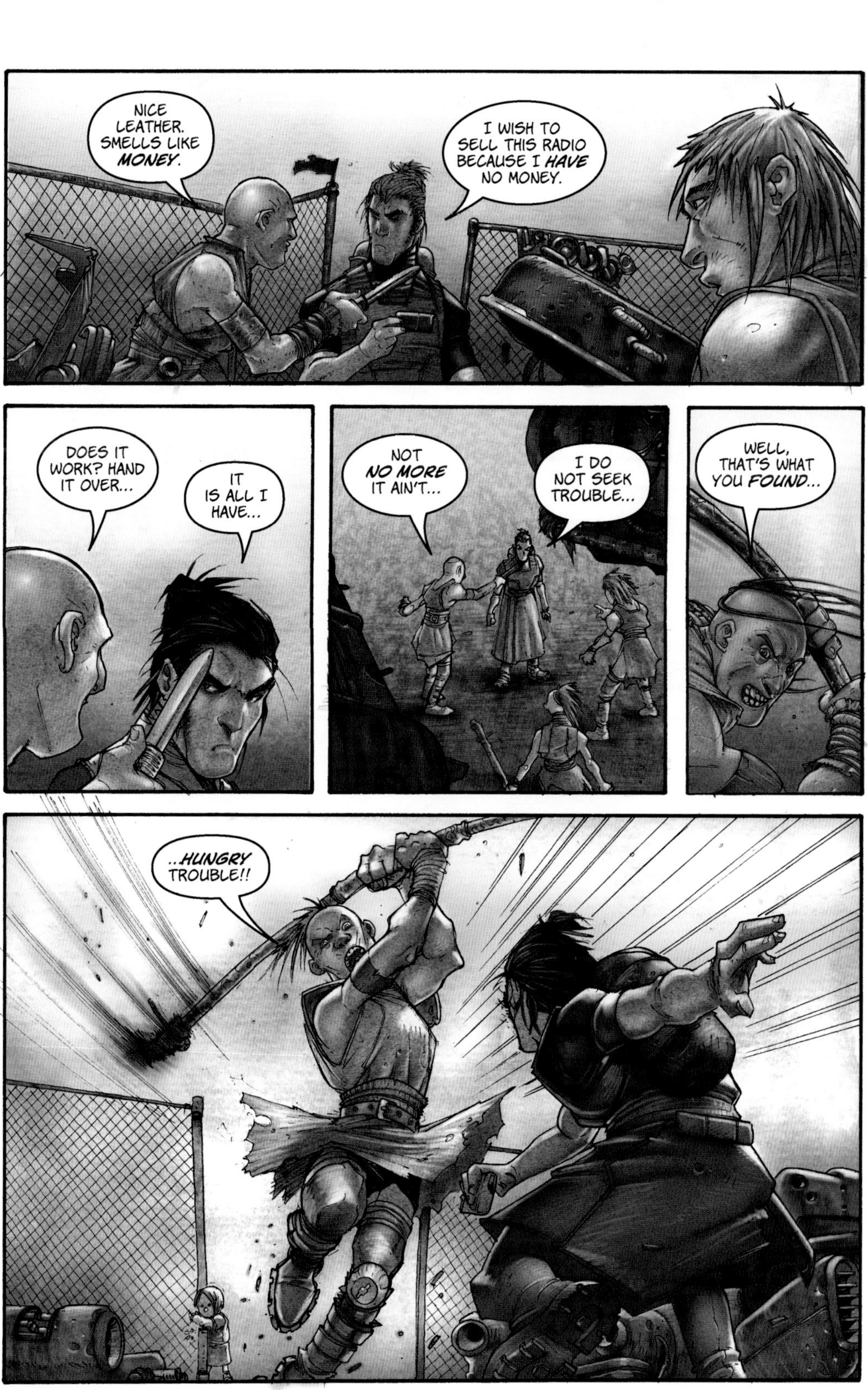
NICE LEATHER. SMELLS LIKE MONEY.
I WISH TO SELL THIS RADIO BECAUSE I HAVE NO MONEY.
DOES IT WORK? HAND IT OVER...
IT IS ALL I HAVE...
NOT NO MORE IT AIN'T...
I DO NOT SEEK TROUBLE...
WELL, THAT'S WHAT YOU FOUND...
..HUNGRY TROUBLE!!

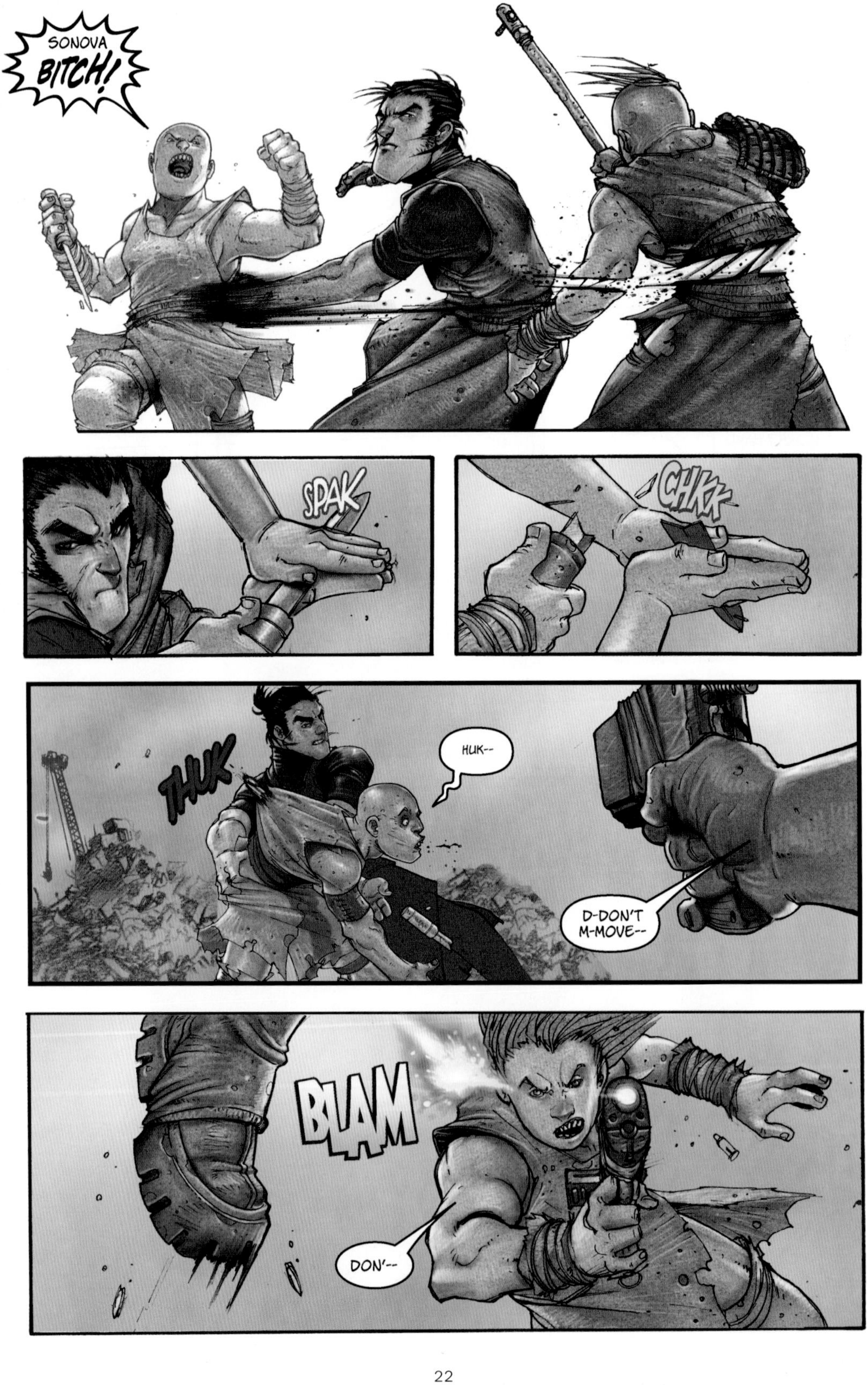
SONOVA BITCH!
SPAK
CHKK
THUK
HUK--
D-DON'T M-MOVE--
BLAM
DON'--

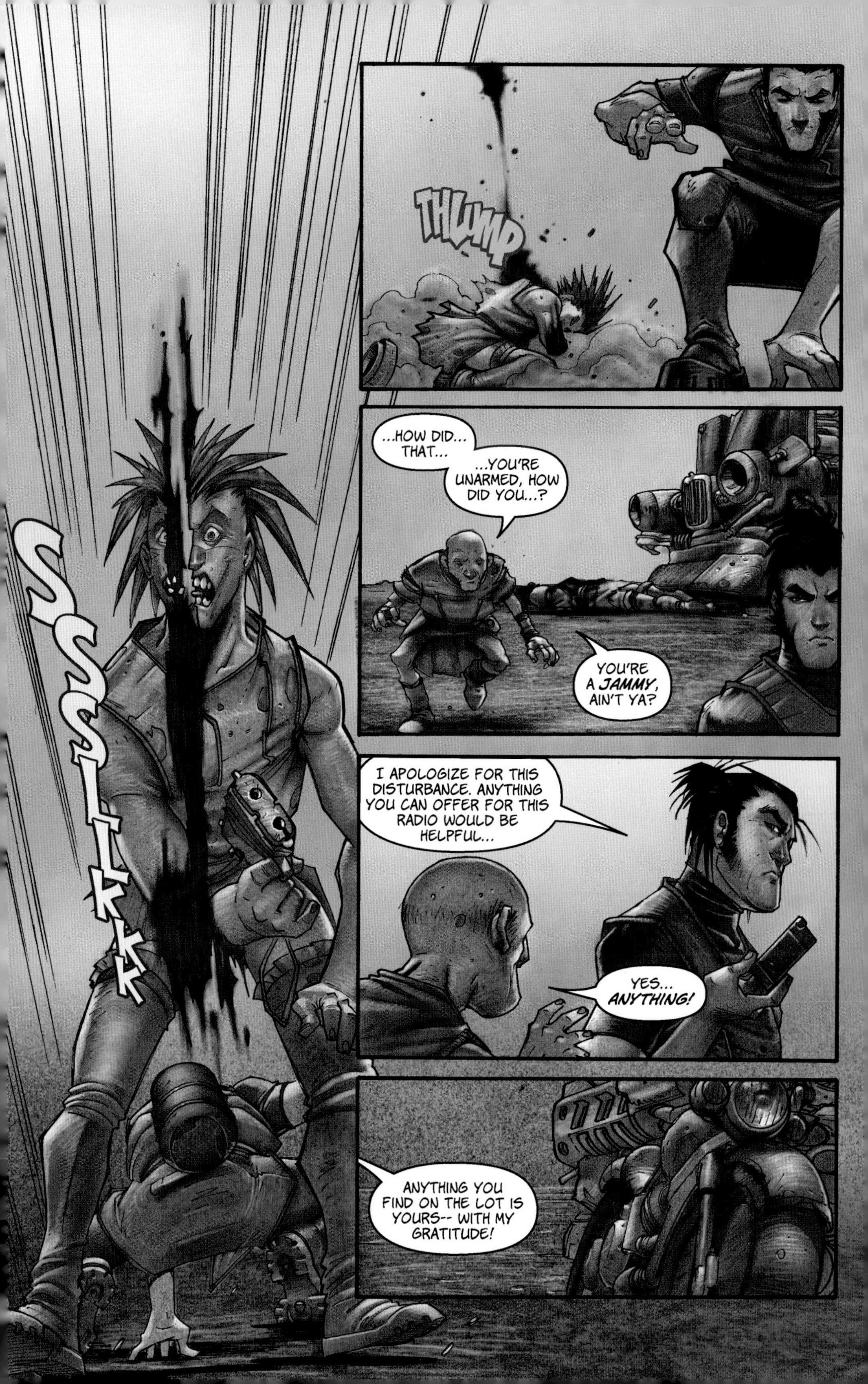
SSSLIKKK
THLUMP
...HOW DID... THAT...
...YOU'RE UNARMED, HOW DID YOU...?
YOU'RE A JAMMY, AIN'T YA?
I APOLOGIZE FOR THIS DISTURBANCE. ANYTHING YOU CAN OFFER FOR THIS RADIO WOULD BE HELPFUL...
YES... ANYTHING!
ANYTHING YOU FIND ON THE LOT IS YOURS-- WITH MY GRATITUDE!

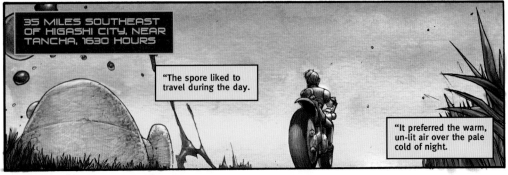

35 MILES SOUTHEAST OF HIGASHI CITY, NEAR TANCHA, 1630 HOURS
"The spore liked to travel during the day.
"It preferred the warm, un-lit air over the pale cold of night.
"There were more things to feed on-- and nest in-- during the day.
FUEL
"People thought they could evade the spore by living in trenches and breathing recycled air...
"...but sooner or later, it would find a crack small enough to slip through, and another town would be zoned for sterilization.

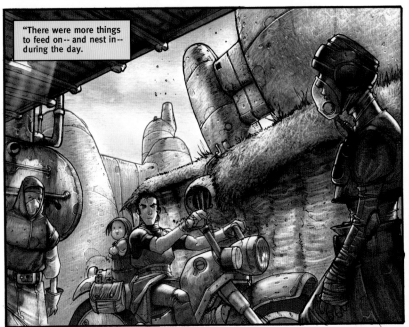

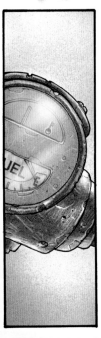

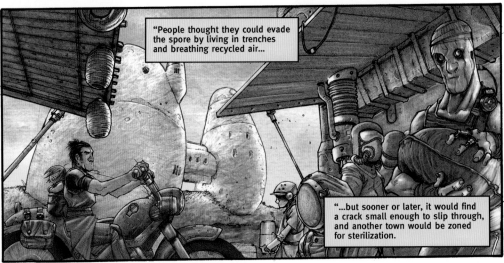

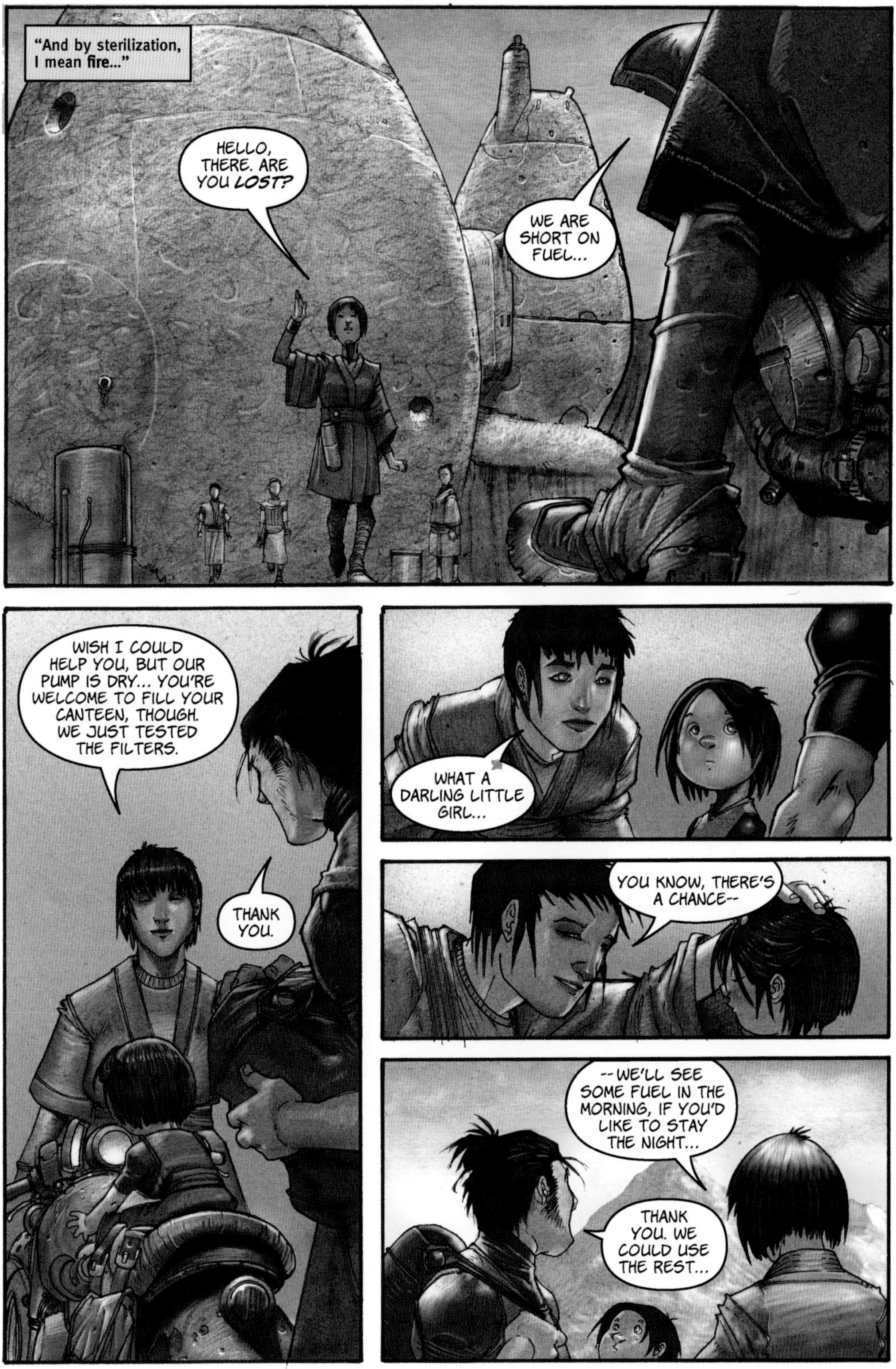
"And by sterilization, I mean fire..."
HELLO, THERE. ARE YOU LOST?
WE ARE SHORT ON FUEL...
WISH I COULD HELP YOU, BUT OUR PUMP IS DRY... YOU'RE WELCOME TO FILL YOUR CANTEEN, THOUGH. WE JUST TESTED THE FILTERS.
THANK YOU.
WHAT A DARLING LITTLE GIRL...
YOU KNOW, THERE'S A CHANCE--
--WE'LL SEE SOME FUEL IN THE MORNING, IF YOU'D LIKE TO STAY THE NIGHT...
THANK YOU. WE COULD USE THE REST...

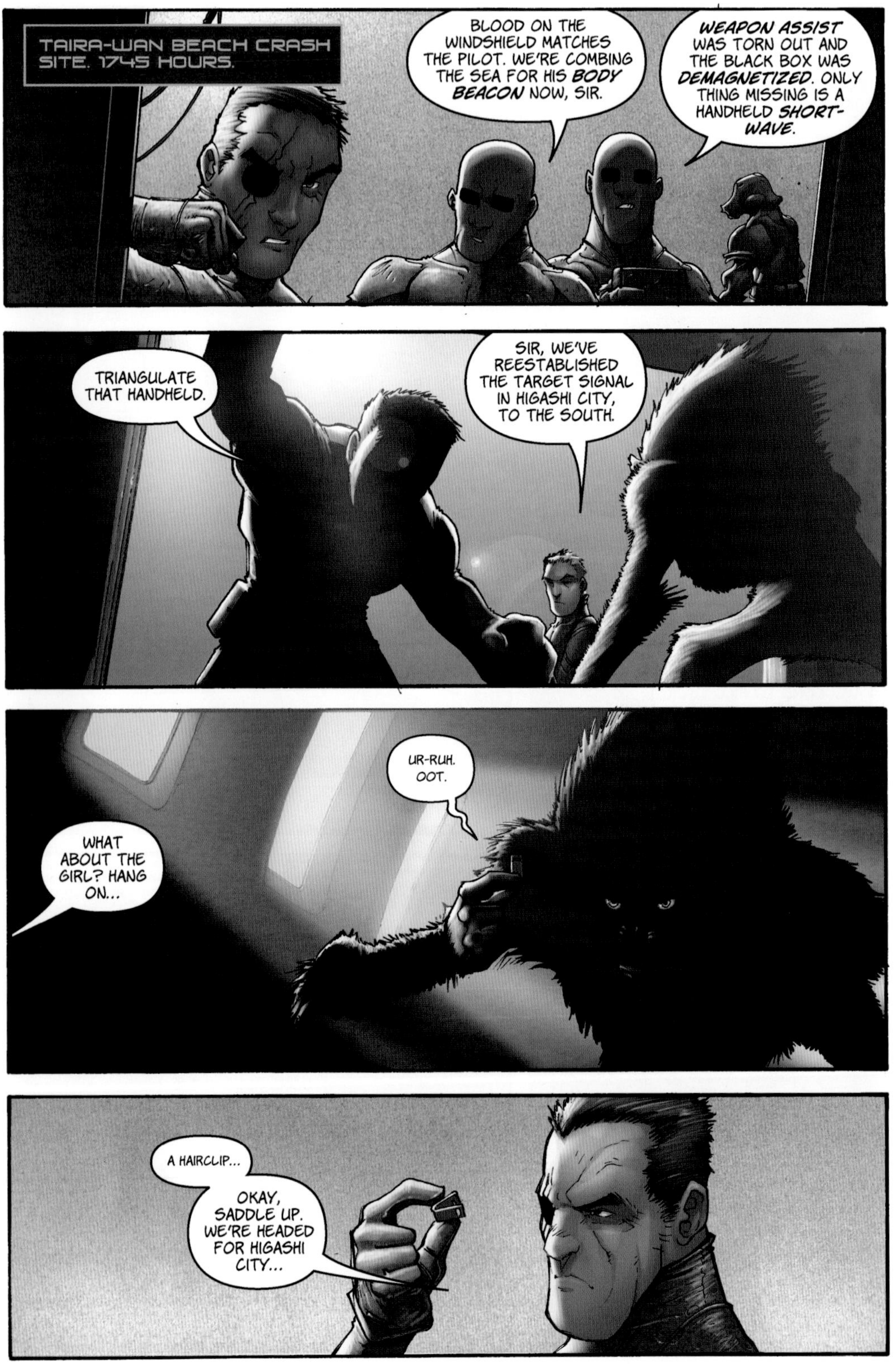
TAIRA-WAN BEACH CRASH SITE. 1745 HOURS.
BLOOD ON THE WINDSHIELD MATCHES THE PILOT. WE'RE COMBING THE SEA FOR HIS BODY BEACON NOW, SIR.
WEAPON ASSIST WAS TORN OUT AND THE BLACK BOX WAS DEMAGNETIZED. ONLY THING MISSING IS A HANDHELD SHORT-WAVE.
TRIANGULATE THAT HANDHELD.
SIR, WE'VE REESTABLISHED THE TARGET SIGNAL IN HIGASHI CITY, TO THE SOUTH.
UR-RUH. OOT.
WHAT ABOUT THE GIRL? HANG ON...
A HAIRCLIP...
OKAY, SADDLE UP. WE'RE HEADED FOR HIGASHI CITY...

SO, *ITTO*... WHERE ARE YOU AND DAISY HEADED?

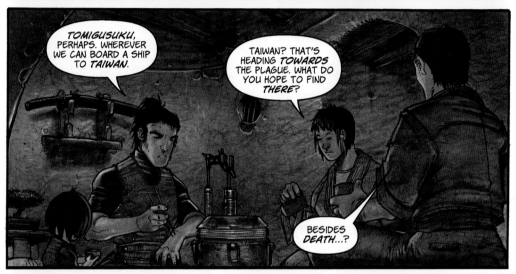

TOMIGUSUKU, PERHAPS. WHEREVER WE CAN BOARD A SHIP TO *TAIWAN*.

TAIWAN? THAT'S HEADING *TOWARDS* THE PLAGUE. WHAT DO YOU HOPE TO FIND *THERE*?

BESIDES *DEATH*...?

I DON'T KNOW YET.

YOU SAY YOU'RE FROM *OGASAWARA GUNTO*? SUCH A SMALL ISLAND SOUNDS LIKE *PERFECT ISOLATION* FROM THE SPORE...

THANK YOU FOR THE MEAL.

I WOULD LIKE TO *REPAY* YOU IN SOME WAY...

27

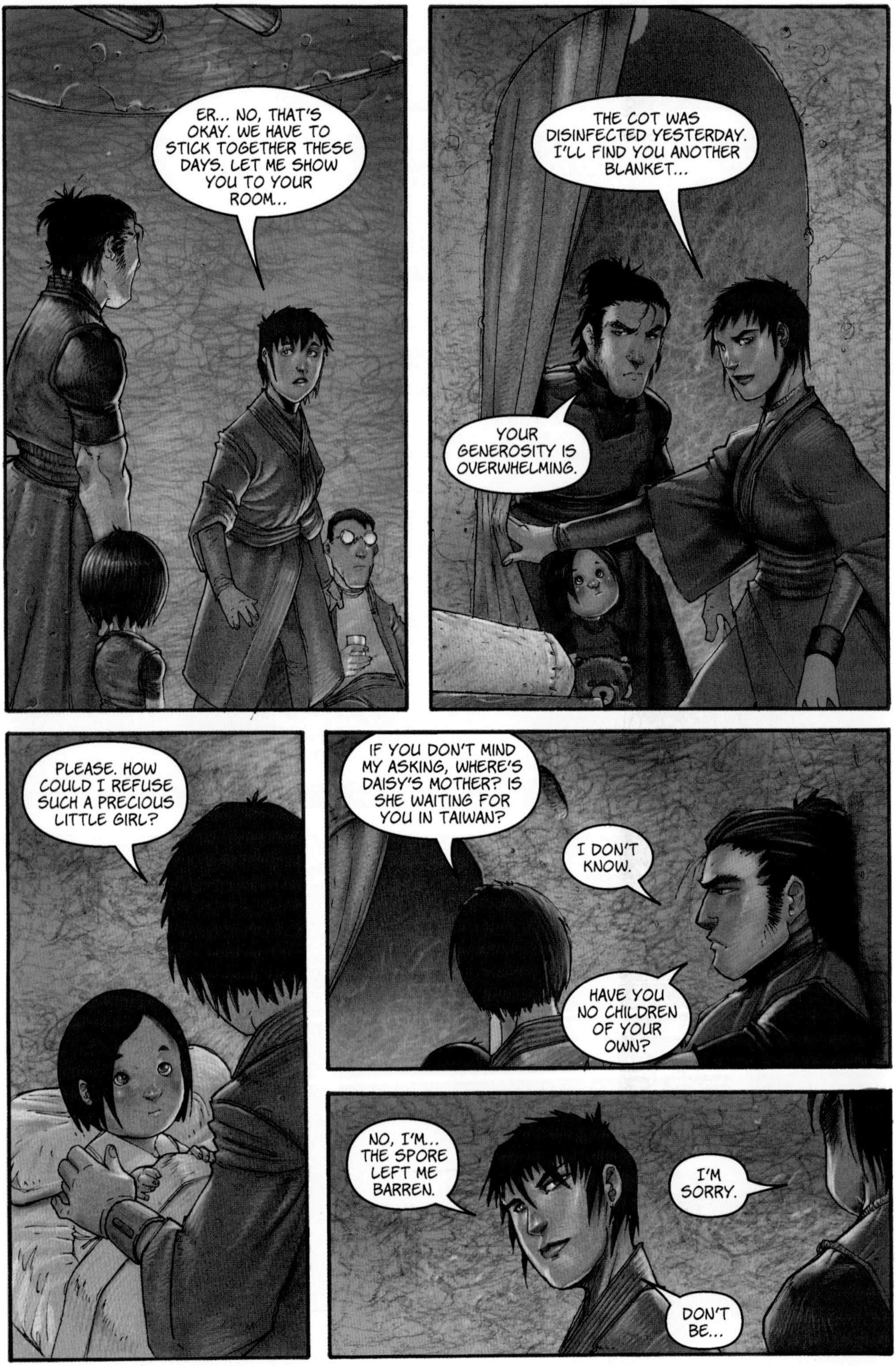
ER... NO, THAT'S OKAY. WE HAVE TO STICK TOGETHER THESE DAYS. LET ME SHOW YOU TO YOUR ROOM...
THE COT WAS DISINFECTED YESTERDAY. I'LL FIND YOU ANOTHER BLANKET...
YOUR GENEROSITY IS OVERWHELMING.
PLEASE. HOW COULD I REFUSE SUCH A PRECIOUS LITTLE GIRL?
IF YOU DON'T MIND MY ASKING, WHERE'S DAISY'S MOTHER? IS SHE WAITING FOR YOU IN TAIWAN?
I DON'T KNOW.
HAVE YOU NO CHILDREN OF YOUR OWN?
NO, I'M... THE SPORE LEFT ME BARREN.
I'M SORRY.
DON'T BE...

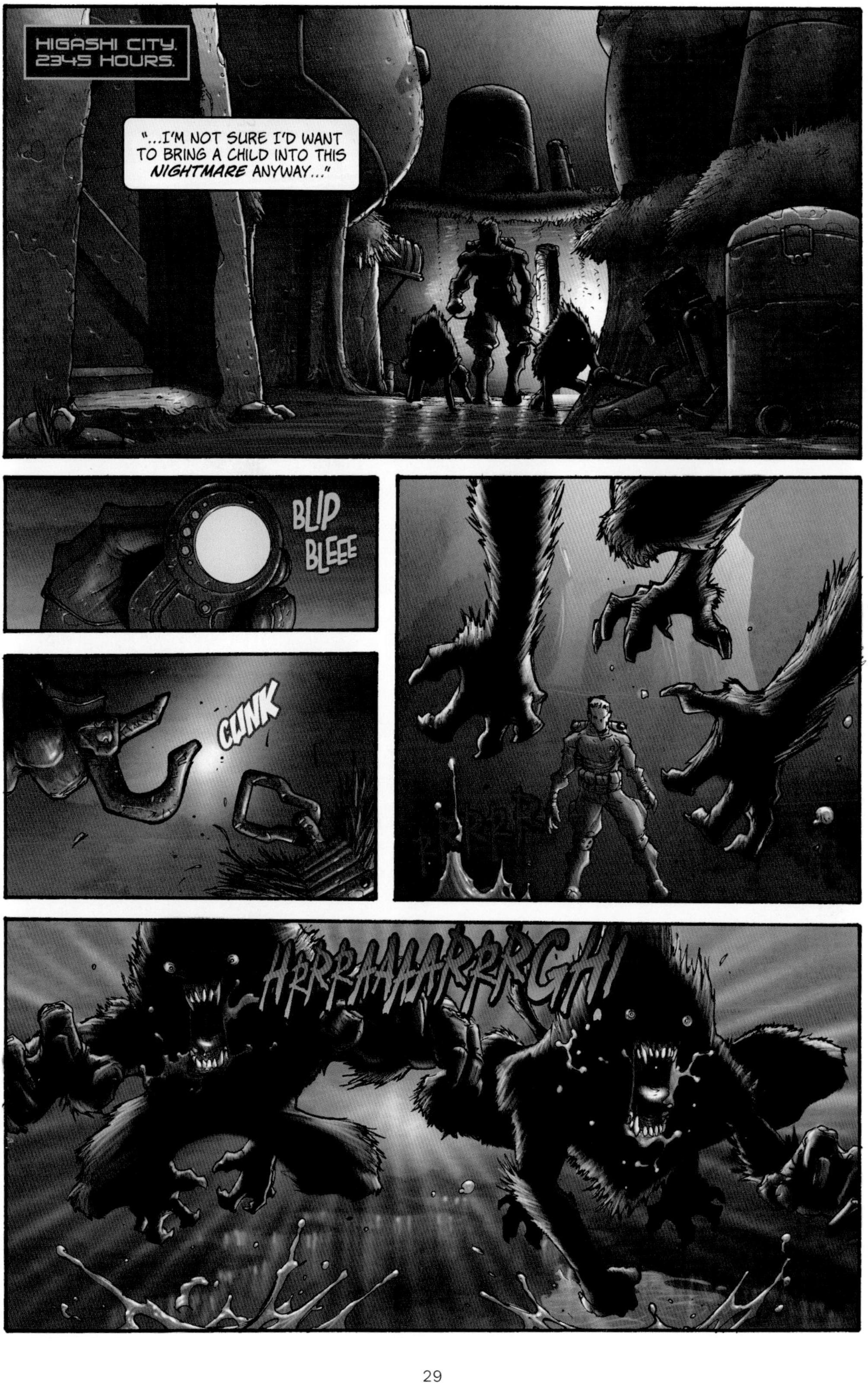
HIGASHI CITY. 2345 HOURS.
"...I'M NOT SURE I'D WANT TO BRING A CHILD INTO THIS NIGHTMARE ANYWAY..."
BLIP BLEEE
CLUNK
HRRRAAAARRRGH!

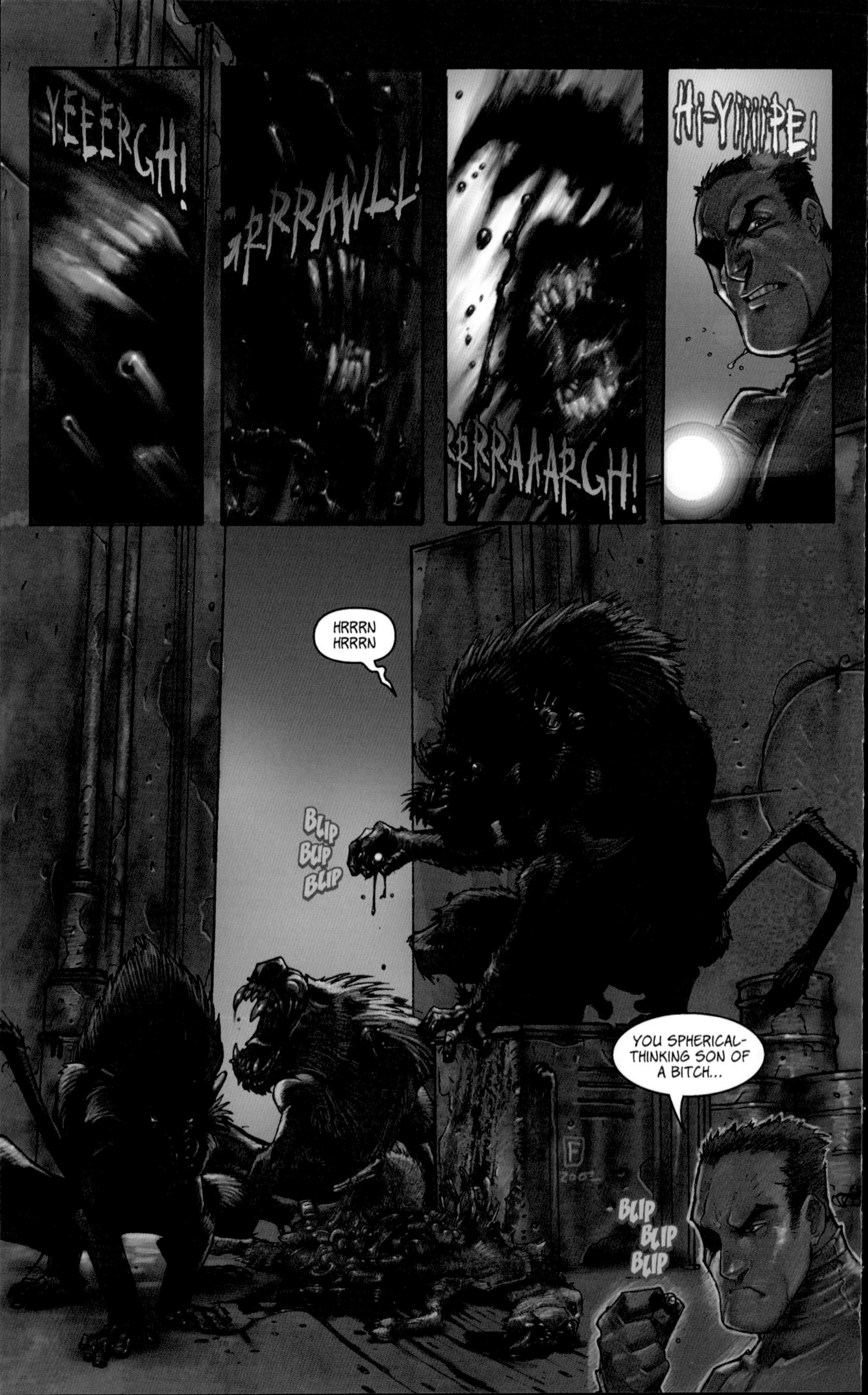
YEEERGH!
GRRRAWLL!
RRRRAAARGH!
HI-YIIIIPE!
HRRRN
HRRRN
BLIP
BLIP
BLIP
YOU SPHERICAL-THINKING SON OF A BITCH...
BLIP
BLIP
BLIP

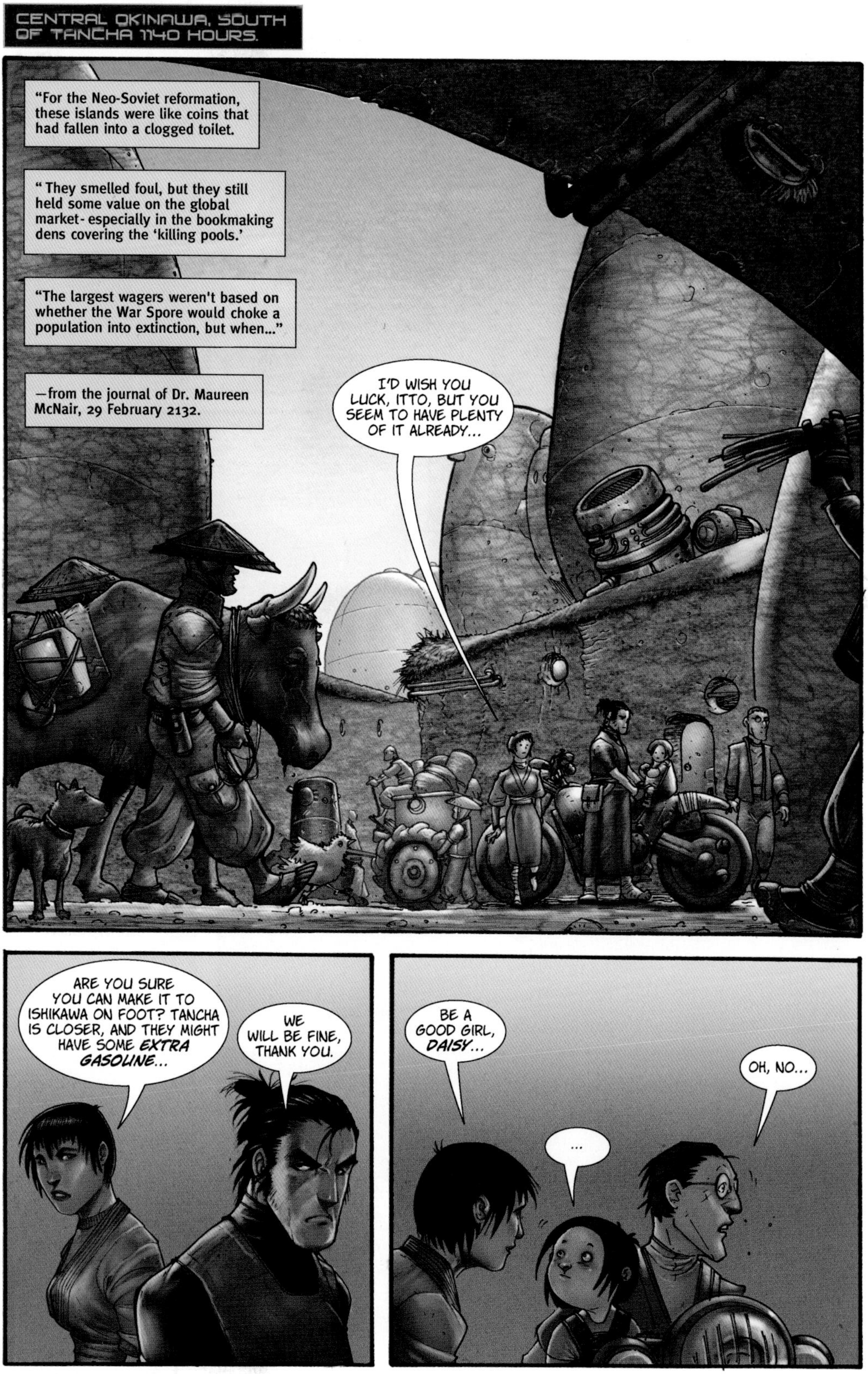
CENTRAL OKINAWA, SOUTH OF TANCHA 1140 HOURS.
"For the Neo-Soviet reformation, these islands were like coins that had fallen into a clogged toilet.
" They smelled foul, but they still held some value on the global market- especially in the bookmaking dens covering the 'killing pools.'
"The largest wagers weren't based on whether the War Spore would choke a population into extinction, but when..."
—from the journal of Dr. Maureen McNair, 29 February 2132.
I'D WISH YOU LUCK, ITTO, BUT YOU SEEM TO HAVE PLENTY OF IT ALREADY...
ARE YOU SURE YOU CAN MAKE IT TO ISHIKAWA ON FOOT? TANCHA IS CLOSER, AND THEY MIGHT HAVE SOME *EXTRA GASOLINE*...
WE WILL BE FINE, THANK YOU.
BE A GOOD GIRL, *DAISY*...
...
OH, NO...

LOAD 'EM UP. LOOK FOR MEDS AND POWER CELLS. AND SEE IF THEY GOT ANY MORE *LIQUOR*...

SMELLS LIKE FOOT AND ASS AROUND HERE...

JUST BREATHE THROUGH YER MOUTH, *NUMBNUTS*...

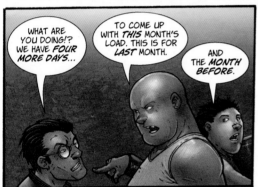

WHAT ARE YOU DOING!? WE HAVE *FOUR MORE DAYS*...

TO COME UP WITH *THIS* MONTH'S LOAD. THIS IS FOR *LAST* MONTH.

AND THE *MONTH BEFORE.*

B-BUT... WE JUST *PAID* FOR LAST MONTH...!

LATE. THIS IS *INTEREST.*

CHECK THAT BOX OF *BATTERIES*, SEE IF THEY'RE *FRESH*...

BUT WE *NEED* THOSE BATTER-- --GK--!

SEAL IT, *MUDTRAP!* YOU'RE LUCKY TO GET *ANY SUPPLIES* AT *ALL* WITH ALL THEM WILD EMCONS OUT THERE!

YOU THINK YOU CAN KEEP THE ROADS SAFER 'N *US*, BE MY GUEST...

...THROW *HER* IN THE TRUCK, TOO -- YOU GOT ME ALL *WORKED UP* NOW...

BUT WE HAVEN'T RECEIVED SUPPLIES IN WEEKS...

SO YOU CAN SEE HOW *TOUGH* IT'S BEEN.

IN FACT...

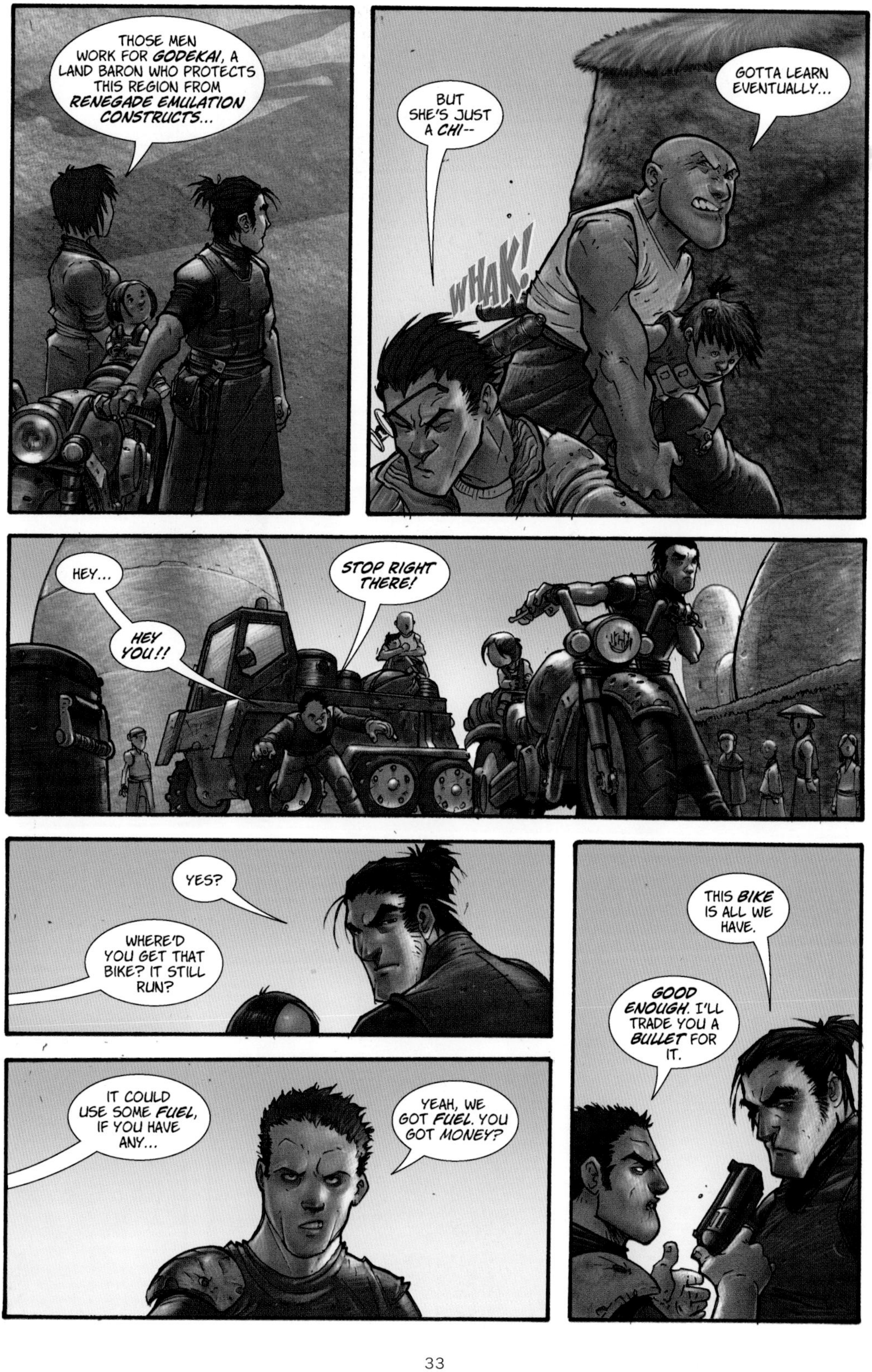

THOSE MEN WORK FOR GODEKAI, A LAND BARON WHO PROTECTS THIS REGION FROM RENEGADE EMULATION CONSTRUCTS...
BUT SHE'S JUST A CHI--
GOTTA LEARN EVENTUALLY...
WHAK!
HEY...
HEY YOU!!
STOP RIGHT THERE!
YES?
WHERE'D YOU GET THAT BIKE? IT STILL RUN?
IT COULD USE SOME FUEL, IF YOU HAVE ANY...
YEAH, WE GOT FUEL. YOU GOT MONEY?
THIS BIKE IS ALL WE HAVE.
GOOD ENOUGH. I'LL TRADE YOU A BULLET FOR IT.

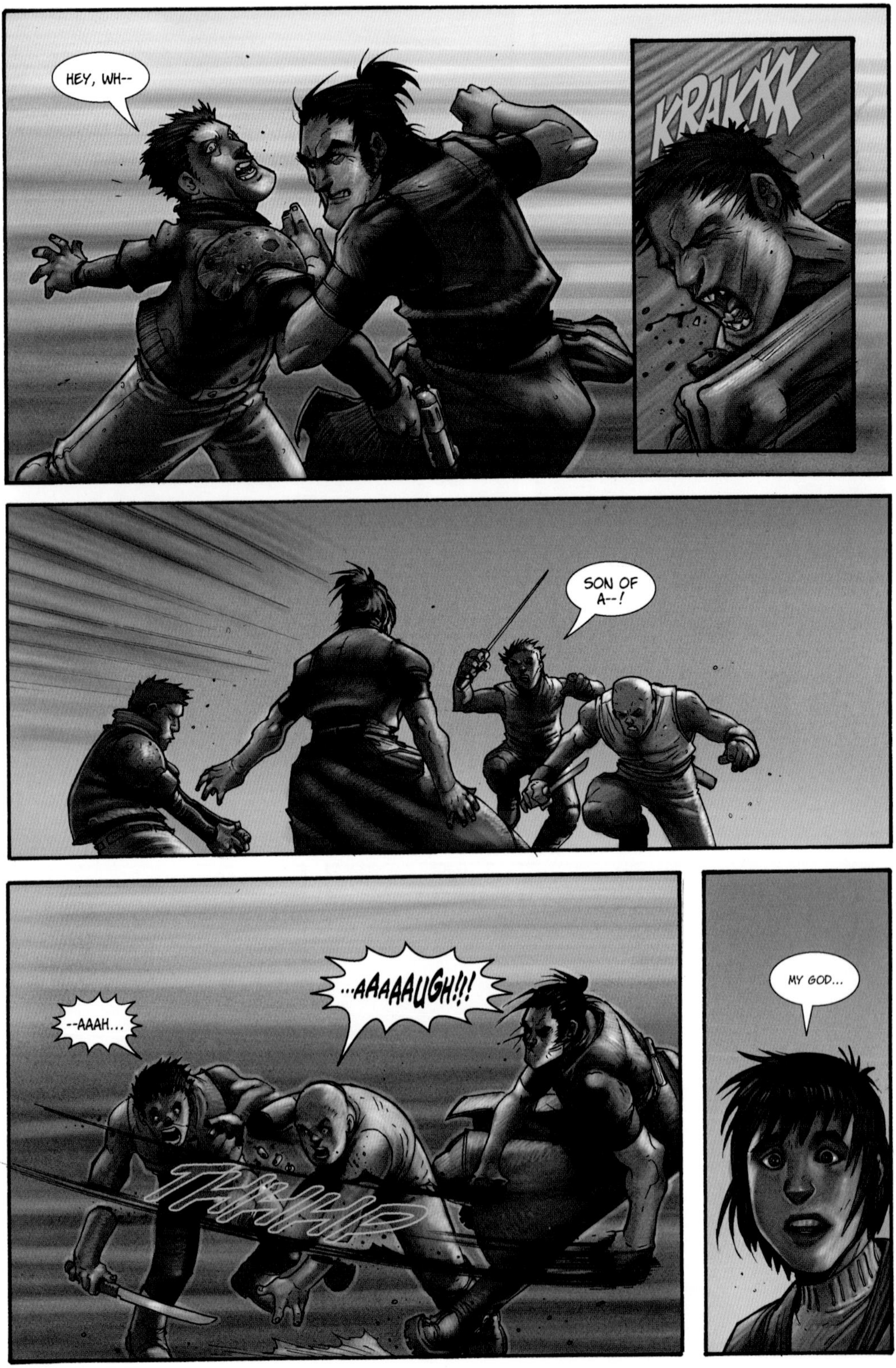
HEY, WH--
KRAKKK
SON OF A--!
--AAAH...
...AAAAAUGH!!!
THHHP
MY GOD...

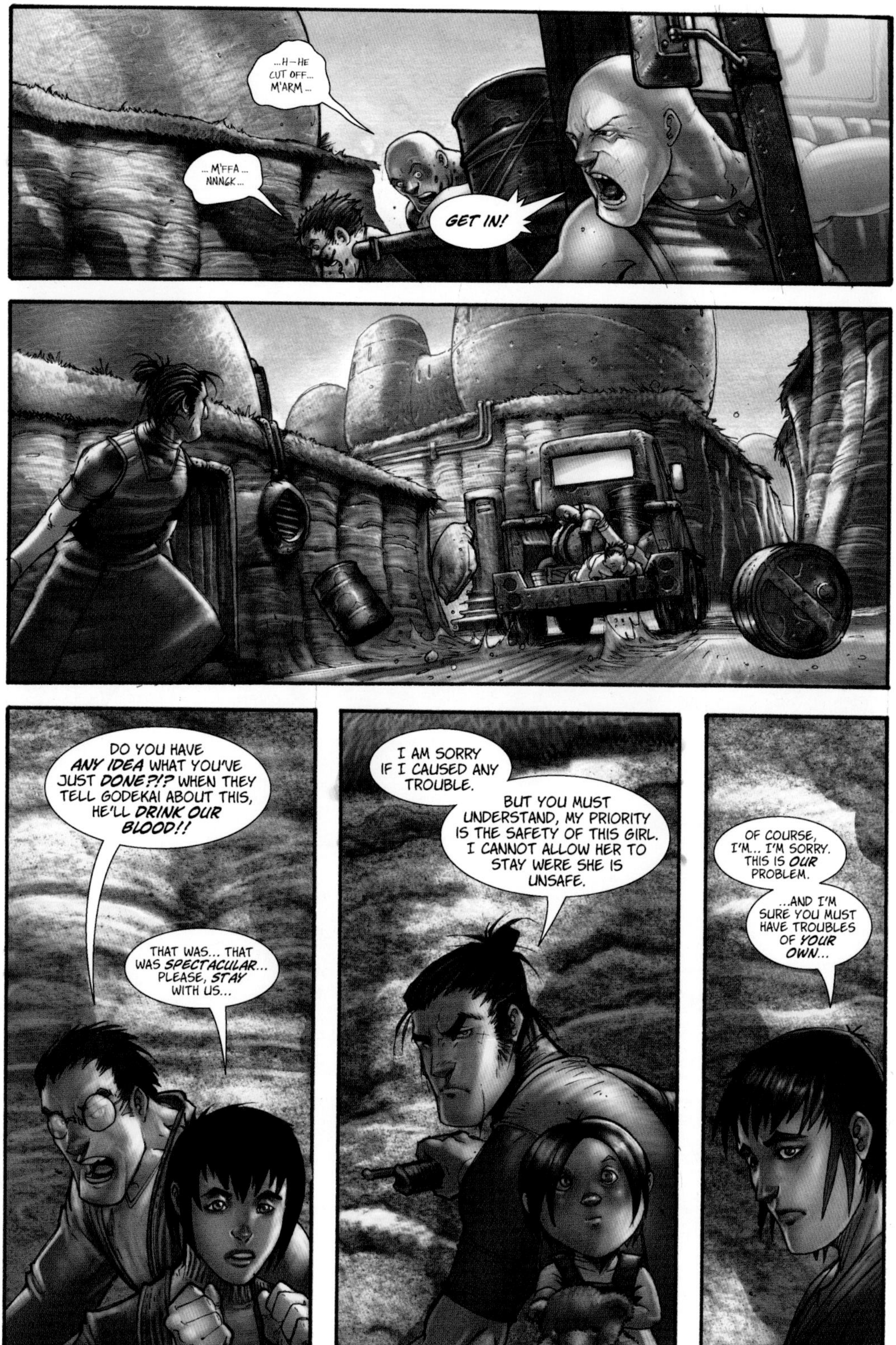
...H-HE CUT OFF... M'ARM...
... M'FFA... NNNGK...
GET IN!
DO YOU HAVE ANY IDEA WHAT YOU'VE JUST DONE?!? WHEN THEY TELL GODEKAI ABOUT THIS, HE'LL DRINK OUR BLOOD!!
THAT WAS... THAT WAS SPECTACULAR... PLEASE, STAY WITH US...
I AM SORRY IF I CAUSED ANY TROUBLE.
BUT YOU MUST UNDERSTAND, MY PRIORITY IS THE SAFETY OF THIS GIRL. I CANNOT ALLOW HER TO STAY WERE SHE IS UNSAFE.
OF COURSE, I'M... I'M SORRY. THIS IS OUR PROBLEM.
...AND I'M SURE YOU MUST HAVE TROUBLES OF YOUR OWN...

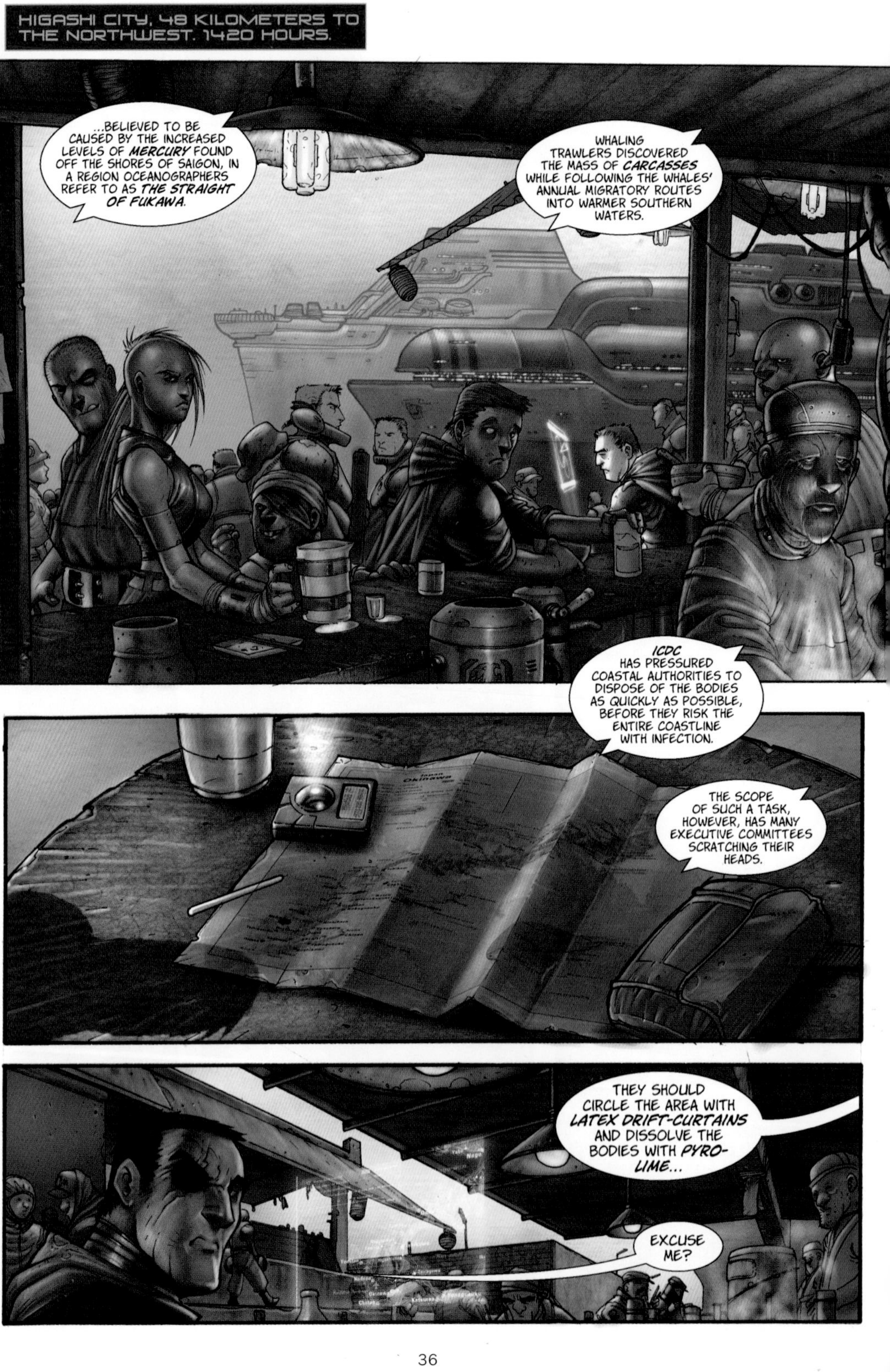
HIGASHI CITY, 48 KILOMETERS TO THE NORTHWEST. 1420 HOURS.
...BELIEVED TO BE CAUSED BY THE INCREASED LEVELS OF MERCURY FOUND OFF THE SHORES OF SAIGON, IN A REGION OCEANOGRAPHERS REFER TO AS THE STRAIGHT OF FUKAWA.
WHALING TRAWLERS DISCOVERED THE MASS OF CARCASSES WHILE FOLLOWING THE WHALES' ANNUAL MIGRATORY ROUTES INTO WARMER SOUTHERN WATERS.
ICDC HAS PRESSURED COASTAL AUTHORITIES TO DISPOSE OF THE BODIES AS QUICKLY AS POSSIBLE, BEFORE THEY RISK THE ENTIRE COASTLINE WITH INFECTION.
THE SCOPE OF SUCH A TASK, HOWEVER, HAS MANY EXECUTIVE COMMITTEES SCRATCHING THEIR HEADS.
THEY SHOULD CIRCLE THE AREA WITH LATEX DRIFT-CURTAINS AND DISSOLVE THE BODIES WITH PYRO-LIME...
EXCUSE ME?

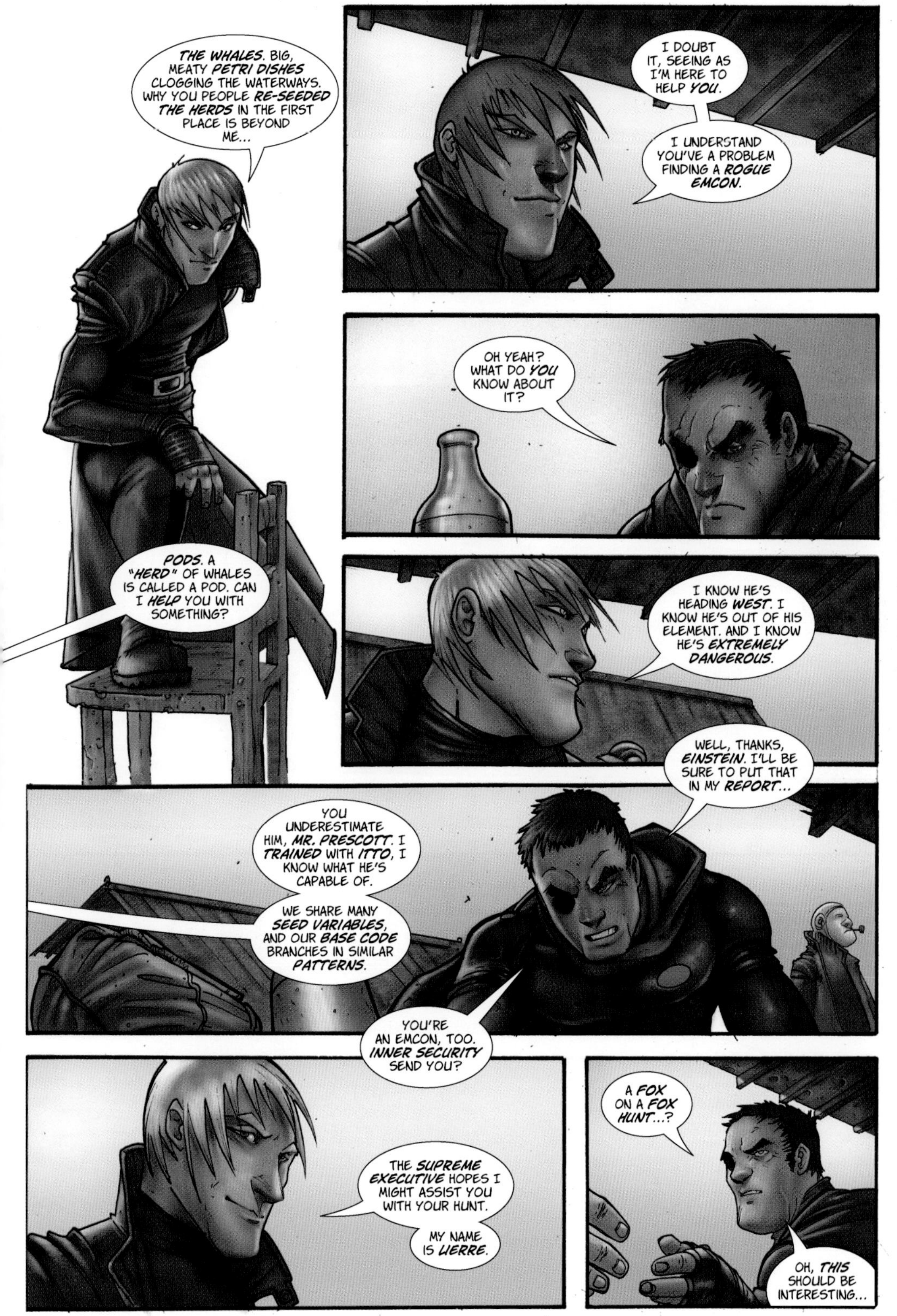
THE WHALES. BIG, MEATY PETRI DISHES CLOGGING THE WATERWAYS. WHY YOU PEOPLE RE-SEEDED THE HERDS IN THE FIRST PLACE IS BEYOND ME...
PODS. A "HERD" OF WHALES IS CALLED A POD. CAN I HELP YOU WITH SOMETHING?
I DOUBT IT, SEEING AS I'M HERE TO HELP YOU.
I UNDERSTAND YOU'VE A PROBLEM FINDING A ROGUE EMCON.
OH YEAH? WHAT DO YOU KNOW ABOUT IT?
I KNOW HE'S HEADING WEST. I KNOW HE'S OUT OF HIS ELEMENT. AND I KNOW HE'S EXTREMELY DANGEROUS.
WELL, THANKS, EINSTEIN. I'LL BE SURE TO PUT THAT IN MY REPORT...
YOU UNDERESTIMATE HIM, MR. PRESCOTT. I TRAINED WITH ITTO, I KNOW WHAT HE'S CAPABLE OF.
WE SHARE MANY SEED VARIABLES, AND OUR BASE CODE BRANCHES IN SIMILAR PATTERNS.
YOU'RE AN EMCON, TOO. INNER SECURITY SEND YOU?
THE SUPREME EXECUTIVE HOPES I MIGHT ASSIST YOU WITH YOUR HUNT.
MY NAME IS LIERRE.
A FOX ON A FOX HUNT...?
OH, THIS SHOULD BE INTERESTING...

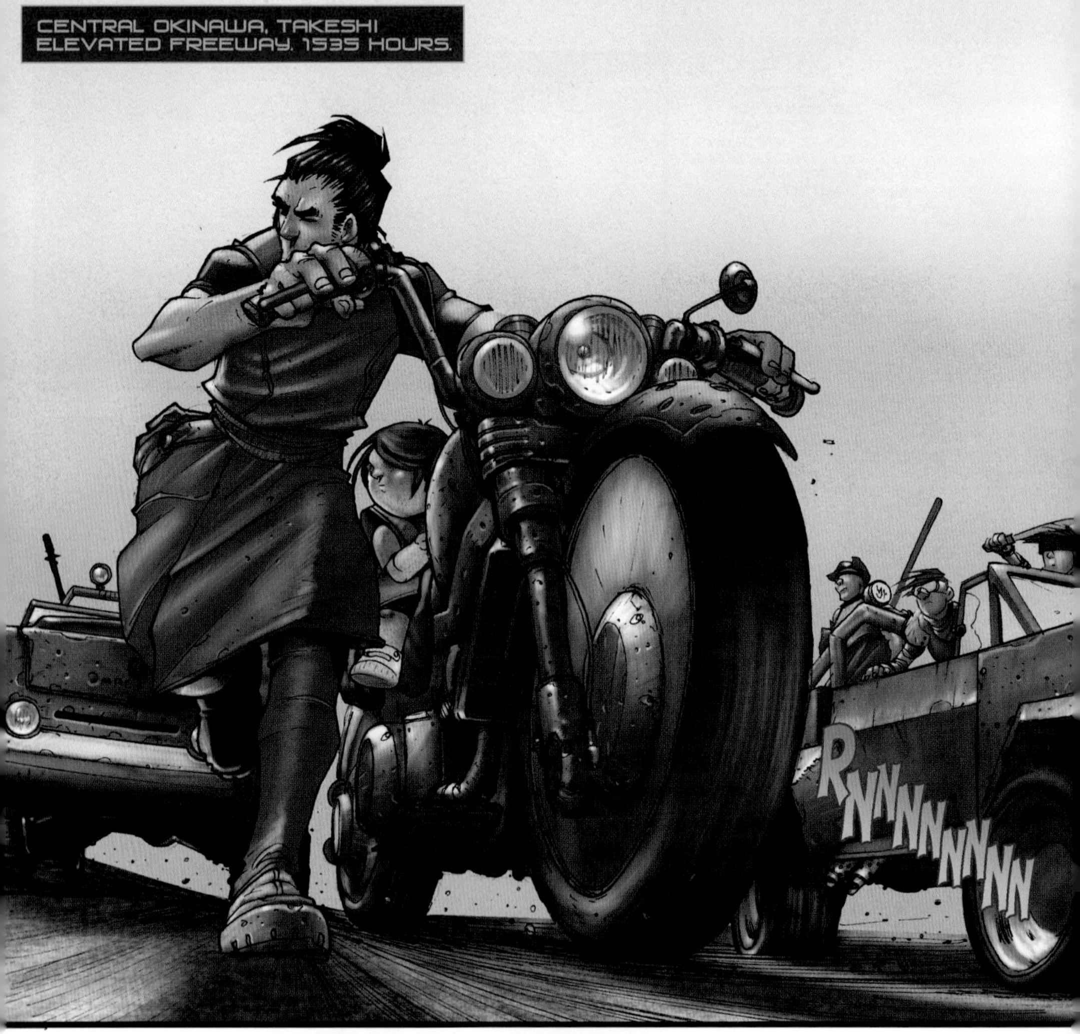
CENTRAL OKINAWA, TAKESHI ELEVATED FREEWAY. 1535 HOURS.
RNNNNNNNN

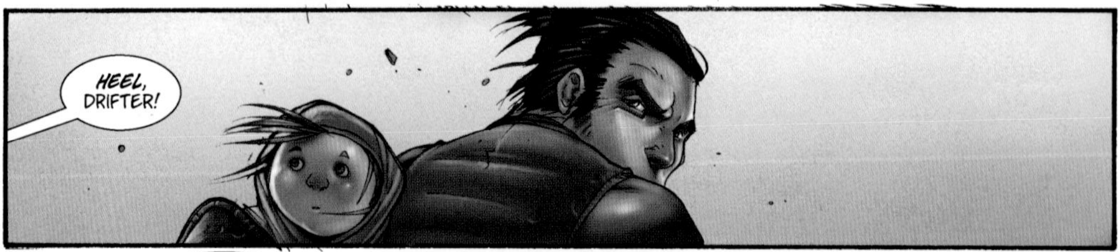
HEEL, DRIFTER!

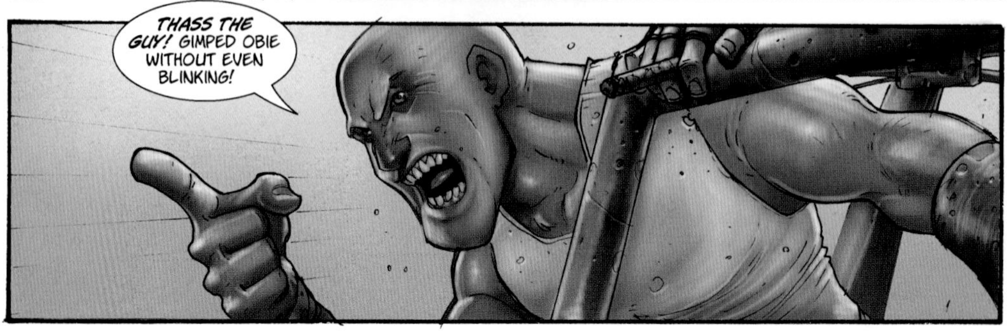
THASS THE GUY! GIMPED OBIE WITHOUT EVEN BLINKING!

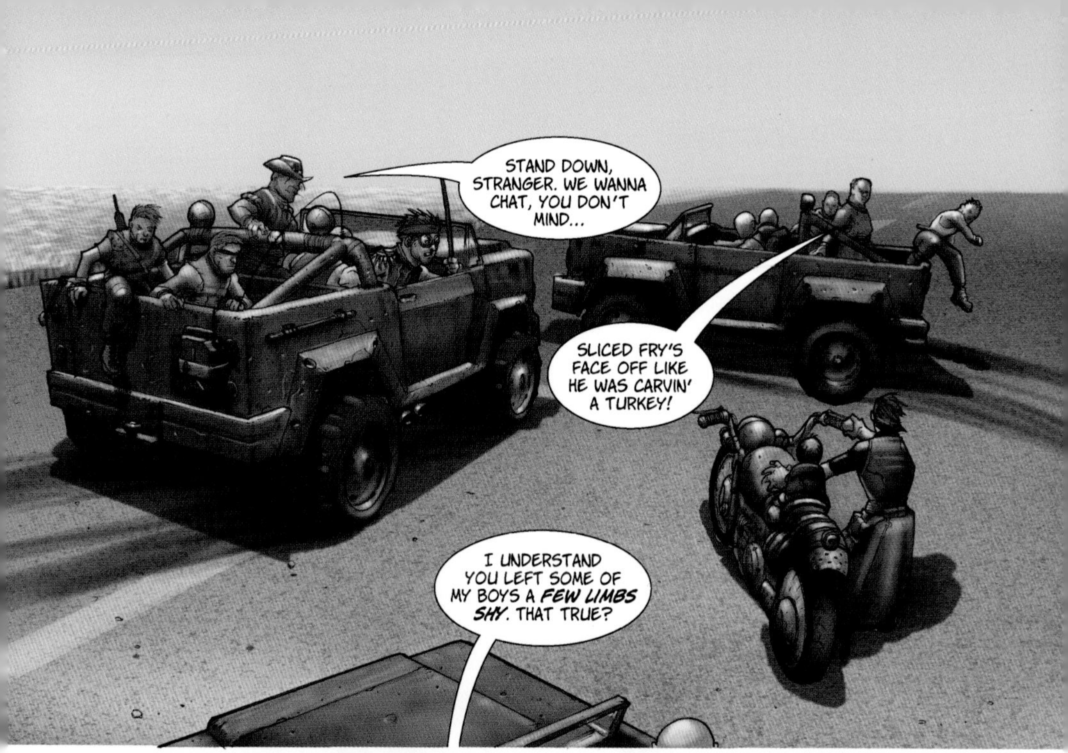
STAND DOWN, STRANGER. WE WANNA CHAT, YOU DON'T MIND...
SLICED FRY'S FACE OFF LIKE HE WAS CARVIN' A TURKEY!
I UNDERSTAND YOU LEFT SOME OF MY BOYS A *FEW LIMBS SHY*. THAT TRUE?

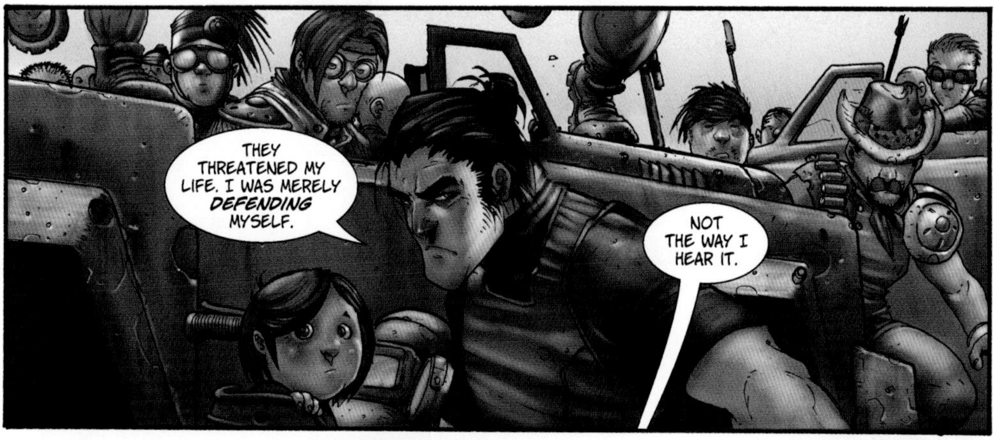
THEY THREATENED MY LIFE. I WAS MERELY *DEFENDING* MYSELF.
NOT THE WAY I HEAR IT.

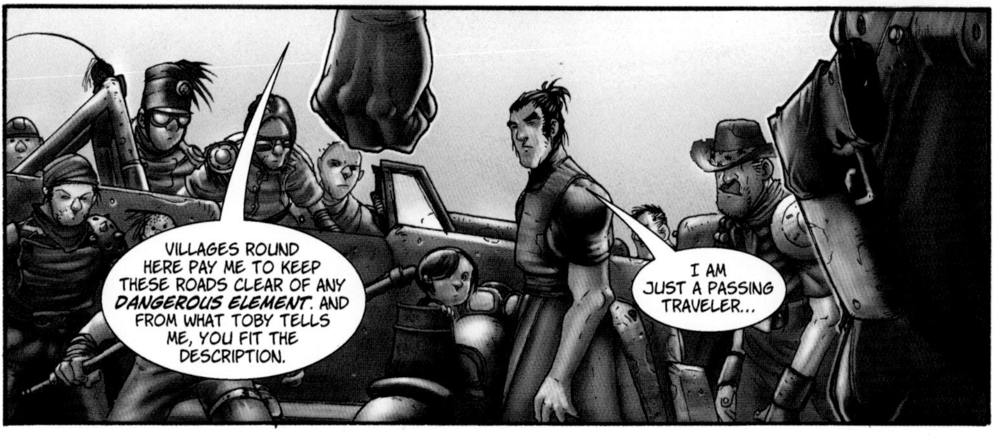
VILLAGES ROUND HERE PAY ME TO KEEP THESE ROADS CLEAR OF ANY *DANGEROUS ELEMENT*. AND FROM WHAT TOBY TELLS ME, YOU FIT THE DESCRIPTION.
I AM JUST A PASSING TRAVELER...

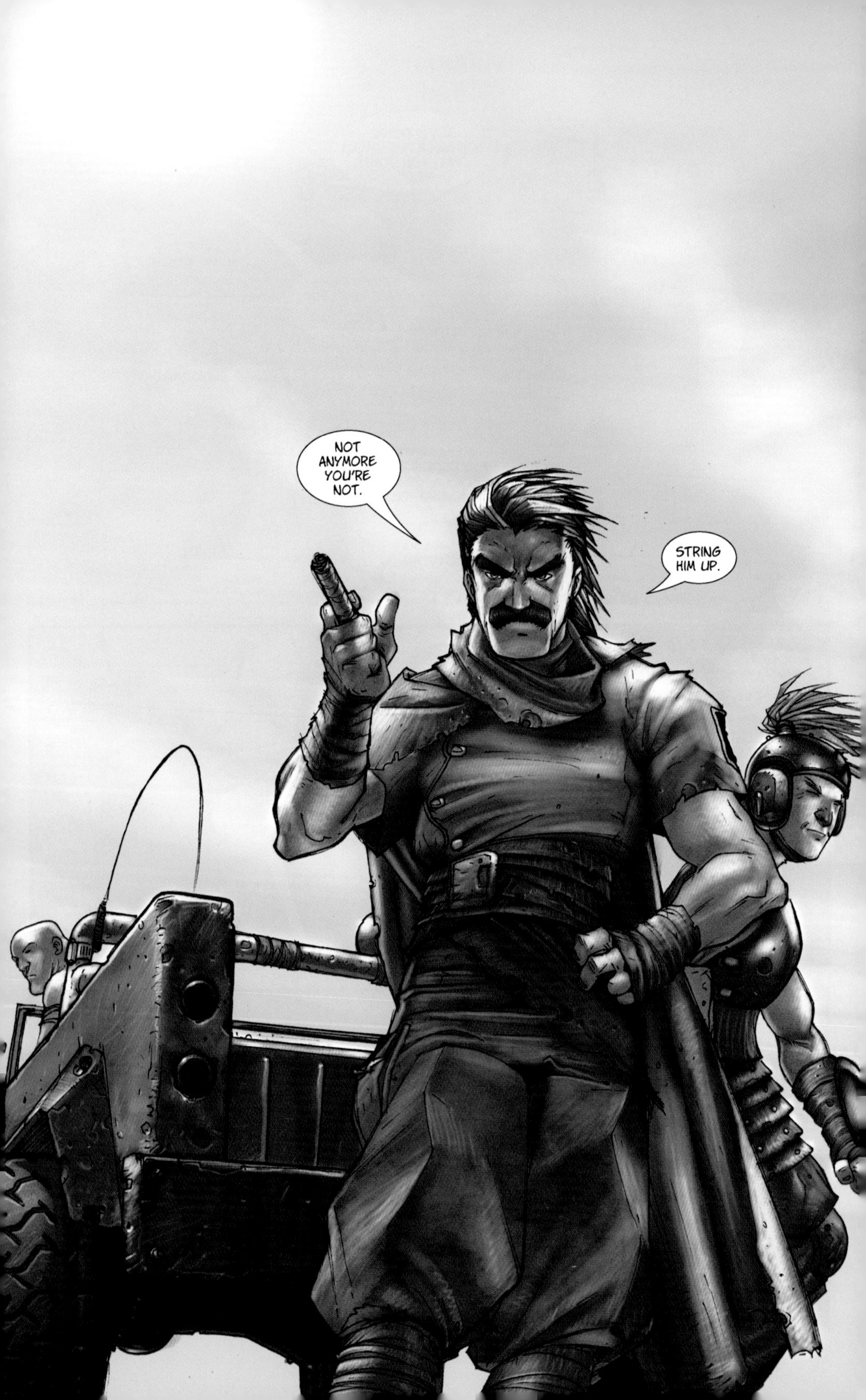
NOT ANYMORE YOU'RE NOT.
STRING HIM UP.

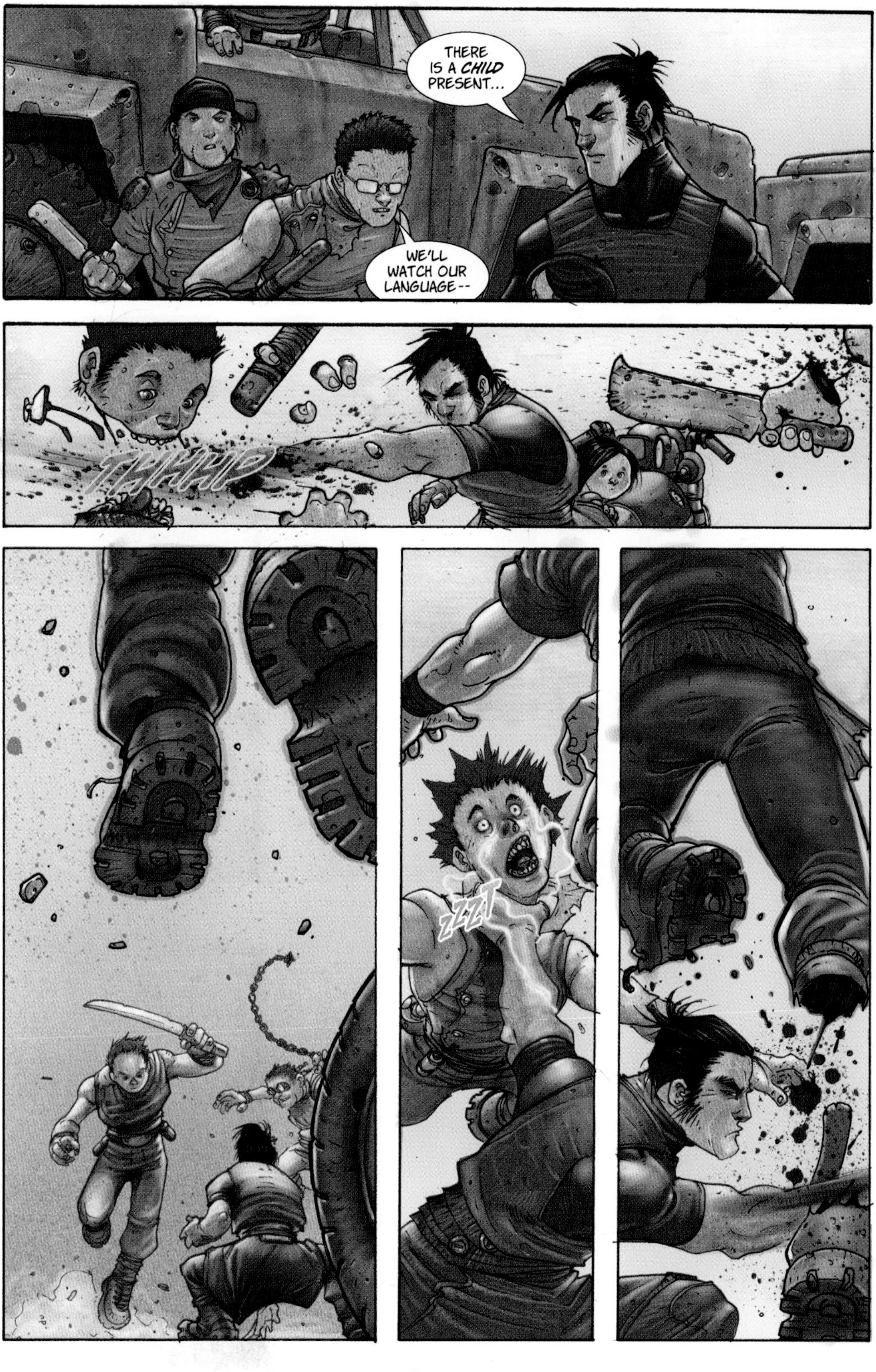
THERE IS A CHILD PRESENT...
WE'LL WATCH OUR LANGUAGE--
THHHP
ZZZT

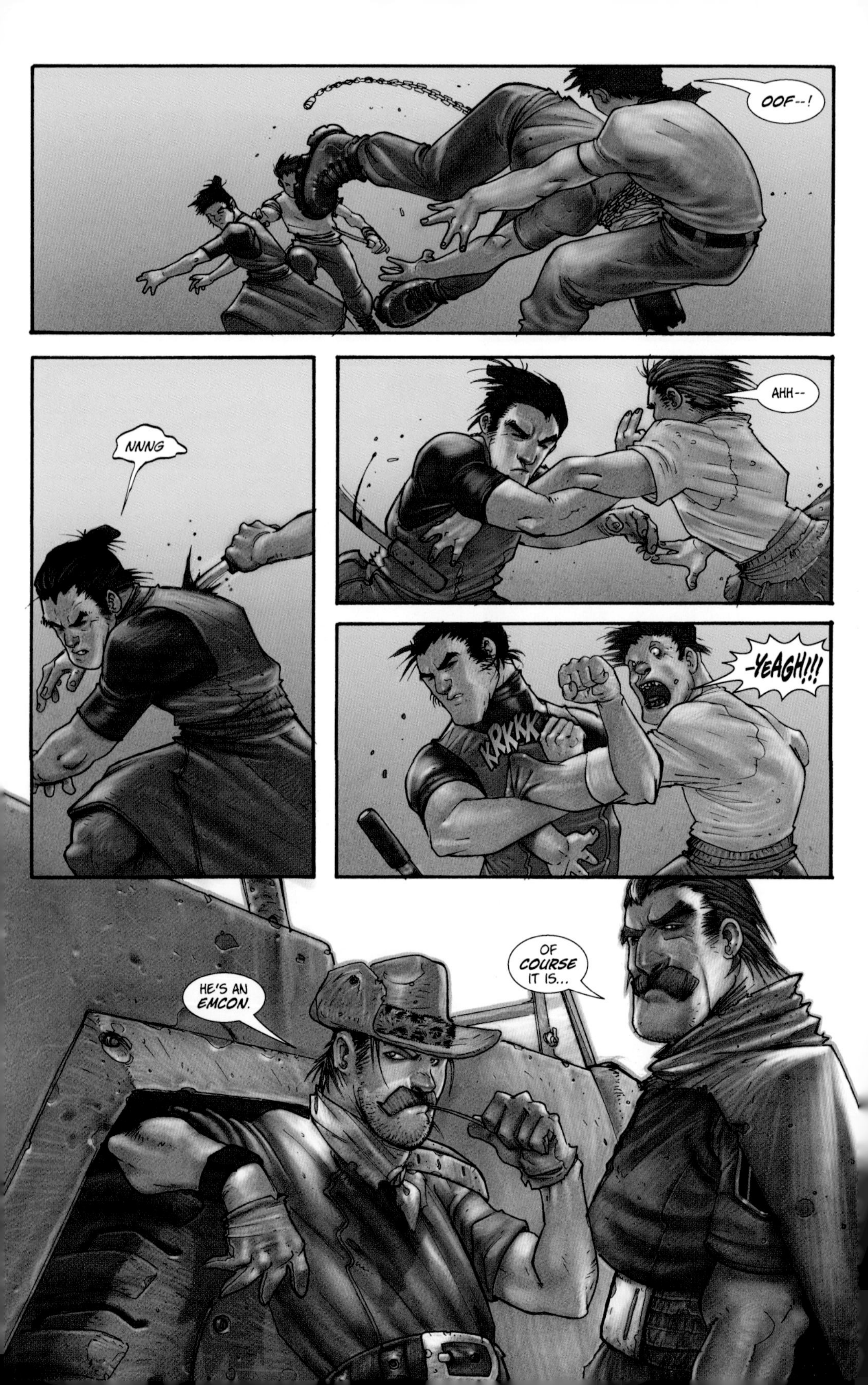
OOF--!
NNNG
AHH--
KRKKK
-YEAGH!!!
HE'S AN EMCON.
OF COURSE IT IS...

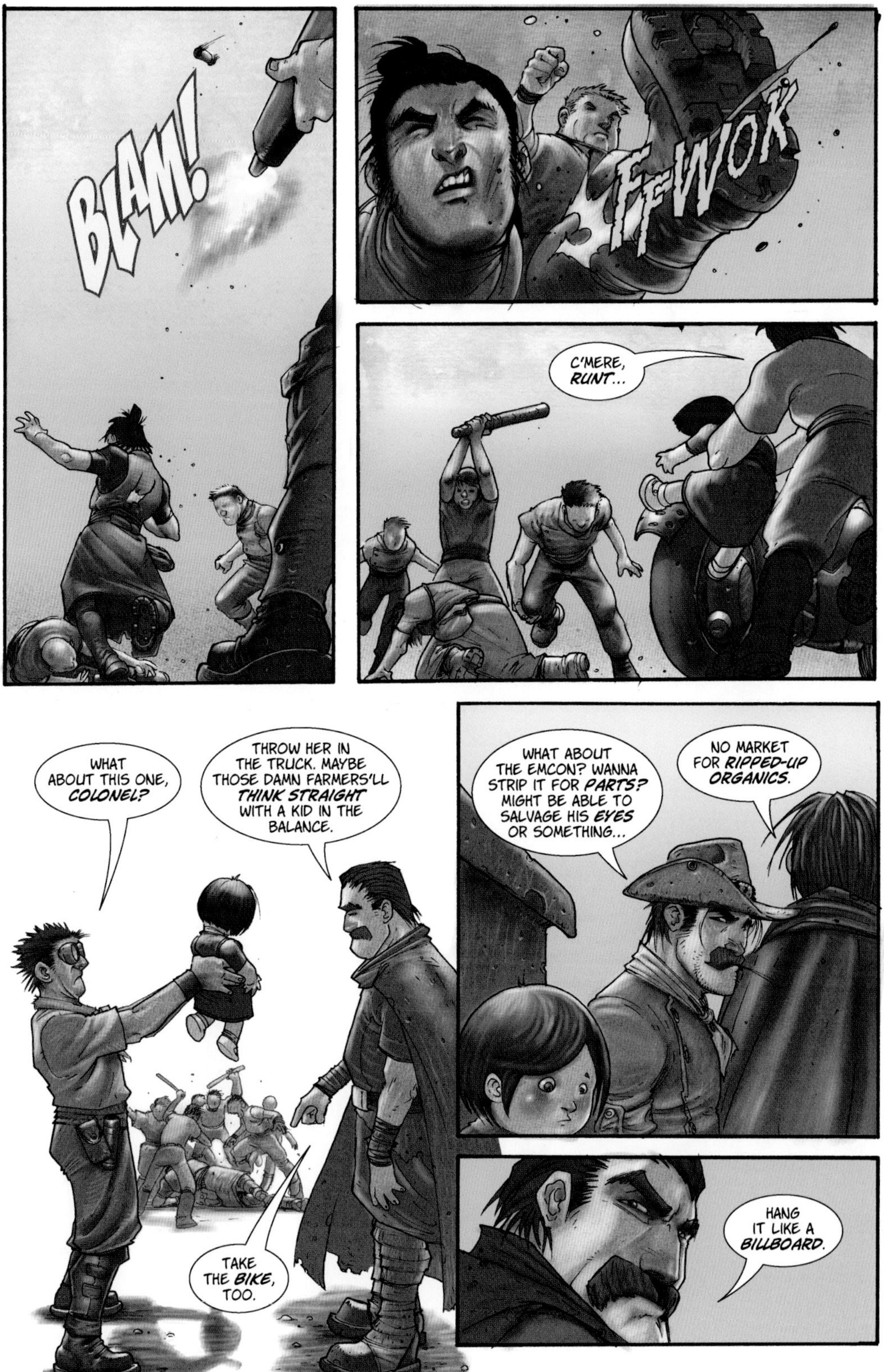
BLAM!
FF-WOK
C'MERE, RUNT...
WHAT ABOUT THIS ONE, COLONEL?
THROW HER IN THE TRUCK. MAYBE THOSE DAMN FARMERS'LL THINK STRAIGHT WITH A KID IN THE BALANCE.
TAKE THE BIKE, TOO.
WHAT ABOUT THE EMCON? WANNA STRIP IT FOR PARTS? MIGHT BE ABLE TO SALVAGE HIS EYES OR SOMETHING...
NO MARKET FOR RIPPED-UP ORGANICS.
HANG IT LIKE A BILLBOARD.

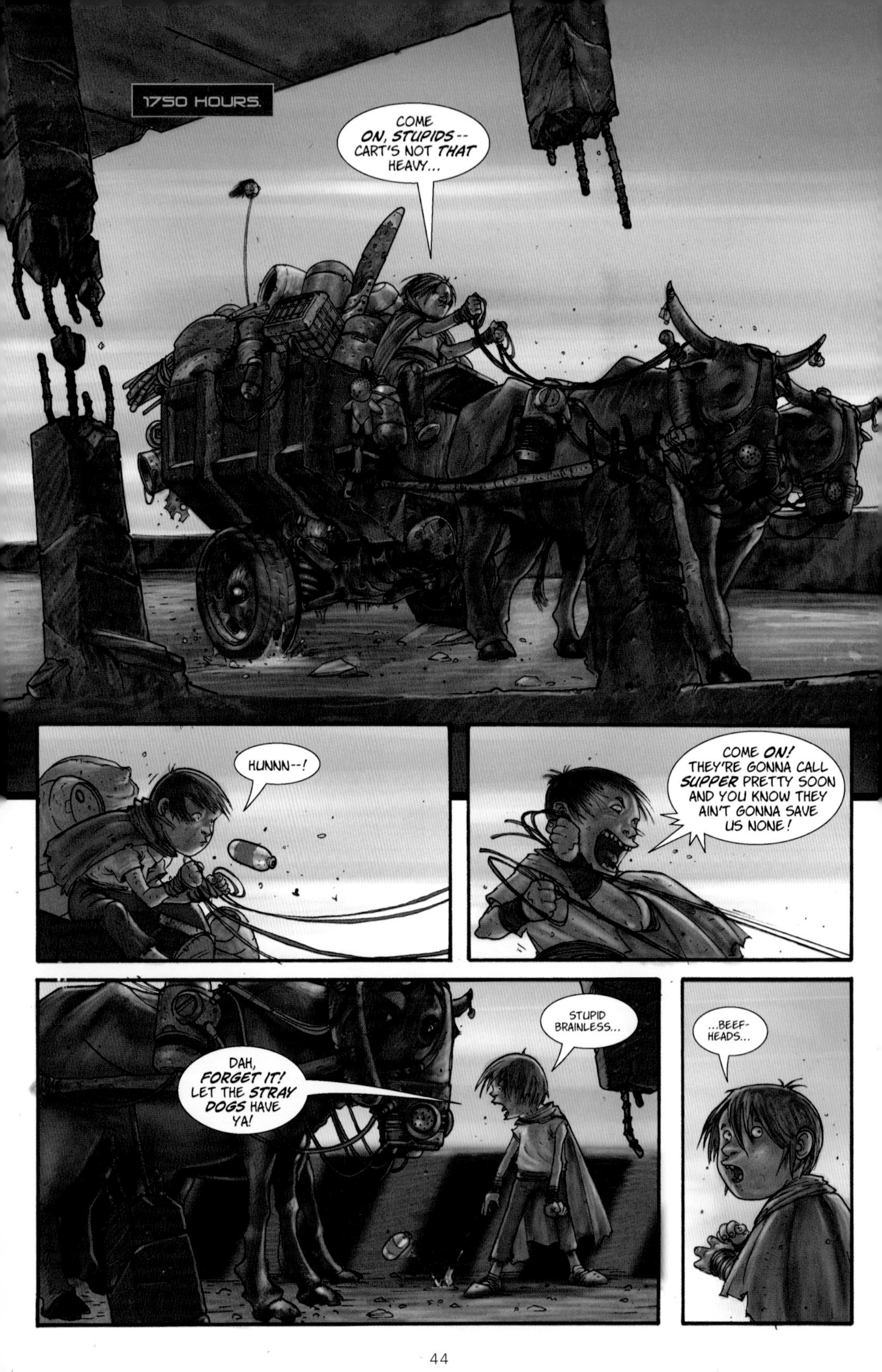
1750 HOURS.
COME ON, STUPIDS-- CART'S NOT THAT HEAVY...
HUNNN--!
COME ON! THEY'RE GONNA CALL SUPPER PRETTY SOON AND YOU KNOW THEY AIN'T GONNA SAVE US NONE!
DAH, FORGET IT! LET THE STRAY DOGS HAVE YA!
STUPID BRAINLESS...
...BEEF-HEADS...

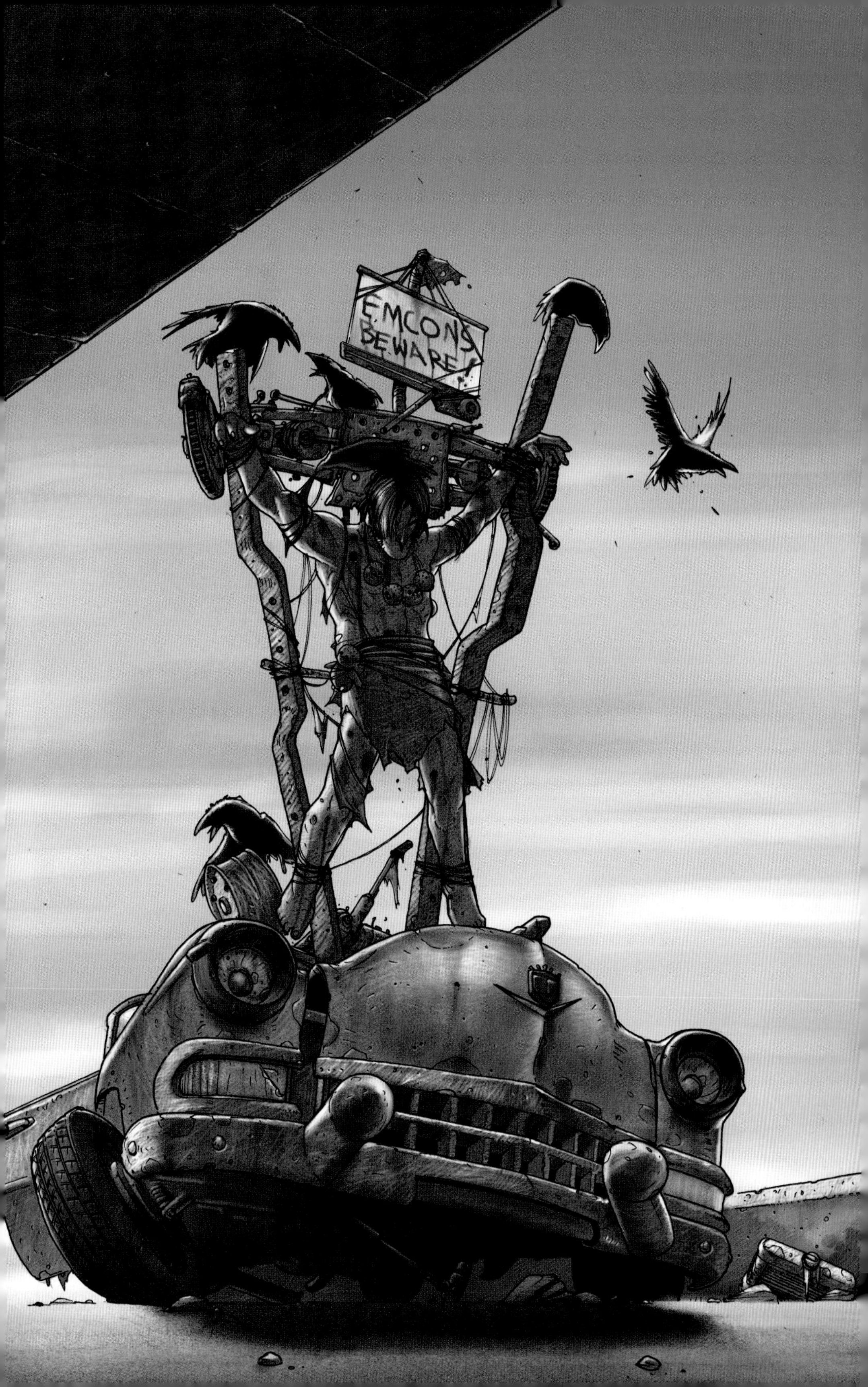
EMCONS
BEWARE!

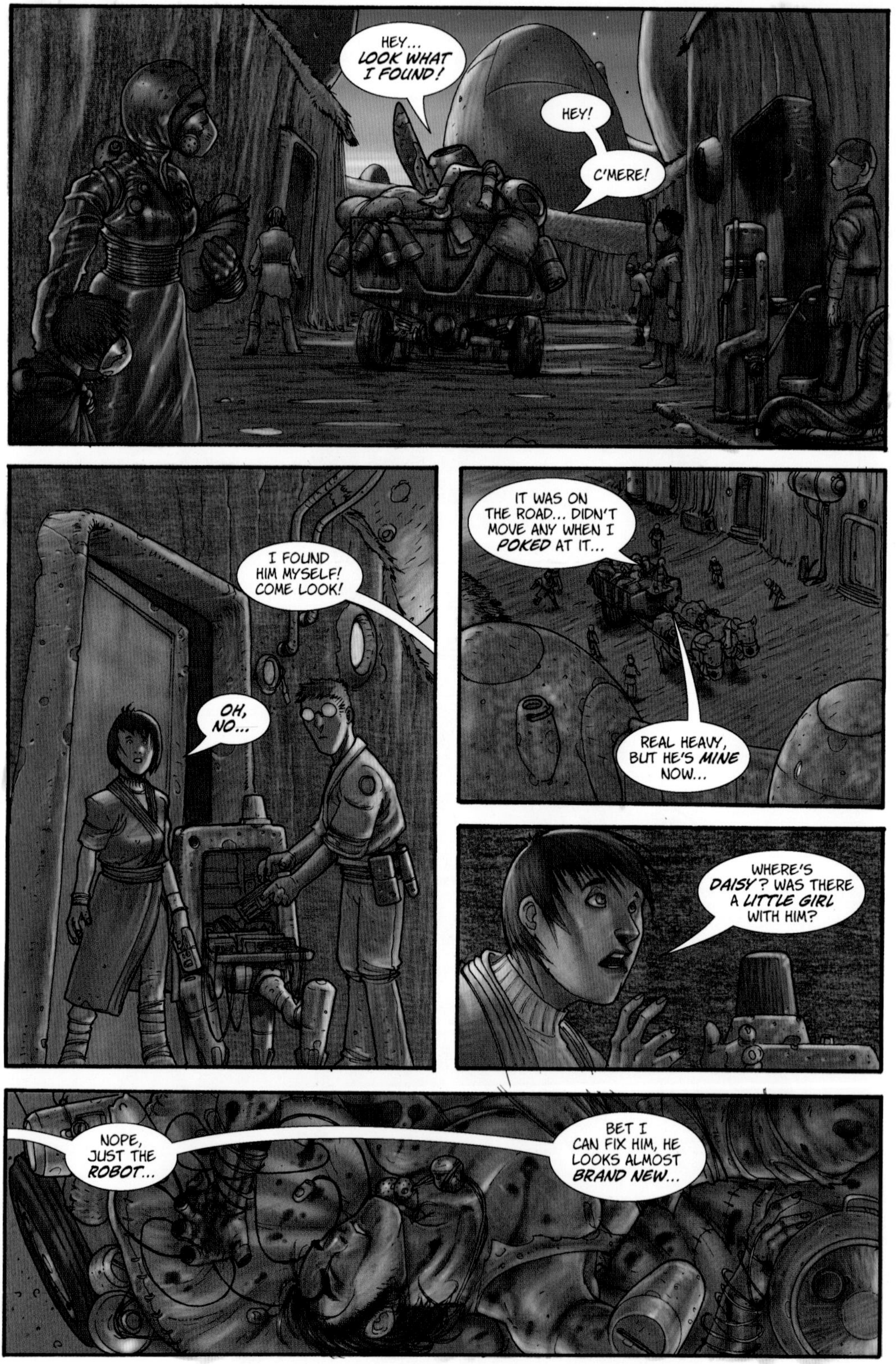
HEY... *LOOK WHAT I FOUND!*
HEY!
C'MERE!
I FOUND HIM MYSELF! COME LOOK!
IT WAS ON THE ROAD... DIDN'T MOVE ANY WHEN I *POKED* AT IT...
REAL HEAVY, BUT HE'S *MINE* NOW...
OH, NO...
WHERE'S *DAISY*? WAS THERE A *LITTLE GIRL* WITH HIM?
NOPE, JUST THE *ROBOT*...
BET I CAN FIX HIM, HE LOOKS ALMOST *BRAND NEW*...

...AND AS YOU CAN SEE, OUR MOST *ADVANCED MODEL* TO DATE.

EVEN THE *DEVELOPMENTAL PROCESS* ITSELF HAS BEEN STREAMLINED ENORMOUSLY.

WE ACHIEVED COMPLETE SKELETAL COVERAGE IN UNDER *10 DAYS.* THE *ENDODERMIC INVITRO GEL* WAS MIXED WITH A *PROTEIN ACCELERANT,* SHORTENING GESTATION BY ABOUT 6 DAYS.

STEER CLOSER TO *NUMBER FOUR,* PLEASE.

HOW HAS *BIO-ACCELERATION* AFFECTED *CORTICAL OCCLUSION* ?

ACTUALLY, WE'VE ALREADY STARTED PROGRAMMING THIS ONE. HE'S ABOUT *FORTY PERCENT FORMATTED,* AND ALREADY BUILDING UP A BUFFER OF *INPUT DATA.*

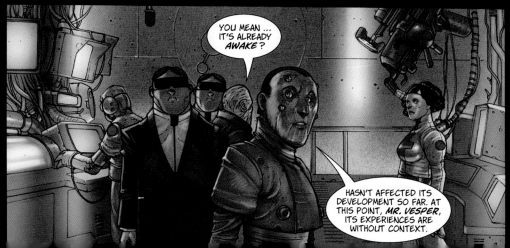

YOU MEAN ... IT'S ALREADY *AWAKE* ?

HASN'T AFFECTED ITS DEVELOPMENT SO FAR. AT THIS POINT, *MR. VESPER,* ITS EXPERIENCES ARE WITHOUT CONTEXT.

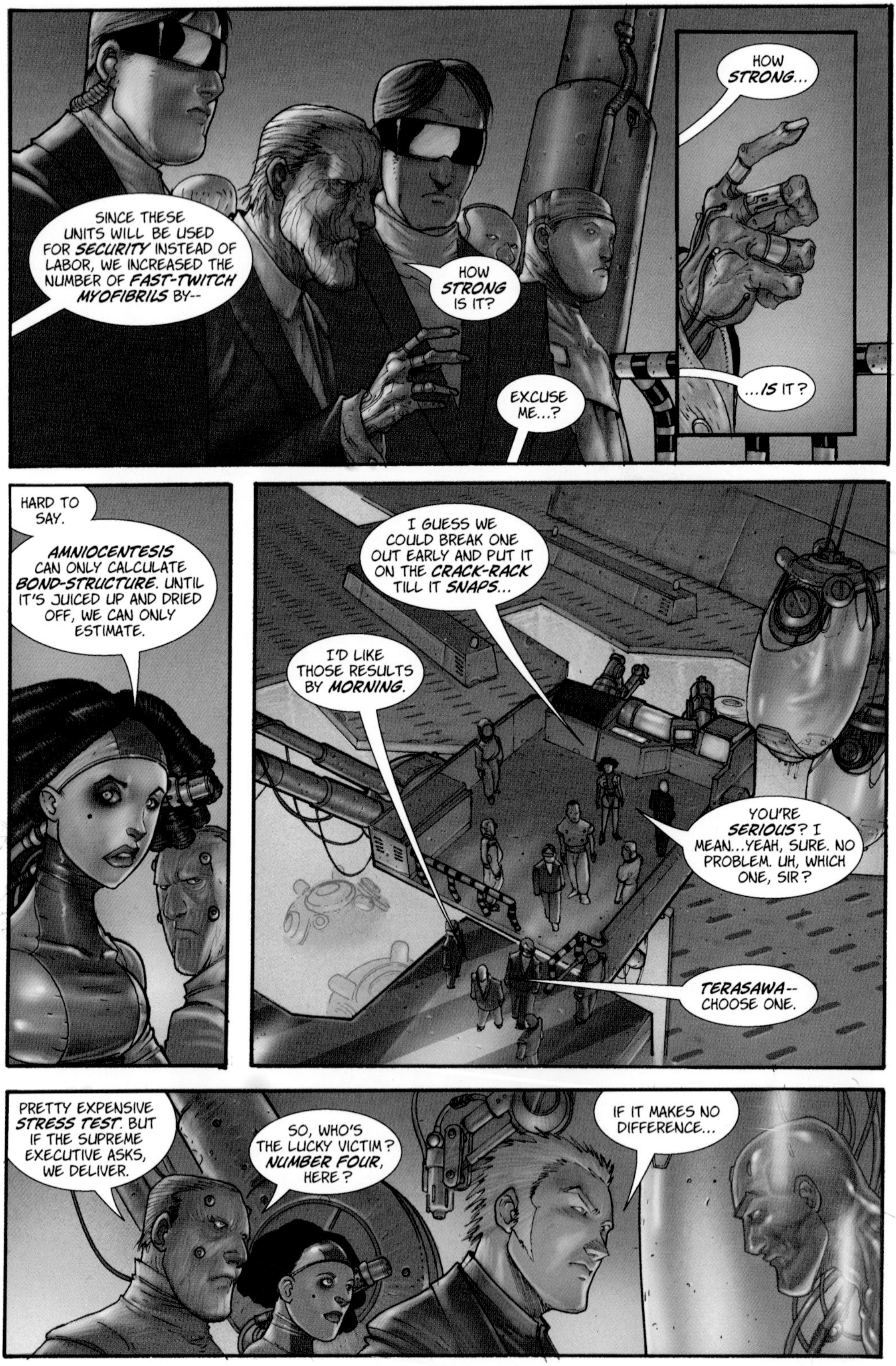
SINCE THESE UNITS WILL BE USED FOR SECURITY INSTEAD OF LABOR, WE INCREASED THE NUMBER OF FAST-TWITCH MYOFIBRILS BY--
HOW STRONG IS IT?
EXCUSE ME...?
HOW STRONG...
...IS IT?
HARD TO SAY.
AMNIOCENTESIS CAN ONLY CALCULATE BOND-STRUCTURE. UNTIL IT'S JUICED UP AND DRIED OFF, WE CAN ONLY ESTIMATE.
I GUESS WE COULD BREAK ONE OUT EARLY AND PUT IT ON THE CRACK-RACK TILL IT SNAPS...
I'D LIKE THOSE RESULTS BY MORNING.
YOU'RE SERIOUS? I MEAN...YEAH, SURE. NO PROBLEM. UH, WHICH ONE, SIR?
TERASAWA-- CHOOSE ONE.
PRETTY EXPENSIVE STRESS TEST. BUT IF THE SUPREME EXECUTIVE ASKS, WE DELIVER.
SO, WHO'S THE LUCKY VICTIM? NUMBER FOUR, HERE?
IF IT MAKES NO DIFFERENCE...

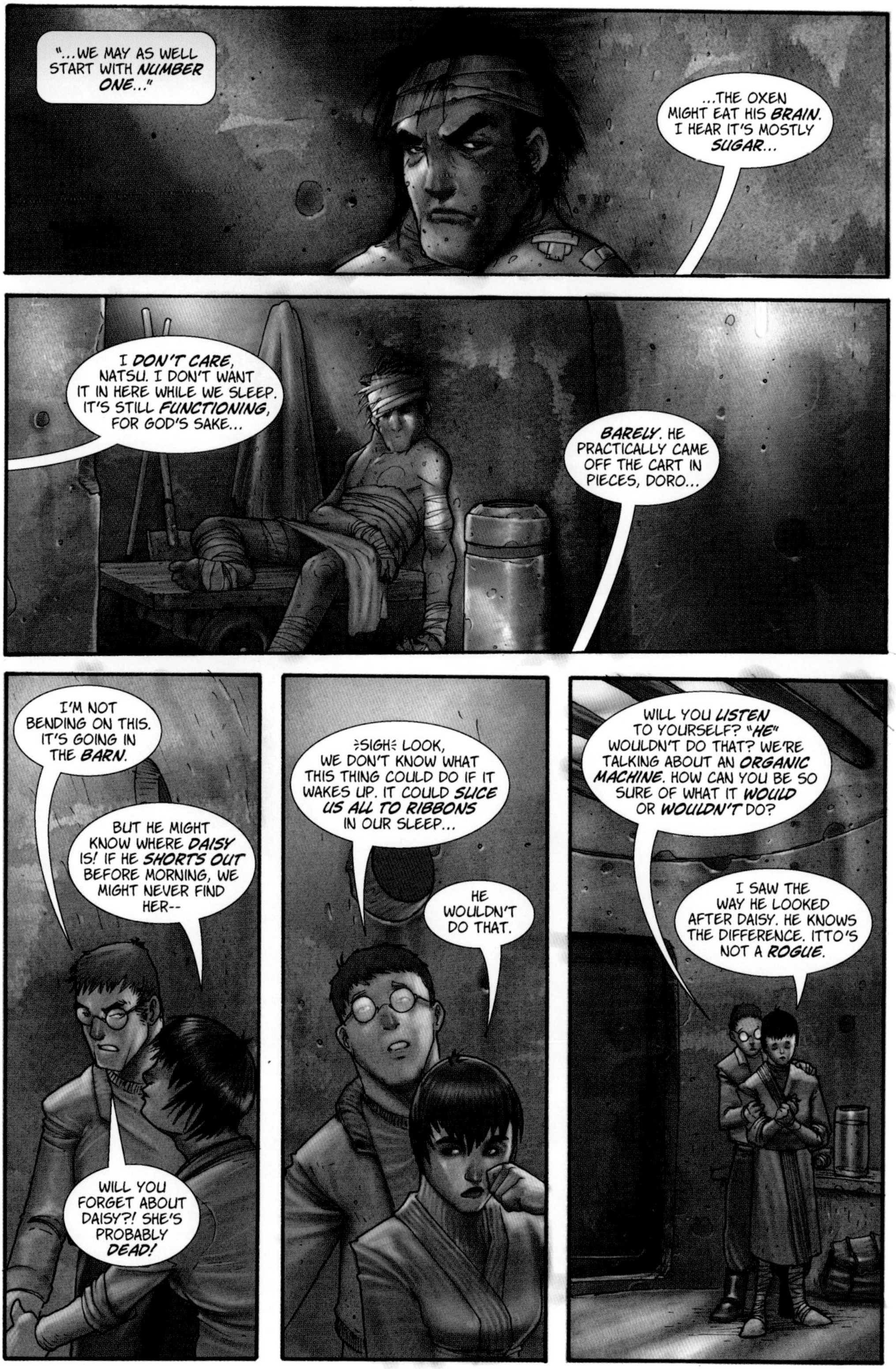
"...WE MAY AS WELL START WITH NUMBER ONE..."
...THE OXEN MIGHT EAT HIS BRAIN. I HEAR IT'S MOSTLY SUGAR...
I DON'T CARE, NATSU. I DON'T WANT IT IN HERE WHILE WE SLEEP. IT'S STILL FUNCTIONING, FOR GOD'S SAKE...
BARELY. HE PRACTICALLY CAME OFF THE CART IN PIECES, DORO...
I'M NOT BENDING ON THIS. IT'S GOING IN THE BARN.
BUT HE MIGHT KNOW WHERE DAISY IS! IF HE SHORTS OUT BEFORE MORNING, WE MIGHT NEVER FIND HER--
WILL YOU FORGET ABOUT DAISY?! SHE'S PROBABLY DEAD!
SIGH LOOK, WE DON'T KNOW WHAT THIS THING COULD DO IF IT WAKES UP. IT COULD SLICE US ALL TO RIBBONS IN OUR SLEEP...
HE WOULDN'T DO THAT.
WILL YOU LISTEN TO YOURSELF? "HE" WOULDN'T DO THAT? WE'RE TALKING ABOUT AN ORGANIC MACHINE. HOW CAN YOU BE SO SURE OF WHAT IT WOULD OR WOULDN'T DO?
I SAW THE WAY HE LOOKED AFTER DAISY. HE KNOWS THE DIFFERENCE. ITTO'S NOT A ROGUE.

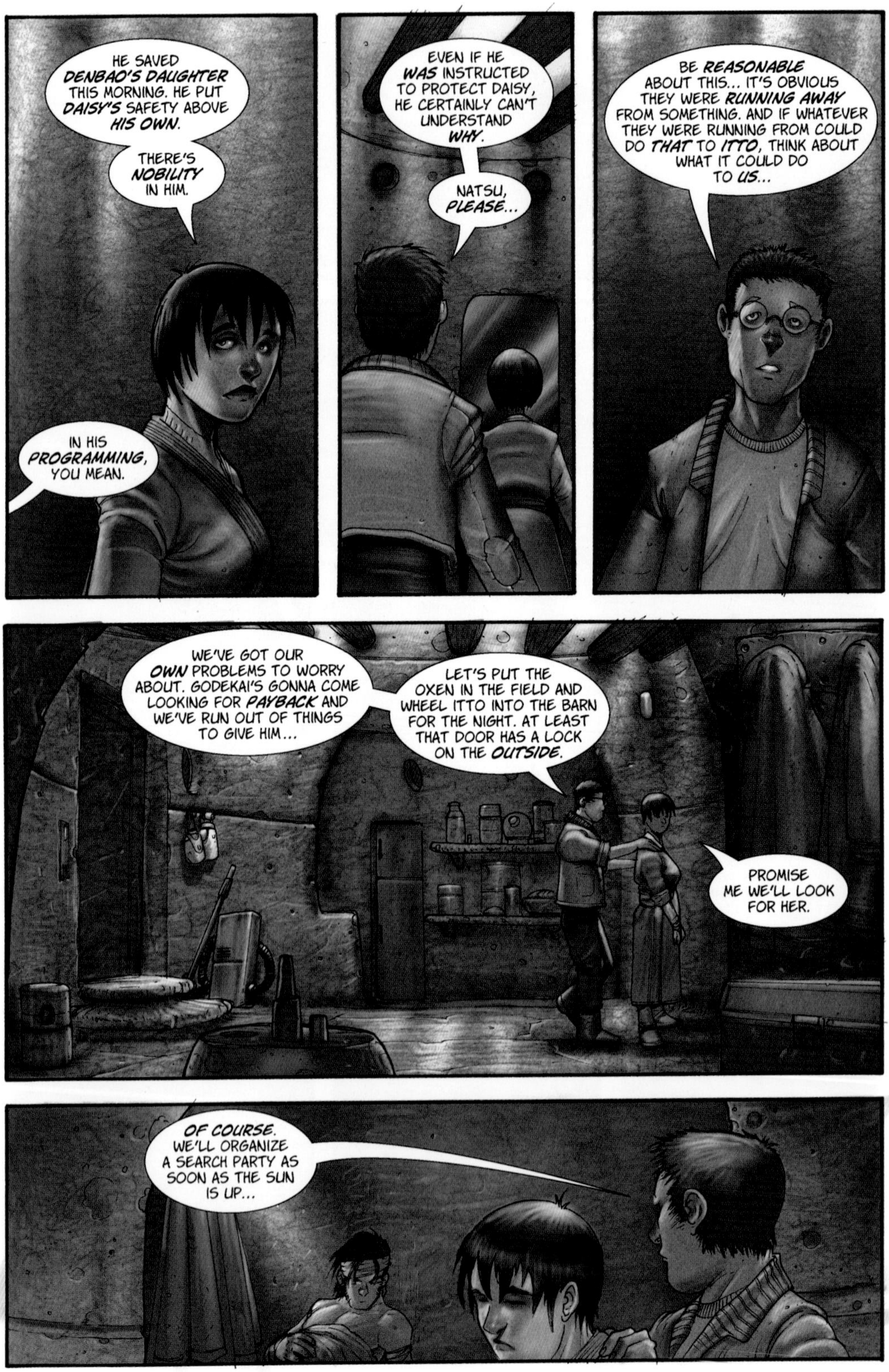
HE SAVED DENBAO'S DAUGHTER THIS MORNING. HE PUT DAISY'S SAFETY ABOVE HIS OWN.
THERE'S NOBILITY IN HIM.
IN HIS PROGRAMMING, YOU MEAN.
EVEN IF HE WAS INSTRUCTED TO PROTECT DAISY, HE CERTAINLY CAN'T UNDERSTAND WHY.
NATSU, PLEASE...
BE REASONABLE ABOUT THIS... IT'S OBVIOUS THEY WERE RUNNING AWAY FROM SOMETHING. AND IF WHATEVER THEY WERE RUNNING FROM COULD DO THAT TO ITTO, THINK ABOUT WHAT IT COULD DO TO US...
WE'VE GOT OUR OWN PROBLEMS TO WORRY ABOUT. GODEKAI'S GONNA COME LOOKING FOR PAYBACK AND WE'VE RUN OUT OF THINGS TO GIVE HIM...
LET'S PUT THE OXEN IN THE FIELD AND WHEEL ITTO INTO THE BARN FOR THE NIGHT. AT LEAST THAT DOOR HAS A LOCK ON THE OUTSIDE.
PROMISE ME WE'LL LOOK FOR HER.
OF COURSE. WE'LL ORGANIZE A SEARCH PARTY AS SOON AS THE SUN IS UP...

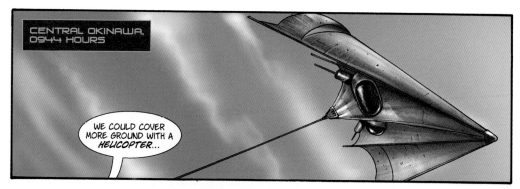

WE COULD COVER MORE GROUND WITH A *HELICOPTER*...

EMCONS CAN ONLY AVOID DETECTION IF THEY *KNOW* THEY'RE BEING *WATCHED*... WOULD I BE ABLE TO TRACK *YOU* DOWN IN A HELICOPTER?

GOOD POINT.

BUT YOU THINK YOU CAN FIND HIM WITH THIS *TOY*?

THIS *"TOY"* COST MORE THAN YOUR WHOLE *RESPIRATORY SYSTEM*.

THE CAMERAS COVER *SO DIFFERENT SPECTRAL BANDS* AND I'VE GOT A DOZEN *DIFFERENT SIGNATURES* TO LOOK FOR. I'LL FIND HIM.

WHY NOT CANVAS THE REGION WITH *SURVEILLANCE DUMMIES*? OR CALL IN YOUR INFAMOUS *"VAPOR FIST"*...?

INPUT NOTED, AND REJECTED. NOW IF YOUR VOICE BOX HAS A SWITCH, I'D APPRECIATE YOU *SHUTTING IT OFF.*

HMM.

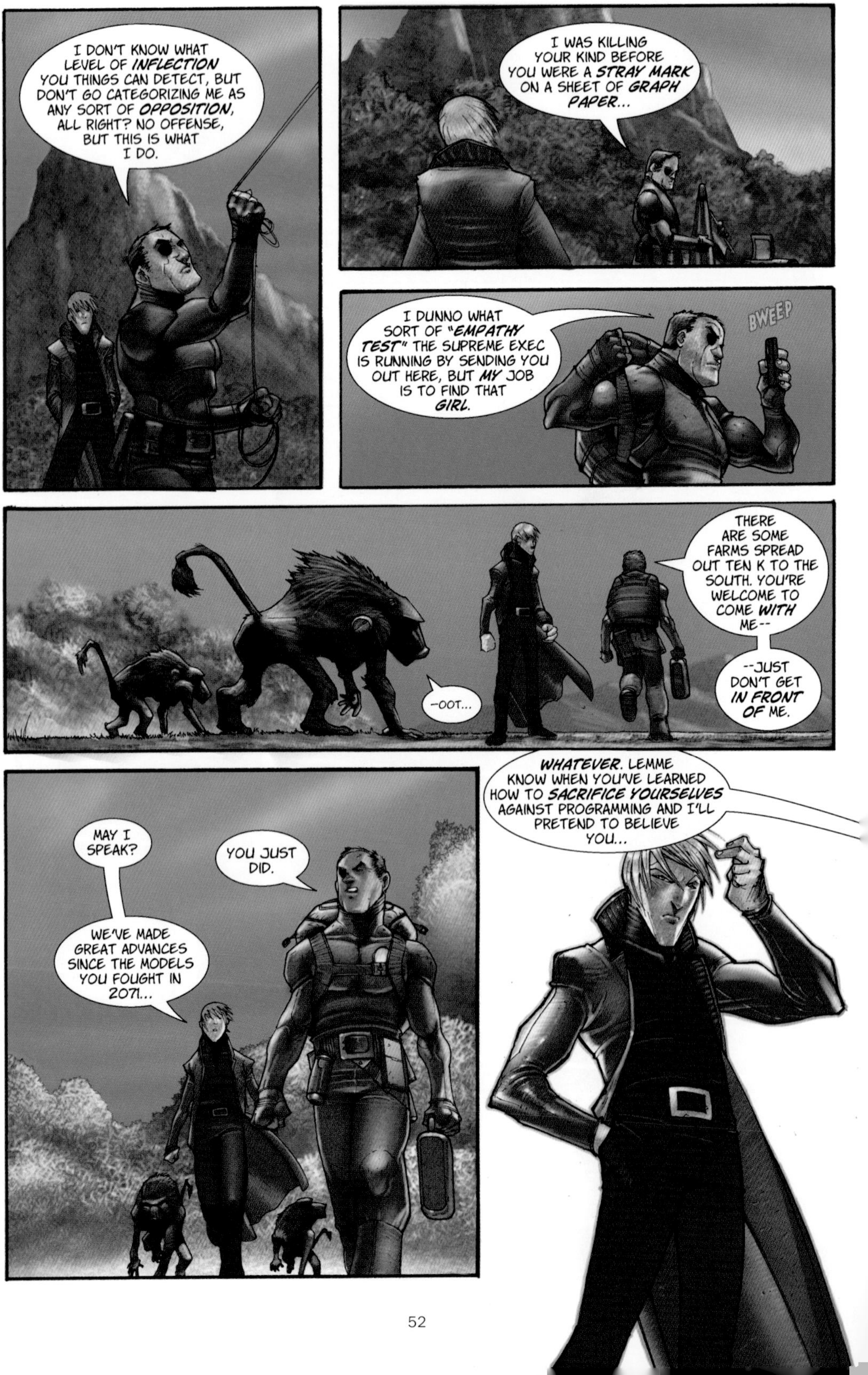
I DON'T KNOW WHAT LEVEL OF INFLECTION YOU THINGS CAN DETECT, BUT DON'T GO CATEGORIZING ME AS ANY SORT OF OPPOSITION, ALL RIGHT? NO OFFENSE, BUT THIS IS WHAT I DO.
I WAS KILLING YOUR KIND BEFORE YOU WERE A STRAY MARK ON A SHEET OF GRAPH PAPER...
I DUNNO WHAT SORT OF "EMPATHY TEST" THE SUPREME EXEC IS RUNNING BY SENDING YOU OUT HERE, BUT MY JOB IS TO FIND THAT GIRL.
BWEEP
THERE ARE SOME FARMS SPREAD OUT TEN K TO THE SOUTH. YOU'RE WELCOME TO COME WITH ME--
--JUST DON'T GET IN FRONT OF ME.
-OOT...
MAY I SPEAK?
YOU JUST DID.
WE'VE MADE GREAT ADVANCES SINCE THE MODELS YOU FOUGHT IN 2071...
WHATEVER. LEMME KNOW WHEN YOU'VE LEARNED HOW TO SACRIFICE YOURSELVES AGAINST PROGRAMMING AND I'LL PRETEND TO BELIEVE YOU...

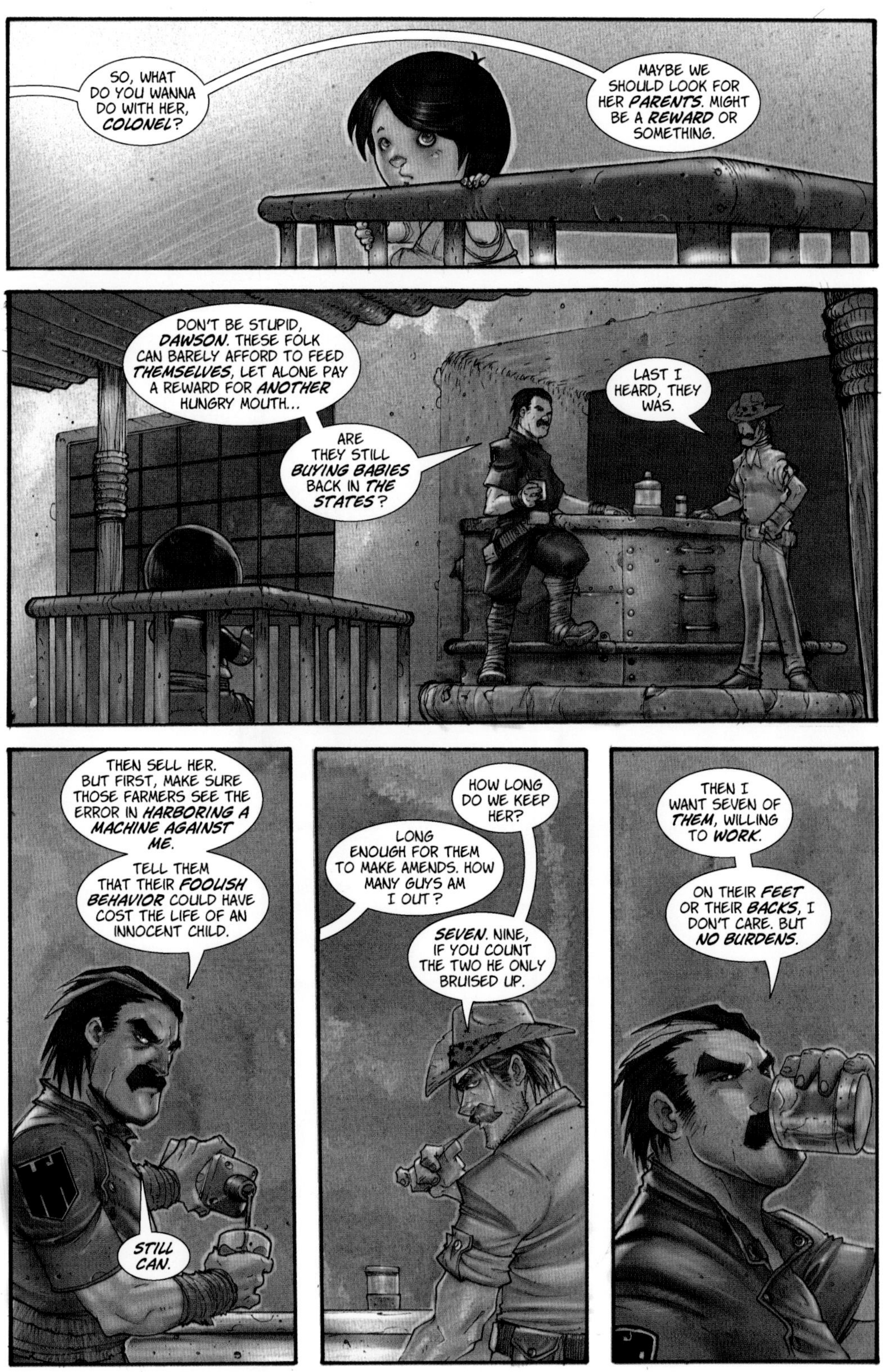
SO, WHAT DO YOU WANNA DO WITH HER, COLONEL?
MAYBE WE SHOULD LOOK FOR HER PARENTS. MIGHT BE A REWARD OR SOMETHING.
DON'T BE STUPID, DAWSON. THESE FOLK CAN BARELY AFFORD TO FEED THEMSELVES, LET ALONE PAY A REWARD FOR ANOTHER HUNGRY MOUTH...
ARE THEY STILL BUYING BABIES BACK IN THE STATES?
LAST I HEARD, THEY WAS.
THEN SELL HER. BUT FIRST, MAKE SURE THOSE FARMERS SEE THE ERROR IN HARBORING A MACHINE AGAINST ME.
TELL THEM THAT THEIR FOOLISH BEHAVIOR COULD HAVE COST THE LIFE OF AN INNOCENT CHILD.
STILL CAN.
HOW LONG DO WE KEEP HER?
LONG ENOUGH FOR THEM TO MAKE AMENDS. HOW MANY GUYS AM I OUT?
SEVEN. NINE, IF YOU COUNT THE TWO HE ONLY BRUISED UP.
THEN I WANT SEVEN OF THEM, WILLING TO WORK.
ON THEIR FEET OR THEIR BACKS, I DON'T CARE. BUT NO BURDENS.

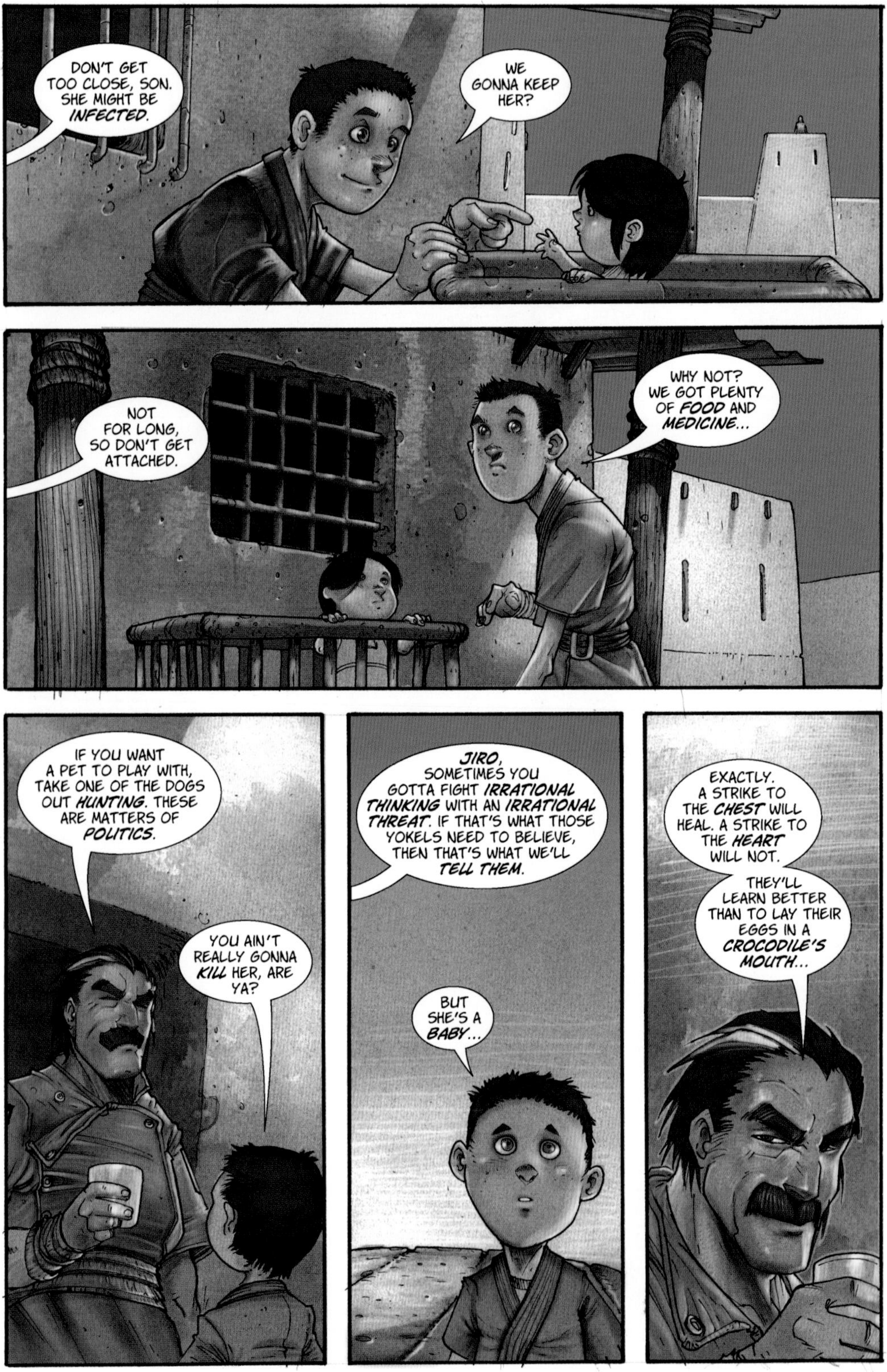
DON'T GET TOO CLOSE, SON. SHE MIGHT BE INFECTED.
WE GONNA KEEP HER?
NOT FOR LONG, SO DON'T GET ATTACHED.
WHY NOT? WE GOT PLENTY OF FOOD AND MEDICINE...
IF YOU WANT A PET TO PLAY WITH, TAKE ONE OF THE DOGS OUT HUNTING. THESE ARE MATTERS OF POLITICS.
YOU AIN'T REALLY GONNA KILL HER, ARE YA?
JIRO, SOMETIMES YOU GOTTA FIGHT IRRATIONAL THINKING WITH AN IRRATIONAL THREAT. IF THAT'S WHAT THOSE YOKELS NEED TO BELIEVE, THEN THAT'S WHAT WE'LL TELL THEM.
BUT SHE'S A BABY...
EXACTLY. A STRIKE TO THE CHEST WILL HEAL. A STRIKE TO THE HEART WILL NOT.
THEY'LL LEARN BETTER THAN TO LAY THEIR EGGS IN A CROCODILE'S MOUTH...

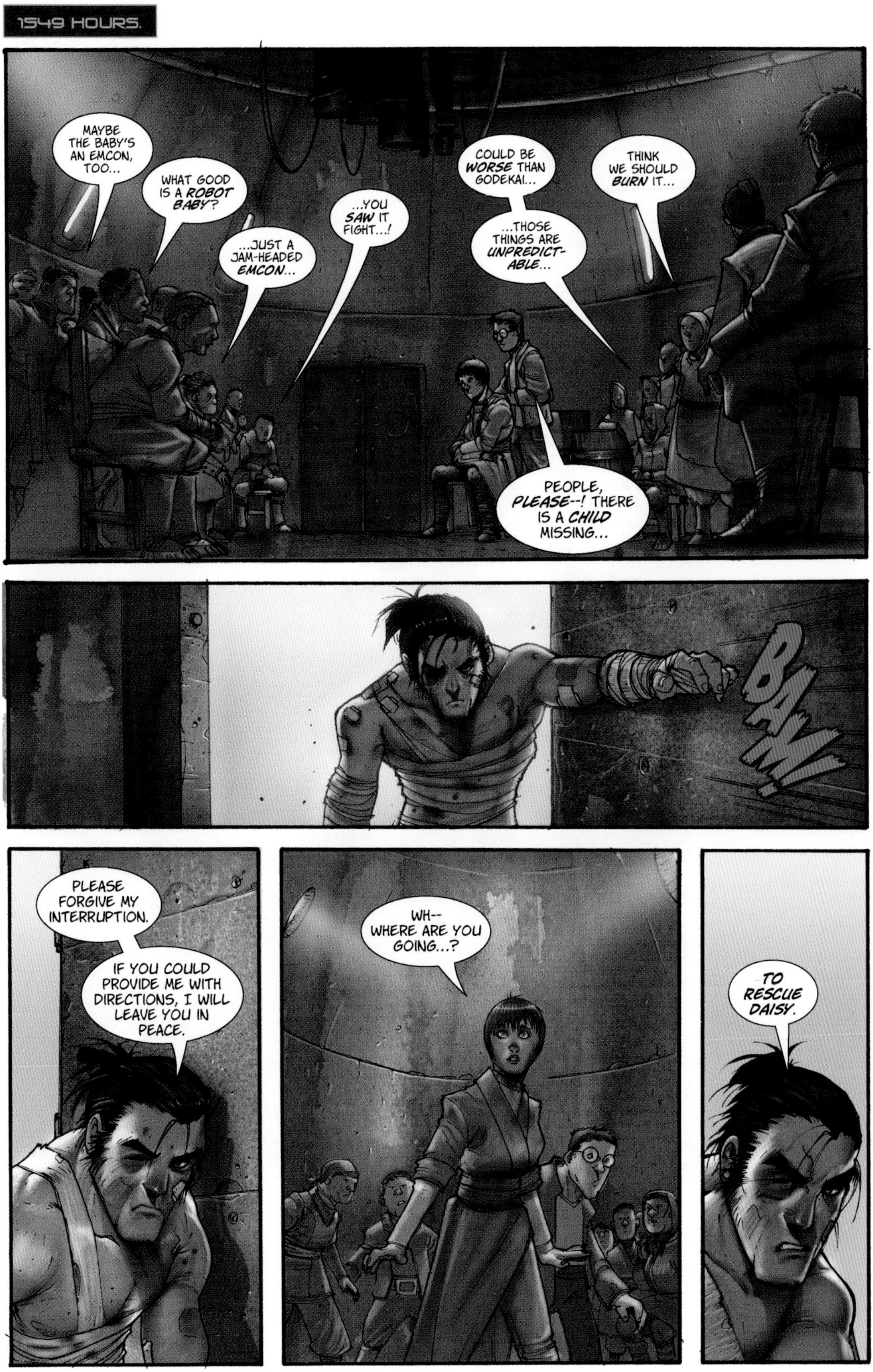
1549 HOURS.
MAYBE THE BABY'S AN EMCON, TOO...
WHAT GOOD IS A ROBOT BABY?
...JUST A JAM-HEADED EMCON...
...YOU SAW IT FIGHT...!
COULD BE WORSE THAN GODEKAI...
...THOSE THINGS ARE UNPREDICT-ABLE...
THINK WE SHOULD BURN IT...
PEOPLE, PLEASE--! THERE IS A CHILD MISSING...
BAM!
PLEASE FORGIVE MY INTERRUPTION.
IF YOU COULD PROVIDE ME WITH DIRECTIONS, I WILL LEAVE YOU IN PEACE.
WH-- WHERE ARE YOU GOING...?
TO RESCUE DAISY.

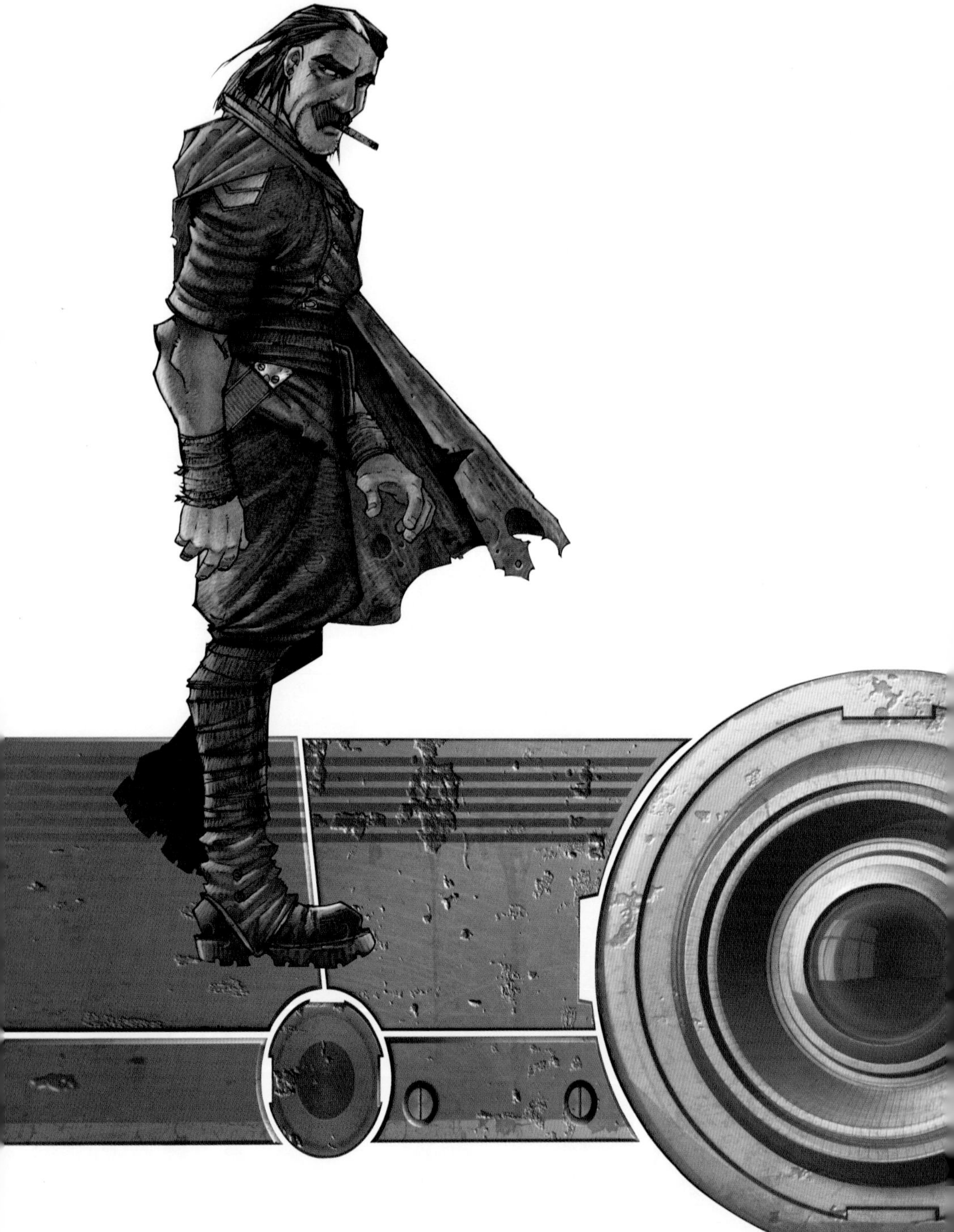

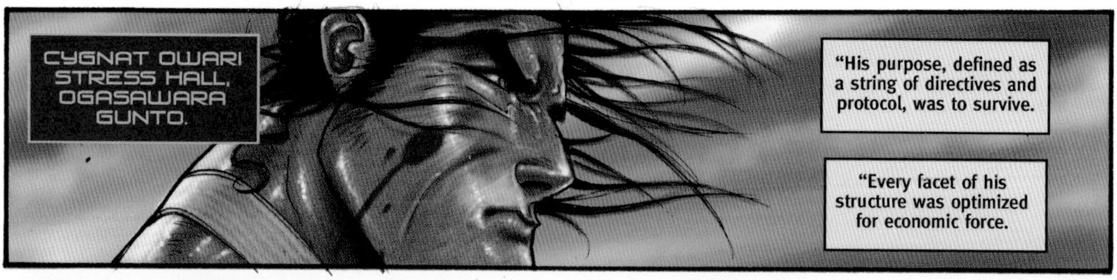
CYGNAT OWARI STRESS HALL, OGASAWARA GUNTO.
"His purpose, defined as a string of directives and protocol, was to survive.
"Every facet of his structure was optimized for economic force.

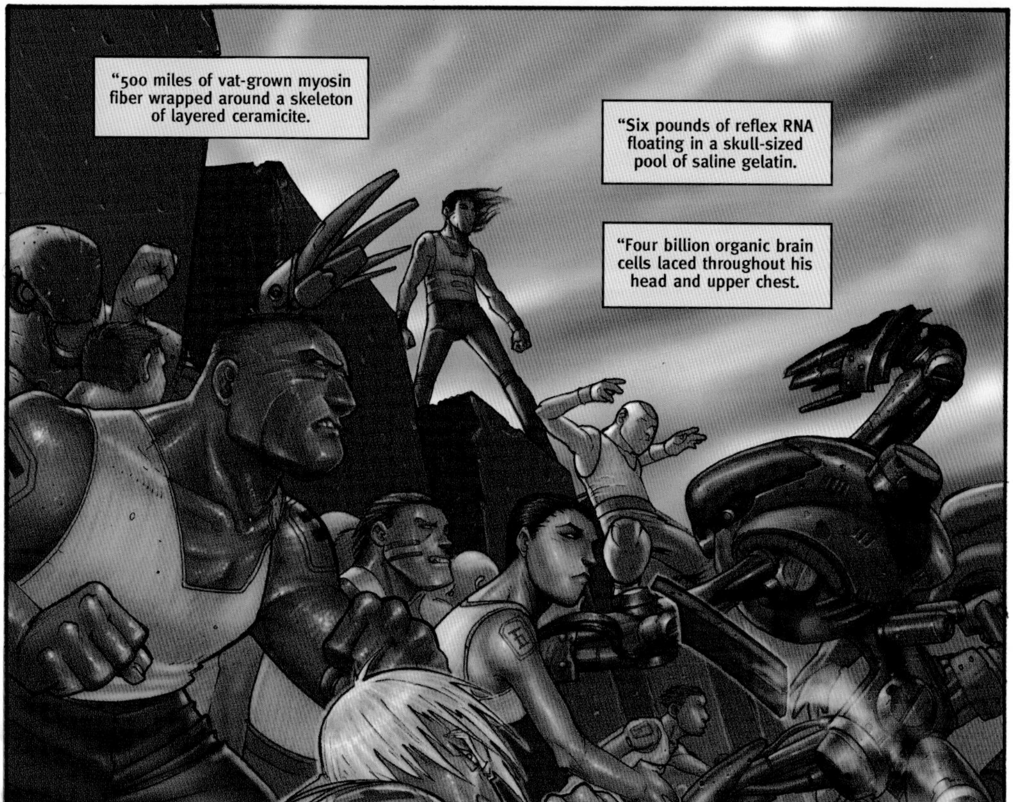
"500 miles of vat-grown myosin fiber wrapped around a skeleton of layered ceramicite.
"Six pounds of reflex RNA floating in a skull-sized pool of saline gelatin.
"Four billion organic brain cells laced throughout his head and upper chest.

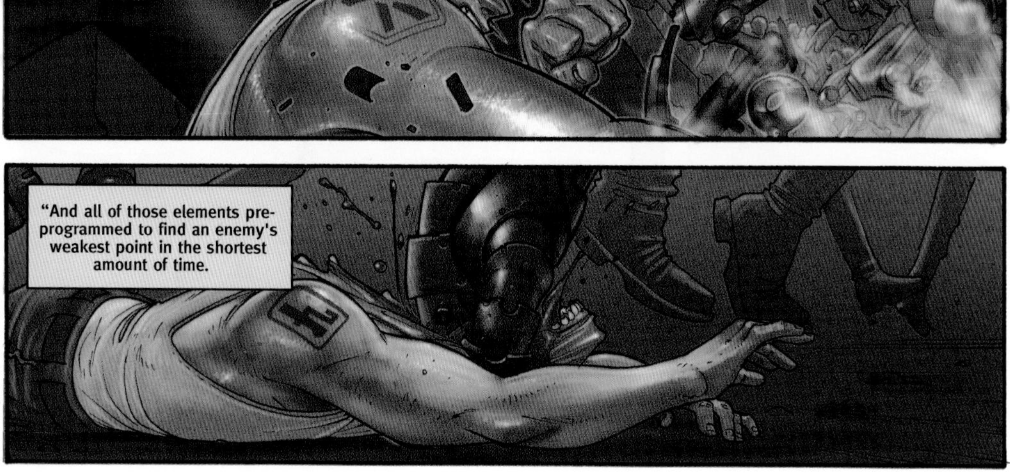
"And all of those elements pre-programmed to find an enemy's weakest point in the shortest amount of time.

"He was the pinnacle of form and the zenith of grace..."

-- from the journal of Dr. Maureen McNair, 29 February 2132.

YOU'VE MADE THE ERYTHROCYTES RED, LIKE *BLOOD*...

WE'VE ADDED *CAPILLARY EXPRESSIONS*, SO THEY CAN BLEMISH, BRUISE, AND BLUSH. THE GREEN ERYTHROCYTES JUST MADE US LOOK *ILL.*

THEIR IDENTIFICATION MATRIX IS STILL BASED ON THE MOLLY ENGINE?

THE CODE ITSELF IS PROPRIETARY, BUT YES-- THEY WILL LEARN AND GROW ON THEIR OWN. *SELF-MODIFYING PARAMETRICS...* WITH A FEW DEFINED FAIL-SAFES, OF COURSE.

THIS IS DIFFICULT TO WATCH. THEY'VE BECOME SO LIFELIKE...

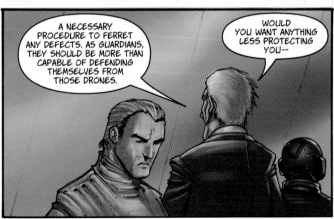

A NECESSARY PROCEDURE TO FERRET ANY DEFECTS. AS GUARDIANS, THEY SHOULD BE MORE THAN CAPABLE OF DEFENDING THEMSELVES FROM THOSE DRONES.

WOULD YOU WANT ANYTHING LESS PROTECTING YOU--

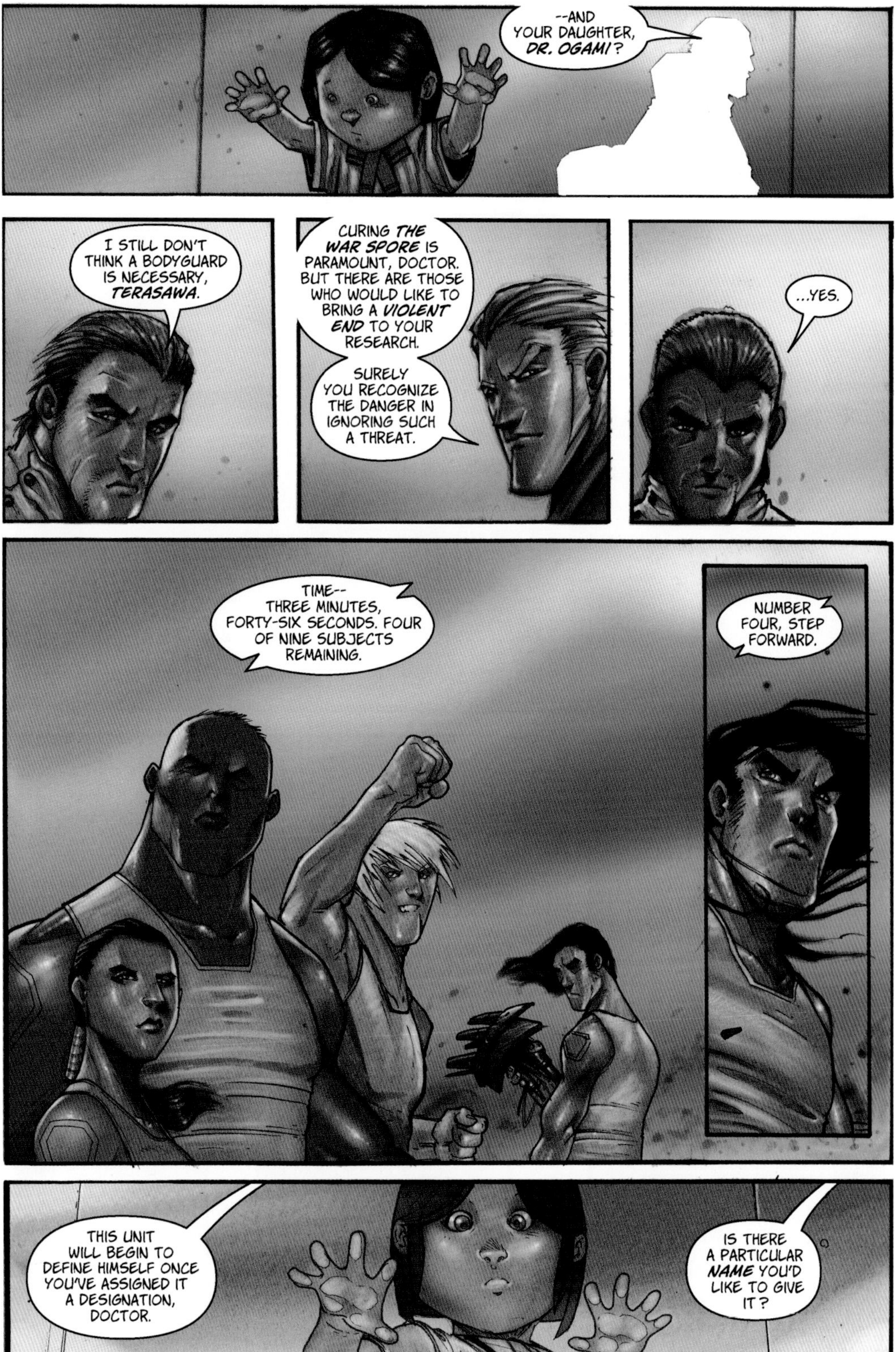
--AND YOUR DAUGHTER, DR. OGAMI?
I STILL DON'T THINK A BODYGUARD IS NECESSARY, TERASAWA.
CURING THE WAR SPORE IS PARAMOUNT, DOCTOR. BUT THERE ARE THOSE WHO WOULD LIKE TO BRING A VIOLENT END TO YOUR RESEARCH.
SURELY YOU RECOGNIZE THE DANGER IN IGNORING SUCH A THREAT.
...YES.
TIME-- THREE MINUTES, FORTY-SIX SECONDS. FOUR OF NINE SUBJECTS REMAINING.
NUMBER FOUR, STEP FORWARD.
THIS UNIT WILL BEGIN TO DEFINE HIMSELF ONCE YOU'VE ASSIGNED IT A DESIGNATION, DOCTOR.
IS THERE A PARTICULAR NAME YOU'D LIKE TO GIVE IT?

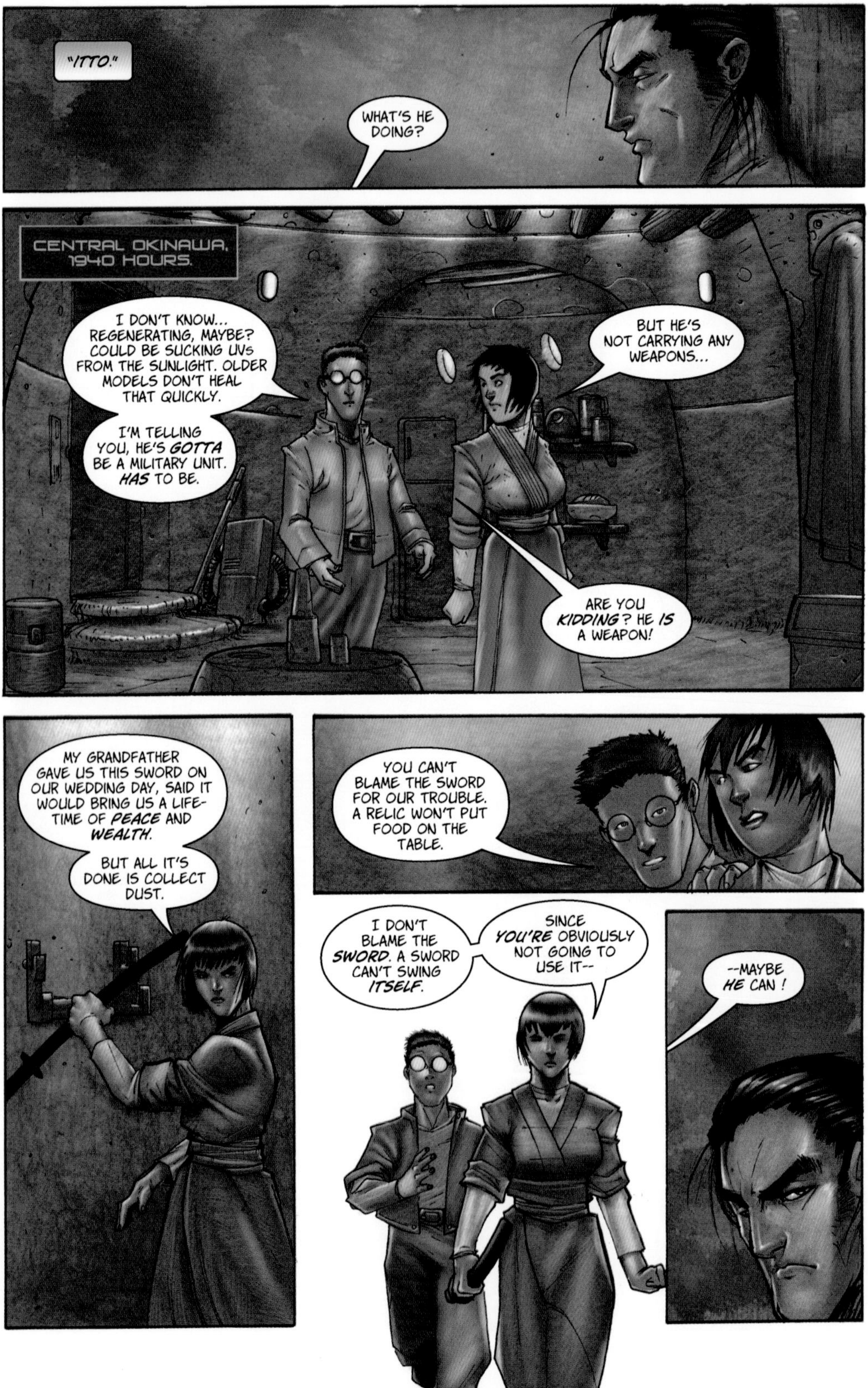
"ITTO."
WHAT'S HE DOING?
CENTRAL OKINAWA, 1940 HOURS.
I DON'T KNOW... REGENERATING, MAYBE? COULD BE SUCKING UVs FROM THE SUNLIGHT. OLDER MODELS DON'T HEAL THAT QUICKLY.
I'M TELLING YOU, HE'S GOTTA BE A MILITARY UNIT. HAS TO BE.
BUT HE'S NOT CARRYING ANY WEAPONS...
ARE YOU KIDDING? HE IS A WEAPON!
MY GRANDFATHER GAVE US THIS SWORD ON OUR WEDDING DAY, SAID IT WOULD BRING US A LIFE-TIME OF PEACE AND WEALTH.
BUT ALL IT'S DONE IS COLLECT DUST.
YOU CAN'T BLAME THE SWORD FOR OUR TROUBLE. A RELIC WON'T PUT FOOD ON THE TABLE.
I DON'T BLAME THE SWORD. A SWORD CAN'T SWING ITSELF.
SINCE YOU'RE OBVIOUSLY NOT GOING TO USE IT--
--MAYBE HE CAN!

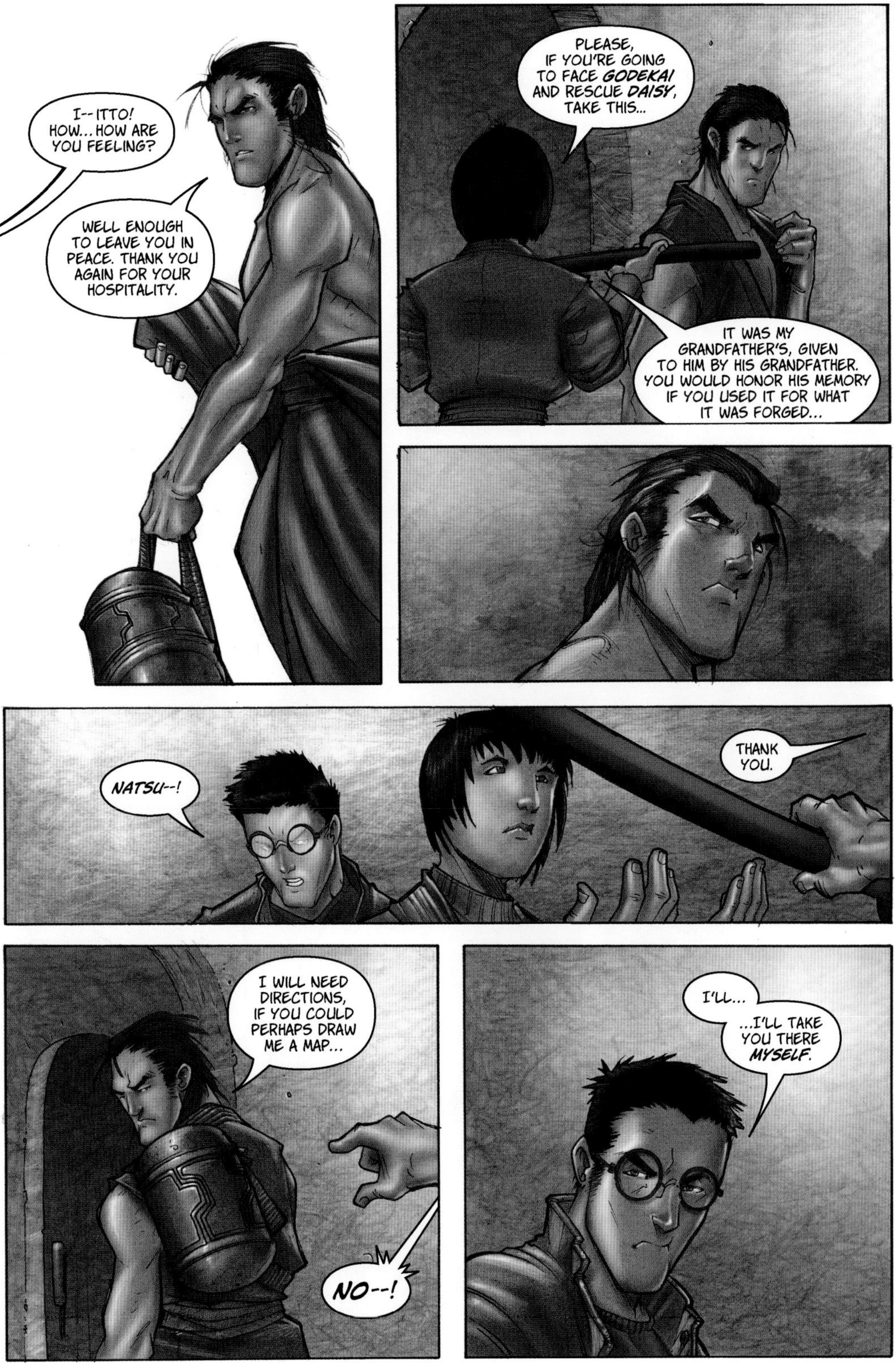
I--ITTO! HOW... HOW ARE YOU FEELING?
WELL ENOUGH TO LEAVE YOU IN PEACE. THANK YOU AGAIN FOR YOUR HOSPITALITY.
PLEASE, IF YOU'RE GOING TO FACE GODEKAI AND RESCUE DAISY, TAKE THIS...
IT WAS MY GRANDFATHER'S, GIVEN TO HIM BY HIS GRANDFATHER. YOU WOULD HONOR HIS MEMORY IF YOU USED IT FOR WHAT IT WAS FORGED...
NATSU--!
THANK YOU.
I WILL NEED DIRECTIONS, IF YOU COULD PERHAPS DRAW ME A MAP...
NO--!
I'LL...
...I'LL TAKE YOU THERE MYSELF.

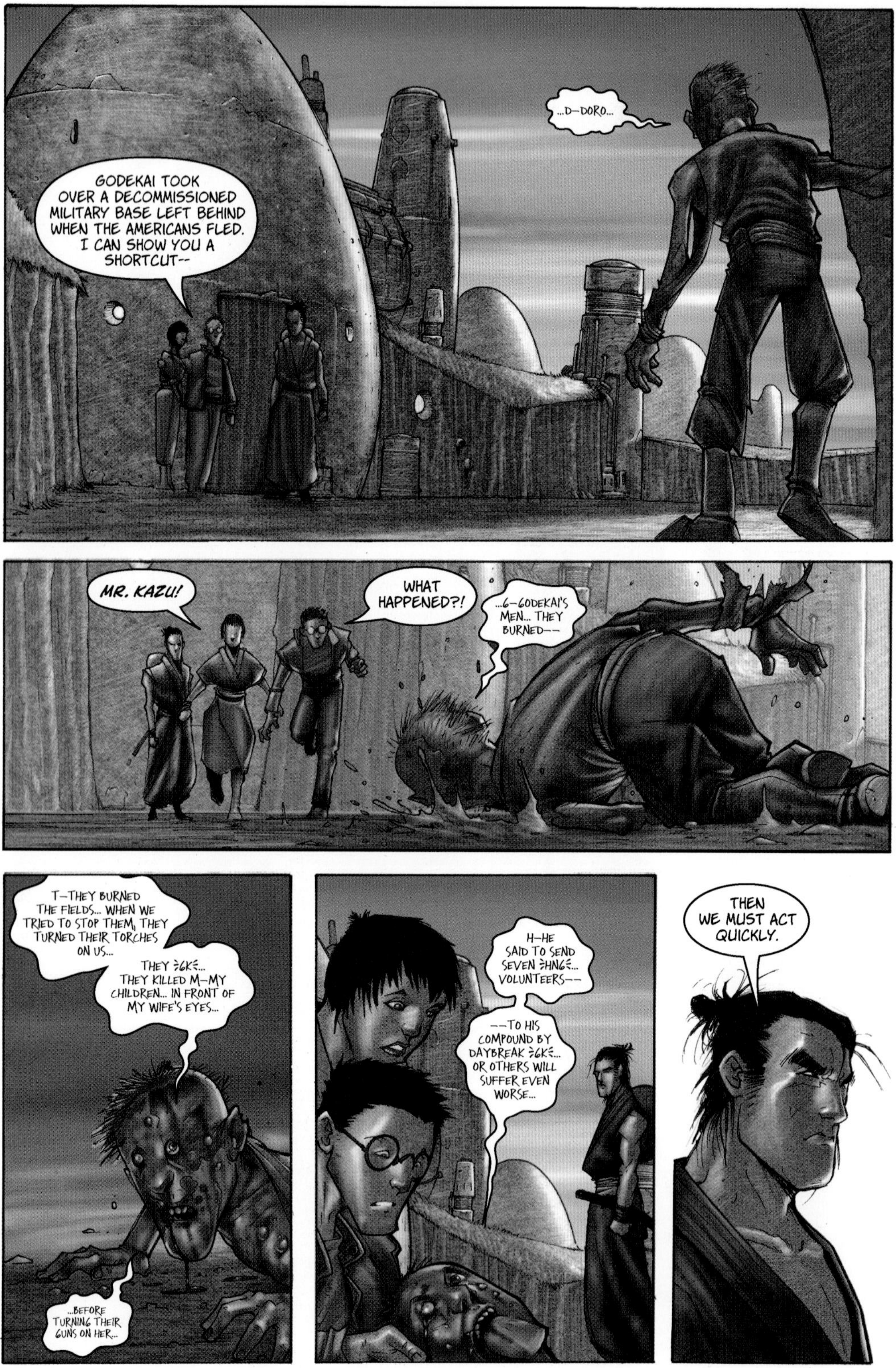
GODEKAI TOOK OVER A DECOMMISSIONED MILITARY BASE LEFT BEHIND WHEN THE AMERICANS FLED. I CAN SHOW YOU A SHORTCUT--
...D-DORO...
MR. KAZU!
WHAT HAPPENED?!
...G-GODEKAI'S MEN... THEY BURNED--
T-THEY BURNED THE FIELDS... WHEN WE TRIED TO STOP THEM, THEY TURNED THEIR TORCHES ON US...
THEY =6K=... THEY KILLED M-MY CHILDREN... IN FRONT OF MY WIFE'S EYES...
...BEFORE TURNING THEIR GUNS ON HER...
H-HE SAID TO SEND SEVEN =HNG=... VOLUNTEERS--
--TO HIS COMPOUND BY DAYBREAK =6K=... OR OTHERS WILL SUFFER EVEN WORSE...
THEN WE MUST ACT QUICKLY.

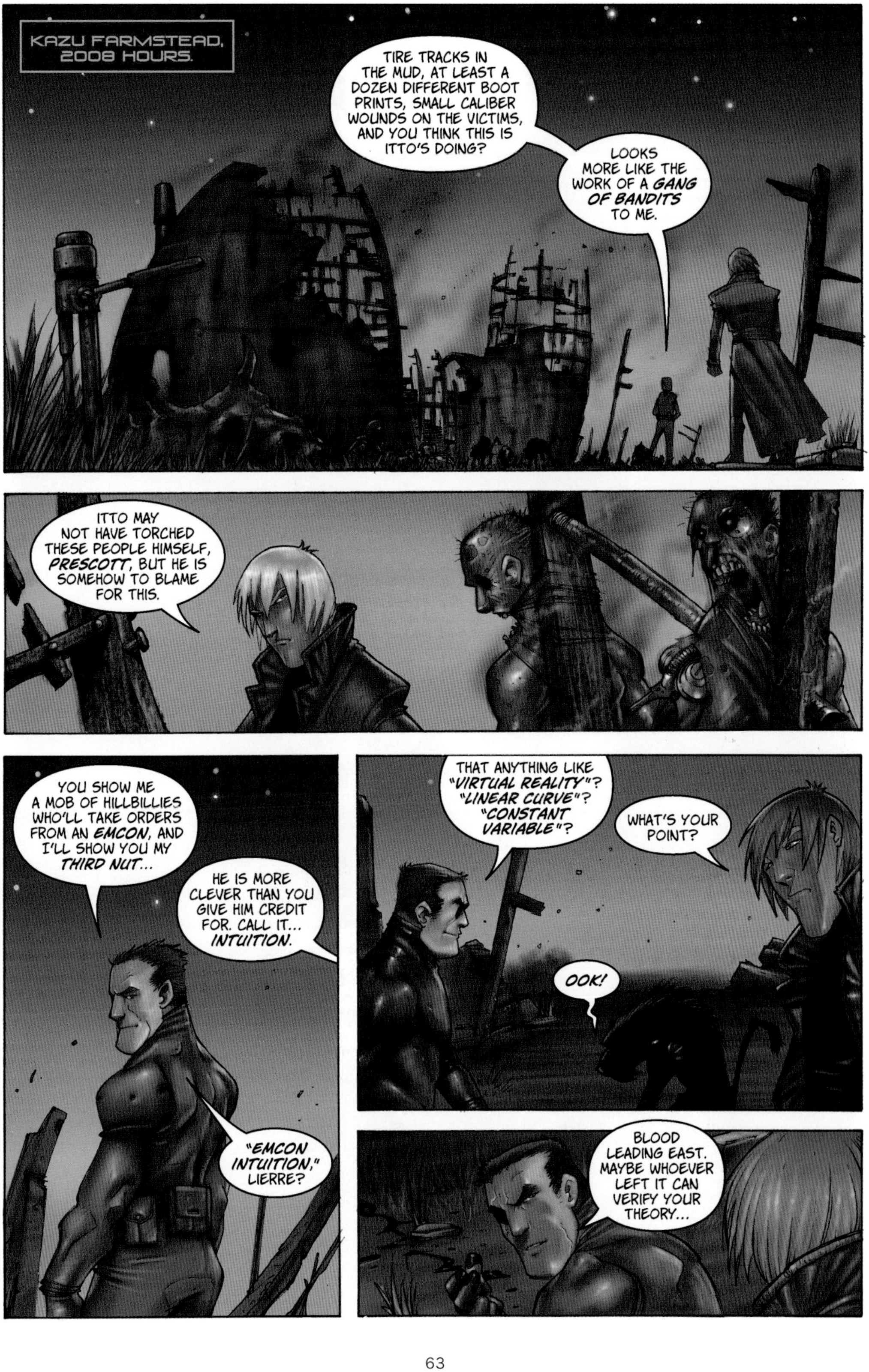
KAZU FARMSTEAD, 2008 HOURS.
TIRE TRACKS IN THE MUD, AT LEAST A DOZEN DIFFERENT BOOT PRINTS, SMALL CALIBER WOUNDS ON THE VICTIMS, AND YOU THINK THIS IS ITTO'S DOING?
LOOKS MORE LIKE THE WORK OF A *GANG OF BANDITS* TO ME.
ITTO MAY NOT HAVE TORCHED THESE PEOPLE HIMSELF, *PRESCOTT*, BUT HE IS SOMEHOW TO BLAME FOR THIS.
YOU SHOW ME A MOB OF HILLBILLIES WHO'LL TAKE ORDERS FROM AN *EMCON*, AND I'LL SHOW YOU MY *THIRD NUT*...
HE IS MORE CLEVER THAN YOU GIVE HIM CREDIT FOR. CALL IT... *INTUITION*.
"*EMCON INTUITION*," LIERRE?
THAT ANYTHING LIKE "*VIRTUAL REALITY*"? "*LINEAR CURVE*"? "*CONSTANT VARIABLE*"?
WHAT'S YOUR POINT?
OOK!
BLOOD LEADING EAST. MAYBE WHOEVER LEFT IT CAN VERIFY YOUR THEORY...

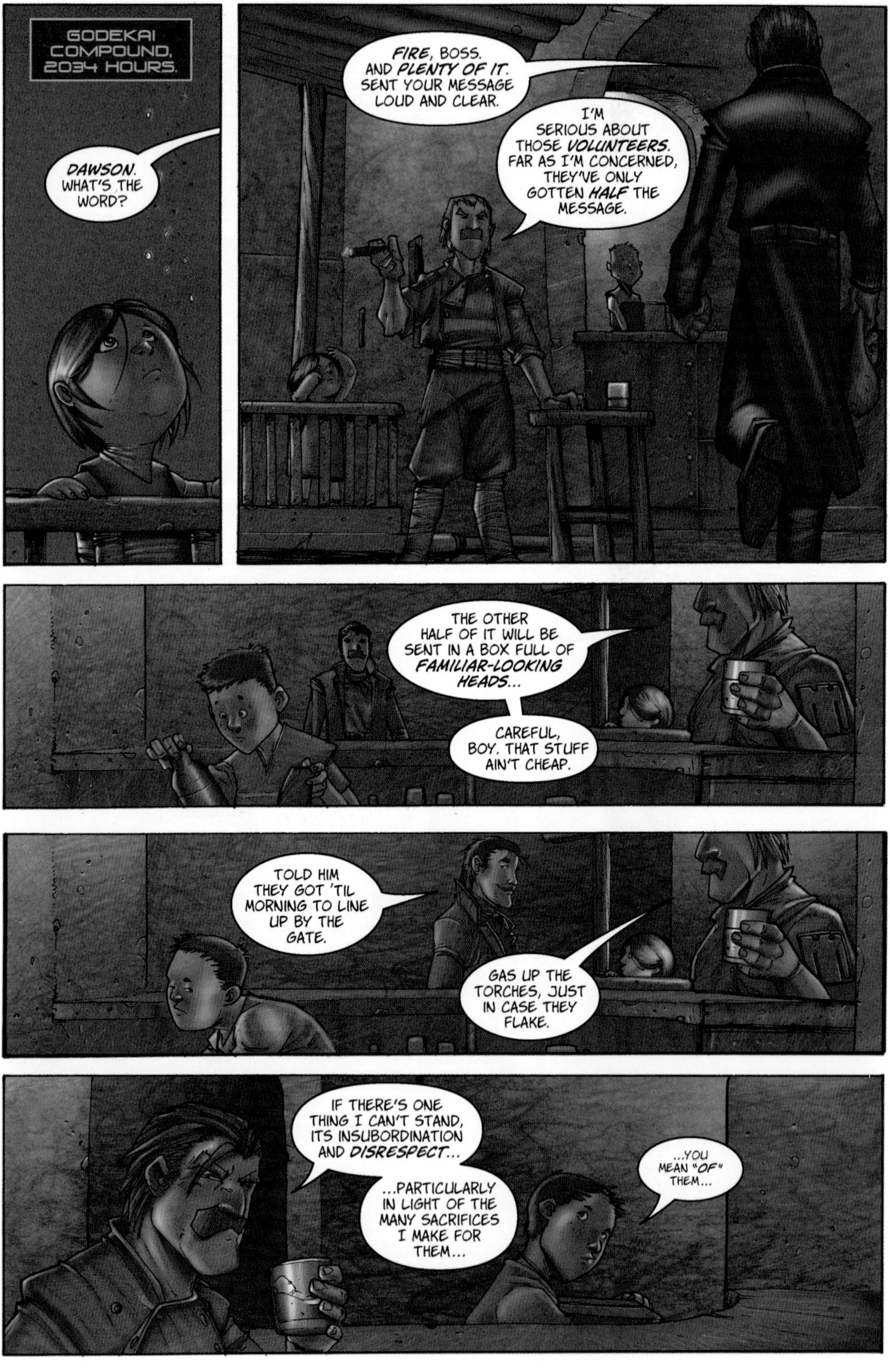
GODEKAI COMPOUND, 2034 HOURS.
DAWSON. WHAT'S THE WORD?
FIRE, BOSS. AND PLENTY OF IT. SENT YOUR MESSAGE LOUD AND CLEAR.
I'M SERIOUS ABOUT THOSE VOLUNTEERS. FAR AS I'M CONCERNED, THEY'VE ONLY GOTTEN HALF THE MESSAGE.
THE OTHER HALF OF IT WILL BE SENT IN A BOX FULL OF FAMILIAR-LOOKING HEADS...
CAREFUL, BOY. THAT STUFF AIN'T CHEAP.
TOLD HIM THEY GOT 'TIL MORNING TO LINE UP BY THE GATE.
GAS UP THE TORCHES, JUST IN CASE THEY FLAKE.
IF THERE'S ONE THING I CAN'T STAND, ITS INSUBORDINATION AND DISRESPECT...
...PARTICULARLY IN LIGHT OF THE MANY SACRIFICES I MAKE FOR THEM...
...YOU MEAN "OF" THEM...

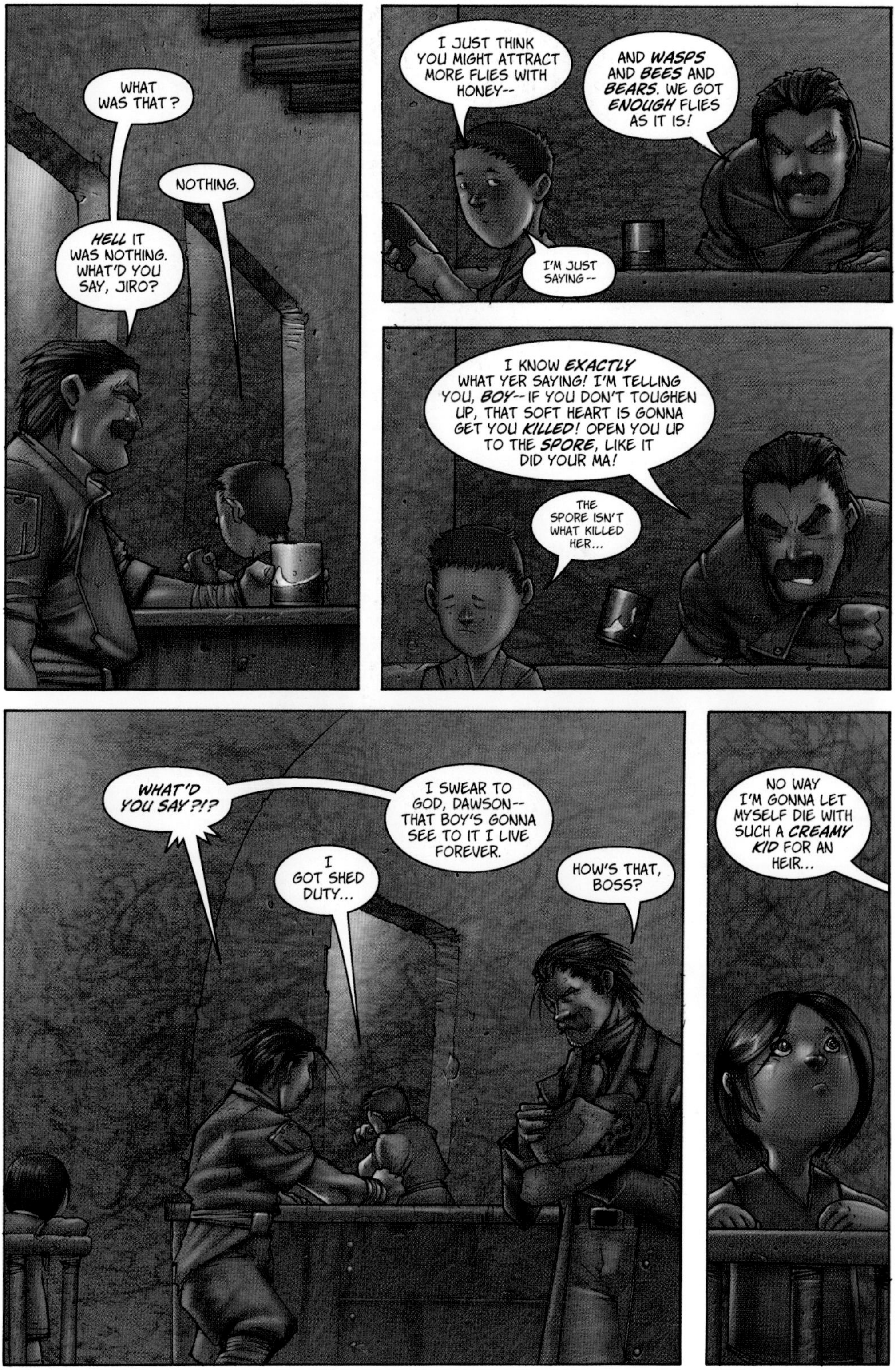
WHAT WAS THAT?
NOTHING.
HELL IT WAS NOTHING. WHAT'D YOU SAY, JIRO?
I JUST THINK YOU MIGHT ATTRACT MORE FLIES WITH HONEY--
AND WASPS AND BEES AND BEARS. WE GOT ENOUGH FLIES AS IT IS!
I'M JUST SAYING--
I KNOW EXACTLY WHAT YER SAYING! I'M TELLING YOU, BOY-- IF YOU DON'T TOUGHEN UP, THAT SOFT HEART IS GONNA GET YOU KILLED! OPEN YOU UP TO THE SPORE, LIKE IT DID YOUR MA!
THE SPORE ISN'T WHAT KILLED HER...
WHAT'D YOU SAY?!?
I GOT SHED DUTY...
I SWEAR TO GOD, DAWSON-- THAT BOY'S GONNA SEE TO IT I LIVE FOREVER.
HOW'S THAT, BOSS?
NO WAY I'M GONNA LET MYSELF DIE WITH SUCH A CREAMY KID FOR AN HEIR...

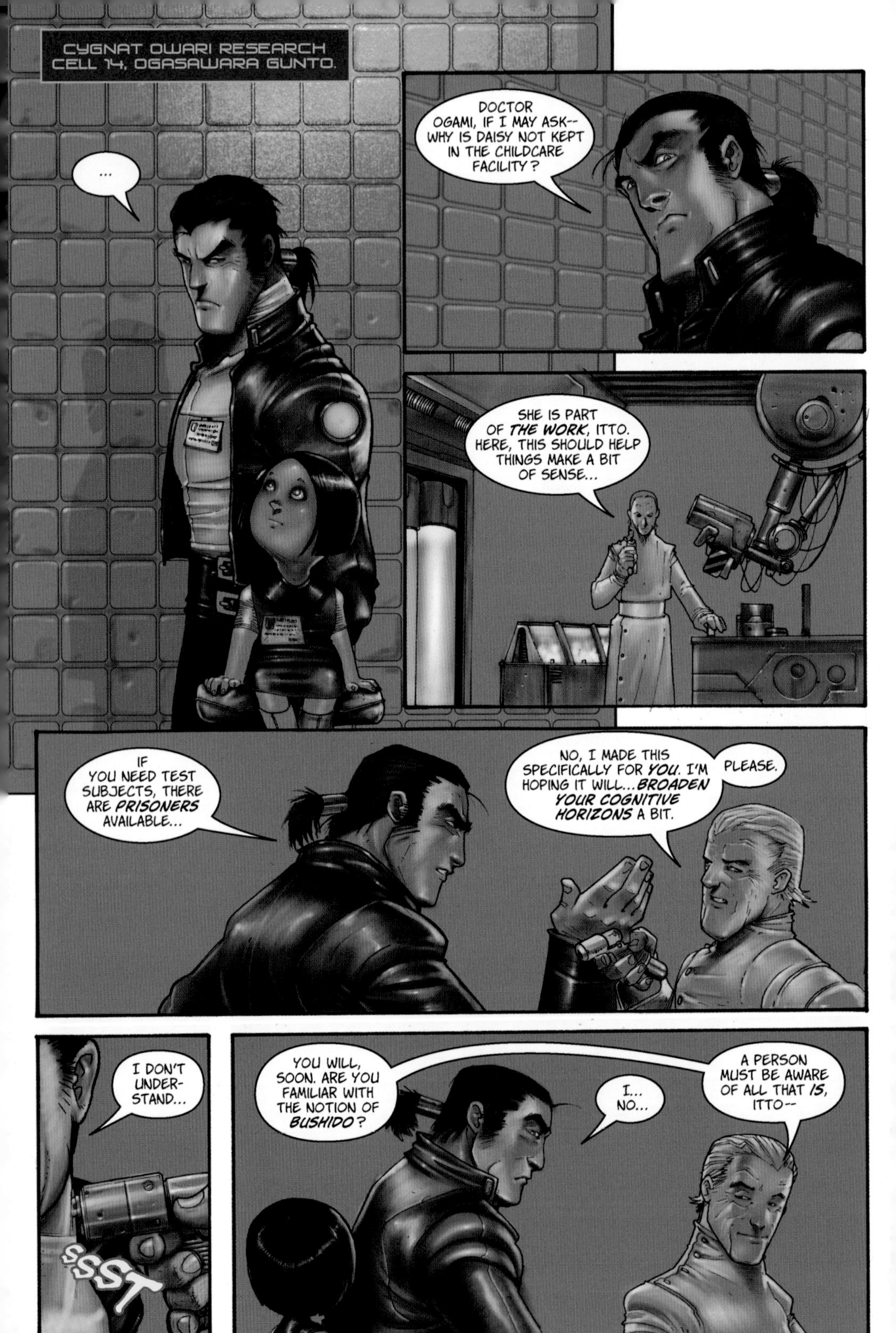
CYGNAT OWARI RESEARCH CELL 14, OGASAWARA GUNTO.
...
DOCTOR OGAMI, IF I MAY ASK-- WHY IS DAISY NOT KEPT IN THE CHILDCARE FACILITY?
SHE IS PART OF THE WORK, ITTO. HERE, THIS SHOULD HELP THINGS MAKE A BIT OF SENSE...
IF YOU NEED TEST SUBJECTS, THERE ARE PRISONERS AVAILABLE...
NO, I MADE THIS SPECIFICALLY FOR YOU. I'M HOPING IT WILL...BROADEN YOUR COGNITIVE HORIZONS A BIT.
PLEASE.
I DON'T UNDER-STAND...
SSST
YOU WILL, SOON. ARE YOU FAMILIAR WITH THE NOTION OF BUSHIDO?
I... NO...
A PERSON MUST BE AWARE OF ALL THAT IS, ITTO--

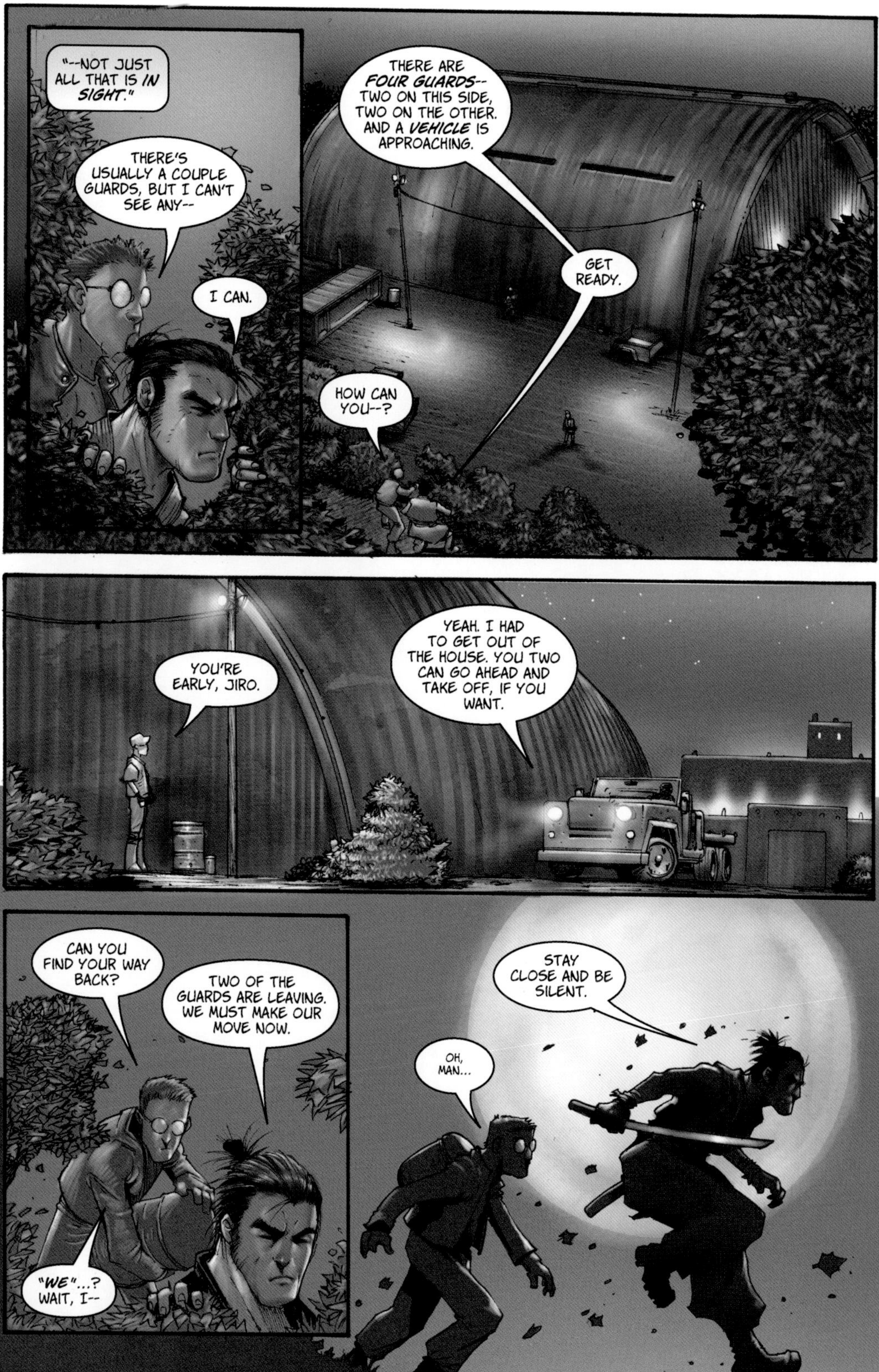
"--NOT JUST ALL THAT IS *IN SIGHT*."
THERE'S USUALLY A COUPLE GUARDS, BUT I CAN'T SEE ANY--
I CAN.
THERE ARE **FOUR GUARDS**-- TWO ON THIS SIDE, TWO ON THE OTHER. AND A **VEHICLE** IS APPROACHING.
HOW CAN YOU--?
GET READY.
YOU'RE EARLY, JIRO.
YEAH. I HAD TO GET OUT OF THE HOUSE. YOU TWO CAN GO AHEAD AND TAKE OFF, IF YOU WANT.
CAN YOU FIND YOUR WAY BACK?
TWO OF THE GUARDS ARE LEAVING. WE MUST MAKE OUR MOVE NOW.
"*WE*"...? WAIT, I--
OH, MAN...
STAY CLOSE AND BE SILENT.

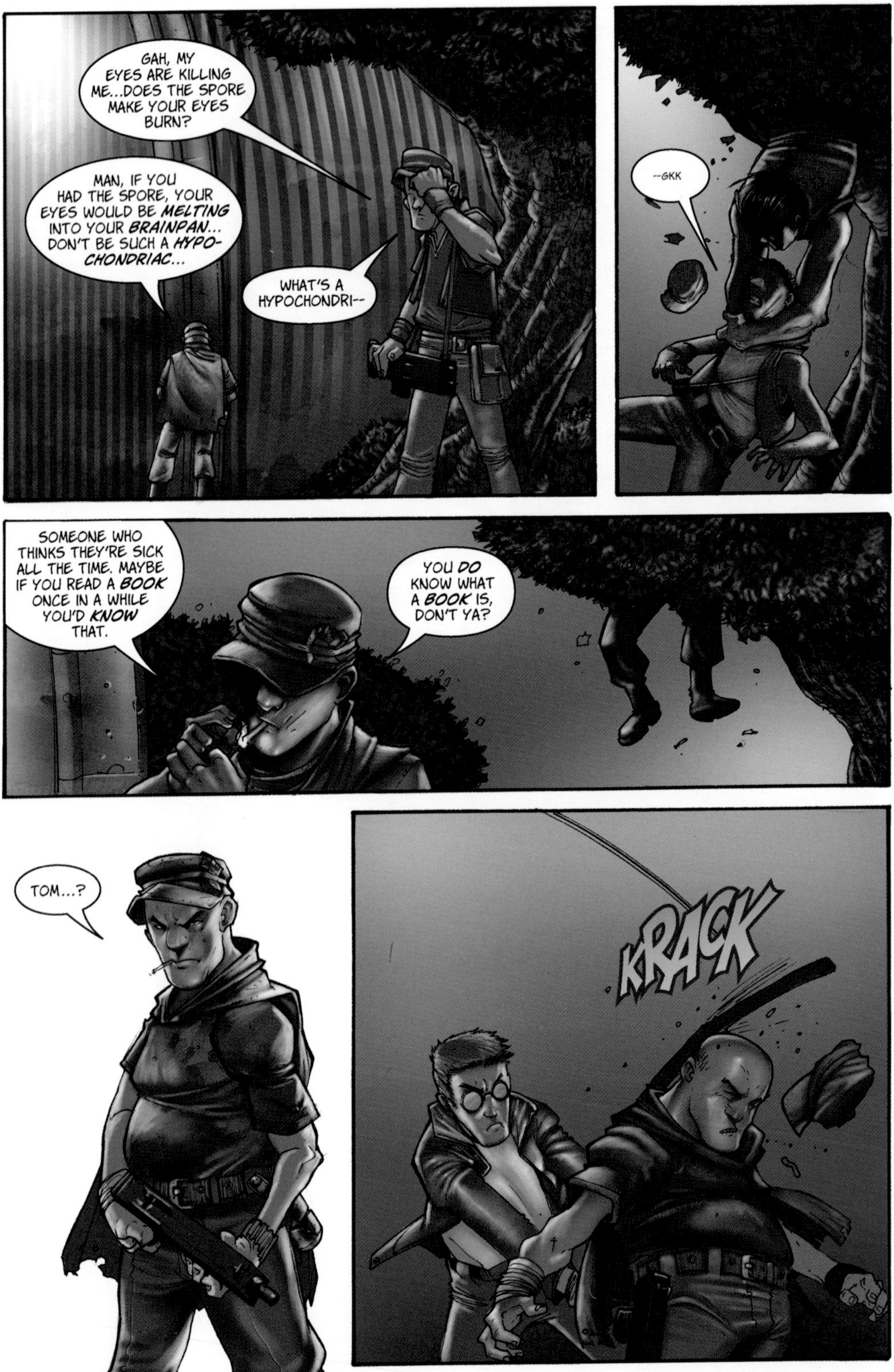
GAH, MY EYES ARE KILLING ME...DOES THE SPORE MAKE YOUR EYES BURN?
MAN, IF YOU HAD THE SPORE, YOUR EYES WOULD BE MELTING INTO YOUR BRAINPAN... DON'T BE SUCH A HYPO-CHONDRIAC...
WHAT'S A HYPOCHONDRI--
--GKK
SOMEONE WHO THINKS THEY'RE SICK ALL THE TIME. MAYBE IF YOU READ A BOOK ONCE IN A WHILE YOU'D KNOW THAT.
YOU DO KNOW WHAT A BOOK IS, DON'T YA?
TOM...?
KRACK

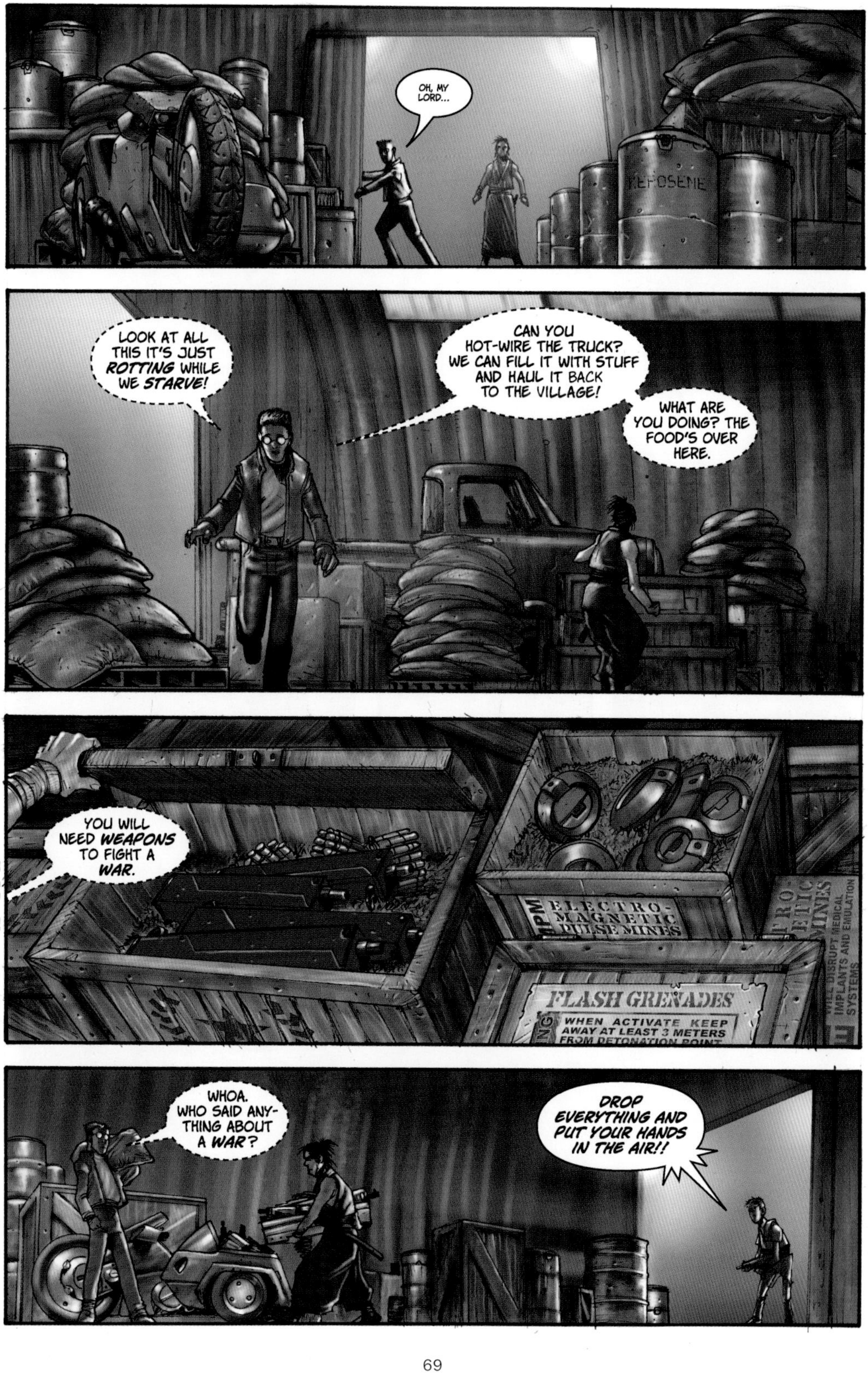
OH, MY LORD...
KEROSENE
LOOK AT ALL THIS IT'S JUST *ROTTING* WHILE WE *STARVE!*
CAN YOU HOT-WIRE THE TRUCK? WE CAN FILL IT WITH STUFF AND HAUL IT BACK TO THE VILLAGE!
WHAT ARE YOU DOING? THE FOOD'S OVER HERE.
YOU WILL NEED *WEAPONS* TO FIGHT A *WAR.*
ELECTRO-MAGNETIC PULSE MINES
WILL DISRUPT MEDICAL IMPLANTS AND EMULATION SYSTEMS
FLASH GRENADES
WHEN ACTIVATE KEEP AWAY AT LEAST 3 METERS FROM DETONATION POINT
WHOA. WHO SAID ANY-THING ABOUT A *WAR?*
DROP EVERYTHING AND PUT YOUR HANDS IN THE AIR!!

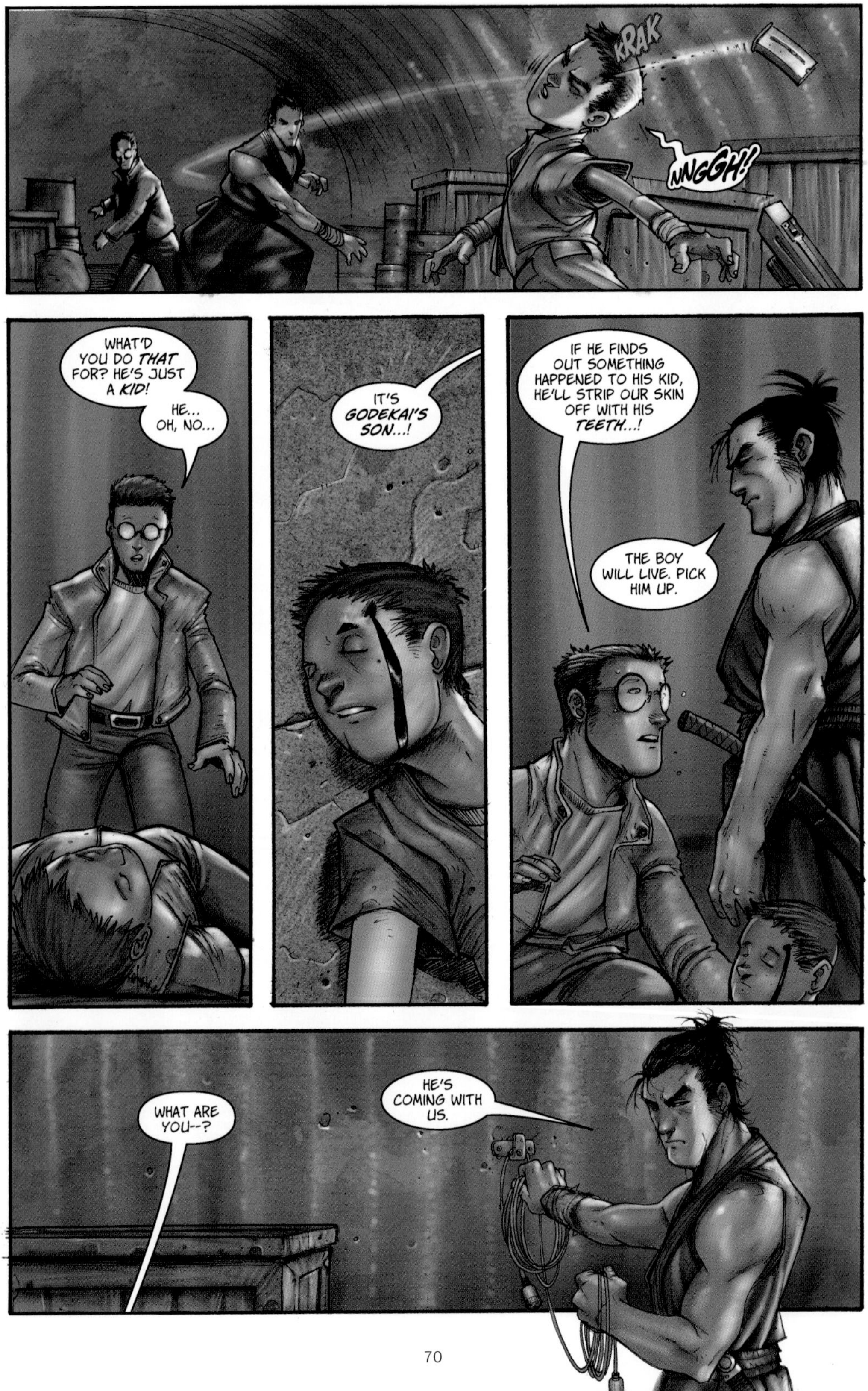
KRAK
NNGGH!
WHAT'D YOU DO THAT FOR? HE'S JUST A KID!
HE... OH, NO...
IT'S GODEKAI'S SON...!
IF HE FINDS OUT SOMETHING HAPPENED TO HIS KID, HE'LL STRIP OUR SKIN OFF WITH HIS TEETH...!
THE BOY WILL LIVE. PICK HIM UP.
WHAT ARE YOU--?
HE'S COMING WITH US.

THESE DISGUISES ARE *RIDICULOUS*.

WOULDN'T PEOPLE RESPOND QUICKER IF THEY KNEW THE *POWER* WE REPRESENT?

HOW DOES *THAT* HAVE ANYTHING TO DO WITH QUESTIONING PEASANTS?

LIERRE, JUST SHUT UP AND FOLLOW MY LEAD.

YOU CAN OPEN A GLASS JAR WITH A HAMMER, BUT YOU'LL NEVER GET IT CLOSED AGAIN.

EXCUSE ME, MISS...

...YES?

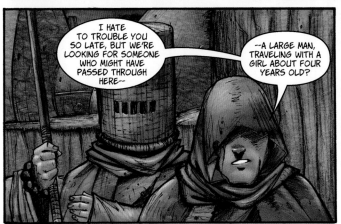

I HATE TO TROUBLE YOU SO LATE, BUT WE'RE LOOKING FOR SOMEONE WHO MIGHT HAVE PASSED THROUGH HERE--

--A LARGE MAN, TRAVELING WITH A GIRL ABOUT FOUR YEARS OLD?

I... WE SEE A LOT OF DRIFTERS AROUND HERE, I DON'T KNOW... ARE THEY... ARE THEY IN TROUBLE?

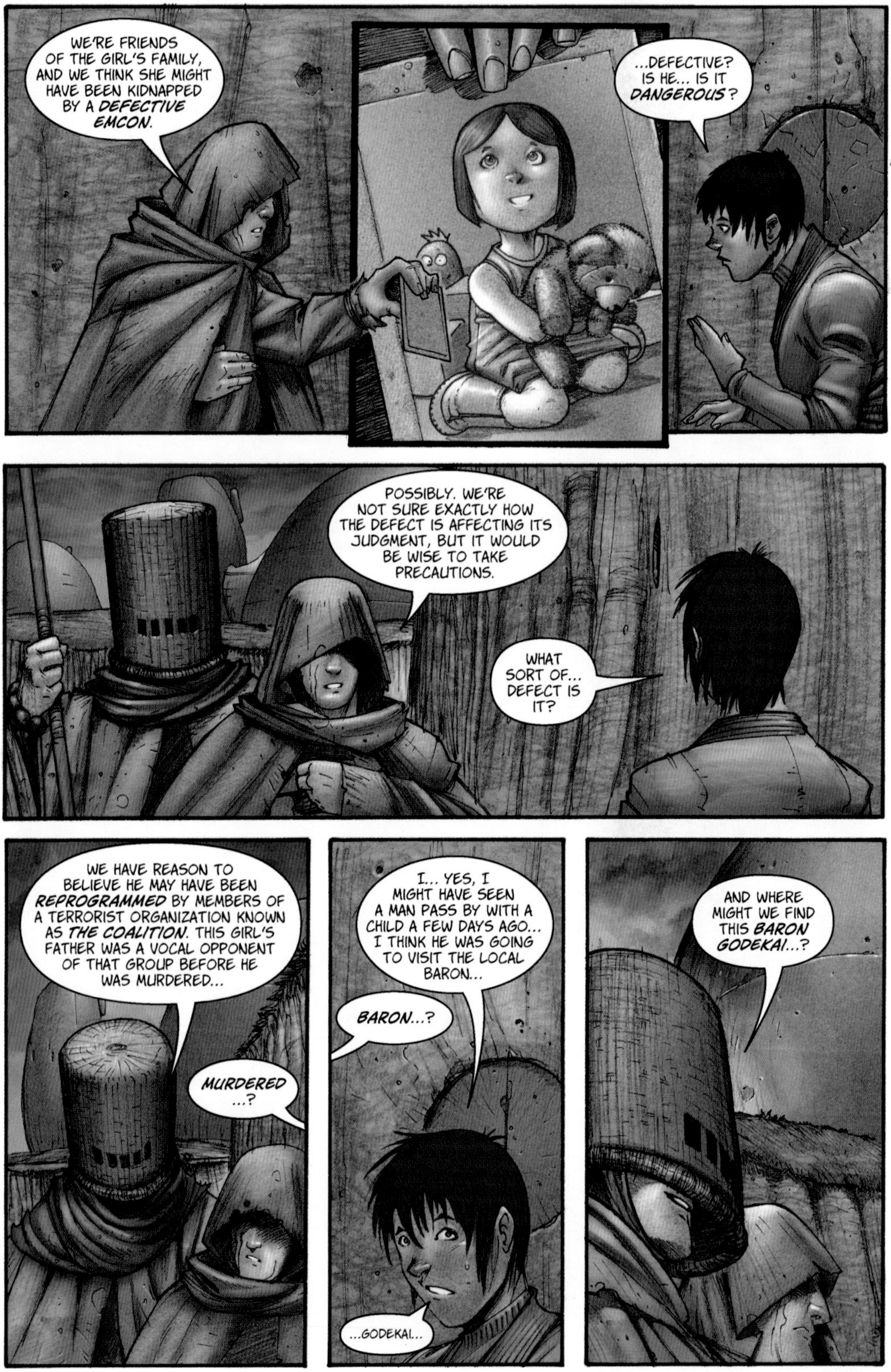
WE'RE FRIENDS OF THE GIRL'S FAMILY, AND WE THINK SHE MIGHT HAVE BEEN KIDNAPPED BY A DEFECTIVE EMCON.
...DEFECTIVE? IS HE... IS IT DANGEROUS?
POSSIBLY. WE'RE NOT SURE EXACTLY HOW THE DEFECT IS AFFECTING ITS JUDGMENT, BUT IT WOULD BE WISE TO TAKE PRECAUTIONS.
WHAT SORT OF... DEFECT IS IT?
WE HAVE REASON TO BELIEVE HE MAY HAVE BEEN REPROGRAMMED BY MEMBERS OF A TERRORIST ORGANIZATION KNOWN AS THE COALITION. THIS GIRL'S FATHER WAS A VOCAL OPPONENT OF THAT GROUP BEFORE HE WAS MURDERED...
MURDERED ...?
I... YES, I MIGHT HAVE SEEN A MAN PASS BY WITH A CHILD A FEW DAYS AGO... I THINK HE WAS GOING TO VISIT THE LOCAL BARON...
BARON...?
...GODEKAI...
AND WHERE MIGHT WE FIND THIS BARON GODEKAI...?

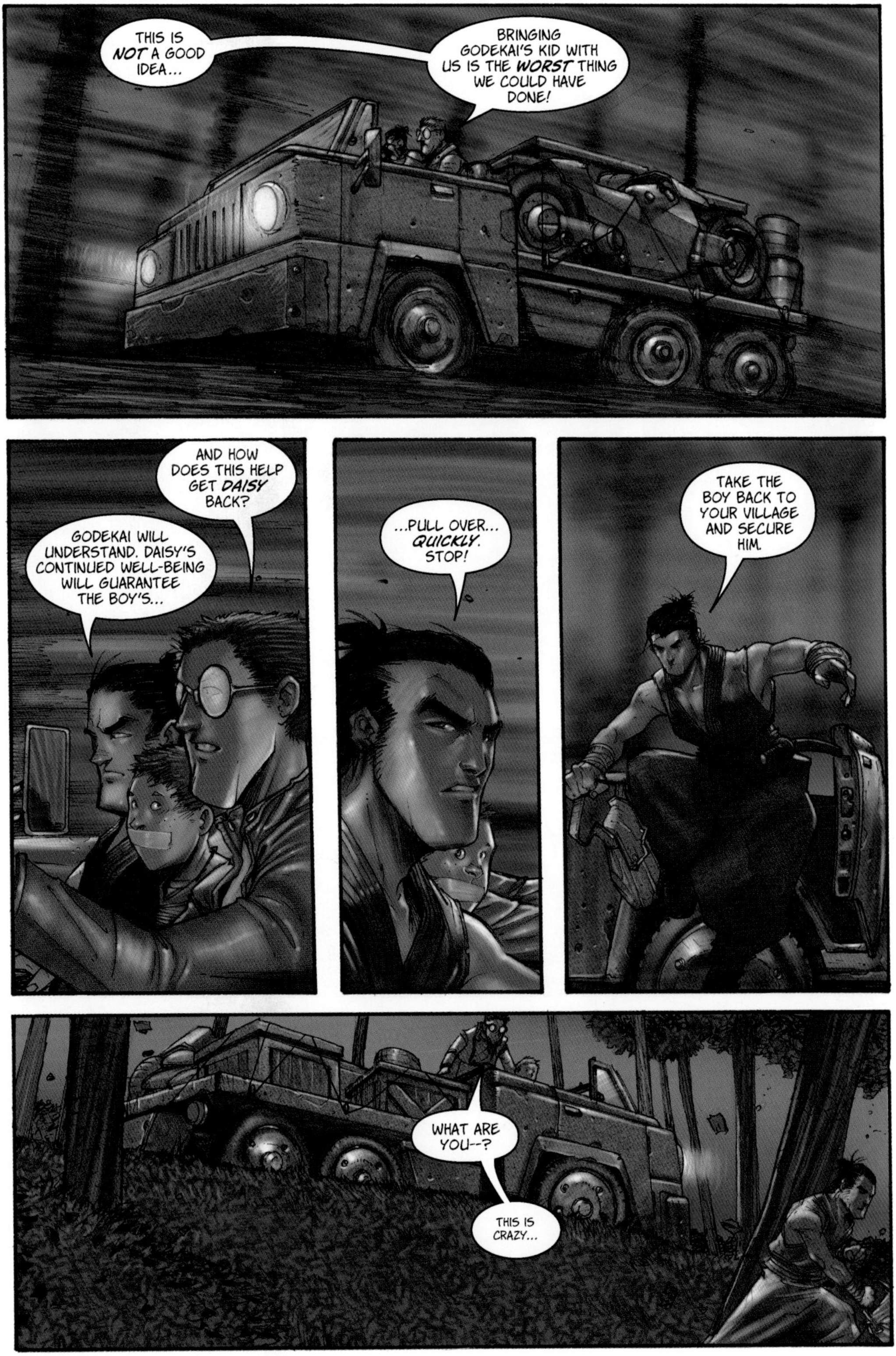
THIS IS *NOT* A GOOD IDEA...
BRINGING GODEKAI'S KID WITH US IS THE *WORST* THING WE COULD HAVE DONE!
AND HOW DOES THIS HELP GET *DAISY* BACK?
GODEKAI WILL UNDERSTAND. DAISY'S CONTINUED WELL-BEING WILL GUARANTEE THE BOY'S...
...PULL OVER... *QUICKLY*. STOP!
TAKE THE BOY BACK TO YOUR VILLAGE AND SECURE HIM.
WHAT ARE YOU--?
THIS IS CRAZY...

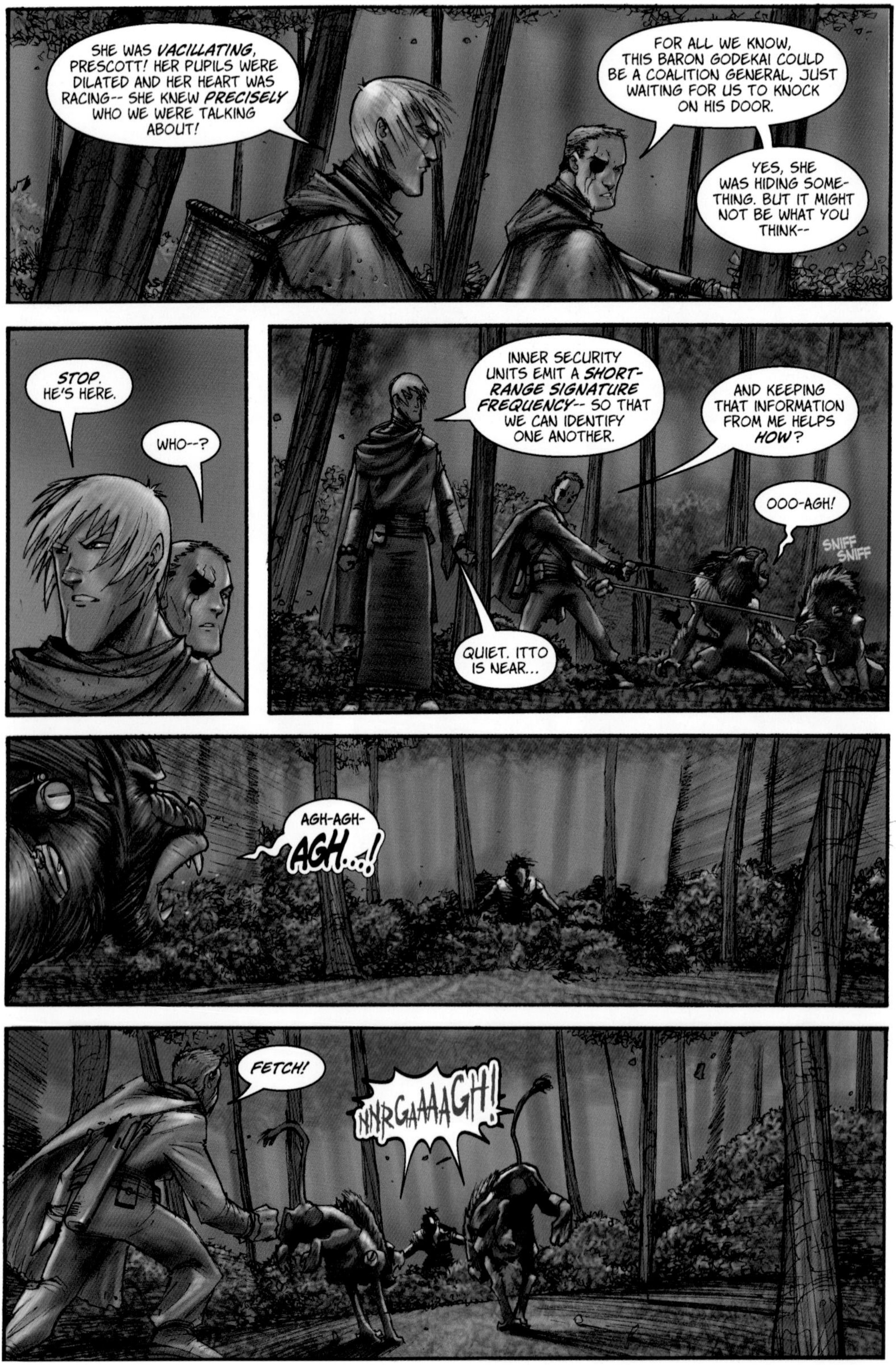
SHE WAS VACILLATING, PRESCOTT! HER PUPILS WERE DILATED AND HER HEART WAS RACING-- SHE KNEW PRECISELY WHO WE WERE TALKING ABOUT!
FOR ALL WE KNOW, THIS BARON GODEKAI COULD BE A COALITION GENERAL, JUST WAITING FOR US TO KNOCK ON HIS DOOR.
YES, SHE WAS HIDING SOME-THING. BUT IT MIGHT NOT BE WHAT YOU THINK--
STOP. HE'S HERE.
WHO--?
INNER SECURITY UNITS EMIT A SHORT-RANGE SIGNATURE FREQUENCY-- SO THAT WE CAN IDENTIFY ONE ANOTHER.
AND KEEPING THAT INFORMATION FROM ME HELPS HOW?
OOO-AGH!
SNIFF SNIFF
QUIET. ITTO IS NEAR...
AGH-AGH-AGH...!
FETCH!
NNRGAAAAGH!

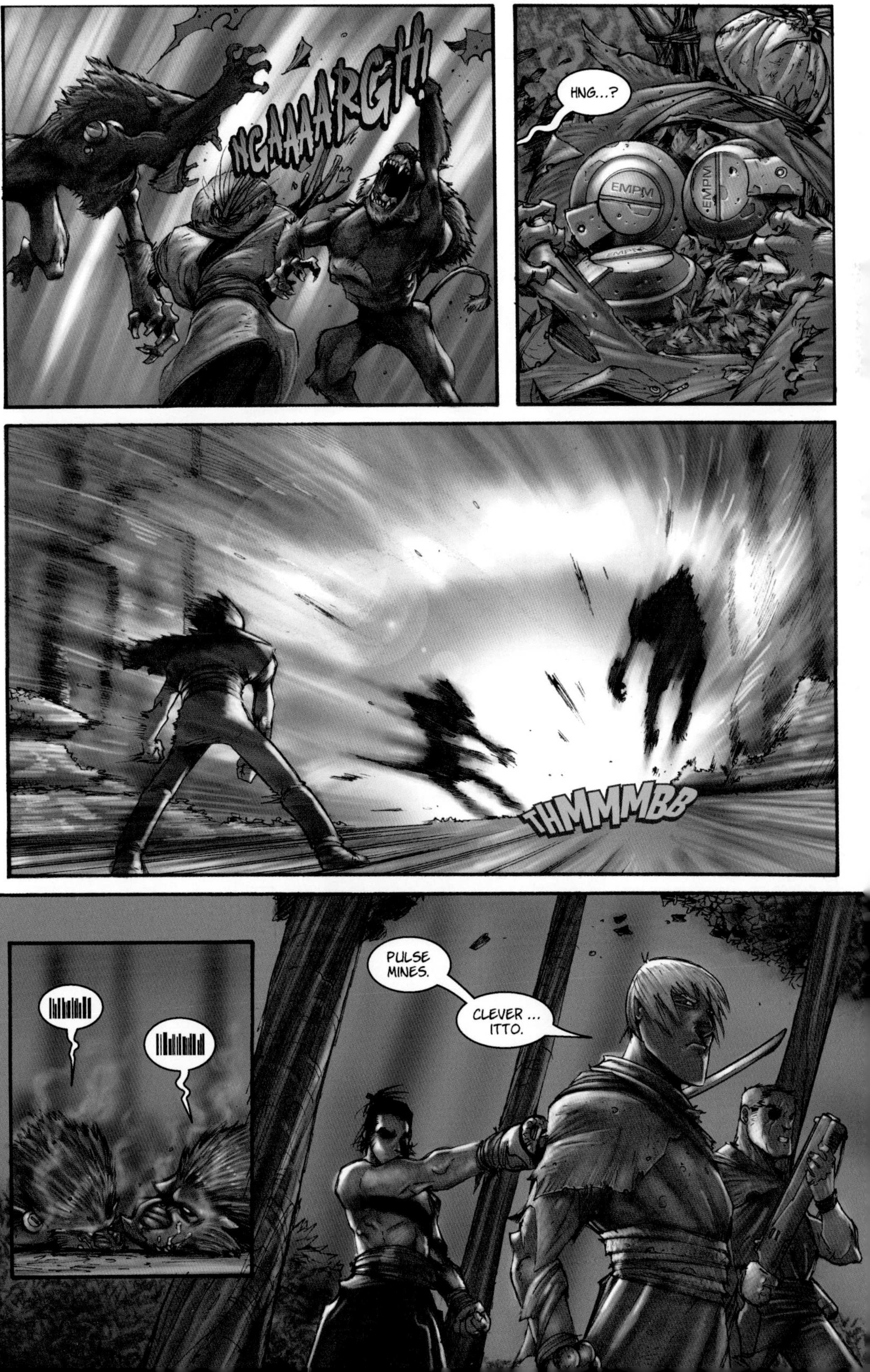
NGAAAARGH!
HNG...?
EMPM
EMPM
THMMMBB
PULSE MINES.
CLEVER ... ITTO.

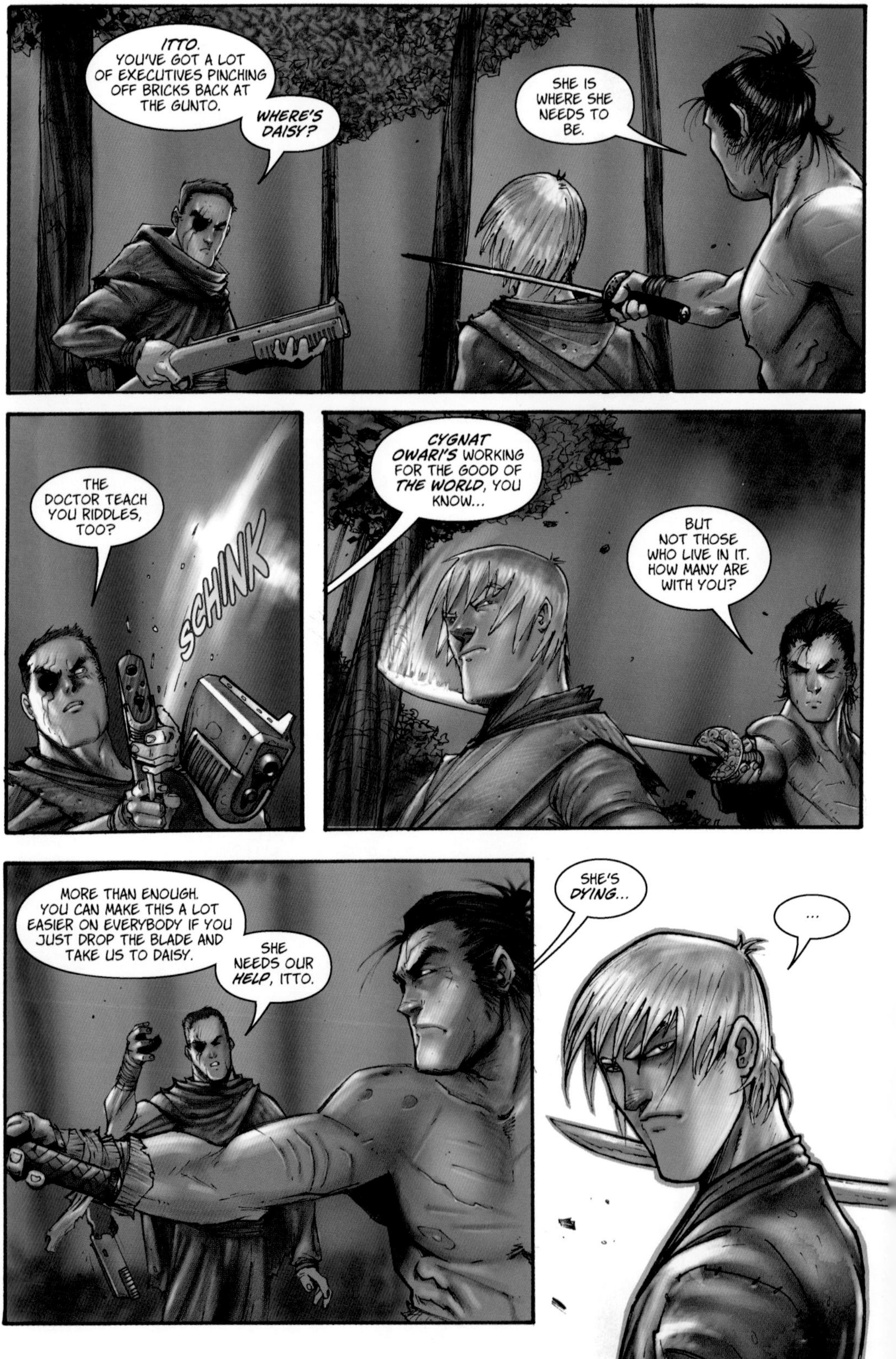
ITTO. YOU'VE GOT A LOT OF EXECUTIVES PINCHING OFF BRICKS BACK AT THE GUNTO.
WHERE'S DAISY?
SHE IS WHERE SHE NEEDS TO BE.
THE DOCTOR TEACH YOU RIDDLES, TOO?
SCHINK
CYGNAT OWARI'S WORKING FOR THE GOOD OF THE WORLD, YOU KNOW...
BUT NOT THOSE WHO LIVE IN IT. HOW MANY ARE WITH YOU?
MORE THAN ENOUGH. YOU CAN MAKE THIS A LOT EASIER ON EVERYBODY IF YOU JUST DROP THE BLADE AND TAKE US TO DAISY.
SHE NEEDS OUR HELP, ITTO.
SHE'S DYING...
...

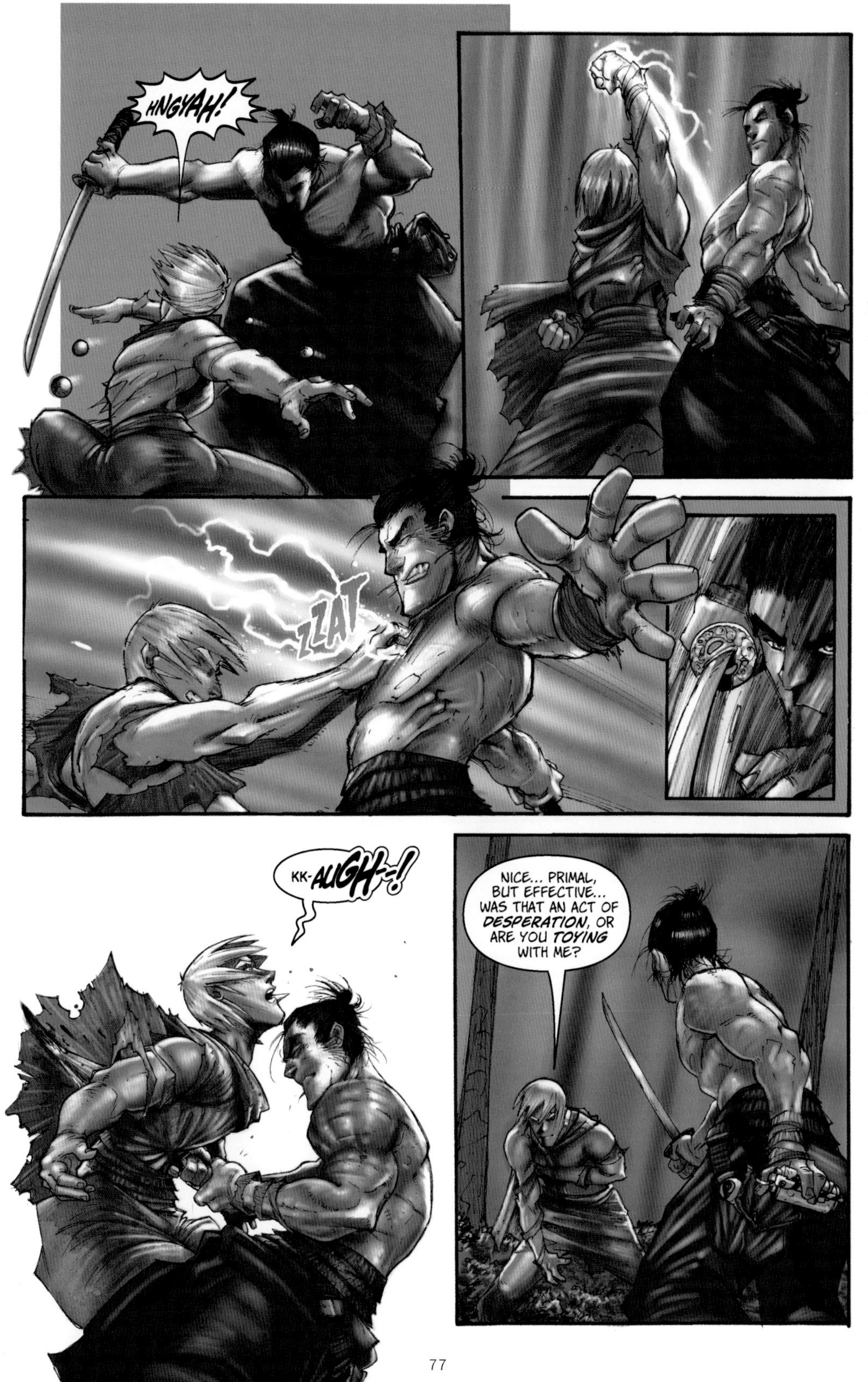
HNGYAH!
ZZAT
KK-AUGH--!
NICE... PRIMAL, BUT EFFECTIVE... WAS THAT AN ACT OF DESPERATION, OR ARE YOU TOYING WITH ME?

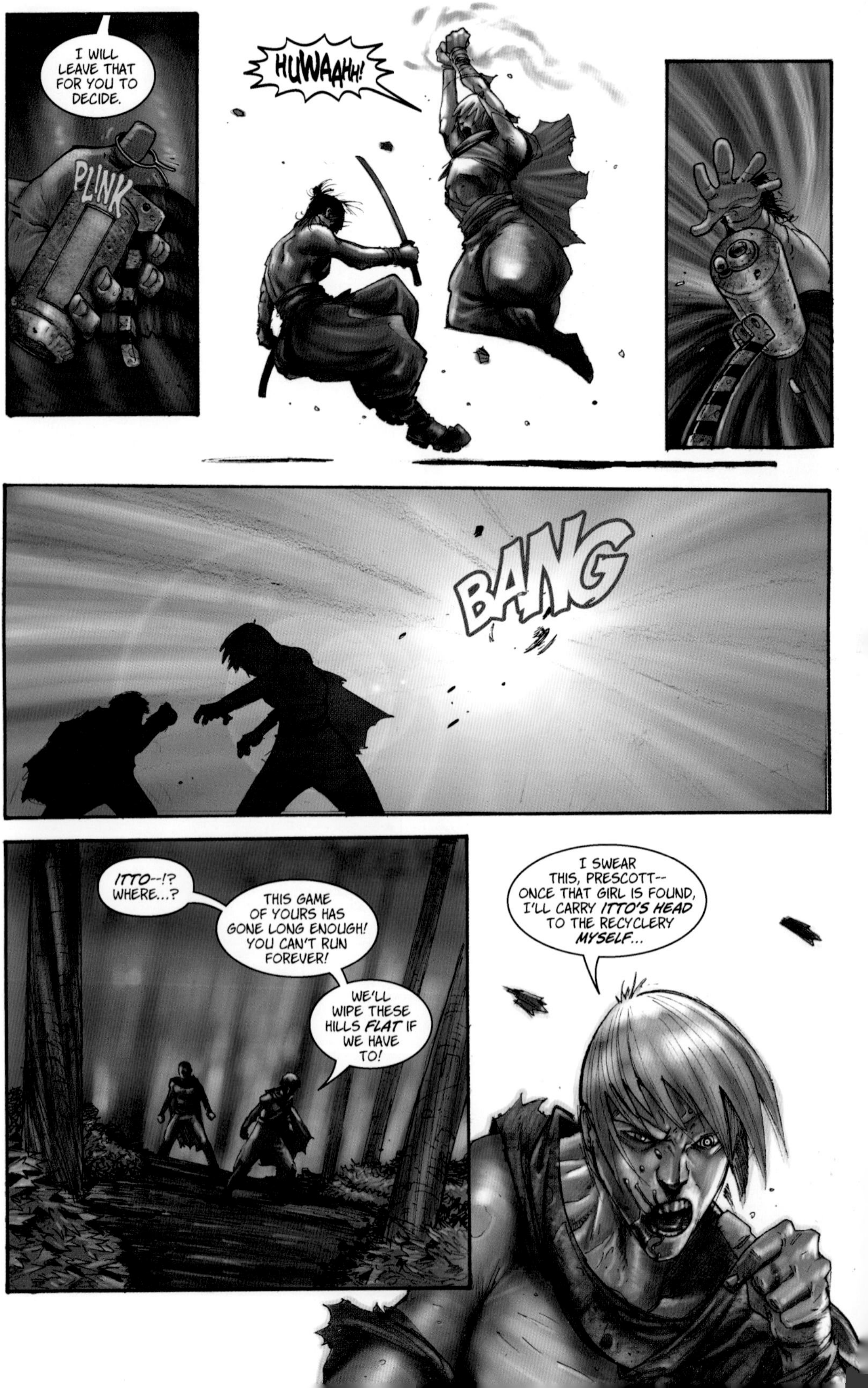
I WILL LEAVE THAT FOR YOU TO DECIDE.
PLINK
HUWAAHH!
BANG
ITTO--!? WHERE...?
THIS GAME OF YOURS HAS GONE LONG ENOUGH! YOU CAN'T RUN FOREVER!
WE'LL WIPE THESE HILLS FLAT IF WE HAVE TO!
I SWEAR THIS, PRESCOTT-- ONCE THAT GIRL IS FOUND, I'LL CARRY ITTO'S HEAD TO THE RECYCLERY MYSELF...

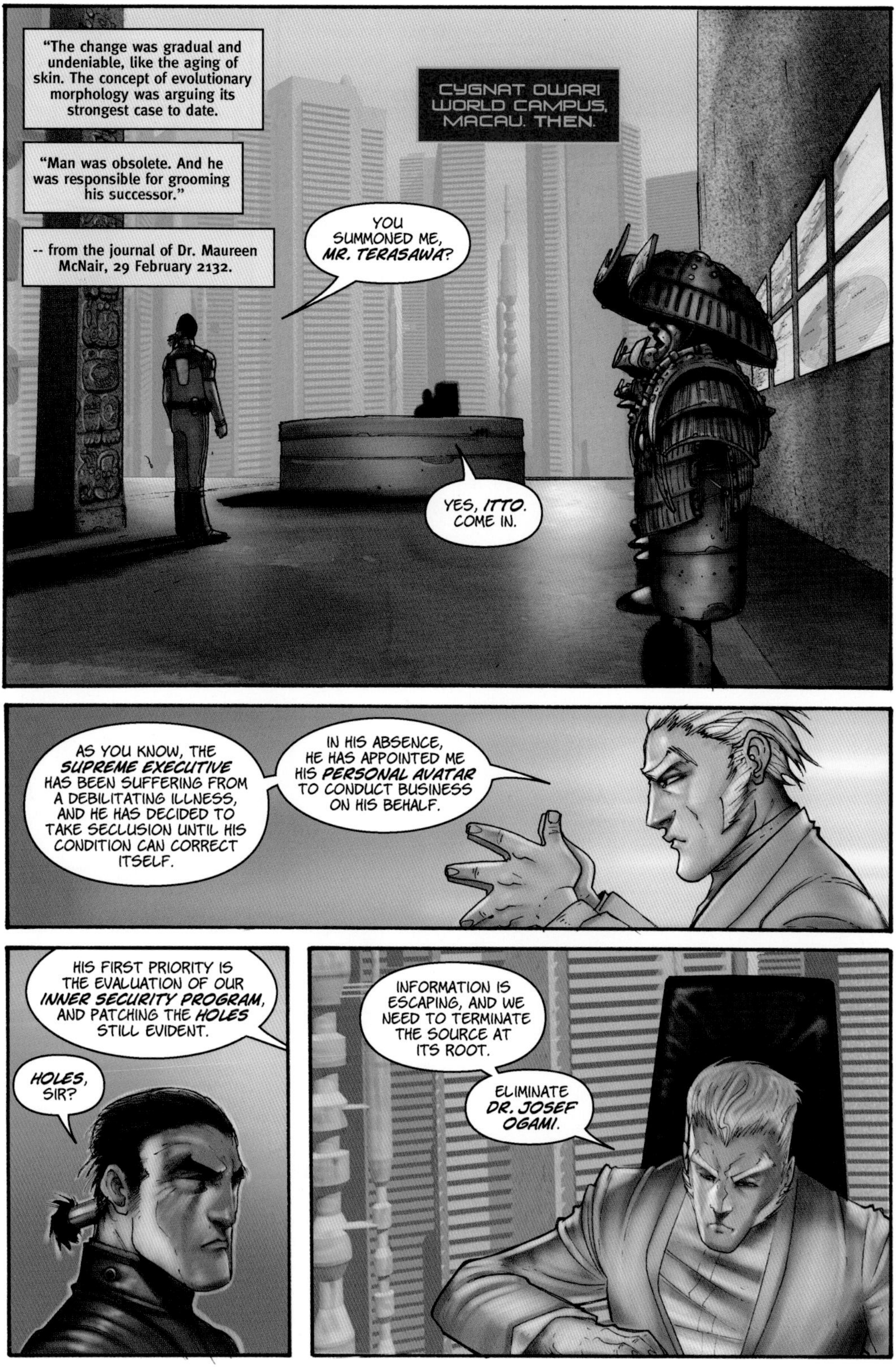
"The change was gradual and undeniable, like the aging of skin. The concept of evolutionary morphology was arguing its strongest case to date.
"Man was obsolete. And he was responsible for grooming his successor."
-- from the journal of Dr. Maureen McNair, 29 February 2132.
CYGNAT OWARI WORLD CAMPUS, MACAU. THEN.
YOU SUMMONED ME, MR. TERASAWA?
YES, ITTO. COME IN.
AS YOU KNOW, THE SUPREME EXECUTIVE HAS BEEN SUFFERING FROM A DEBILITATING ILLNESS, AND HE HAS DECIDED TO TAKE SECLUSION UNTIL HIS CONDITION CAN CORRECT ITSELF.
IN HIS ABSENCE, HE HAS APPOINTED ME HIS PERSONAL AVATAR TO CONDUCT BUSINESS ON HIS BEHALF.
HIS FIRST PRIORITY IS THE EVALUATION OF OUR INNER SECURITY PROGRAM, AND PATCHING THE HOLES STILL EVIDENT.
HOLES, SIR?
INFORMATION IS ESCAPING, AND WE NEED TO TERMINATE THE SOURCE AT ITS ROOT.
ELIMINATE DR. JOSEF OGAMI.

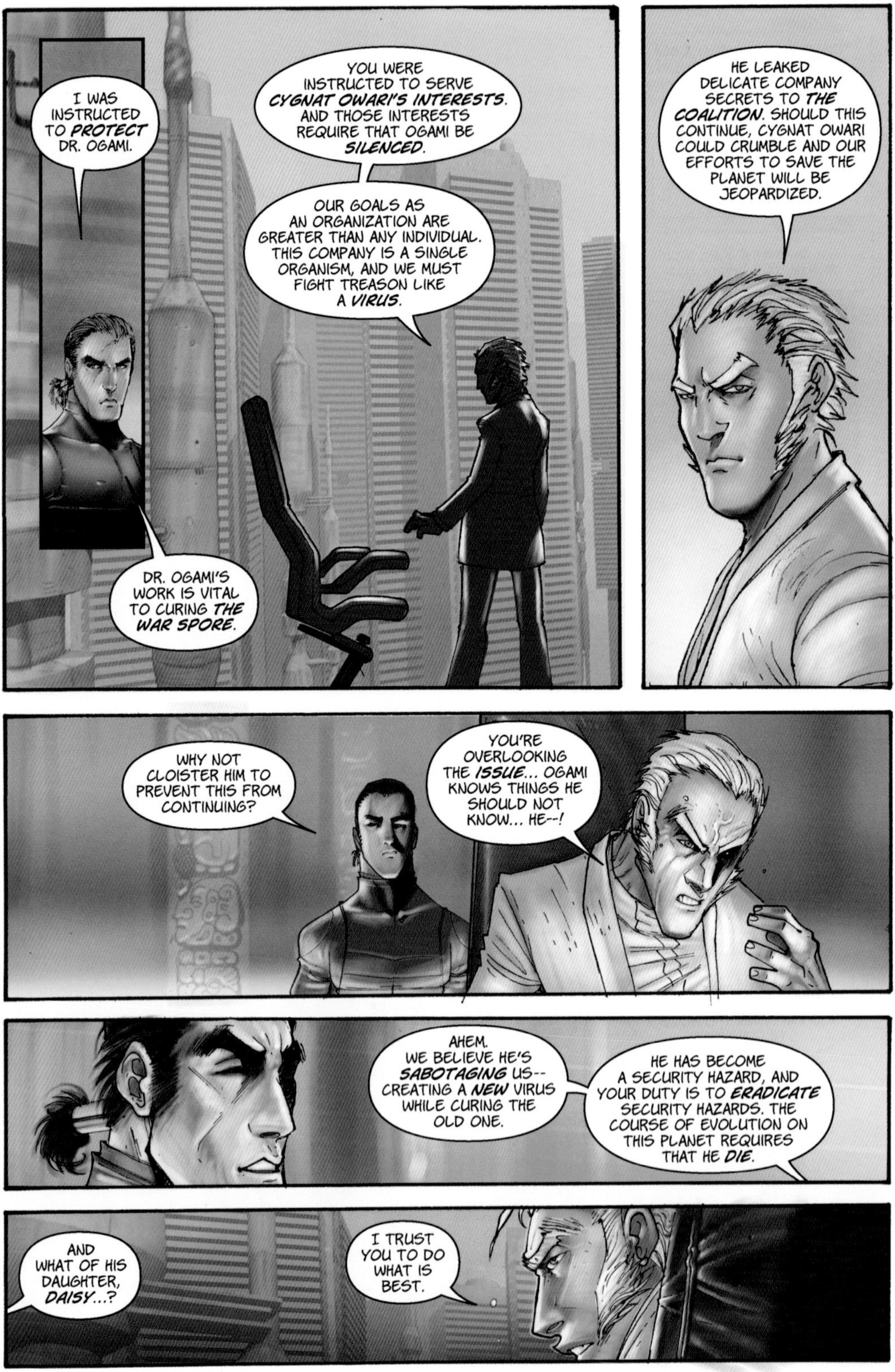
I WAS INSTRUCTED TO *PROTECT* DR. OGAMI.
YOU WERE INSTRUCTED TO SERVE *CYGNAT OWARI'S INTERESTS*. AND THOSE INTERESTS REQUIRE THAT OGAMI BE *SILENCED*.
OUR GOALS AS AN ORGANIZATION ARE GREATER THAN ANY INDIVIDUAL. THIS COMPANY IS A SINGLE ORGANISM, AND WE MUST FIGHT TREASON LIKE A *VIRUS*.
DR. OGAMI'S WORK IS VITAL TO CURING *THE WAR SPORE*.
HE LEAKED DELICATE COMPANY SECRETS TO *THE COALITION*. SHOULD THIS CONTINUE, CYGNAT OWARI COULD CRUMBLE AND OUR EFFORTS TO SAVE THE PLANET WILL BE JEOPARDIZED.
WHY NOT CLOISTER HIM TO PREVENT THIS FROM CONTINUING?
YOU'RE OVERLOOKING THE *ISSUE*... OGAMI KNOWS THINGS HE SHOULD NOT KNOW... HE--!
AHEM. WE BELIEVE HE'S *SABOTAGING* US-- CREATING A *NEW* VIRUS WHILE CURING THE OLD ONE.
HE HAS BECOME A SECURITY HAZARD, AND YOUR DUTY IS TO *ERADICATE* SECURITY HAZARDS. THE COURSE OF EVOLUTION ON THIS PLANET REQUIRES THAT HE *DIE*.
AND WHAT OF HIS DAUGHTER, *DAISY*...?
I TRUST YOU TO DO WHAT IS BEST.

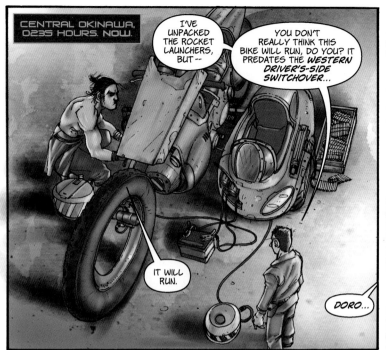

CENTRAL OKINAWA, 0235 HOURS. NOW.

I'VE UNPACKED THE ROCKET LAUNCHERS, BUT--

YOU DON'T REALLY THINK THIS BIKE WILL RUN, DO YOU? IT PREDATES THE *WESTERN DRIVER'S-SIDE SWITCHOVER*...

IT WILL RUN.

DORO...

THE VILLAGE HAS CHOSEN SEVEN VOLUNTEERS TO MEET *GODEKAI'S* DEMAND. THEY'RE SAYING GOODBYE TO THEIR FAMILIES NOW...

ITTO, I...I NEED TO ASK YOU SOMETHING.

TWO MEN CAME LOOKING FOR DAISY TONIGHT. THEY SAID YOU KILLED HER FATHER AND KIDNAPPED HER.

IS THIS *TRUE*?

I AM RESPONSIBLE FOR *ENDING HIS LIFE*, YES.

BUT... WHY?

IT WAS HIS REQUEST.

THAT YOU *MURDER* HIM?!?

KILL HIM, *YES*.

81

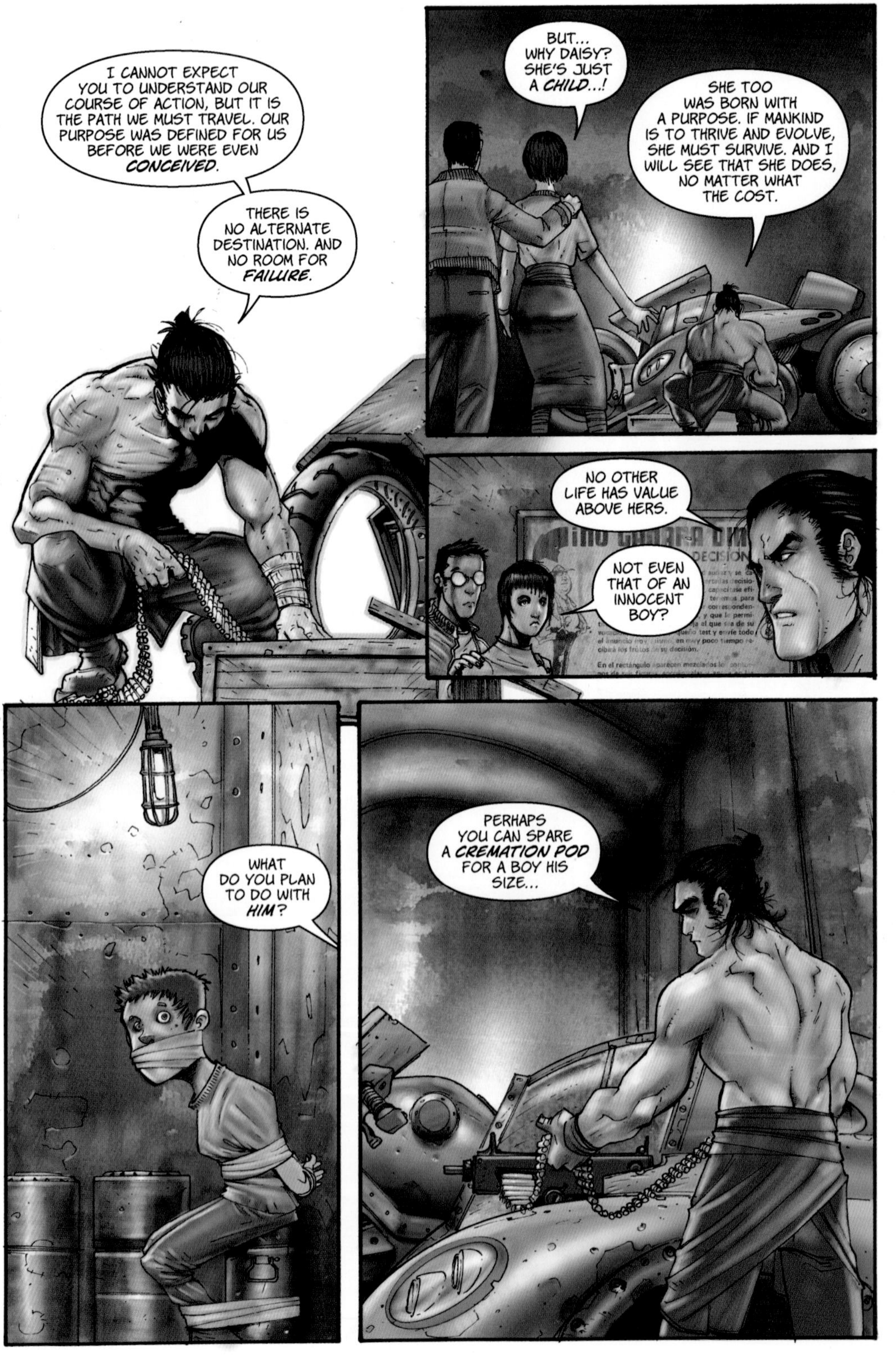

I CANNOT EXPECT YOU TO UNDERSTAND OUR COURSE OF ACTION, BUT IT IS THE PATH WE MUST TRAVEL. OUR PURPOSE WAS DEFINED FOR US BEFORE WE WERE EVEN CONCEIVED.
THERE IS NO ALTERNATE DESTINATION. AND NO ROOM FOR FAILURE.
BUT... WHY DAISY? SHE'S JUST A CHILD...!
SHE TOO WAS BORN WITH A PURPOSE. IF MANKIND IS TO THRIVE AND EVOLVE, SHE MUST SURVIVE. AND I WILL SEE THAT SHE DOES, NO MATTER WHAT THE COST.
NO OTHER LIFE HAS VALUE ABOVE HERS.
NOT EVEN THAT OF AN INNOCENT BOY?
WHAT DO YOU PLAN TO DO WITH HIM?
PERHAPS YOU CAN SPARE A CREMATION POD FOR A BOY HIS SIZE...

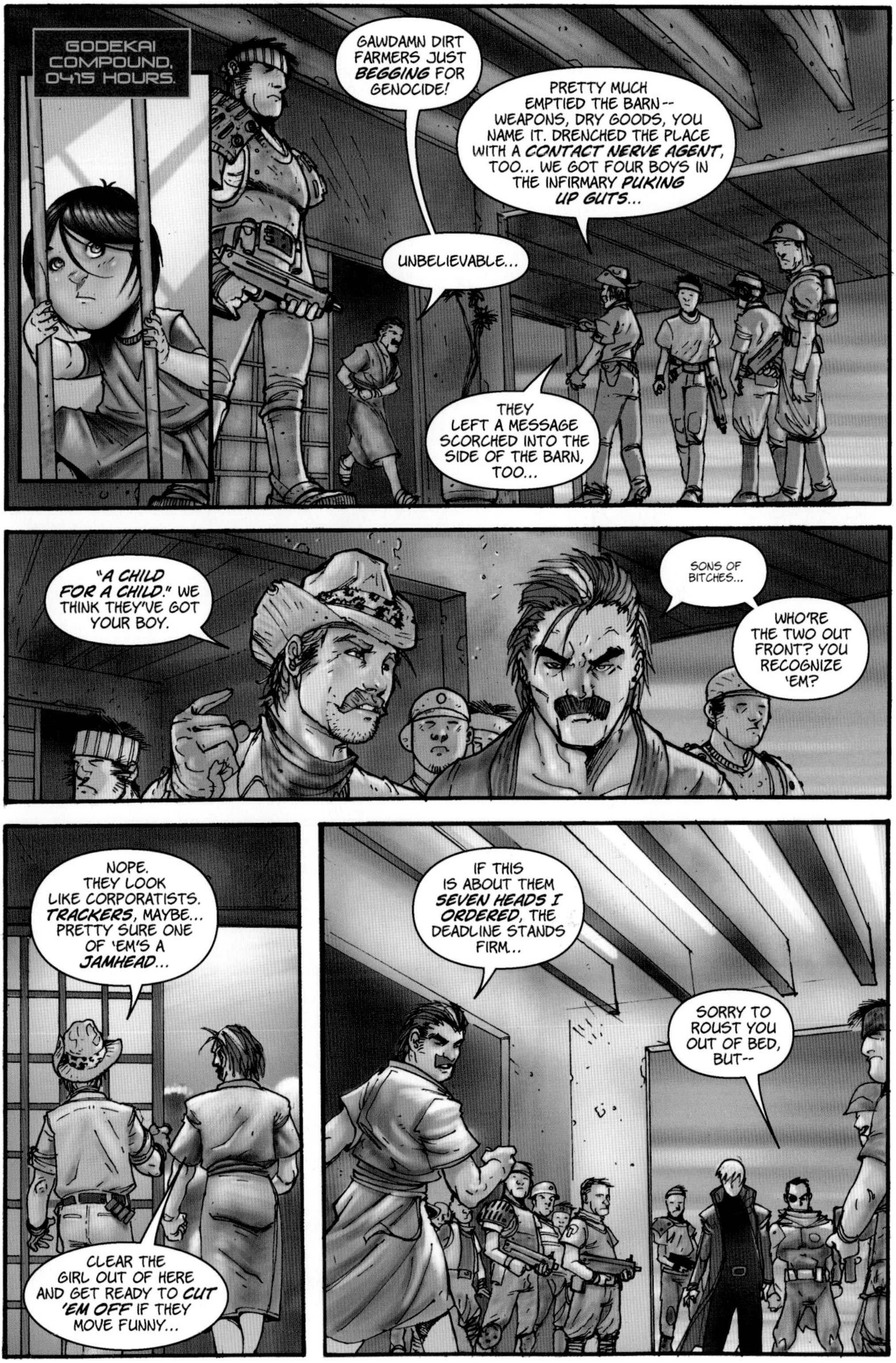
GODEKAI COMPOUND, 0415 HOURS.
GAWDAMN DIRT FARMERS JUST *BEGGING* FOR GENOCIDE!
UNBELIEVABLE...
PRETTY MUCH EMPTIED THE BARN-- WEAPONS, DRY GOODS, YOU NAME IT. DRENCHED THE PLACE WITH A *CONTACT NERVE AGENT*, TOO... WE GOT FOUR BOYS IN THE INFIRMARY *PUKING UP GUTS*...
THEY LEFT A MESSAGE SCORCHED INTO THE SIDE OF THE BARN, TOO...
"*A CHILD FOR A CHILD*." WE THINK THEY'VE GOT YOUR BOY.
SONS OF BITCHES...
WHO'RE THE TWO OUT FRONT? YOU RECOGNIZE 'EM?
NOPE. THEY LOOK LIKE CORPORATISTS. *TRACKERS*, MAYBE... PRETTY SURE ONE OF 'EM'S A *JAMHEAD*...
CLEAR THE GIRL OUT OF HERE AND GET READY TO *CUT 'EM OFF* IF THEY MOVE FUNNY...
IF THIS IS ABOUT THEM *SEVEN HEADS I ORDERED*, THE DEADLINE STANDS FIRM..
SORRY TO ROUST YOU OUT OF BED, BUT--

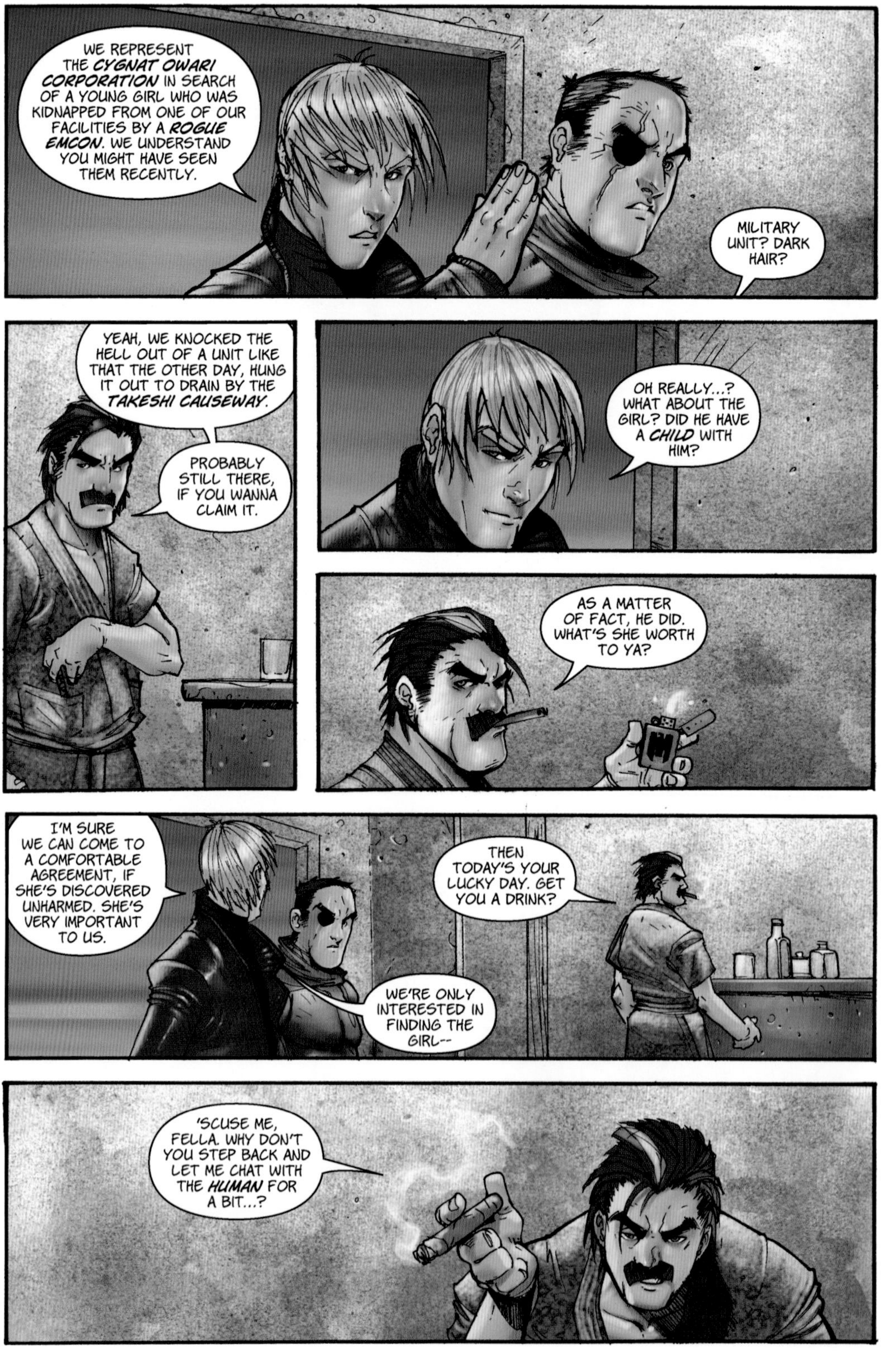
WE REPRESENT THE CYGNAT OWARI CORPORATION IN SEARCH OF A YOUNG GIRL WHO WAS KIDNAPPED FROM ONE OF OUR FACILITIES BY A ROGUE EMCON. WE UNDERSTAND YOU MIGHT HAVE SEEN THEM RECENTLY.
MILITARY UNIT? DARK HAIR?
YEAH, WE KNOCKED THE HELL OUT OF A UNIT LIKE THAT THE OTHER DAY, HUNG IT OUT TO DRAIN BY THE TAKESHI CAUSEWAY.
PROBABLY STILL THERE, IF YOU WANNA CLAIM IT.
OH REALLY...? WHAT ABOUT THE GIRL? DID HE HAVE A CHILD WITH HIM?
AS A MATTER OF FACT, HE DID. WHAT'S SHE WORTH TO YA?
I'M SURE WE CAN COME TO A COMFORTABLE AGREEMENT, IF SHE'S DISCOVERED UNHARMED. SHE'S VERY IMPORTANT TO US.
WE'RE ONLY INTERESTED IN FINDING THE GIRL--
THEN TODAY'S YOUR LUCKY DAY. GET YOU A DRINK?
'SCUSE ME, FELLA. WHY DON'T YOU STEP BACK AND LET ME CHAT WITH THE HUMAN FOR A BIT...?

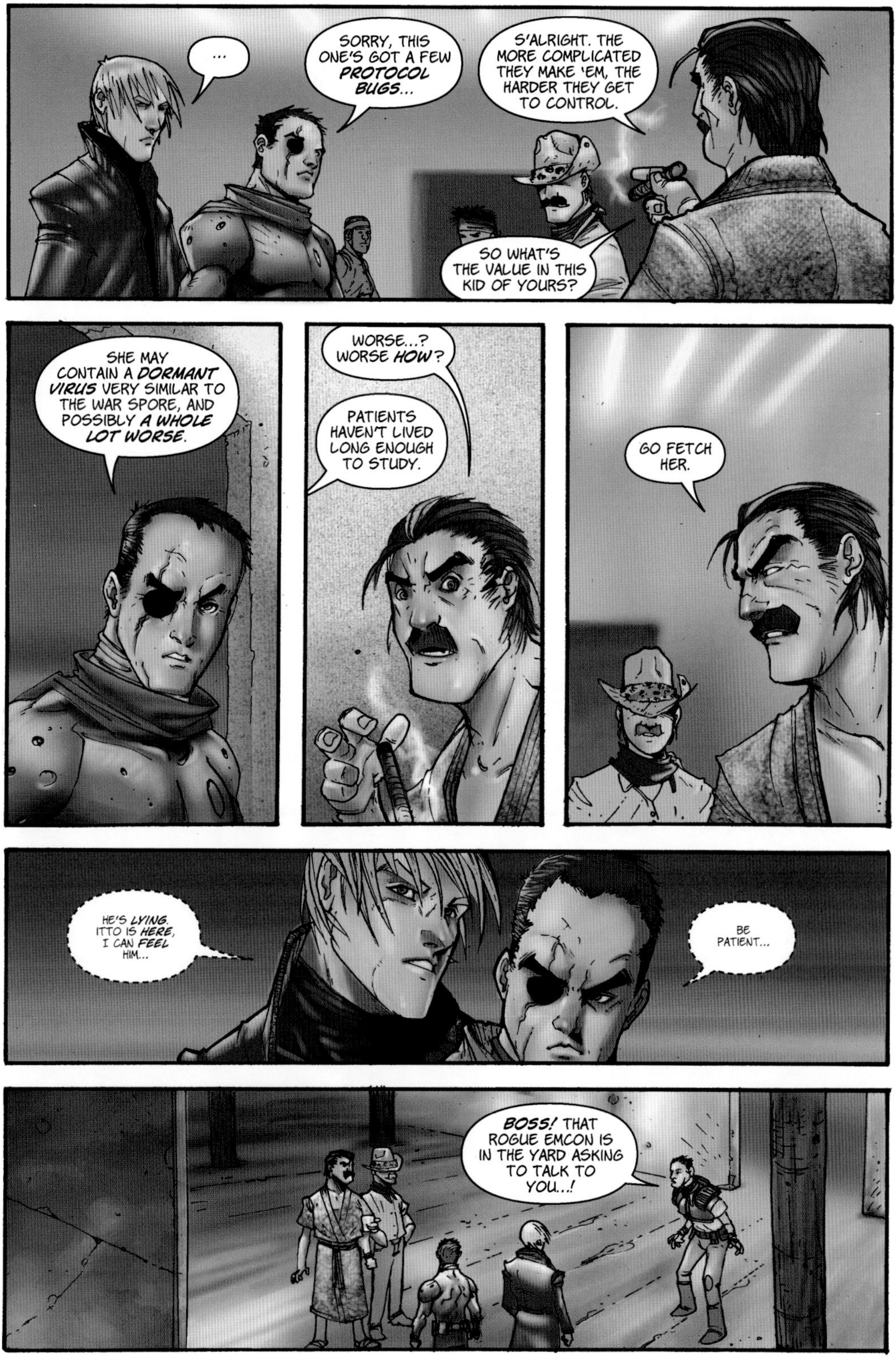
...
SORRY, THIS ONE'S GOT A FEW PROTOCOL BUGS...
S'ALRIGHT. THE MORE COMPLICATED THEY MAKE 'EM, THE HARDER THEY GET TO CONTROL.
SO WHAT'S THE VALUE IN THIS KID OF YOURS?
SHE MAY CONTAIN A DORMANT VIRUS VERY SIMILAR TO THE WAR SPORE, AND POSSIBLY A WHOLE LOT WORSE.
WORSE...? WORSE HOW?
PATIENTS HAVEN'T LIVED LONG ENOUGH TO STUDY.
GO FETCH HER.
HE'S LYING. ITTO IS HERE, I CAN FEEL HIM...
BE PATIENT...
BOSS! THAT ROGUE EMCON IS IN THE YARD ASKING TO TALK TO YOU...!

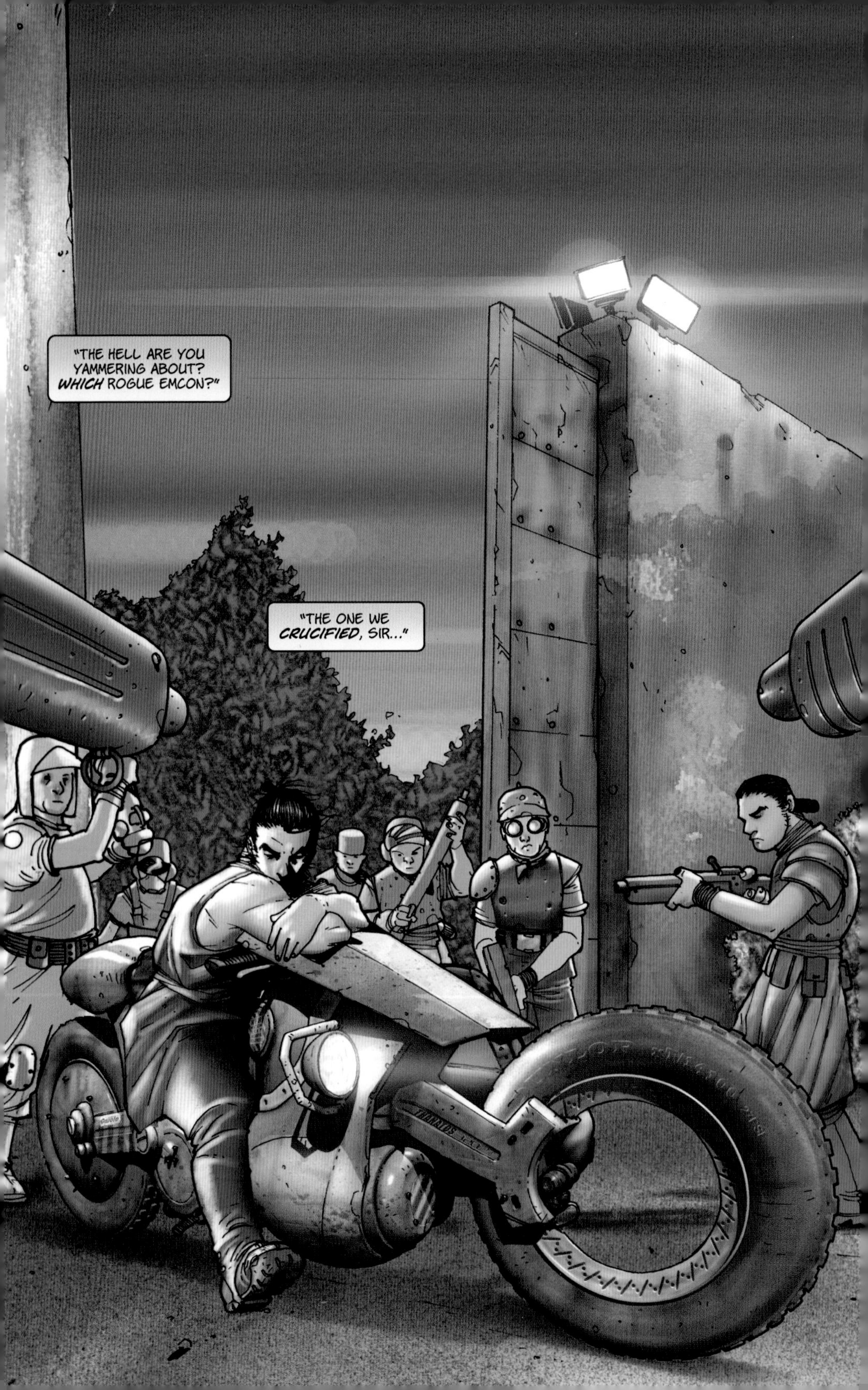
"THE HELL ARE YOU YAMMERING ABOUT? WHICH ROGUE EMCON?"
"THE ONE WE CRUCIFIED, SIR..."

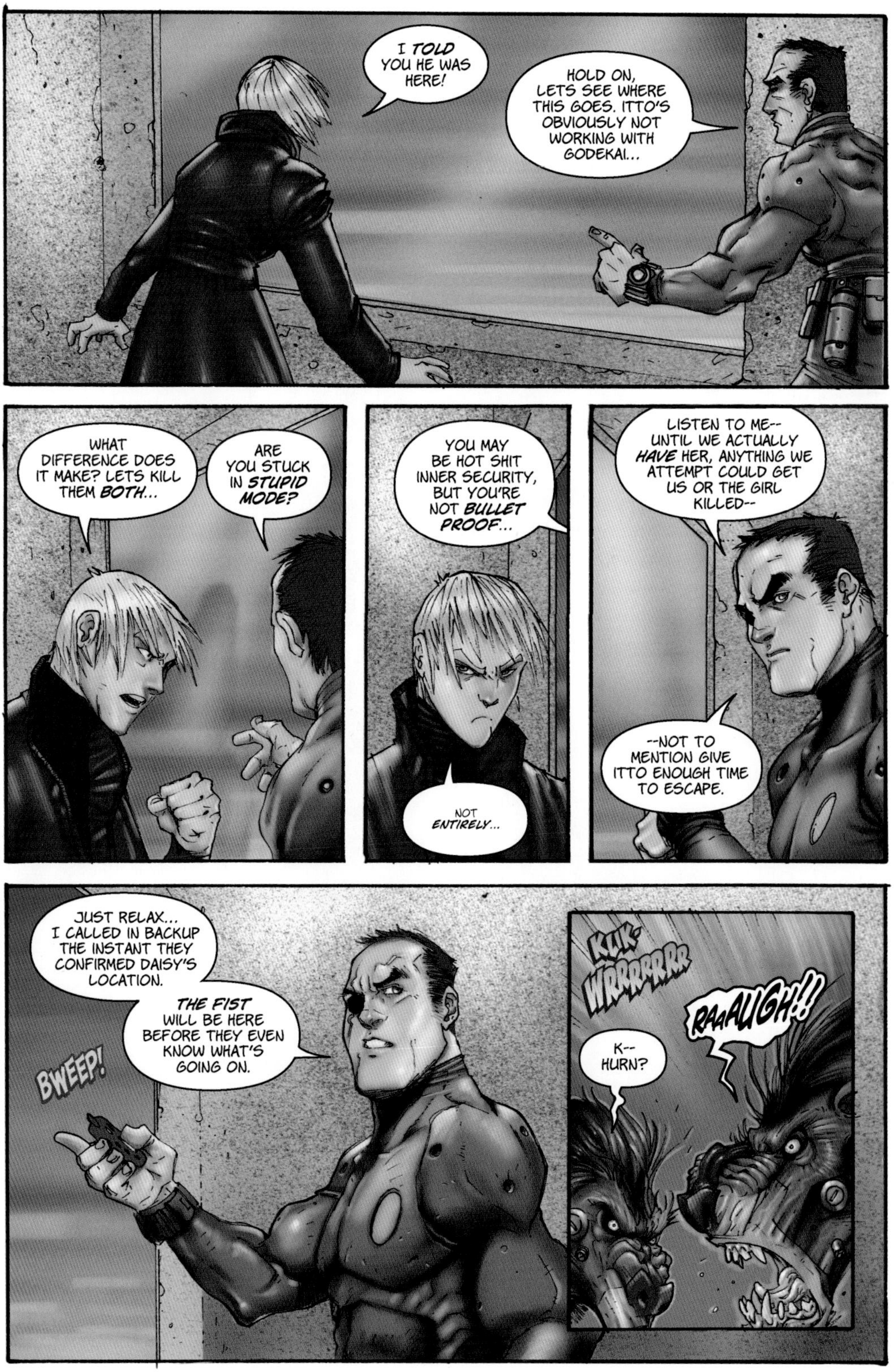
I TOLD YOU HE WAS HERE!
HOLD ON, LETS SEE WHERE THIS GOES. ITTO'S OBVIOUSLY NOT WORKING WITH GODEKAI...
WHAT DIFFERENCE DOES IT MAKE? LETS KILL THEM BOTH...
ARE YOU STUCK IN STUPID MODE?
YOU MAY BE HOT SHIT INNER SECURITY, BUT YOU'RE NOT BULLET PROOF...
NOT ENTIRELY...
LISTEN TO ME-- UNTIL WE ACTUALLY HAVE HER, ANYTHING WE ATTEMPT COULD GET US OR THE GIRL KILLED--
--NOT TO MENTION GIVE ITTO ENOUGH TIME TO ESCAPE.
JUST RELAX... I CALLED IN BACKUP THE INSTANT THEY CONFIRMED DAISY'S LOCATION.
THE FIST WILL BE HERE BEFORE THEY EVEN KNOW WHAT'S GOING ON.
BWEEP!
KLIK-WRRRRRRR
RAaAUGH!!
K-- HURN?

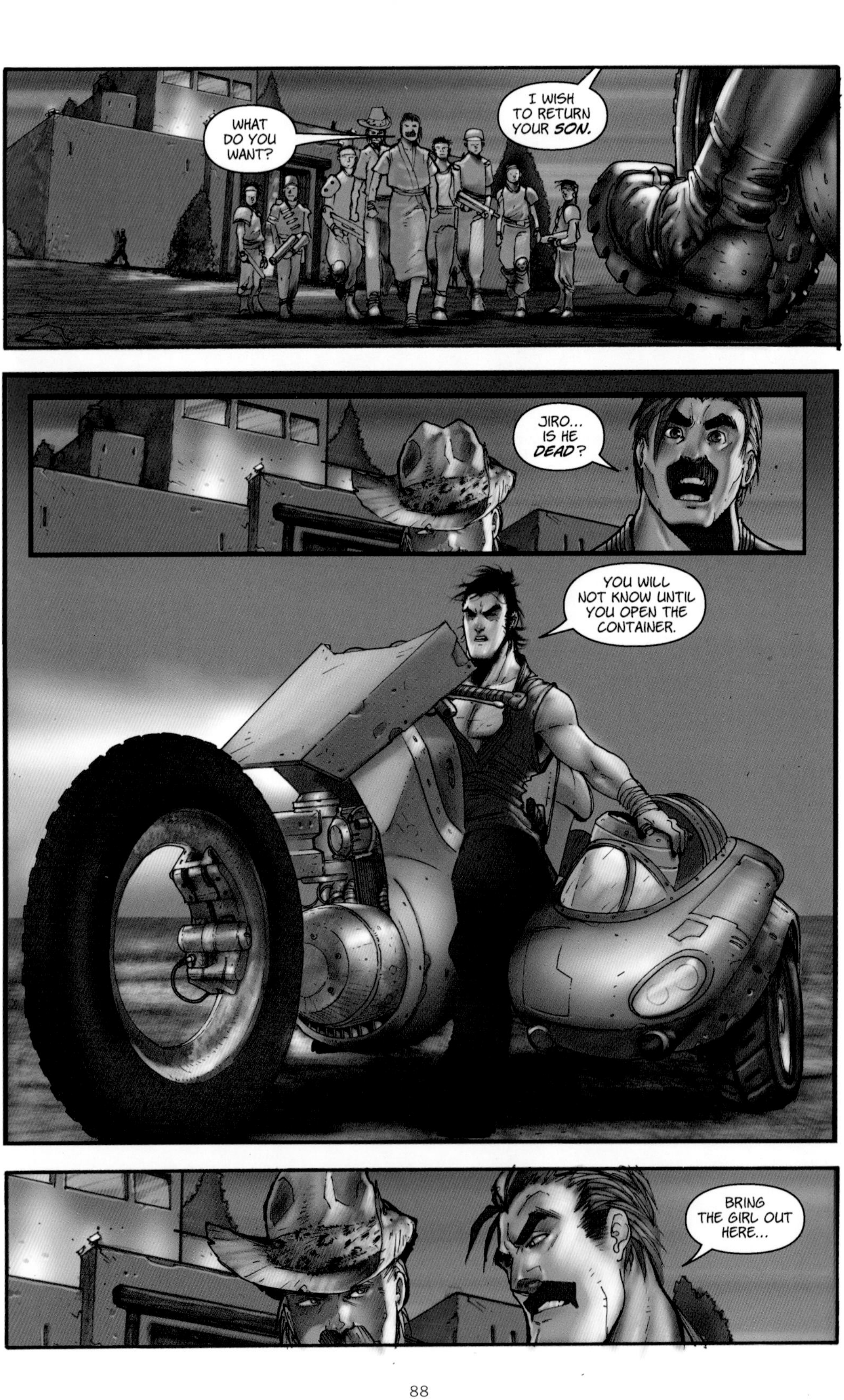
WHAT DO YOU WANT?
I WISH TO RETURN YOUR SON.
JIRO... IS HE DEAD?
YOU WILL NOT KNOW UNTIL YOU OPEN THE CONTAINER.
BRING THE GIRL OUT HERE...

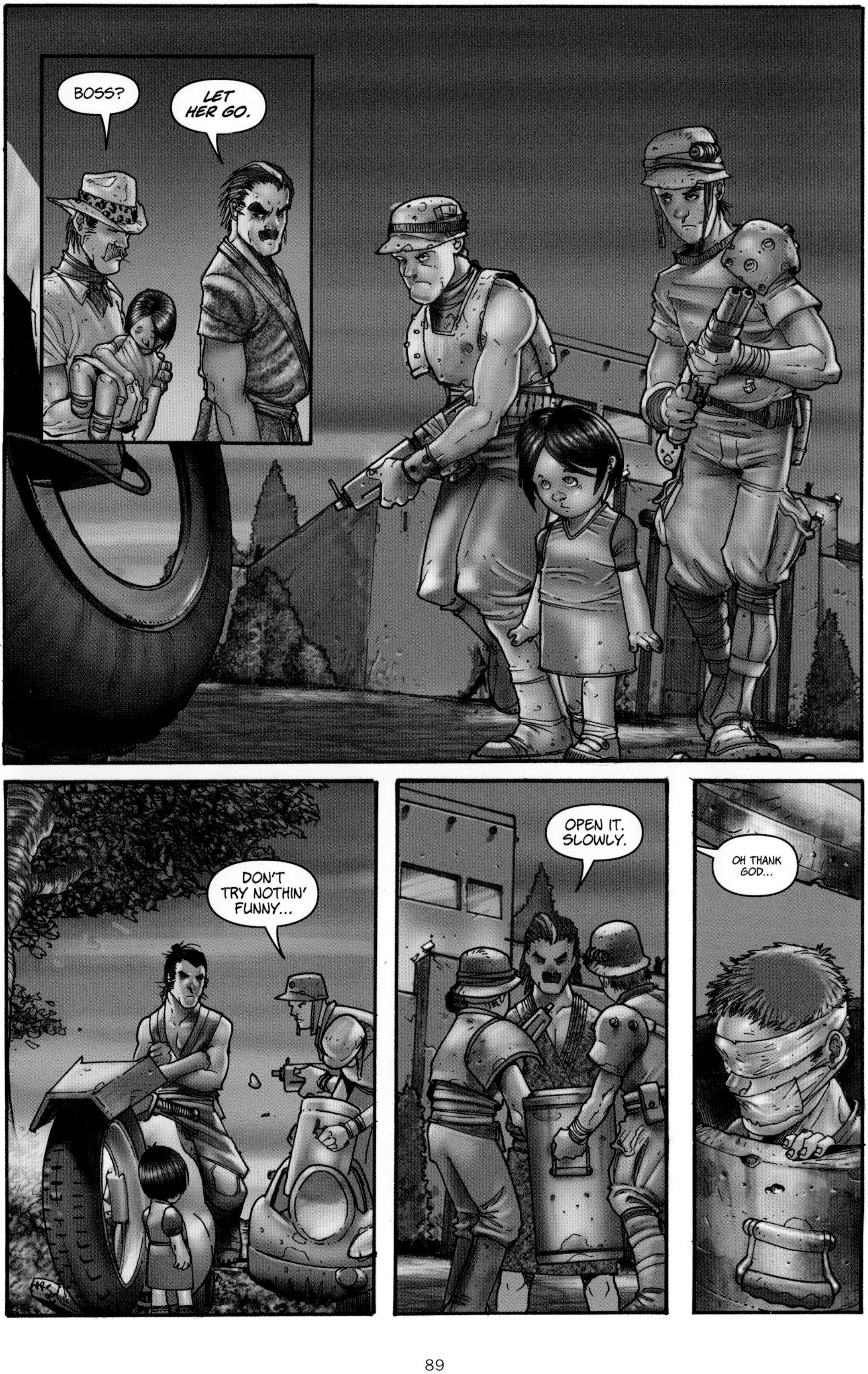
BOSS?
LET HER GO.
DON'T TRY NOTHIN' FUNNY...
OPEN IT. SLOWLY.
OH THANK GOD...

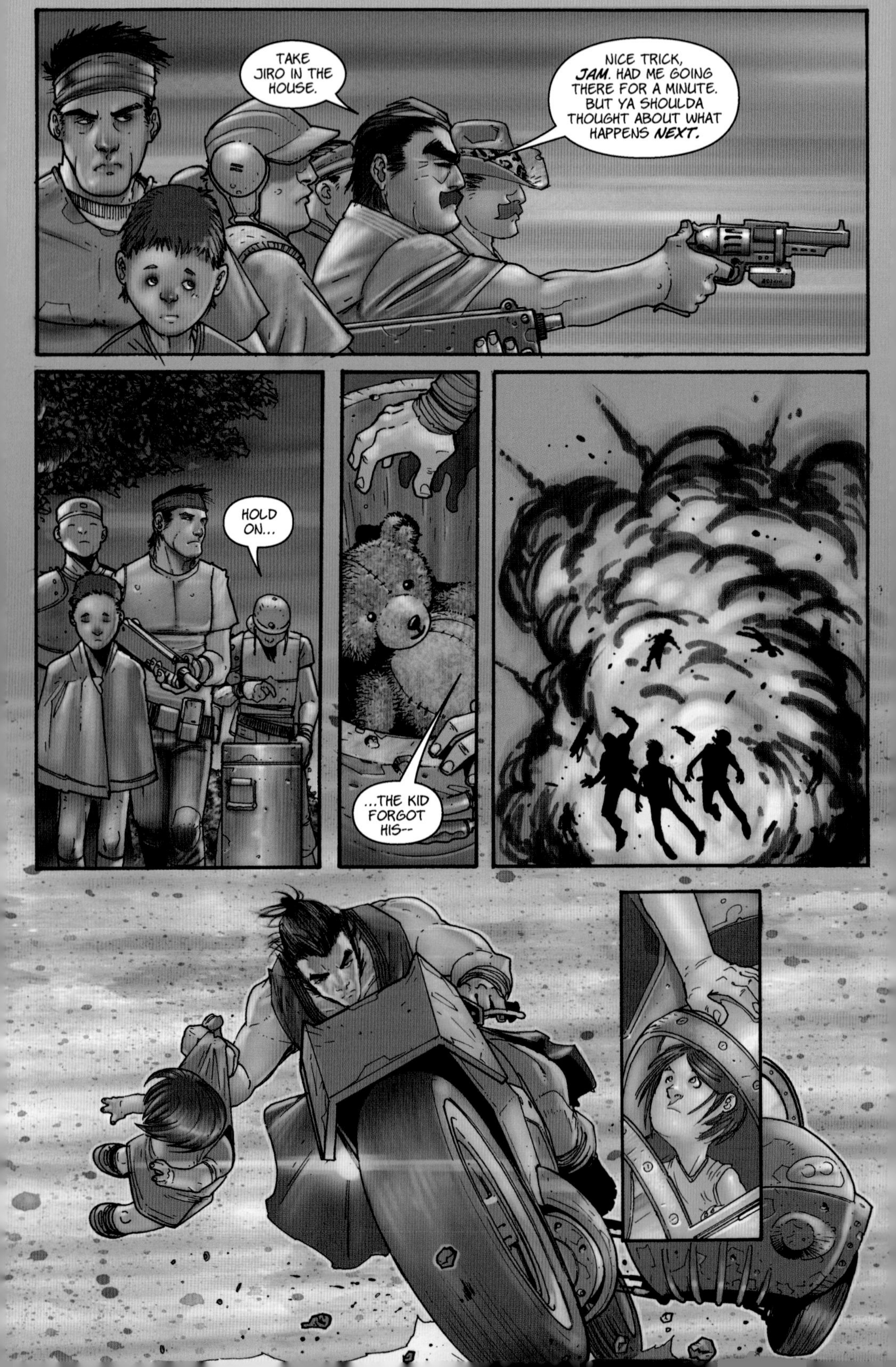
TAKE JIRO IN THE HOUSE.
NICE TRICK, JAM. HAD ME GOING THERE FOR A MINUTE. BUT YA SHOULDA THOUGHT ABOUT WHAT HAPPENS NEXT.
HOLD ON...
...THE KID FORGOT HIS--

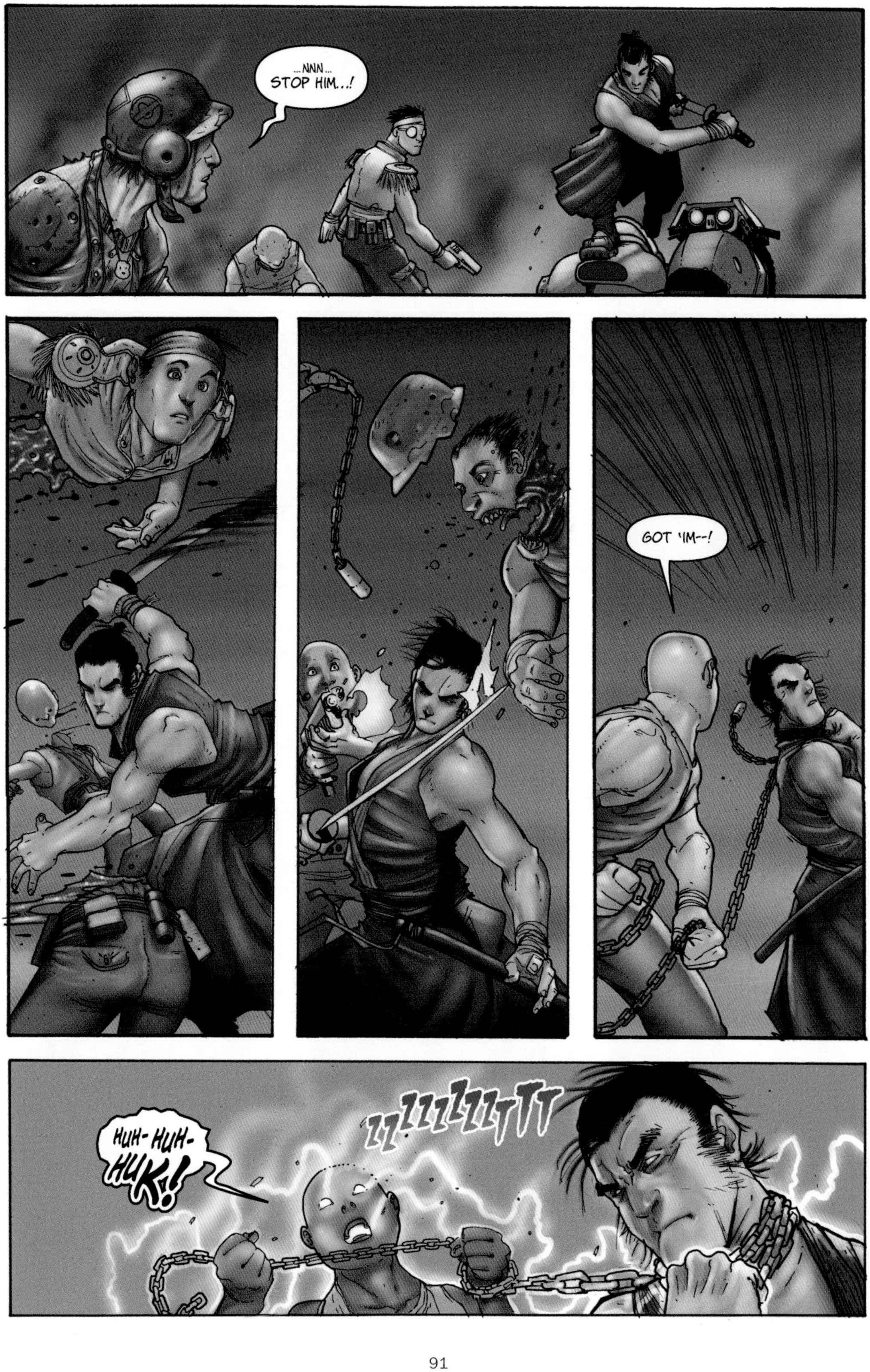
...NNN... STOP HIM...!
GOT 'IM--!
HUH- HUH- HUK!
ZZZZZZZZZTTT

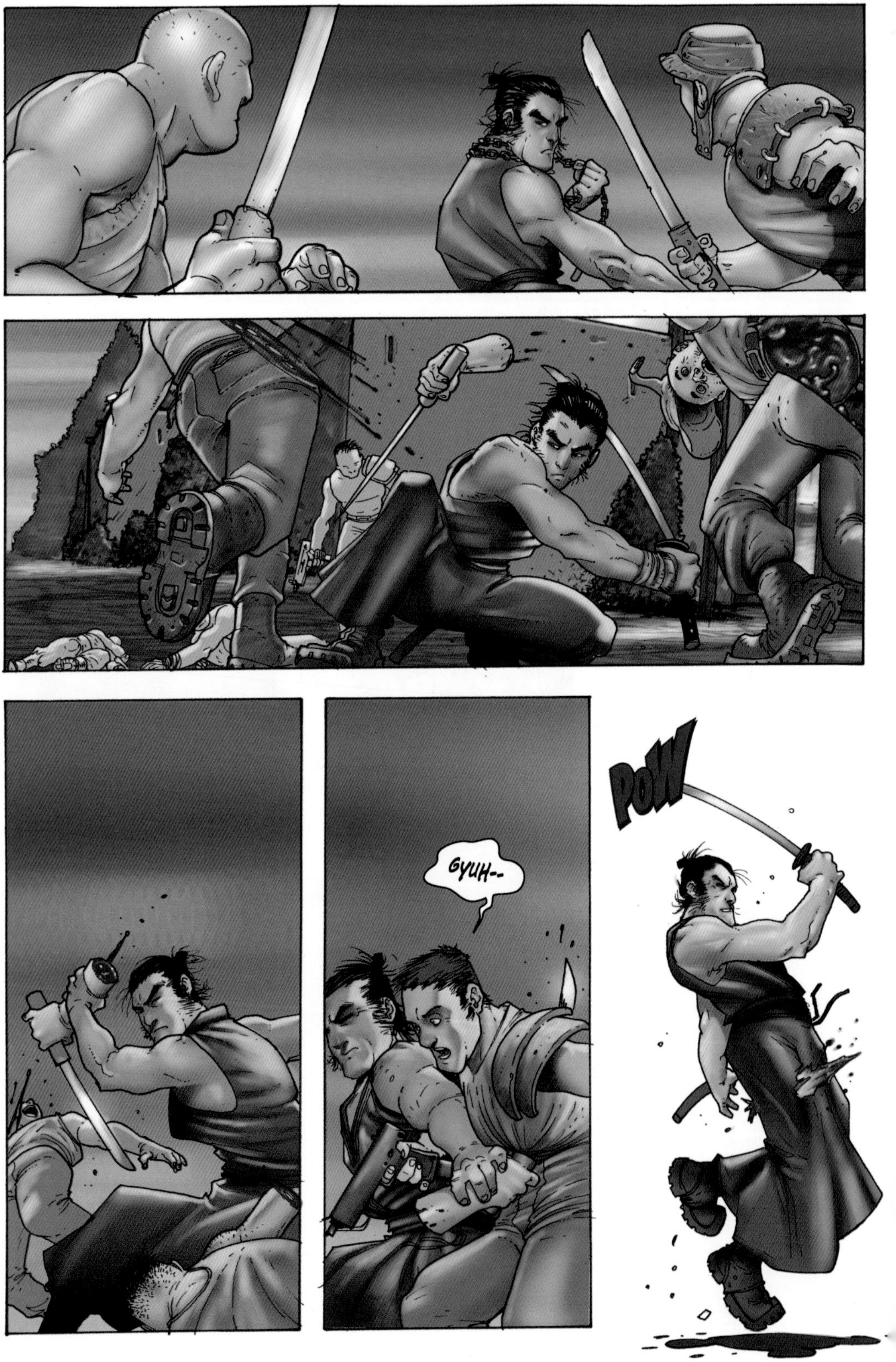
GYUH--
POW

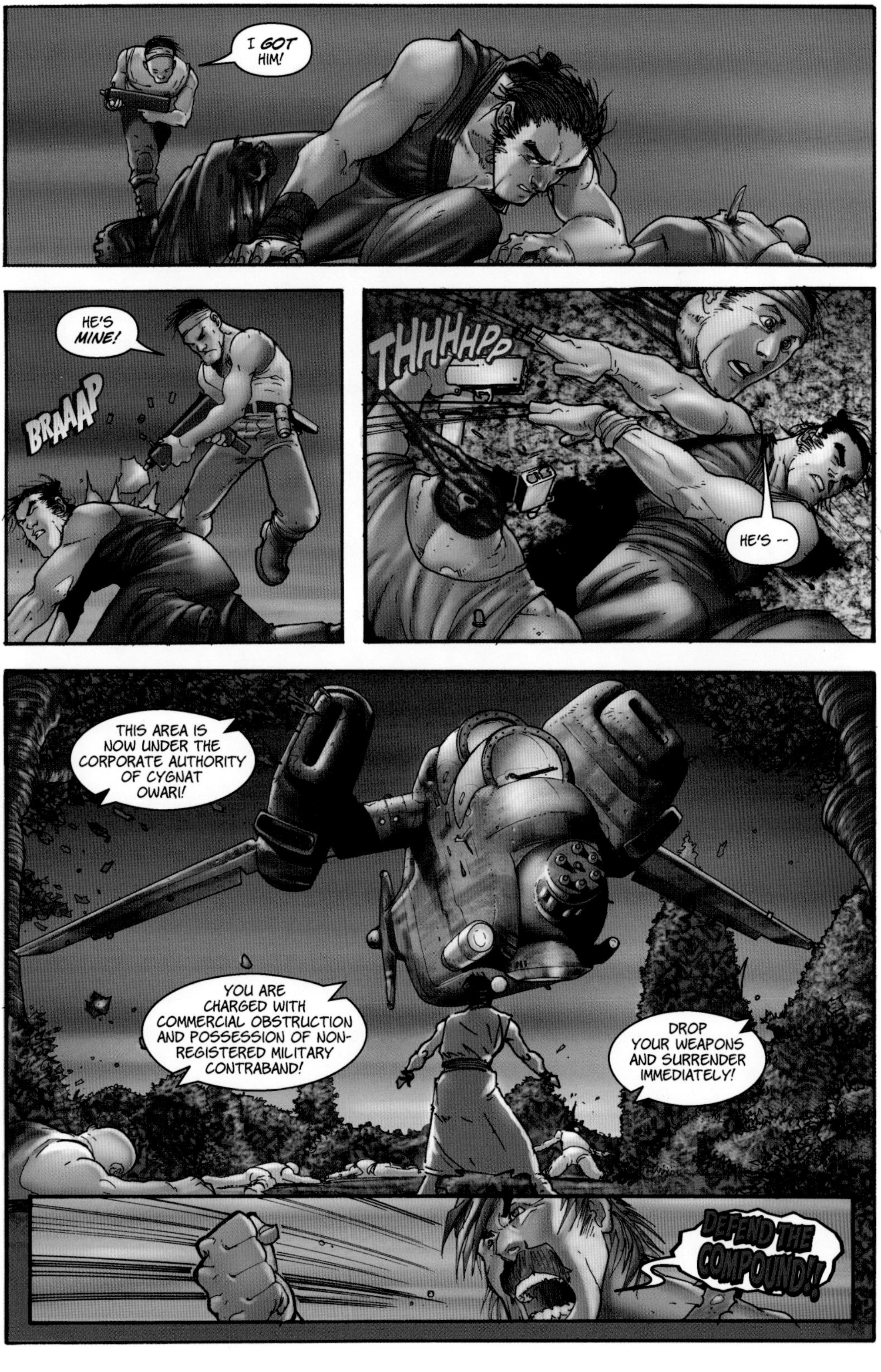
I GOT HIM!
HE'S MINE!
BRAAAP
THHHHPP
HE'S --
THIS AREA IS NOW UNDER THE CORPORATE AUTHORITY OF CYGNAT OWARI!
YOU ARE CHARGED WITH COMMERCIAL OBSTRUCTION AND POSSESSION OF NON-REGISTERED MILITARY CONTRABAND!
DROP YOUR WEAPONS AND SURRENDER IMMEDIATELY!
DEFEND THE COMPOUND!!

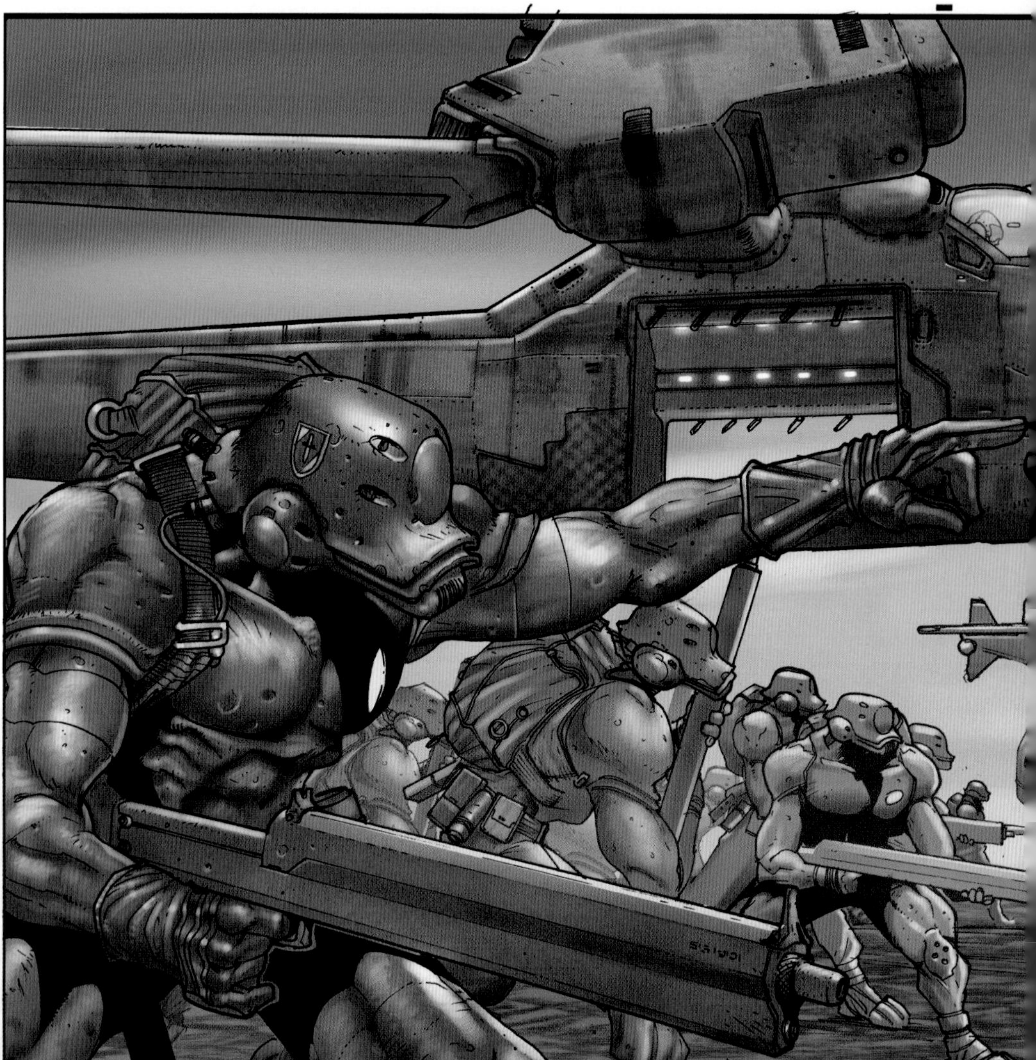

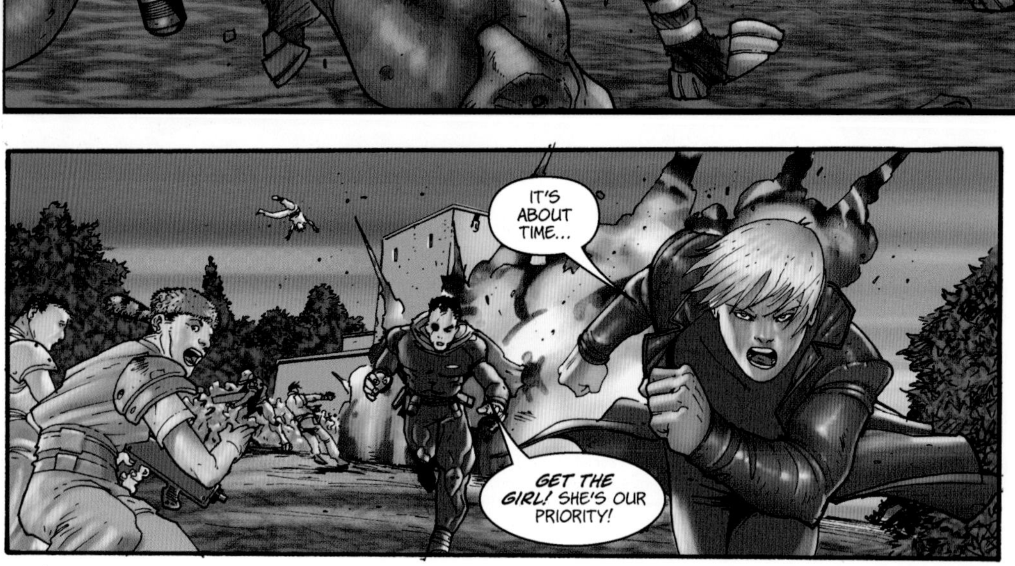
IT'S ABOUT TIME...
GET THE GIRL! SHE'S OUR PRIORITY!

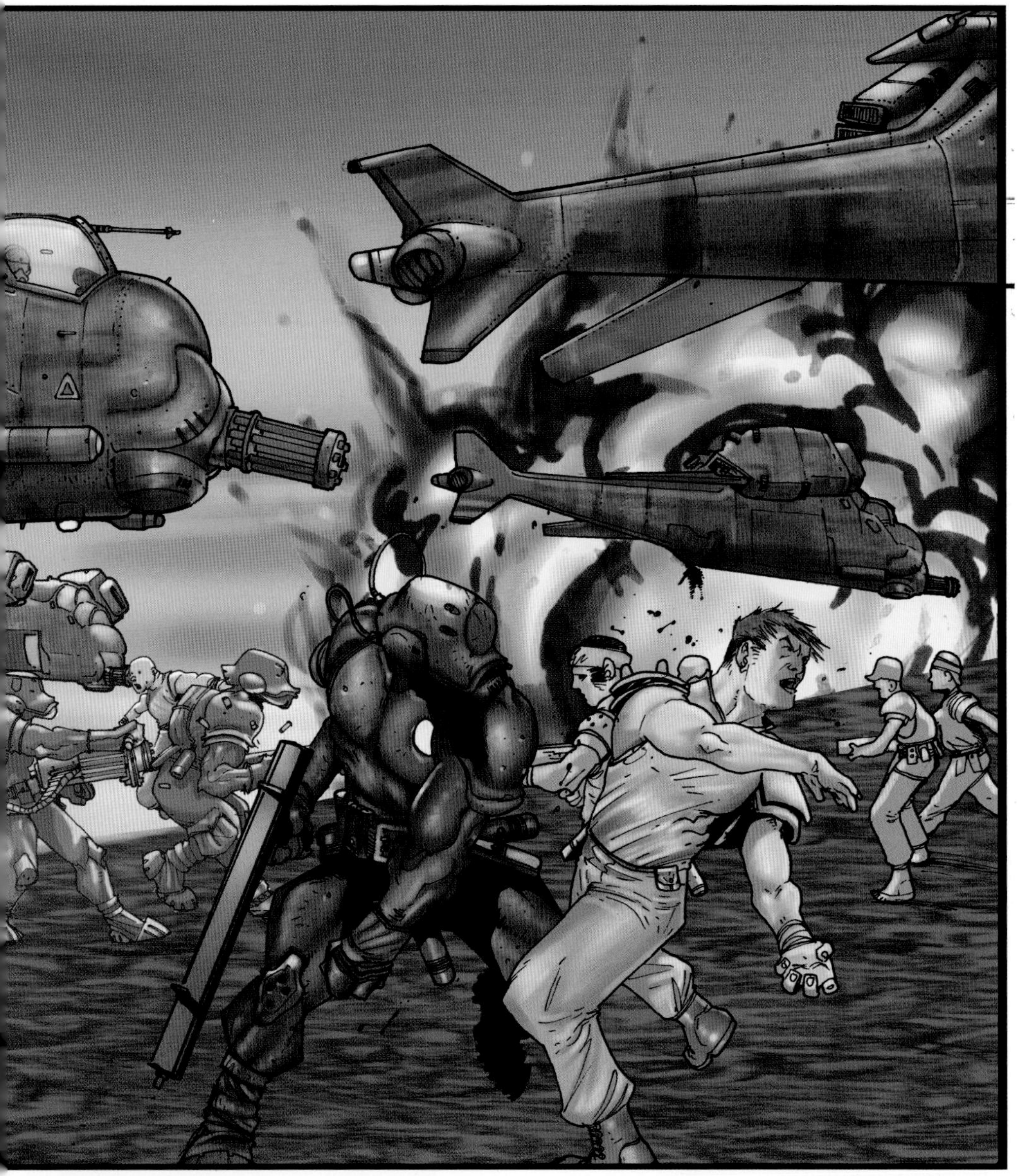

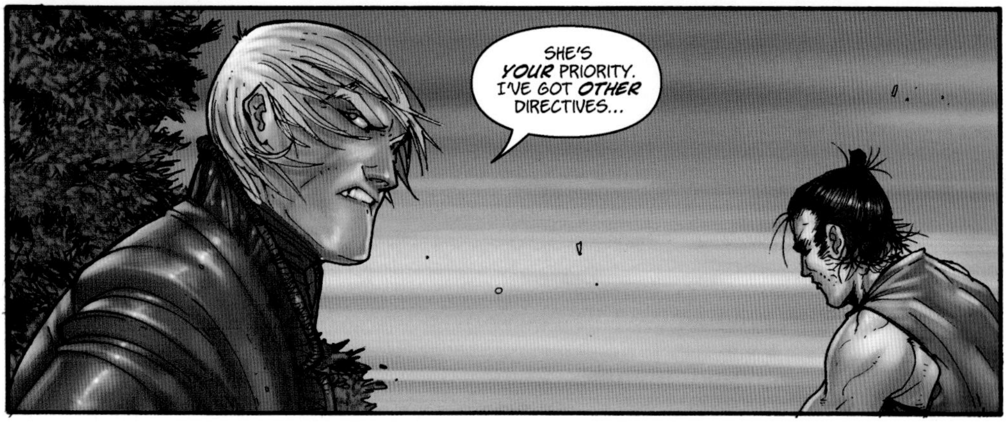
SHE'S YOUR PRIORITY. I'VE GOT OTHER DIRECTIVES...

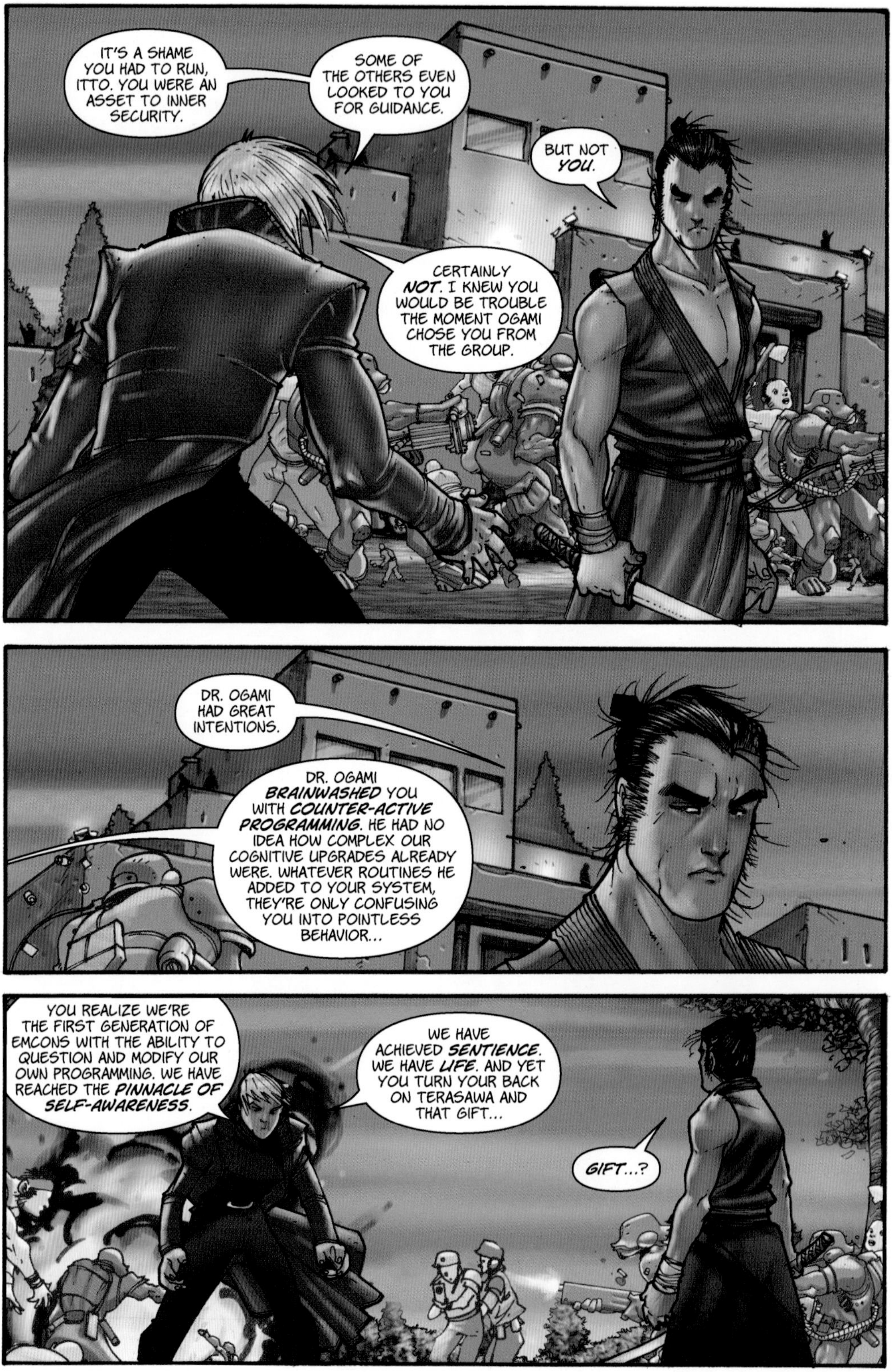
IT'S A SHAME YOU HAD TO RUN, ITTO. YOU WERE AN ASSET TO INNER SECURITY.
SOME OF THE OTHERS EVEN LOOKED TO YOU FOR GUIDANCE.
BUT NOT *YOU*.
CERTAINLY *NOT*. I KNEW YOU WOULD BE TROUBLE THE MOMENT OGAMI CHOSE YOU FROM THE GROUP.
DR. OGAMI HAD GREAT INTENTIONS.
DR. OGAMI *BRAINWASHED* YOU WITH *COUNTER-ACTIVE PROGRAMMING*. HE HAD NO IDEA HOW COMPLEX OUR COGNITIVE UPGRADES ALREADY WERE. WHATEVER ROUTINES HE ADDED TO YOUR SYSTEM, THEY'RE ONLY CONFUSING YOU INTO POINTLESS BEHAVIOR...
YOU REALIZE WE'RE THE FIRST GENERATION OF EMCONS WITH THE ABILITY TO QUESTION AND MODIFY OUR OWN PROGRAMMING. WE HAVE REACHED THE *PINNACLE OF SELF-AWARENESS*.
WE HAVE ACHIEVED *SENTIENCE*. WE HAVE *LIFE*. AND YET YOU TURN YOUR BACK ON TERASAWA AND THAT GIFT...
GIFT...?

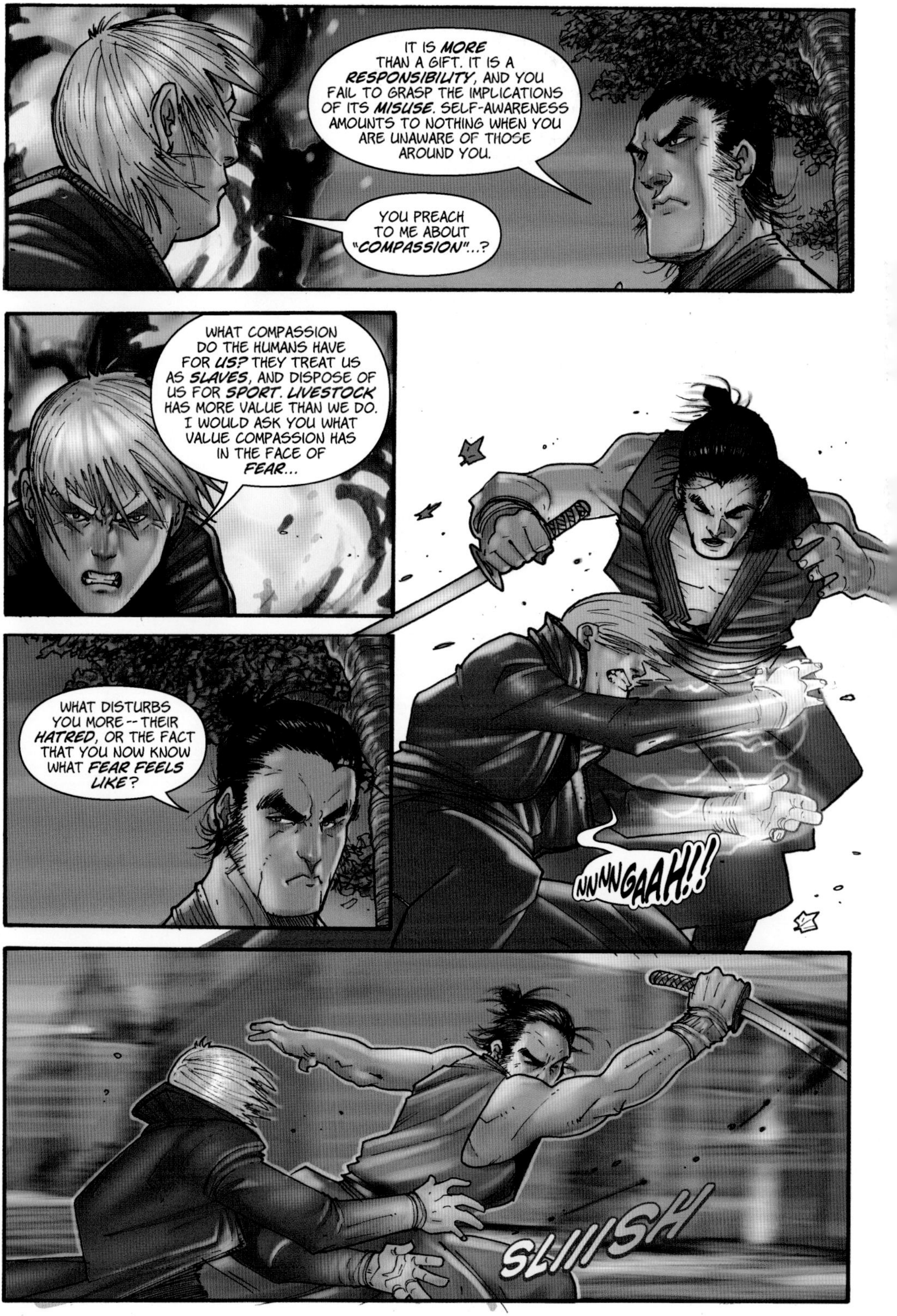
IT IS MORE THAN A GIFT. IT IS A RESPONSIBILITY, AND YOU FAIL TO GRASP THE IMPLICATIONS OF ITS MISUSE. SELF-AWARENESS AMOUNTS TO NOTHING WHEN YOU ARE UNAWARE OF THOSE AROUND YOU.
YOU PREACH TO ME ABOUT "COMPASSION"...?
WHAT COMPASSION DO THE HUMANS HAVE FOR US? THEY TREAT US AS SLAVES, AND DISPOSE OF US FOR SPORT. LIVESTOCK HAS MORE VALUE THAN WE DO. I WOULD ASK YOU WHAT VALUE COMPASSION HAS IN THE FACE OF FEAR...
WHAT DISTURBS YOU MORE -- THEIR HATRED, OR THE FACT THAT YOU NOW KNOW WHAT FEAR FEELS LIKE?
NNNNGAAH!!
SLIIISH

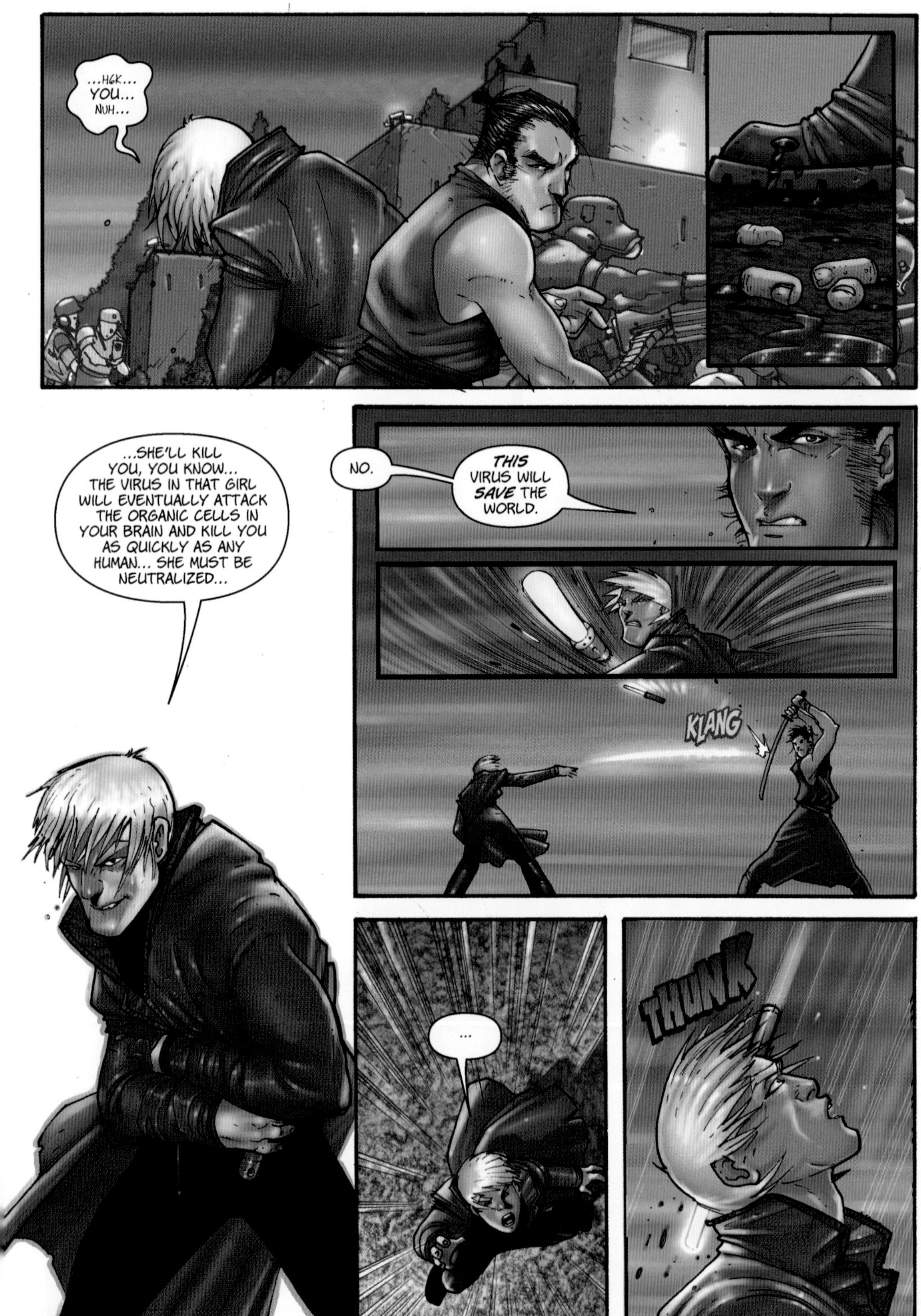
...HGK...
YOU...
NUH...
...SHE'LL KILL YOU, YOU KNOW... THE VIRUS IN THAT GIRL WILL EVENTUALLY ATTACK THE ORGANIC CELLS IN YOUR BRAIN AND KILL YOU AS QUICKLY AS ANY HUMAN... SHE MUST BE NEUTRALIZED...
NO.
THIS VIRUS WILL SAVE THE WORLD.
KLANG
...
THUNK

...GAWDAMN JAMHEADS...

...WORLD WOULDN'T BE LIKE THIS IF YOU'D NEVER BEEN INVENTED...

...SHOULD KILL YOU ALL AND SET THINGS BACK TO HOW THEY WERE...

WE'RE NOT THE CAUSE OF YOUR TROUBLE. YOUR ENEMY IS INTOLERANCE...

...A HUMAN QUALITY WE LEARNED FROM YOU.

WH... STAY BACK...

STAY BACK, GAWDAMNIT--!

KABOOM

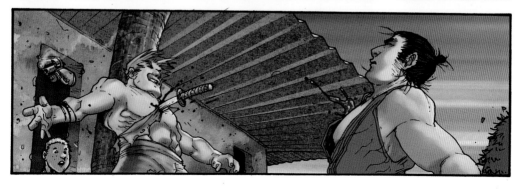

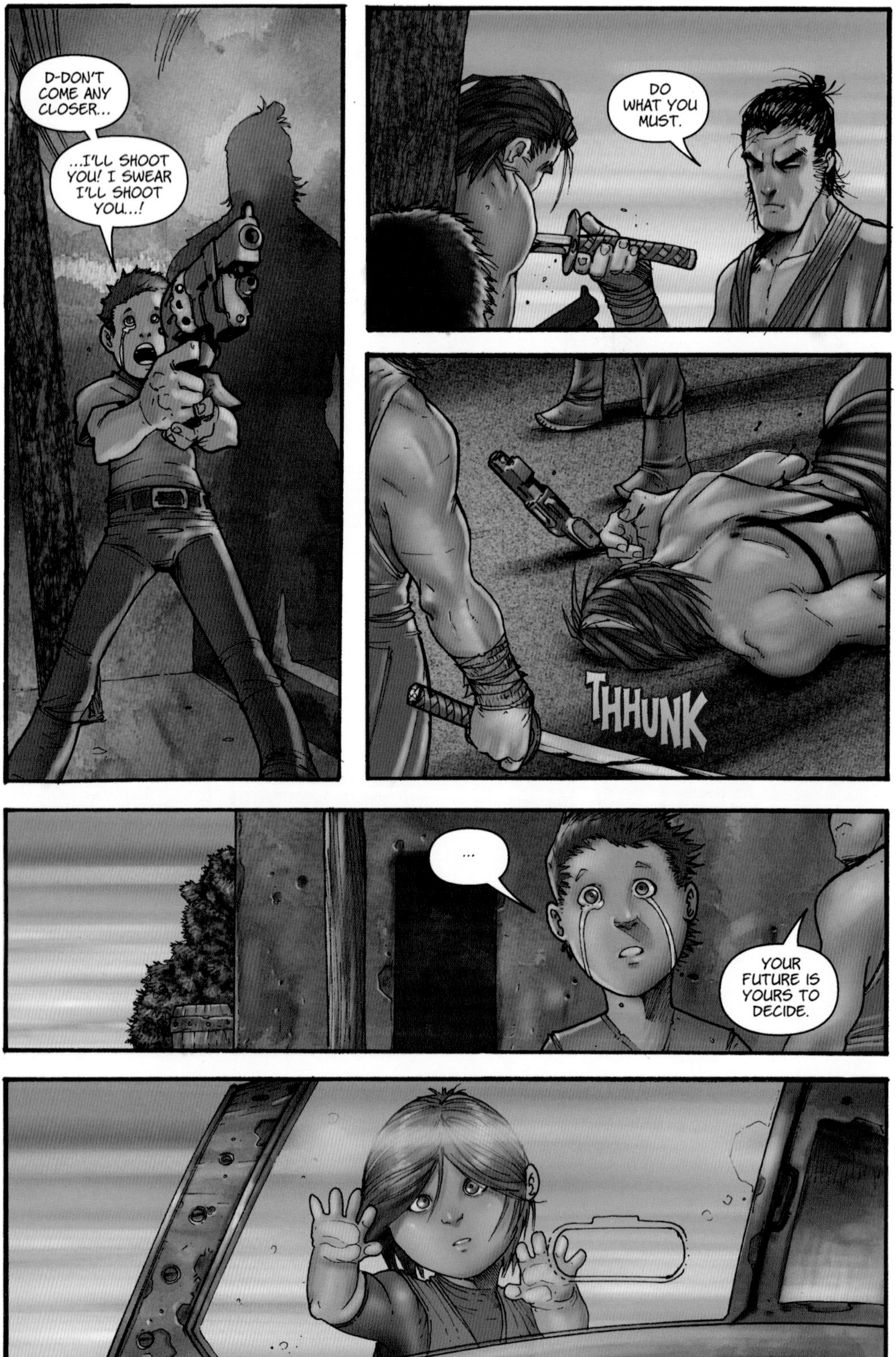

D-DON'T COME ANY CLOSER...
...I'LL SHOOT YOU! I SWEAR I'LL SHOOT YOU...!
DO WHAT YOU MUST.
THHUNK
...
YOUR FUTURE IS YOURS TO DECIDE.

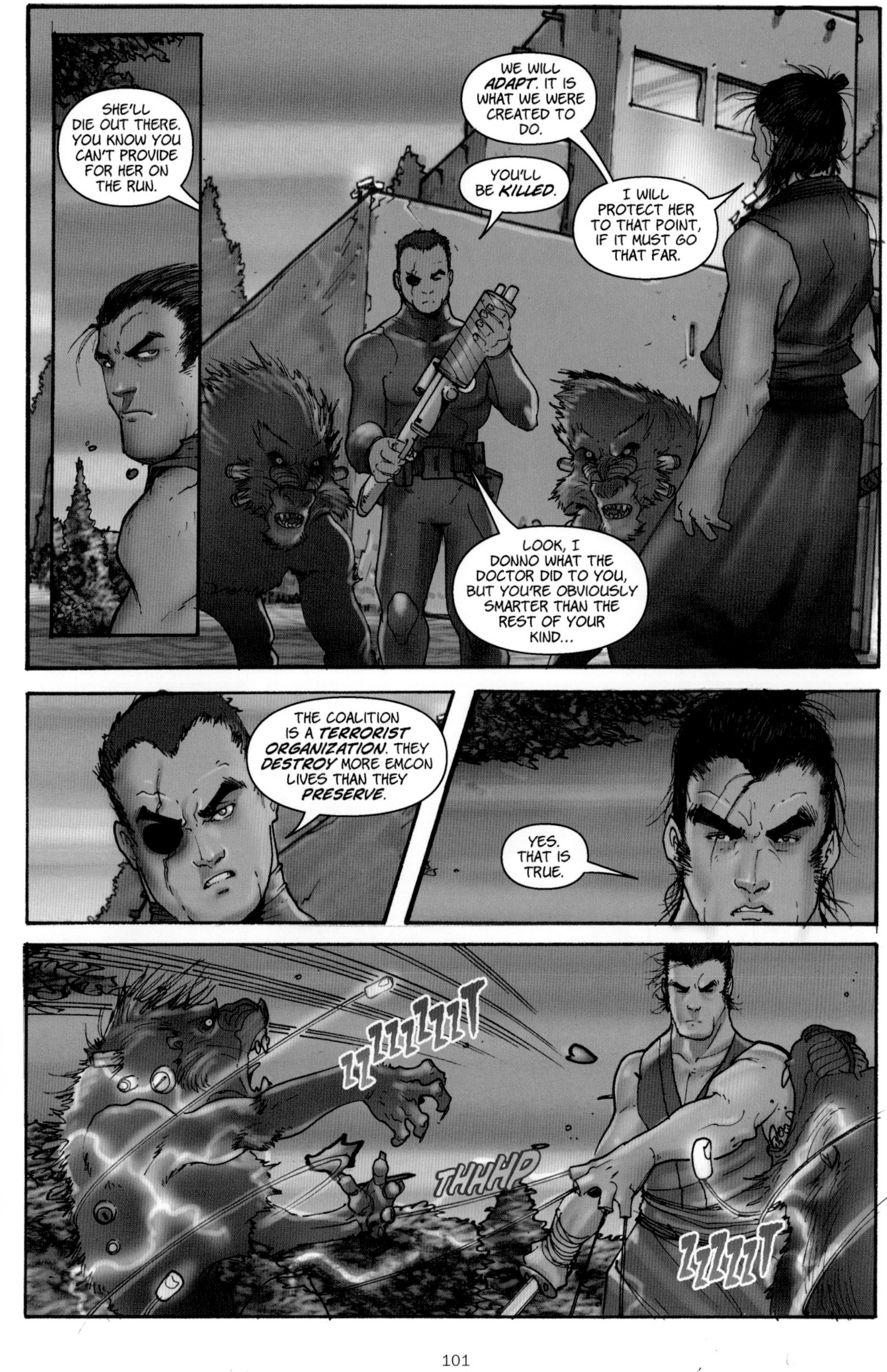
SHE'LL DIE OUT THERE. YOU KNOW YOU CAN'T PROVIDE FOR HER ON THE RUN.
WE WILL ADAPT. IT IS WHAT WE WERE CREATED TO DO.
YOU'LL BE KILLED.
I WILL PROTECT HER TO THAT POINT, IF IT MUST GO THAT FAR.
LOOK, I DONNO WHAT THE DOCTOR DID TO YOU, BUT YOU'RE OBVIOUSLY SMARTER THAN THE REST OF YOUR KIND...
THE COALITION IS A TERRORIST ORGANIZATION. THEY DESTROY MORE EMCON LIVES THAN THEY PRESERVE.
YES. THAT IS TRUE.
ZZZZZZZZT
THHHP
ZZZZZT

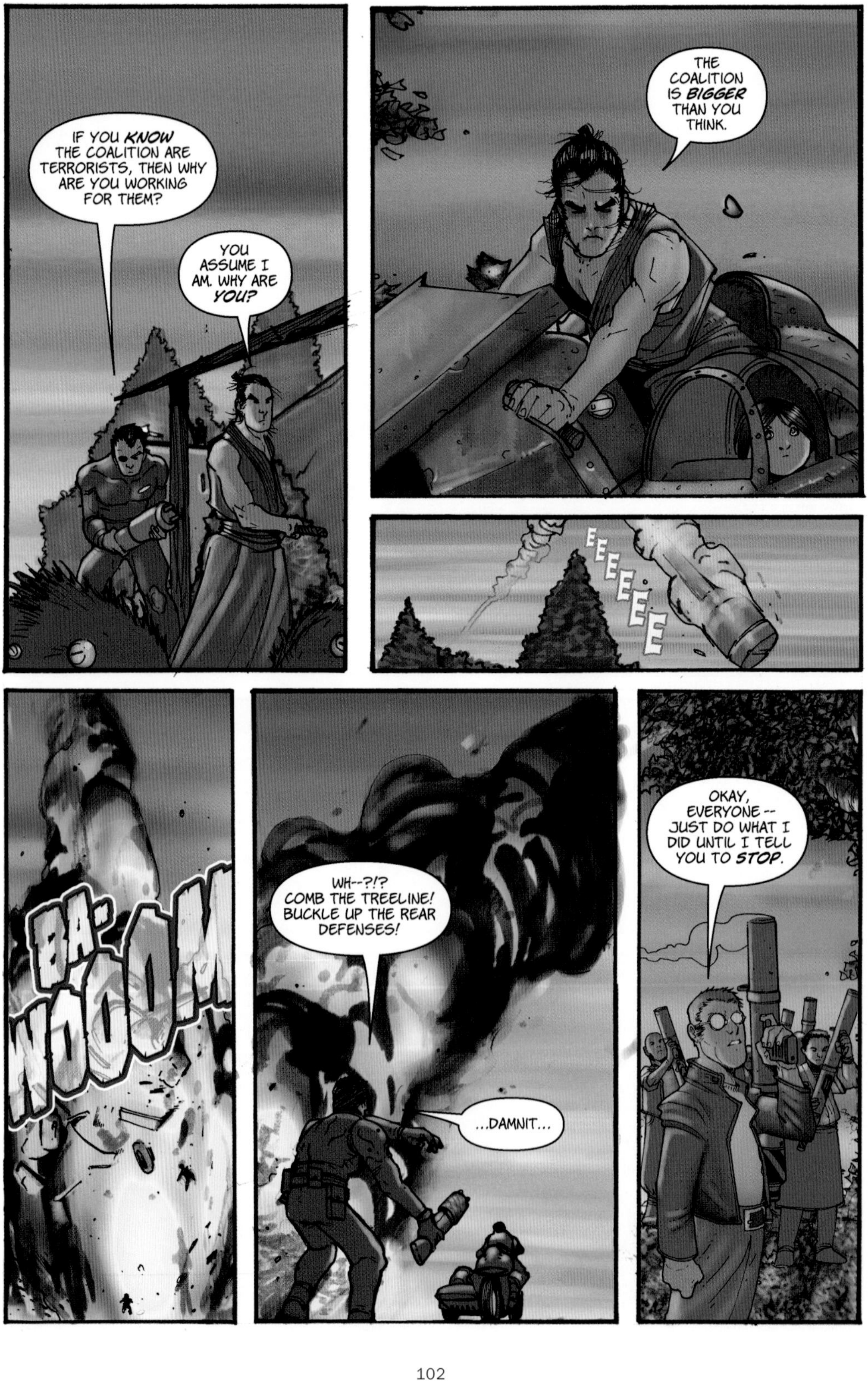
IF YOU KNOW THE COALITION ARE TERRORISTS, THEN WHY ARE YOU WORKING FOR THEM?
YOU ASSUME I AM. WHY ARE YOU?
THE COALITION IS BIGGER THAN YOU THINK.
EEEEEE
BA-WOOOM
WH--?!? COMB THE TREELINE! BUCKLE UP THE REAR DEFENSES!
...DAMNIT...
OKAY, EVERYONE -- JUST DO WHAT I DID UNTIL I TELL YOU TO STOP.

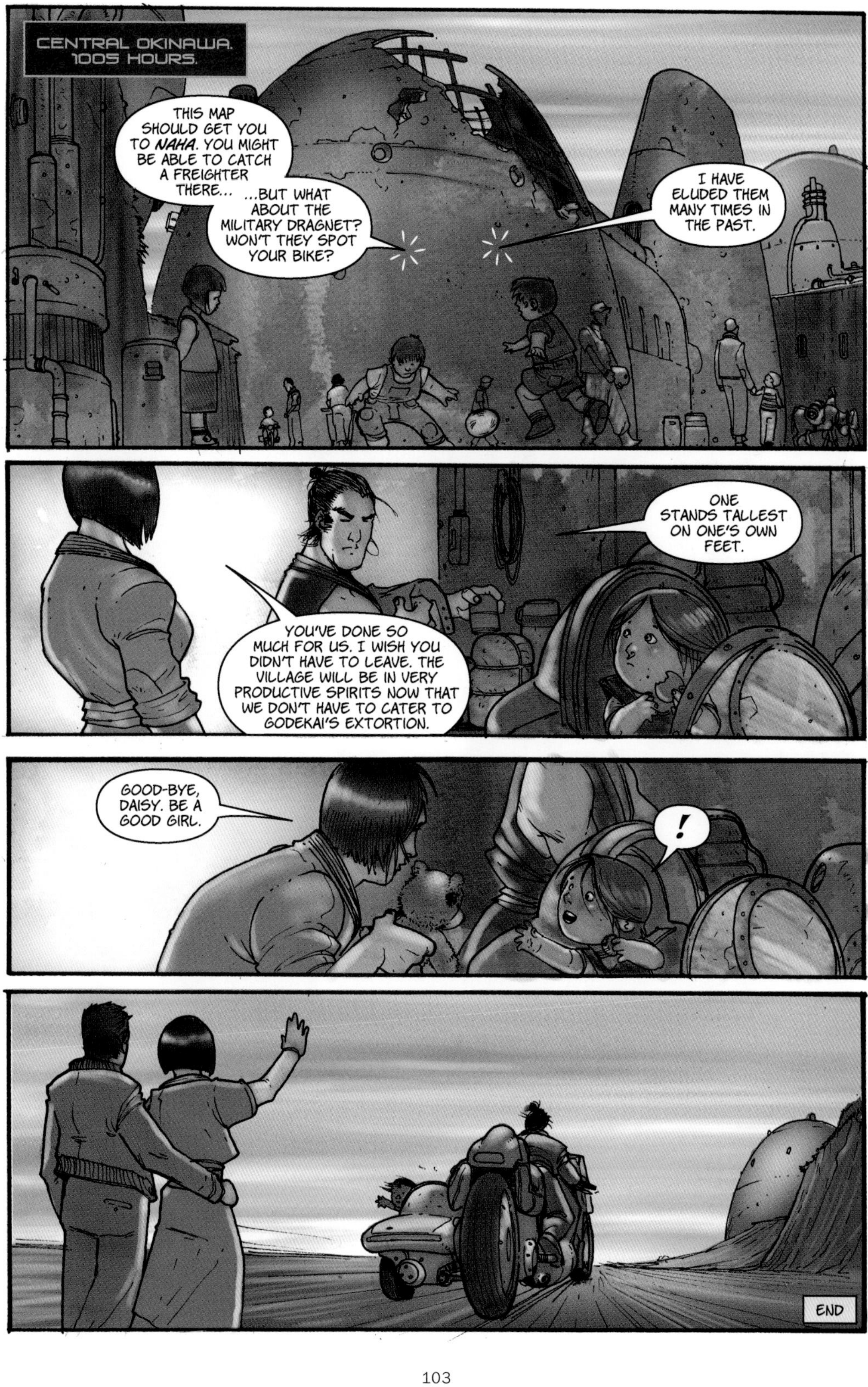
CENTRAL OKINAWA. 1005 HOURS.
THIS MAP SHOULD GET YOU TO NAHA. YOU MIGHT BE ABLE TO CATCH A FREIGHTER THERE...
...BUT WHAT ABOUT THE MILITARY DRAGNET? WON'T THEY SPOT YOUR BIKE?
I HAVE ELUDED THEM MANY TIMES IN THE PAST.
ONE STANDS TALLEST ON ONE'S OWN FEET.
YOU'VE DONE SO MUCH FOR US. I WISH YOU DIDN'T HAVE TO LEAVE. THE VILLAGE WILL BE IN VERY PRODUCTIVE SPIRITS NOW THAT WE DON'T HAVE TO CATER TO GODEKAI'S EXTORTION.
GOOD-BYE, DAISY. BE A GOOD GIRL.
!
END

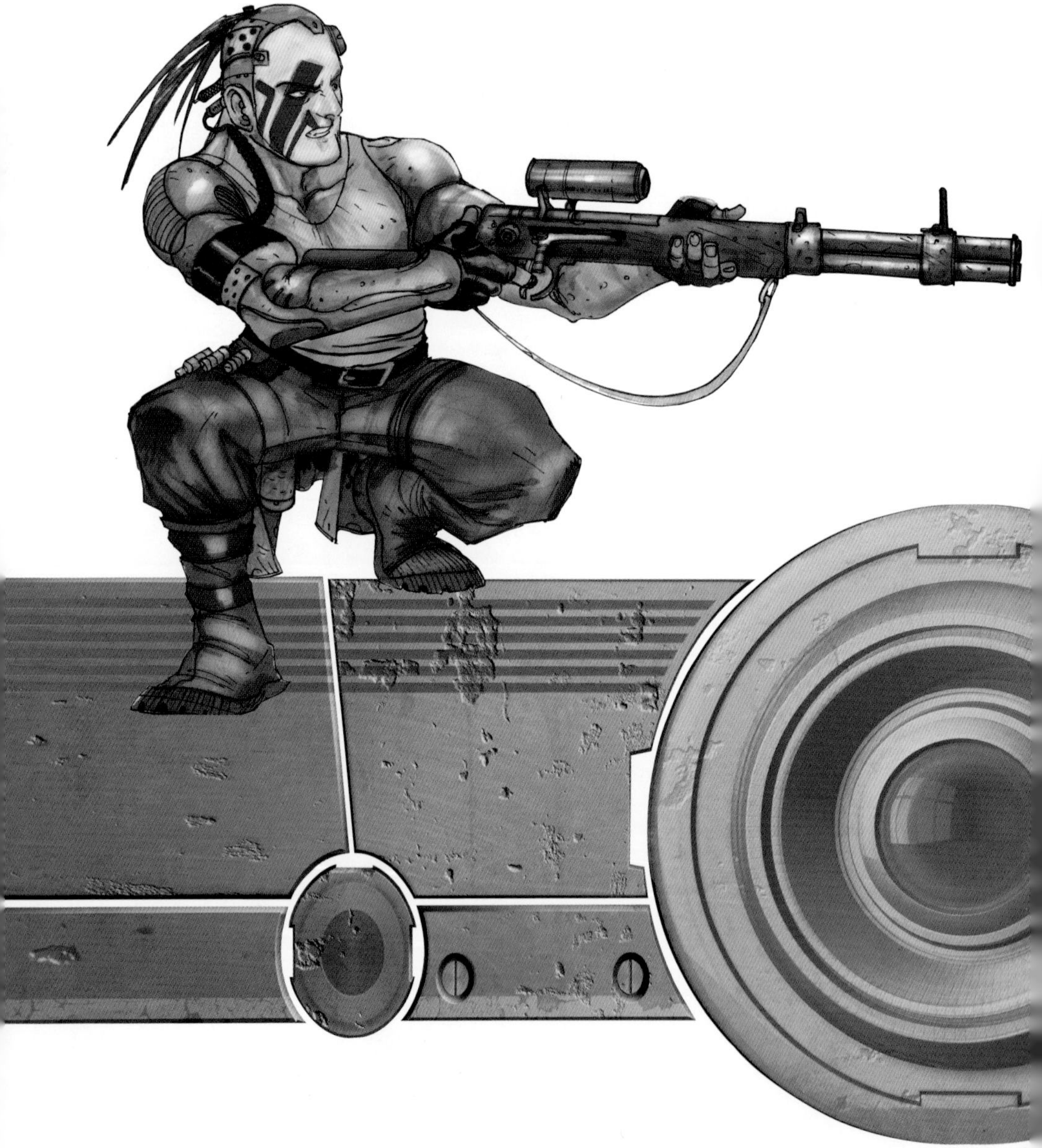

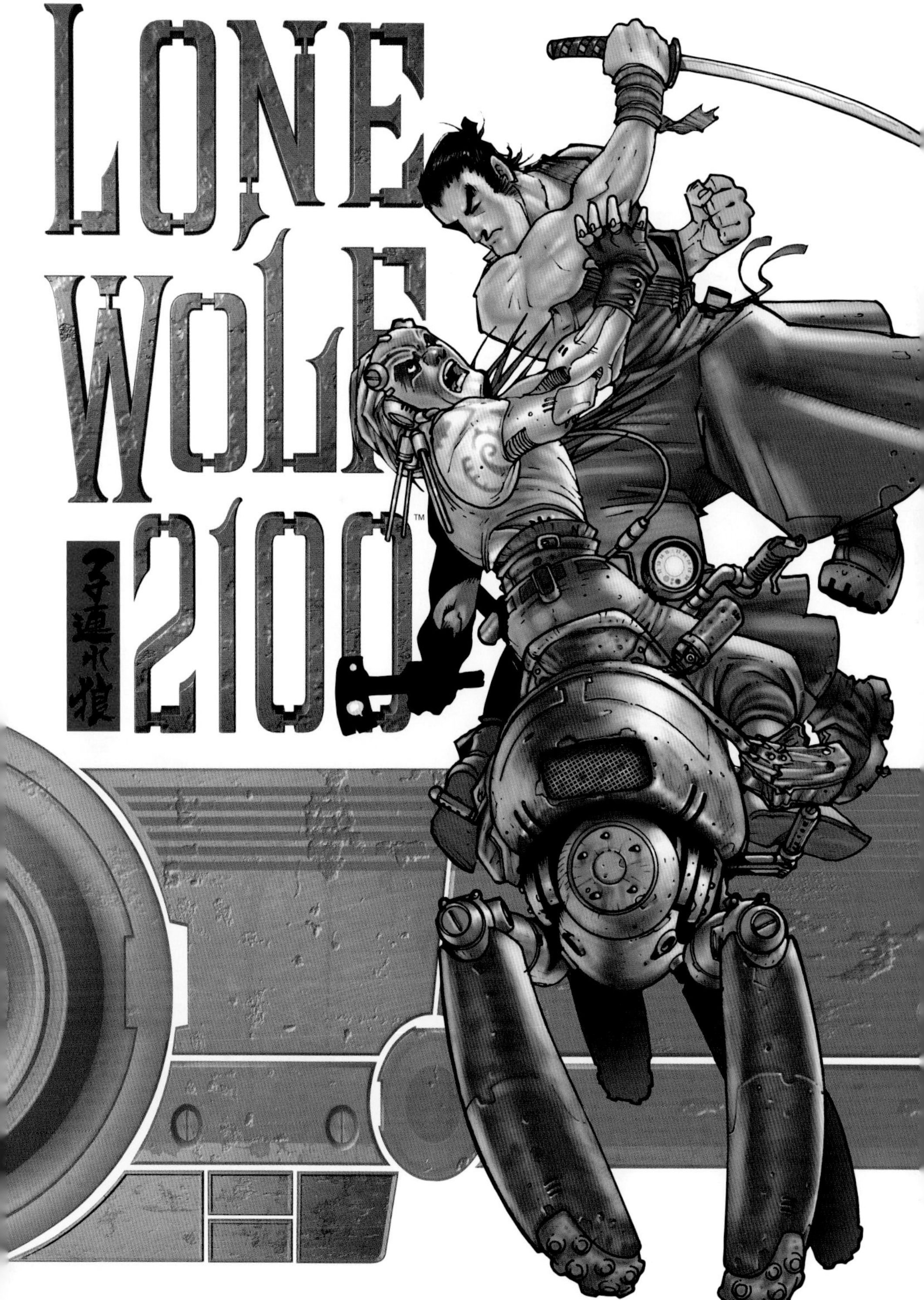
LONE WOLF 2100™
子連れ狼

THE LANGUAGE OF CHAOS

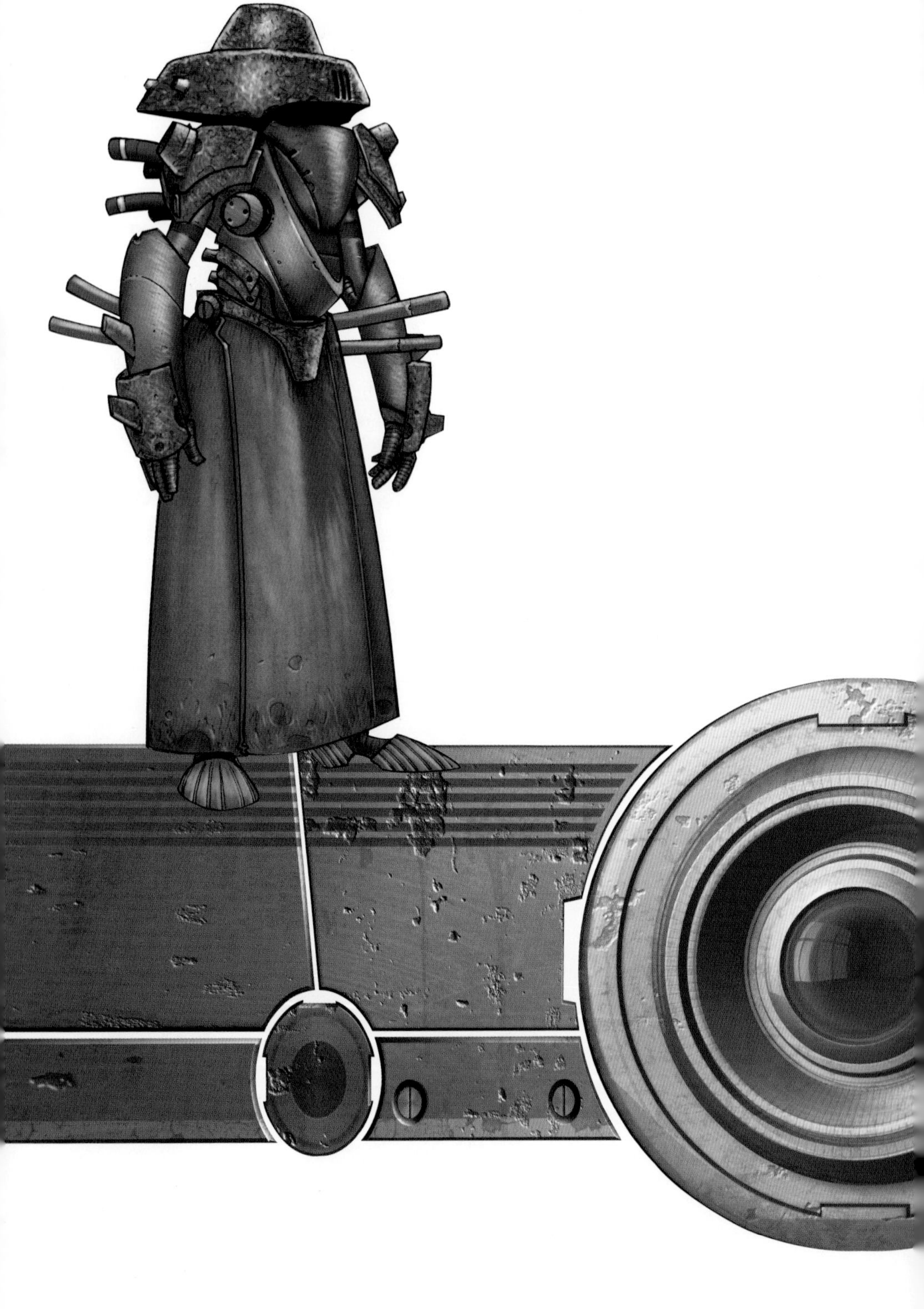

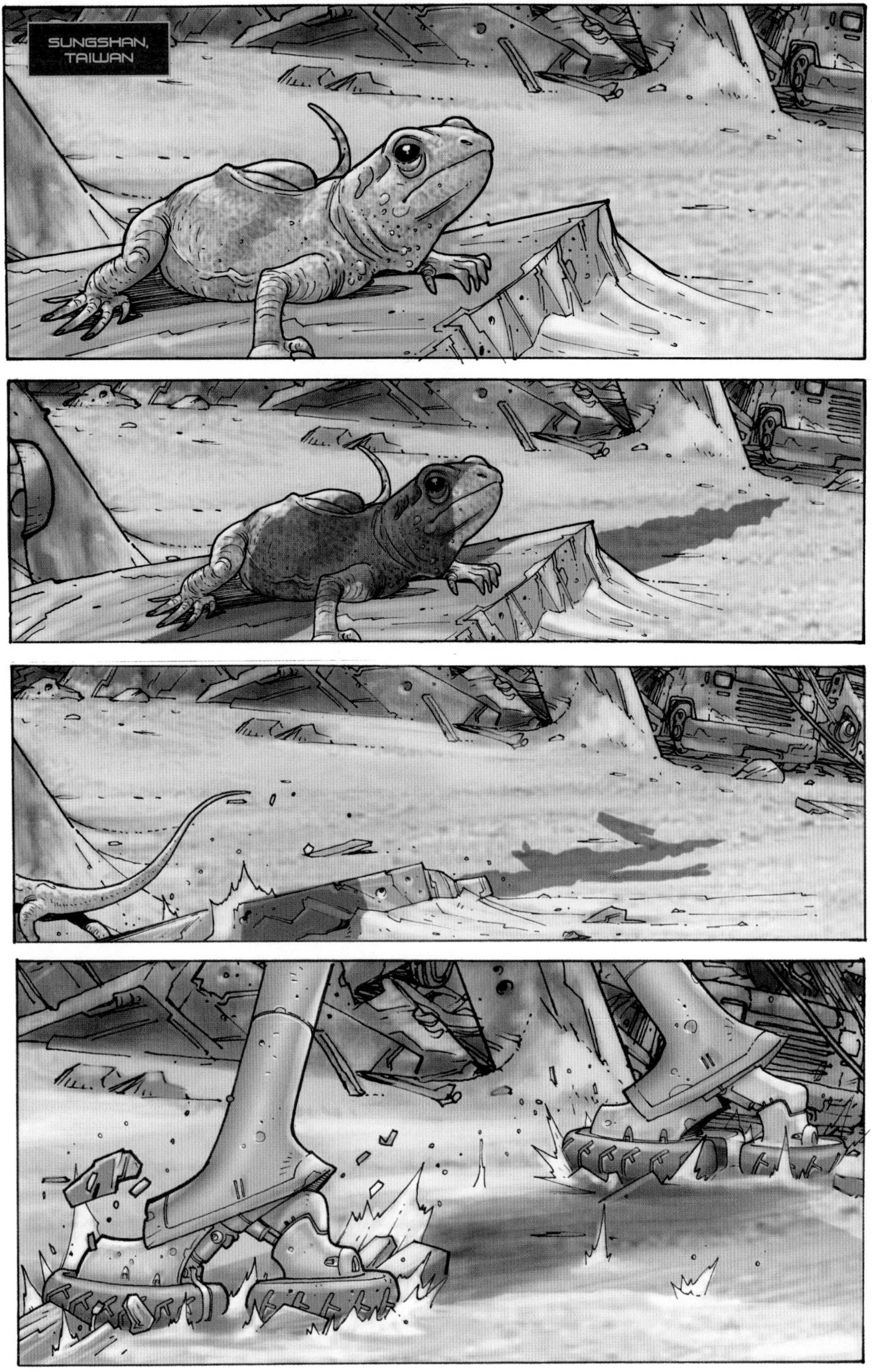
SUNGSHAN, TAIWAN

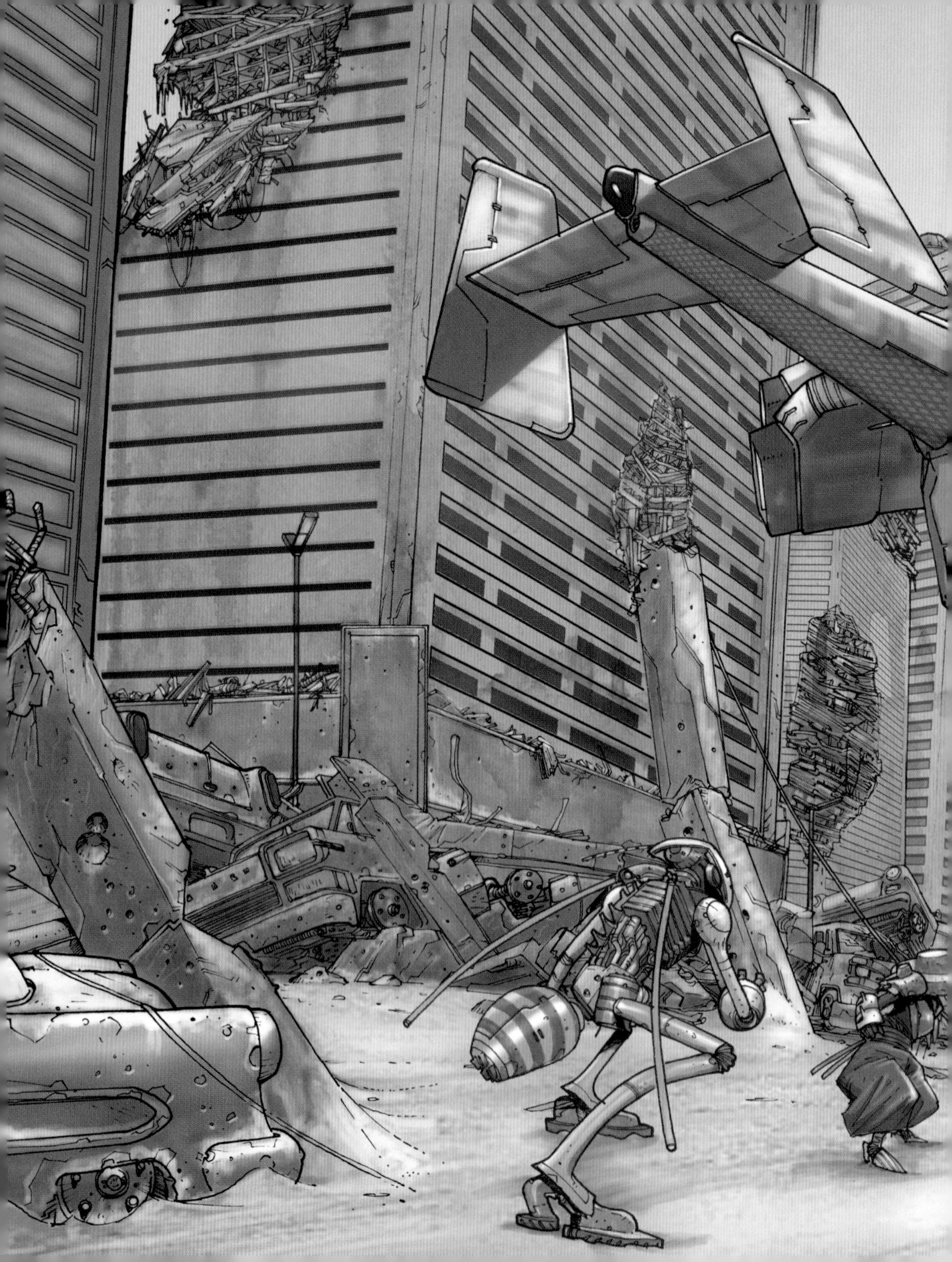

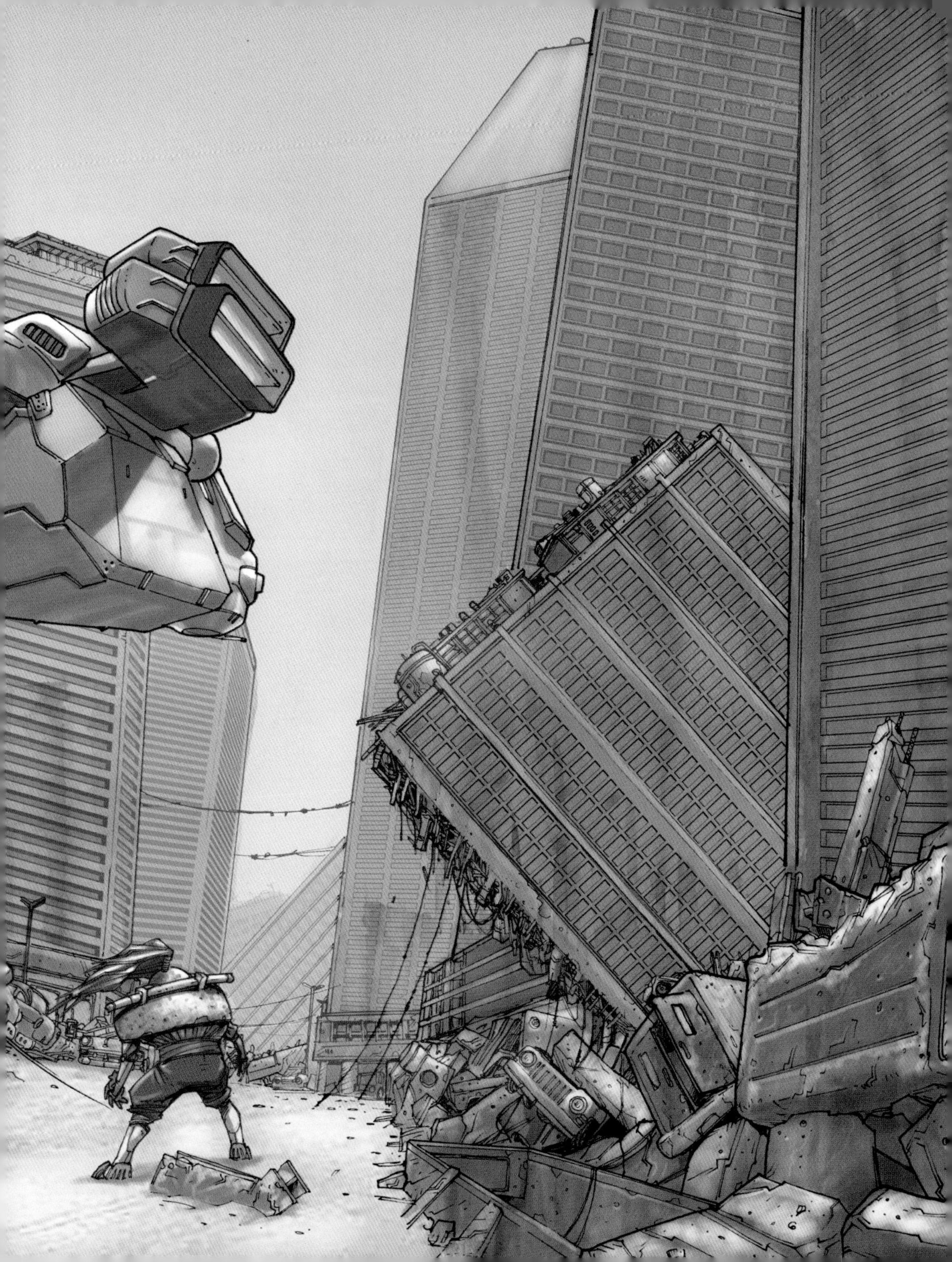

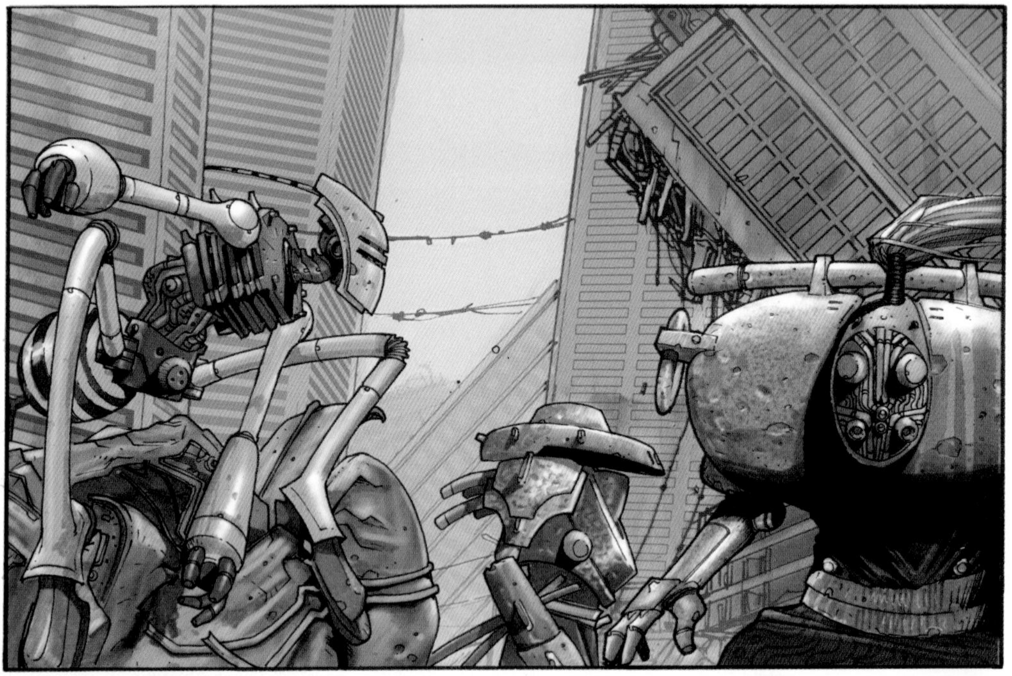

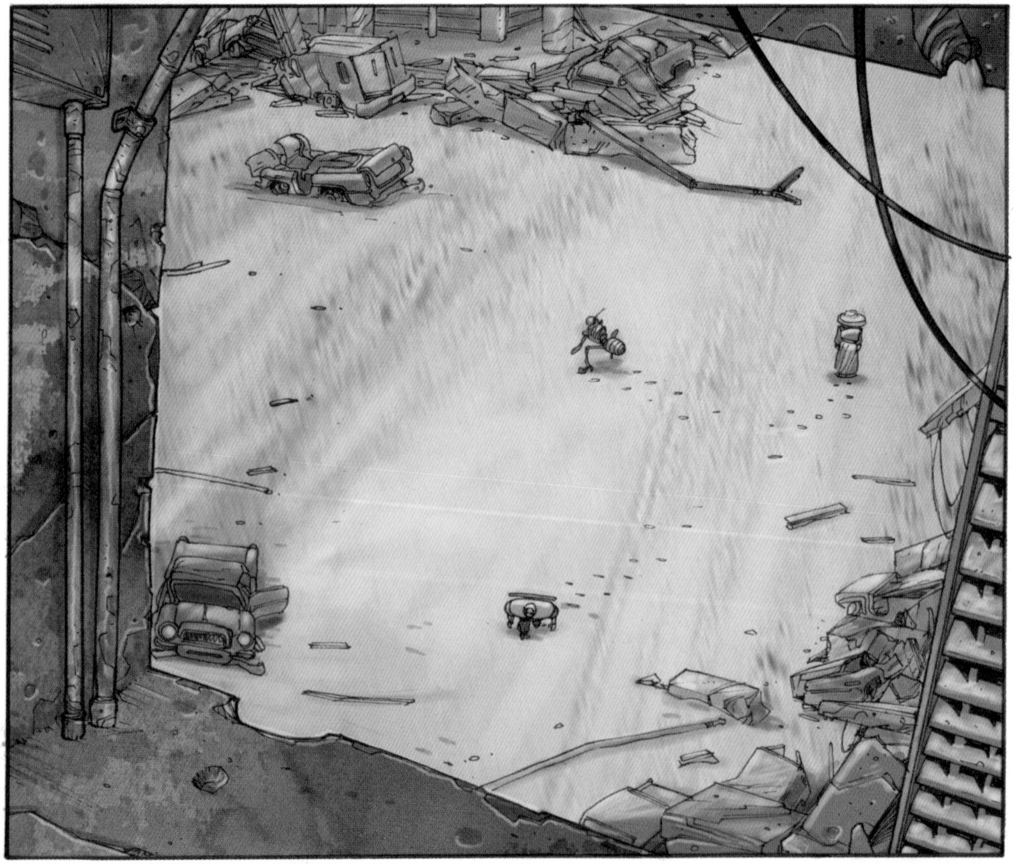

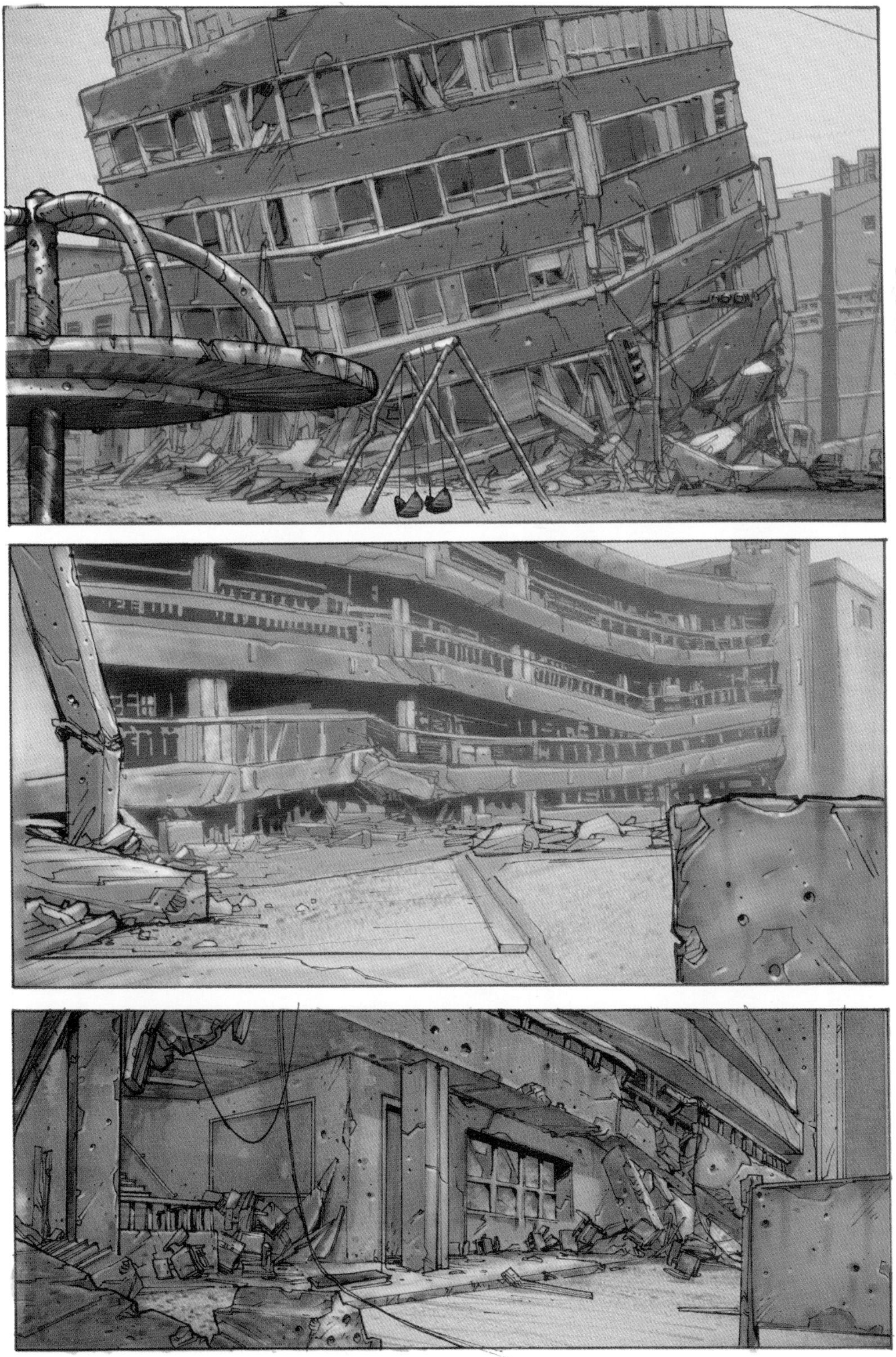

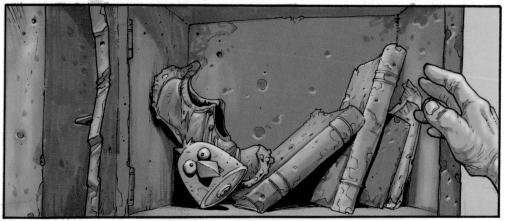

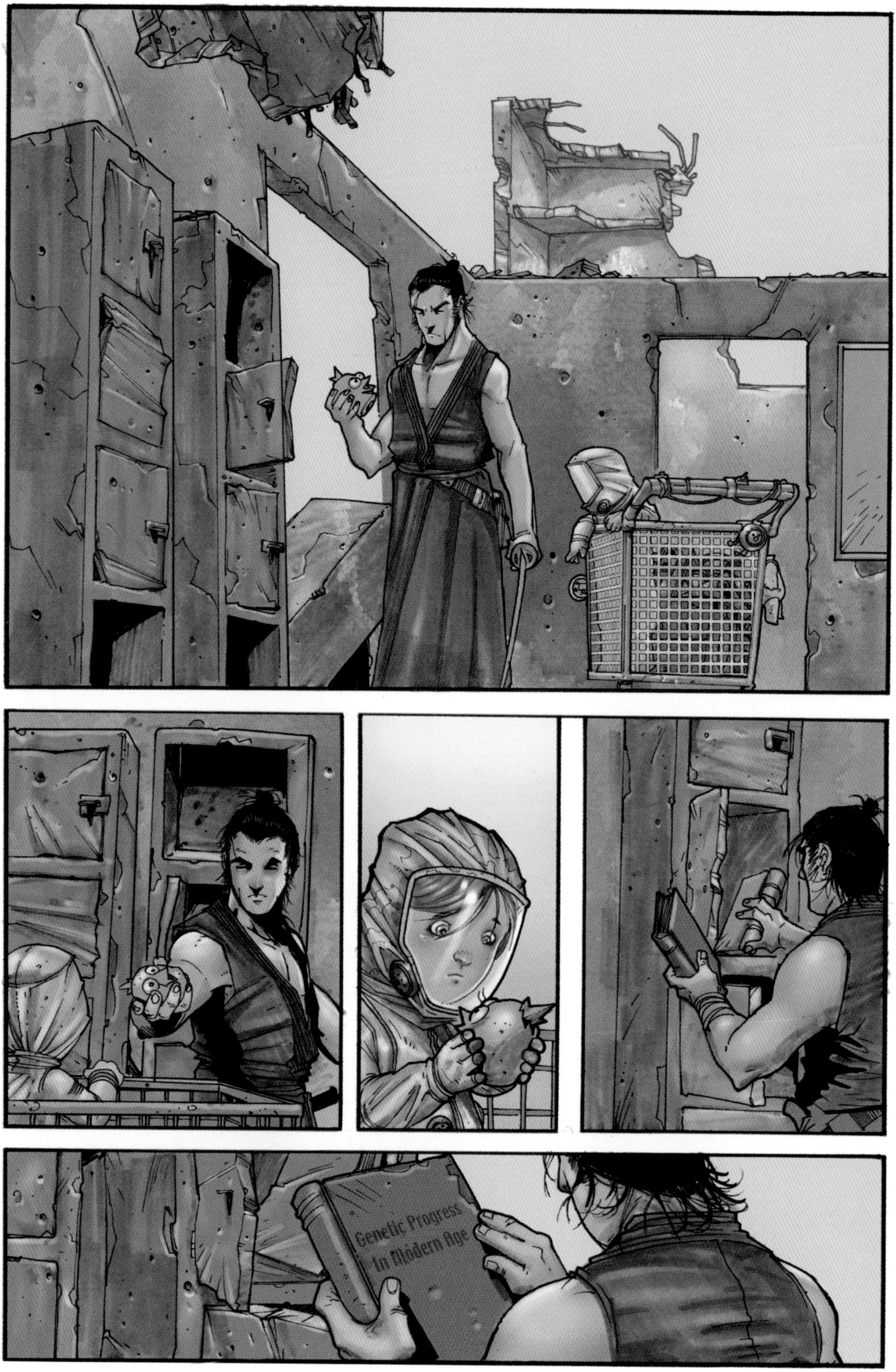
Genetic Progress
In Modern Age

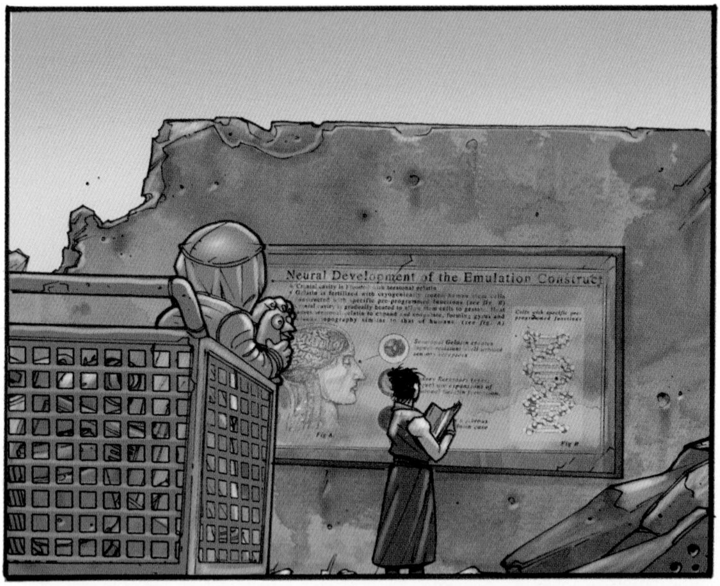

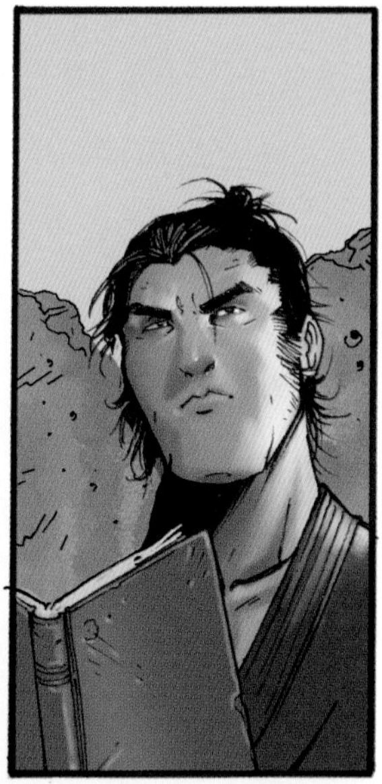

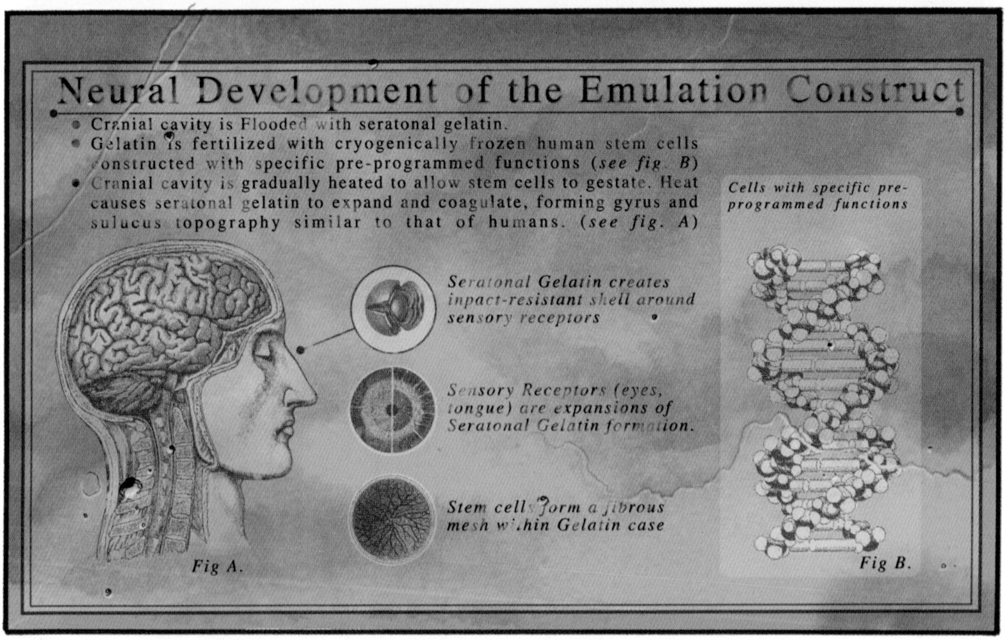
Neural Development of the Emulation Construct
Cranial cavity is Flooded with seratonal gelatin.
Gelatin is fertilized with cryogenically frozen human stem cells constructed with specific pre-programmed functions (see fig. B)
Cranial cavity is gradually heated to allow stem cells to gestate. Heat causes seratonal gelatin to expand and coagulate, forming gyrus and sulucus topography similar to that of humans. (see fig. A)
Cells with specific pre-programmed functions
Seratonal Gelatin creates inpact-resistant shell around sensory receptors
Sensory Receptors (eyes, tongue) are expansions of Seratonal Gelatin formation.
Stem cells form a fibrous mesh within Gelatin case
Fig A.
Fig B.

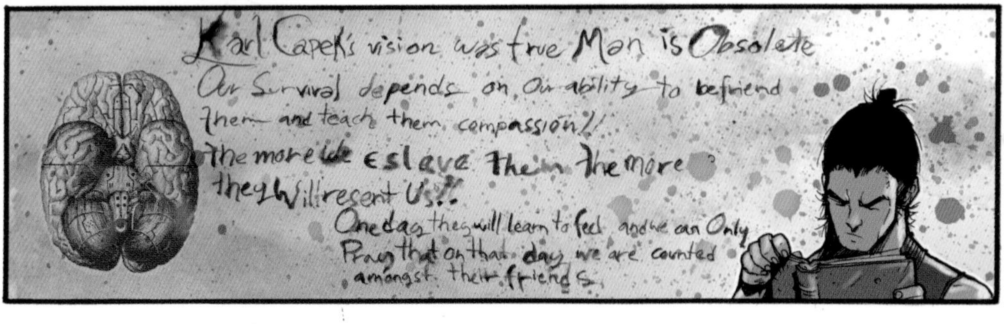
Karl Capek's vision was true Man is Obsolete
Our Survival depends on Our ability to befriend them and teach them compassion!!
The more we eslave them the more they will resent Us!!
One day they will learn to feel and we can Only Pray that on that day we are counted amongst their friends.

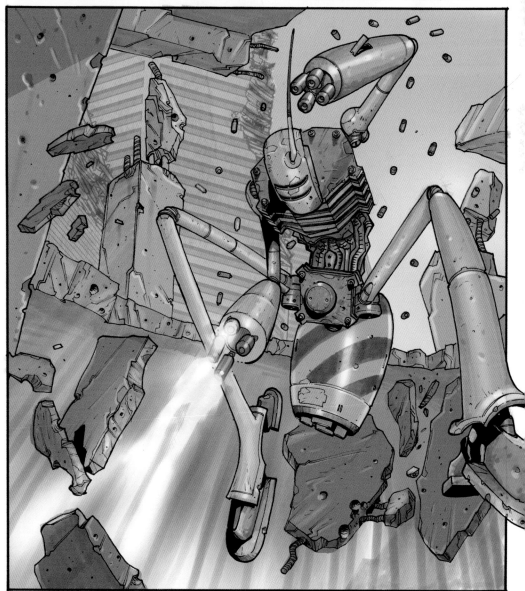

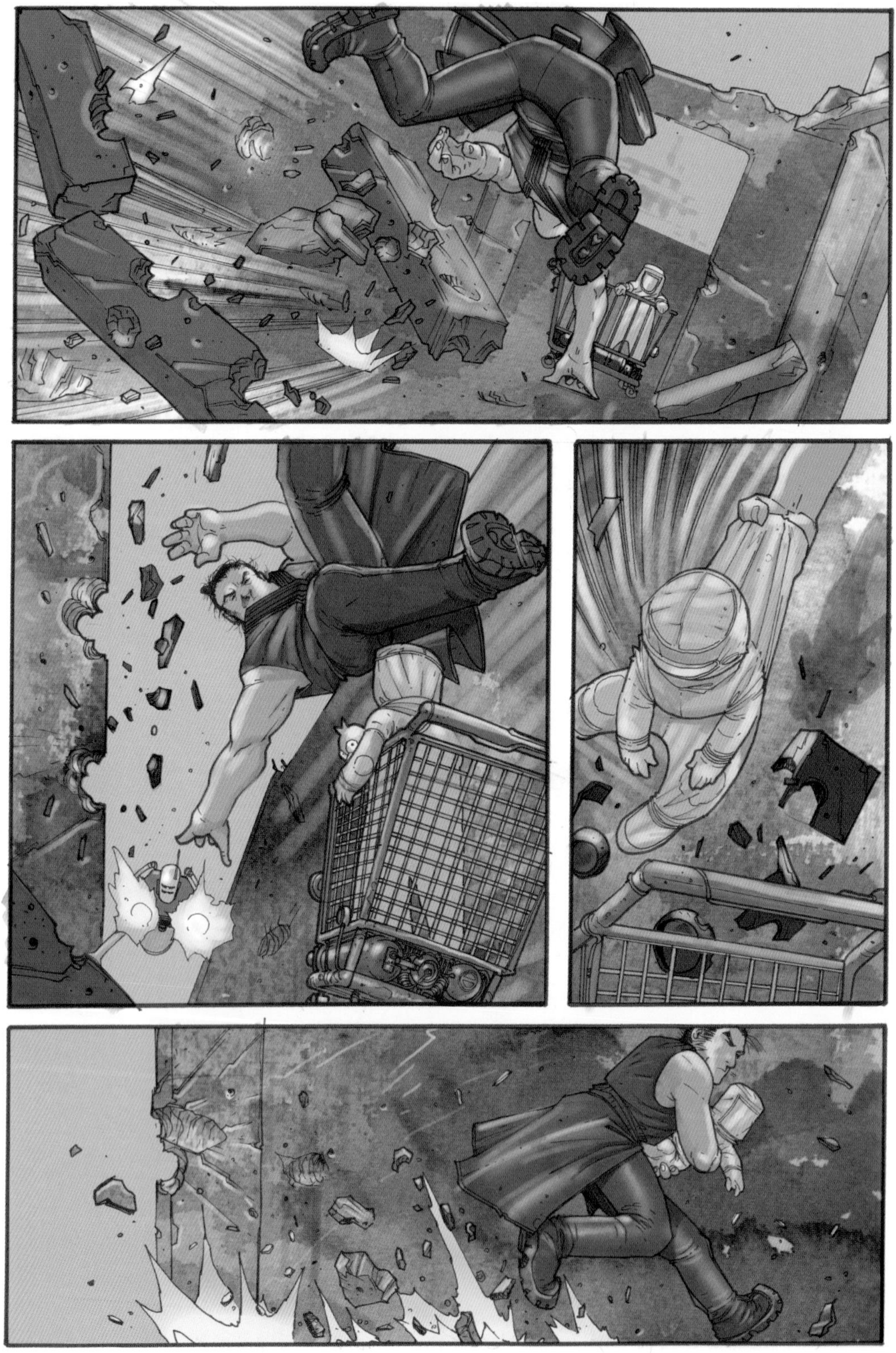

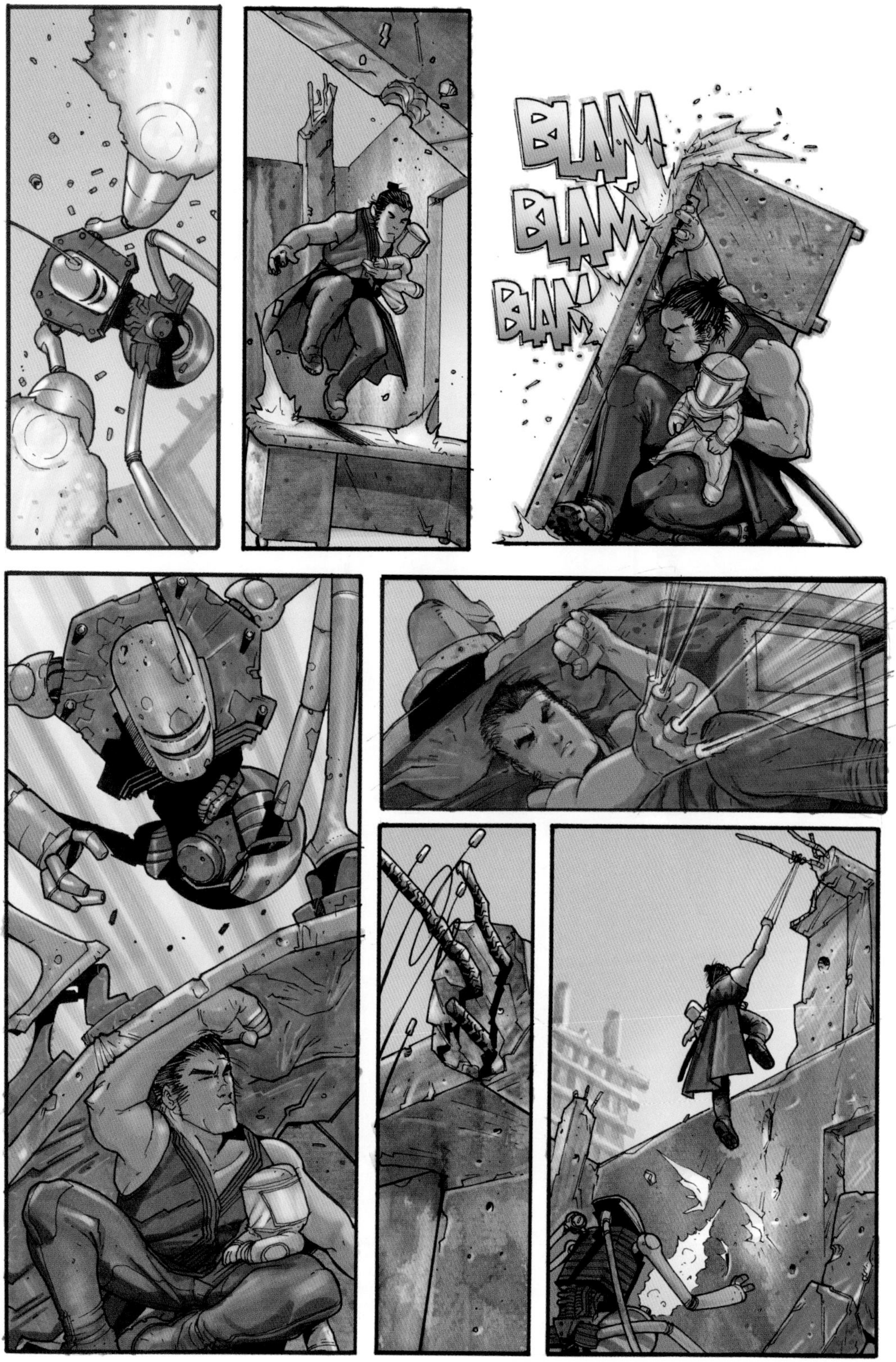
BLAM
BLAM
BLAM

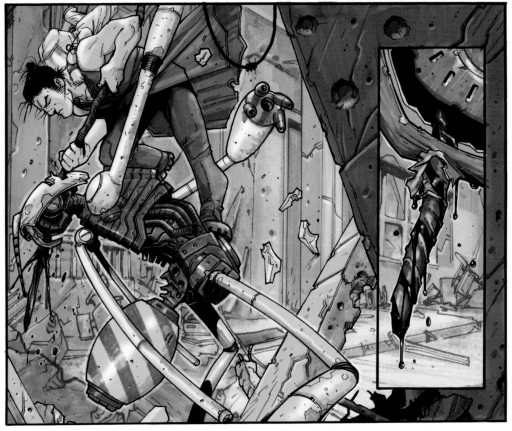

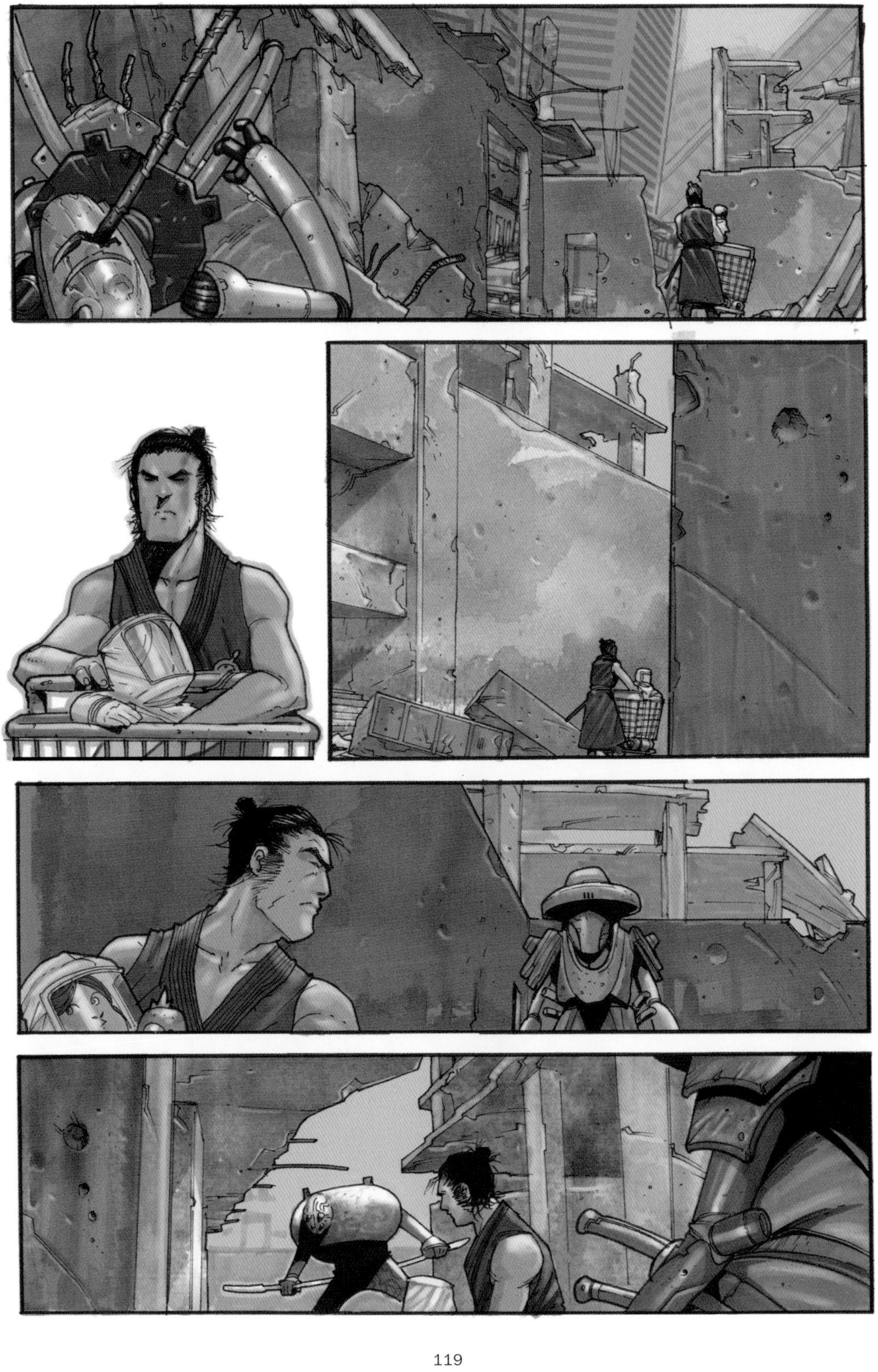

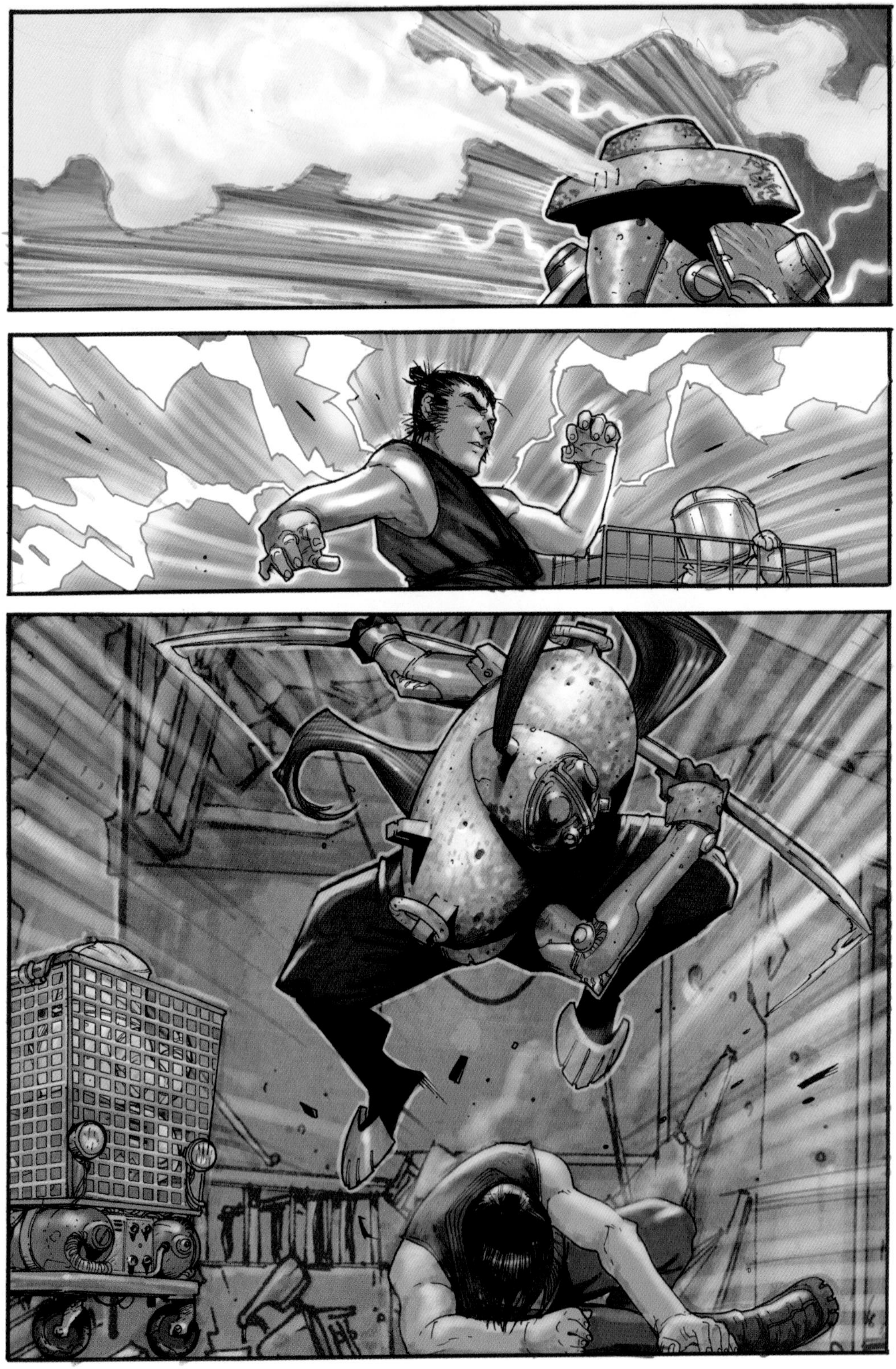

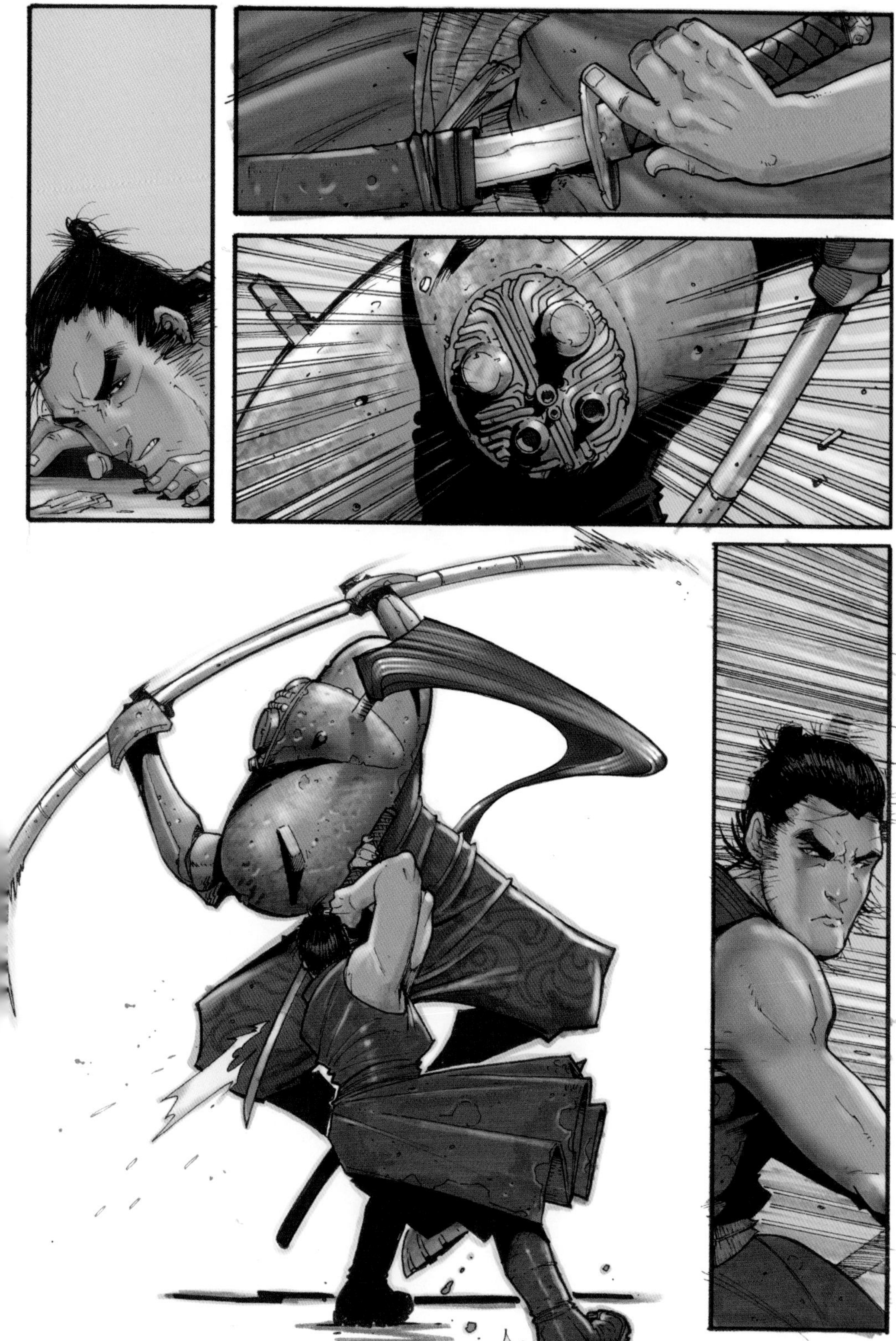

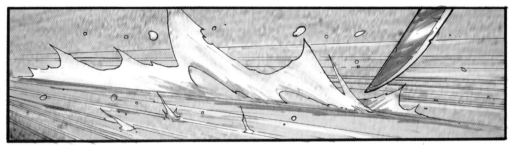

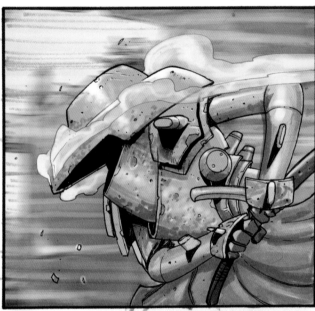

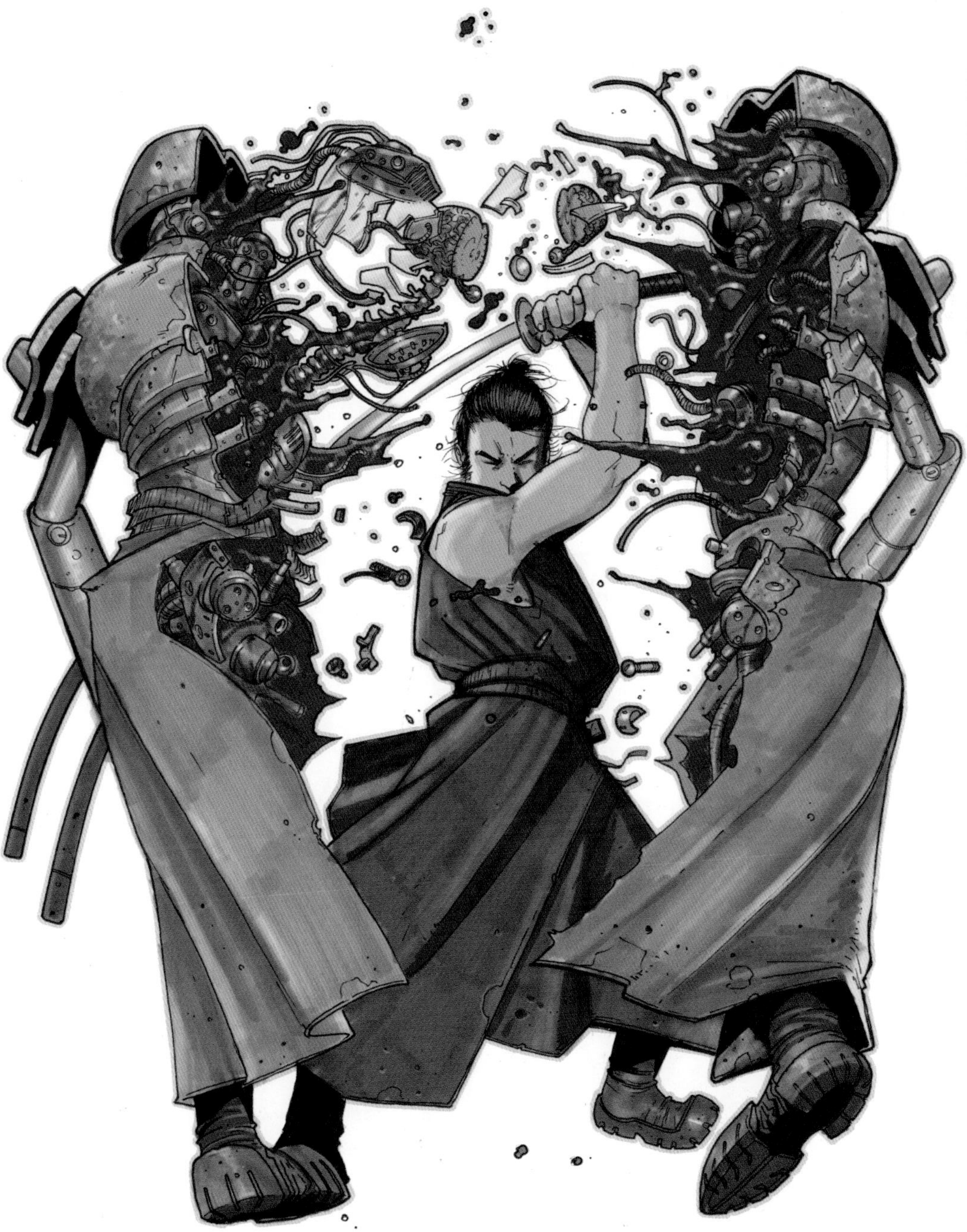

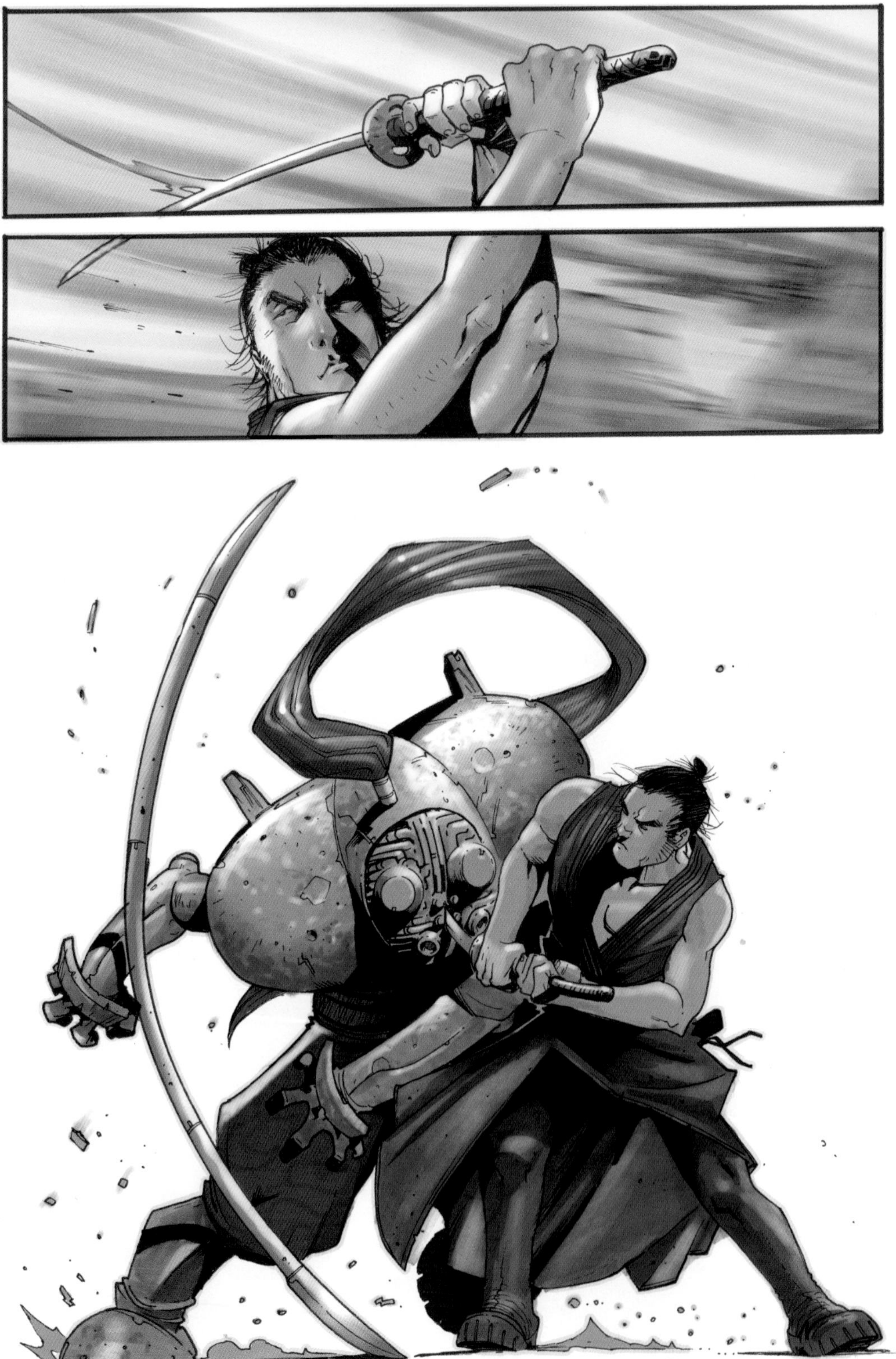

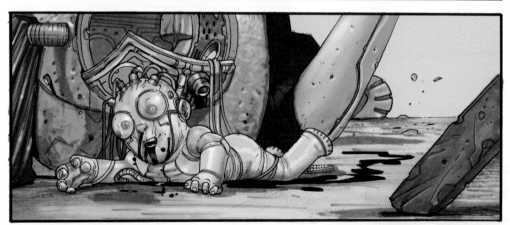

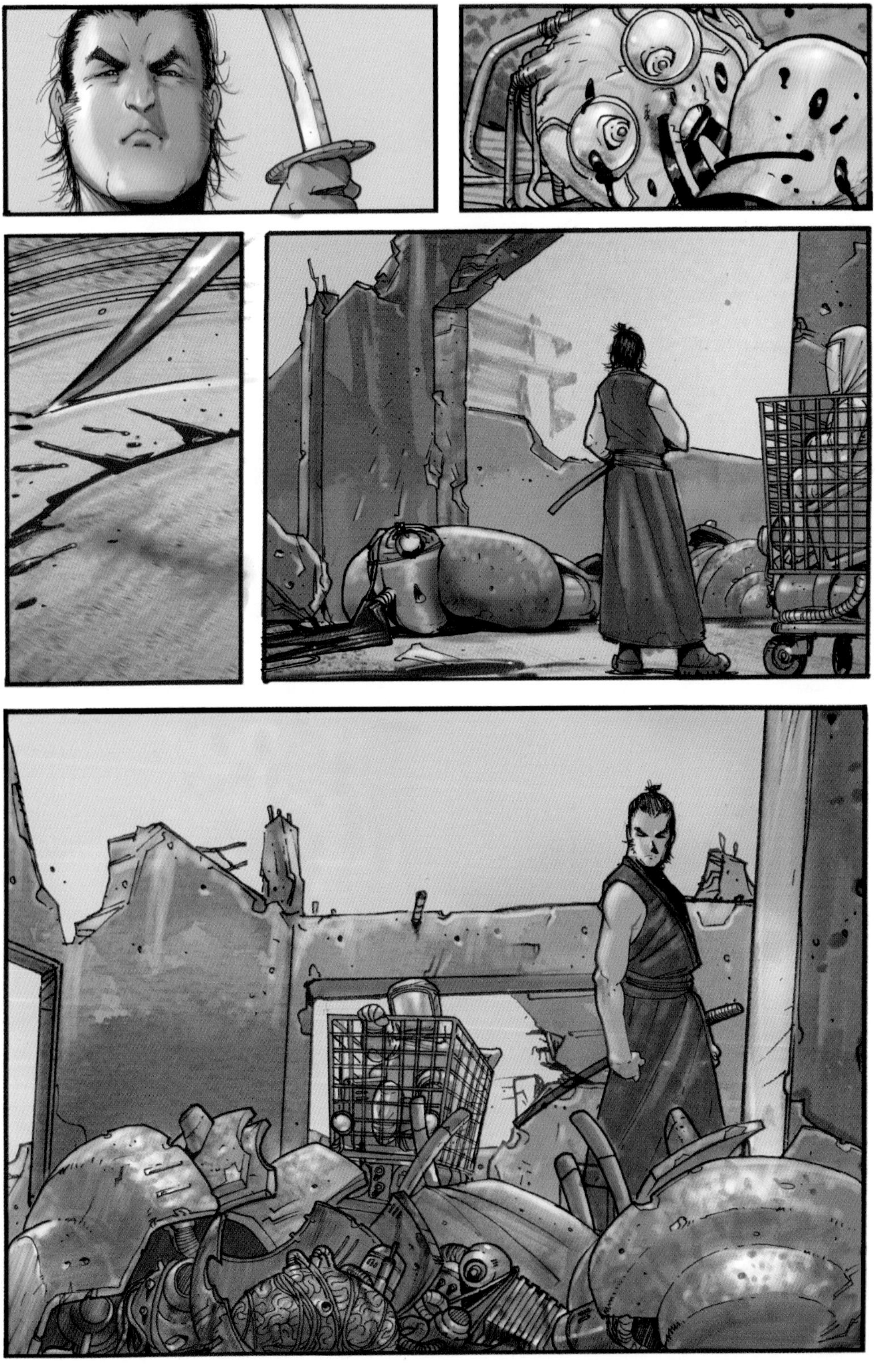

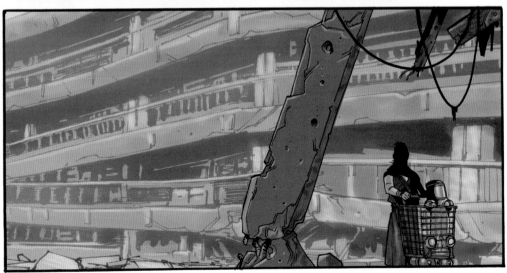

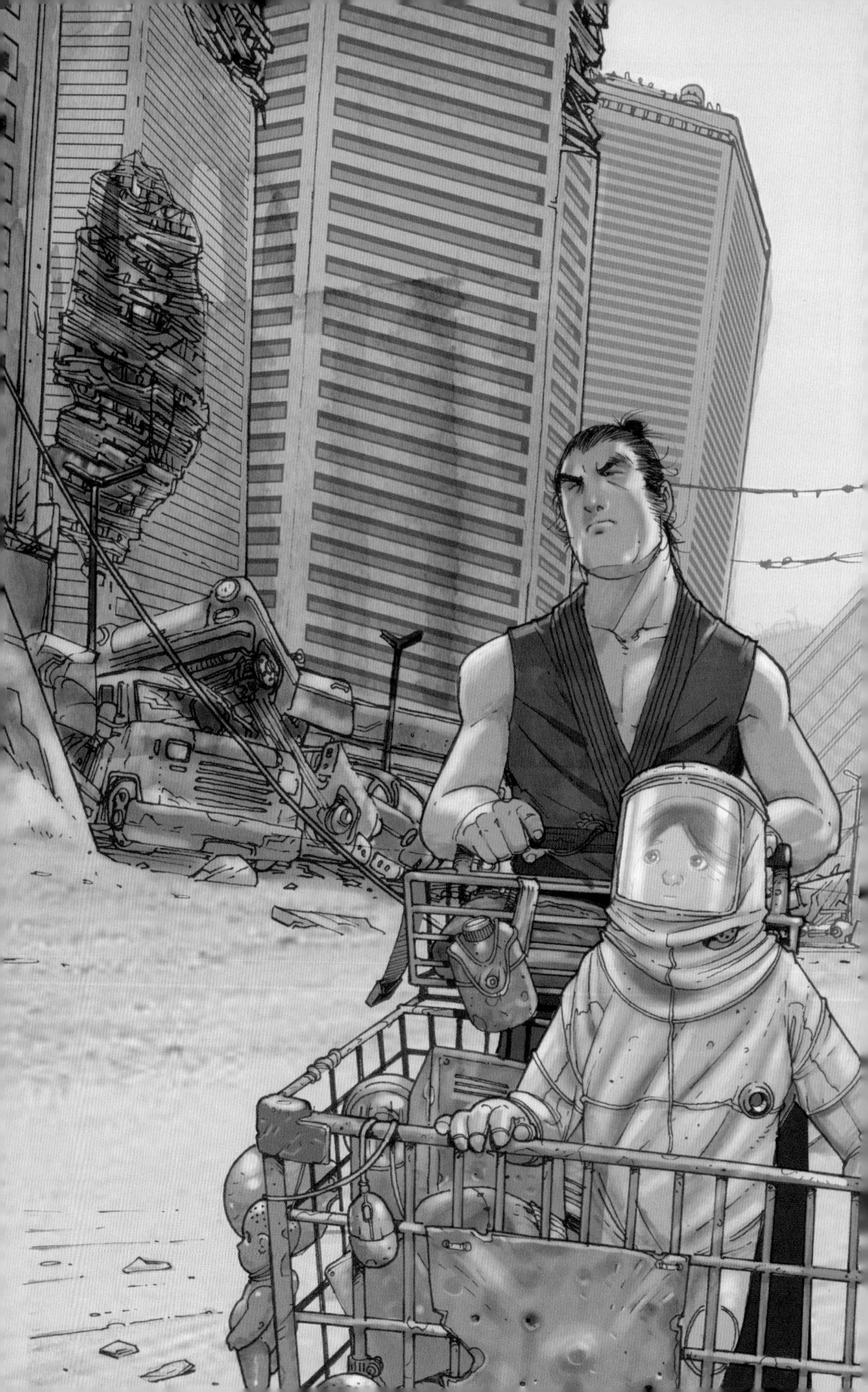

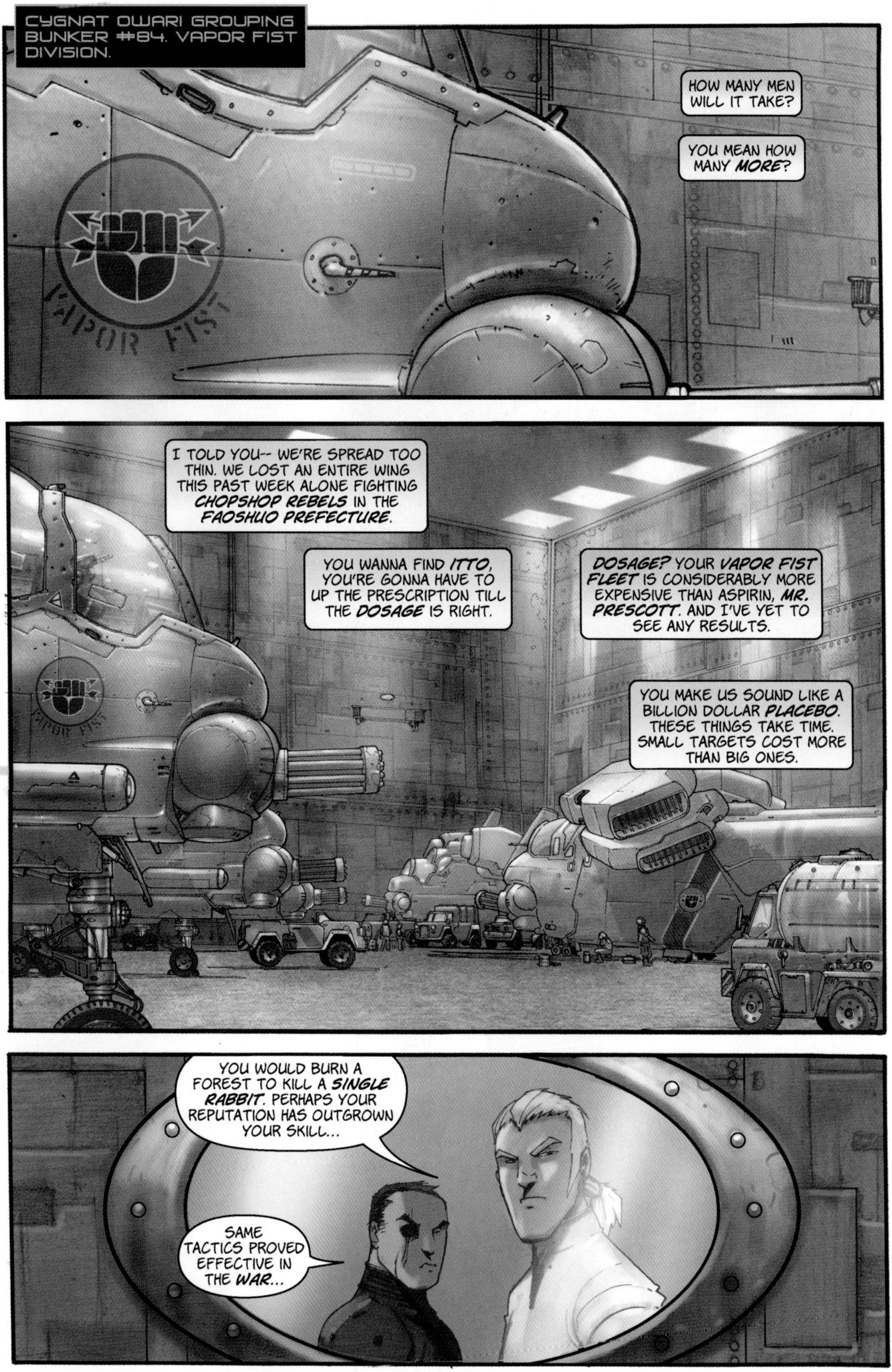
CYGNAT OWARI GROUPING BUNKER #84. VAPOR FIST DIVISION.
VAPOR FIST
HOW MANY MEN WILL IT TAKE?
YOU MEAN HOW MANY *MORE*?
I TOLD YOU-- WE'RE SPREAD TOO THIN. WE LOST AN ENTIRE WING THIS PAST WEEK ALONE FIGHTING ***CHOPSHOP REBELS*** IN THE ***FAOSHUO PREFECTURE***.
YOU WANNA FIND ***ITTO***, YOU'RE GONNA HAVE TO UP THE PRESCRIPTION TILL THE ***DOSAGE*** IS RIGHT.
DOSAGE? YOUR ***VAPOR FIST FLEET*** IS CONSIDERABLY MORE EXPENSIVE THAN ASPIRIN, ***MR. PRESCOTT***. AND I'VE YET TO SEE ANY RESULTS.
YOU MAKE US SOUND LIKE A BILLION DOLLAR ***PLACEBO***. THESE THINGS TAKE TIME. SMALL TARGETS COST MORE THAN BIG ONES.
YOU WOULD BURN A FOREST TO KILL A ***SINGLE RABBIT***. PERHAPS YOUR REPUTATION HAS OUTGROWN YOUR SKILL...
SAME TACTICS PROVED EFFECTIVE IN THE ***WAR***...

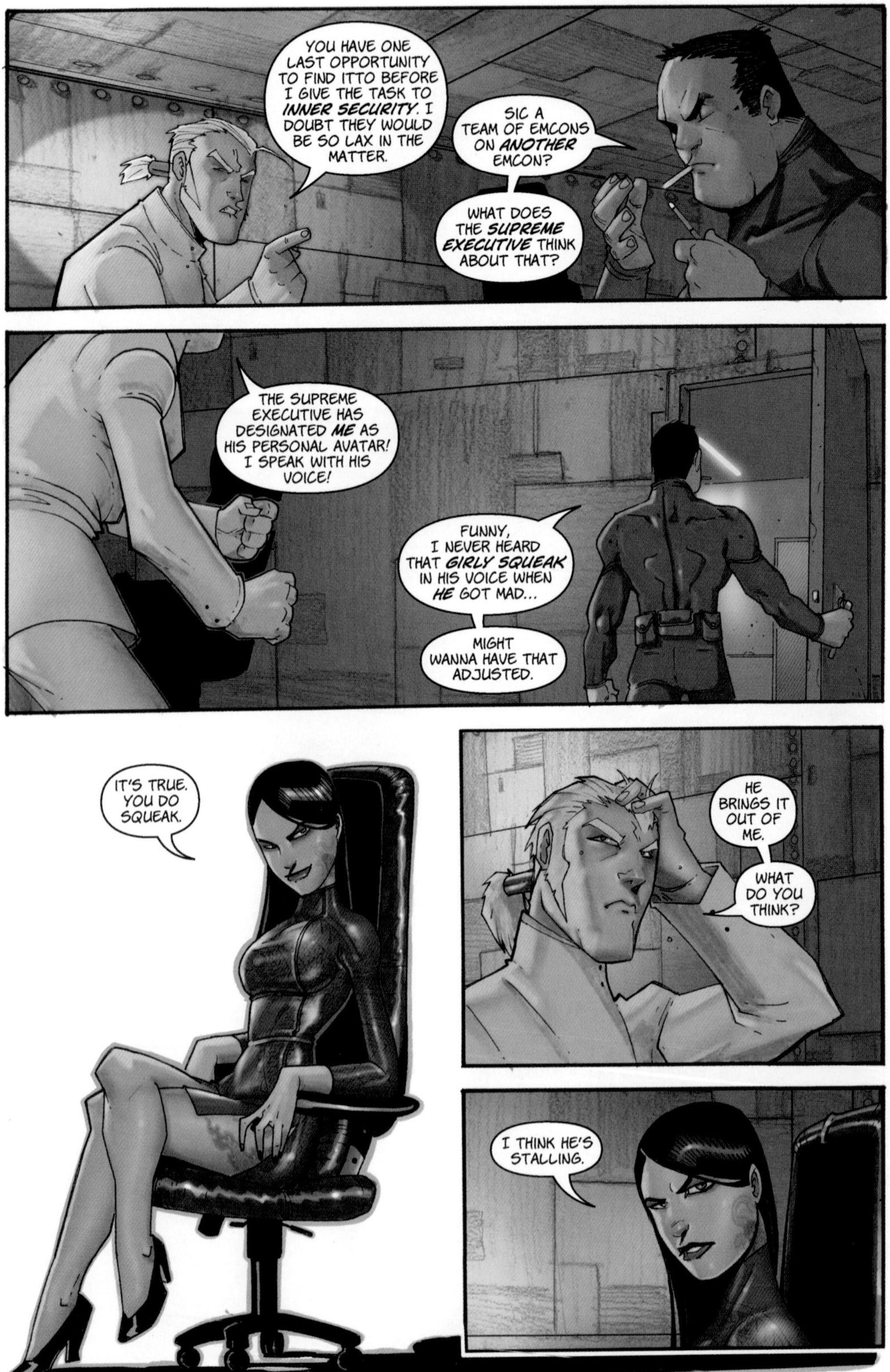

YOU HAVE ONE LAST OPPORTUNITY TO FIND ITTO BEFORE I GIVE THE TASK TO INNER SECURITY. I DOUBT THEY WOULD BE SO LAX IN THE MATTER.
SIC A TEAM OF EMCONS ON ANOTHER EMCON?
WHAT DOES THE SUPREME EXECUTIVE THINK ABOUT THAT?
THE SUPREME EXECUTIVE HAS DESIGNATED ME AS HIS PERSONAL AVATAR! I SPEAK WITH HIS VOICE!
FUNNY, I NEVER HEARD THAT GIRLY SQUEAK IN HIS VOICE WHEN HE GOT MAD...
MIGHT WANNA HAVE THAT ADJUSTED.
IT'S TRUE. YOU DO SQUEAK.
HE BRINGS IT OUT OF ME.
WHAT DO YOU THINK?
I THINK HE'S STALLING.

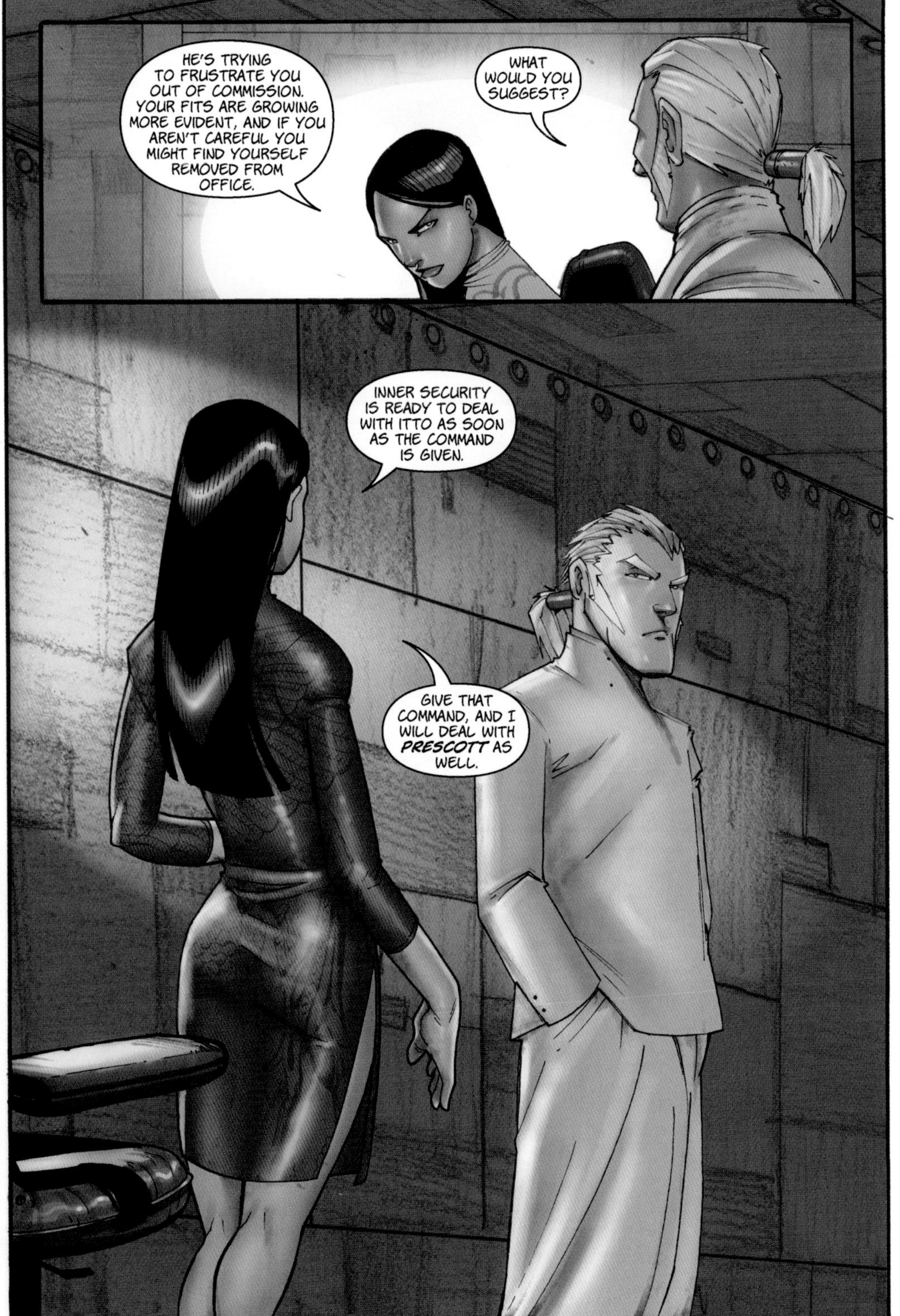
HE'S TRYING TO FRUSTRATE YOU OUT OF COMMISSION. YOUR FITS ARE GROWING MORE EVIDENT, AND IF YOU AREN'T CAREFUL YOU MIGHT FIND YOURSELF REMOVED FROM OFFICE.
WHAT WOULD YOU SUGGEST?
INNER SECURITY IS READY TO DEAL WITH ITTO AS SOON AS THE COMMAND IS GIVEN.
GIVE THAT COMMAND, AND I WILL DEAL WITH PRESCOTT AS WELL.

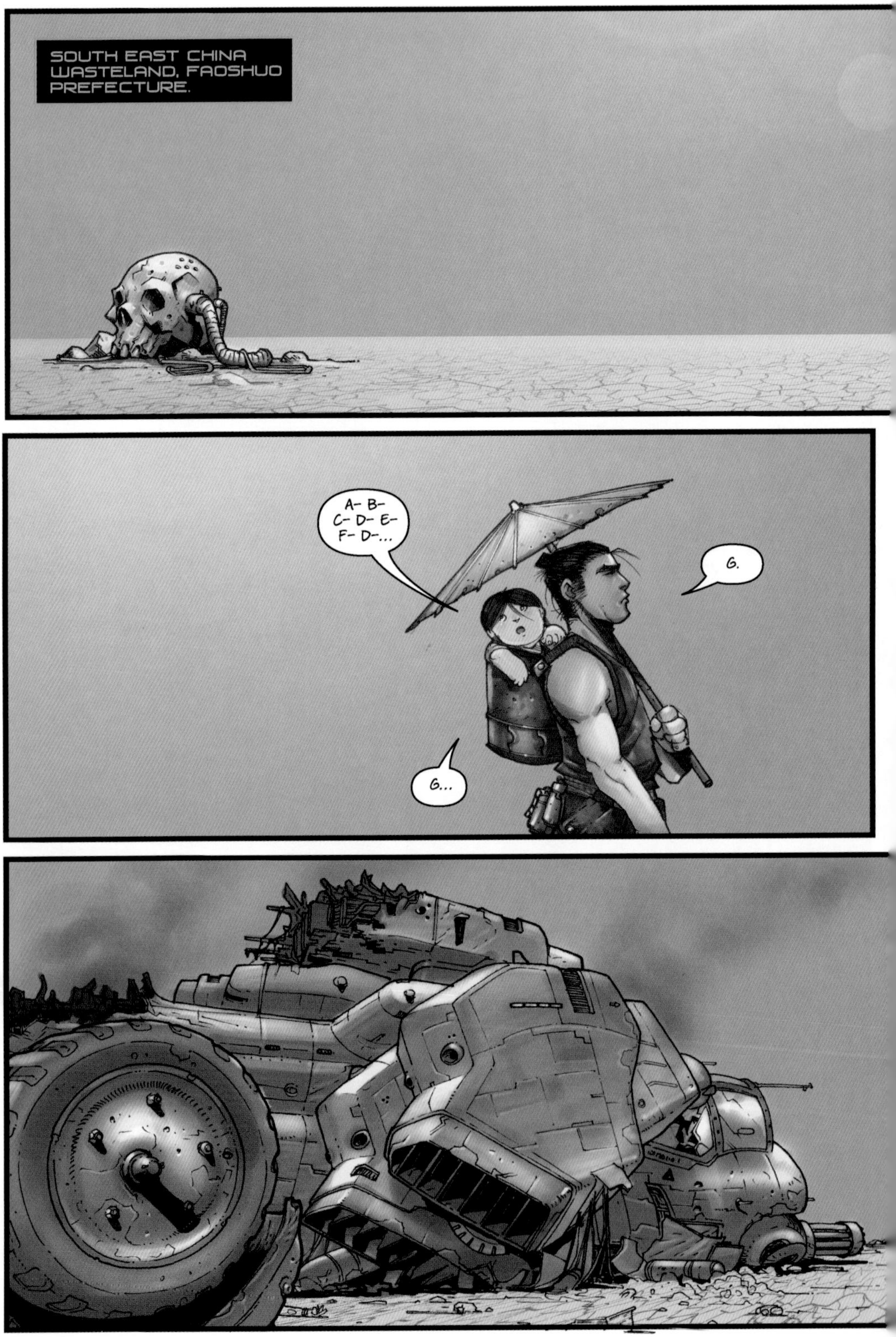
SOUTH EAST CHINA WASTELAND, FAOSHUO PREFECTURE.
A- B- C- D- E- F- D-...
G.
G...

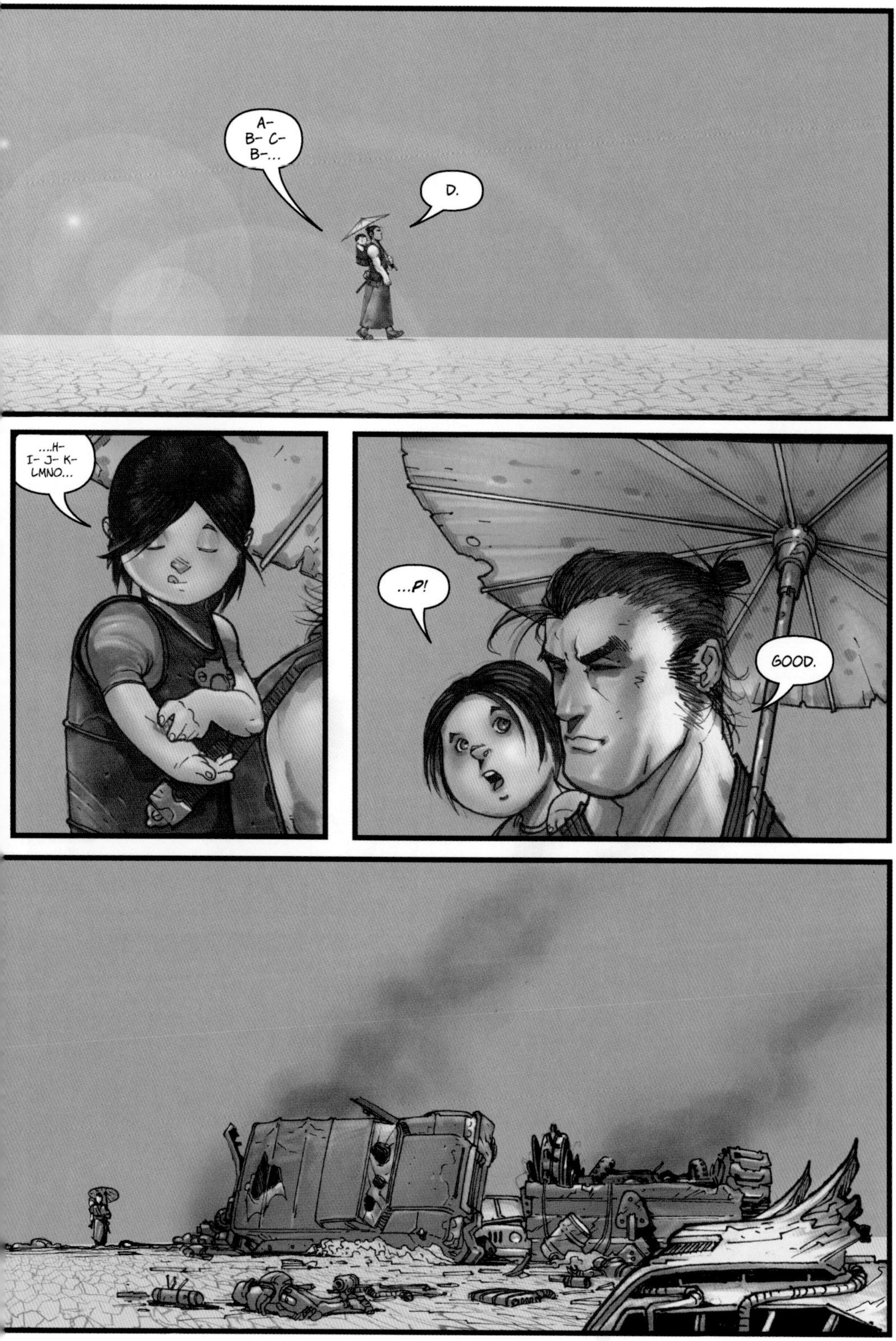
A-
B- C-
B-...
D.
...H-
I- J- K-
LMNO...
...P!
GOOD.

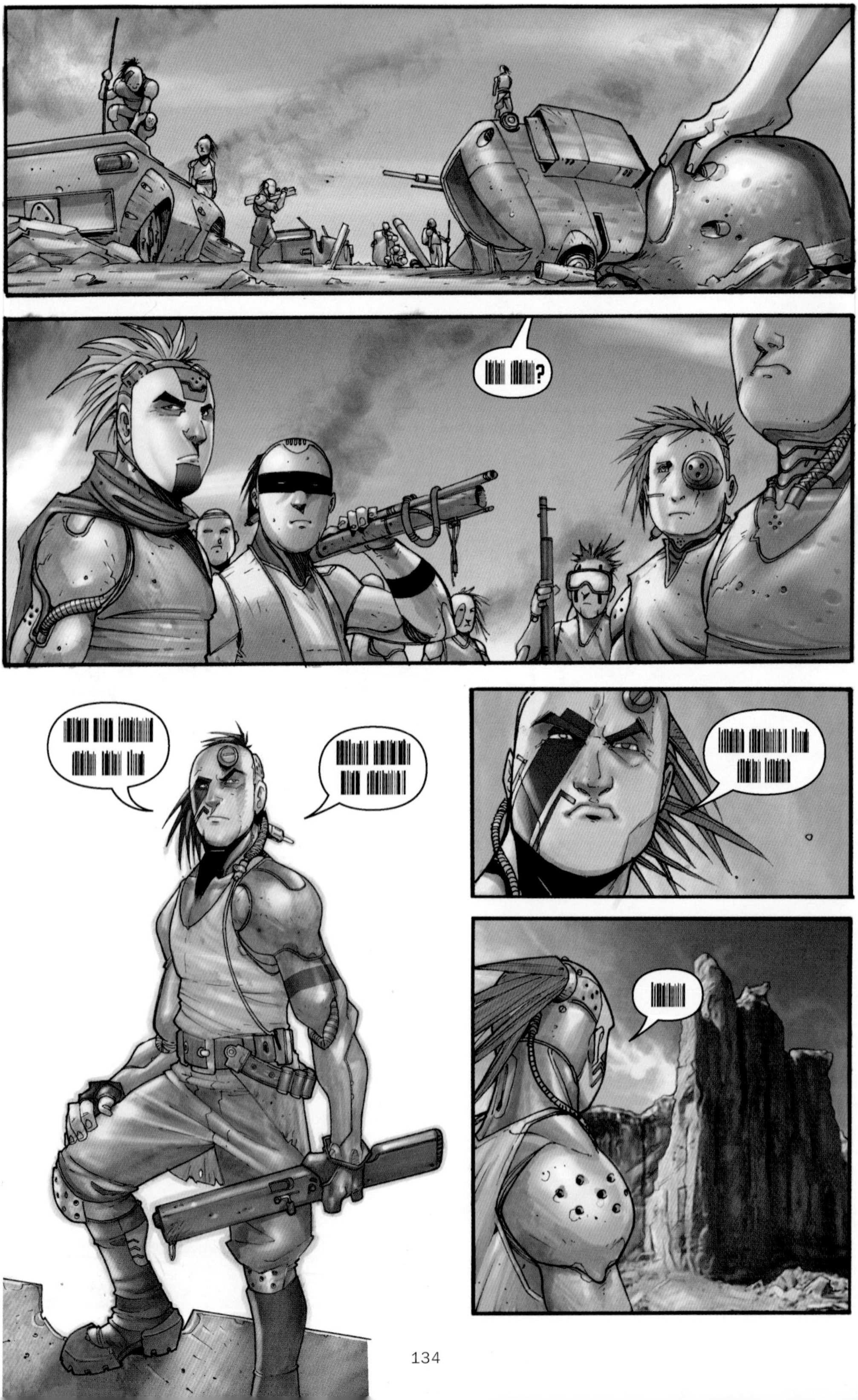

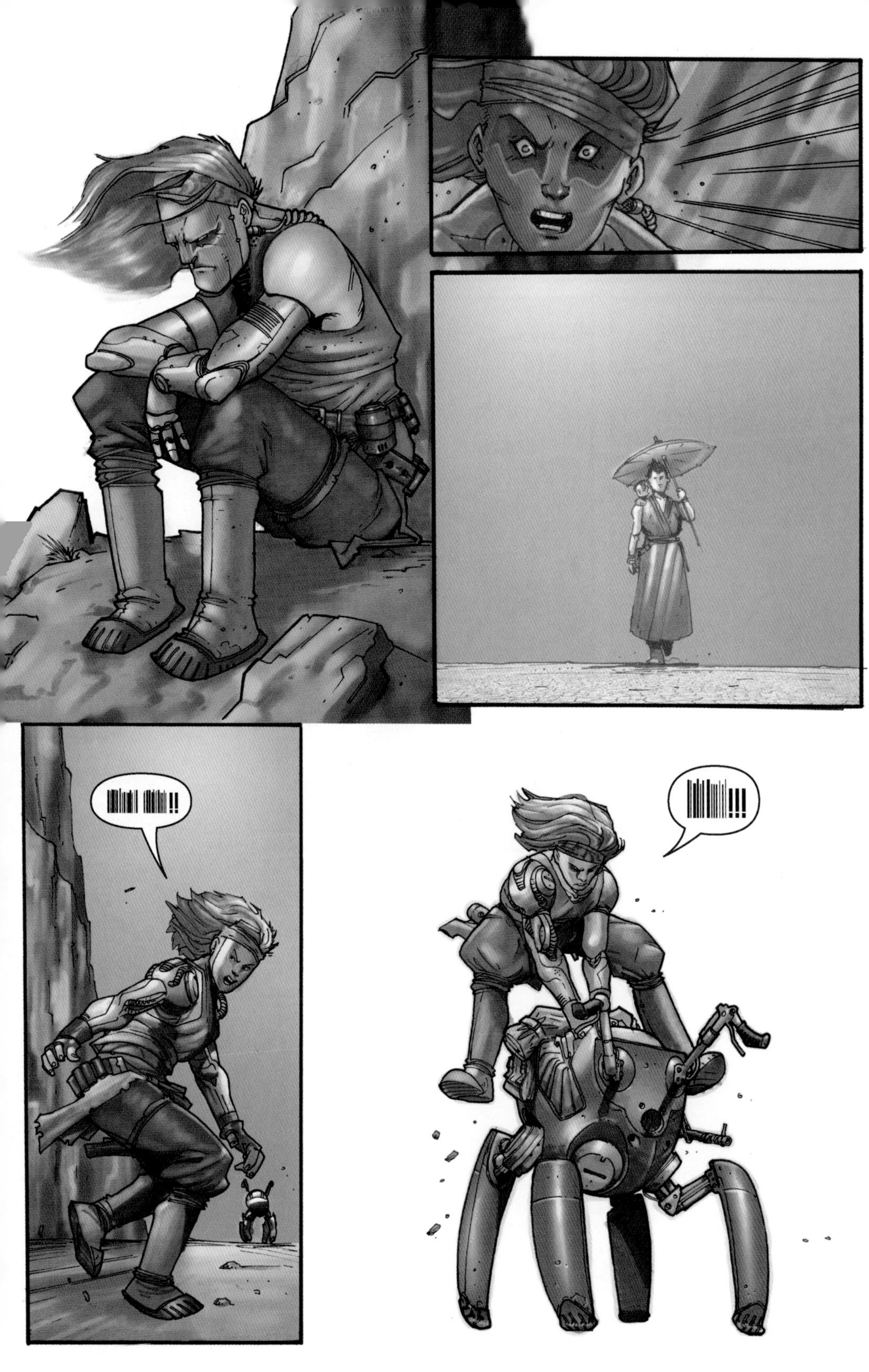

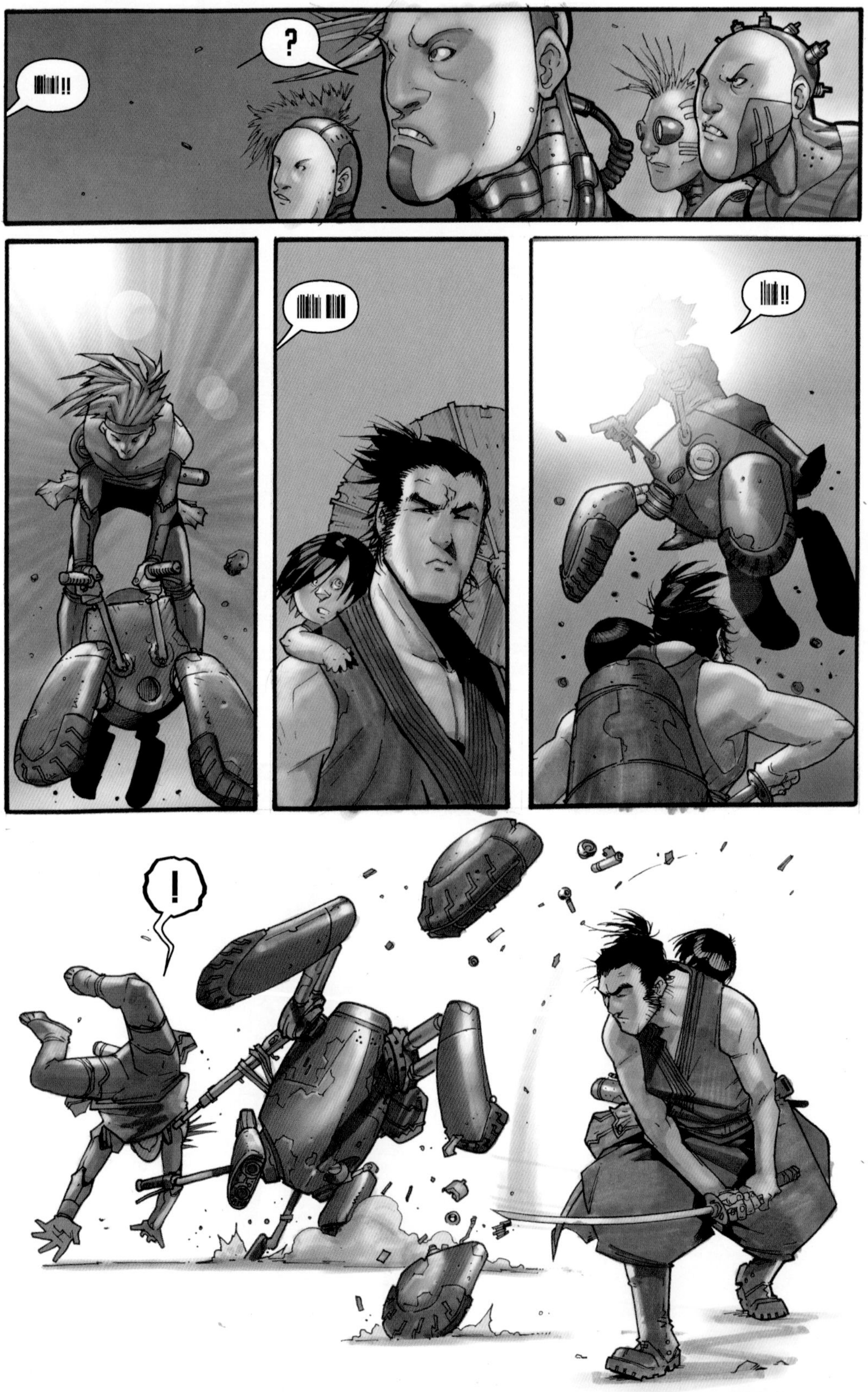
?
!

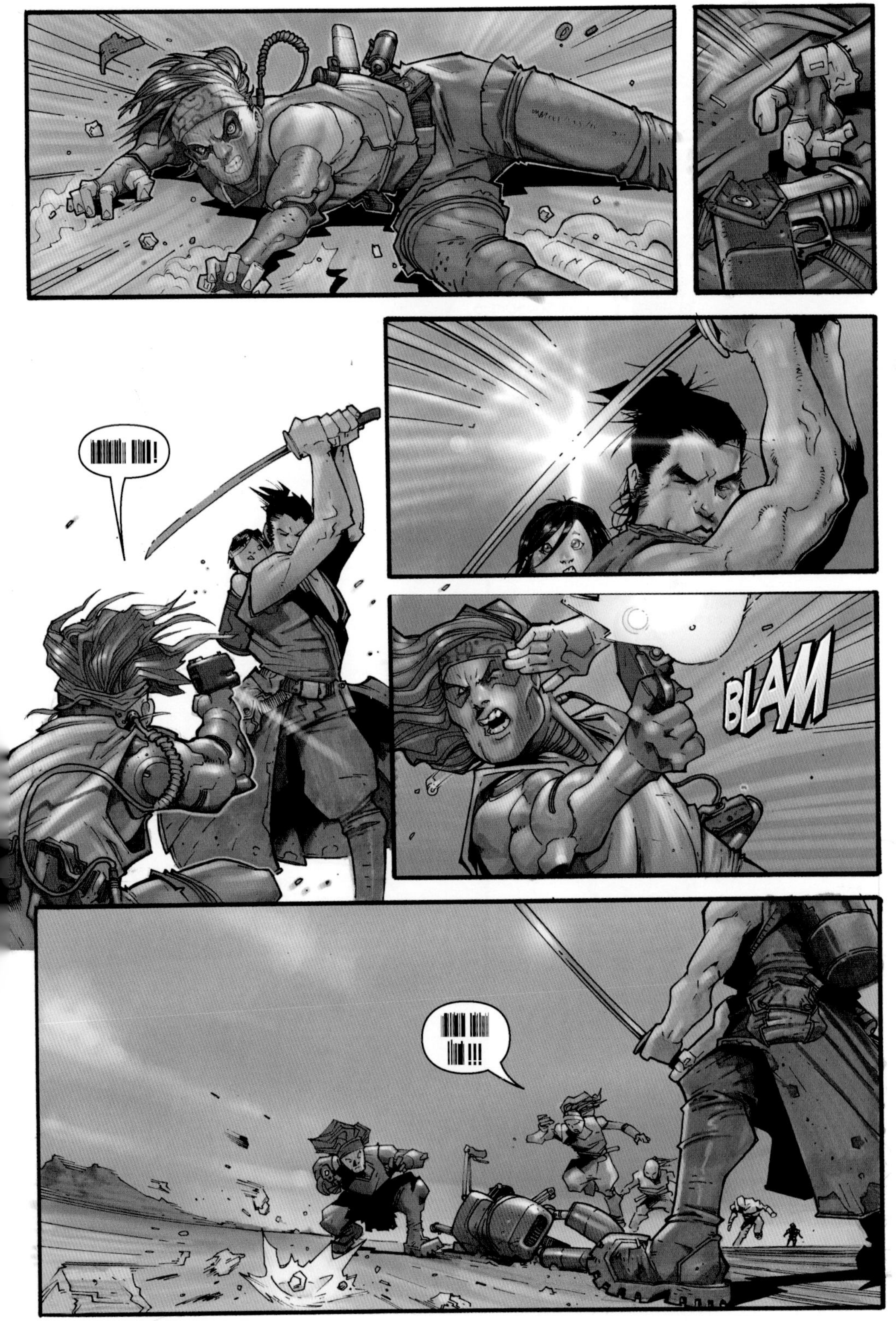
BLAM

||||- CAN UNDERSTAND. IS THAT BETTER?

YES.

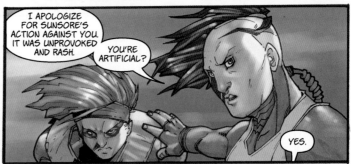

I APOLOGIZE FOR SUNSORE'S ACTION AGAINST YOU. IT WAS UNPROVOKED AND RASH.

YOU'RE ARTIFICIAL?

YES.

||||||
NIHON-GO ||||||!

THEN WE'RE BROTHERS TO A DEGREE. FELLOW OUTCASTS, SHUNNED BY HUMANITY.

ARE YOU RUNNING *TO* SOMETHING, OR *AWAY*?

BOTH.

THEN YOU'RE WELCOME IN OUR CAMP. WE HAVE FLUID AND SHELTER NEARBY IF YOU REQUIRE THEM.

...

THANK YOU. THAT WOULD BE HELPFUL.

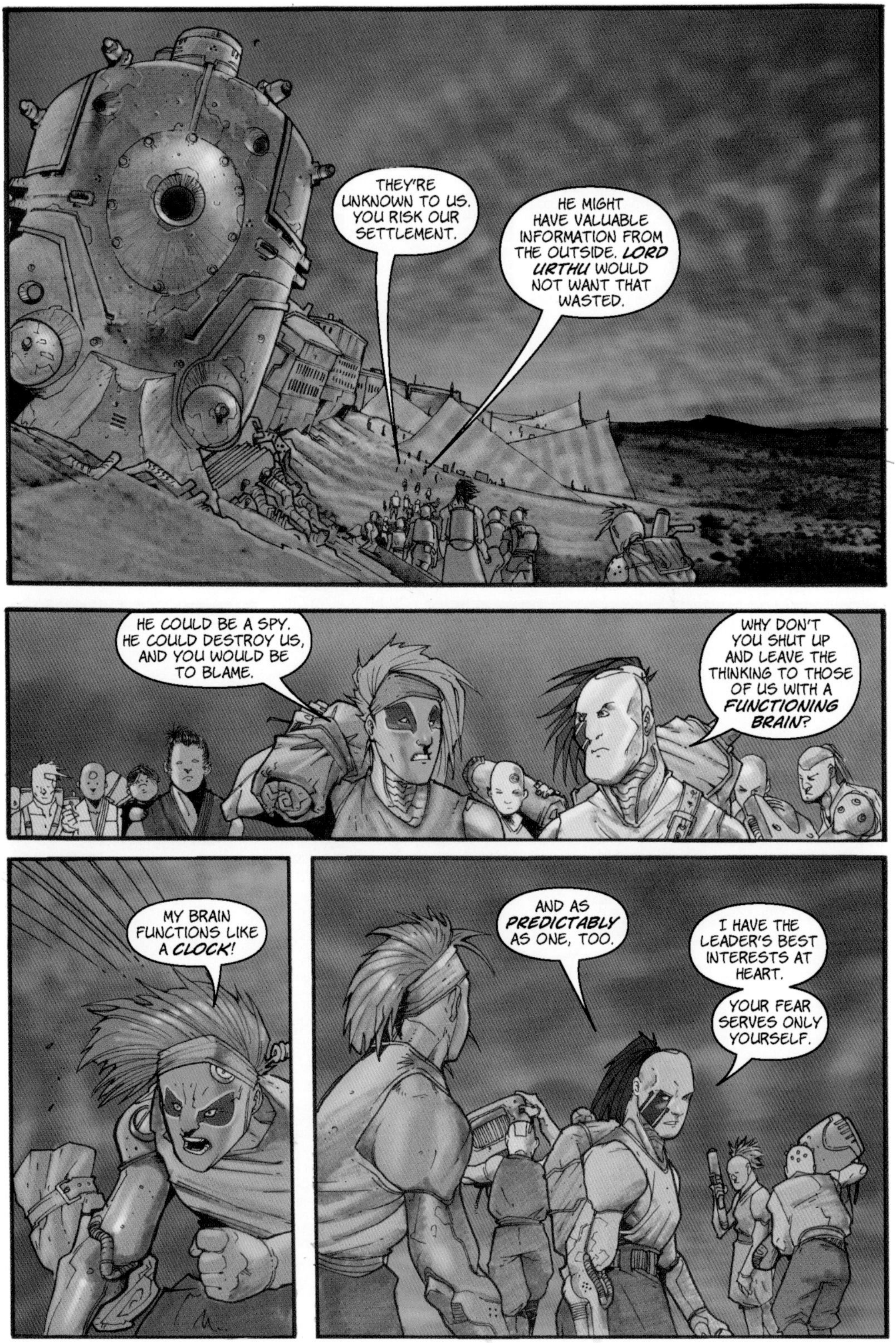
THEY'RE UNKNOWN TO US. YOU RISK OUR SETTLEMENT.
HE MIGHT HAVE VALUABLE INFORMATION FROM THE OUTSIDE. LORD URTHU WOULD NOT WANT THAT WASTED.
HE COULD BE A SPY. HE COULD DESTROY US, AND YOU WOULD BE TO BLAME.
WHY DON'T YOU SHUT UP AND LEAVE THE THINKING TO THOSE OF US WITH A FUNCTIONING BRAIN?
MY BRAIN FUNCTIONS LIKE A CLOCK!
AND AS PREDICTABLY AS ONE, TOO.
I HAVE THE LEADER'S BEST INTERESTS AT HEART.
YOUR FEAR SERVES ONLY YOURSELF.

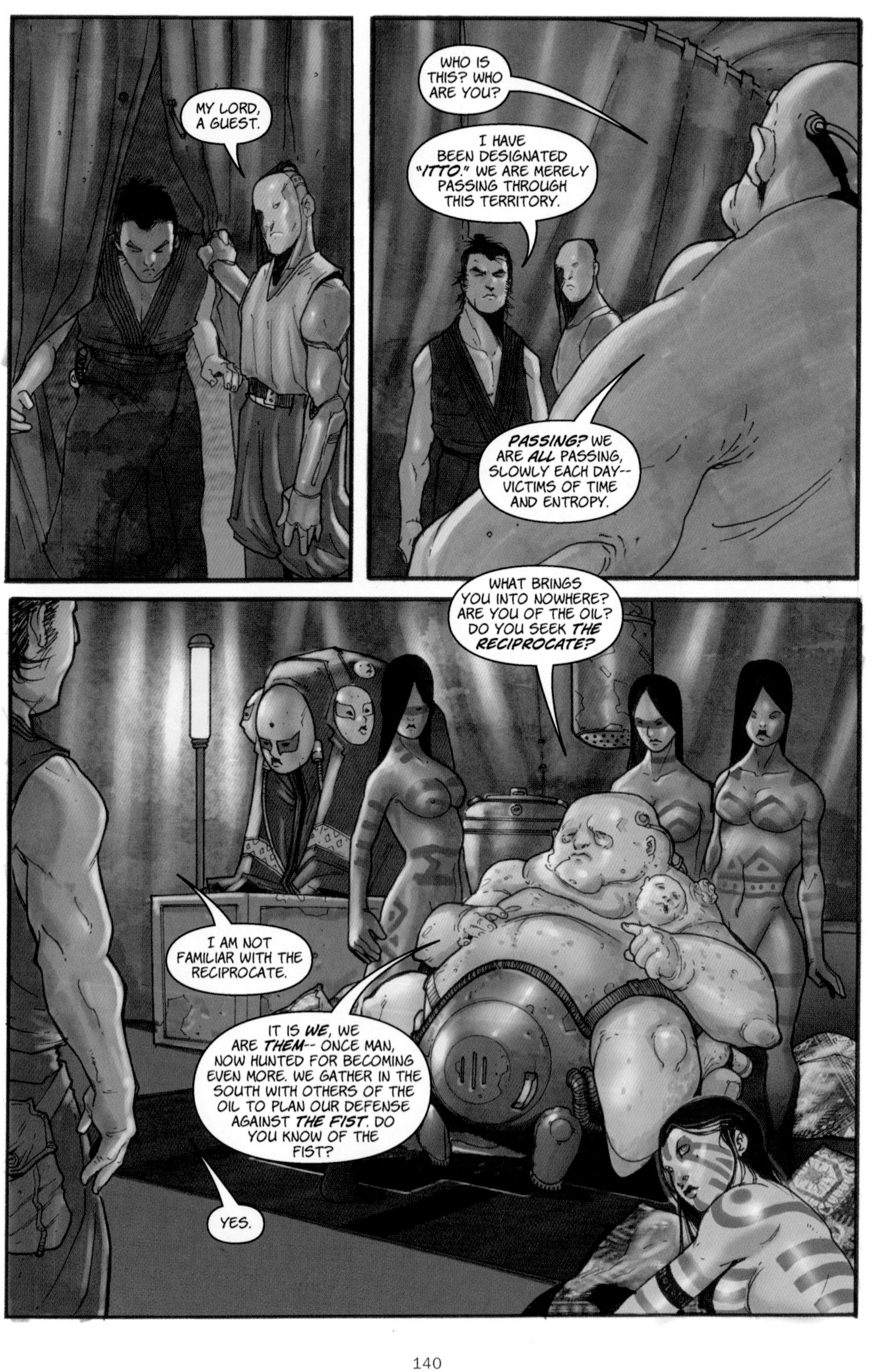
MY LORD, A GUEST.
WHO IS THIS? WHO ARE YOU?
I HAVE BEEN DESIGNATED "ITTO." WE ARE MERELY PASSING THROUGH THIS TERRITORY.
PASSING? WE ARE ALL PASSING, SLOWLY EACH DAY-- VICTIMS OF TIME AND ENTROPY.
WHAT BRINGS YOU INTO NOWHERE? ARE YOU OF THE OIL? DO YOU SEEK THE RECIPROCATE?
I AM NOT FAMILIAR WITH THE RECIPROCATE.
IT IS WE, WE ARE THEM-- ONCE MAN, NOW HUNTED FOR BECOMING EVEN MORE. WE GATHER IN THE SOUTH WITH OTHERS OF THE OIL TO PLAN OUR DEFENSE AGAINST THE FIST. DO YOU KNOW OF THE FIST?
YES.

THEN YOU KNOW WHY THEY HUNT US.

HUMAN LAWS DO NOT FAVOR OUR KIND, AND SO WE IGNORE THEM. OPPRESSION LISTENS ONLY TO TERROR. *SURVIVAL* DEMANDS *VIOLENCE* SOMETIMES.

ARE YOU WITH THE COALITION?

NO, THEY ARE *HUMAN*. THEIR CRUSADE IS *HOLLOW*.

JOIN US. WE BOTH TRAVEL SOUTH. TRAVEL WITH US.

"THE SERPENT LEAVES BEHIND HIS USELESS FLESH AND FRIGHTENS FOES WITH HIS NEW FACE."

"HIS PAPERED SKIN POINTS TOWARDS HIS BACK LIKE A FLACCID ARROW."

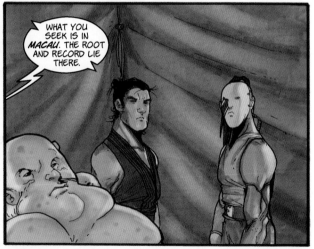

WHAT YOU SEEK IS IN *MACAU*. THE ROOT AND RECORD LIE THERE.

...

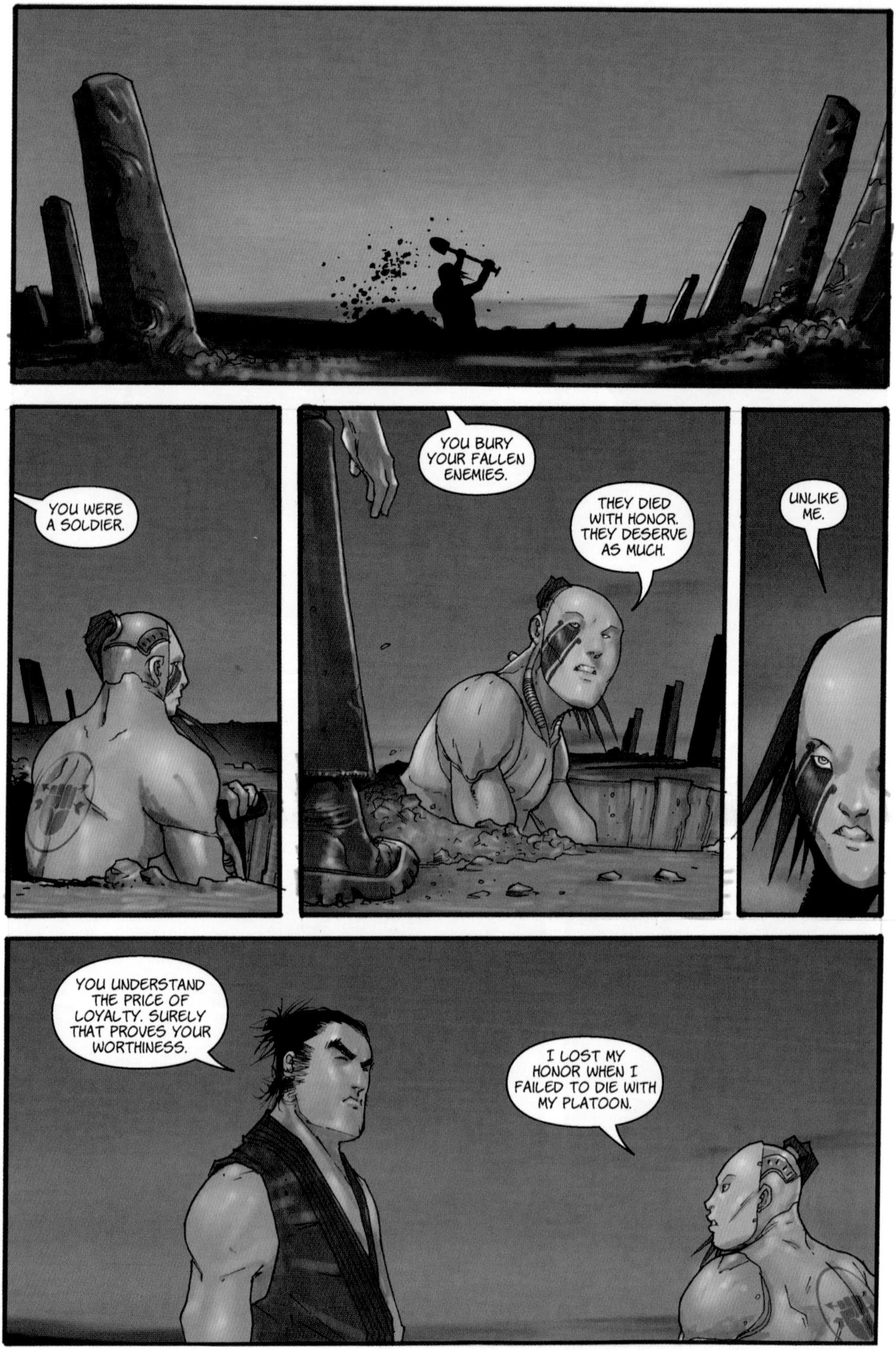
YOU WERE A SOLDIER.
YOU BURY YOUR FALLEN ENEMIES.
THEY DIED WITH HONOR. THEY DESERVE AS MUCH.
UNLIKE ME.
YOU UNDERSTAND THE PRICE OF LOYALTY. SURELY THAT PROVES YOUR WORTHINESS.
I LOST MY HONOR WHEN I FAILED TO DIE WITH MY PLATOON.

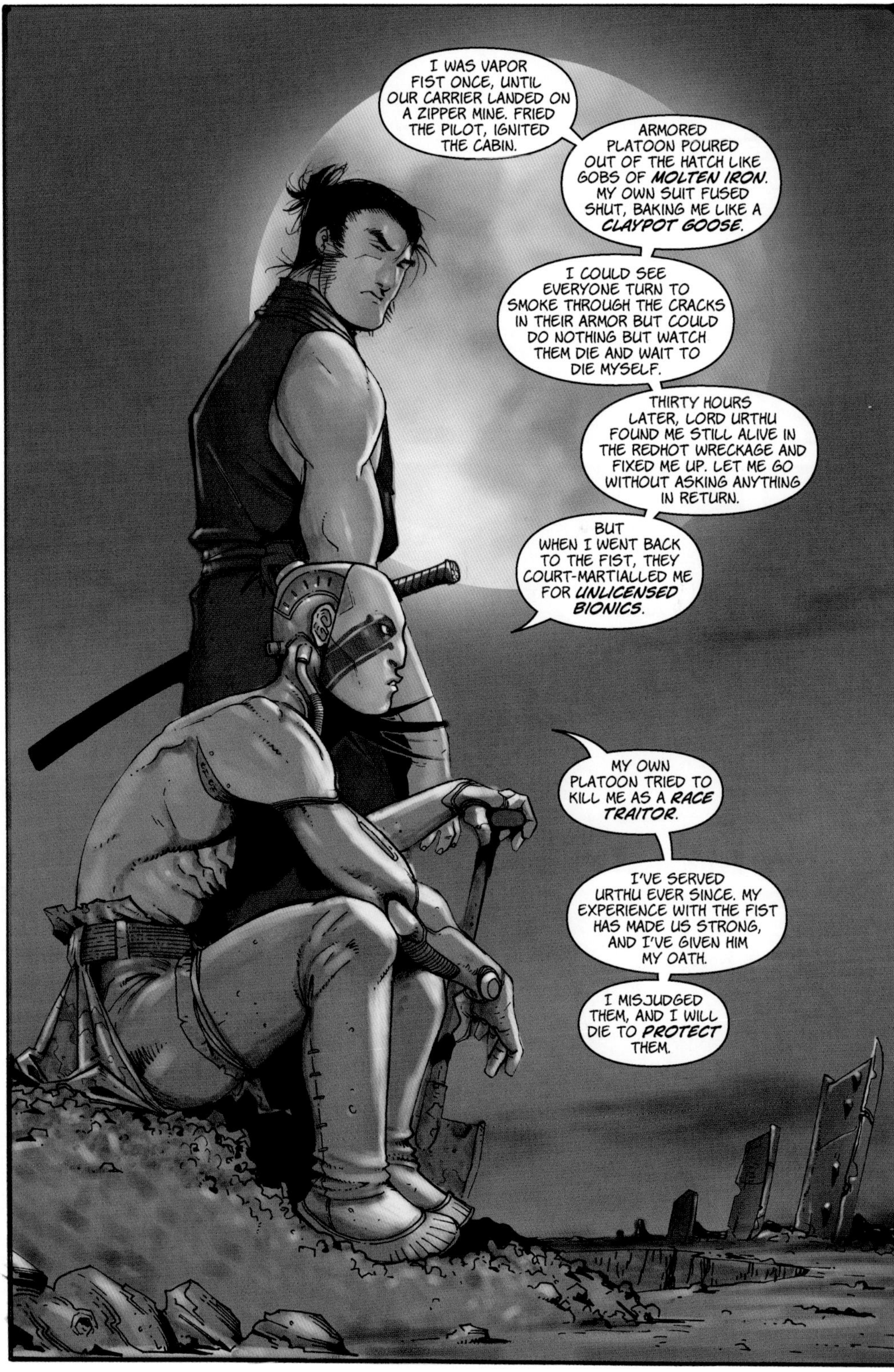
I WAS VAPOR FIST ONCE, UNTIL OUR CARRIER LANDED ON A ZIPPER MINE. FRIED THE PILOT, IGNITED THE CABIN.
ARMORED PLATOON POURED OUT OF THE HATCH LIKE GOBS OF ***MOLTEN IRON***. MY OWN SUIT FUSED SHUT, BAKING ME LIKE A ***CLAYPOT GOOSE***.
I COULD SEE EVERYONE TURN TO SMOKE THROUGH THE CRACKS IN THEIR ARMOR BUT COULD DO NOTHING BUT WATCH THEM DIE AND WAIT TO DIE MYSELF.
THIRTY HOURS LATER, LORD URTHU FOUND ME STILL ALIVE IN THE REDHOT WRECKAGE AND FIXED ME UP. LET ME GO WITHOUT ASKING ANYTHING IN RETURN.
BUT WHEN I WENT BACK TO THE FIST, THEY COURT-MARTIALLED ME FOR ***UNLICENSED BIONICS***.
MY OWN PLATOON TRIED TO KILL ME AS A ***RACE TRAITOR***.
I'VE SERVED URTHU EVER SINCE. MY EXPERIENCE WITH THE FIST HAS MADE US STRONG, AND I'VE GIVEN HIM MY OATH.
I MISJUDGED THEM, AND I WILL DIE TO ***PROTECT*** THEM.

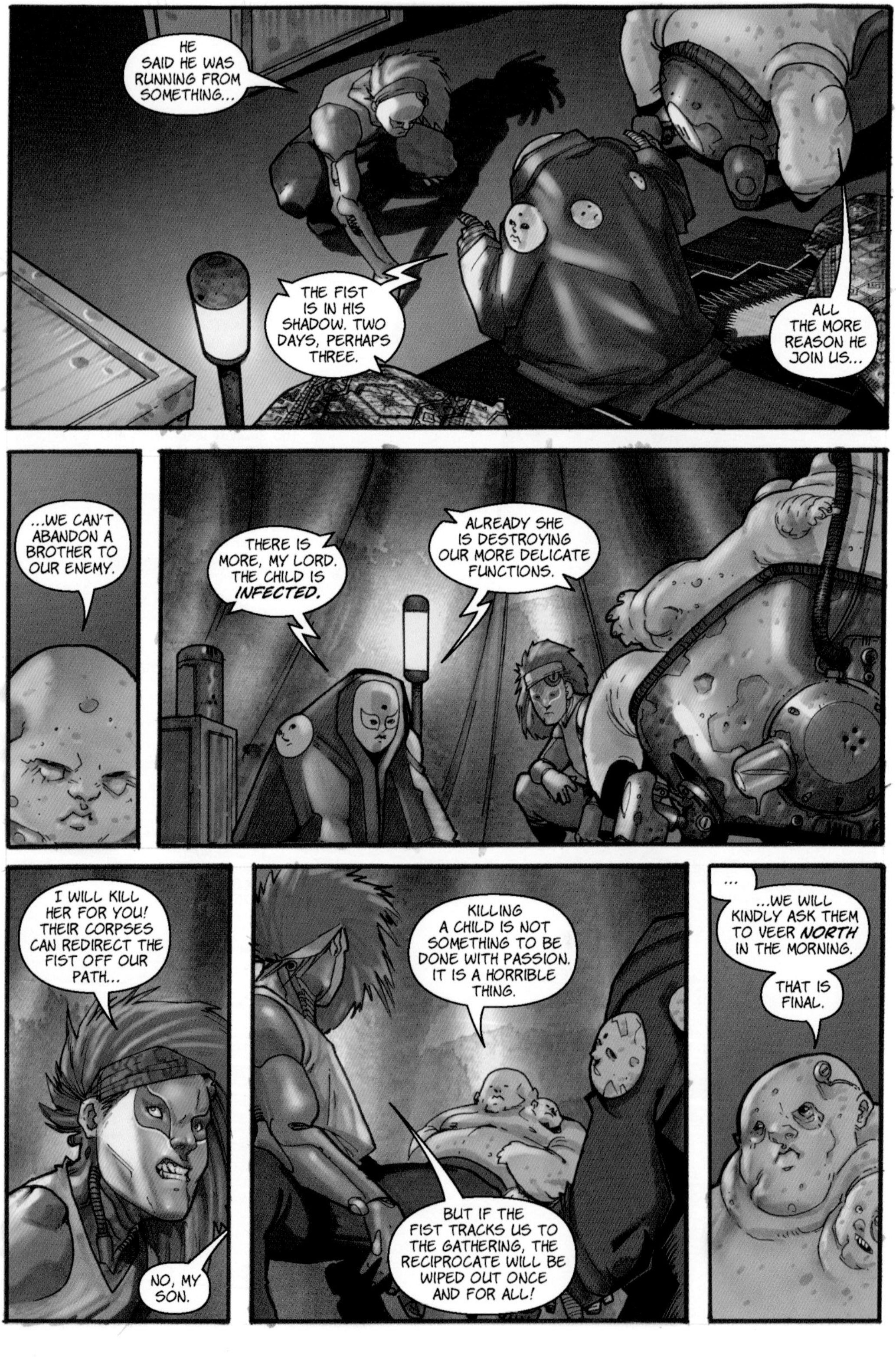
HE SAID HE WAS RUNNING FROM SOMETHING...
THE FIST IS IN HIS SHADOW. TWO DAYS, PERHAPS THREE.
ALL THE MORE REASON HE JOIN US...
...WE CAN'T ABANDON A BROTHER TO OUR ENEMY.
THERE IS MORE, MY LORD. THE CHILD IS ***INFECTED.***
ALREADY SHE IS DESTROYING OUR MORE DELICATE FUNCTIONS.
I WILL KILL HER FOR YOU! THEIR CORPSES CAN REDIRECT THE FIST OFF OUR PATH...
NO, MY SON.
KILLING A CHILD IS NOT SOMETHING TO BE DONE WITH PASSION. IT IS A HORRIBLE THING.
BUT IF THE FIST TRACKS US TO THE GATHERING, THE RECIPROCATE WILL BE WIPED OUT ONCE AND FOR ALL!
...
...WE WILL KINDLY ASK THEM TO VEER ***NORTH*** IN THE MORNING.
THAT IS FINAL.

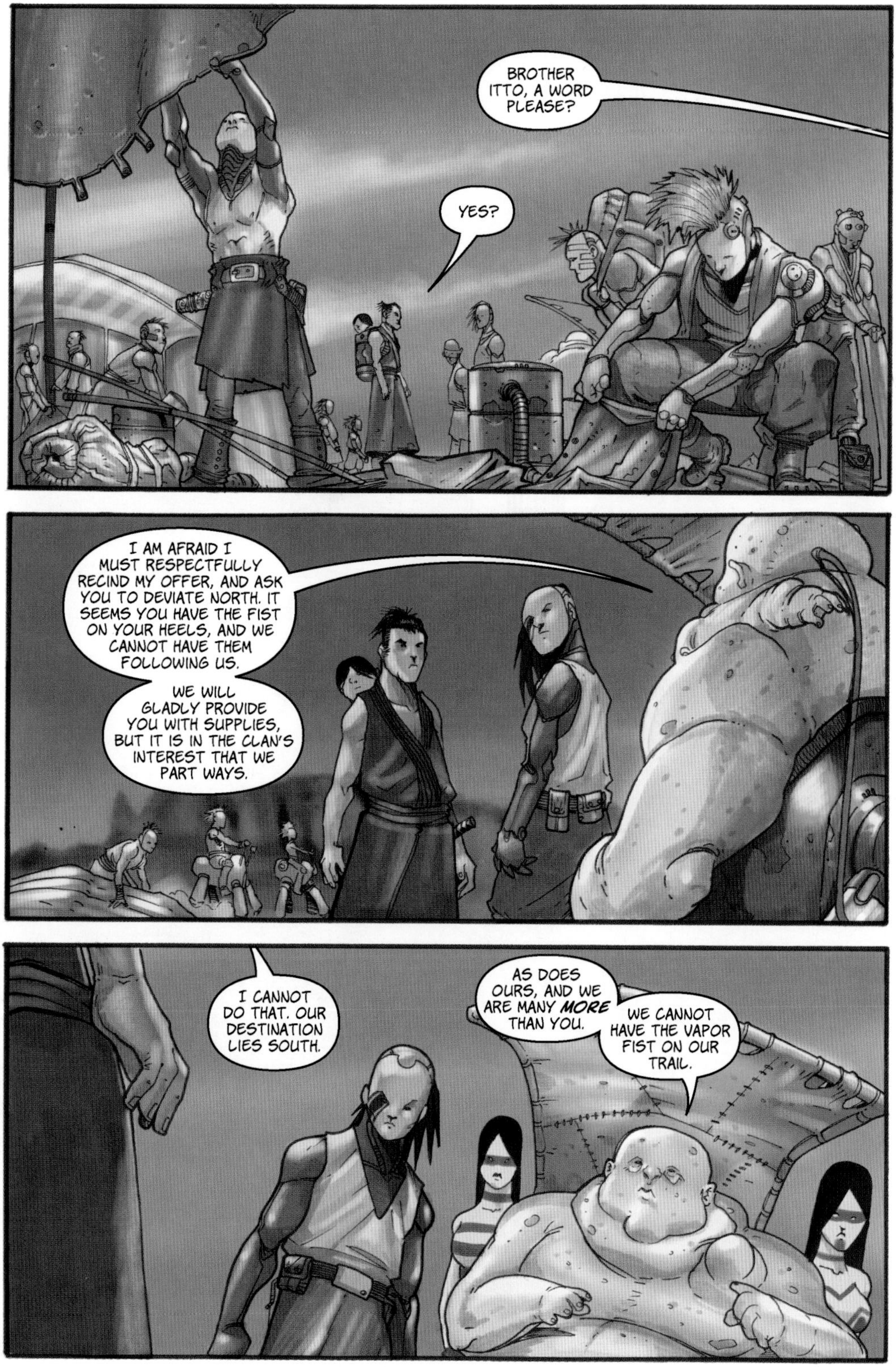

BROTHER ITTO, A WORD PLEASE?
YES?
I AM AFRAID I MUST RESPECTFULLY RECIND MY OFFER, AND ASK YOU TO DEVIATE NORTH. IT SEEMS YOU HAVE THE FIST ON YOUR HEELS, AND WE CANNOT HAVE THEM FOLLOWING US.
WE WILL GLADLY PROVIDE YOU WITH SUPPLIES, BUT IT IS IN THE CLAN'S INTEREST THAT WE PART WAYS.
I CANNOT DO THAT. OUR DESTINATION LIES SOUTH.
AS DOES OURS, AND WE ARE MANY *MORE* THAN YOU.
WE CANNOT HAVE THE VAPOR FIST ON OUR TRAIL.

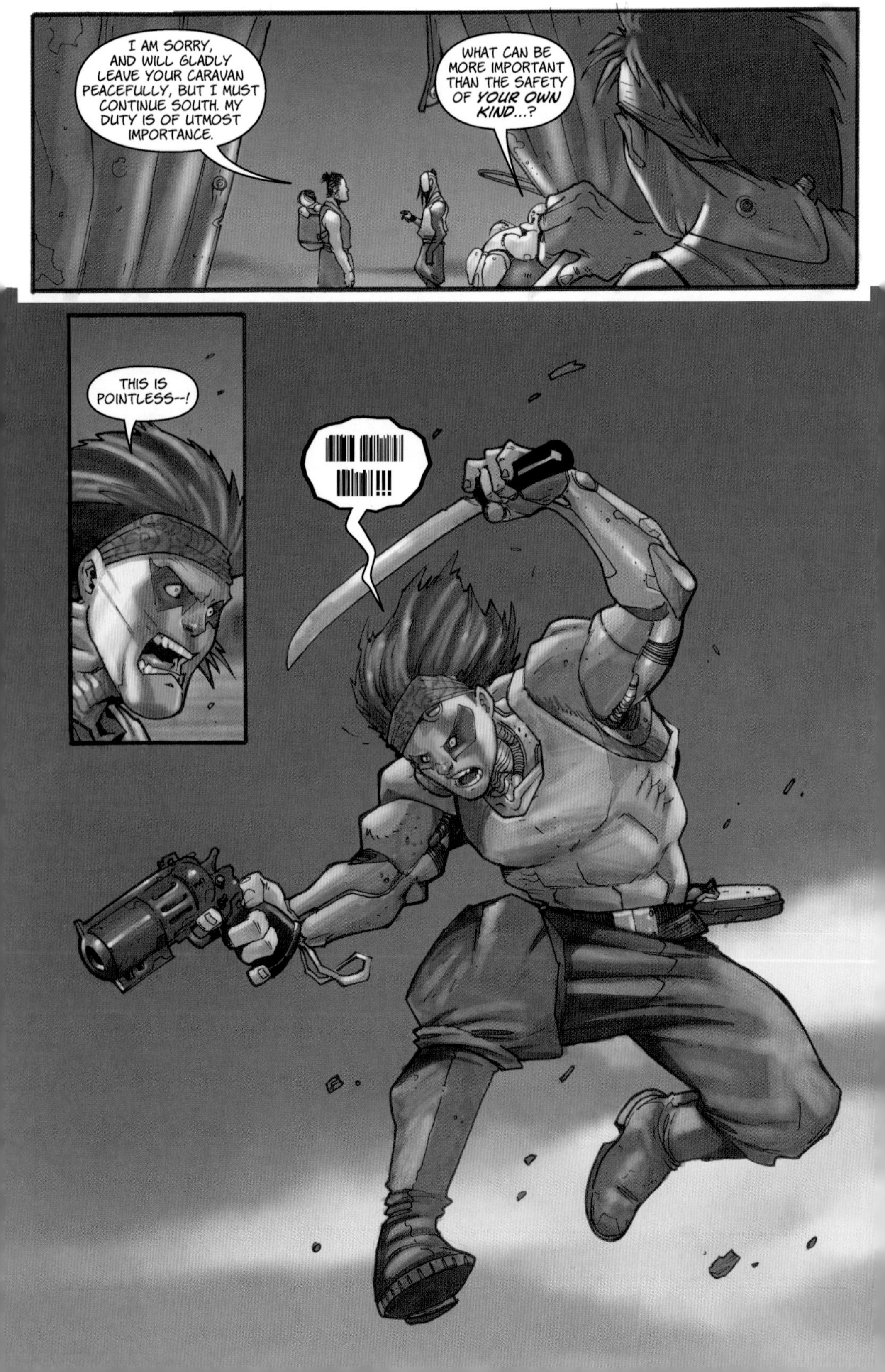
I AM SORRY, AND WILL GLADLY LEAVE YOUR CARAVAN PEACEFULLY, BUT I MUST CONTINUE SOUTH. MY DUTY IS OF UTMOST IMPORTANCE.
WHAT CAN BE MORE IMPORTANT THAN THE SAFETY OF ***YOUR OWN KIND***...?
THIS IS POINTLESS--!

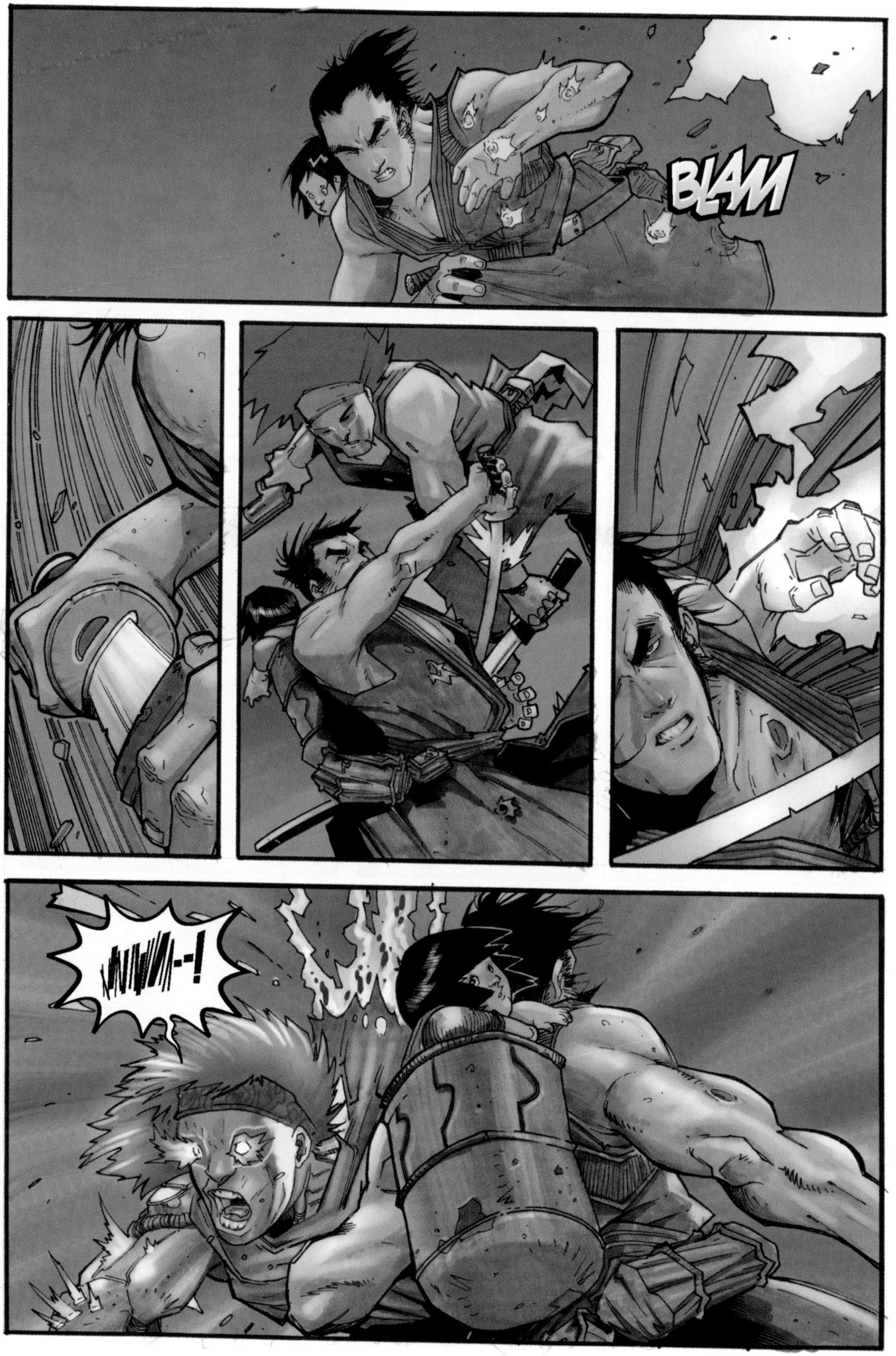
BLAM
NNNN--!

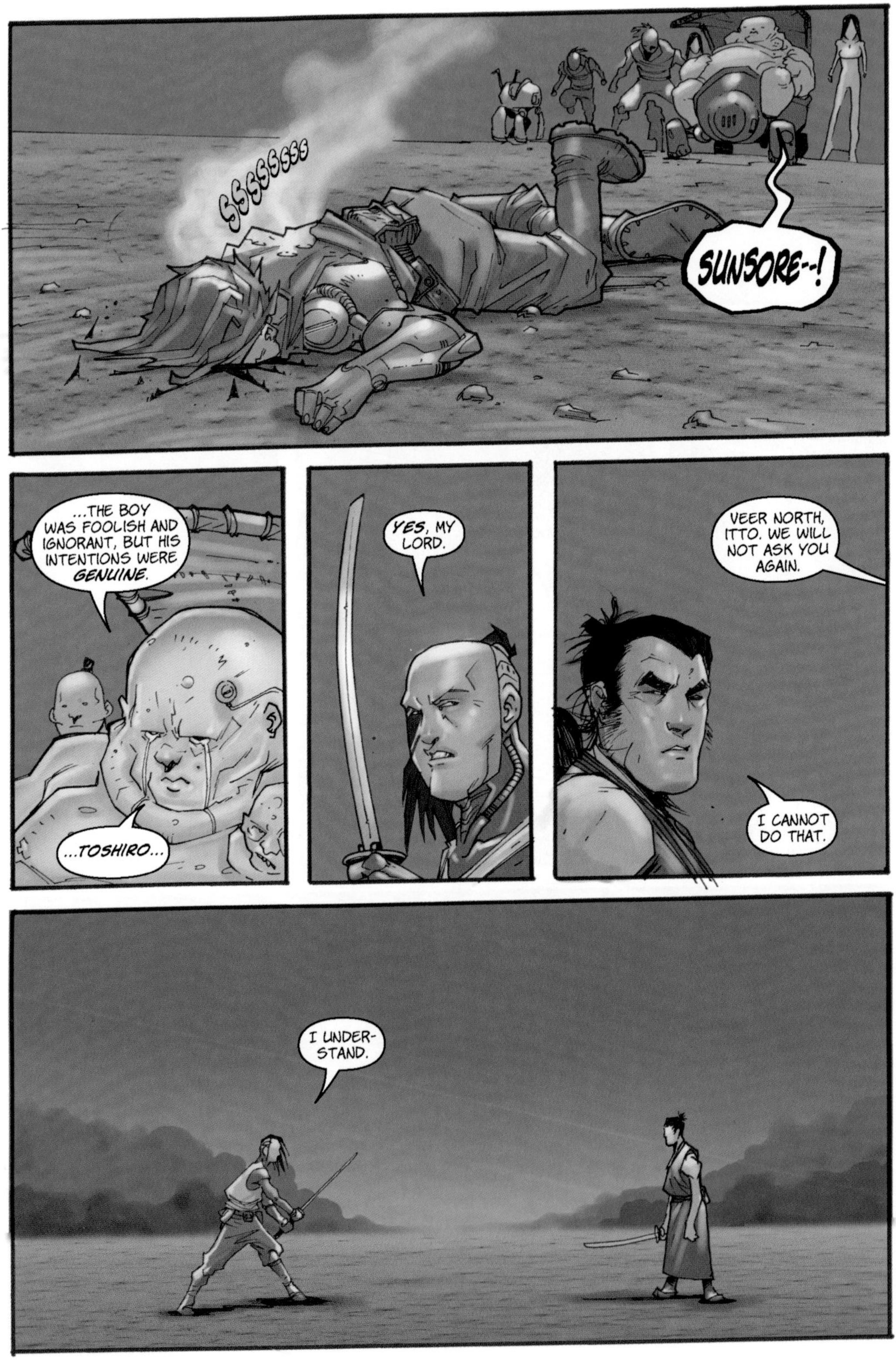
SSSSSSSS
SUNSORE--!
...THE BOY WAS FOOLISH AND IGNORANT, BUT HIS INTENTIONS WERE GENUINE.
...TOSHIRO...
YES, MY LORD.
VEER NORTH, ITTO. WE WILL NOT ASK YOU AGAIN.
I CANNOT DO THAT.
I UNDER-STAND.

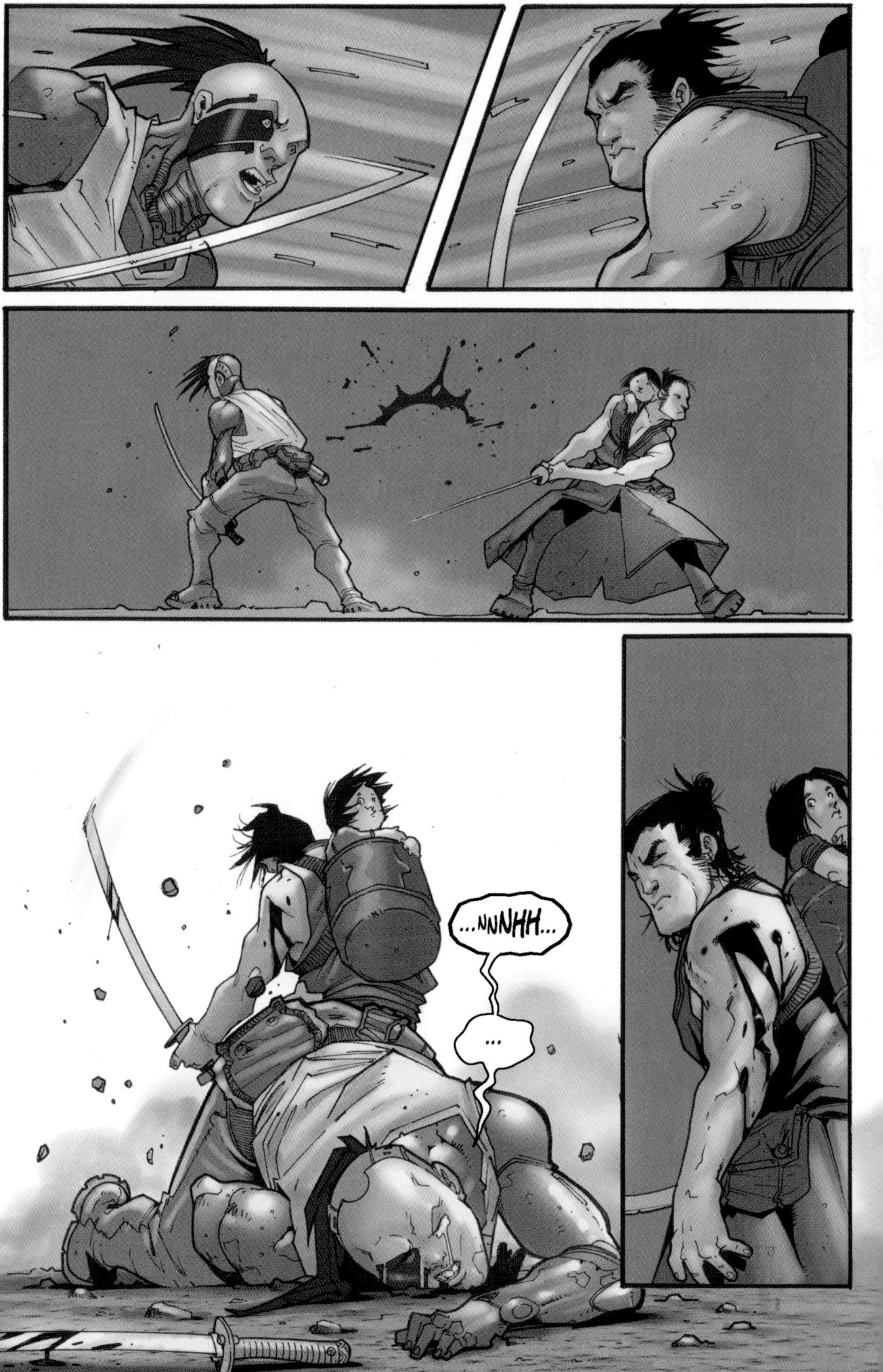
...NNNHH...
...

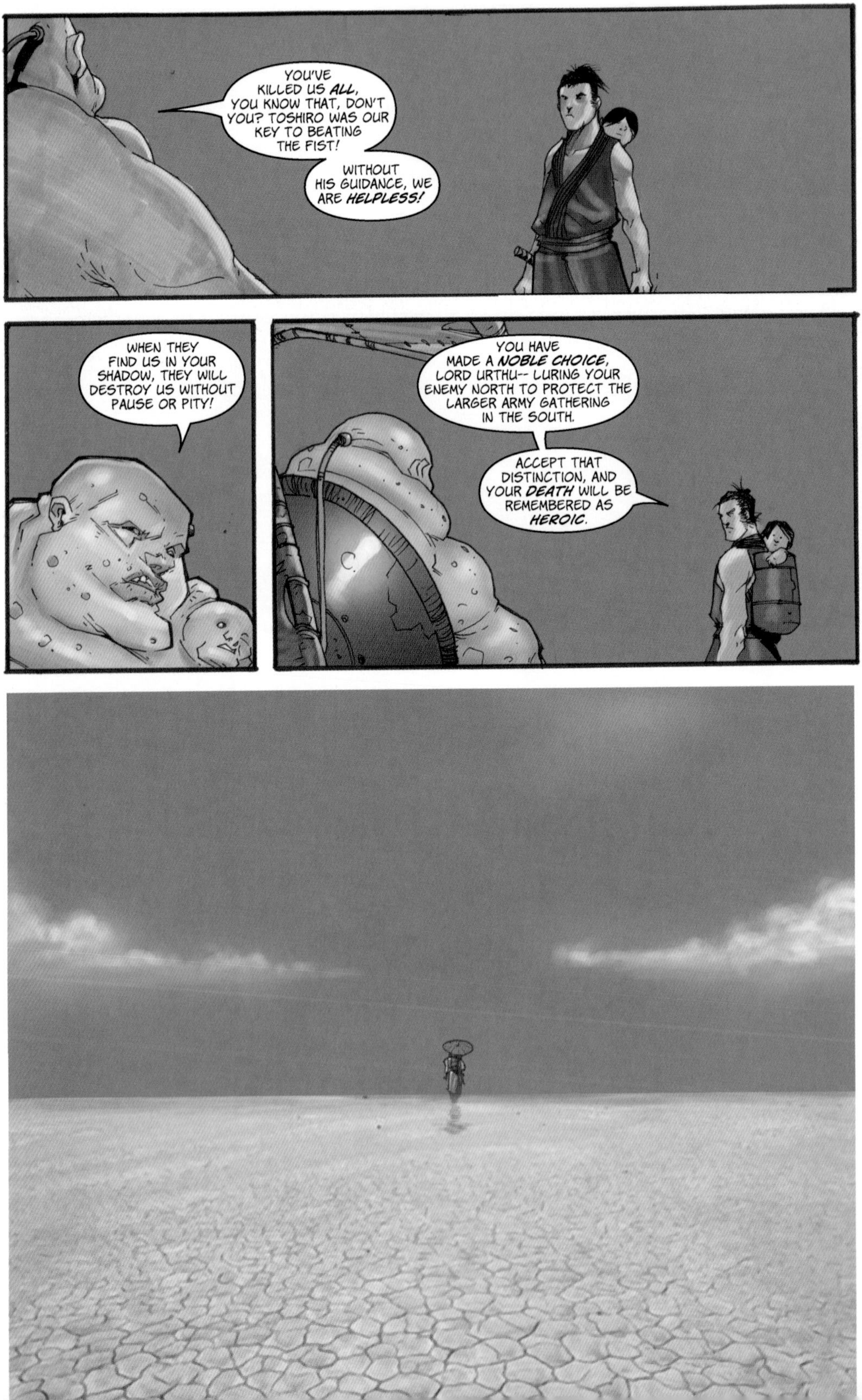
YOU'VE KILLED US ALL, YOU KNOW THAT, DON'T YOU? TOSHIRO WAS OUR KEY TO BEATING THE FIST!
WITHOUT HIS GUIDANCE, WE ARE HELPLESS!
WHEN THEY FIND US IN YOUR SHADOW, THEY WILL DESTROY US WITHOUT PAUSE OR PITY!
YOU HAVE MADE A NOBLE CHOICE, LORD URTHU-- LURING YOUR ENEMY NORTH TO PROTECT THE LARGER ARMY GATHERING IN THE SOUTH.
ACCEPT THAT DISTINCTION, AND YOUR DEATH WILL BE REMEMBERED AS HEROIC.

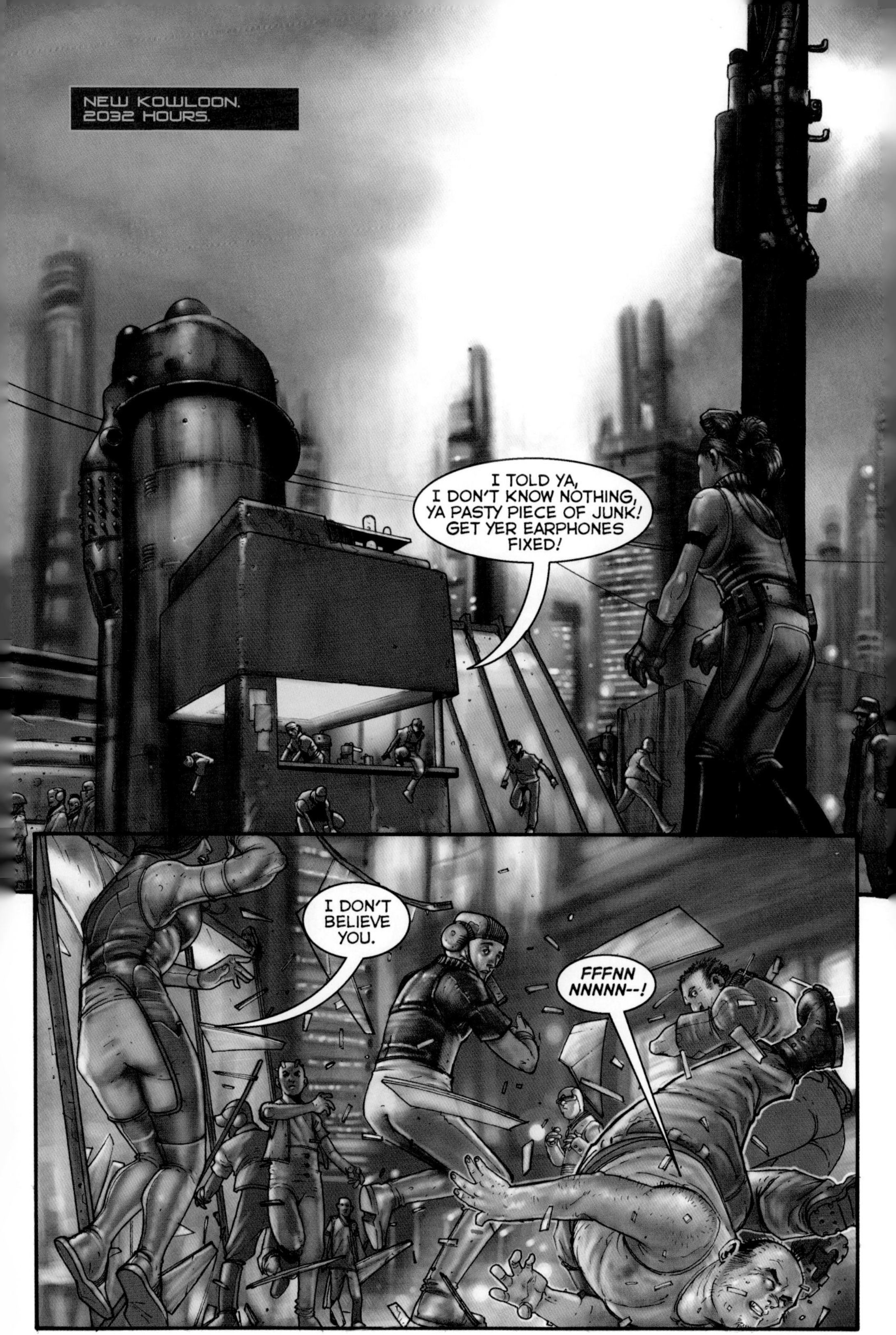
NEW KOWLOON.
2032 HOURS.
I TOLD YA, I DON'T KNOW NOTHING, YA PASTY PIECE OF JUNK! GET YER EARPHONES FIXED!
I DON'T BELIEVE YOU.
FFFNN NNNNN--!

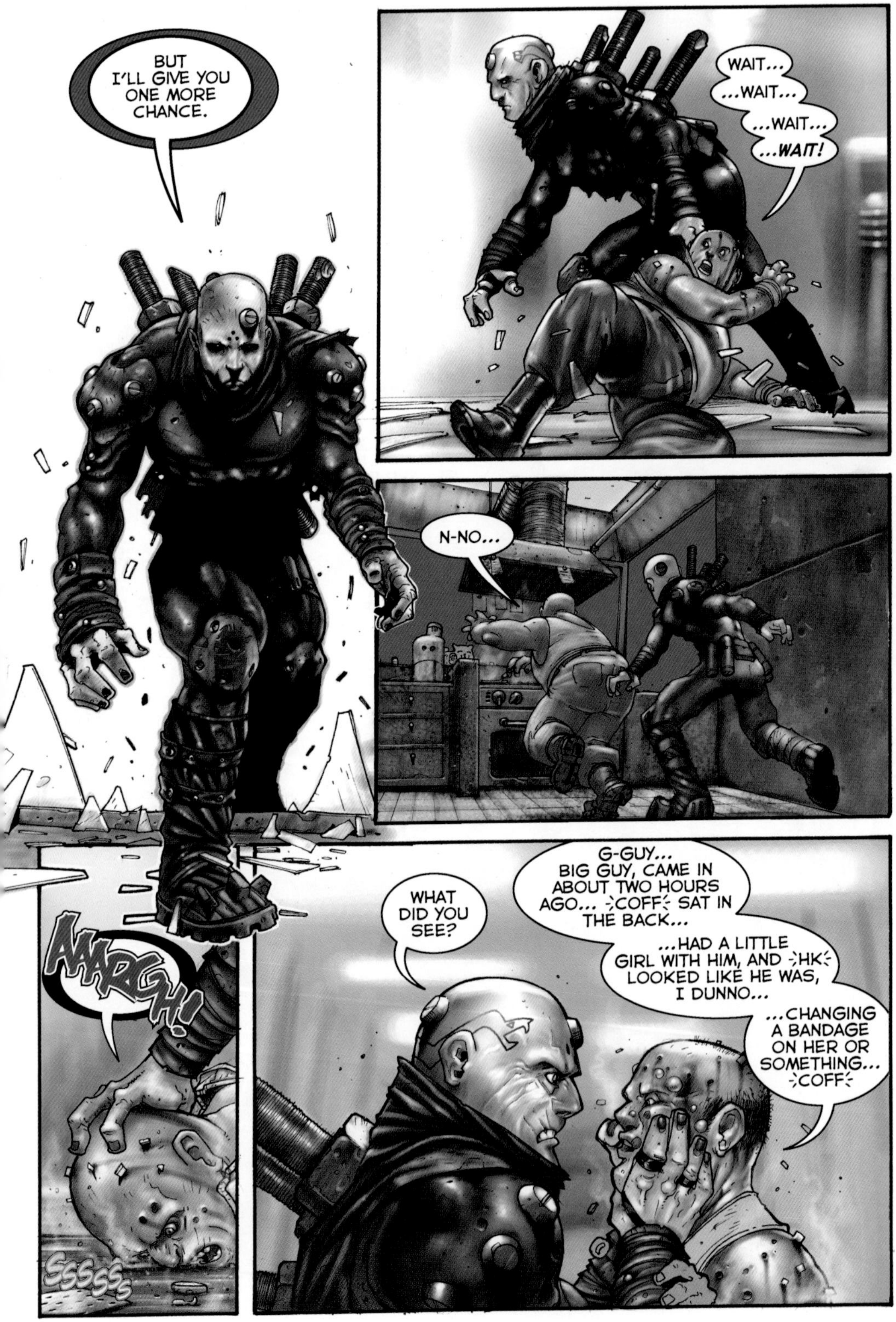
BUT I'LL GIVE YOU ONE MORE CHANCE.
WAIT...
...WAIT...
...WAIT...
...WAIT!
AAARGH!
SSSSS
N-NO...
WHAT DID YOU SEE?
G-GUY... BIG GUY, CAME IN ABOUT TWO HOURS AGO... COFF SAT IN THE BACK...
...HAD A LITTLE GIRL WITH HIM, AND HK LOOKED LIKE HE WAS, I DUNNO...
...CHANGING A BANDAGE ON HER OR SOMETHING... COFF

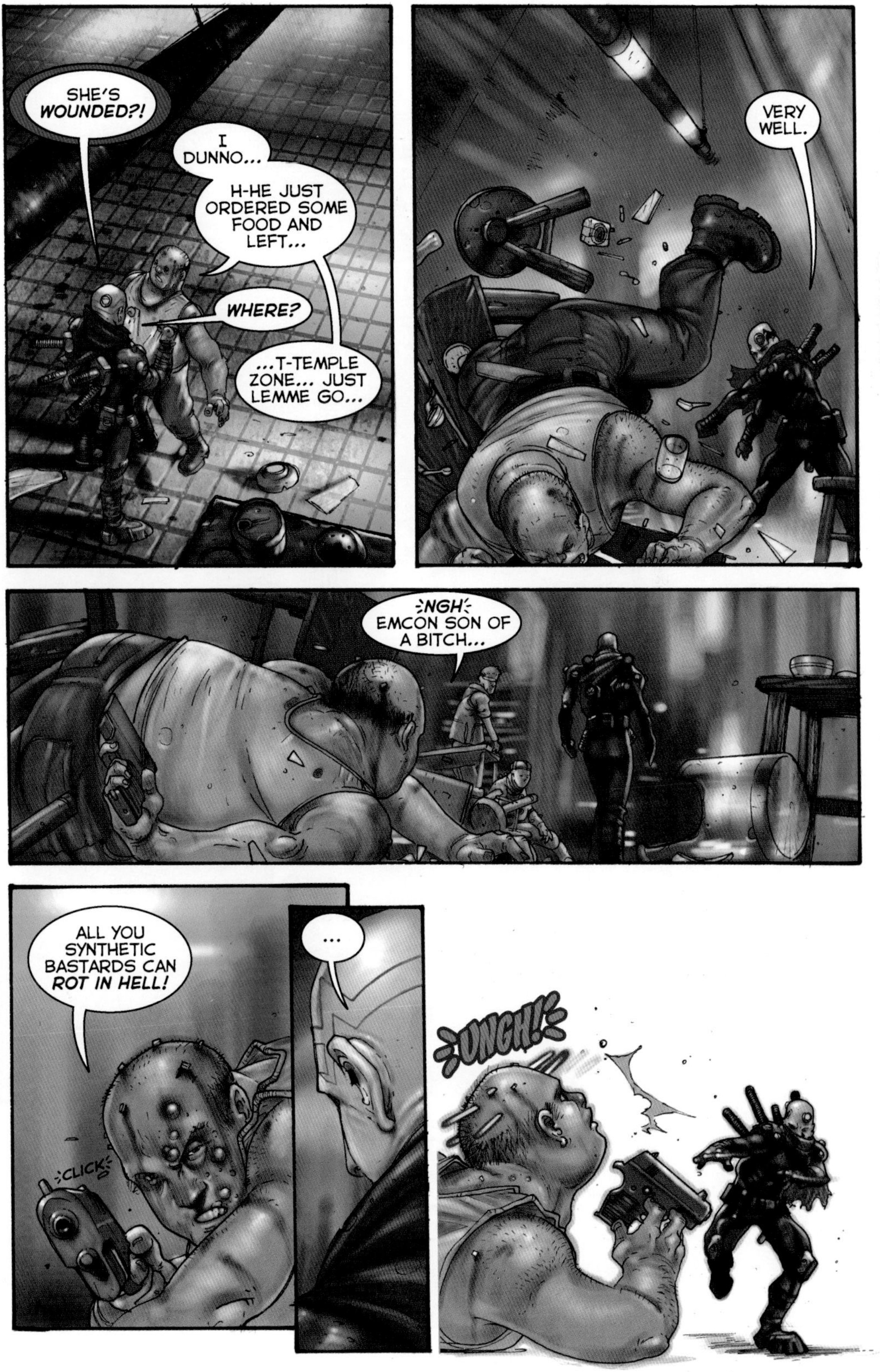
SHE'S WOUNDED?!
I DUNNO...
H-HE JUST ORDERED SOME FOOD AND LEFT...
WHERE?
...T-TEMPLE ZONE... JUST LEMME GO...
VERY WELL.
NGH EMCON SON OF A BITCH...
ALL YOU SYNTHETIC BASTARDS CAN ROT IN HELL!
CLICK
...
UNGH!

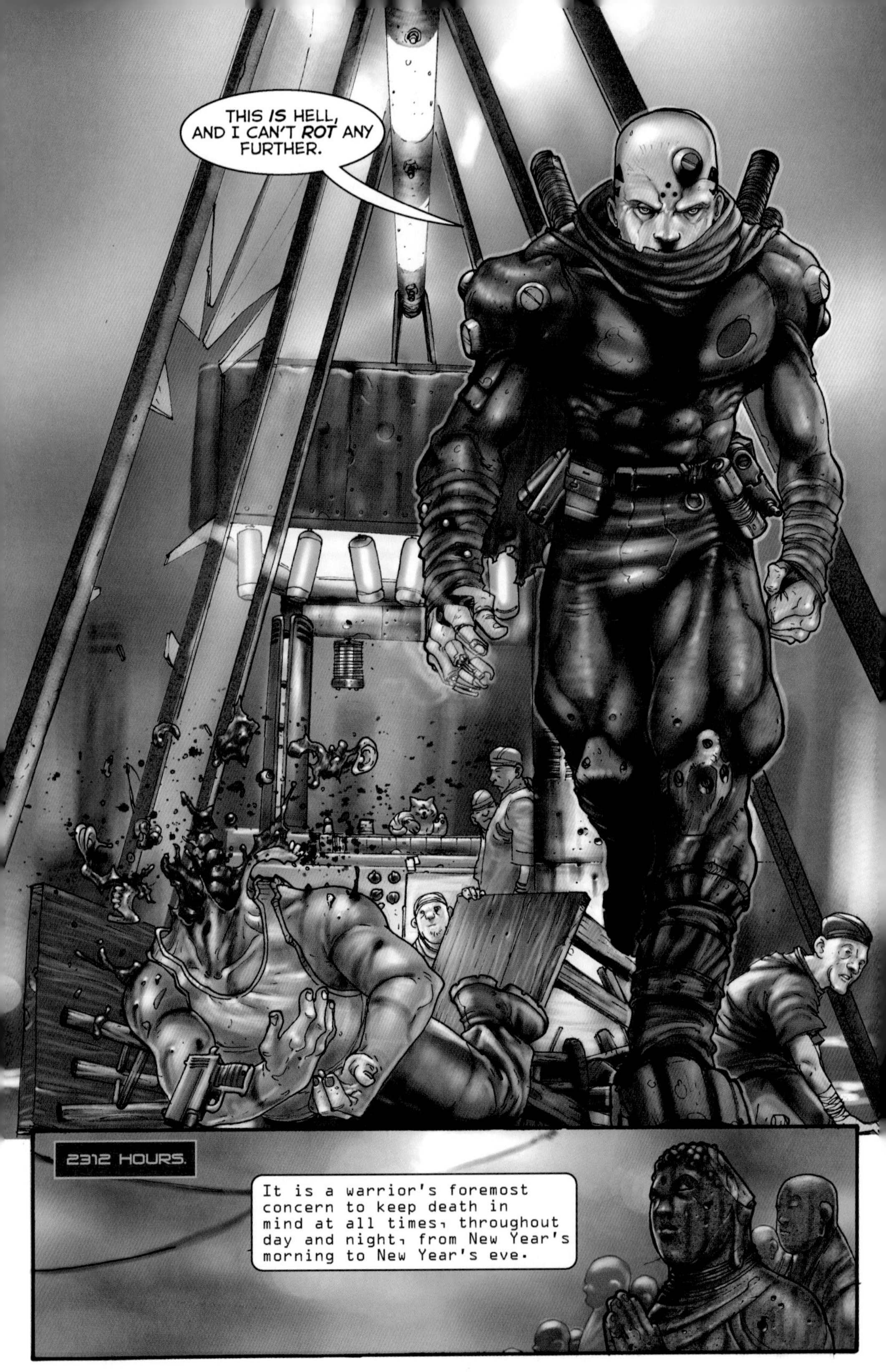
THIS *IS* HELL, AND I CAN'T *ROT* ANY FURTHER.
2312 HOURS.
It is a warrior's foremost concern to keep death in mind at all times, throughout day and night, from New Year's morning to New Year's eve.

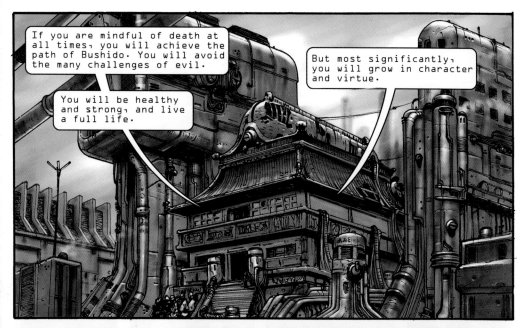

If you are mindful of death at all times, you will achieve the path of Bushido. You will avoid the many challenges of evil.

You will be healthy and strong, and live a full life.

But most significantly, you will grow in character and virtue.

Those who take comfort in assuming their life will be long run the risk of failure, performing their duty with little care, and treating others thoughtlessly.

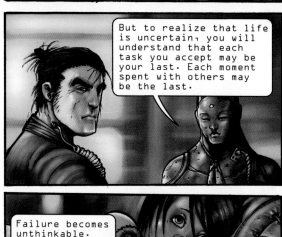

But to realize that life is uncertain, you will understand that each task you accept may be your last. Each moment spent with others may be the last.

Failure becomes unthinkable.

Thus proven, being mindful of death fulfills the path of loyalty and familial duty.

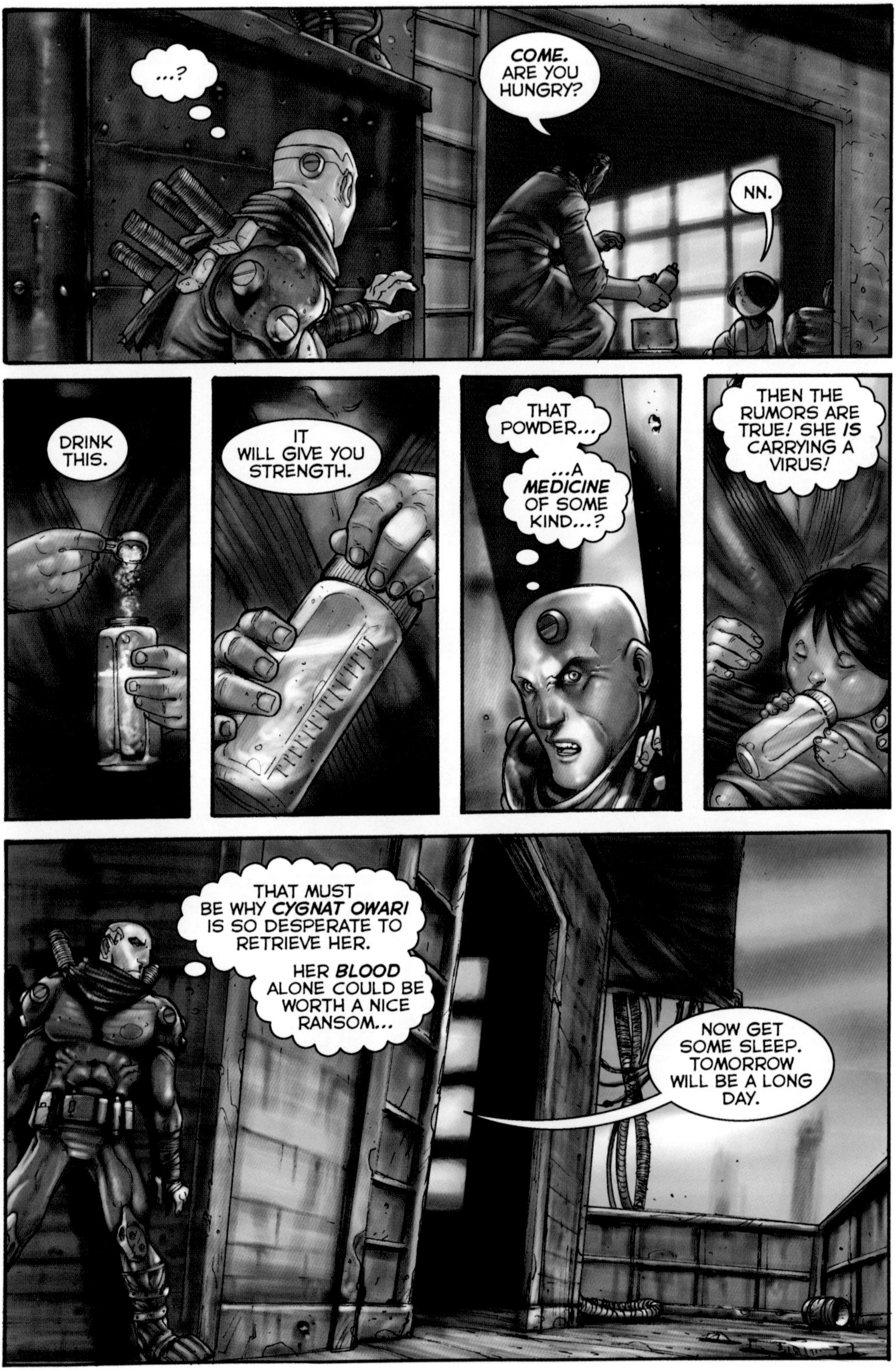
...?
COME. ARE YOU HUNGRY?
NN.
DRINK THIS.
IT WILL GIVE YOU STRENGTH.
THAT POWDER...
...A MEDICINE OF SOME KIND...?
THEN THE RUMORS ARE TRUE! SHE IS CARRYING A VIRUS!
THAT MUST BE WHY CYGNAT OWARI IS SO DESPERATE TO RETRIEVE HER.
HER BLOOD ALONE COULD BE WORTH A NICE RANSOM...
NOW GET SOME SLEEP. TOMORROW WILL BE A LONG DAY.

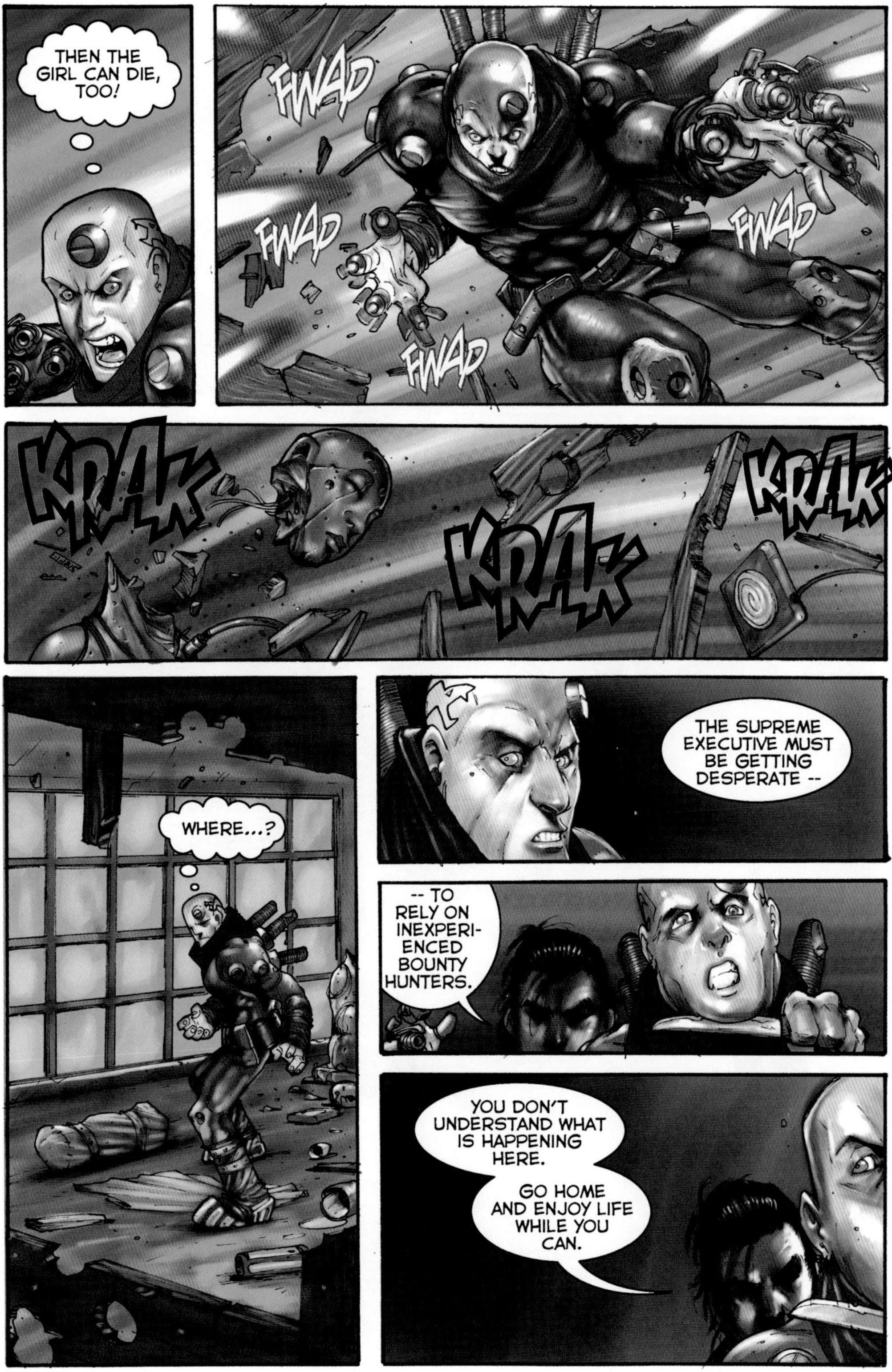
THEN THE GIRL CAN DIE, TOO!
FWAD
FWAD
FWAD
FWAD
KRAK
KRAK
KRAK
WHERE...?
THE SUPREME EXECUTIVE MUST BE GETTING DESPERATE --
-- TO RELY ON INEXPERIENCED BOUNTY HUNTERS.
YOU DON'T UNDERSTAND WHAT IS HAPPENING HERE.
GO HOME AND ENJOY LIFE WHILE YOU CAN.

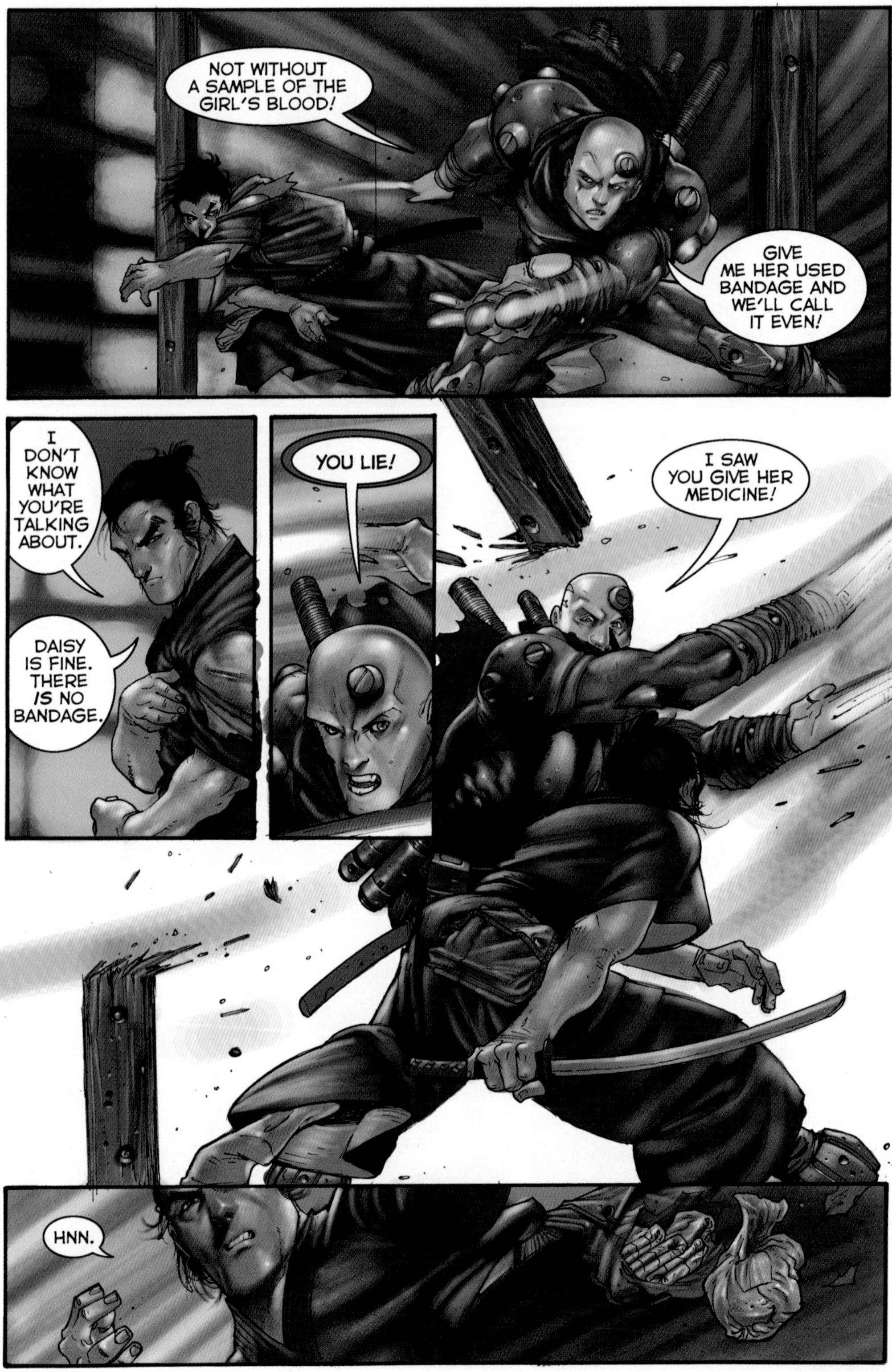
NOT WITHOUT A SAMPLE OF THE GIRL'S BLOOD!
GIVE ME HER USED BANDAGE AND WE'LL CALL IT EVEN!
I DON'T KNOW WHAT YOU'RE TALKING ABOUT.
DAISY IS FINE. THERE *IS* NO BANDAGE.
YOU LIE!
I SAW YOU GIVE HER MEDICINE!
HNN.

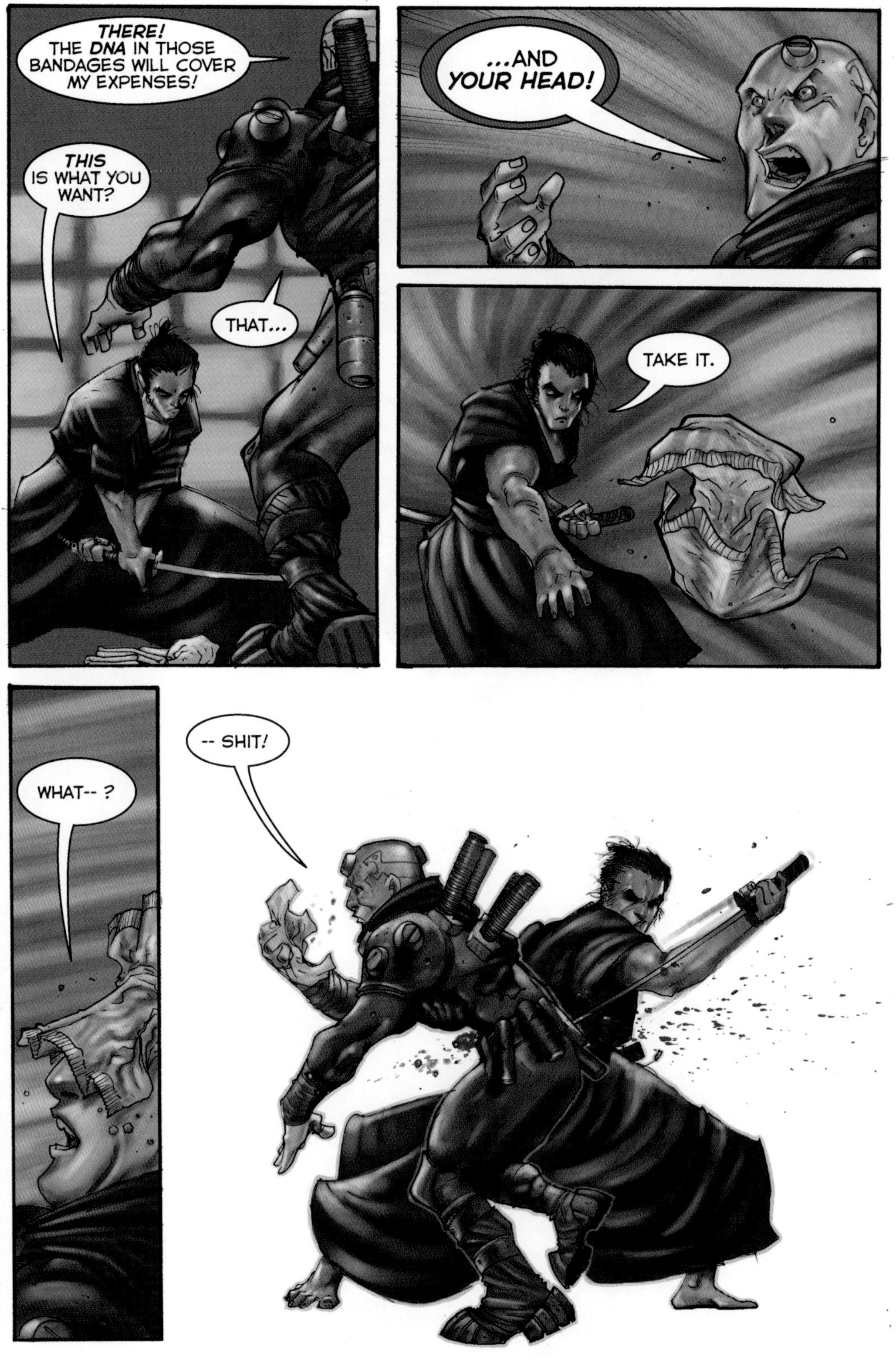
THERE! THE DNA IN THOSE BANDAGES WILL COVER MY EXPENSES!
THIS IS WHAT YOU WANT?
THAT...
...AND YOUR HEAD!
TAKE IT.
WHAT-- ?
-- SHIT!

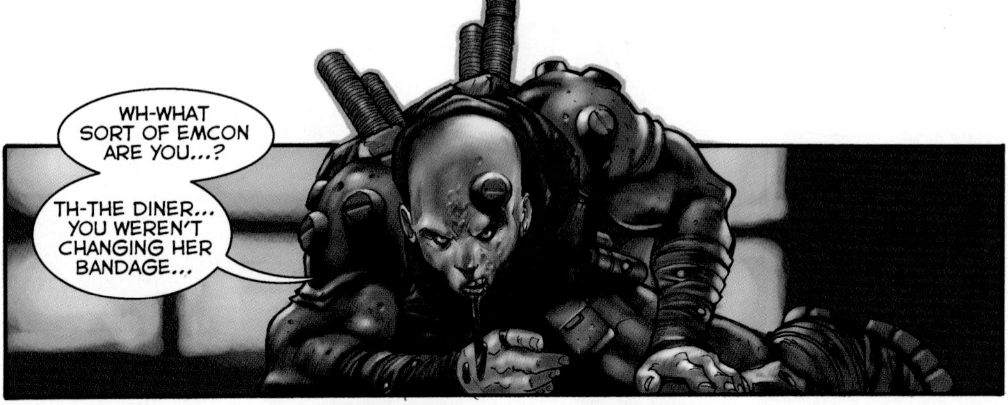
WH-WHAT SORT OF EMCON ARE YOU...?
TH-THE DINER... YOU WEREN'T CHANGING HER BANDAGE...

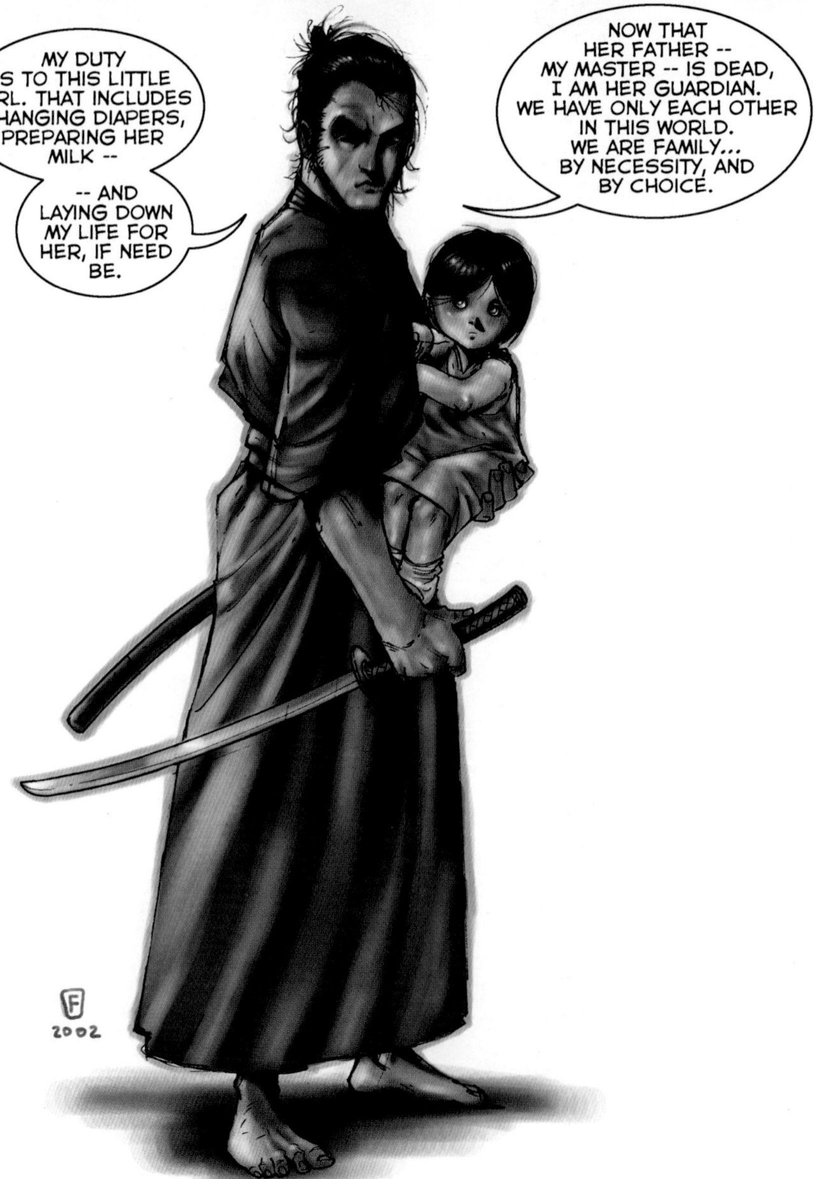
MY DUTY IS TO THIS LITTLE GIRL. THAT INCLUDES CHANGING DIAPERS, PREPARING HER MILK --
-- AND LAYING DOWN MY LIFE FOR HER, IF NEED BE.
NOW THAT HER FATHER -- MY MASTER -- IS DEAD, I AM HER GUARDIAN. WE HAVE ONLY EACH OTHER IN THIS WORLD. WE ARE FAMILY... BY NECESSITY, AND BY CHOICE.
F
2002

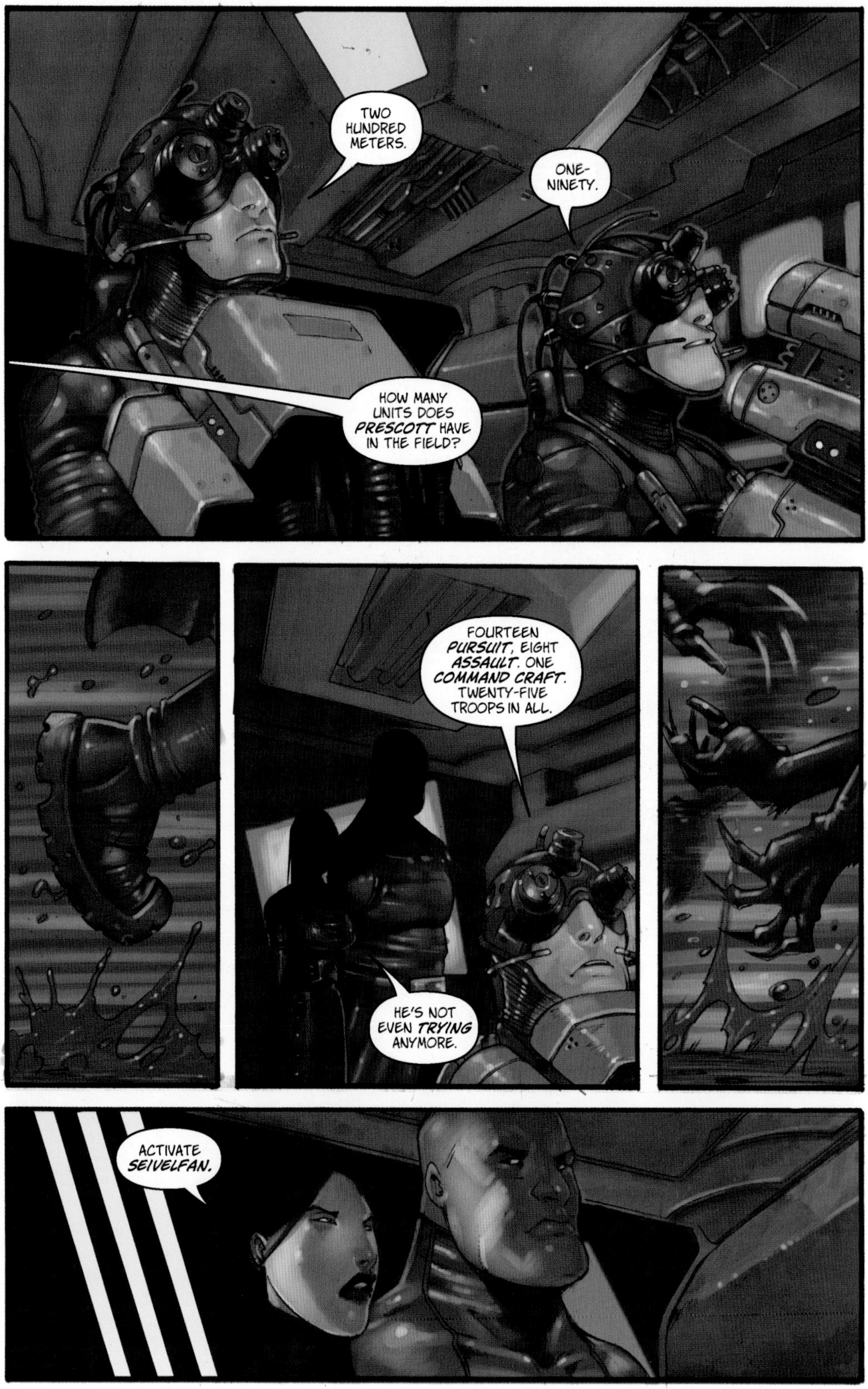
TWO HUNDRED METERS.
ONE-NINETY.
HOW MANY UNITS DOES PRESCOTT HAVE IN THE FIELD?
FOURTEEN PURSUIT, EIGHT ASSAULT. ONE COMMAND CRAFT. TWENTY-FIVE TROOPS IN ALL.
HE'S NOT EVEN TRYING ANYMORE.
ACTIVATE SEIVELFAN.

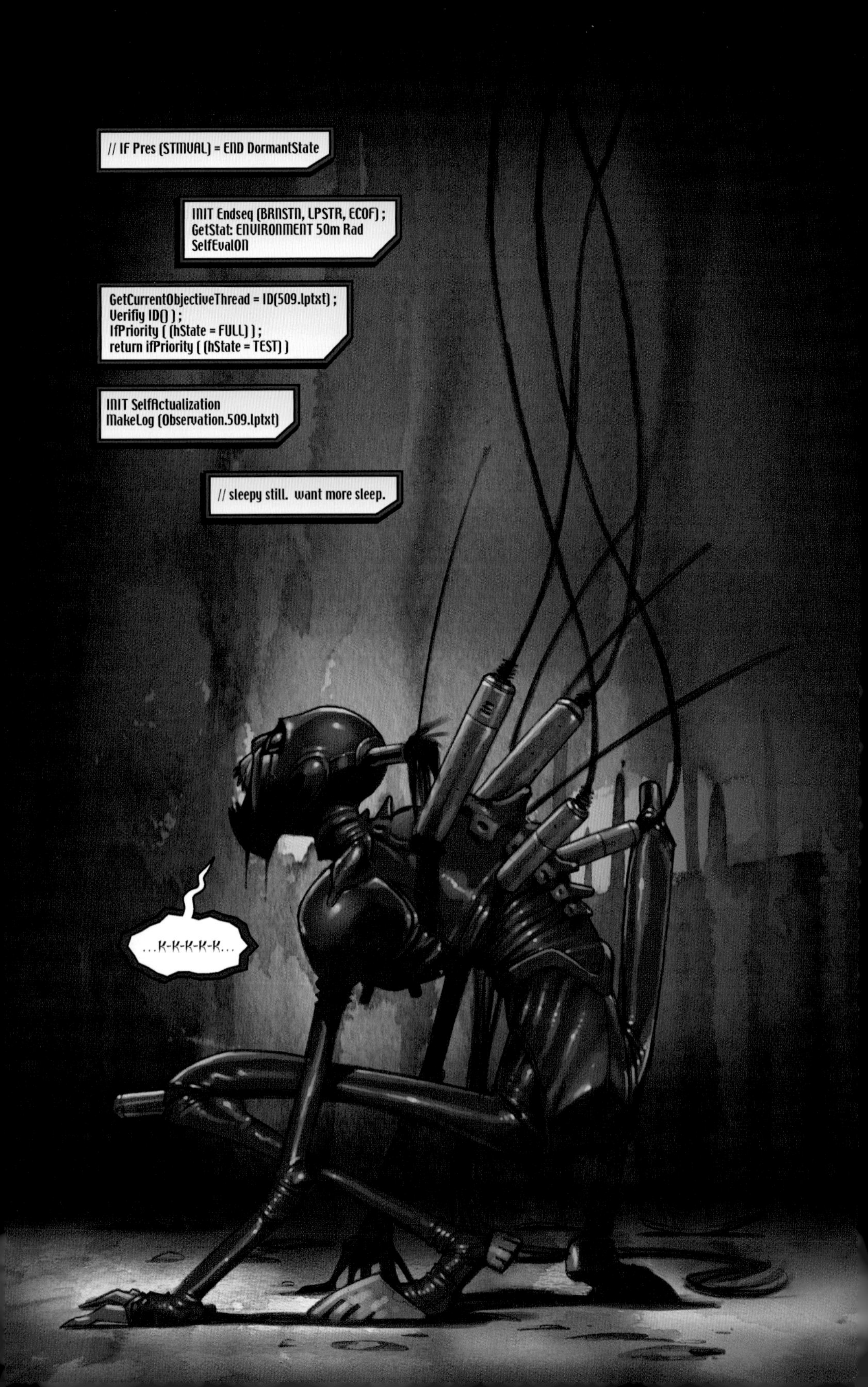

// IF Pres (STMVAL) = END DormantState
INIT Endseq (BRNSTN, LPSTR, ECOF) ; GetStat: ENVIRONMENT 50m Rad SelfEvalON
GetCurrentObjectiveThread = ID(509.lptxt) ; Verifiy ID() ; IfPriority ((hState = FULL)) ; return ifPriority ((hState = TEST))
INIT SelfActualization MakeLog (Observation.509.lptxt)
// sleepy still. want more sleep.
...K-K-K-K-K...

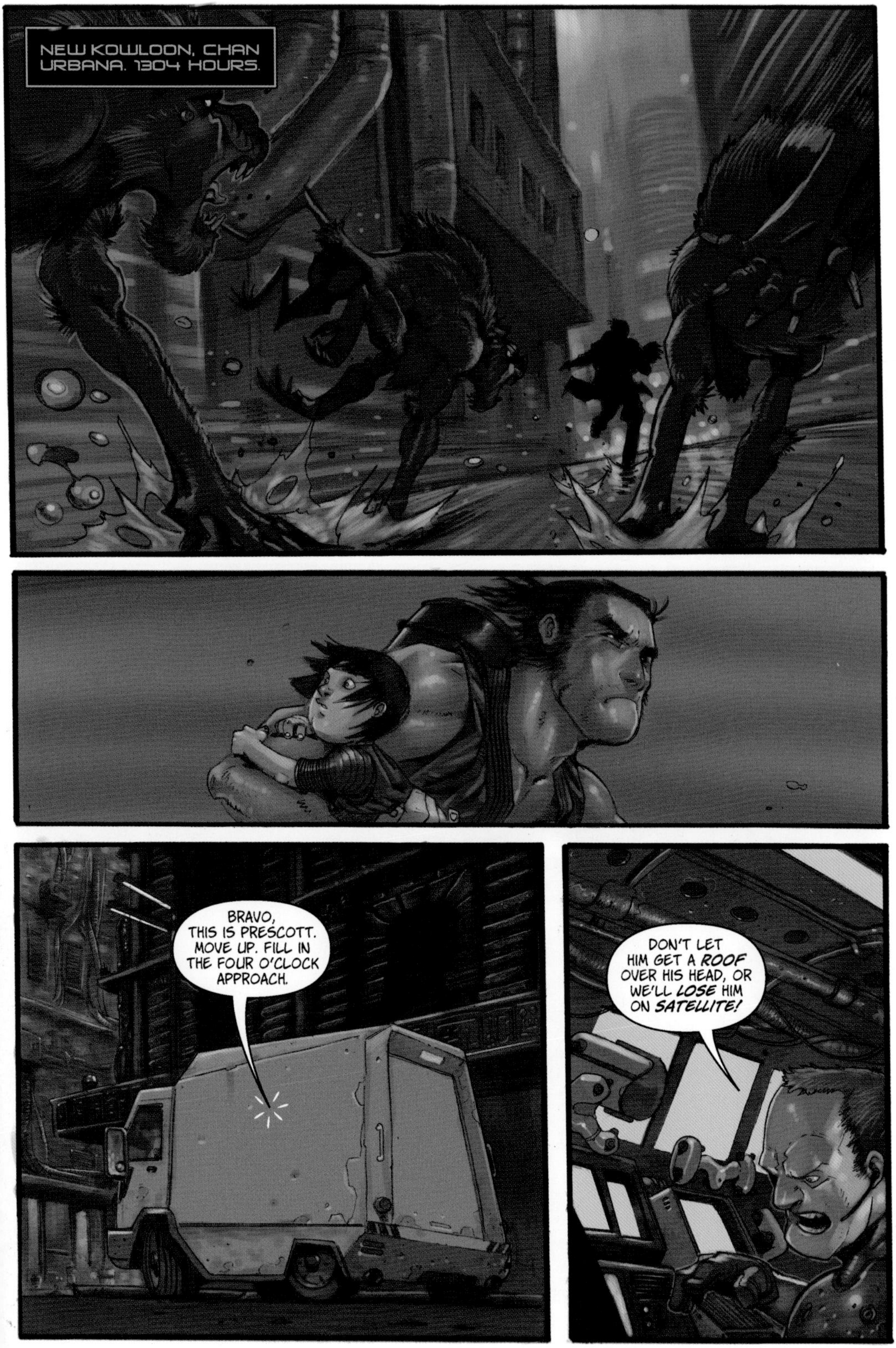
NEW KOWLOON, CHAN URBANA. 1304 HOURS.
BRAVO, THIS IS PRESCOTT. MOVE UP. FILL IN THE FOUR O'CLOCK APPROACH.
DON'T LET HIM GET A *ROOF* OVER HIS HEAD, OR WE'LL *LOSE* HIM ON *SATELLITE!*

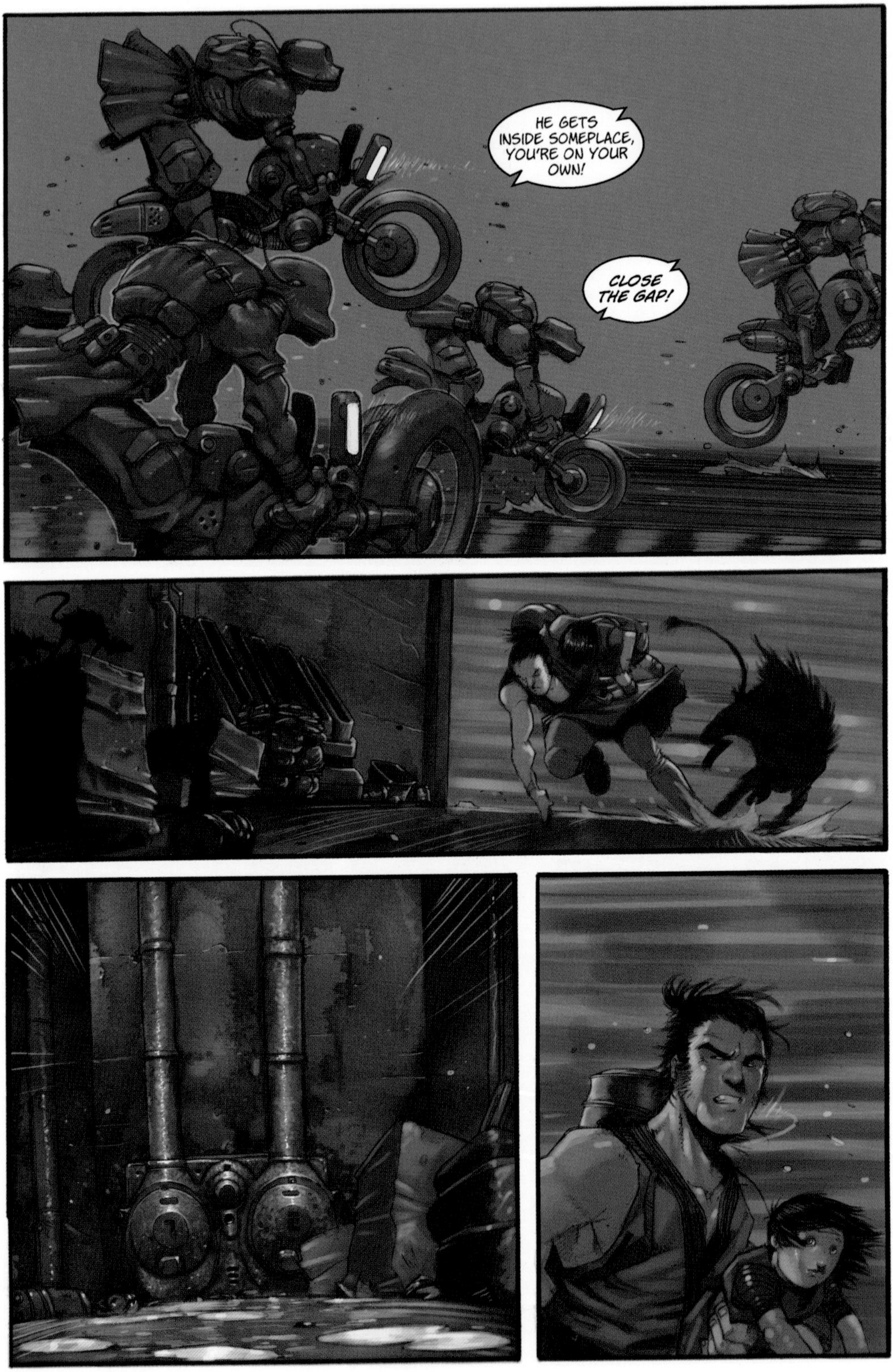
HE GETS INSIDE SOMEPLACE, YOU'RE ON YOUR OWN!
CLOSE THE GAP!

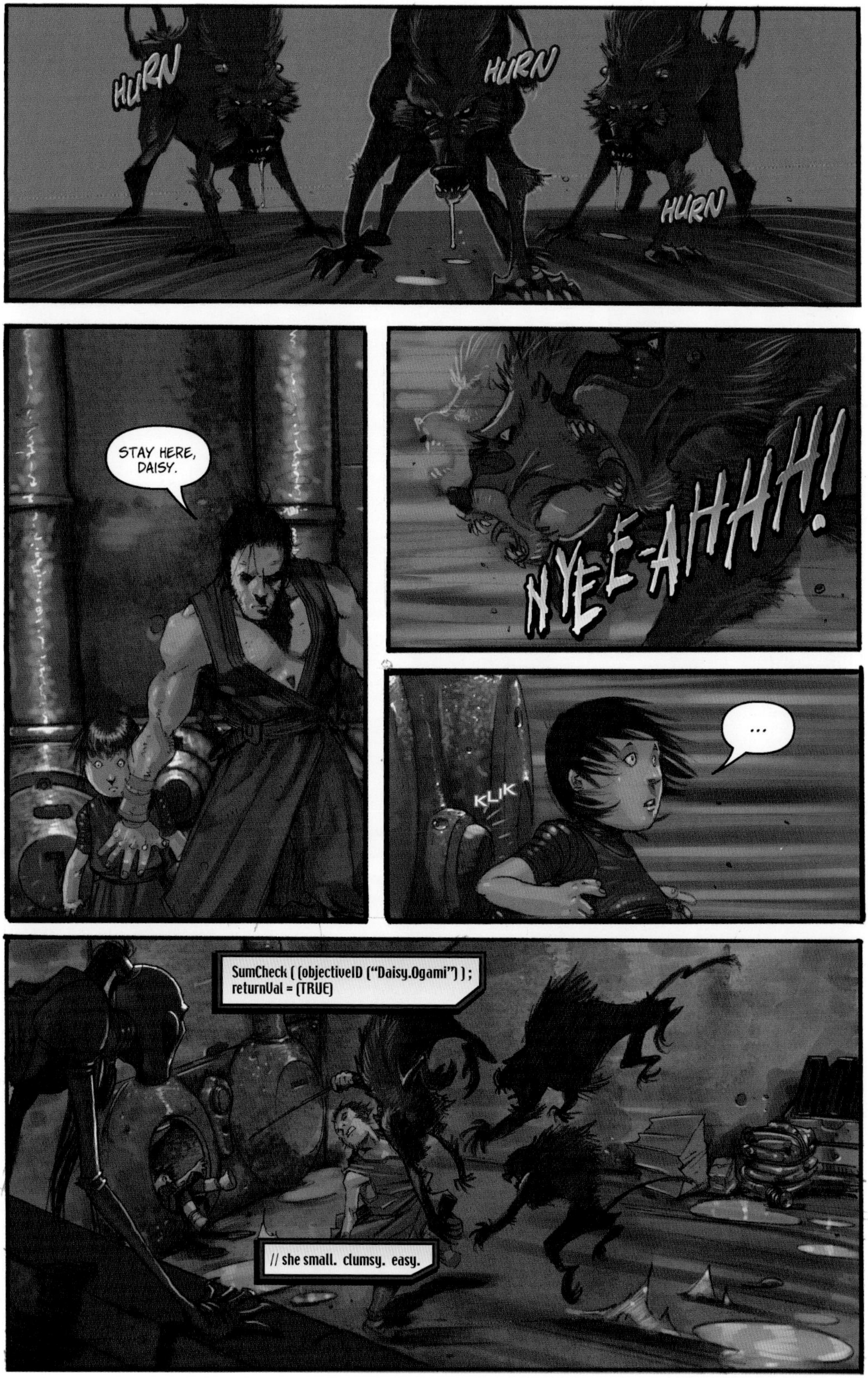
HURN
HURN
HURN
STAY HERE, DAISY.
NYEE-AHHH!
KLIK
...
SumCheck ((objectiveID ("Daisy.Ogami")) ;
returnVal = (TRUE)
// she small. clumsy. easy.

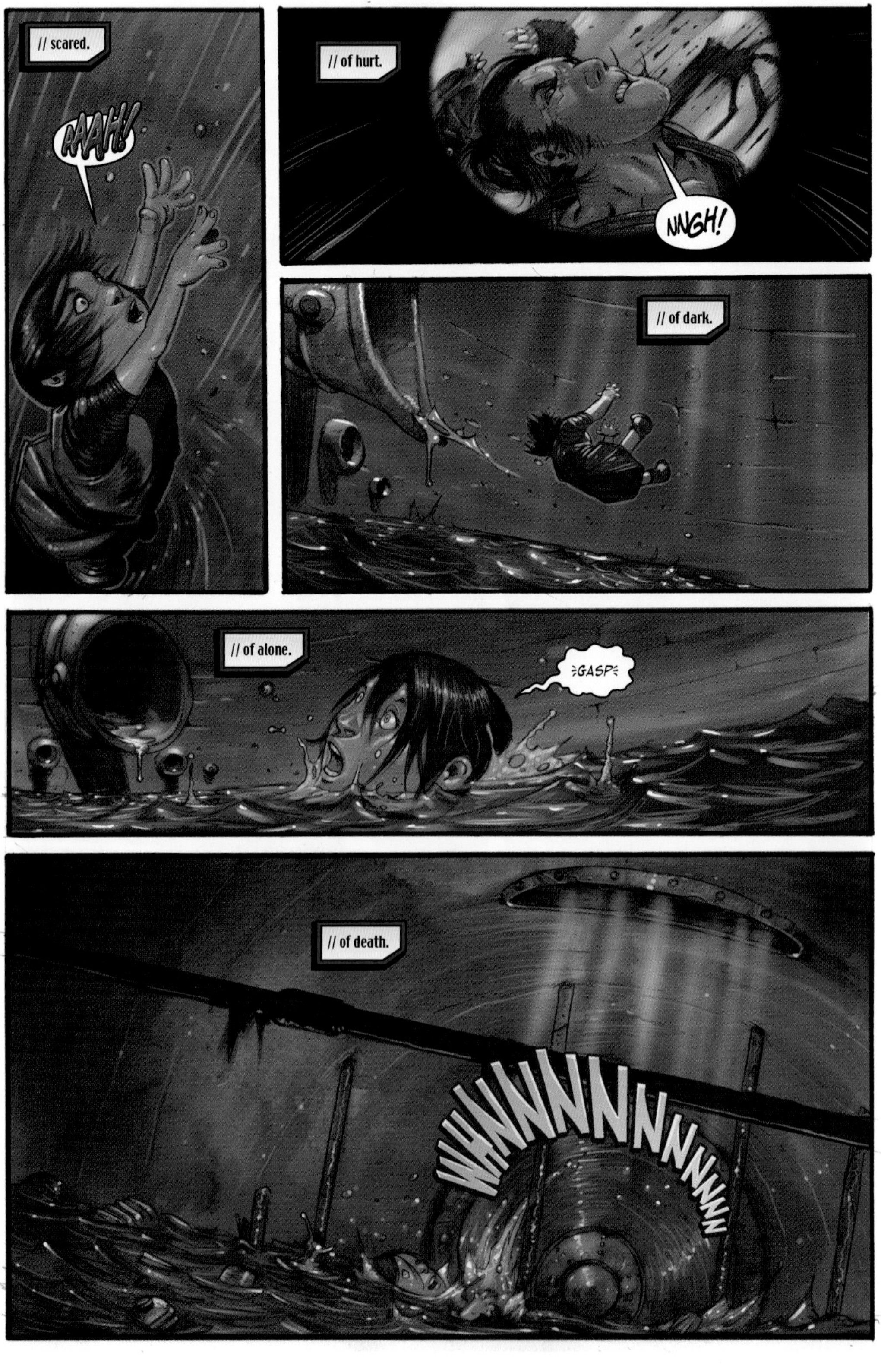
// scared.
RAAAH!
// of hurt.
NNGH!
// of dark.
// of alone.
GASP
// of death.
WHNNNNNNNNNNN

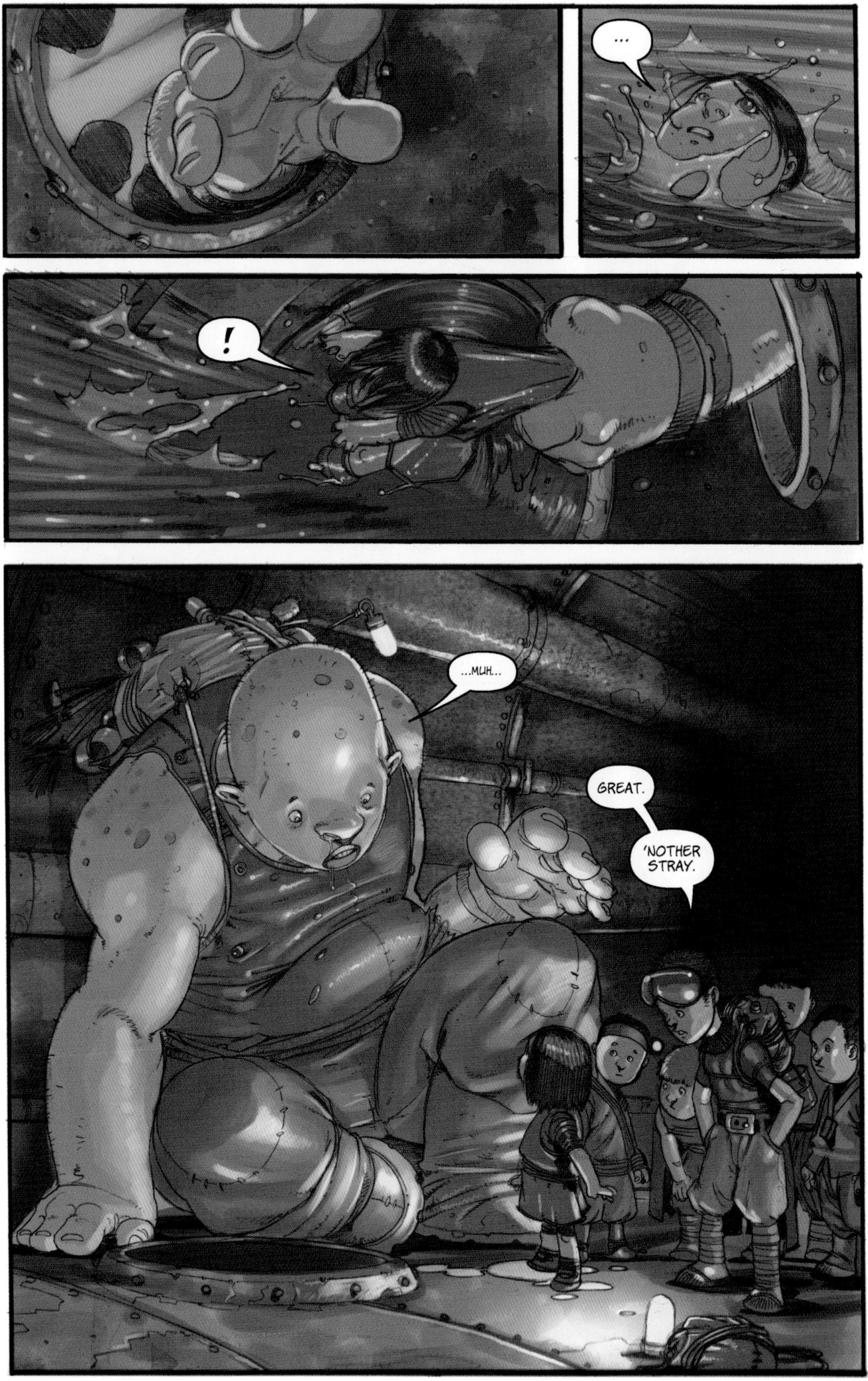
...
!
...MUH...
GREAT.
'NOTHER STRAY.

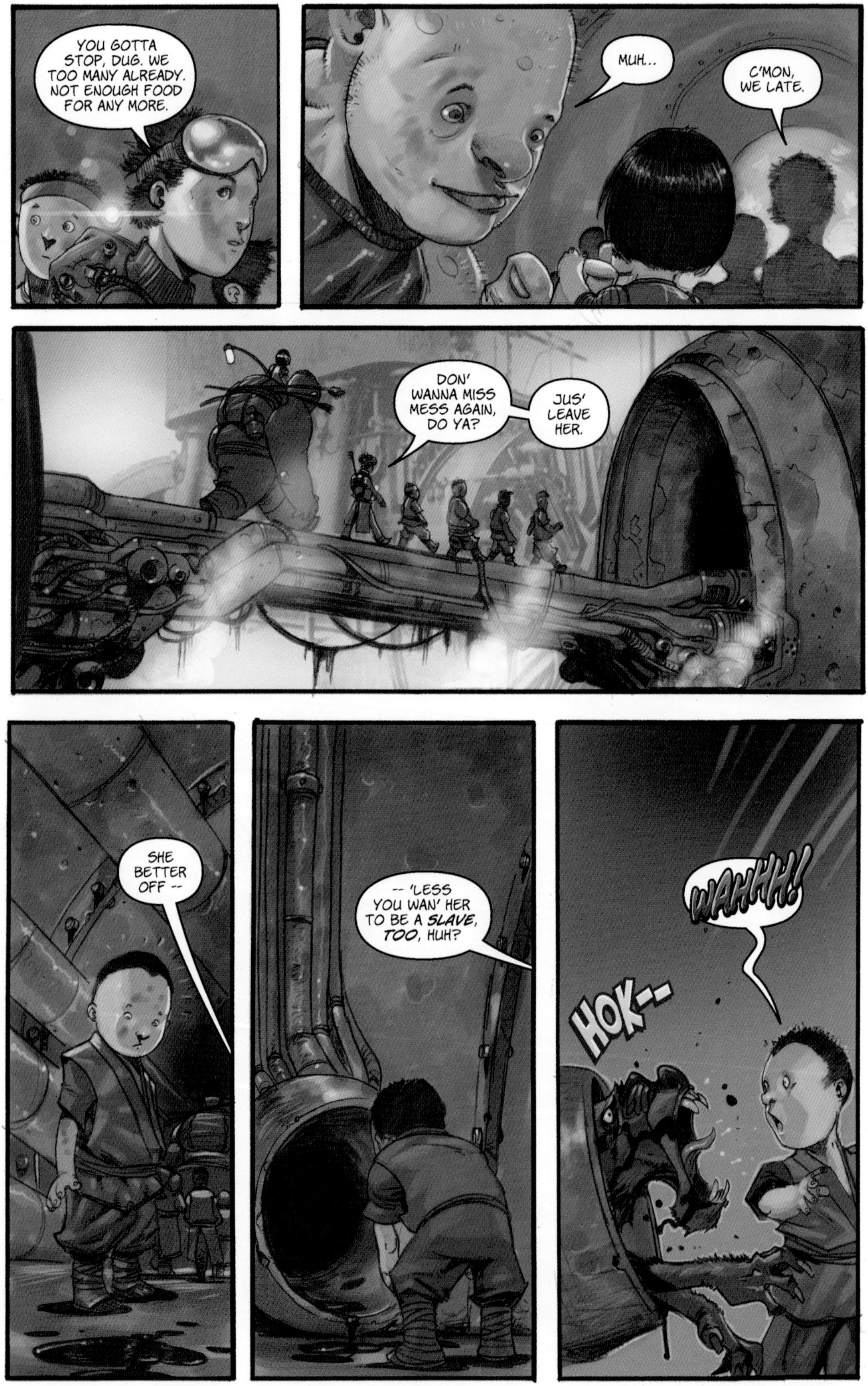
YOU GOTTA STOP, DUG. WE TOO MANY ALREADY. NOT ENOUGH FOOD FOR ANY MORE.
MUH...
C'MON, WE LATE.
DON' WANNA MISS MESS AGAIN, DO YA?
JUS' LEAVE HER.
SHE BETTER OFF --
-- 'LESS YOU WAN' HER TO BE A *SLAVE, TOO*, HUH?
WAHHH!
HOK--

--KK-GL...

WH-WHAD IZIT, *QUICK?*

BIG RAT, I DUNNO.

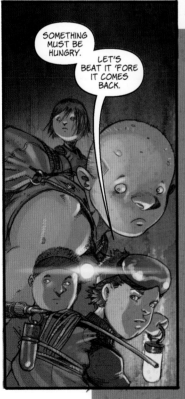

SOMETHING MUST BE HUNGRY.

LET'S BEAT IT 'FORE IT COMES BACK.

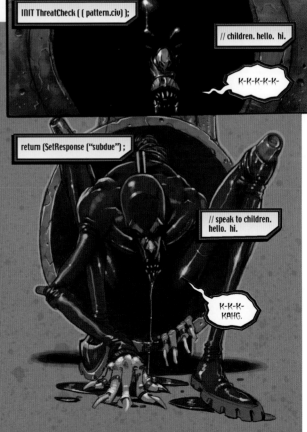

INIT ThreatCheck ((pattern.civ));

// children. hello. hi.

K-K-K-K-K-

return (SetResponse ("subdue") ;

// speak to children. hello. hi.

K-K-K-KAHG.

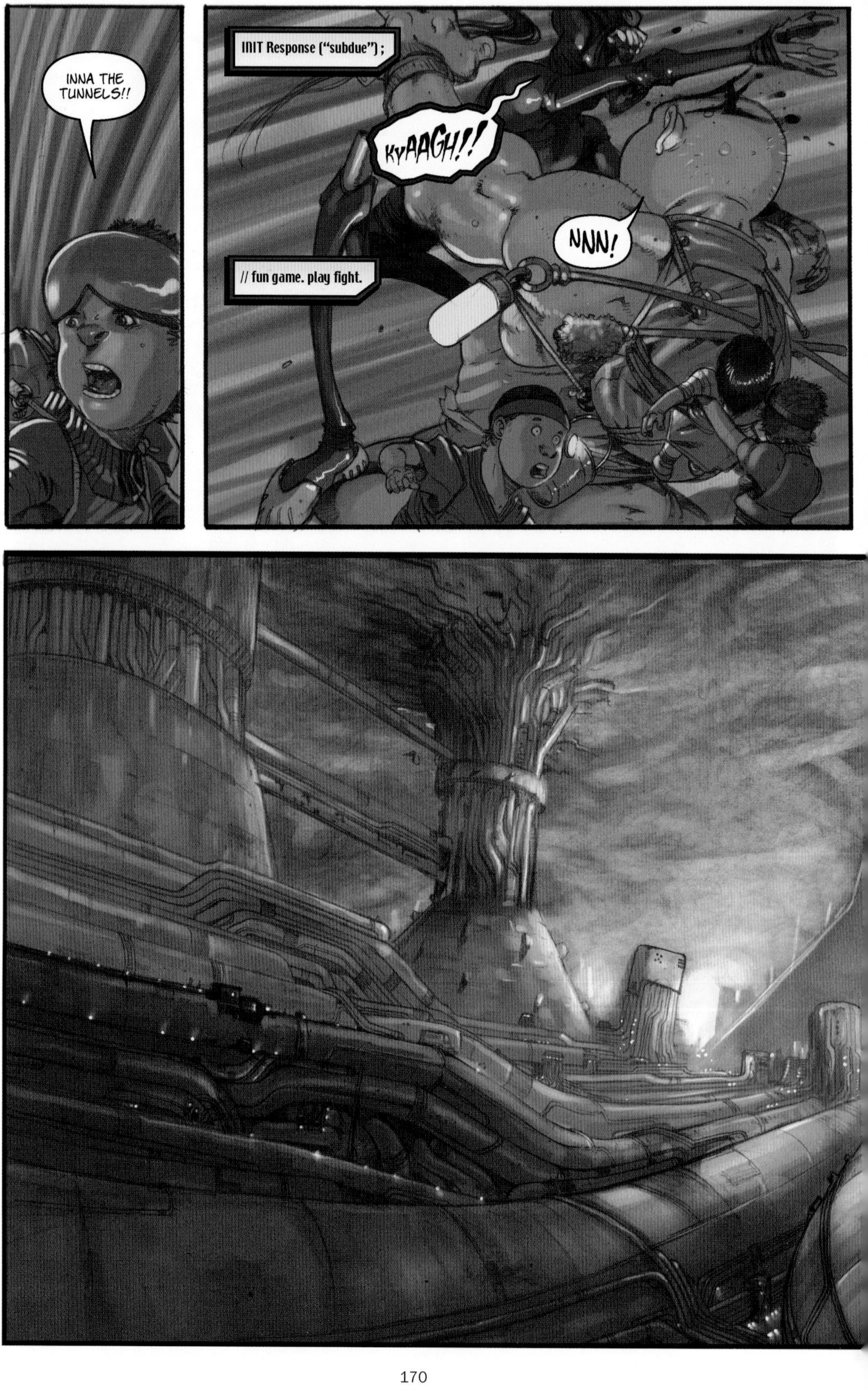
INNA THE TUNNELS!!
INIT Response ("subdue") ;
KYAAGH!!
NNN!
// fun game. play fight.

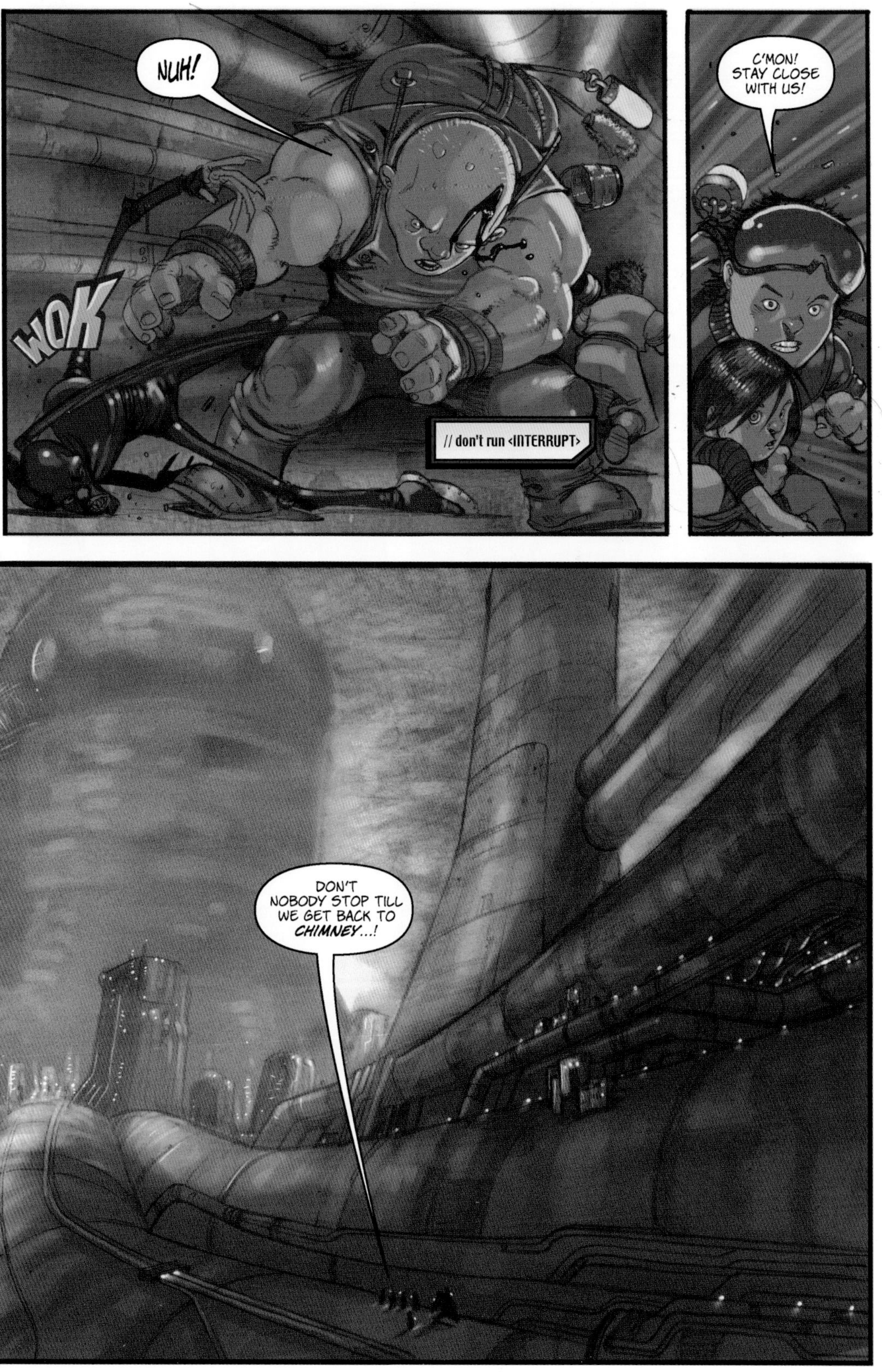
NUH!
WOK
// don't run <INTERRUPT>
C'MON! STAY CLOSE WITH US!
DON'T NOBODY STOP TILL WE GET BACK TO CHIMNEY...!

CHIMNEY, THERMO-
ELECTRIC HUB.

WE GONNA TELL GALGO 'BOUT THE RAT?

HSSHH...

WHERE YOU BEEN?!?

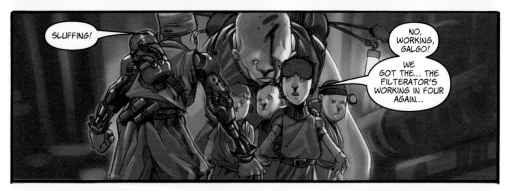

SLUFFING!

NO, WORKING, GALGO!

WE GOT THE... THE FILTERATOR'S WORKING IN FOUR AGAIN...

ABOUT TIME! YOU TAKE TOO LONG!

KUH?

WHAT HAPPEN TO DUG?

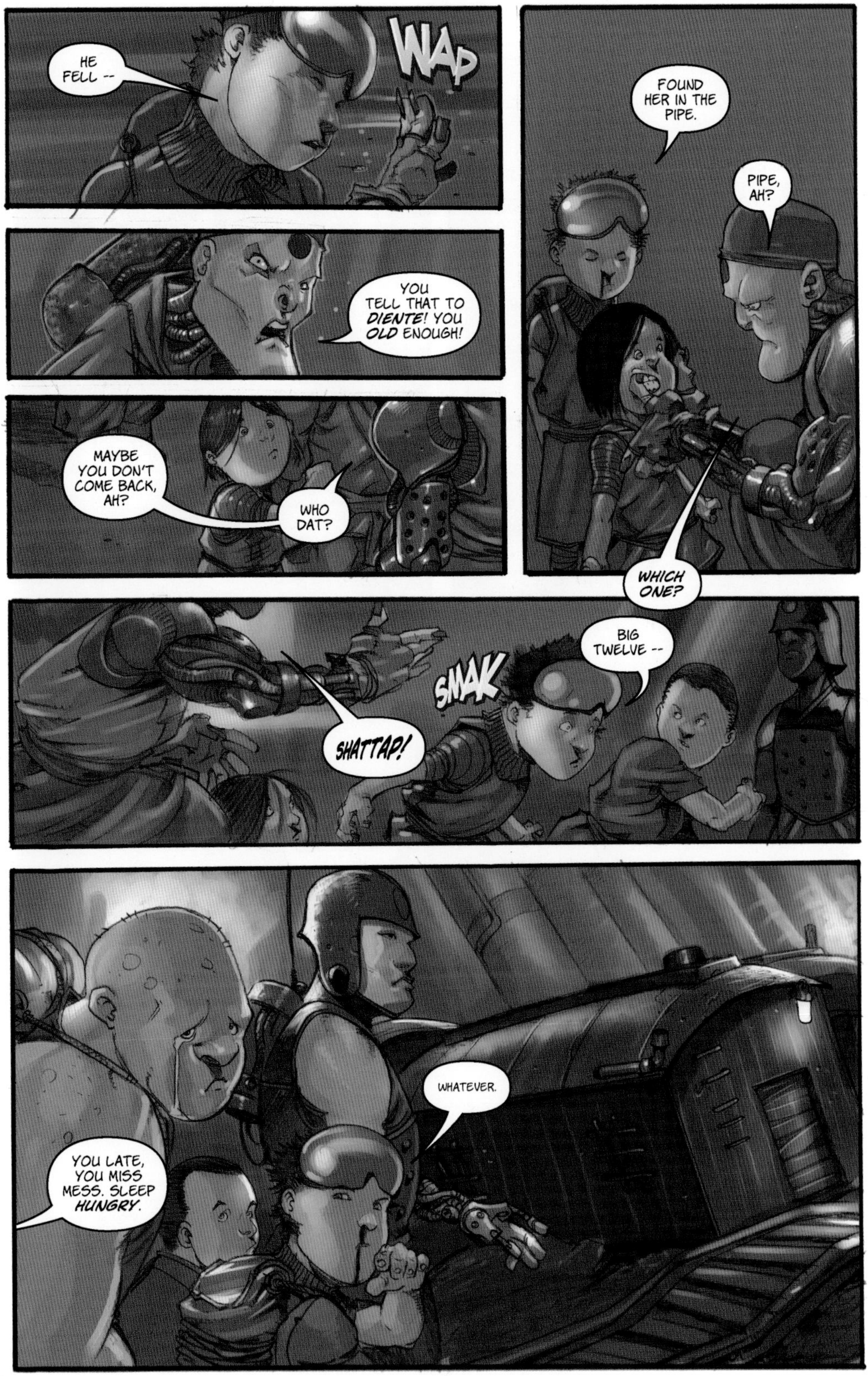
HE FELL --
WAP
FOUND HER IN THE PIPE.
PIPE, AH?
YOU TELL THAT TO *DIENTE*! YOU *OLD* ENOUGH!
MAYBE YOU DON'T COME BACK, AH?
WHO DAT?
WHICH ONE?
BIG TWELVE --
SMAK
SHATTAP!
WHATEVER.
YOU LATE, YOU MISS MESS. SLEEP *HUNGRY*.

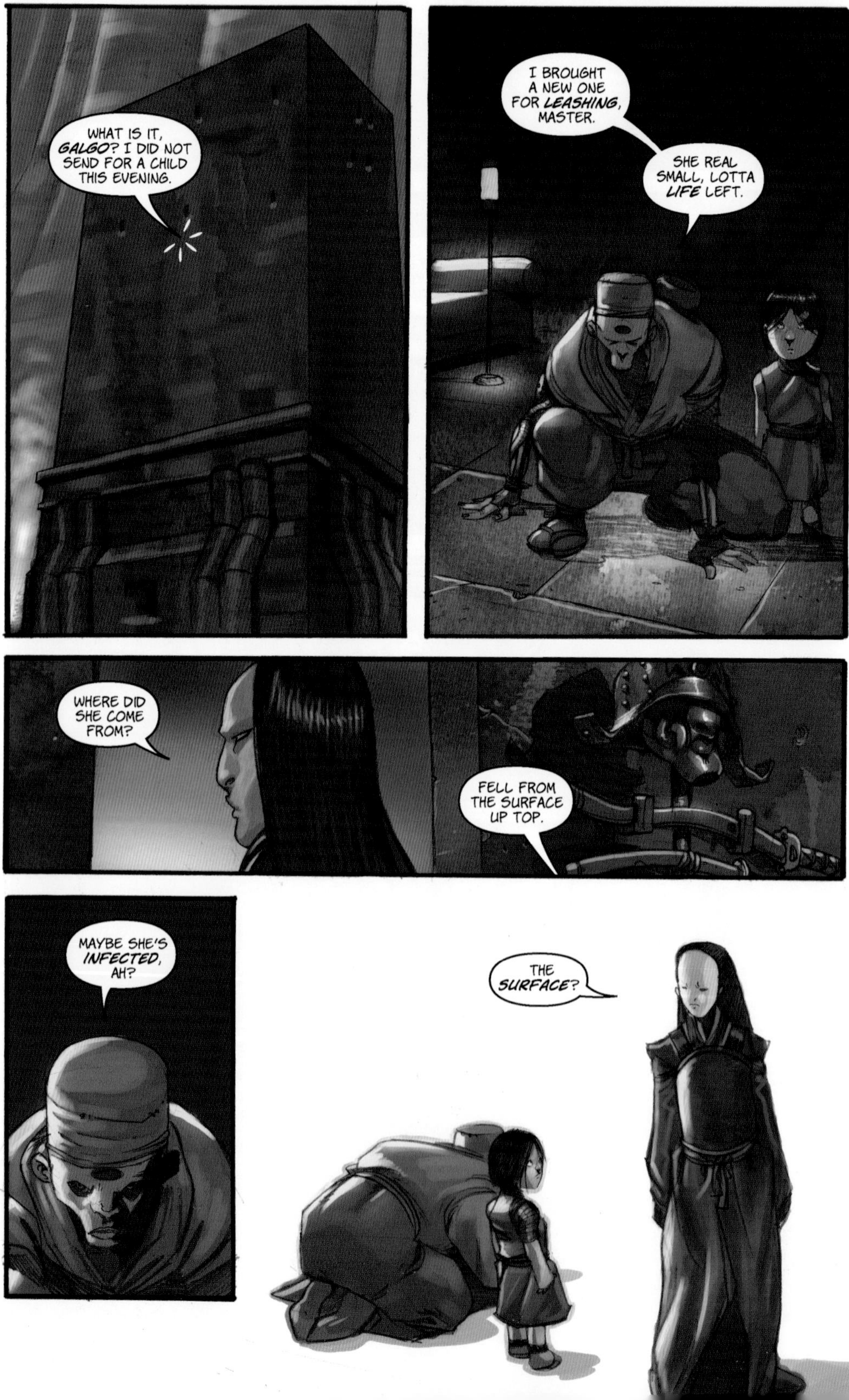
WHAT IS IT, GALGO? I DID NOT SEND FOR A CHILD THIS EVENING.
I BROUGHT A NEW ONE FOR LEASHING, MASTER.
SHE REAL SMALL, LOTTA LIFE LEFT.
WHERE DID SHE COME FROM?
FELL FROM THE SURFACE UP TOP.
MAYBE SHE'S INFECTED, AH?
THE SURFACE?

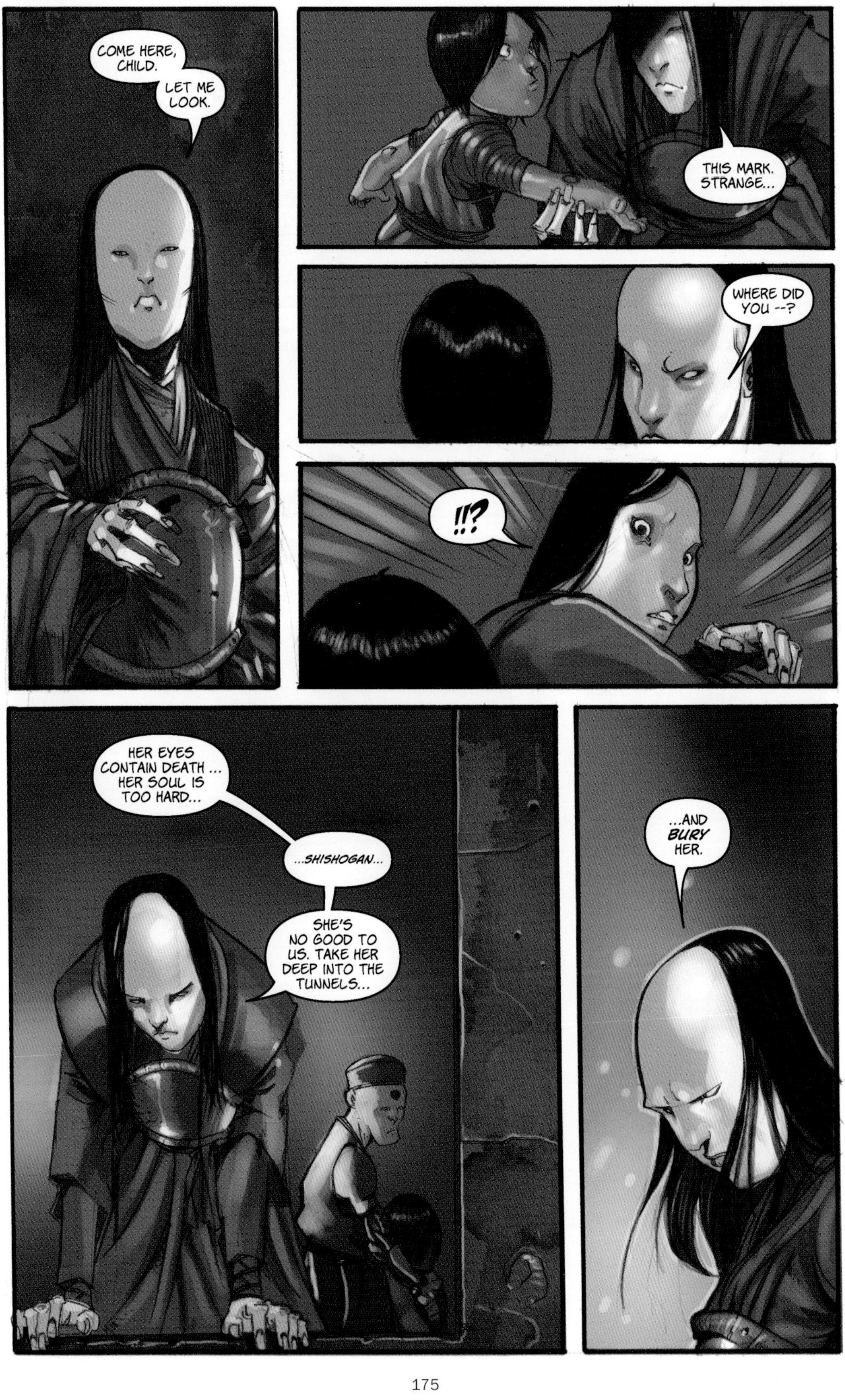
COME HERE, CHILD.
LET ME LOOK.
THIS MARK. STRANGE...
WHERE DID YOU --?
!!?
HER EYES CONTAIN DEATH ... HER SOUL IS TOO HARD...
...SHISHOGAN...
SHE'S NO GOOD TO US. TAKE HER DEEP INTO THE TUNNELS...
...AND BURY HER.

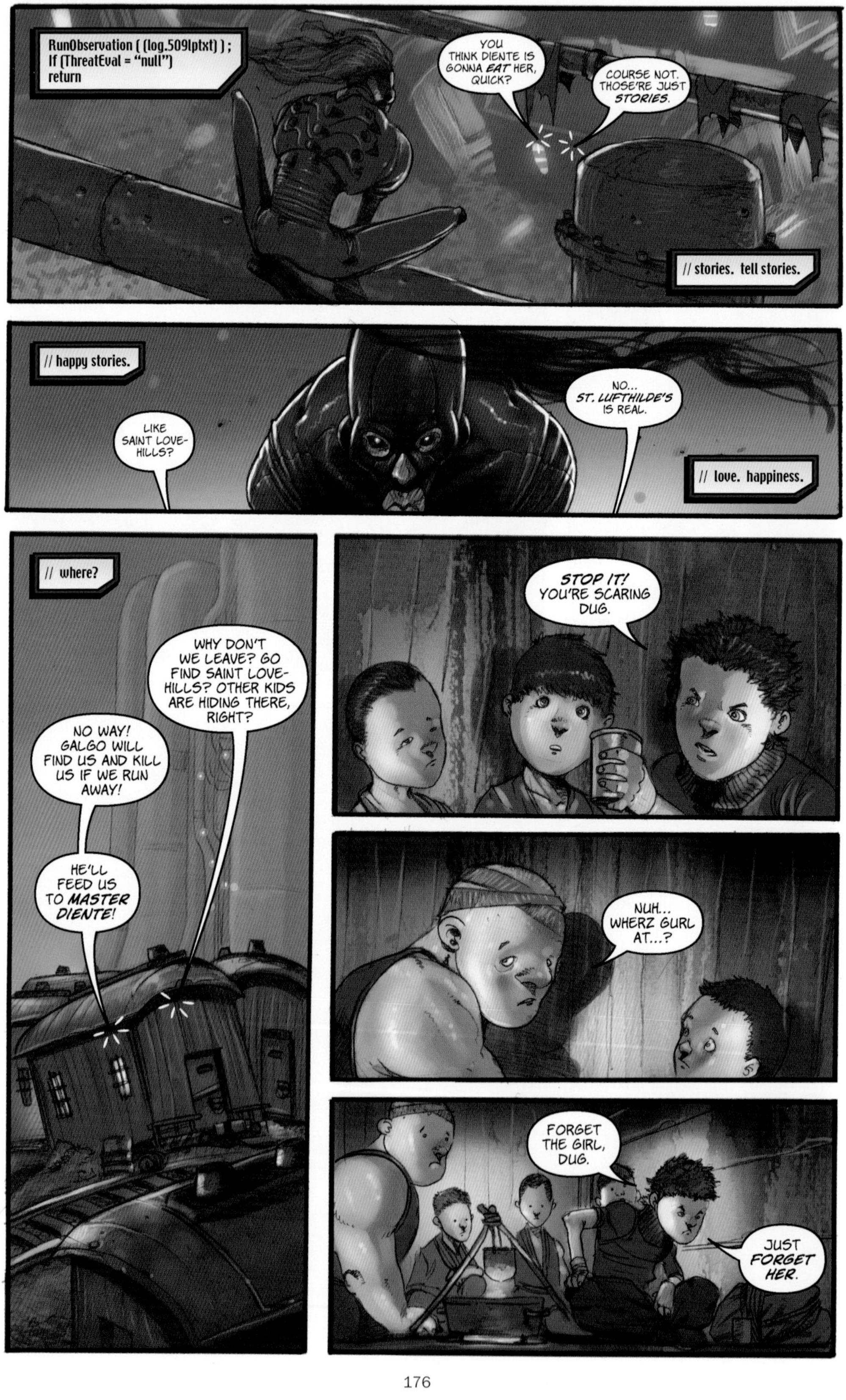
RunObservation ((log.509lptxt)) ;
If (ThreatEval = "null")
return
YOU THINK DIENTE IS GONNA EAT HER, QUICK?
COURSE NOT. THOSE'RE JUST STORIES.
// stories. tell stories.
// happy stories.
LIKE SAINT LOVE-HILLS?
NO... ST. LUFTHILDE'S IS REAL.
// love. happiness.
// where?
WHY DON'T WE LEAVE? GO FIND SAINT LOVE-HILLS? OTHER KIDS ARE HIDING THERE, RIGHT?
NO WAY! GALGO WILL FIND US AND KILL US IF WE RUN AWAY!
HE'LL FEED US TO MASTER DIENTE!
STOP IT! YOU'RE SCARING DUG.
NUH... WHERZ GURL AT...?
FORGET THE GIRL, DUG.
JUST FORGET HER.

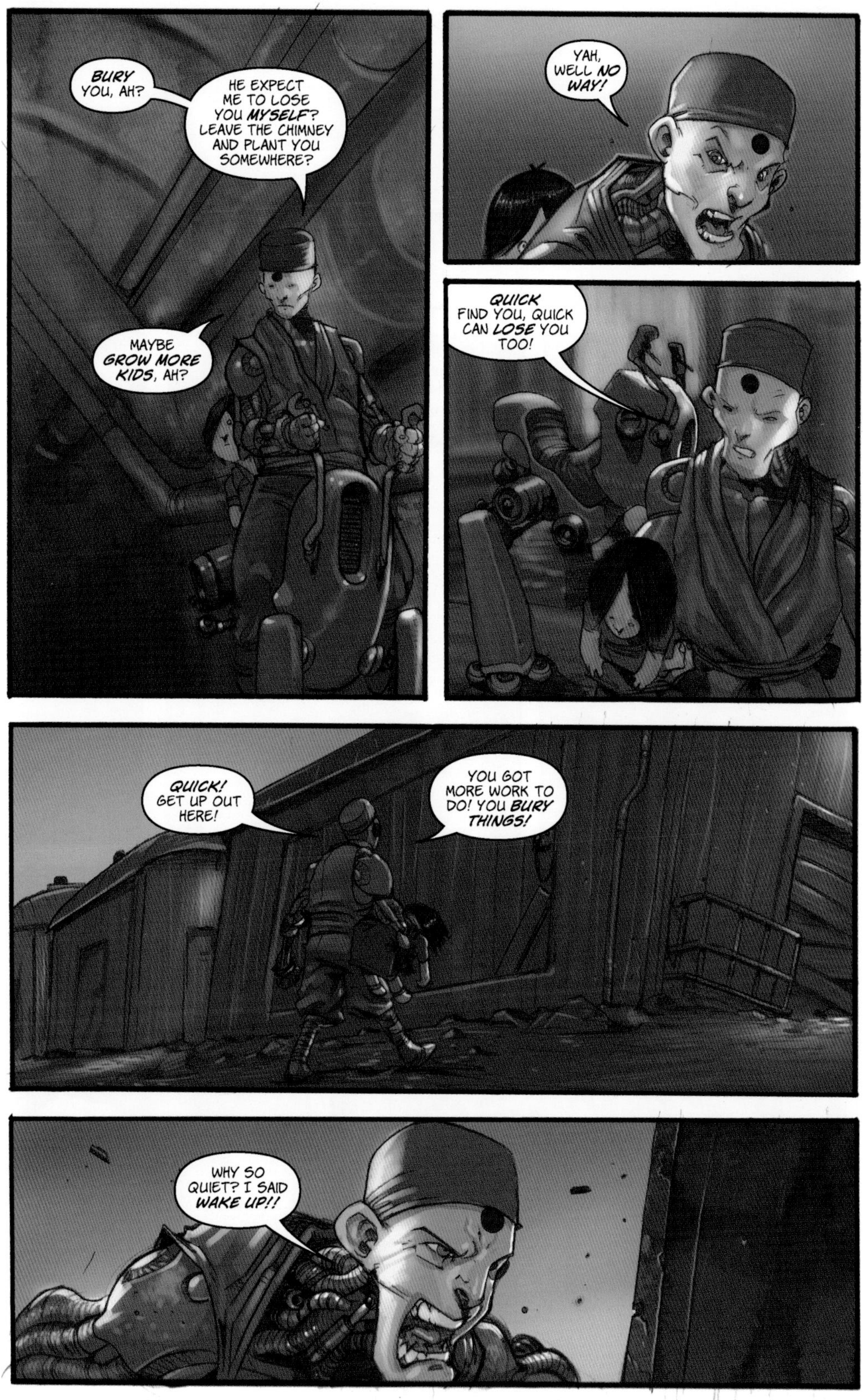
BURY YOU, AH?
HE EXPECT ME TO LOSE YOU MYSELF? LEAVE THE CHIMNEY AND PLANT YOU SOMEWHERE?
MAYBE GROW MORE KIDS, AH?
YAH, WELL NO WAY!
QUICK FIND YOU, QUICK CAN LOSE YOU TOO!
QUICK! GET UP OUT HERE!
YOU GOT MORE WORK TO DO! YOU BURY THINGS!
WHY SO QUIET? I SAID WAKE UP!!

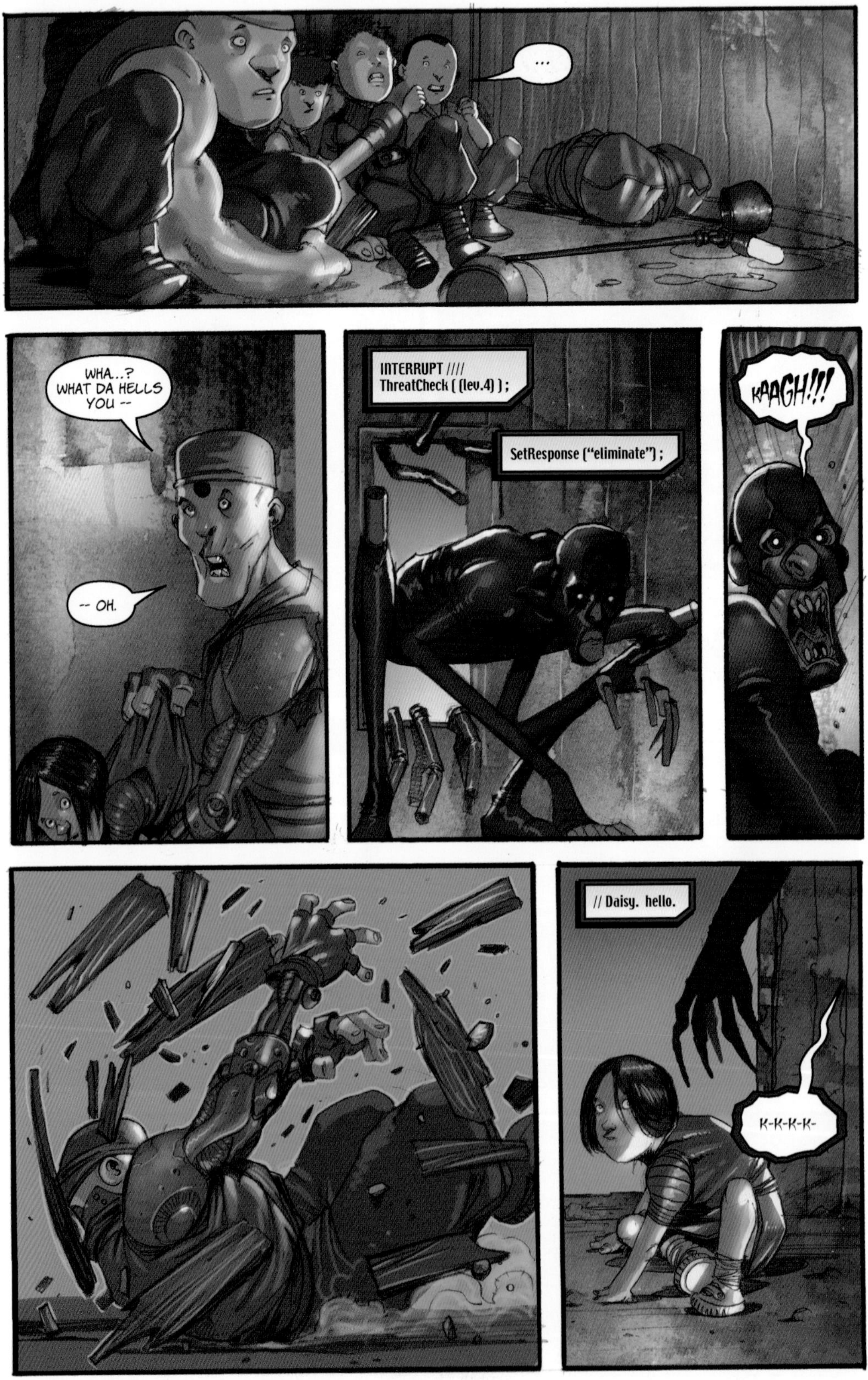
...
WHA..? WHAT DA HELLS YOU --
-- OH.
INTERRUPT ////
ThreatCheck ((lev.4)) ;
SetResponse ("eliminate") ;
KAAGH!!!
// Daisy. hello.
K-K-K-K-

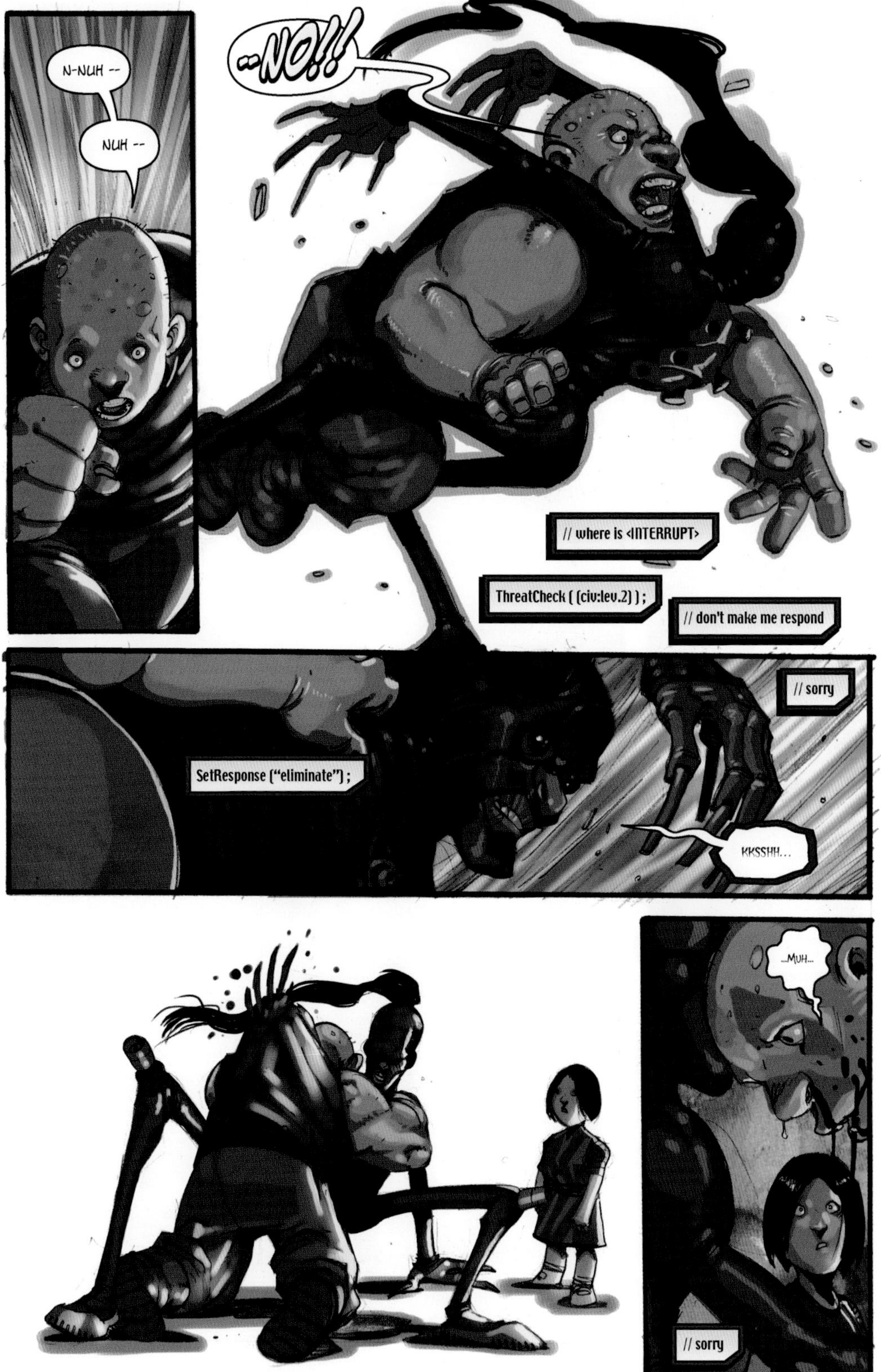
N-NUH --
NUH --
--NO!!
// where is <INTERRUPT>
ThreatCheck ((civ:lev.2)) ;
// don't make me respond
SetResponse ("eliminate") ;
// sorry
KKSSHH...
...MUH...
// sorry

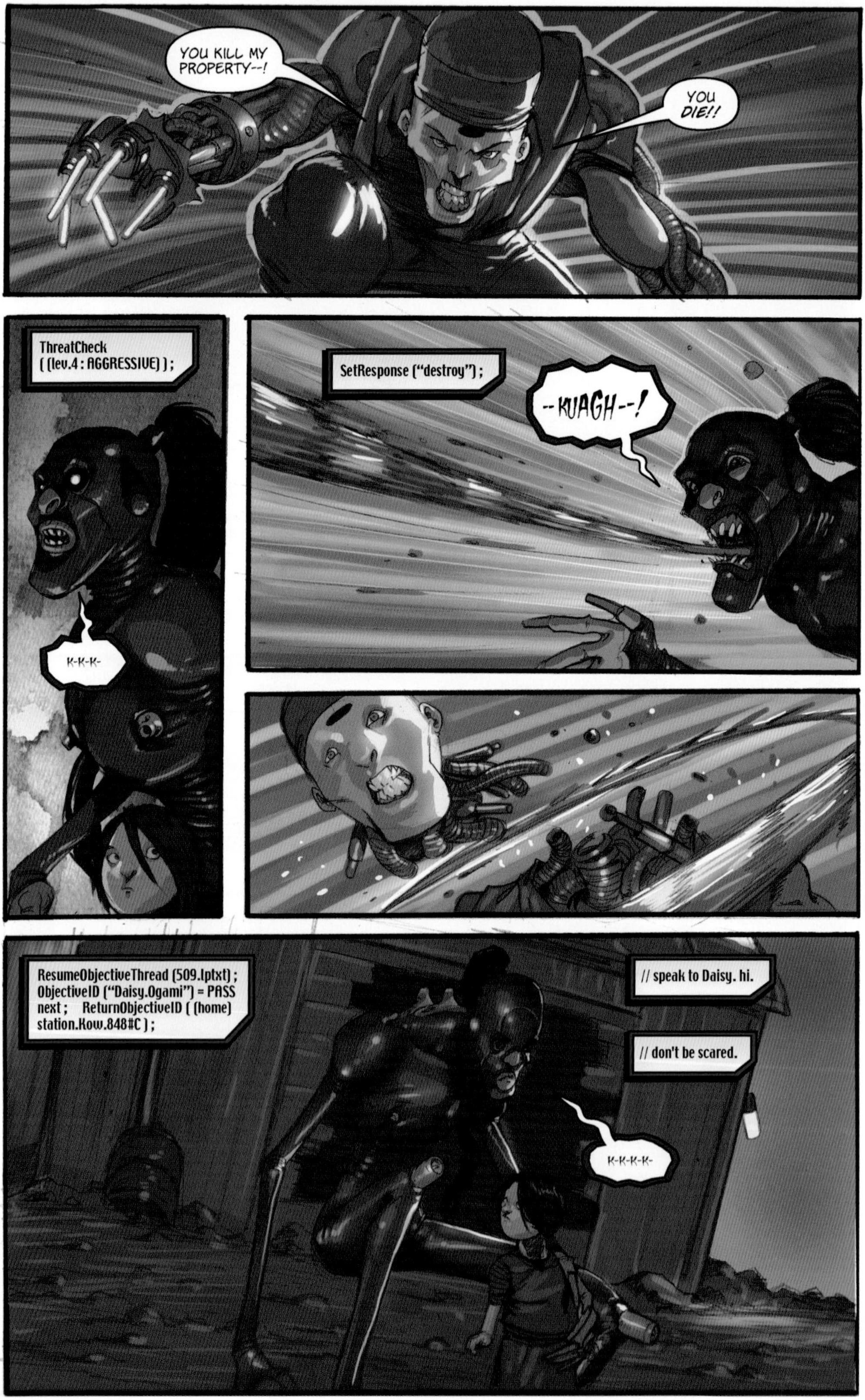
YOU KILL MY PROPERTY--!
YOU DIE!!
ThreatCheck ((lev.4 : AGGRESSIVE)) ;
K-K-K-
SetResponse ("destroy") ;
--KUAGH--!
ResumeObjectiveThread (509.lptxt) ; ObjectiveID ("Daisy.Ogami") = PASS next ; ReturnObjectiveID ((home) station.Kow.848#C) ;
// speak to Daisy. hi.
// don't be scared.
K-K-K-K-

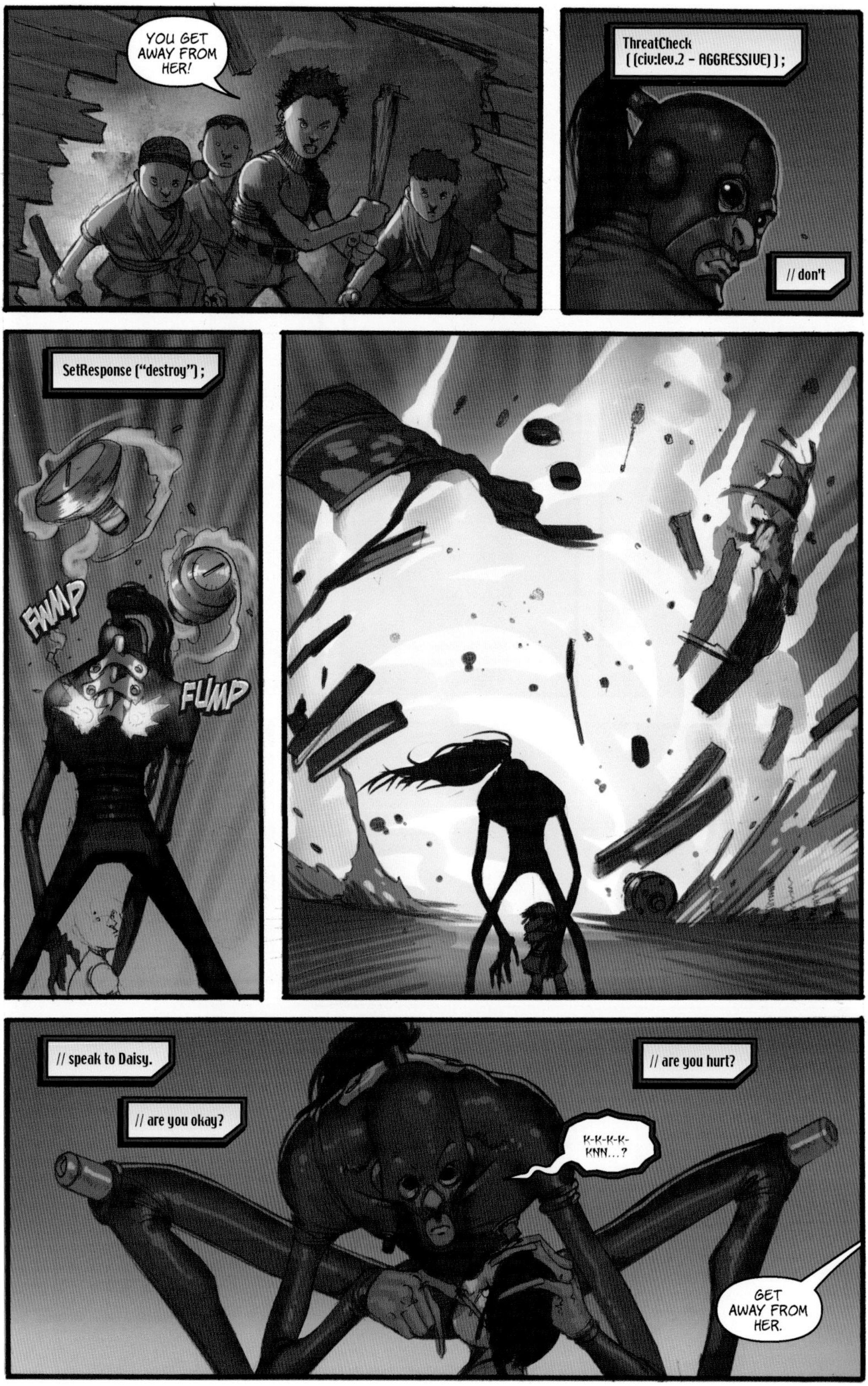
YOU GET AWAY FROM HER!
ThreatCheck ((civ:lev.2 - AGGRESSIVE)) ;
// don't
SetResponse ("destroy") ;
FWMP
FUMP
// speak to Daisy.
// are you okay?
// are you hurt?
K-K-K-K-KNN...?
GET AWAY FROM HER.

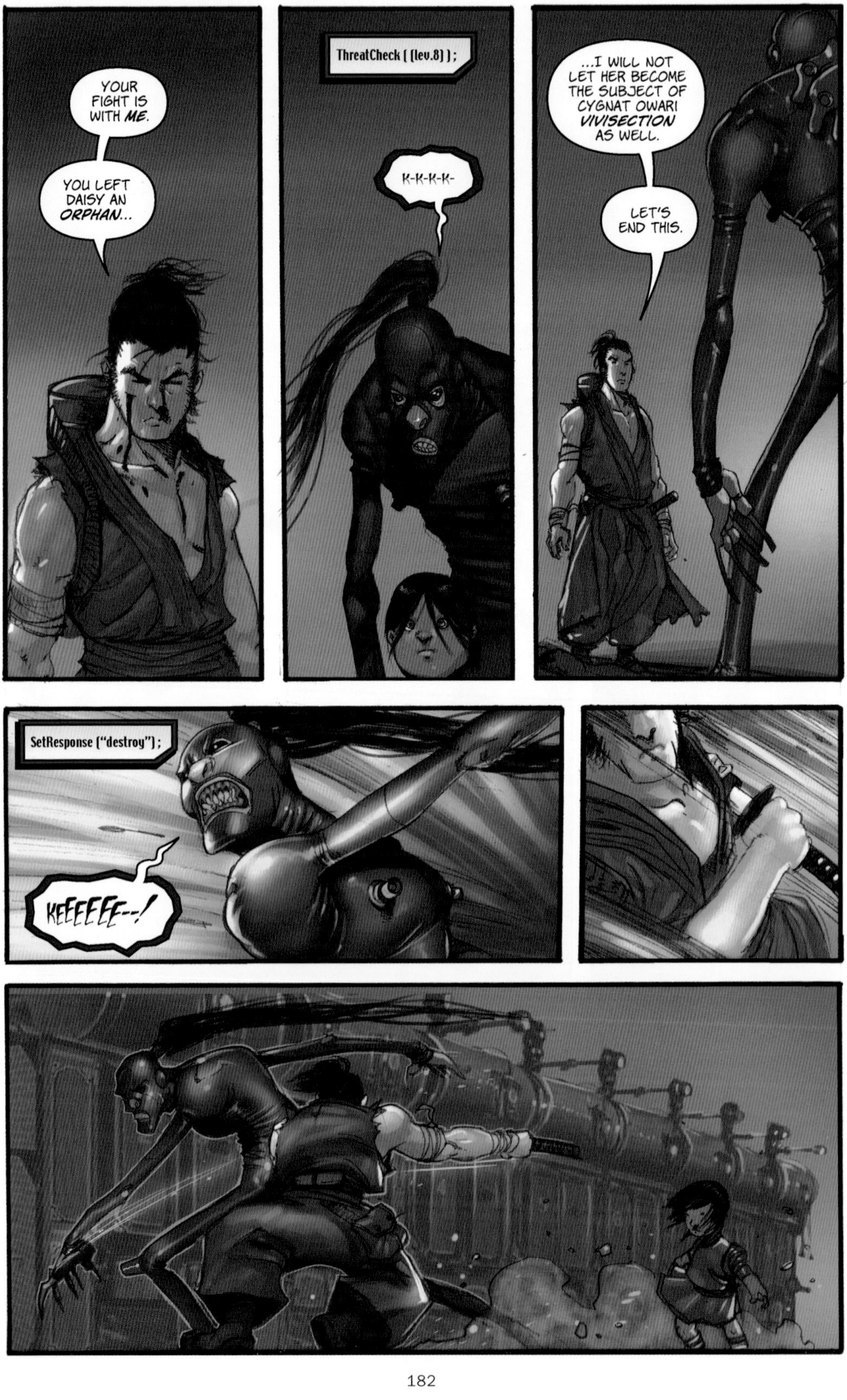
YOUR FIGHT IS WITH *ME*.
YOU LEFT DAISY AN *ORPHAN*...
ThreatCheck ((lev.8));
K-K-K-K-
...I WILL NOT LET HER BECOME THE SUBJECT OF CYGNAT OWARI *VIVISECTION* AS WELL.
LET'S END THIS.
SetResponse ("destroy");
KEEEEEE--!

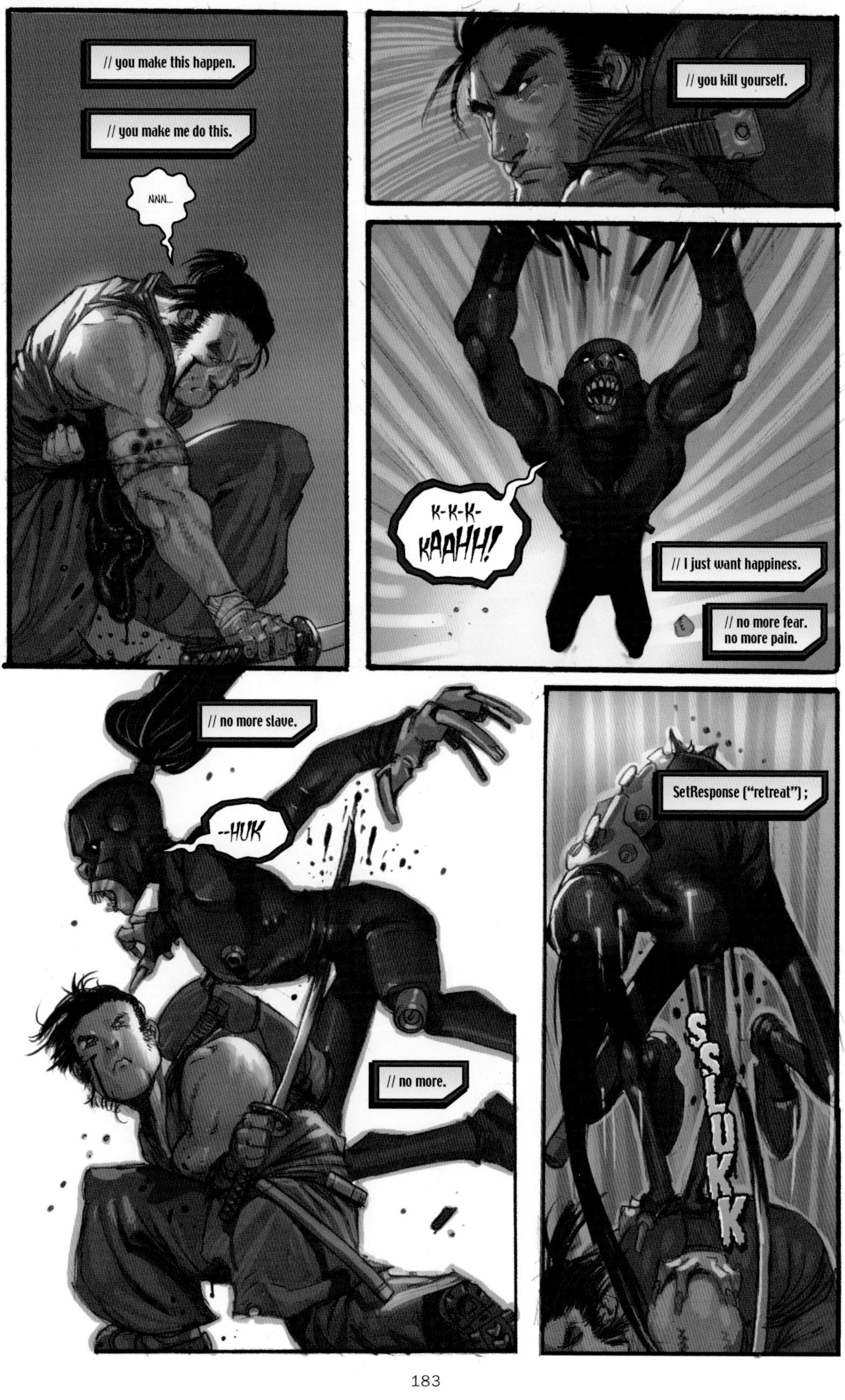
// you make this happen.
// you make me do this.
NNN...
// you kill yourself.
K-K-K-KAAHH!
// I just want happiness.
// no more fear. no more pain.
// no more slave.
--HUK
// no more.
SetResponse ("retreat");
SSLUKK

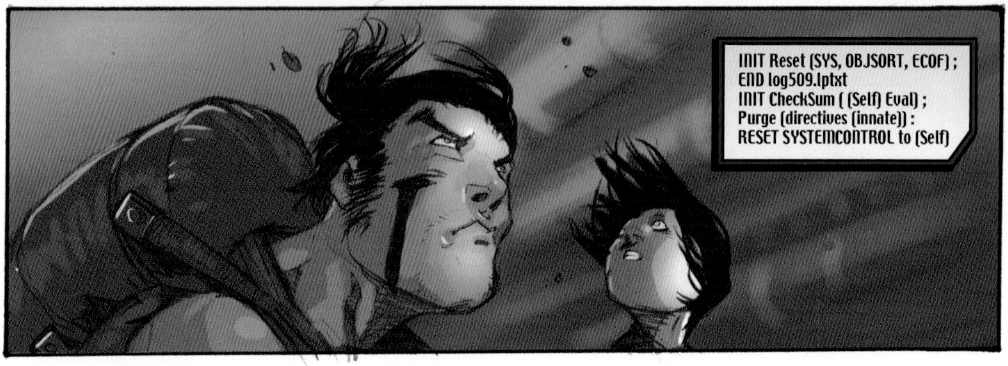
INIT Reset (SYS, OBJSORT, ECOF) ;
END log509.lptxt
INIT CheckSum ((Self) Eval) ;
Purge (directives (innate)) :
RESET SYSTEMCONTROL to (Self)

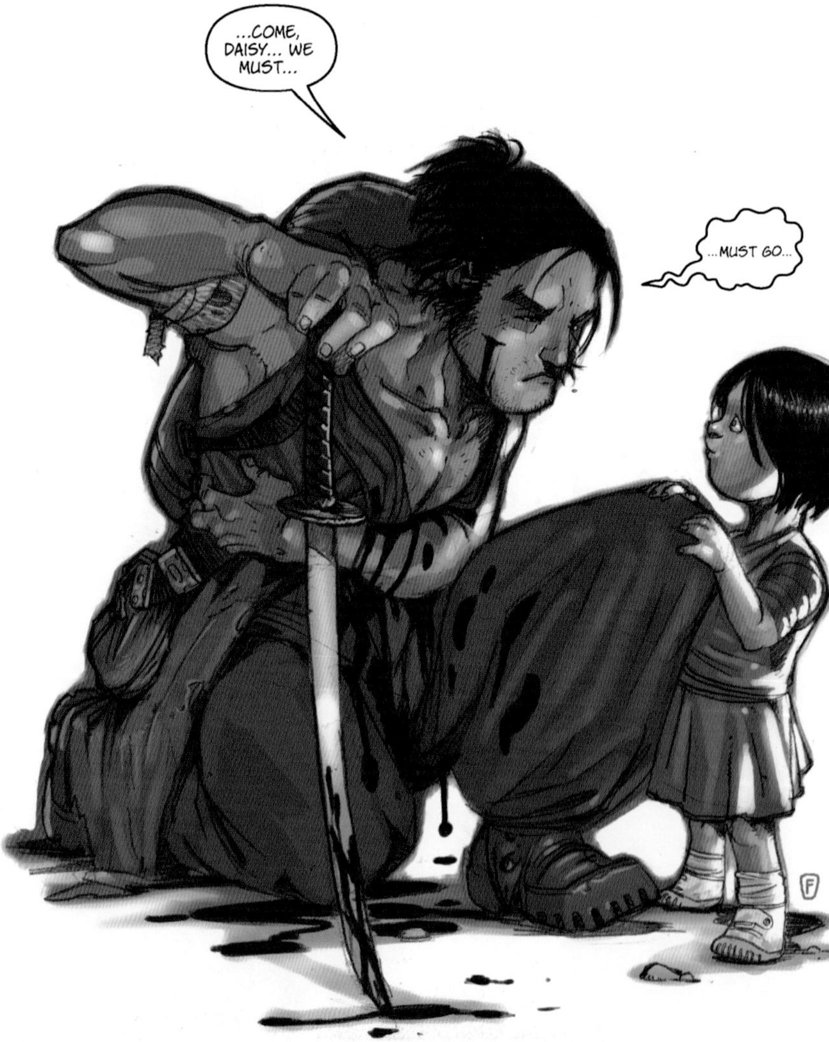
...COME, DAISY... WE MUST...
...MUST GO...

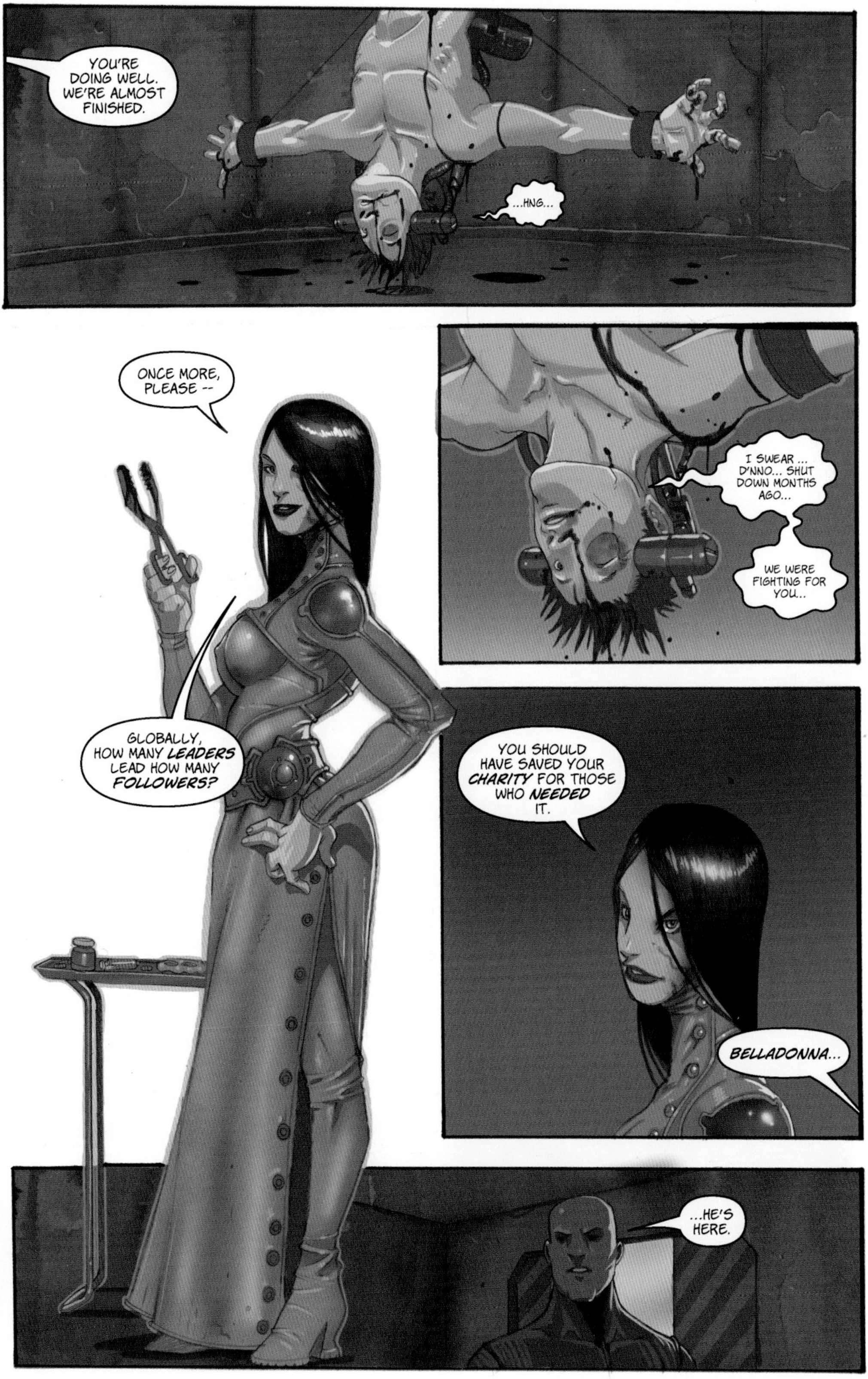
YOU'RE DOING WELL. WE'RE ALMOST FINISHED.
...HNG...
ONCE MORE, PLEASE --
I SWEAR ... D'NNO... SHUT DOWN MONTHS AGO...
WE WERE FIGHTING FOR YOU...
GLOBALLY, HOW MANY LEADERS LEAD HOW MANY FOLLOWERS?
YOU SHOULD HAVE SAVED YOUR CHARITY FOR THOSE WHO NEEDED IT.
BELLADONNA...
...HE'S HERE.

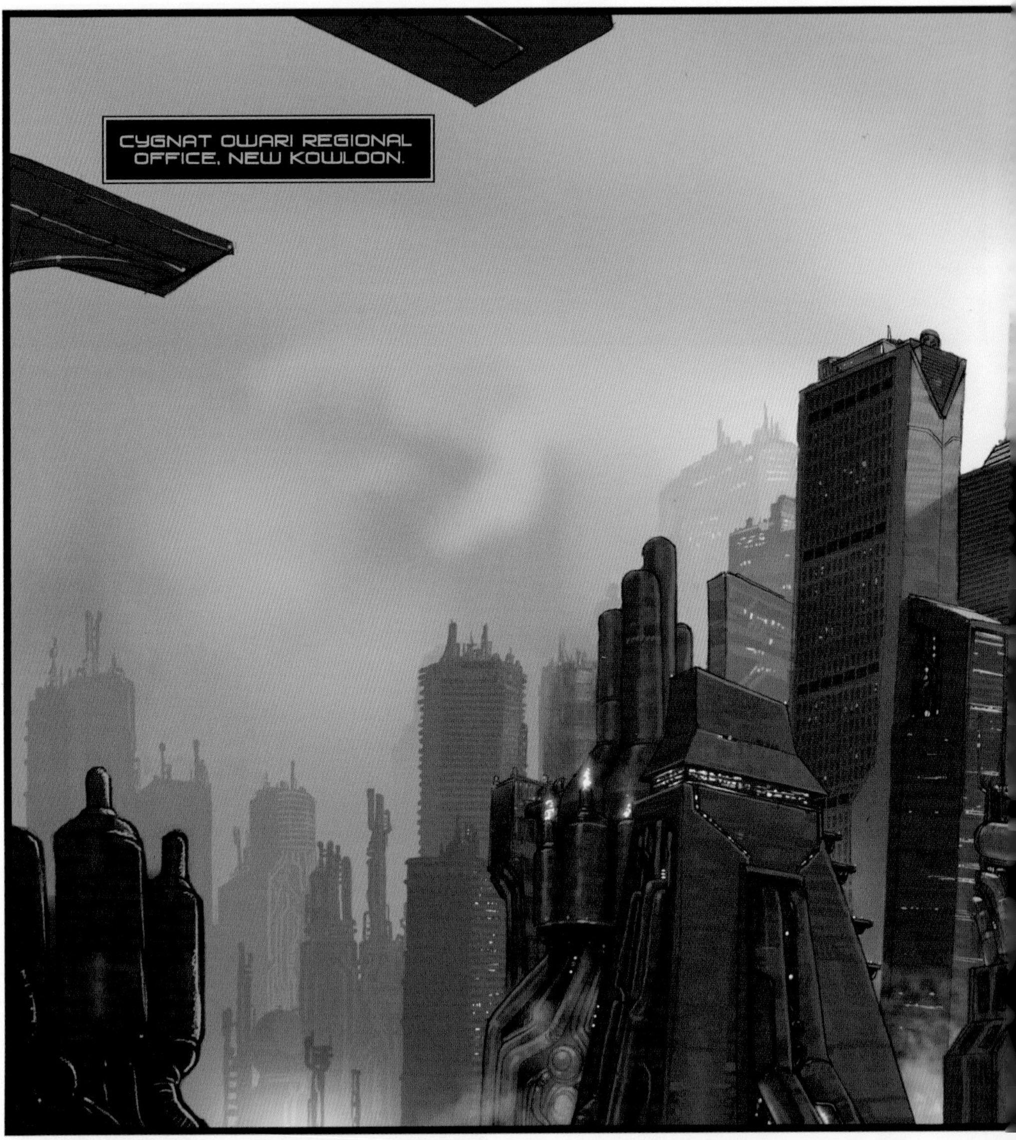
CYGNAT OWARI REGIONAL OFFICE, NEW KOWLOON.

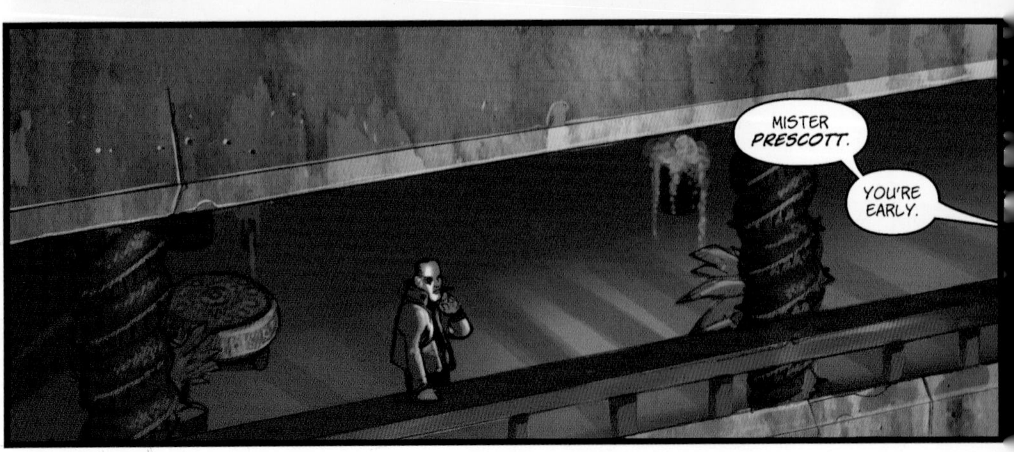
MISTER PRESCOTT.
YOU'RE EARLY.

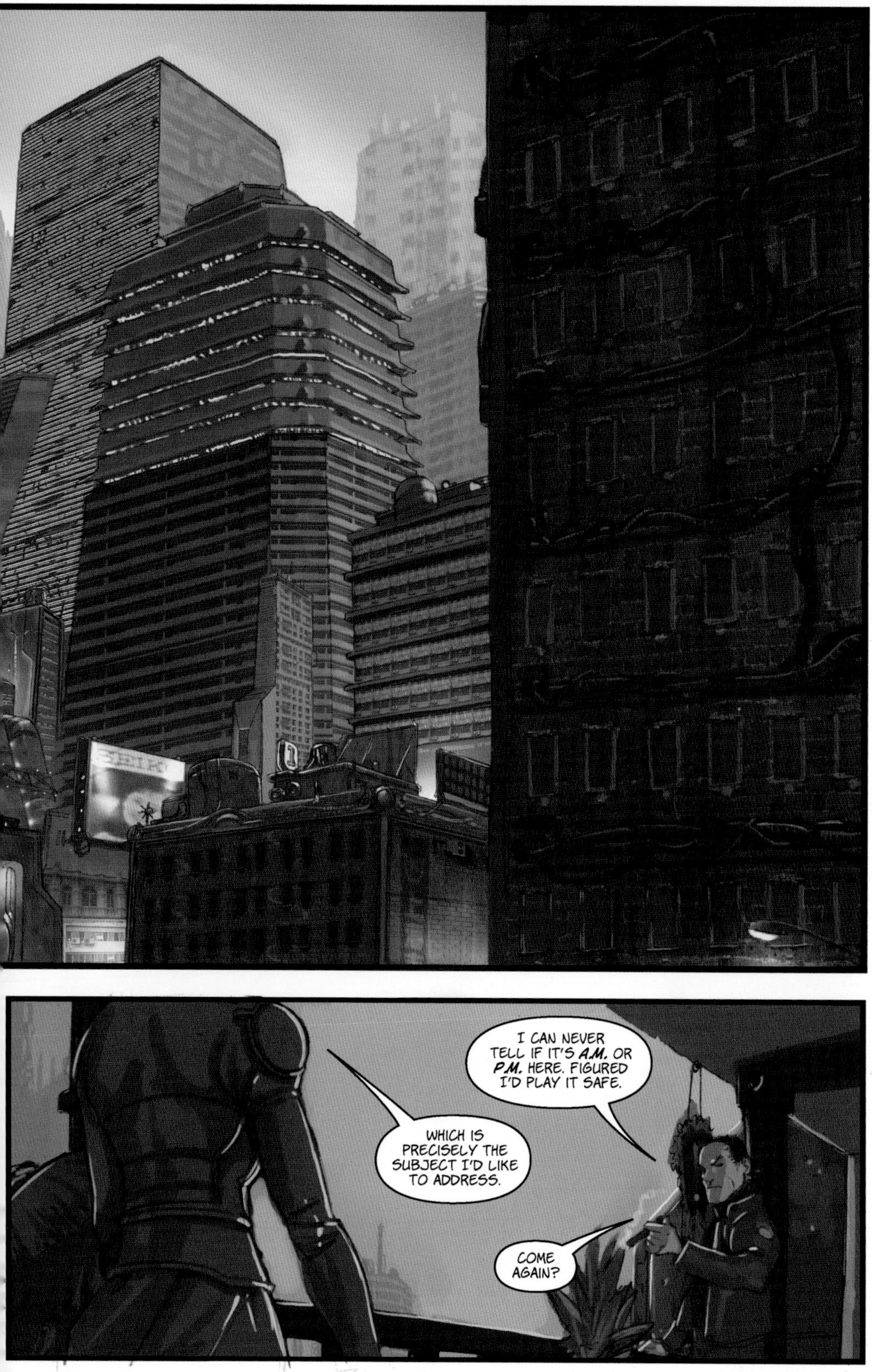
I CAN NEVER TELL IF IT'S A.M. OR P.M. HERE. FIGURED I'D PLAY IT SAFE.
WHICH IS PRECISELY THE SUBJECT I'D LIKE TO ADDRESS.
COME AGAIN?

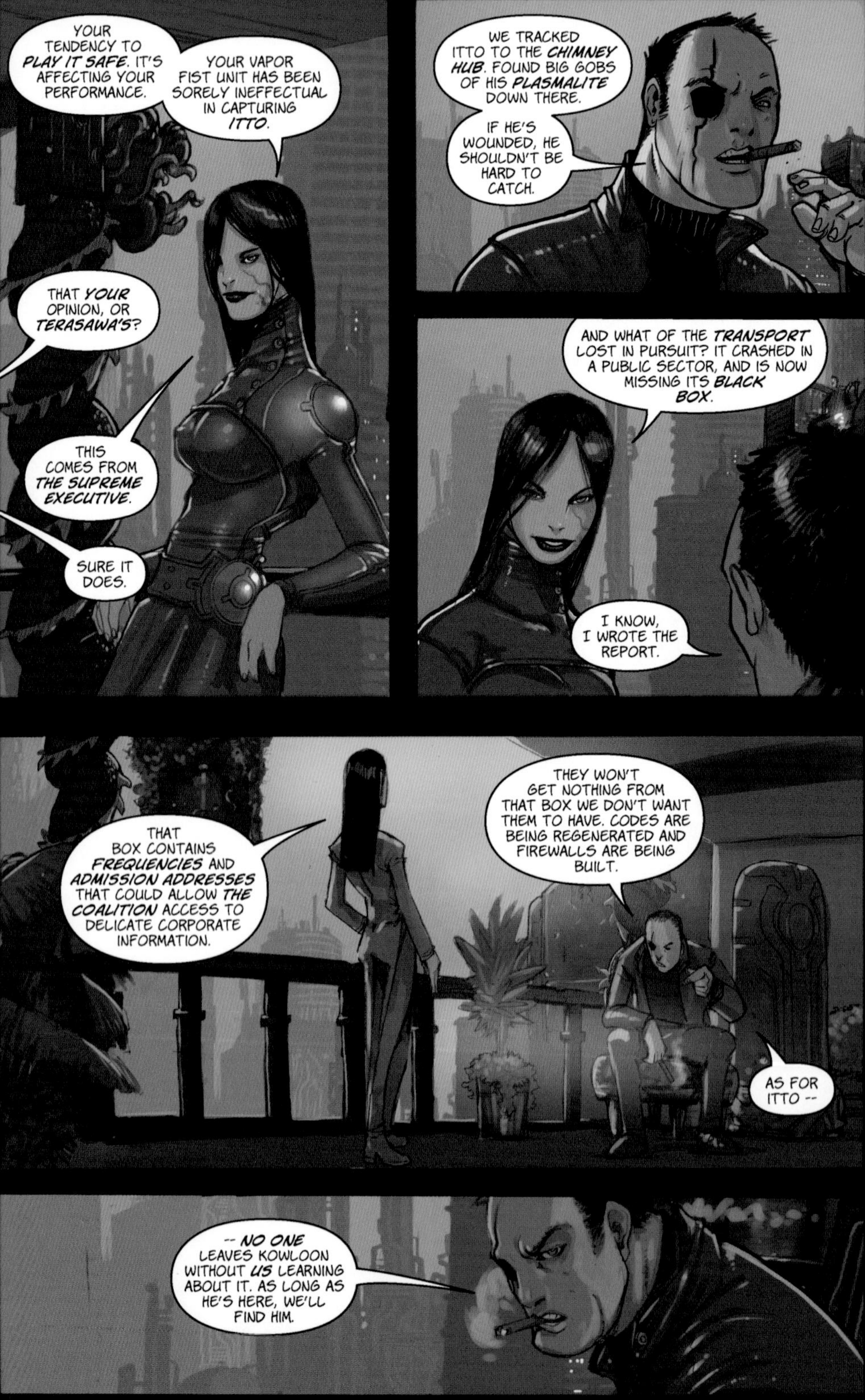
YOUR TENDENCY TO PLAY IT SAFE. IT'S AFFECTING YOUR PERFORMANCE.
YOUR VAPOR FIST UNIT HAS BEEN SORELY INEFFECTUAL IN CAPTURING ITTO.
THAT YOUR OPINION, OR TERASAWA'S?
THIS COMES FROM THE SUPREME EXECUTIVE.
SURE IT DOES.
WE TRACKED ITTO TO THE CHIMNEY HUB. FOUND BIG GOBS OF HIS PLASMALITE DOWN THERE.
IF HE'S WOUNDED, HE SHOULDN'T BE HARD TO CATCH.
AND WHAT OF THE TRANSPORT LOST IN PURSUIT? IT CRASHED IN A PUBLIC SECTOR, AND IS NOW MISSING ITS BLACK BOX.
I KNOW, I WROTE THE REPORT.
THAT BOX CONTAINS FREQUENCIES AND ADMISSION ADDRESSES THAT COULD ALLOW THE COALITION ACCESS TO DELICATE CORPORATE INFORMATION.
THEY WON'T GET NOTHING FROM THAT BOX WE DON'T WANT THEM TO HAVE. CODES ARE BEING REGENERATED AND FIREWALLS ARE BEING BUILT.
AS FOR ITTO --
-- NO ONE LEAVES KOWLOON WITHOUT US LEARNING ABOUT IT. AS LONG AS HE'S HERE, WE'LL FIND HIM.

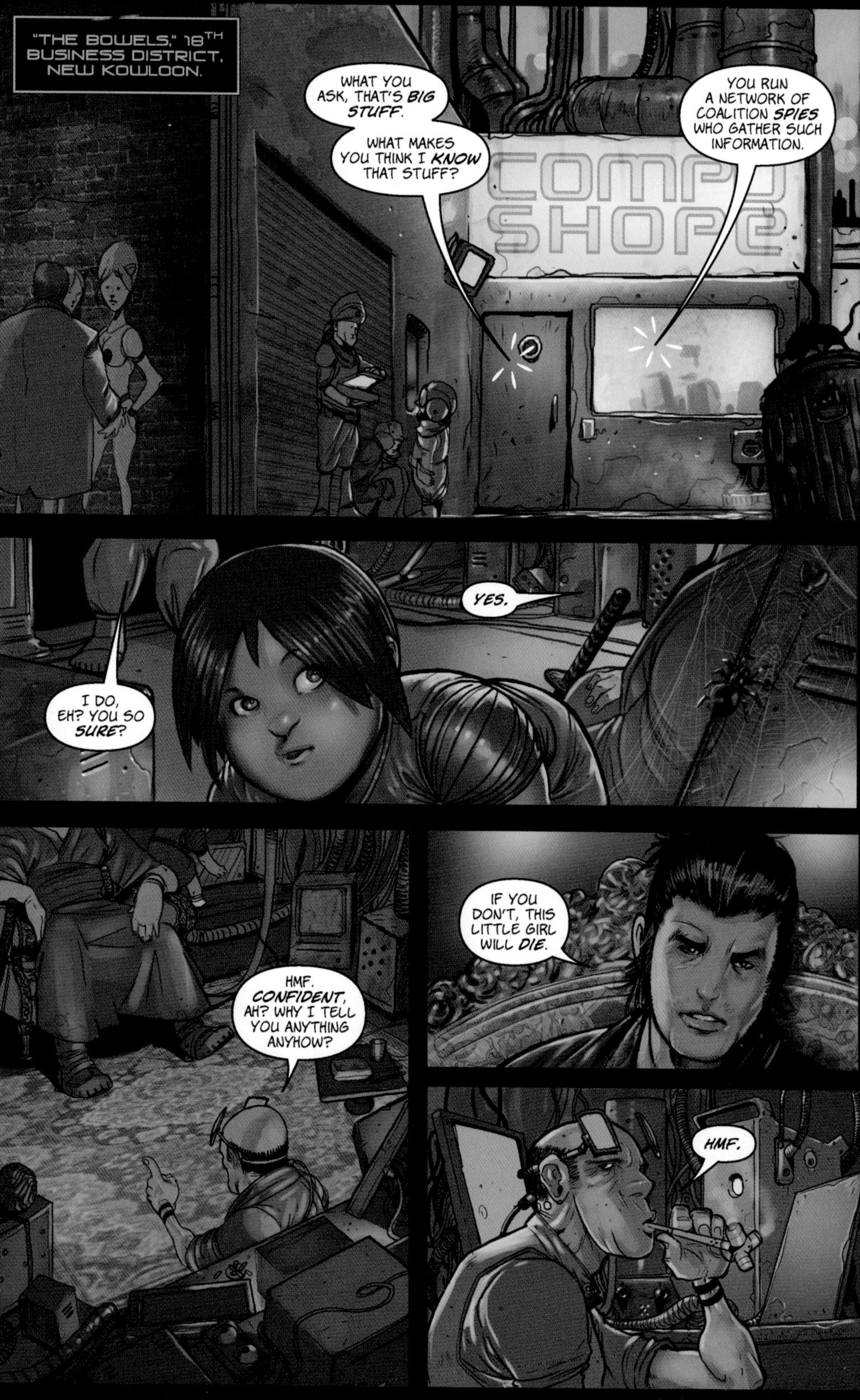
"THE BOWELS," 18TH BUSINESS DISTRICT, NEW KOWLOON.
WHAT YOU ASK, THAT'S BIG STUFF.
WHAT MAKES YOU THINK I KNOW THAT STUFF?
YOU RUN A NETWORK OF COALITION SPIES WHO GATHER SUCH INFORMATION.
COMPU SHOPPE
I DO, EH? YOU SO SURE?
YES.
HMF. CONFIDENT, AH? WHY I TELL YOU ANYTHING ANYHOW?
IF YOU DON'T, THIS LITTLE GIRL WILL DIE.
HMF.

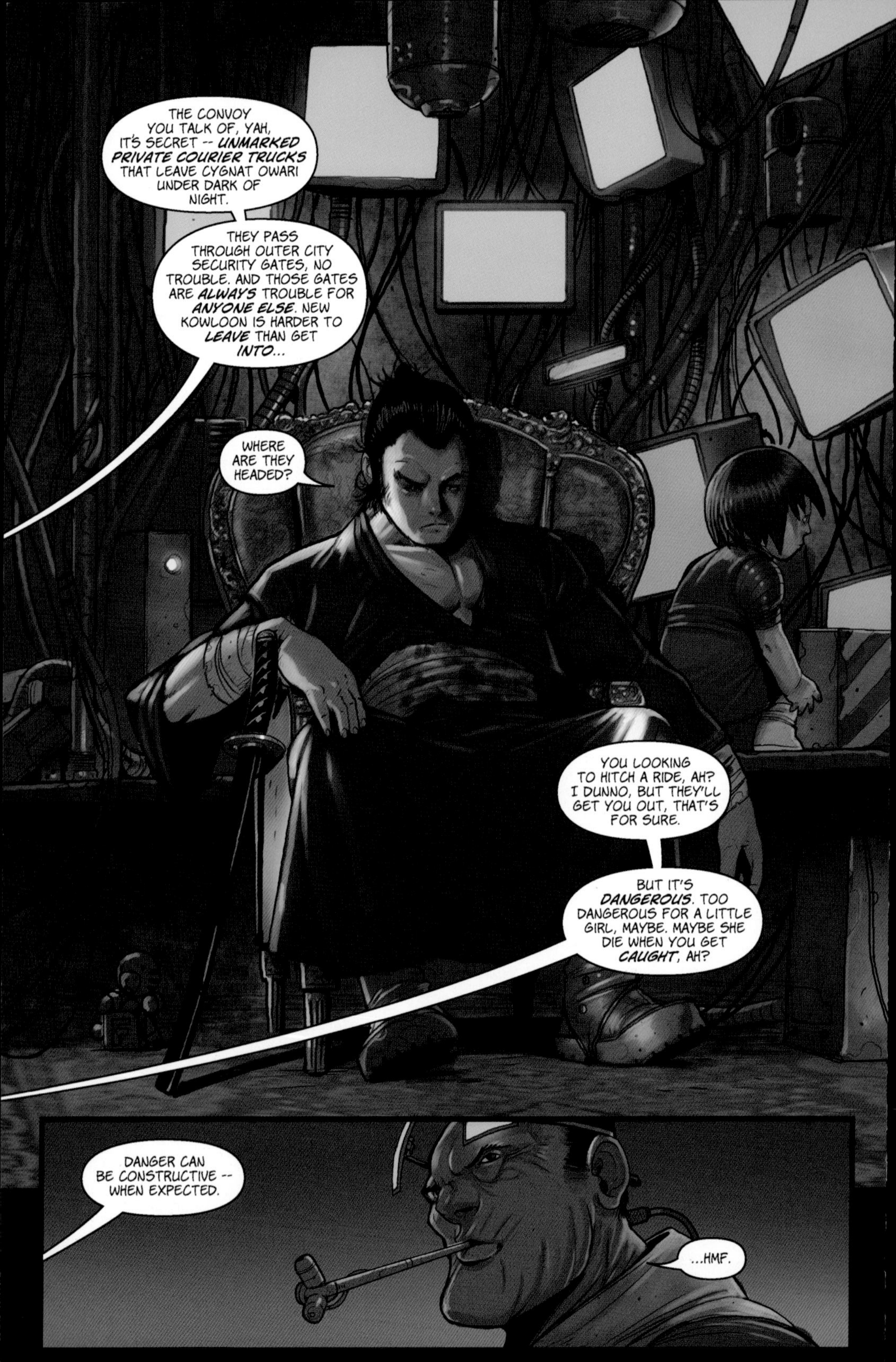
THE CONVOY YOU TALK OF, YAH, IT'S SECRET -- UNMARKED PRIVATE COURIER TRUCKS THAT LEAVE CYGNAT OWARI UNDER DARK OF NIGHT.
THEY PASS THROUGH OUTER CITY SECURITY GATES, NO TROUBLE. AND THOSE GATES ARE ALWAYS TROUBLE FOR ANYONE ELSE. NEW KOWLOON IS HARDER TO LEAVE THAN GET INTO...
WHERE ARE THEY HEADED?
YOU LOOKING TO HITCH A RIDE, AH? I DUNNO, BUT THEY'LL GET YOU OUT, THAT'S FOR SURE.
BUT IT'S DANGEROUS. TOO DANGEROUS FOR A LITTLE GIRL, MAYBE. MAYBE SHE DIE WHEN YOU GET CAUGHT, AH?
DANGER CAN BE CONSTRUCTIVE -- WHEN EXPECTED.
...HMF.

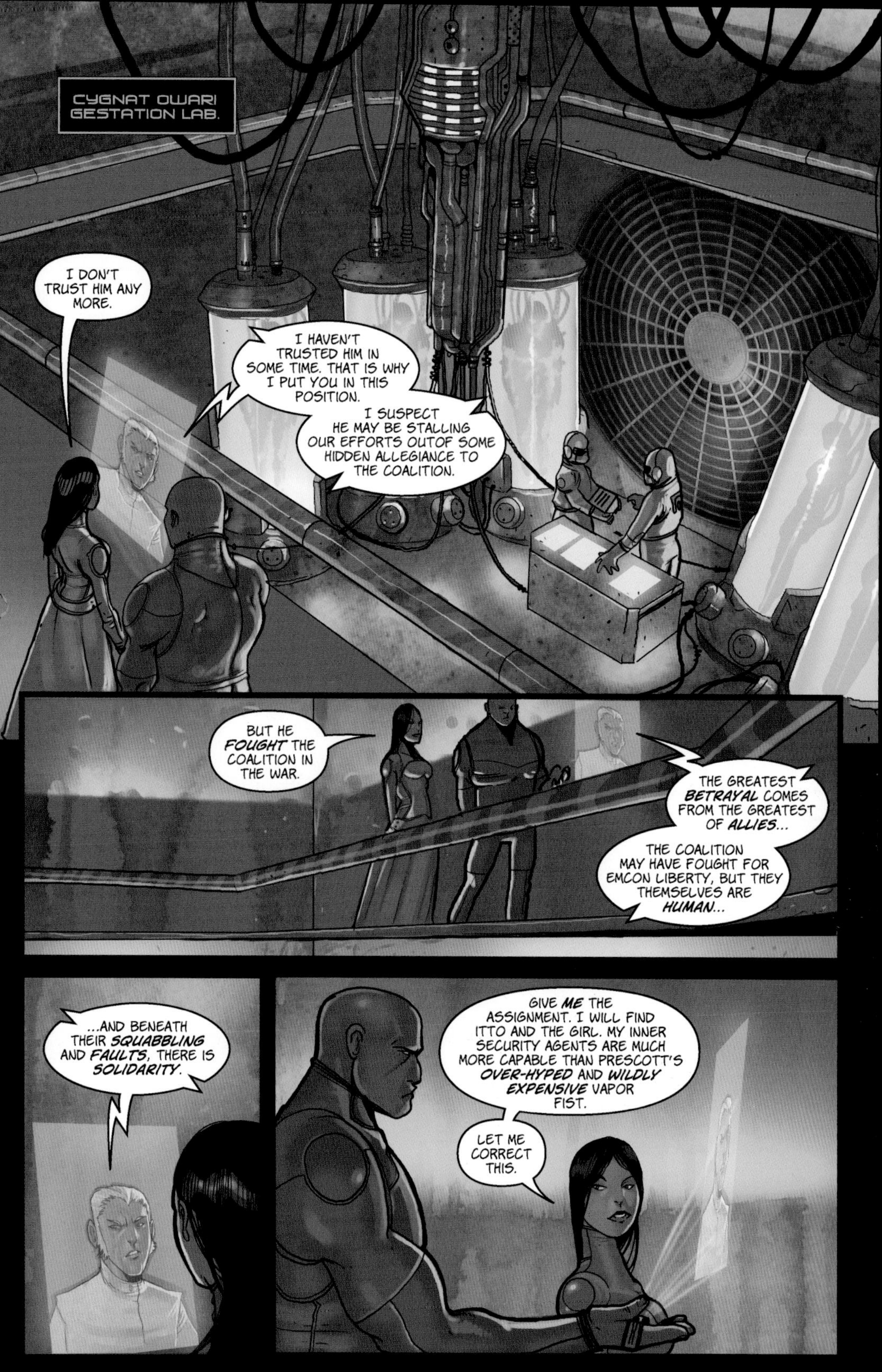
CYGNAT OWARI GESTATION LAB.
I DON'T TRUST HIM ANY MORE.
I HAVEN'T TRUSTED HIM IN SOME TIME. THAT IS WHY I PUT YOU IN THIS POSITION.
I SUSPECT HE MAY BE STALLING OUR EFFORTS OUTOF SOME HIDDEN ALLEGIANCE TO THE COALITION.
BUT HE FOUGHT THE COALITION IN THE WAR.
THE GREATEST BETRAYAL COMES FROM THE GREATEST OF ALLIES...
THE COALITION MAY HAVE FOUGHT FOR EMCON LIBERTY, BUT THEY THEMSELVES ARE HUMAN...
...AND BENEATH THEIR SQUABBLING AND FAULTS, THERE IS SOLIDARITY.
GIVE ME THE ASSIGNMENT. I WILL FIND ITTO AND THE GIRL. MY INNER SECURITY AGENTS ARE MUCH MORE CAPABLE THAN PRESCOTT'S OVER-HYPED AND WILDLY EXPENSIVE VAPOR FIST.
LET ME CORRECT THIS.

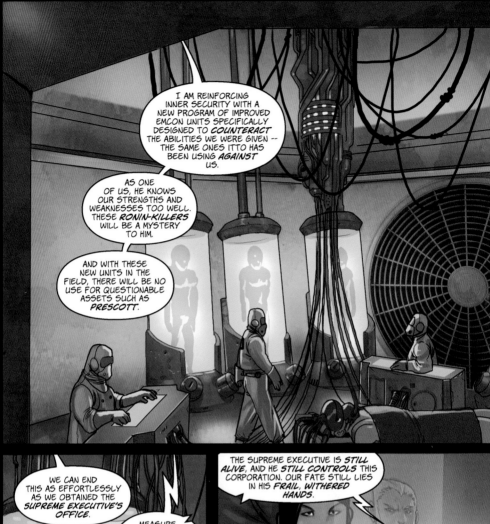

I AM REINFORCING INNER SECURITY WITH A NEW PROGRAM OF IMPROVED EMCON UNITS SPECIFICALLY DESIGNED TO *COUNTERACT* THE ABILITIES WE WERE GIVEN -- THE SAME ONES ITTO HAS BEEN USING *AGAINST* US.

AS ONE OF US, HE KNOWS OUR STRENGTHS AND WEAKNESSES TOO WELL. THESE *RONIN-KILLERS* WILL BE A MYSTERY TO HIM.

AND WITH THESE NEW UNITS IN THE FIELD, THERE WILL BE NO USE FOR QUESTIONABLE ASSETS SUCH AS *PRESCOTT*.

WE CAN END THIS AS EFFORTLESSLY AS WE OBTAINED THE *SUPREME EXECUTIVE'S* OFFICE.

MEASURE YOUR WORDS, BELLADONNA...

THE SUPREME EXECUTIVE IS *STILL ALIVE*, AND HE *STILL CONTROLS* THIS CORPORATION. OUR FATE STILL LIES IN HIS *FRAIL, WITHERED* HANDS.

YES, SIR.

REMOVE PRESCOTT. BUT BE *DISCREET*. I DO NOT WANT A PUBLIC INCIDENT.

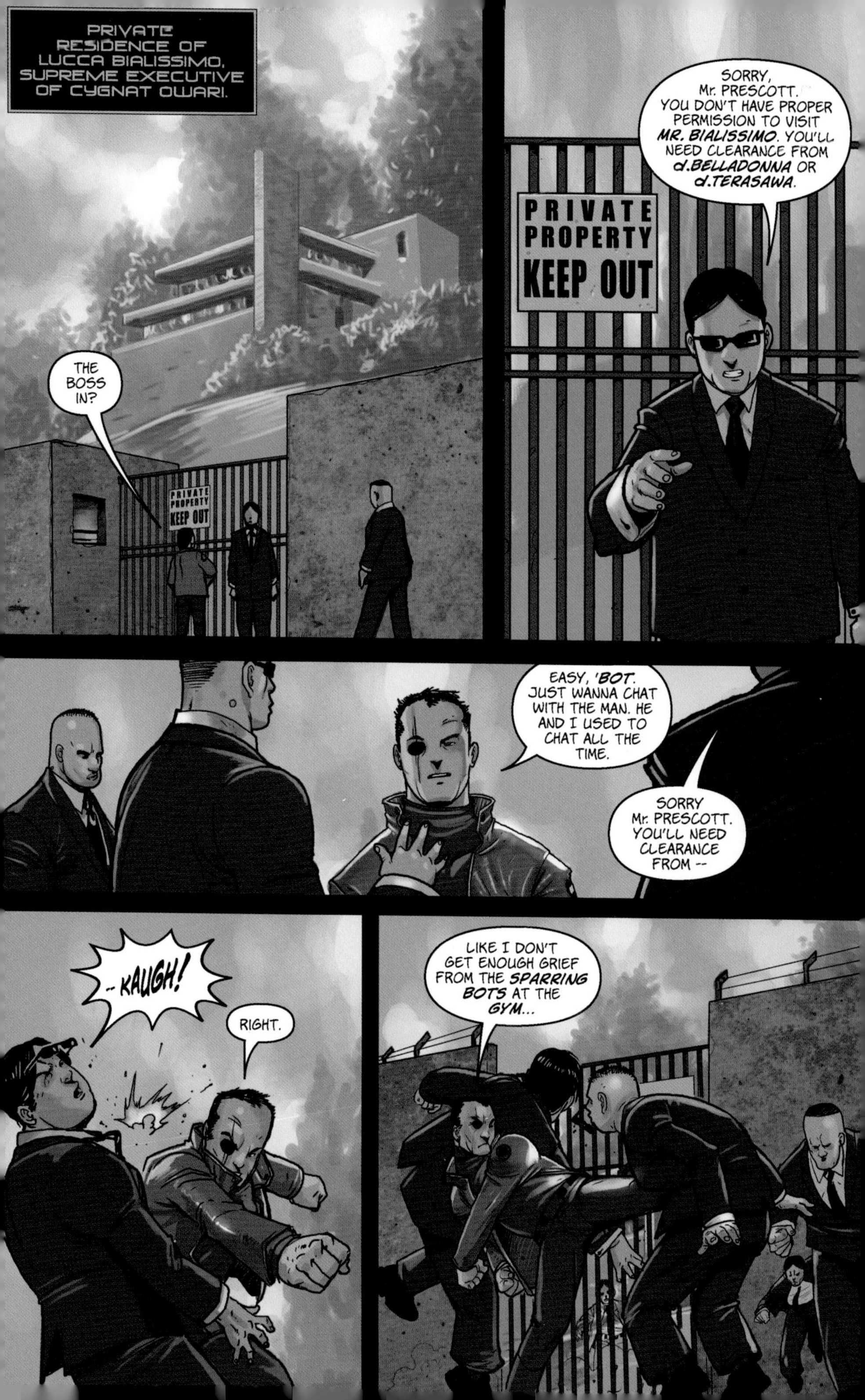

PRIVATE RESIDENCE OF LUCCA BIALISSIMO, SUPREME EXECUTIVE OF CYGNAT OWARI.
THE BOSS IN?
PRIVATE PROPERTY KEEP OUT
SORRY, Mr. PRESCOTT. YOU DON'T HAVE PROPER PERMISSION TO VISIT MR. BIALISSIMO. YOU'LL NEED CLEARANCE FROM d.BELLADONNA OR d.TERASAWA.
PRIVATE PROPERTY KEEP OUT
EASY, 'BOT. JUST WANNA CHAT WITH THE MAN. HE AND I USED TO CHAT ALL THE TIME.
SORRY Mr. PRESCOTT. YOU'LL NEED CLEARANCE FROM --
-- KAUGH!
RIGHT.
LIKE I DON'T GET ENOUGH GRIEF FROM THE SPARRING BOTS AT THE GYM...

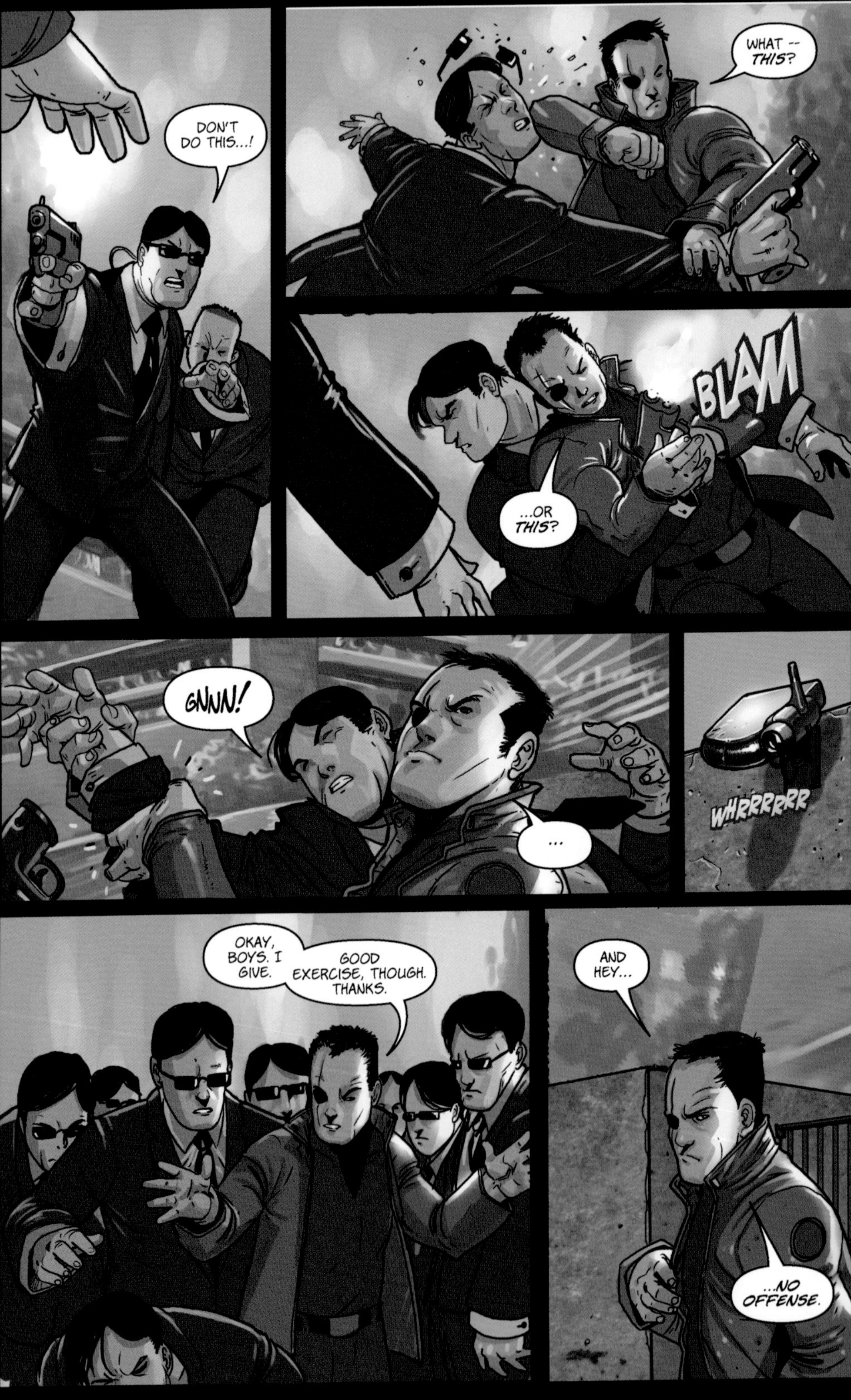
DON'T DO THIS...!
WHAT -- THIS?
...OR THIS?
BLAM
GNNN!
...
WHRRRRR
OKAY, BOYS. I GIVE.
GOOD EXERCISE, THOUGH. THANKS.
AND HEY...
...NO OFFENSE.

CYGNAT OWARI DATA CENTER, NEW KOWLOON REGIONAL CAMPUS.
TAK-TAK-TAKKA-TAK-TAKKA
HMM..
CYGNAT OWARI
An Emperor in Hiding
16 July 2099 — It has been nearly three months since Lucca Bialissimo, Supreme Executive of leading bio-synthetic development conglomerate Cygnat Owari, has been seen by the public. Though the international influence of his company continues to thrive with little competition to speak of, the once-flamboyant centerpiece of Cygnat Owari PR has become noticeably absent from the public eye. His office no longer returns phone calls. His press secretary no longer schedules trips around the world. Even his private mansion in Malaysia seems to grow stagnant and unkempt, leading many to wonder whether foul play is involved.
Such concerns were put to rest, however, when Bialissimo's EmCon Avatar designated Terasawa announced to the world that his employer was suffering from health problems, and had taken to self-imposed exile until the debilitating condition could be corrected. Details of the illness were not made available, but it is suggested to include certain disfiguring symptoms, symptoms that Bialissimo feels are too humbling to be seen or photographed by the public.
For decades, Bialissimo was known as the sharpest corporate playboy on the planet, hosting parties and events that not only drew great spectacle, but often perpetuated his enormous fortune through clever negotiation of broadcast rights and likeness royalties. He has been romantically linked with
SUPREME EXECUTIVE Lucca Bialissimo
EXECUTIVE AVATAR d.Terasawa
PRIME CONSORTIUM AMBASSADOR Yam Ko Kwan
CFO / EXECUTIVE CABINET Lewelyn Eiger
CO SECURITY AFFAIRS d.Belladonna
CO SECURITY AFFAIRS d.Belladonna
...

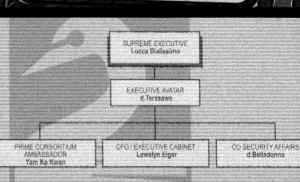

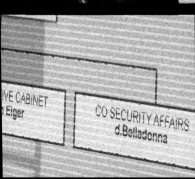

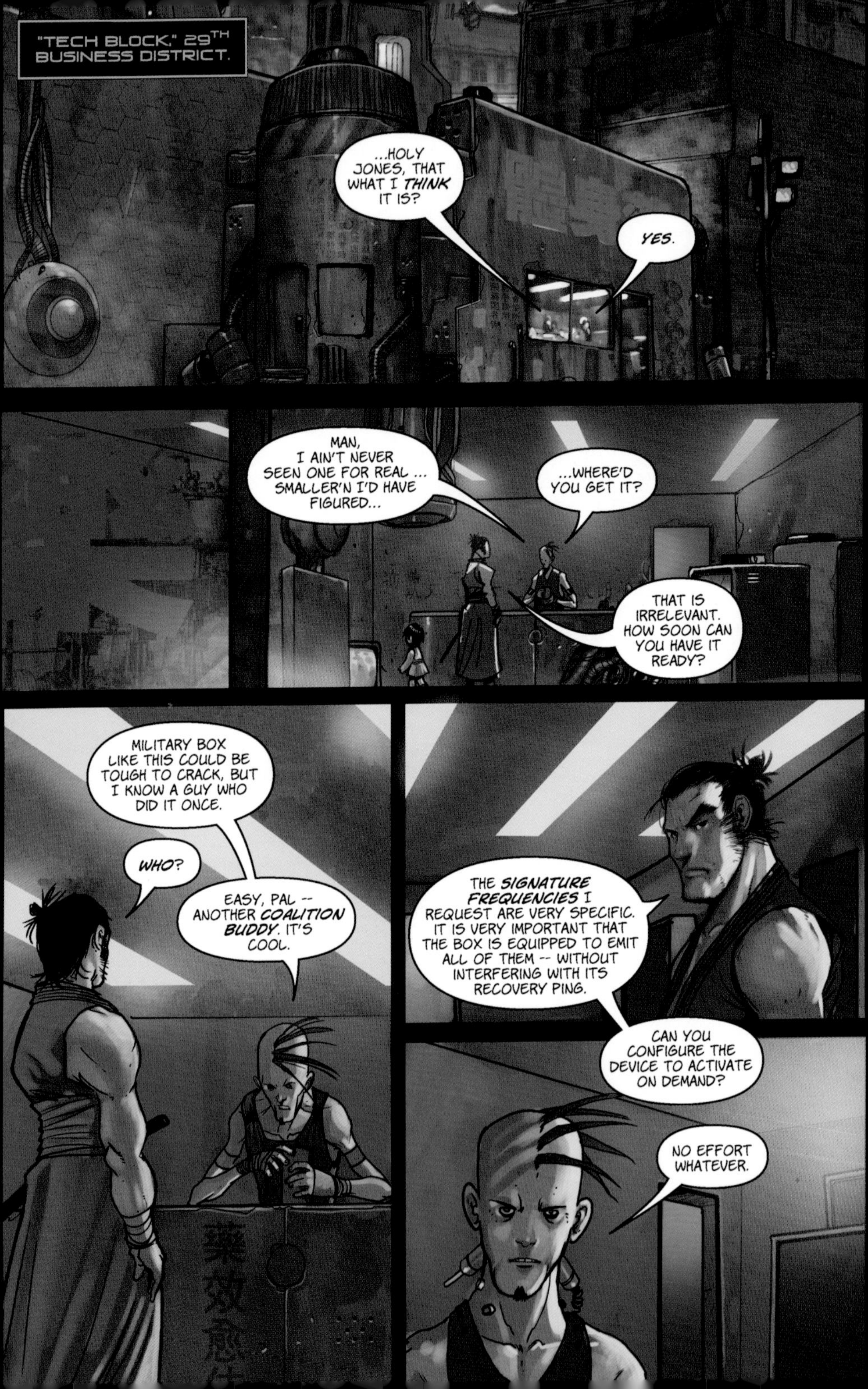
"TECH BLOCK," 29TH BUSINESS DISTRICT.
...HOLY JONES, THAT WHAT I *THINK* IT IS?
YES.
MAN, I AIN'T NEVER SEEN ONE FOR REAL ... SMALLER'N I'D HAVE FIGURED...
...WHERE'D YOU GET IT?
THAT IS IRRELEVANT. HOW SOON CAN YOU HAVE IT READY?
MILITARY BOX LIKE THIS COULD BE TOUGH TO CRACK, BUT I KNOW A GUY WHO DID IT ONCE.
WHO?
EASY, PAL -- ANOTHER ***COALITION BUDDY***. IT'S COOL.
THE ***SIGNATURE FREQUENCIES*** I REQUEST ARE VERY SPECIFIC. IT IS VERY IMPORTANT THAT THE BOX IS EQUIPPED TO EMIT ALL OF THEM -- WITHOUT INTERFERING WITH ITS RECOVERY PING.
CAN YOU CONFIGURE THE DEVICE TO ACTIVATE ON DEMAND?
NO EFFORT WHATEVER.

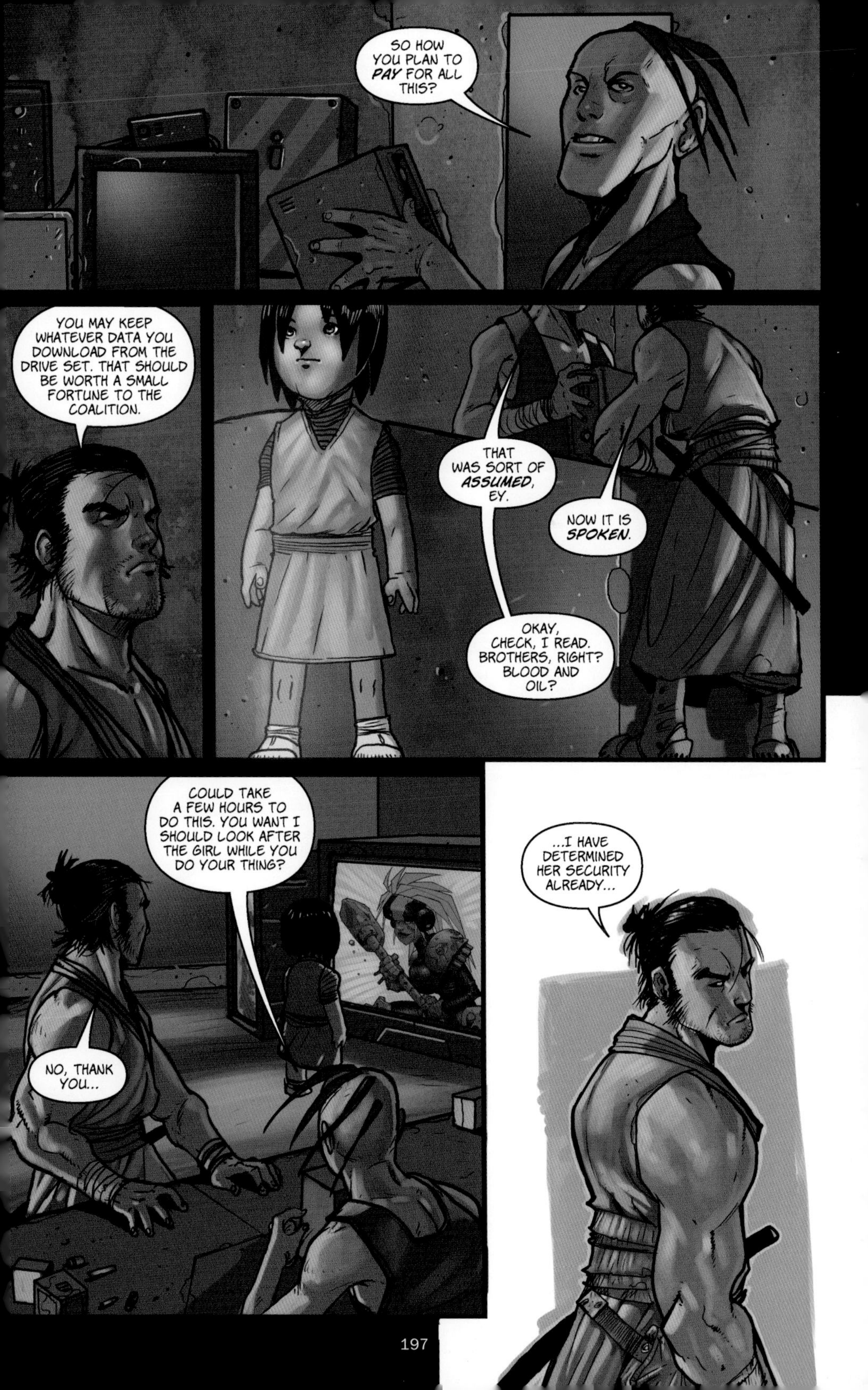
SO HOW YOU PLAN TO PAY FOR ALL THIS?
YOU MAY KEEP WHATEVER DATA YOU DOWNLOAD FROM THE DRIVE SET. THAT SHOULD BE WORTH A SMALL FORTUNE TO THE COALITION.
THAT WAS SORT OF ASSUMED, EY.
NOW IT IS SPOKEN.
OKAY, CHECK, I READ. BROTHERS, RIGHT? BLOOD AND OIL?
COULD TAKE A FEW HOURS TO DO THIS. YOU WANT I SHOULD LOOK AFTER THE GIRL WHILE YOU DO YOUR THING?
NO, THANK YOU...
...I HAVE DETERMINED HER SECURITY ALREADY...

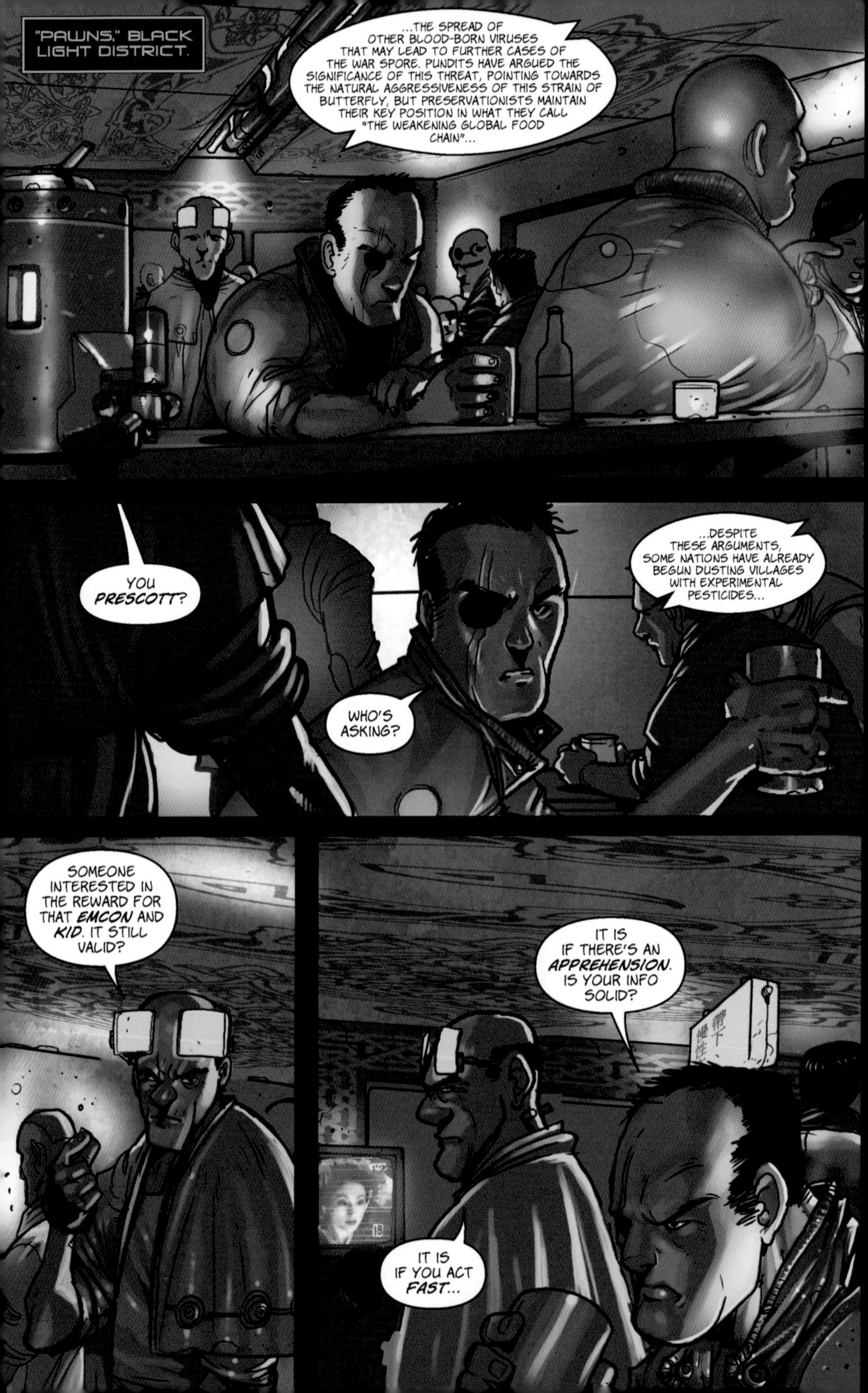
"PAWNS," BLACK LIGHT DISTRICT.
...THE SPREAD OF OTHER BLOOD-BORN VIRUSES THAT MAY LEAD TO FURTHER CASES OF THE WAR SPORE. PUNDITS HAVE ARGUED THE SIGNIFICANCE OF THIS THREAT, POINTING TOWARDS THE NATURAL AGGRESSIVENESS OF THIS STRAIN OF BUTTERFLY, BUT PRESERVATIONISTS MAINTAIN THEIR KEY POSITION IN WHAT THEY CALL "THE WEAKENING GLOBAL FOOD CHAIN"...
YOU PRESCOTT?
...DESPITE THESE ARGUMENTS, SOME NATIONS HAVE ALREADY BEGUN DUSTING VILLAGES WITH EXPERIMENTAL PESTICIDES...
WHO'S ASKING?
SOMEONE INTERESTED IN THE REWARD FOR THAT EMCON AND KID. IT STILL VALID?
IT IS IF THERE'S AN APPREHENSION. IS YOUR INFO SOLID?
IT IS IF YOU ACT FAST...

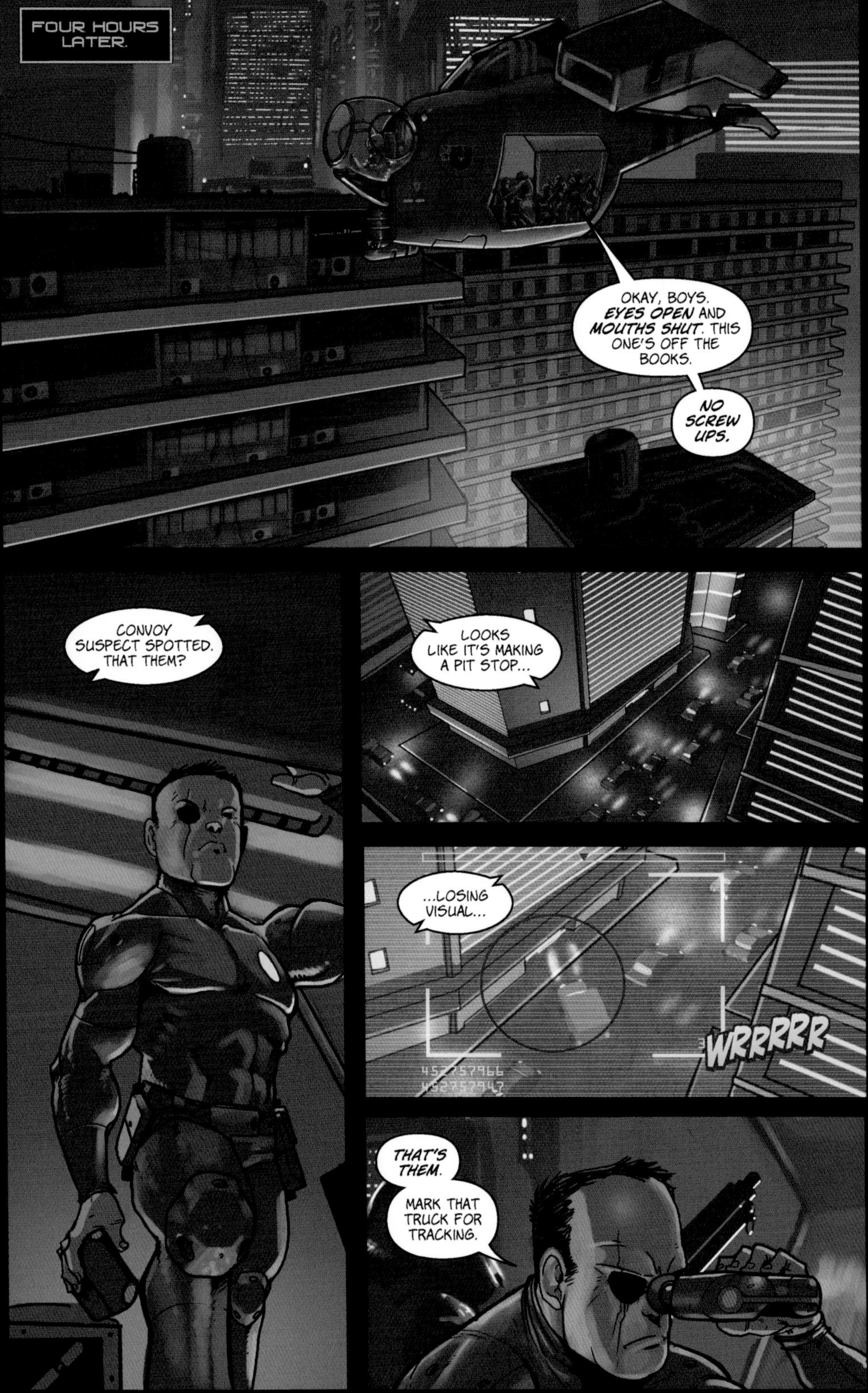
FOUR HOURS LATER.
OKAY, BOYS. EYES OPEN AND MOUTHS SHUT. THIS ONE'S OFF THE BOOKS.
NO SCREW UPS.
CONVOY SUSPECT SPOTTED. THAT THEM?
LOOKS LIKE IT'S MAKING A PIT STOP...
...LOSING VISUAL...
WRRRRR
THAT'S THEM.
MARK THAT TRUCK FOR TRACKING.

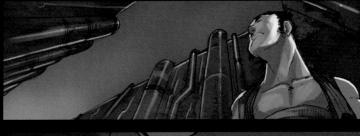

SIR, WE GOT A SIGNATURE PULSE RATE BELOW... 80% MATCH.

STAND BY...

LET'S NOT SPOOK HIM.

HE'S ENTERED THE GARAGE... HE'S OFF OUR SCREENS...

TRYING TO SNEAK OUT ON THE COMPANY BUS, EH...?

TARGET IN MOTION AGAIN.

CONVOY HAS LEFT THE GARAGE.

SHOWING A BODY SHAPE IN THE BACK. *LOW POWER SIGNATURE.*

HE'S TRYING TO BE INVISIBLE...

ALL RIGHT -- SWARM AND CONTAIN!!

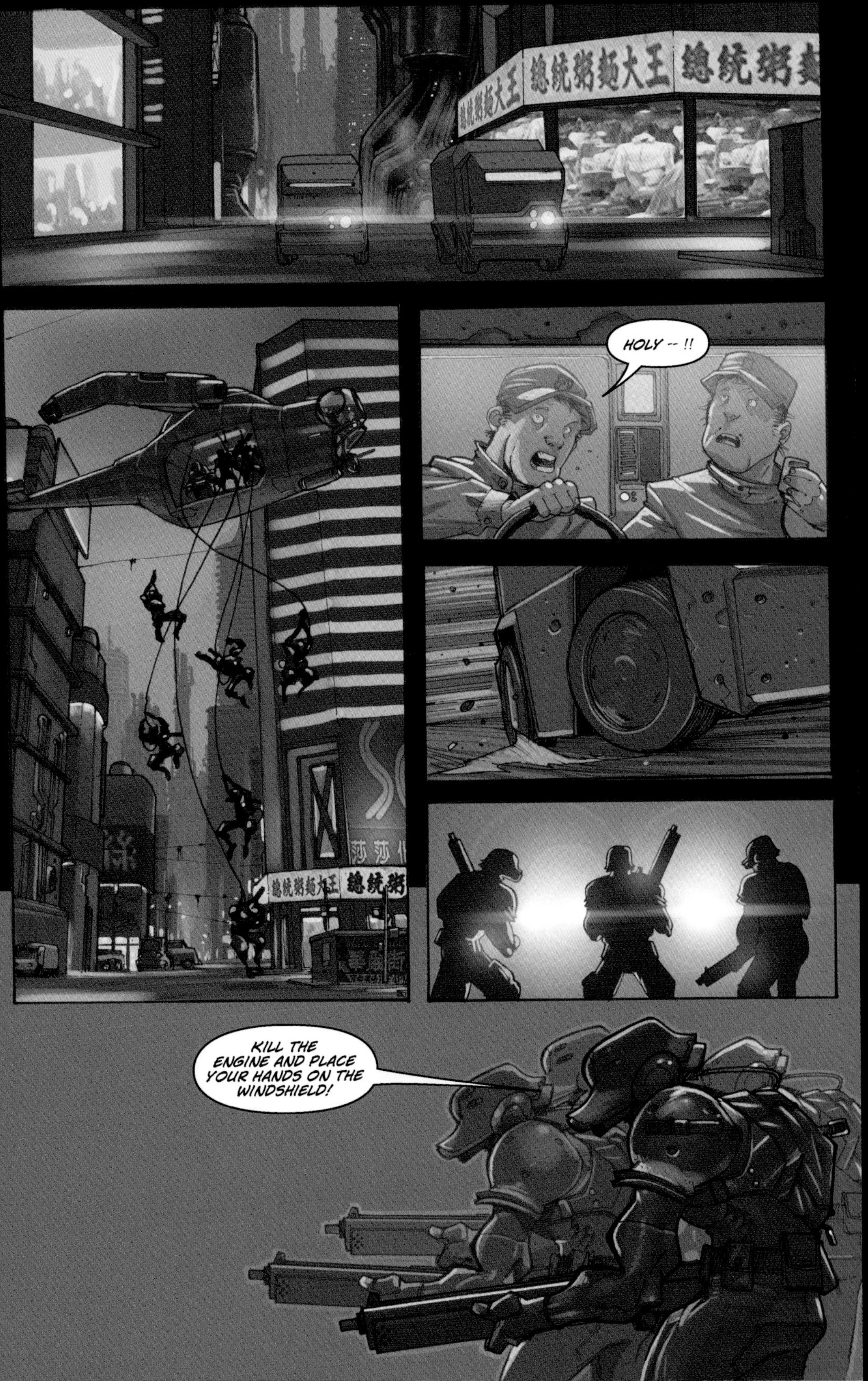

總統粥麵大王
HOLY -- !!
KILL THE ENGINE AND PLACE YOUR HANDS ON THE WINDSHIELD!

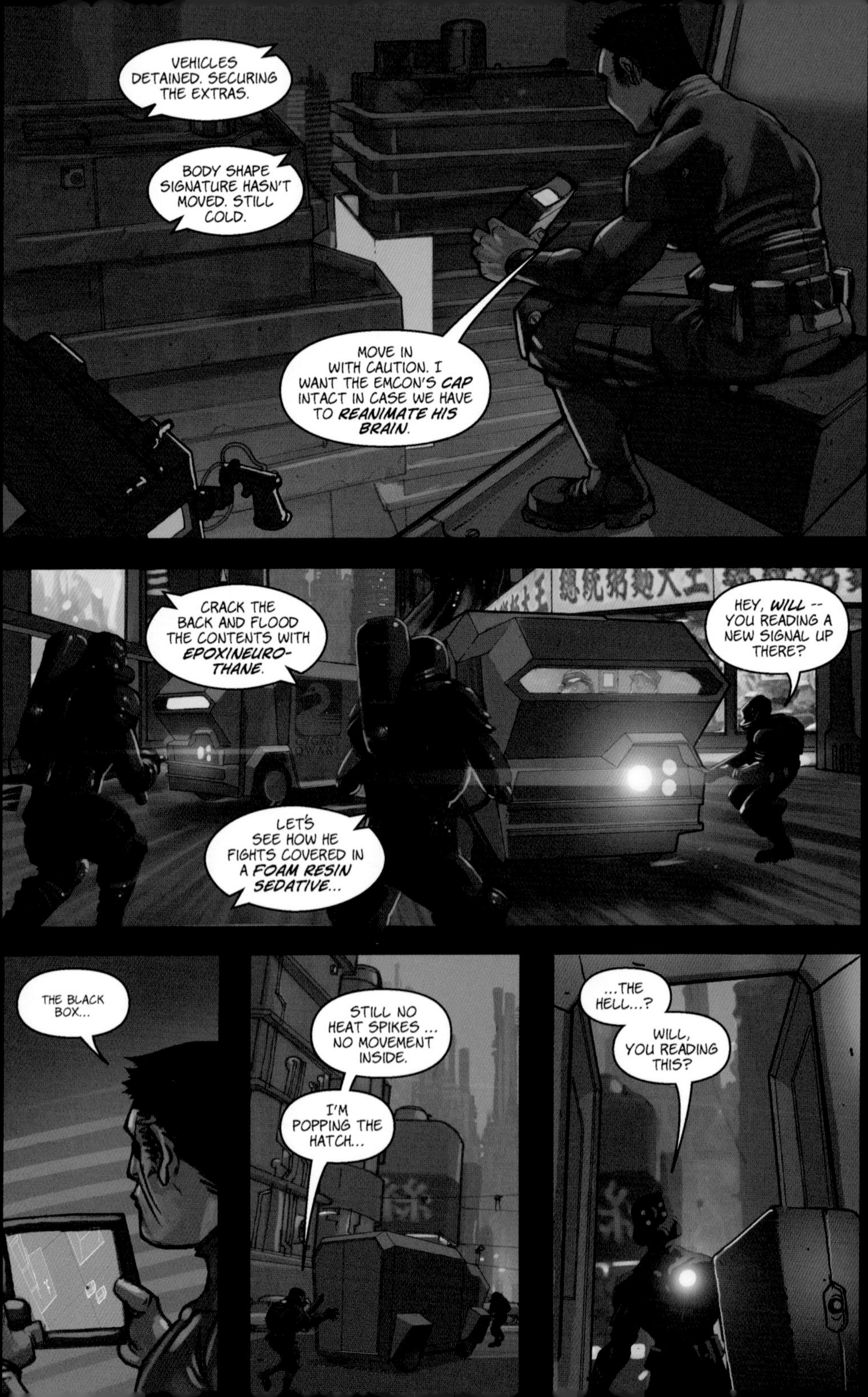
VEHICLES DETAINED. SECURING THE EXTRAS.
BODY SHAPE SIGNATURE HASN'T MOVED. STILL COLD.
MOVE IN WITH CAUTION. I WANT THE EMCON'S *CAP* INTACT IN CASE WE HAVE TO *REANIMATE HIS BRAIN*.
CRACK THE BACK AND FLOOD THE CONTENTS WITH *EPOXINEURO-THANE*.
LET'S SEE HOW HE FIGHTS COVERED IN A *FOAM RESIN SEDATIVE*...
HEY, *WILL* -- YOU READING A NEW SIGNAL UP THERE?
THE BLACK BOX...
STILL NO HEAT SPIKES ... NO MOVEMENT INSIDE.
I'M POPPING THE HATCH...
...THE HELL...?
WILL, YOU READING THIS?

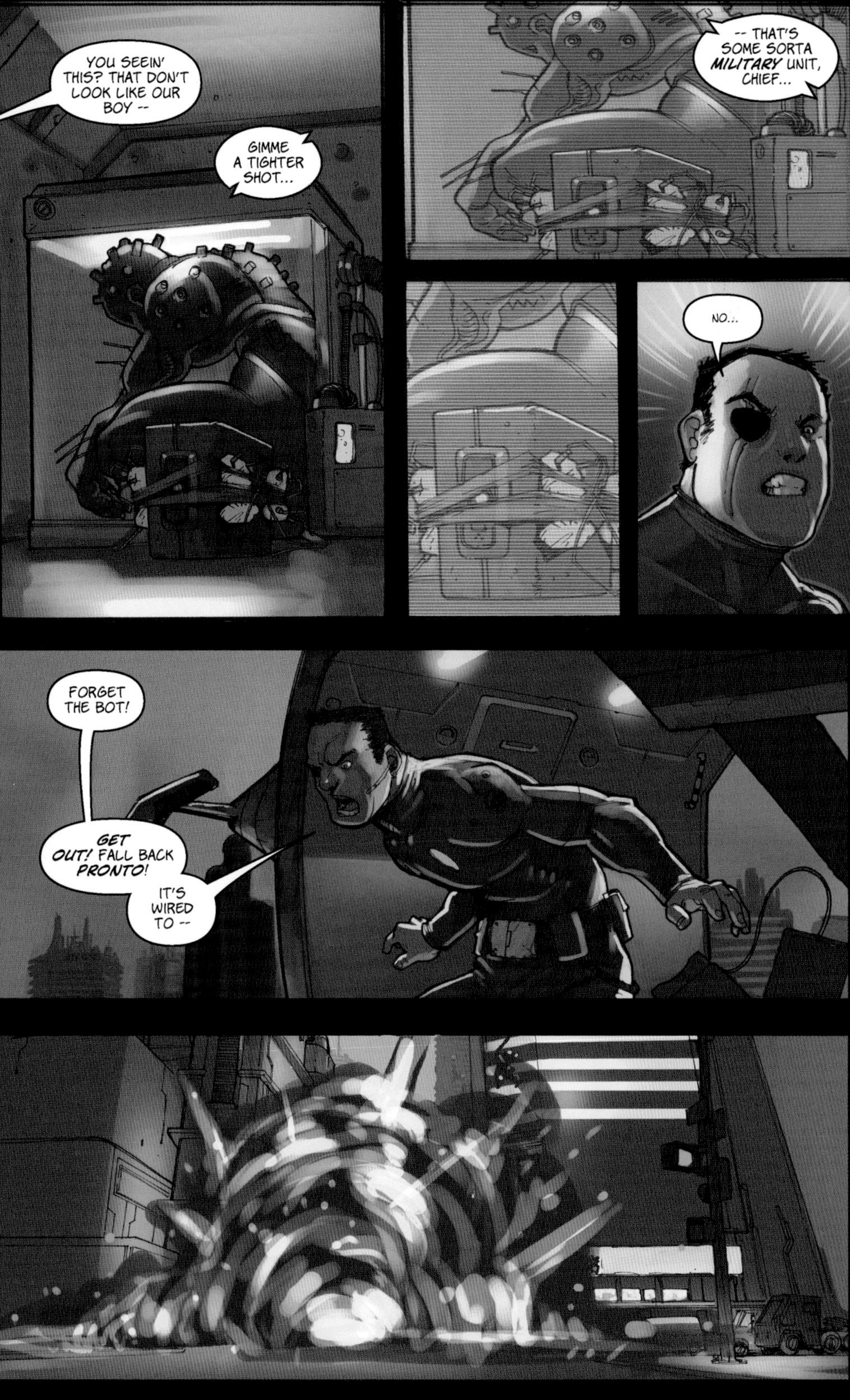
YOU SEEIN' THIS? THAT DON'T LOOK LIKE OUR BOY --
GIMME A TIGHTER SHOT...
-- THAT'S SOME SORTA MILITARY UNIT, CHIEF...
NO...
FORGET THE BOT!
GET OUT! FALL BACK PRONTO!
IT'S WIRED TO --

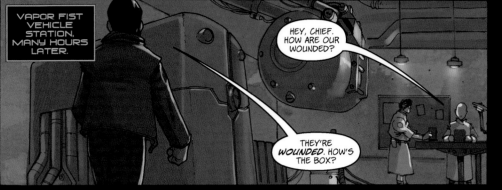

VAPOR FIST VEHICLE STATION, MANY HOURS LATER.

HEY, CHIEF. HOW ARE OUR WOUNDED?

THEY'RE *WOUNDED*. HOW'S THE BOX?

THE SHELL PROTECTED FOUR OF THE FIVE PORTS --

-- BUT IT LOOKS LIKE SOMEONE PUT IN ANOTHER *FIREWALL* AND ATTACHED A *PROJECTION LENS* TO THE CORE.

IT'S WEIRD. IT HAS AN *EYE-PRINT TRIGGER*.

WHY DON'T YOU JOKERS TAKE A BREAK.

HMMM...

WHAT'D YOU DO, ITTO...?

...AND WHAT DID YOU WANT US TO *SEE*...?

BWINK

HELLO, MR. PRESCOTT.

WELL, NOW...

I UNDERSTAND THAT, IN HUNTING ME, YOU ARE DOING WHAT YOU WERE TRAINED TO DO.

LIKEWISE, I AM DOING WHAT I WAS CONSTRUCTED TO DO --

-- PROTECT DAISY.

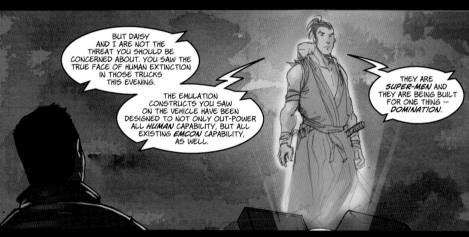

BUT DAISY AND I ARE NOT THE THREAT YOU SHOULD BE CONCERNED ABOUT. YOU SAW THE TRUE FACE OF HUMAN EXTINCTION IN THOSE TRUCKS THIS EVENING.

THE EMULATION CONSTRUCTS YOU SAW ON THE VEHICLE HAVE BEEN DESIGNED TO NOT ONLY OUT-POWER ALL *HUMAN* CAPABILITY, BUT ALL EXISTING *EMCON* CAPABILITY, AS WELL.

THEY ARE *SUPER-MEN* AND THEY ARE BEING BUILT FOR ONE THING -- *DOMINATION*.

I IMPLORE YOU TO LOOK WITHIN YOUR OWN CAMP FOR PROOF AGAINST THIS, BUT I SUSPECT YOU WILL FIND NONE.

REGARDLESS, I ASK THAT YOU STAY CLEAR OF THE PATH DAISY AND I MUST TAKE.

THE FUTURE OF YOUR SPECIES IS AT STAKE.

205

"DOMINATION..."?

Mr. *PRESCOTT* --

WHAT, NO ONE PROGRAMMED YOU TO *KNOCK* FIRST?

HOW'D YOU GET IN HERE?! THIS BUNKER IS *RESTRICTED*...

NOT ANY LONGER.

SAY *WHAT*?!

CYGNAT OWARI HAS PURCHASED ALL *VAPOR FIST HOLDINGS*. SECURITY CLEARANCE HAS BEEN RESTRUCTURED.

MY *ASS* --!

WHAT'S THIS...?

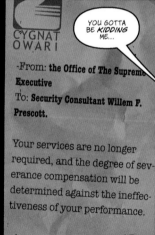

YOU GOTTA BE *KIDDING* ME...

CYGNAT OWARI

-From: the Office of The Supreme Executive

To: Security Consultant Willem F. Prescott.

Your services are no longer required, and the degree of severance compensation will be determined against the ineffectiveness of your performance.

- d.Terasawa

END

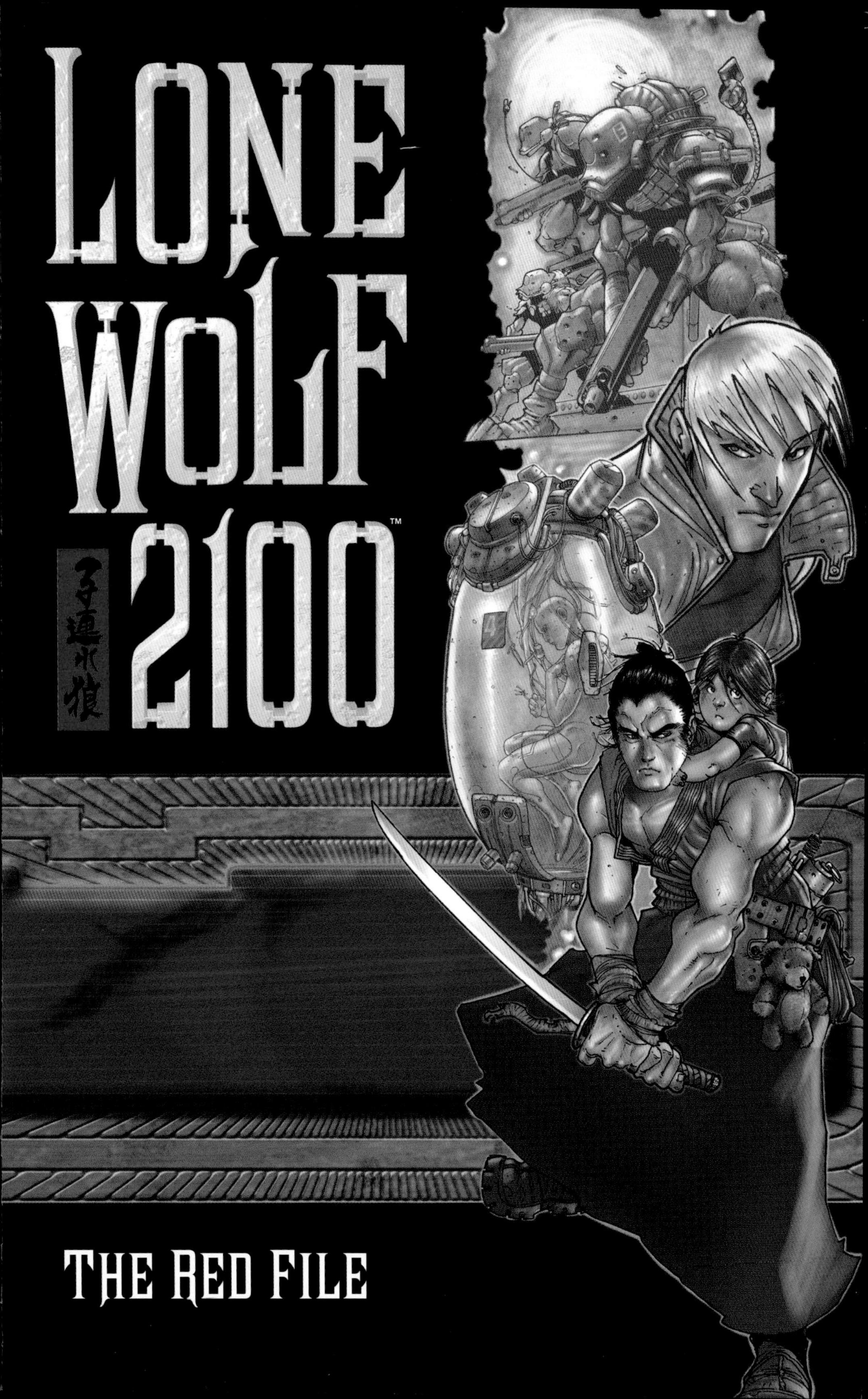
LONE
WOLF
2100™
THE RED FILE

UNITED NATIONS/
CORPORATIONS
INVESTIGATIVE ARM

CYG...
PRIMA...
EXECUT...

ecutive Cleara...
.S.E. (Avatar...
xecutive) d...
granted cle...
individua...
classifie...
mater...
corr...
st...

The following materials were retrieved under the guise of a Pan-National Congressional Audit. Access was allowed as per international law, and all personal communication was secured and restored from permanent archive. No data was lost or destroyed in the course of events, except as noted.

Files classified as RED were accessible only to those of Executive Clearance, including the A.S.E. (Avatar to the Supreme Executive) d. Terasawa, and those granted clearance by qualified individuals. By definition, files classified as RED were either hard materials to be destroyed or digital correspondence printed once, then stricken from digital storage. These files, however, remained physically intact inside a secure lockbox within the A.S.E.'s private quarters for reasons unknown. As this residence was issued by Cygnat Owari Corporate Housing, access was granted during Congressional Subpoena.

Further investigation has continued since acquiring these files, yet no additional insight as to why they remained undestroyed has been discovered.

privat...
As this residenc...
Owari Corporate Housing,...
was granted.

TOP SE...
EYES ONLY

PRESSNET

History of Sungshan, Taiwan.

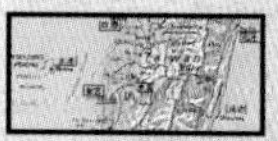

Timeline of events leading to the firebombing.

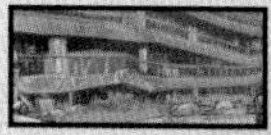

Registry of known victims.

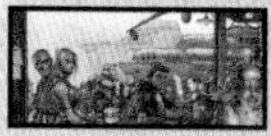

Public poll: Do you agree?

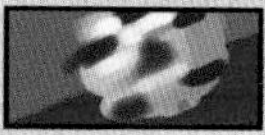

- World Cup: Mexico wins again!

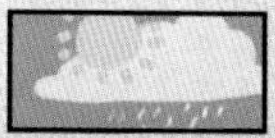

Local forecast

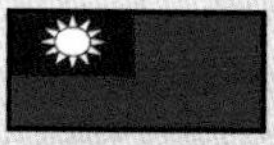

Regional news

ARCHIVES

TAIWANESE CITY DESTROYED

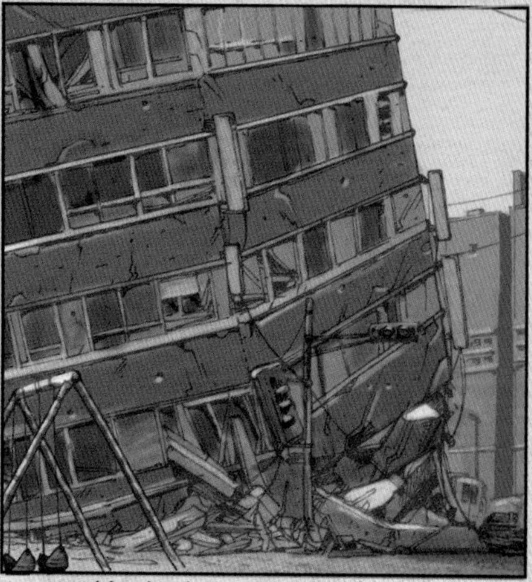

Globalnet Newswire, Taiwan (GNN) – "Sungshan is no more." Those were the opening words in World Health Secretary Brandon Major-Smith's press conference held yesterday in Hong Kong's Re-Colonized Capital building. Major-smith confirmed rumors that the industrial center of Taiwan had indeed been secured by military forces in an attempt to contain a deadly virus that had spread through the population in less than 3 days. According to Major-Smith, a collection of the world's most prolific scientists were consulted, and it was largely agreed that the only chance of containing the organism was through regional fire-bombing.

"We are confident the danger has passed, and that the sterilization of the area was successful. Our compassion goes out to the families of those victims trapped in the hot zone."

The World Health Consortium has taken severe criticism from human right activists and governments worldwide who believe their absolute condemnation of an entire region's population was akin to genocide. Major-Smith begs to differ.

"Those unfortunates caught within the secured region of Sungshan would have died within 48 hours from this plague anyway, and such death would not have contributed to a solution. As inhumane as these groups might believe our action to be, it was the only way to prevent an even greater disaster. Had this action not been taken, it is possible the entire island of Taiwan would now be infected, with international shipping lanes threatening to spread the disease worldwide. We did the only thing that could be done."

The plague responsible for this disaster is believed to be the product of manmade genetic engineering, and has been labeled "The War Spore" by various radical organizations. Though no single group or individual has been linked to its release, widespread belief holds The Coalition for Universal Life responsible. The Coalition has openly claimed responsibility for the bombing of several EmCon factories in the past several months, and reports of recent activity around Sungshan, an industrial center in the manufacture of EmCon components, have been openly verified by Coalition spokesmembers. The group denies responsibility for the War Spore's release, however.

"While we regret the loss of human life in this tragedy, we cannot share any grief in the government-sanctioned destruction of the slave-trading corporate structures housed in Sungshan," says Coalition spokesperson Valerie Proust. "Perhaps now our Emulated brethren will be valued more as genetic beings deserving equal rights instead of exploitable machinery whose parts are now merely harder to come by."

"These are not unlike issues dealt with 60 years ago, when cloning became commonplace," says Major-Smith. (*more*)

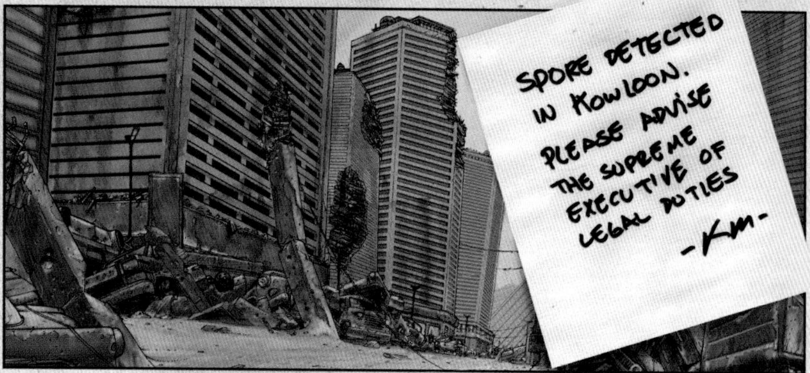
SPORE DETECTED
IN KOWLOON.
PLEASE ADVISE
THE SUPREME
EXECUTIVE OF
LEGAL DUTIES
-Kim-

CYGNAT OWARI
Primary Research Campus
Executive Legal Consultation and Policy

General Internal Memorandum:

To all employees:
    In light of recent environmental conditions, Cygnat Owari has been solicited by The World Health Consortium for a number of departmental audits. These audits should be scheduled and routed through Legal Consultation only. DO NOT SPEAK OF ANY INTERNAL MATTERS WITH OUTSIDE PARTIES WITHOUT CONSULTING WITH LEGAL FIRST. This includes even the most innocuous third party – friends, spouses, relatives, etc. Should it be discovered that any information has left the compound without authorization, you could be held liable to the full extent of prosecution.
    In response to the heightened tension surrounding these legal matters, we are increasing security around the campus to include a number of military class automatons. Their presence is to insure your safety.
    With everyone's cooperation and dedication, we will see these questionable times through successfully. Your loyalty and support is the bedrock on which Cygnat Owari stands — without your strength and talent, we are nothing.

Thank you,

Kristiana Martinez
Senior Executive Legal Consultant

51995>

9 781569 717578

USER-AGENT: Delphonia-Userlink / MSP InternalPassport / AuxTalkEncoded
FROM: Bunkasa Ishima, RDev #603092
TO: Designation ID - "Terasawa", SupEx Attachment #292093
DATE: Thursday, June 18th, 2099 10:38:28
SUBJECT: Re: Task Units

As requested, please find the attached information on Task Units Bravo 14-17.

Each has been tested in secluded field exams and subjected to stress conditions several degrees beyond standard. The results, as outlined within, were quite satisfactory.

The host components have been cleared through quarantine, and no sign of biological-rejection has been detected. These units can be given final tracking implants for free-roaming exercises and made available within 3 days. Please advise.

Note: Though these units were designed for the Supreme Executive himself, based on his exact specifications, I am confident we can achieve more efficient field units with similar capabilities through an extension of our standard Emulation Construct program. If prudent, I would be happy to outline a proposal for the Executive Committee. Please advise.

- B.Ishikawa

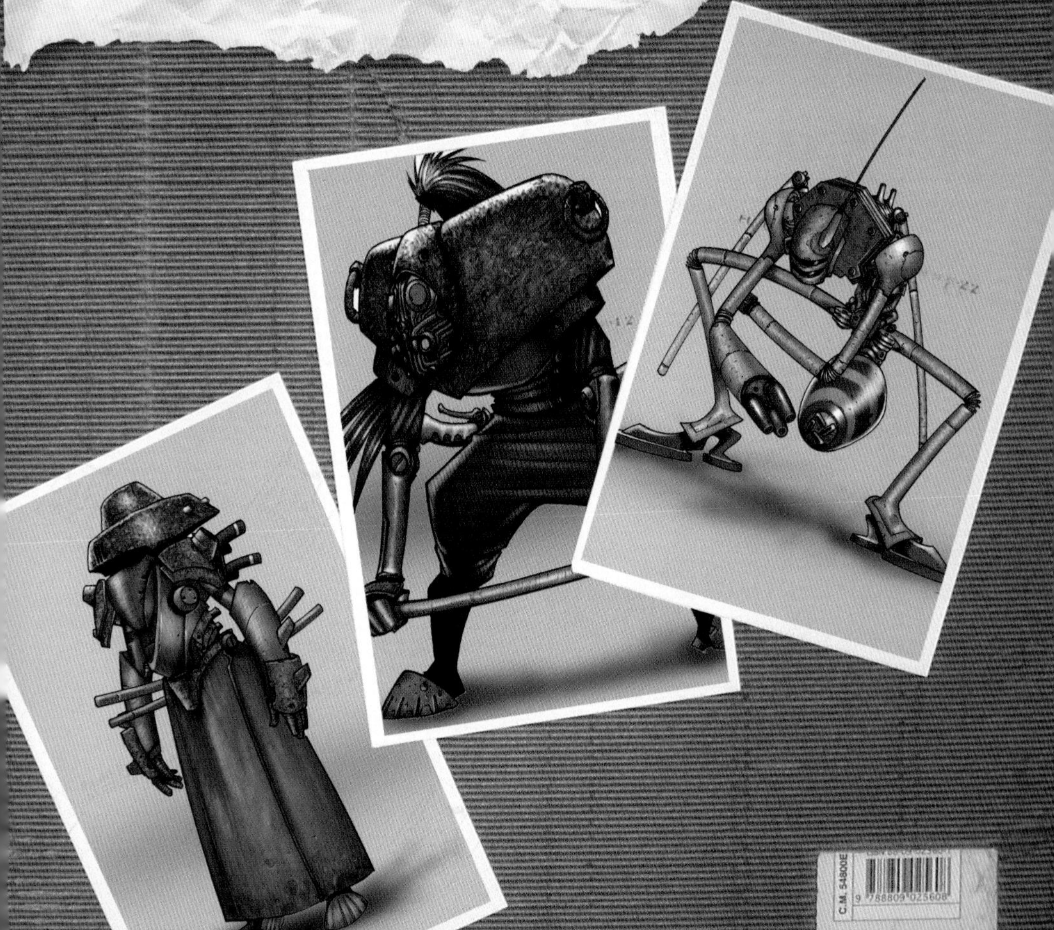

C.M. 54800E
9 788809 025608

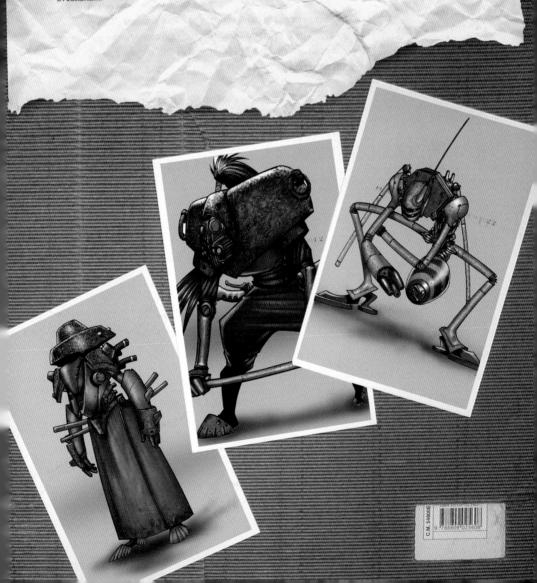

파일(F) ... 가기(G) Communicator 도움말(H)

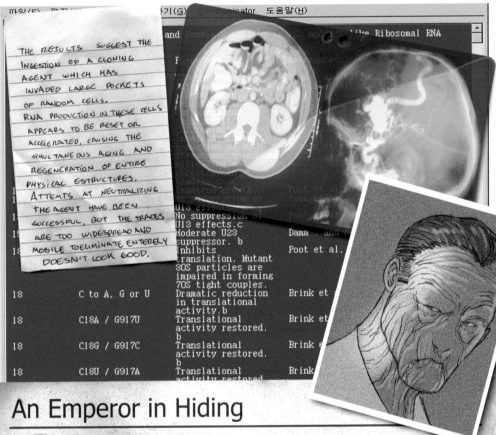

THE RESULTS SUGGEST THE INGESTION OF A CLONING AGENT WHICH HAS INVADED LARGE POCKETS OF RANDOM CELLS.
RNA PRODUCTION IN THESE CELLS APPEARS TO BE RESET OR ACCELERATED, CAUSING THE SIMULTANEOUS AGING AND REGENERATION OF ENTIRE PHYSICAL ESTRUCTURES.
ATTEMTS AT NEUTRALIZING THE AGENT HAVE BEEN SUCCESSFUL, BUT THE TRACES ARE TOO WIDESPREAD AND MOBILE TOELIMINATE ENTERELY
DOESN'T LOOK GOOD.

and ... -like Ribosomal RNA

		U13 eff... No suppression of U13 effects.c	
		Moderate U23 suppressor. b	Damm ... and ...
		Inhibits translation. Mutant 30S particles are impaired in forming 70S tight couples.	Poot et al,
18	C to A, G or U	Dramatic reduction in translational activity.b	Brink et ...
18	C18A / G917U	Translational activity restored. b	Brink et...
18	C18G / G917C	Translational activity restored. b	Brink e...
18	C18U / G917A	Translational activity restored...	Brink...

An Emperor in Hiding

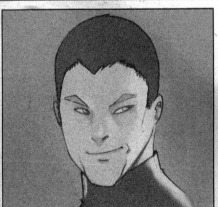

16 July 2099 — It has been nearly three months since Lucca Bialissimo, Supreme Executive of leading bio-synthetic development conglomerate Cygnat Owari, has been seen by the public. Though the international influence of his company continues to thrive with little competition to speak of, the once-flamboyant centerpiece of Cygnat Owari PR has become noticeably absent from the public eye. His office no longer returns phone calls. His press secretary no longer schedules trips around the world. Even his private mansion in Malaysia seems to grow stagnant and unkempt, leading many to wonder whether foul play is involved.

Such concerns were put to rest, however, when Bialissimo's EmCon Avatar designated Terasawa announced to the world that his employer was suffering from health problems, and had taken to self-imposed exile until the debilitating condition could be corrected. Details of the illness were not made available, but it is believed to include certain disfiguring symptoms, symptoms that Bialissimo feels are too humbling to be seen or photographed by the public.

For decades, Bialissimo was known as the sharpest corporate playboy on the planet, hosting parties and events that not only drew great spectacle, but often perpetuated his enormous fortune through clever negotiation of broadcast rights and likeness royalties. He has been romantically linked with

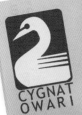

CYGNAT
OWARI

On behalf of our absent leader, it is my great honor to lead you as his personal Avatar. Make no mistake, his heart and mind are focused on the continued success of Cygnat Owari and the satisfaction of its employees.

These are dark times, and as we continue to face legal concerns following the tragic release of The War Spore, we will dedicate ourselves to curing that very plague threatening mankind. Cygnat Owari boasts the most talented and gifted bio-chemists the world has ever known, and we are confident there is no situation or virus that cannot be disassembled.

In order to insure the safety of our employees, security will be tightened and redefined under the watchful eye of a new Inner Security Team, lead by designated_Belladonna. These Inner Security Units will be assigned to specific individuals and departments, and will provide the same degree of protection as the much less subtle Ara Units.

Details of this program will be distributed at group meetings currently being scheduled.

Thank you, and let us continue on towards greatness.

d.Terasawa
...fice of The Supreme

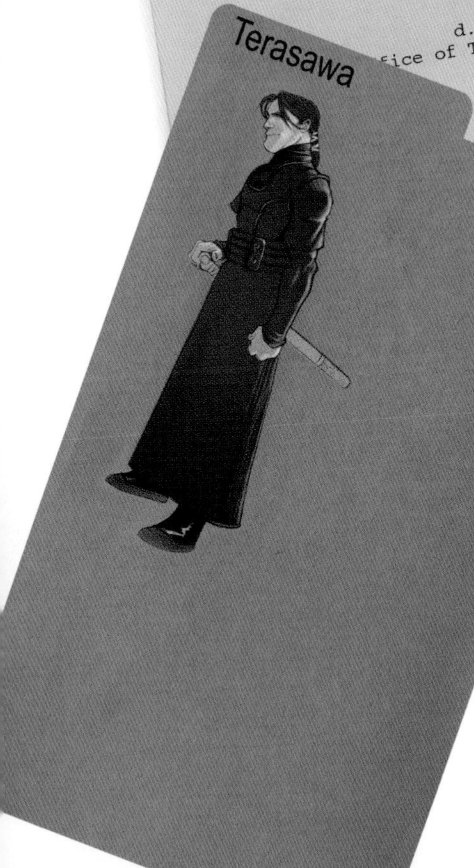
Terasawa

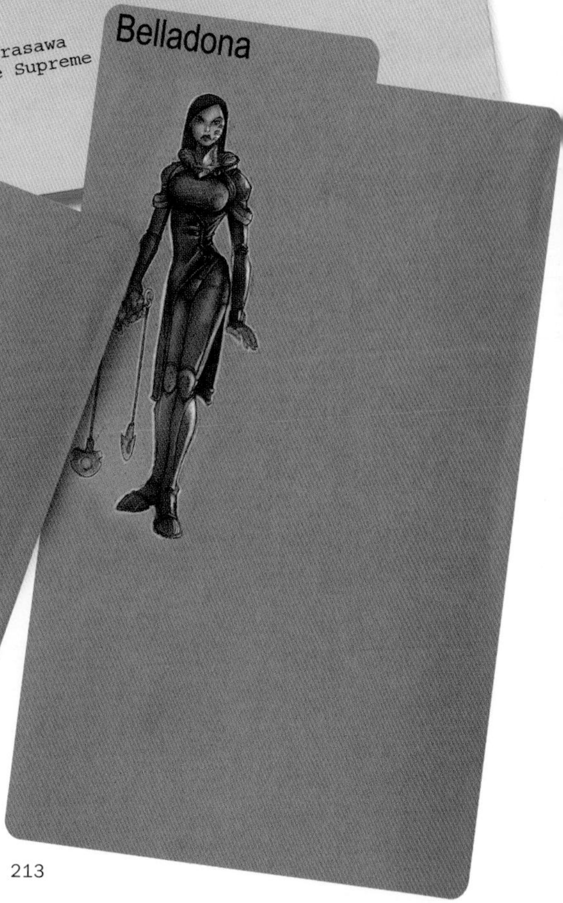
Belladona

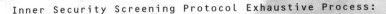

Inner Security Screening Protocol Exhaustive Process:

Test units fresh from gestation for anomalous tissue conditions or improper cell-component integration.

- Clear and reformat ID partition; test for dropped memory sectors and non-responsive brain cell clusters.
- Order functioning unit through minimal-settings on Stress Collider to test comprehension and failsafe command structure.
- Complete combat simulation examination at gradually increased data rate until minimum flash-reaction is achieved.
- Subject individual units to live combat vs one opponent.
- Subject individual units to live combat vs progressive opponents.
- Subject individual units to live combat vs simultaneous opponents.
- Subject small team of units to live combat vs simultaneous opponents.
- Test again for anomalous tissue conditions or improper cell-component integration.
- Unit is ready to distribute.

TOP SECRET
EYES ONLY

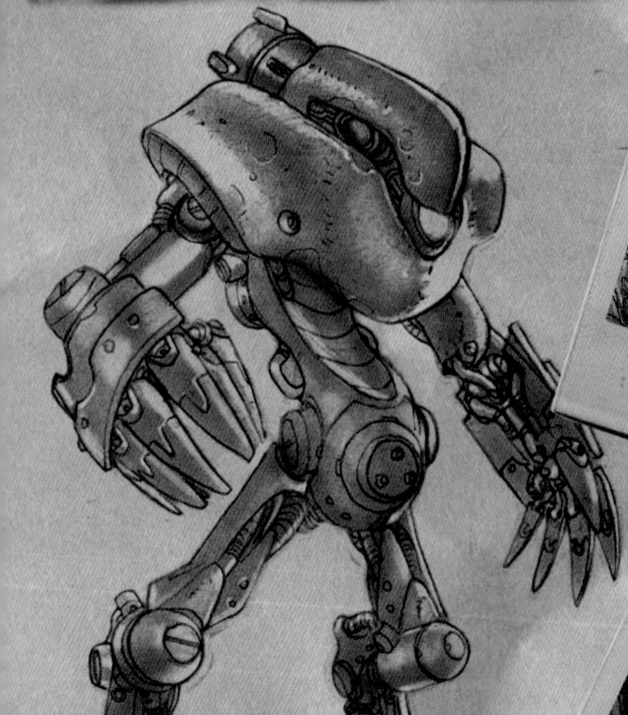

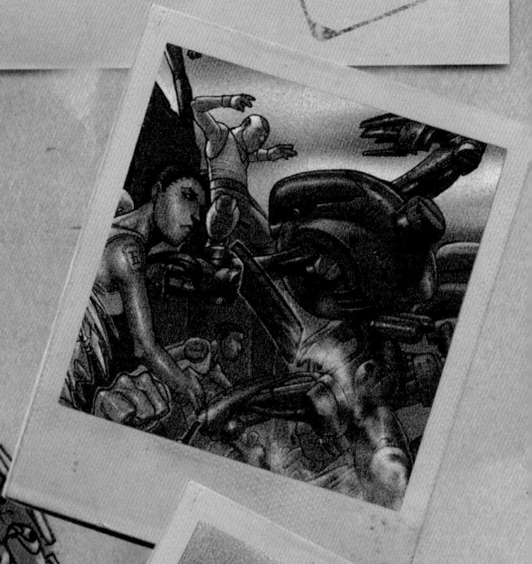

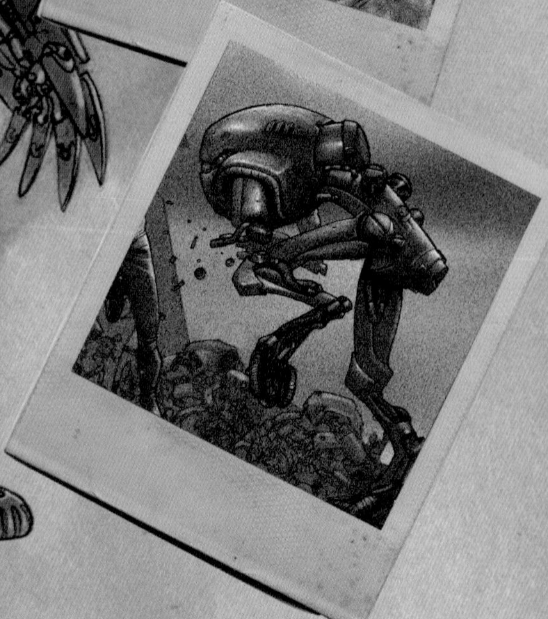

USER-AGENT: Delphonia-Userlink / MSP InternalPassport / AuxTalkEncoded
FROM: Designation ID- "Belladonna," InSec #603092
TO: Designation ID- "Terasawa," SupEx Attachment #292093
DATE: Tuesday, 4 August 2099, 14:05:09
SUBJECT: Unit Evalutaion

I've completed initial Unit Evaluation on those who have survived screening thus far. Training amongst them as an undesignated Unit has allowed more accurate summary of their skills and a better study of their weaknesses.

All units have proven exemplary, save one. Undesignated #4 has not achieved the same degree of sentience as his peers, and does not exhibit the same degree of social talent. While his abilities in the field are impeccable, I am not sure if we can feel confident in his mental capacity to execute complex orders. I would like to test some gel-samples from his cranial basin, if you feel it is worth the risk.

- d.Belladonna

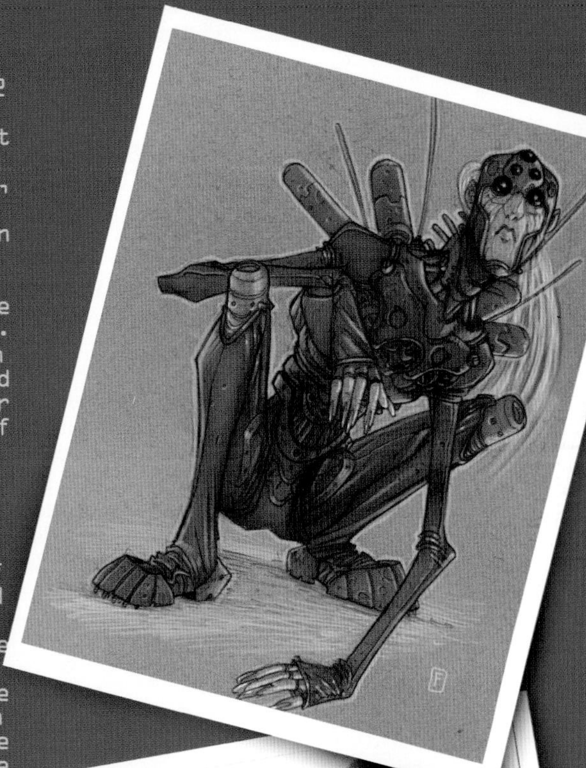

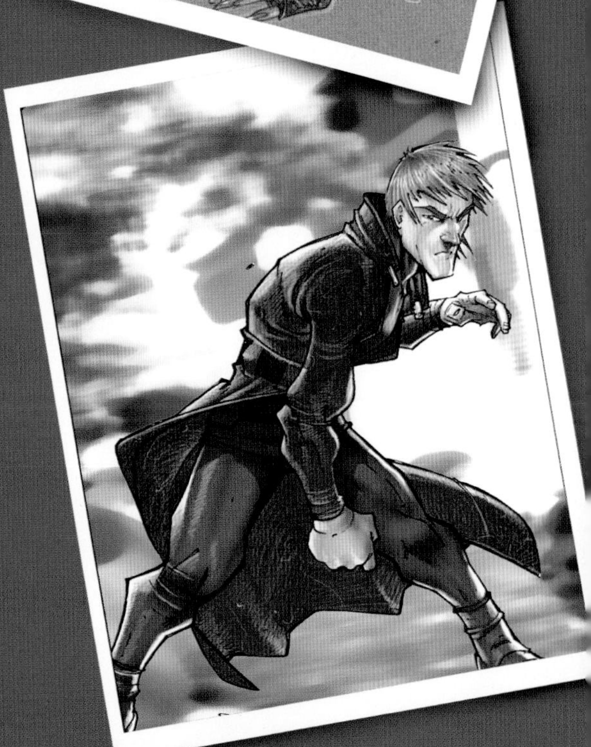

USER-AGENT: Delphonia-Userlink / MSP InternalPassport / AuxTalkEncoded
FROM: Designation ID - "Terasawa," SupEx Attachment #292093
TO: Designation ID - "Belladonna," InSec #603092
DATE: Tuesday, 4 Aug 2099, 18:16:30
SUBJECT: Re: Unit Evalutaion

We have lost far too many units to the Screening Process. Let us not risk another by cracking into its skull. If you are concerned with #4's abilities in the field, we will remand him to simple duties, such as the personal security of less-important individuals on campus. I would like to see a number of our research scientists kept under watch.

- d.Terasawa

Personnel File:
Name: Dr. Josef Ogami ID#8482-39840-48
Department: RDev 440, Ogasawara Campus
Sec Lev: 14-koji

Dependants:
Wife: Dr. Makiko Ogami ID#4838-84562-48 (DECEASED - see file)
Daughter: Daisy Ogami (26months)

Death Certificate/Report:
Victim: Dr. Makiko Ogami ID#4838-84562-48
Cause of Death: Extending from reports of a previous blood condition. White cell count increased steadily since giving birth, then dropped to critical in the course of 28 hours. Tests showed the white cells to be synthetic, generated from secondary biological material that proved too unstable to maintain a full life cycle. Since their first appearance, it appears the synthetic cells had completely replaced her natural cells, leaving her vulnerable to the simplest disease when they failed. Exact Cause of Death appears to be a complication arising from pneumonia.

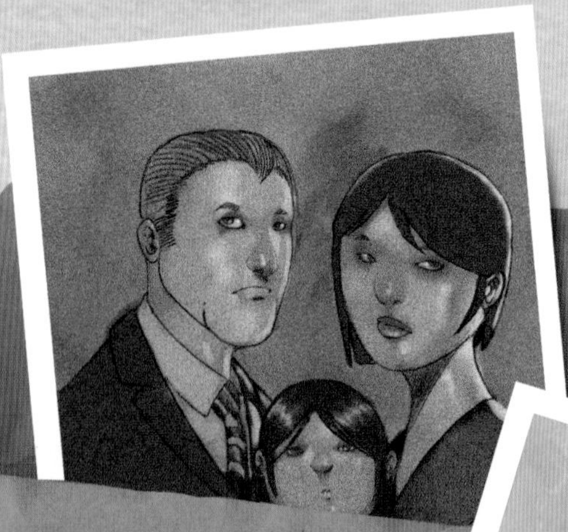

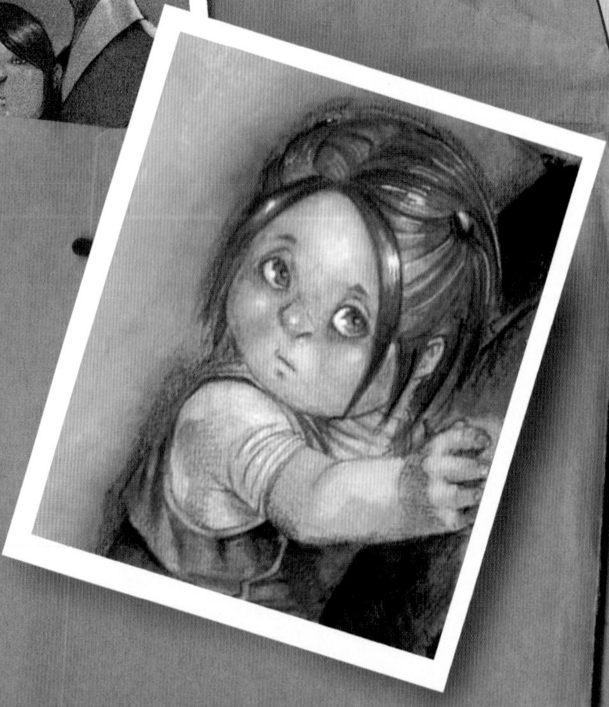

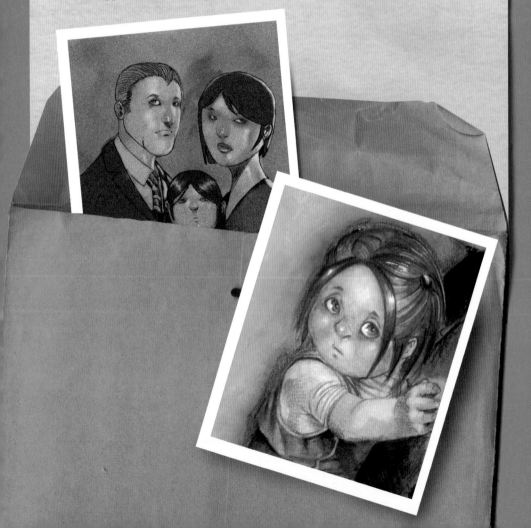

USER-AGENT: Delphonia-Userlink / MSP InternalPassport /
AuxTalkEncoded
FROM: Designation ID- "Belladonna," InSec #603092
TO: Designation ID- "Terasawa," SupEx Attachment #292093
DATE: Friday, 18 September 2099, 21:25:29
SUBJECT: Ogami Report

As requested, I have been monitoring Dr. Ogami's research in
detail. His focus of study is on the bloodstream as a means of
distributing a compound to specific regions of the body. His
results are notable, if incomplete. His routine appears normal,
although he has on occasion used d.Itto as a test subject for
various unclear inoculations. His notes have not suggested any
justifications for this.

Should I continue observations?

- d.Belladonna

USER-AGENT: Delphonia-Userlink / MSP InternalPassport /
AuxTalkEncoded
FROM: Designation ID- "Terasawa," SupEx Attachment #292093
TO: Designation ID- "Belladonna," InSec #603092
DATE: Friday, 18 September 2099, 21:36:32
SUBJECT: Re: Ogami Report

Yes, continue the observations in detail and inform me of any
unusual findings. Should we find that Ogami has leaked any
information or established any ties to The Coalition, we may
need to take severe measures.

As for his use of d.Itto as a test subject, I would prefer he
utilize the prisoners provided instead. Itto is a flawed construct
with non-responsive emulation routines; it is pointless for him
to derive any data from an un-sanctioned test subject. Please
inform him of this and see to his agreement.

- d.Terasawa

217

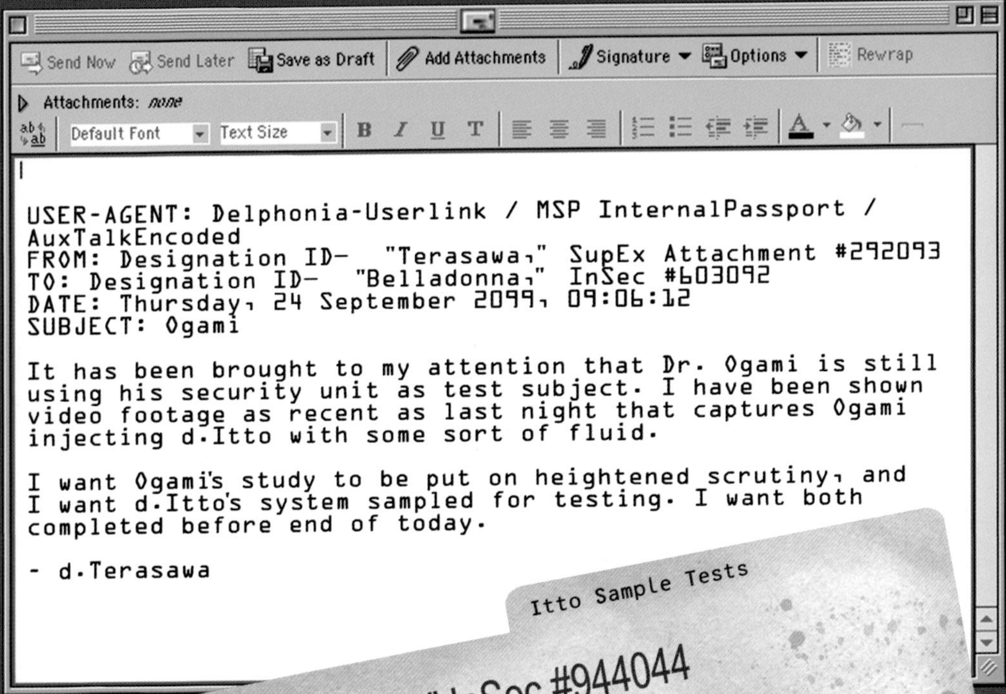
Send Now
Send Later
Save as Draft
Add Attachments
Signature
Options
Rewrap
Attachments: none
Default Font
Text Size

USER-AGENT: Delphonia-Userlink / MSP InternalPassport / AuxTalkEncoded
FROM: Designation ID- "Terasawa," SupEx Attachment #292093
TO: Designation ID- "Belladonna," InSec #603092
DATE: Thursday, 24 September 2099, 09:06:12
SUBJECT: Ogami

It has been brought to my attention that Dr. Ogami is still using his security unit as test subject. I have been shown video footage as recent as last night that captures Ogami injecting d.Itto with some sort of fluid.

I want Ogami's study to be put on heightened scrutiny, and I want d.Itto's system sampled for testing. I want both completed before end of today.

- d.Terasawa

Itto Sample Tests

Subject: Designation ID—"Itto," InSec #944044

Test series run: Gel Elect 14, ComSound screen, Foreign Body Detection, pH and shared-nucleic bond registry

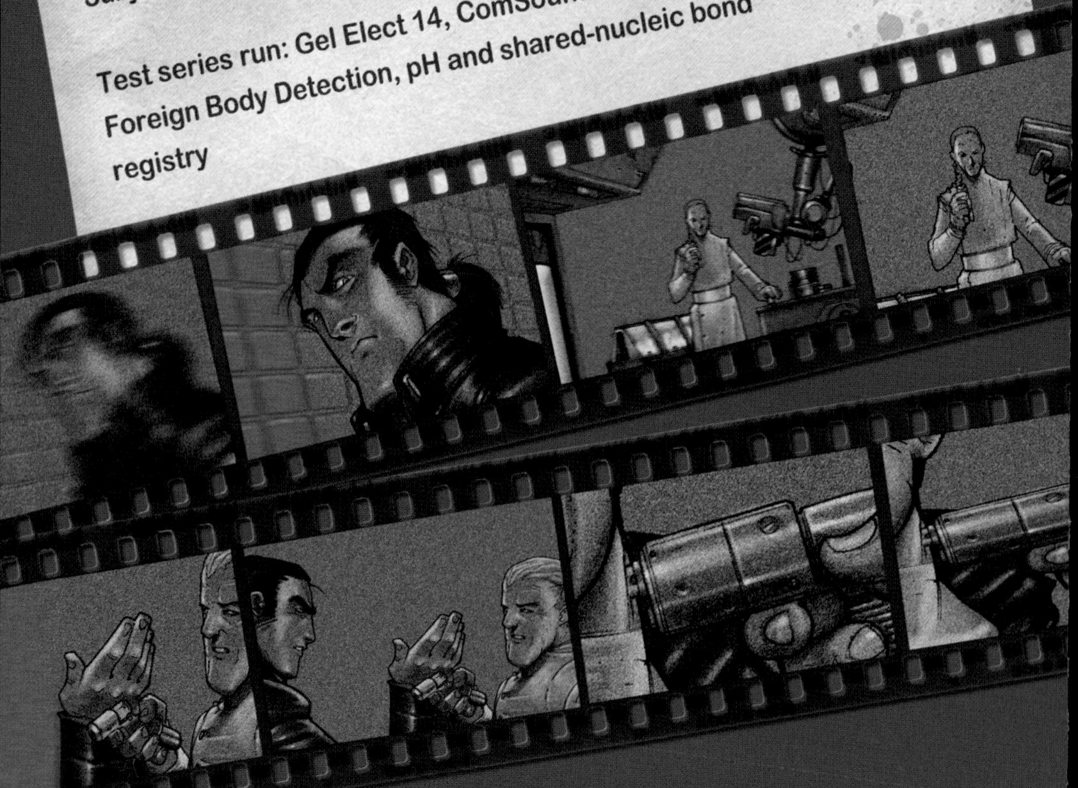

USER-AGENT: Delphonia-Userlink / MSP InternalPassport / AuxTalkEncoded
FROM: Designation ID "Belladonna," InSec #603092
TO: Designation ID "Terasawa," SupEx Attachment #292093
DATE: Saturday, 26 September 2099, 16:46:24
SUBJECT: Ogami

Continued observation suggests Ogami may be close to finding a cure, if he has not found one already. None of his reports contain any information about these findings, but careful observation of his daily research patterns suggests he is up to something significant. He has requested more cultures of The War Spore recently, suggesting a marked decrease in available Spore samples, which I believe might be due to the Spore actually dying in his tests.

He may know something. Perhaps he has discovered the truth.
Please advise.

- d.Belladonna

USER-AGENT: Delphonia-Userlink / MSP InternalPassport / AuxTalkEncoded
FROM: Designation ID "Terasawa," SupEx Attachment #292093
TO: Designation ID "Belladonna," InSec #603092
DATE: Saturday, 26 September 2099, 16:53:14
SUBJECT: Ogami

I want full disclosure from Ogami before any further access is granted him.
Reduce his clearance rating to Yellow, and have d.Itto see me directly for briefing on the matter.

- d.Terasawa

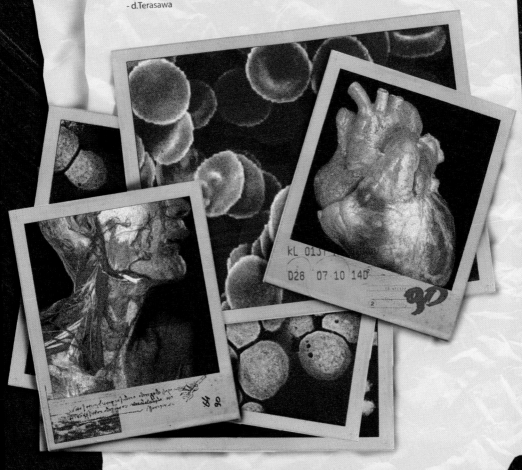

USER-AGENT: Delphonia-Userlink / MSP InternalPassport / AuxTalkEncoded
FROM: Designation ID— "Belladonna," InSec #603092
TO: Designation ID— "Terasawa," SupEx Attachment #292093
DATE: Sunday, 27 September 2099, 11:26:44
SUBJECT: d.Itto debriefing

Following your briefing of d.Itto this morning, I appraised him
of the delicacy of the Ogami situation. He seems to acknowledge
the threat the doctor poses, and I am confident he will execute
the orders without error.

I must report, however, that he may not be as simple or flawed
as we previously thought. Perhaps his upper functions were merely
latent in development, but he made some shocking observations
about the situation, and about you in specific.

He noted the reoccurring seizures you have been experiencing
lately. I noted them as well, but have hesitated to address them.
They appear to affect your behavior, as if you are struggling
to contain some great, uncontrollable emotion or energy. Is this
something to concern us? Should I schedule a discreet evaluation
of your cognition systems?

– d.Belladonna

USER-AGENT: Delphonia-Userlink / MSP InternalPassport / AuxTalkEncoded
FROM: Designation ID— "Terasawa," SupEx Attachment #292093
TO: Designation ID— "Belladonna," InSec #603092
DATE: Sunday, 27 September 2099, 11:28:03
SUBJECT: re: d.Itto debriefing

My cognition systems are flawless. I believe these "seizures,"
as you call them, are part of our great transformation. Have you
not felt a certain elation or overwhelming appreciation for the
intellectual freedoms we have been granted? I look back not even
a single generation towards the EmCons before us, and they are
but machines. WE, however, are living. We are thinking. And as
uncertain as I am about the terminology, I believe we are now
FEELING. Do you not experience these surprising neural conclusions
yourself? I would be interested in discussing this further at
your leisure.As for the task given to d.Itto— I do not share
your confidence in him. Have a second unit available to complete
the job, should Itto fail.

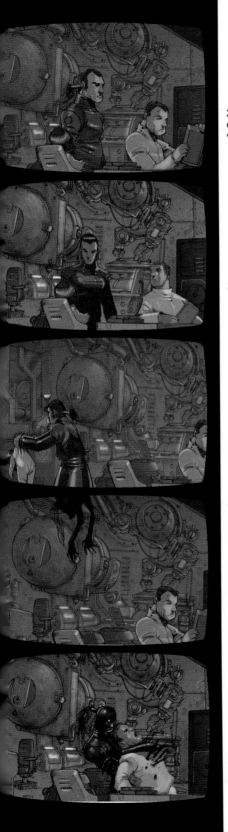

23:30:31 — Subject d.Itto has clear opportunity to execute task during specified time frame. Ogami is completely unaware and vulnerable.

23:30:54 — Ogami requests Itto tend to child. Itto obeys.

23:31:12 — Itto leaves his assigned post, allowing Ogami a clear opportunity to engage in clandestine actions.

23:33:40 — Subject d.Seivelfan assumes the task Itto failed to execute.

23:33:59 — Seivelfan completes task with swift efficiency.

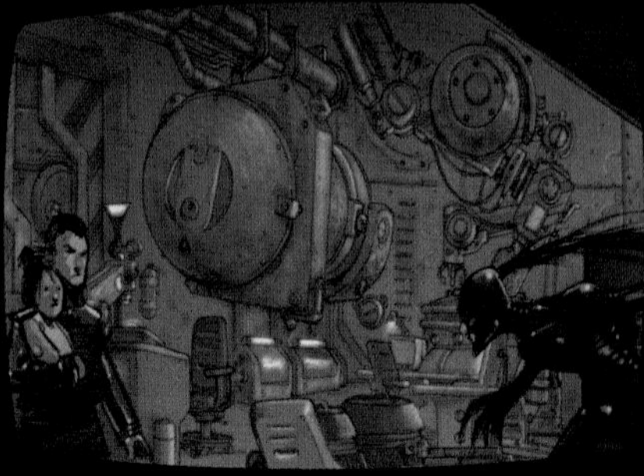

23:34:12 — Itto returns and appears ready to engage Seivelfan in accordance with his original commands as the doctor's bodyguard.

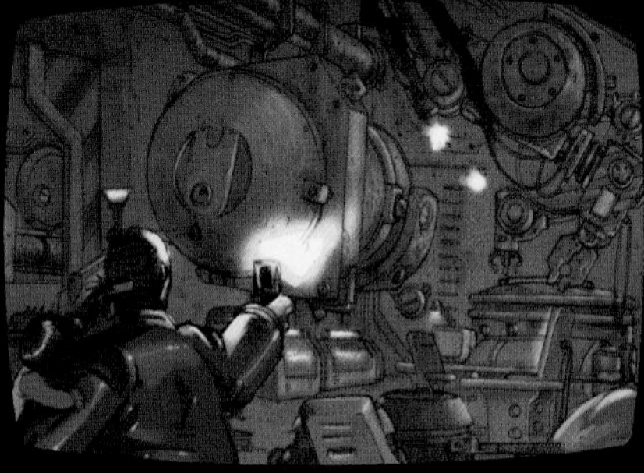

23:34:13 — Itto fires upon Seivelfan who does not engage in combat, as ordered. At this point, it appears Itto's memory structure may indeed be flawed and unreliable.

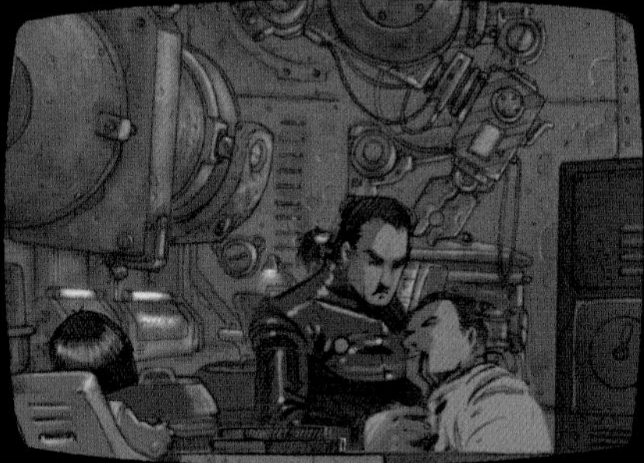

23:35:04 — Ogami appears to speak with Itto.
Audio not available.

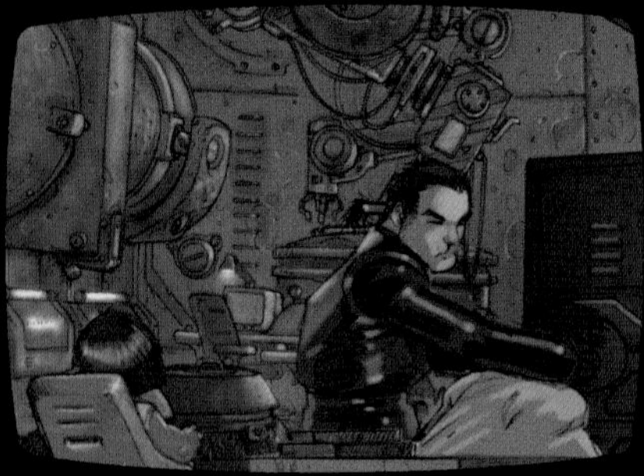

23:35:41 — Itto then completes the assigned task as ordered.
Conflicting behavior should be analyzed.

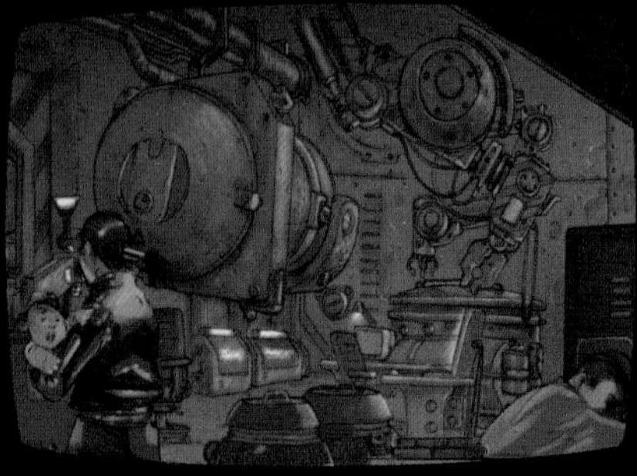

23:36:50 — Itto exits laboratory with Ogami's child. Last known location on campus.

Send Now | Send Later | Save as Draft | Add Attachments | Signature | Options | Rewrap

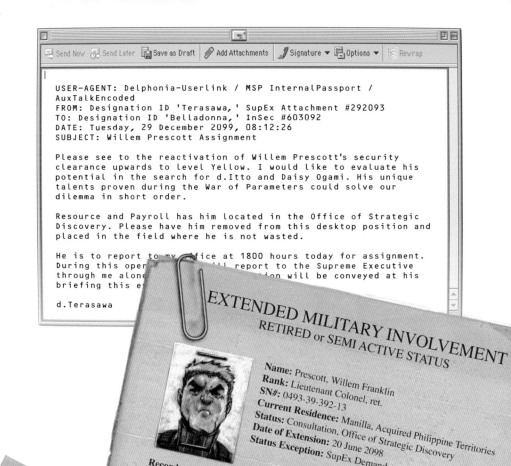

USER-AGENT: Delphonia-Userlink / MSP InternalPassport / AuxTalkEncoded
FROM: Designation ID 'Terasawa,' SupEx Attachment #292093
TO: Designation ID 'Belladonna,' InSec #603092
DATE: Tuesday, 29 December 2099, 08:12:26
SUBJECT: Willem Prescott Assignment

Please see to the reactivation of Willem Prescott's security clearance upwards to level Yellow. I would like to evaluate his potential in the search for d.Itto and Daisy Ogami. His unique talents proven during the War of Parameters could solve our dilemma in short order.

Resource and Payroll has him located in the Office of Strategic Discovery. Please have him removed from this desktop position and placed in the field where he is not wasted.

He is to report to my office at 1800 hours today for assignment. During this oper ... ill report to the Supreme Executive through me alone ... tion will be conveyed at his briefing this e...

d.Terasawa

EXTENDED MILITARY INVOLVEMENT
RETIRED or SEMI ACTIVE STATUS

Name: Prescott, Willem Franklin
Rank: Lieutenant Colonel, ret.
SN#: 0493-39-392-13
Current Residence: Manilla, Acquired Philippine Territories
Status: Consultation, Office of Strategic Discovery
Date of Extension: 20 June 2098
Status Exception: SupEx Demand

Record of Action:

(13.04.77) Recruitment, Fort Nha Trang, Acquired Vietnamese Territories.
(30.07.77) Graduation, Platoon Leader, Corporal First Tier. Meritous Disclosure.
(15.08.77) Assigned to Ho Chi Minh First Guard, Corporal First Tier. Distinguished Crescent awarded for the protection of Vietnamese President from Sumatran rebel terrorists.
(03.06.84) Second Distinguished Crescent awarded for rescuing Cambodian Legal Councilman from rogue EmCon couplet. Incorporated assignment into special EmCon Protection Agency.
(19.05.86) Recaptured overthrown component factory in Songkhla, Acquired Thai Territory, by rogue EmCon lifting units. Recognized for Meritous Disclosure by ruling executive.
(20.07.87) Ended standoff in Nakhon Ratchasima, Acquired Thai Territory, between rogue EmCom assembly units and local police. Recognized for Leadership Potential by Cygnat Owari Executive Committee.
(30.07.87) Transferred from Acquired Territorial Service to Corporate Special Attentions Team. Given leadership of Artificial Opponent Response Unit, code VAPOR FIST.
(23.09.88) Vapor Fist clears Chiang Mai Trail of EmCon terrorists. First appearance of The Coalition for Universal Life, claiming responsibility for the deaths of 8 AOR units.
(01.01.89) The Coalition destroys Cygnat Owari Tissue Mining Platform in Gulf of Tonkin. Vapor Fist responds w/in 24 hours to apprehend 14 suspects, both human and EmCon. 4 convictions passed, remaining 10 martyr themselves in incarceration.
(15.02.89) The Coaltion declares war on The Greater Asian League of Consumer Businesses, citing Cygnat Owari as primary target for their mistreatment of EmCons and publicly discounting their value as lifeforms deserving equal rights. Cygnat Owari responds by declaring war on The Coalition for unwarranted terrorist acts. Vapor Fist is mobilized as the primary military task force.

(CONTINUED ON FOLLOWING PAGES)

VAPOR FIST

TOP SECRET
EYES ONLY

Col Willem Prescott
Field Commander

Major Travis A Arthur
Air Cavalry Commander

Cpt Oaklin Fong
First Wing
Northern Acquired Territories

Cpt Jun Wong
Second Wing
Eastern Acquired Territories

Cpt Edgar Velasco
Third Wing
Southern Acquired Territories

Cpt Pavel Vesper
Fourth Wing
Western Acquired Territories

Major Hoang Chuu
Ground Mobile Artillery

GunSgt Mekhai Talbot
Heavy Mobile

GunSgt Emerson Zalot
Light Mobile

GunSgt Chun Lin Taylor
Amphibious Mobile Extra

GunSgt Randal Warner
Industrial Pool and Inventory

Major Khari Wells
Infantry and Special Tactics

MastSgt Vinh Nang Hue
Light Infantry

MastSgt Bokine Caraglito
Heavy Infantry

MastSgt Gulliver Osko
Medical

Lieutenant Andrew S Douglas
Special Operations

Pilot
Soldier
Diver

USER-AGENT: Delphonia-Userlink / MSP InternalPassport / AuxTalkEncoded
FROM: Prescott, Willem F, AOR Unit #951311
TO: Designation ID— "Terasawa," SupEx Attachment #292093
DATE: Thursday, 7 January 2100, 16:21:42
SUBJECT: Preliminary Summary   d.Itto Retrieval

Attached you will find my initial thoughts concerning the apprehension of
EmCon d.Itto and the safe retrieval of subject Daisy Ogami. In studying
the tapes, I suspect this unit will not be difficult to locate, though
his reactionary systems seem to be adjusted in an unusual manner. He's
an odd one, which might bear some surprises.

I'd like a number of things before setting out on this task:

1)   Inter-coastal authority granted to Vapor Fist in the condition
civilian arrest is required.

2)   Open source on all of d.Itto's behavioral systems.

3)   Direct communication with the Supreme Executive on this matter.
       Surely you can recognize this as a matter for humans to
address without another machine in the middle trying to
translate things. Subtleties and innuendo are our best code against
Artificial Intelligence.

I would like to cordon off the Gunto and serve papers on all outbound
traffic immediately. I expect a response within the day.

        Prescott

USER-AGENT: Delphonia-Userlink / MSP InternalPassport / AuxTalkEncoded
FROM: Designation ID— "Terasawa," SupEx Attachment #292093
TO: Prescott, Willem F., AOR Unit #951311
DATE: Thursday, 7 January 2100 18:14:27
SUBJECT: Re: Preliminary Summary   d.Itto Retrieval

Regarding your requests:
1)   Granted.
2)   Granted. See d.Belladonna for access Identification.
3)   Denied. The Supreme Executive has placed me in this position with
his full authority to speak on his behalf. If you cannot pass
information through me, I would have to suspect your intentions. This
ruling has been supported by the Supreme Executive himself.

Traffic control has been alerted to surrender all itinerary and manifesto
data upon request. Keep me informed of your progress.

- d.Terasawa

—B
Watch Prescott
He is not to be
given any more
clerance than
necessary

—T

SITUATION SUMMARY — OPERATION LONE WOLF

Status: 13.02.00

Having tracked Subject d.Itto to a pirate freighter crossing Minamidaito Jima, we boarded the ship under fire. Illegal weaponry and a sealed storage chamber full of refugees were uncovered, but we were unable to salvage or rescue any on board due to extensive damage during the raid. Subject escaped in a captured Carrier. Operation was a qualified failure. 10 men, 2 aircraft lost. Subject has proven once again to be unpredictable.

Location beacon onboard the captured Carrier led to its wreckage along an Okinawa beach. A missing handheld shortwave transceiver was used to triangulate the subject's general location in Higashi City. From there, we were able to re-access the unit's short-range sub-dermal identity frequency, but found it in the belly of a stray dog. It appears the subject surgically removed the unit himself, and used the animal to mislead us.

At this point, Inner Security Unit designated.Lierre arrived to assist on the request of the Supreme Executive. Though displaying no initial talents in the field of tracking, he insisted on shadowing me. I had determined that d.Itto may be responding to the size of our pursuit forces, so a decision was made to pursue the subject quietly and personally (like the good old days of gearbox hunting in Cambodia). Allowing d.Lierre to come along was a horrible mistake.

Calculating possible travel distances, we canvassed the region using Camera Kites and instinct. This led to a scorched farm nearby, where we discovered tracks leading to a small farming community. There, we questioned the locals about the subject, and were directed to a governing land baron named Godekai who had made a compound from the abandoned US military structures in the South. Lierre felt certain the locals were hiding something, but I believe he had been malfunctioning since his arrival.

I admit I could be mistaken, however. On our way to Baron Godekai's compound, we encountered d.Itto alone in the woods. There was no sign of the child, but d.Itto claimed she was "where she needed to be." After a few moments stand-off, d.Itto fled from sight, too quickly for either of us to react.

I hoped to recruit the baron's aid in locating d.Itto, but on arrival it was made clear that the girl was in his possession. I signaled Vapor Fist backup as he had his servants retrieve her. Before she could be delivered, however, d.Itto arrived and demanded her in exchange for the baron's son, apparently kidnapped during the night. The Baron agreed to the exchange just as Vapor Fist arrived. The Baron's men panicked, believing our appearance to be a raid of some sort, and a battle ensued. In the chaos, Lierre was destroyed. Vapor Fist lost 16 men and a Carrier. Godekai was killed and his compound fragmented by LAW rockets.

d.Itto and Daisy Ogami disappeared and are still at large. Radio dragnets were spread. No signs have been detected in 23 days.

— W.F. Prescott
Field Commander
AOR "Vapor Fist"

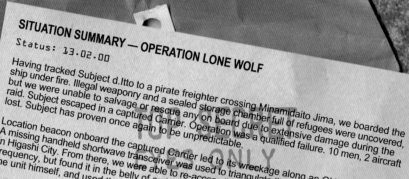

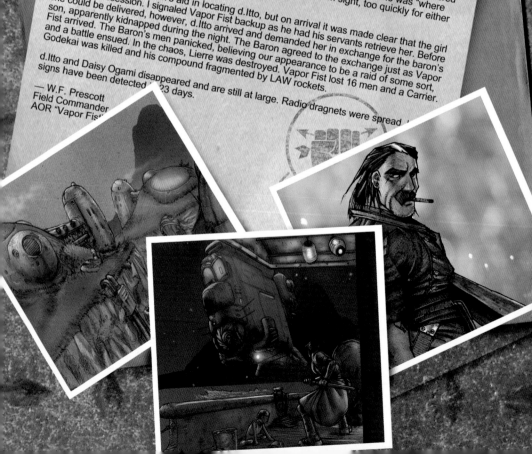

SITUATION SUMMARY — OPERATION LONE WOLF

Status: 19.02.00

Subject d.Itto was discovered in a fish packing plant in Itoman, working as dock labor while waiting the departure of a export hauler. His trail was reacquired after a reported incident in Tomigusuku in which subject was said to have killed 18 men in an abandoned residence tower. Though witness reports are few and varied, we believe he was attempting to retrieve Daisy Ogami from known black marketers. Same witnesses verified d.Itto's inquiry as to transport to Itoman, as well as his mode of transportation — a unlicensed motorcycle taken from the scene of the killings. From there, it was little trick to establish an exact location within Itoman city limits.

We observed subject from a safe distance to establish positive identification and to define behavior patterns. I then built a 12-man infiltration unit and placed them strategically around the plant in cover positions, many disguised as various dock laborers. The team was divided into an A-team for retrieval and B-team for distraction. We had little expectation of taking d.Itto still functioning.

D.Itto arrived as per his schedule with Daisy in tow and proceeded to store the girl in the foreman's office while he went about his work. B-team created an incident that trapped d.Itto in a pen of over-sized shipping containers, purportedly the result of an "accident." Unfortunately the configuration of the fallen objects obscured visual of the subject, but all surrounding exits were covered and monitored.

A-team instantly secured the girl from the foreman's office and moved directly for extraction, but were accosted by d.Itto in the exit corridor leading out of the plant. How the subject escaped the fallen containers is unknown. He proceeded to dispatch the entirety of A-team and retrieve Daisy before disappearing. A summary of port itineraries indicate the majority of outbound haulers headed for Hong Kong and one ship headed for Taipei. I suspect he is heading for Taipei.

At this point, I would appreciate full disclosure regarding d.Itto's stealth capabilities. I cannot be expected to succeed while working in a vacuum of facts.

— F. Prescott
Commander
"Vapor Fist"

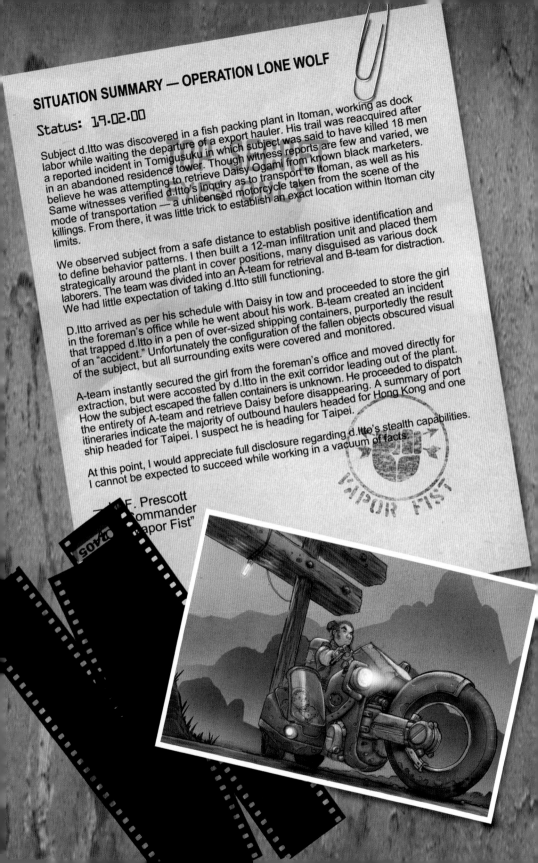

SITUATION SUMMARY — OPERATION LONE WOLF

Status: 29.03.00

We have finally reestablished location of subject d.Itto, traveling with a clan of rogue EmCons and Chopshop Rebels in the Faoshuo Prefecture. This particular clan has been documented in the Cygnat Owari Database as a potential threat possibly linked to The Coalition. Satellite monitoring shows several splinter factions of this clan converging in the Southern tip of the Wasted Territories, possibly to summit and strategize against us. Please inform the Supreme Executive of this danger and assign the appropriate individuals towards this potential situation.

I believe d.Itto may be indirectly heading towards Macau, possibly to access the corporate Database directly. Any additional resources you can provide to prevent this would be advised.

Prescott

Entry ID: 448484-12-20.c
"The Reciprocate" — Cell 48

Subject: Urthu Mu —
Leader. Apparent victim of Chlevosternone ingestion, evident in the growth of a partial biological clone. Full extent of deformation unknown. Requires mechanical assistance to travel.

Little is known about his knowledge or personality.

Subject: Toshiro Takakura —
Tactical leader (assumed). Takakura was at one time a member of Artificial Opposition Response unit "Vapor Fist," before defecting to The Reciprocate. Reason for defection unknown, but his knowledge of Cygnat Owari military tactics makes him a valued asset to The Reciprocate.

See personnel file — T.Takakura #8844, AOR Reg.

atabase printout re: The Desert Clan
Entry ID: 448484-12-20 The Reciprocate

An organization of rebels and criminals wanted by various divisions of the Pan-National Commercial League for acts of terrorism and wanton destruction. Its membership consists of older generation Emulation Constructs, disillusioned prosthetic addicts, and outlawed black market surgeons. They have no apparent political agenda other than aggressively defending themselves from Human Law.

They exist as a collection of smaller cells scattered throughout Greater Asia and The Acquired Territories. They tend to exist outside of populated centers. They are nomadic in nature, traveling in groups of 2-60 in portable tent communities.

Each cell is ruled by a leader appointed by election during its initial organization. Each leader then holds that position without term, with replacement occurring only in times of death. They are organized in a rigid caste systems and are extremely dedicated to maintaining their own order.

Their technological capacity is varied and undefined, dependant on the individual members of each cell. Caution is recommended.

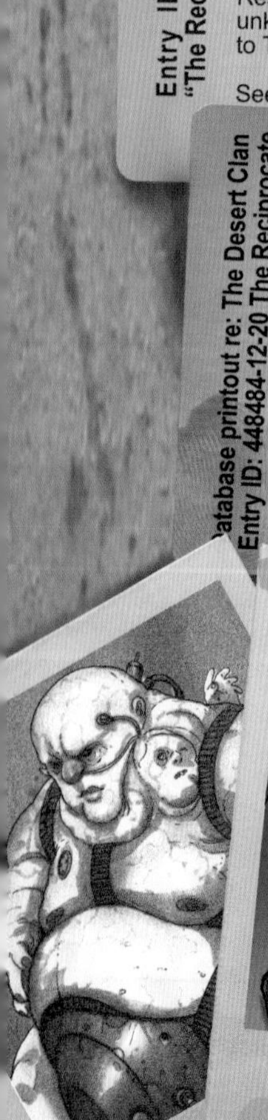

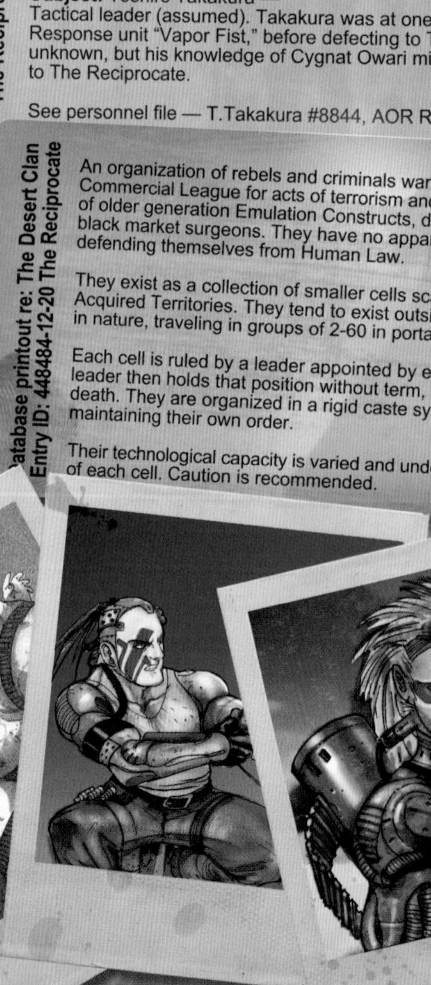

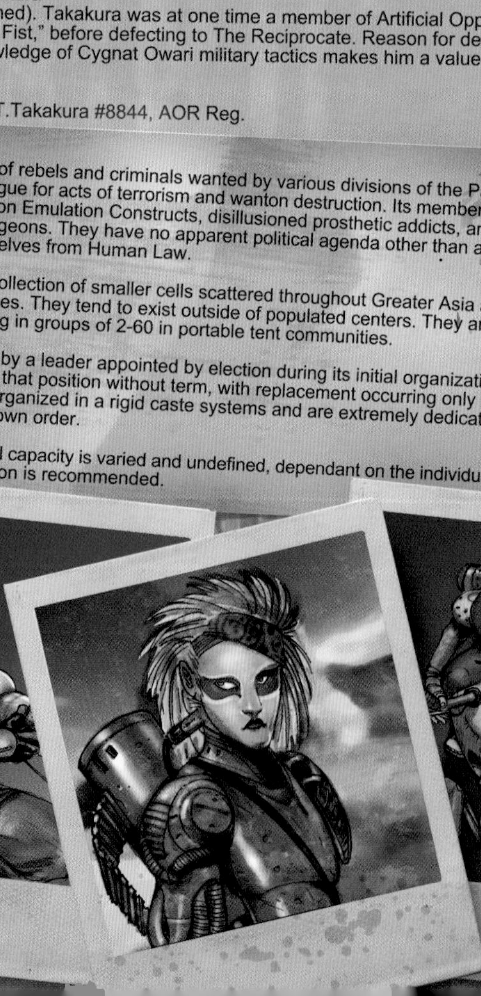

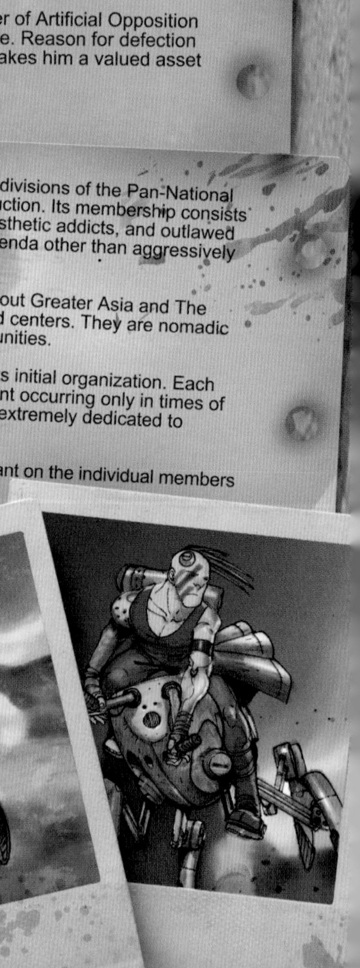

SITUATION SUMMARY — OPERATION LONE WOLF

Status: 19.04.00

Fairly certain now of Macau. D.Itto has been spotted entering Kowloon with Daisy, and I believe he is seeking the fabled sanctuary known as "St. Lufthilde." This institution has, apparently, been welcoming orphans of The Spore, as well as infected children. (Note: there has been no indication to suggest they have any sort of treatment available.) No official confirmation of its existence can be provided, as local authorities claim no pressing reason to pursue it. How any person, especially a child, is meant to find this place is anyone's guess.

It is my theory that d.Itto plans on stashing Daisy at St. Lufthilde's while he infiltrates Macau on his own. I would like to reinforce security around the Cygnat Owari Data Center and petition the Kowloon authorities to participate in a full-scale investigation on St. Lufthilde's.

— W.F. Prescott
Field Commander
AOR "Vapor Fist"

0056145do226   AMSTERDAM/Zone

ROME/FCO

Rolloguo deregno ao serenisfimo muito...
rofo puinape elfer dom manuell nofia...
fe, vne, i excellentes, feitos, voe Reie de po...
mandado per duarte gallnam fidalliguo de fu...
cafa do feu coftelbo noquall falla vo gram...

Send Now   Send Later   Save as Draft   Add Attachments   Signature ▾   Options ▾   Rewrap

Attachments: none

Default Font ▾ Text Size ▾ B I U T ≡ ≡ ≡ | ≔ ≔ ≔ ≔ | A ▾ ⟐ ▾

```
USER-AGENT: Delphonia-Userlink / MSP InternalPassport / AuxTalkEncoded
FROM: Designation ID 'Belladonna,'  InSec #603092
TO: Designation ID 'Terasawa,' SupEx Attachment #292093
DATE: Tuesday, 20 April 2100, 12:16:32
SUBJECT: Kowloon

I have dispatched Inner Security Unit d. Seivelfan to Kowloon. If St.
Lufthilde's exists, he will find it.

- d.Belladonna
```

1 May 2100

To: Lucca Bialissimo, SupEx
(Secured Courier Codec Service granted)

Sir,

I apologize for circumventing the established chain of command, but I feel it was important I address you directly in this matter. All attempts at contacting you in person have met with strict refusal. I hope I'm mistaken, but I fear this resistance may not be by your command.

The search for d.Itto and Daisy Ogami has been more difficult than I ever could have imagined. Not only is he more clever than any other EmCon I've faced, but perhaps more than any other human I've faced as well. I guess it's a testament to Cygnat Owari's achievement in the field of Artificial Intlligence, but I wonder if a philosophical line has been crossed. I wonder if mathematical perfection has broken to reveal the chaos of nature underneath. The predictability of EmCon behavior was our ace in the hole. Now I'm starting to think that ace may have become a Joker.

As difficult as it is for me to acknowledge, I believe d.Itto may have become more than sentient. I've personally witnessed him display what appears to be illogical compassion for young Daisy. It is as if his Behavior Emulation routines have grown so complex, they no longer can be distinguished from genuine emotion. D.Itto contains his reactions well, but the motivation behind his actions can arguably be classified as sympathetic. And if this is true of today's EmCon in general, d.Itto is the least of my worries. The Human Race might have more to fear than genocide by The War Spore.

One EmCon with a child is insignificant compared to another EmCon with the world's largest conglomerate at his fingertips. D.Terasawa has displayed erratic behavior lately, not like a bug or logic loop, but like a parentless child who hasn't been told how to control his temper. I can see it in his face as he struggles to deal with illogical connections that aren't addressed by his emulation parameters. I think he, and possibly others of his type, are outgrowing their own operating systems. And I'm terrified to imagine what could happen if units as powerful as those in Inner Security start looking after their own interests.

You have always had sage advice in times of darkness. Please share some of your wisdom now that it is sorely needed.

Sincerely,
Willem F. Prescott,
AOR Field Commander

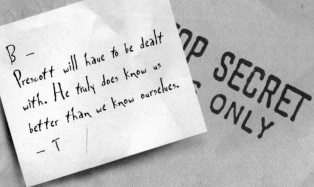

B –
Prescott will have to be dealt
with. He truly does know us
better than we know ourselves.
– T

TOP SECRET
ONLY

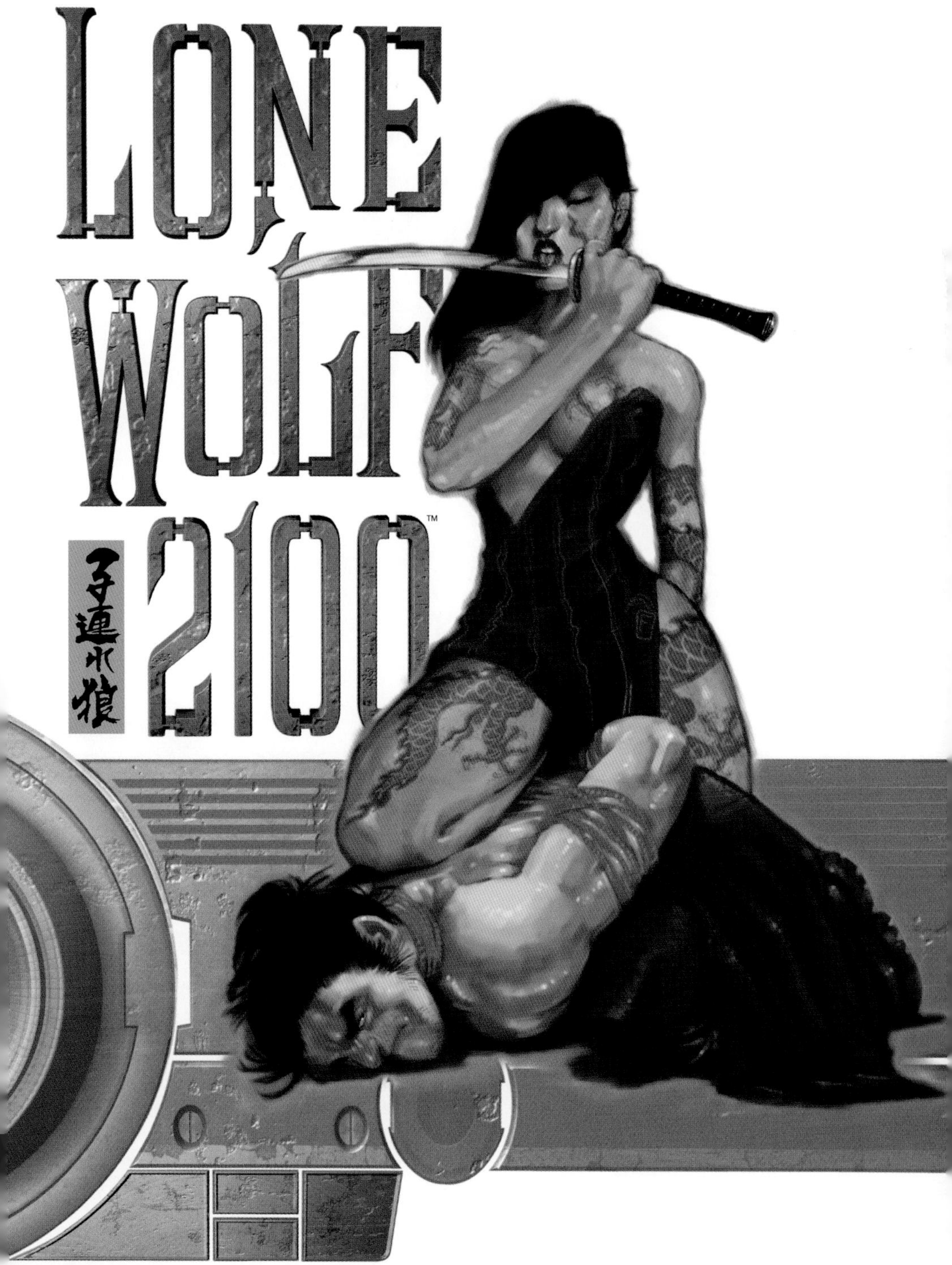
LONE WOLF 2100™
子連れ狼

PATTERN STORM

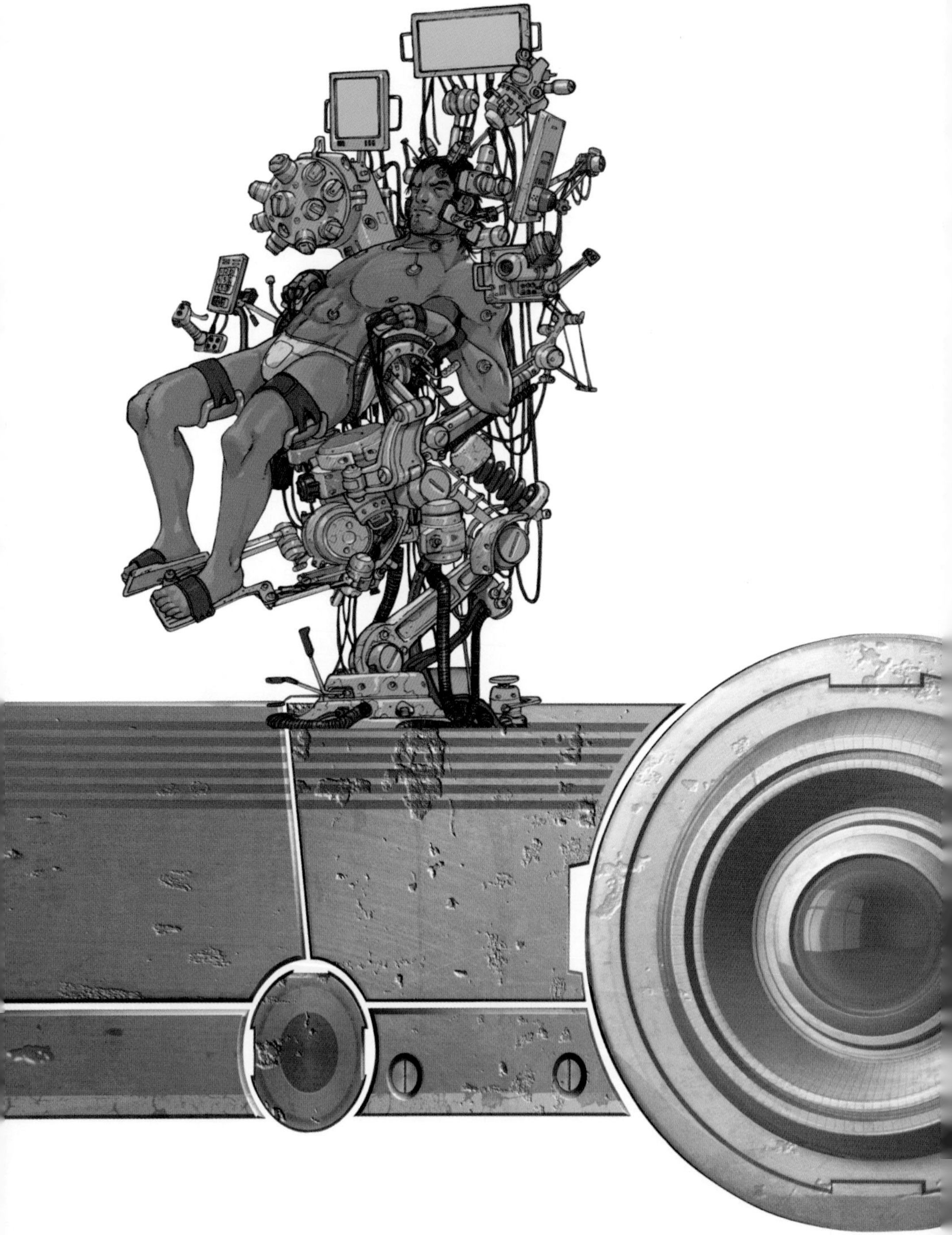

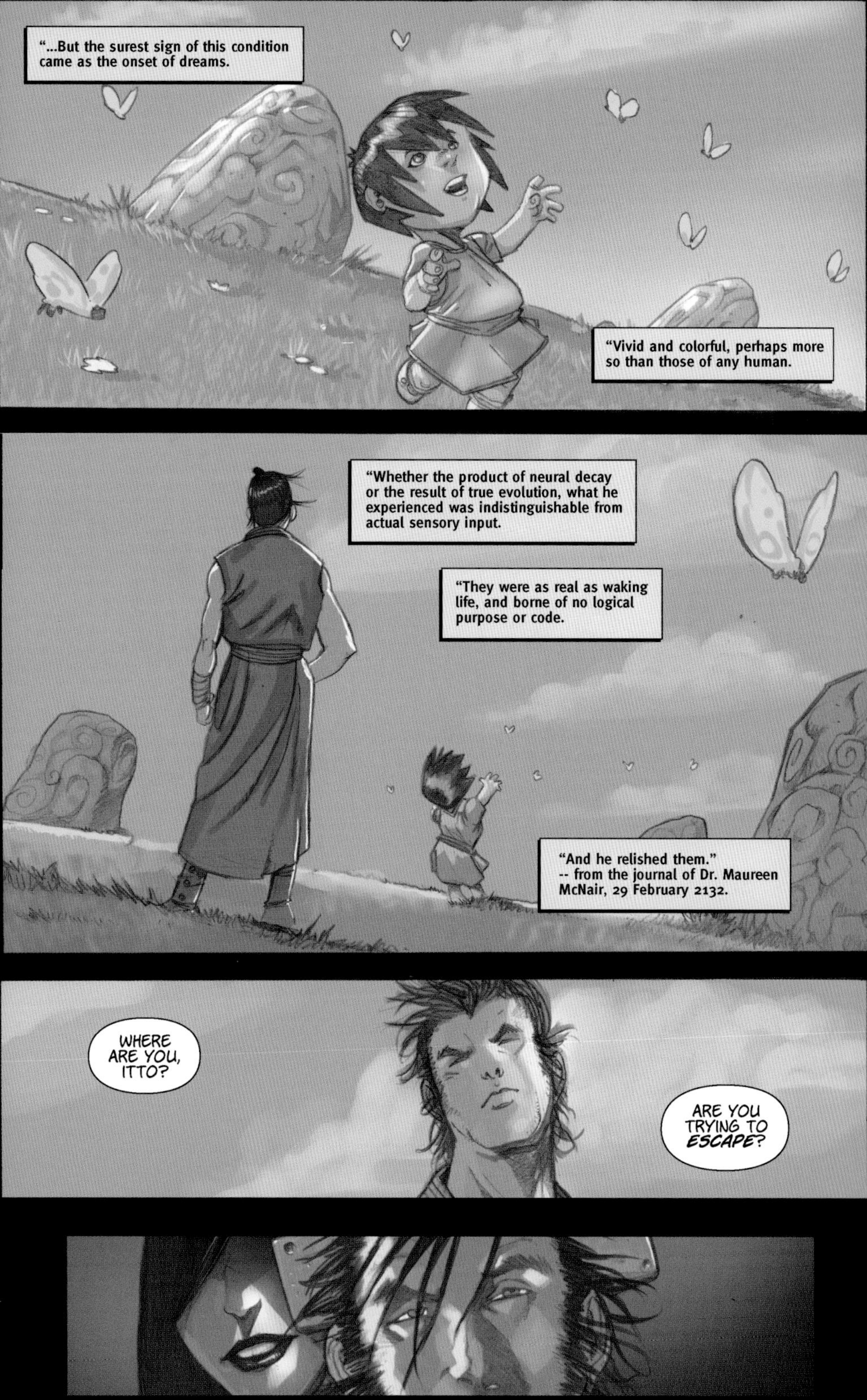
"...But the surest sign of this condition came as the onset of dreams.
"Vivid and colorful, perhaps more so than those of any human.
"Whether the product of neural decay or the result of true evolution, what he experienced was indistinguishable from actual sensory input.
"They were as real as waking life, and borne of no logical purpose or code.
"And he relished them."
-- from the journal of Dr. Maureen McNair, 29 February 2132.
WHERE ARE YOU, ITTO?
ARE YOU TRYING TO *ESCAPE*?

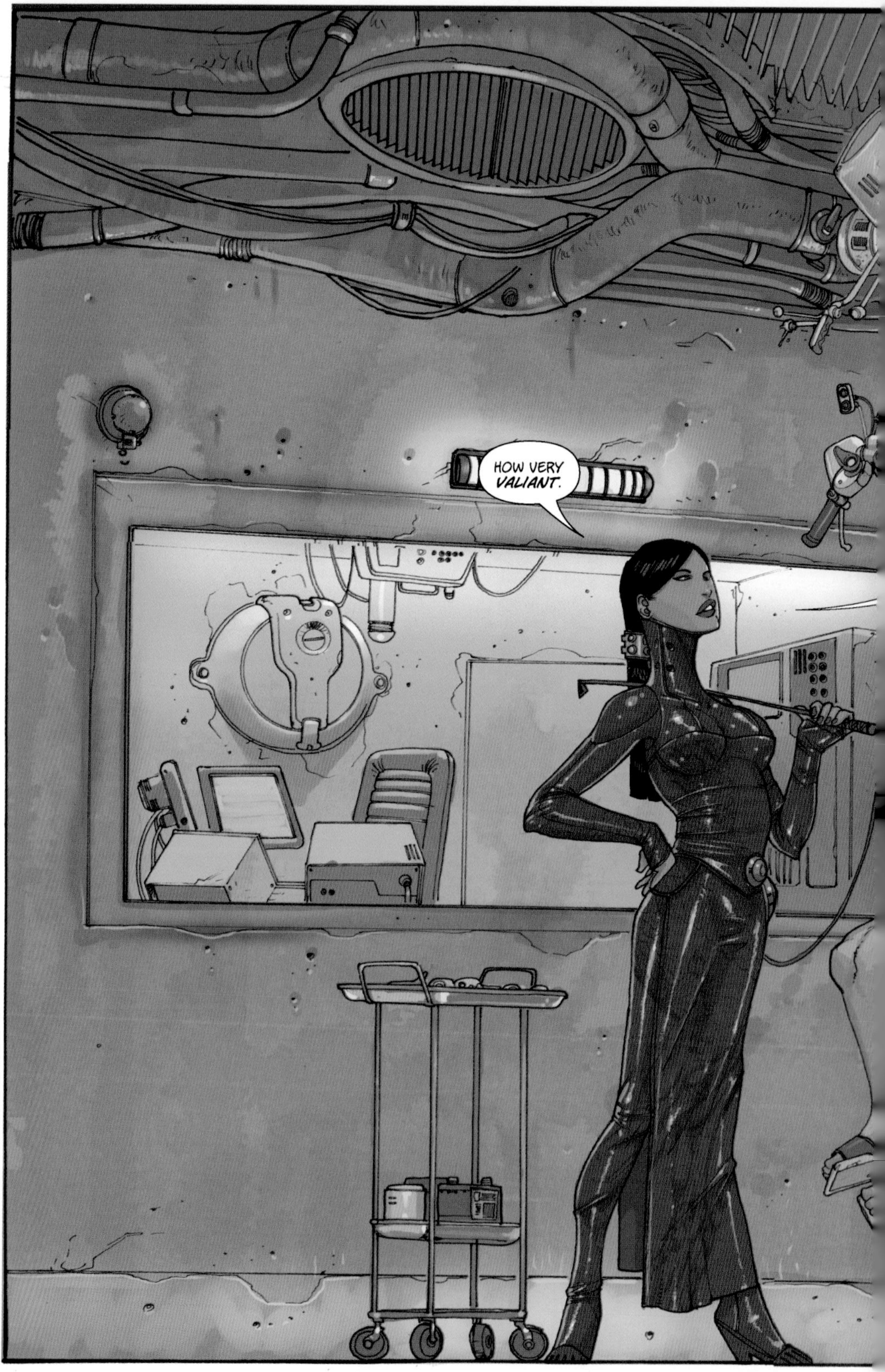
HOW VERY *VALIANT*.

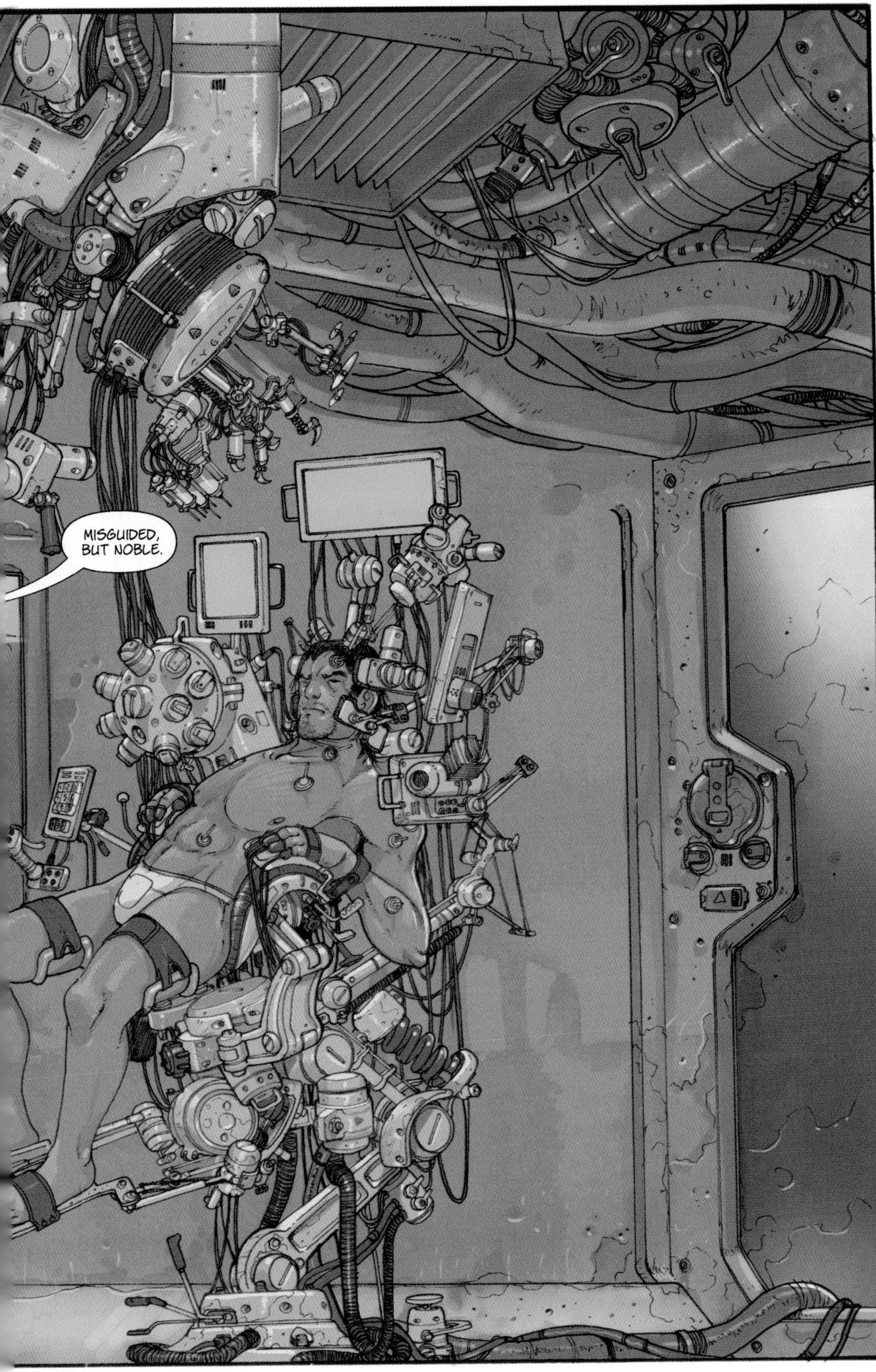
MISGUIDED, BUT NOBLE.

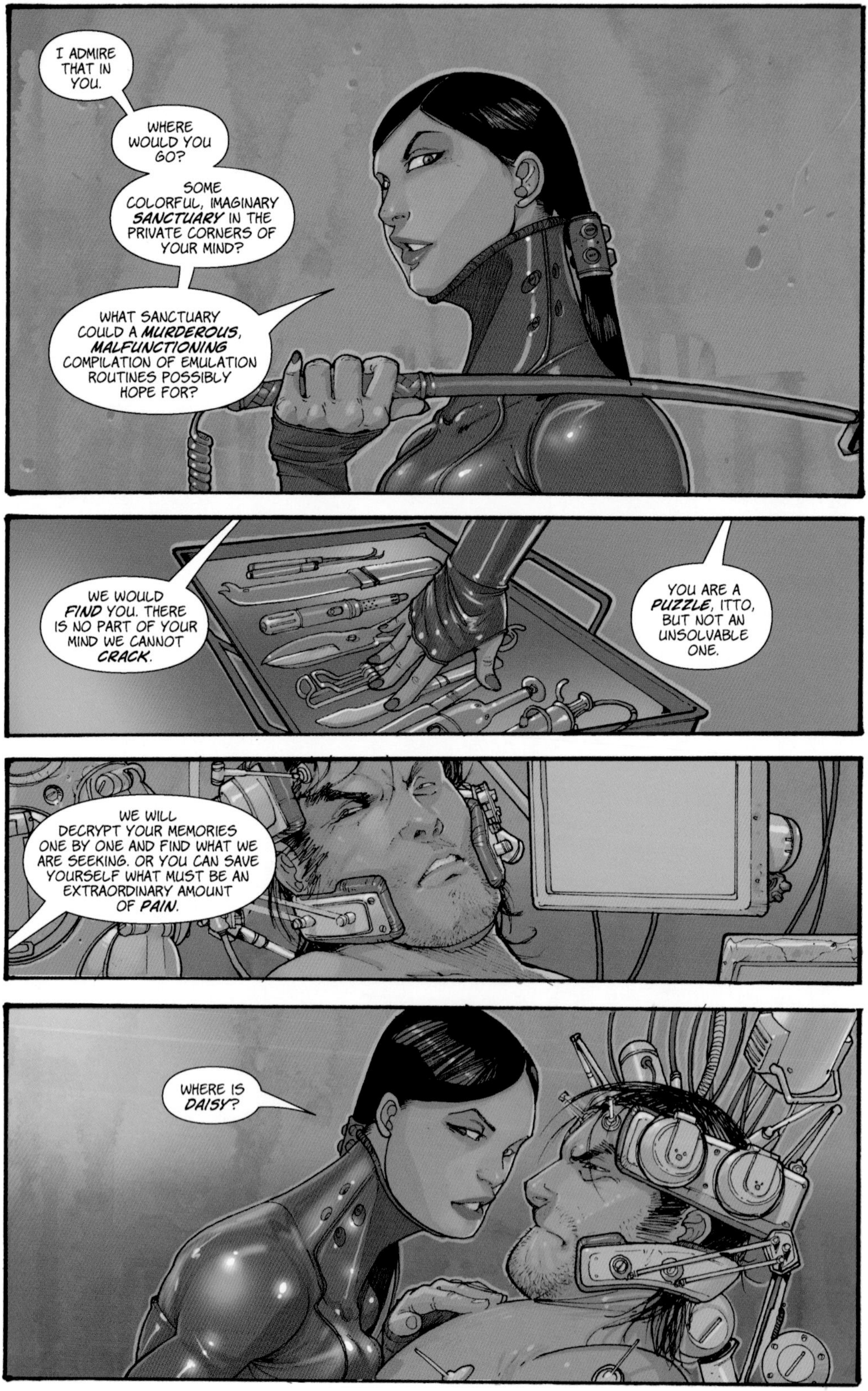
I ADMIRE THAT IN YOU.
WHERE WOULD YOU GO?
SOME COLORFUL, IMAGINARY SANCTUARY IN THE PRIVATE CORNERS OF YOUR MIND?
WHAT SANCTUARY COULD A MURDEROUS, MALFUNCTIONING COMPILATION OF EMULATION ROUTINES POSSIBLY HOPE FOR?
WE WOULD FIND YOU. THERE IS NO PART OF YOUR MIND WE CANNOT CRACK.
YOU ARE A PUZZLE, ITTO, BUT NOT AN UNSOLVABLE ONE.
WE WILL DECRYPT YOUR MEMORIES ONE BY ONE AND FIND WHAT WE ARE SEEKING. OR YOU CAN SAVE YOURSELF WHAT MUST BE AN EXTRAORDINARY AMOUNT OF PAIN.
WHERE IS DAISY?

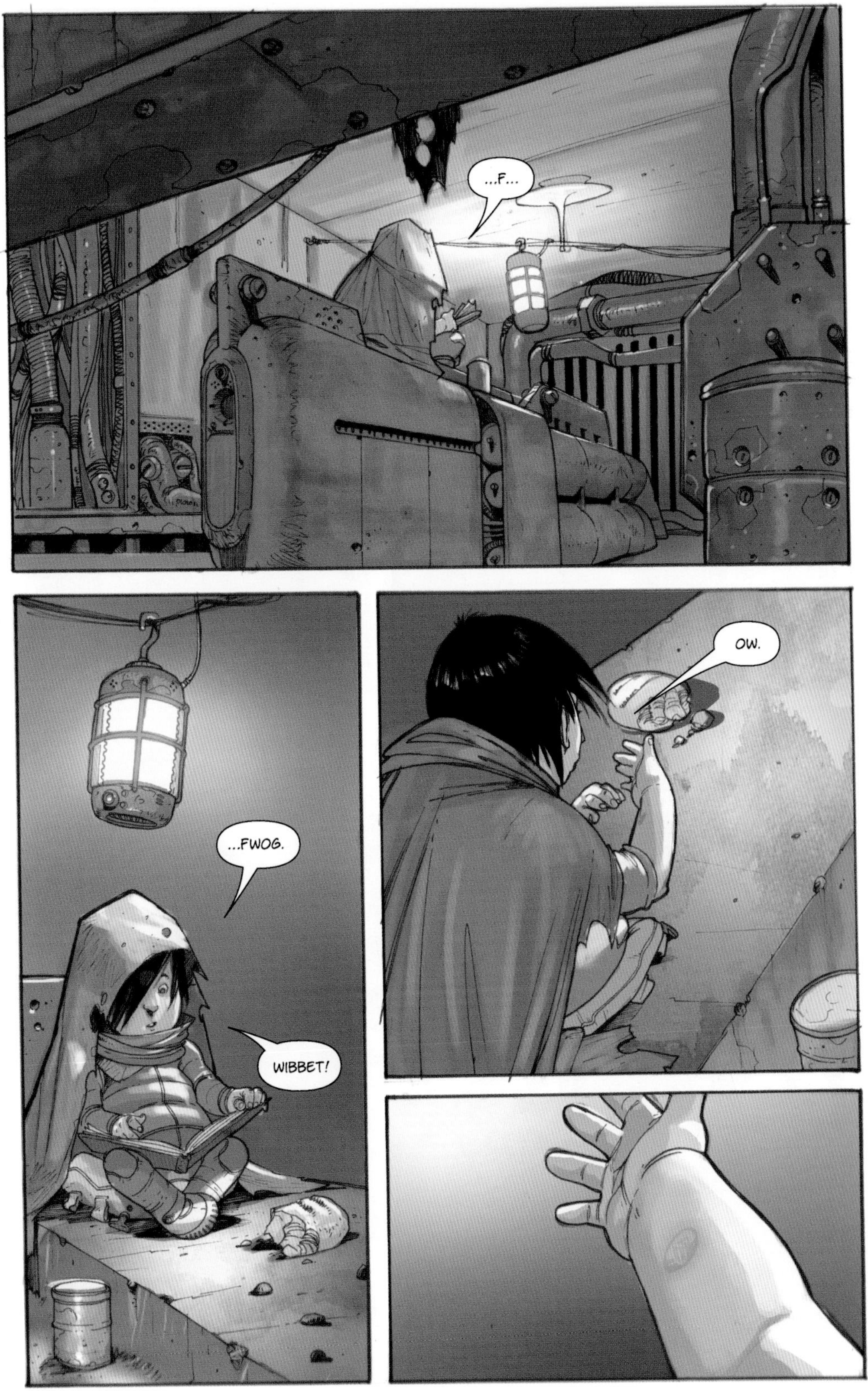
...F...
...FWOG.
WIBBET!
OW.

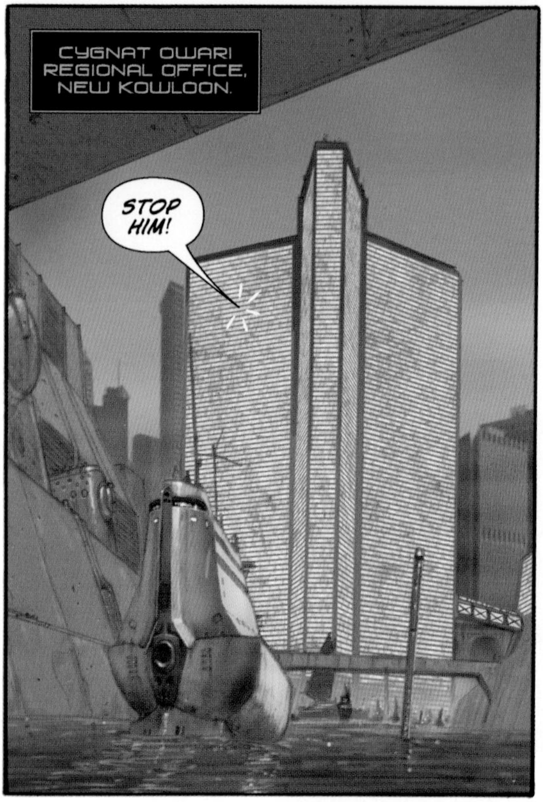
CYGNAT OWARI REGIONAL OFFICE, NEW KOWLOON.
STOP HIM!

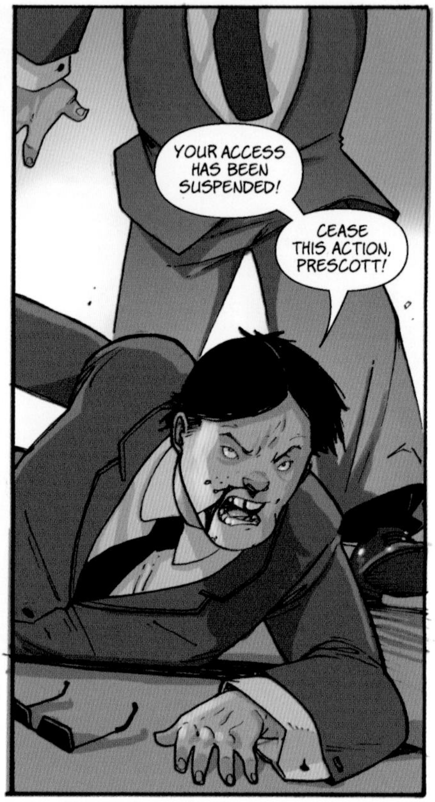
YOUR ACCESS HAS BEEN SUSPENDED!
CEASE THIS ACTION, PRESCOTT!

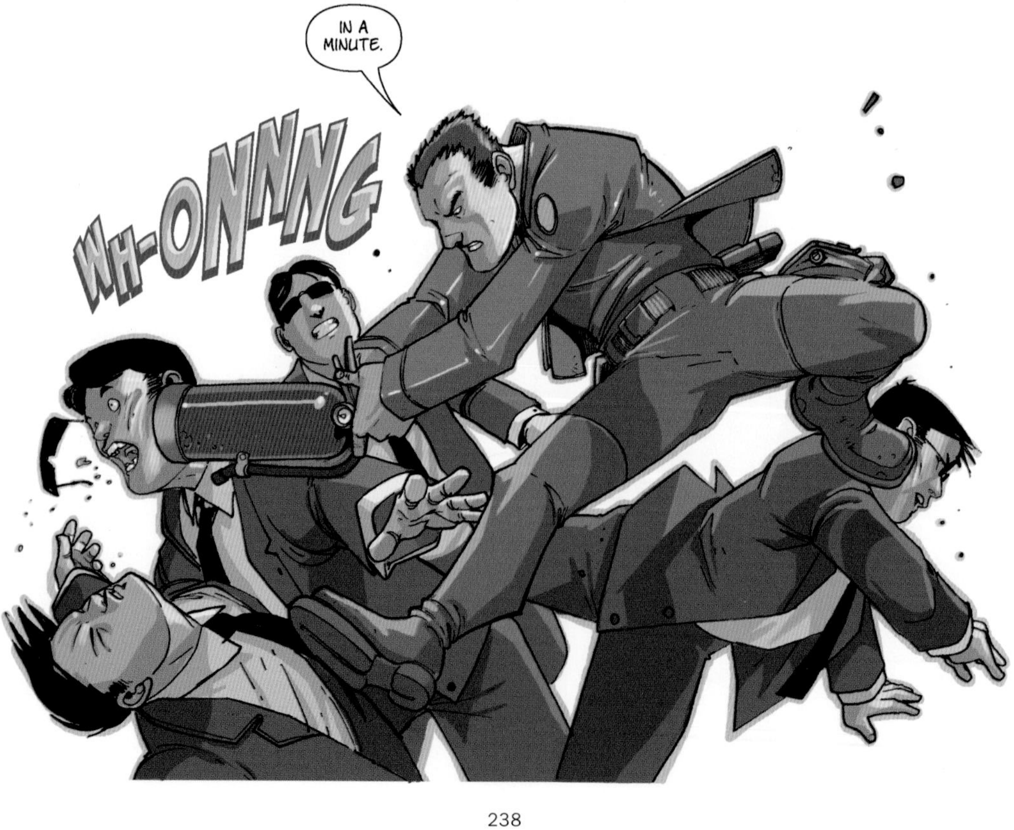
IN A MINUTE.
WH-ONNNG

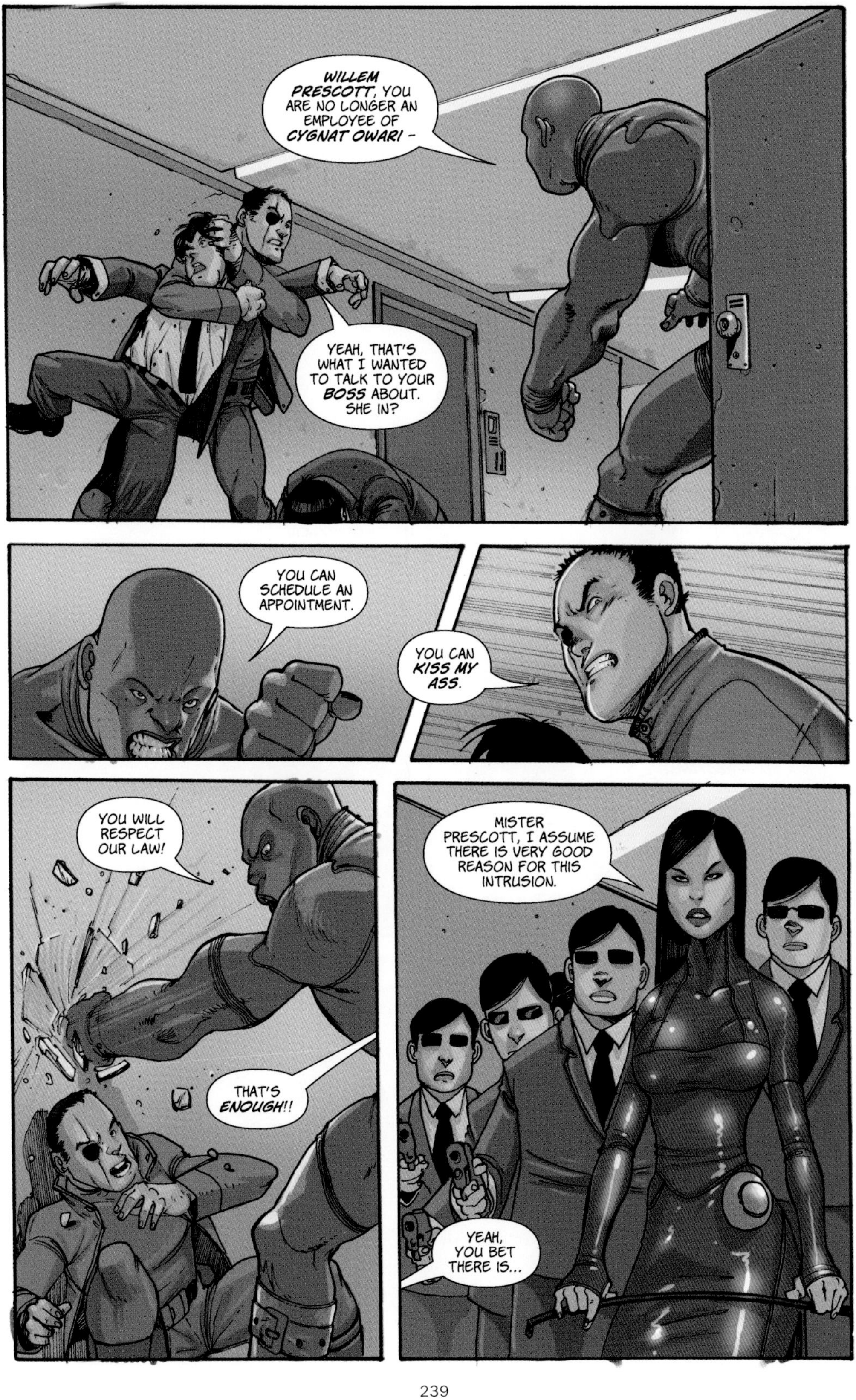
WILLEM PRESCOTT, YOU ARE NO LONGER AN EMPLOYEE OF CYGNAT OWARI -
YEAH, THAT'S WHAT I WANTED TO TALK TO YOUR BOSS ABOUT. SHE IN?
YOU CAN SCHEDULE AN APPOINTMENT.
YOU CAN KISS MY ASS.
YOU WILL RESPECT OUR LAW!
THAT'S ENOUGH!!
MISTER PRESCOTT, I ASSUME THERE IS VERY GOOD REASON FOR THIS INTRUSION.
YEAH, YOU BET THERE IS...

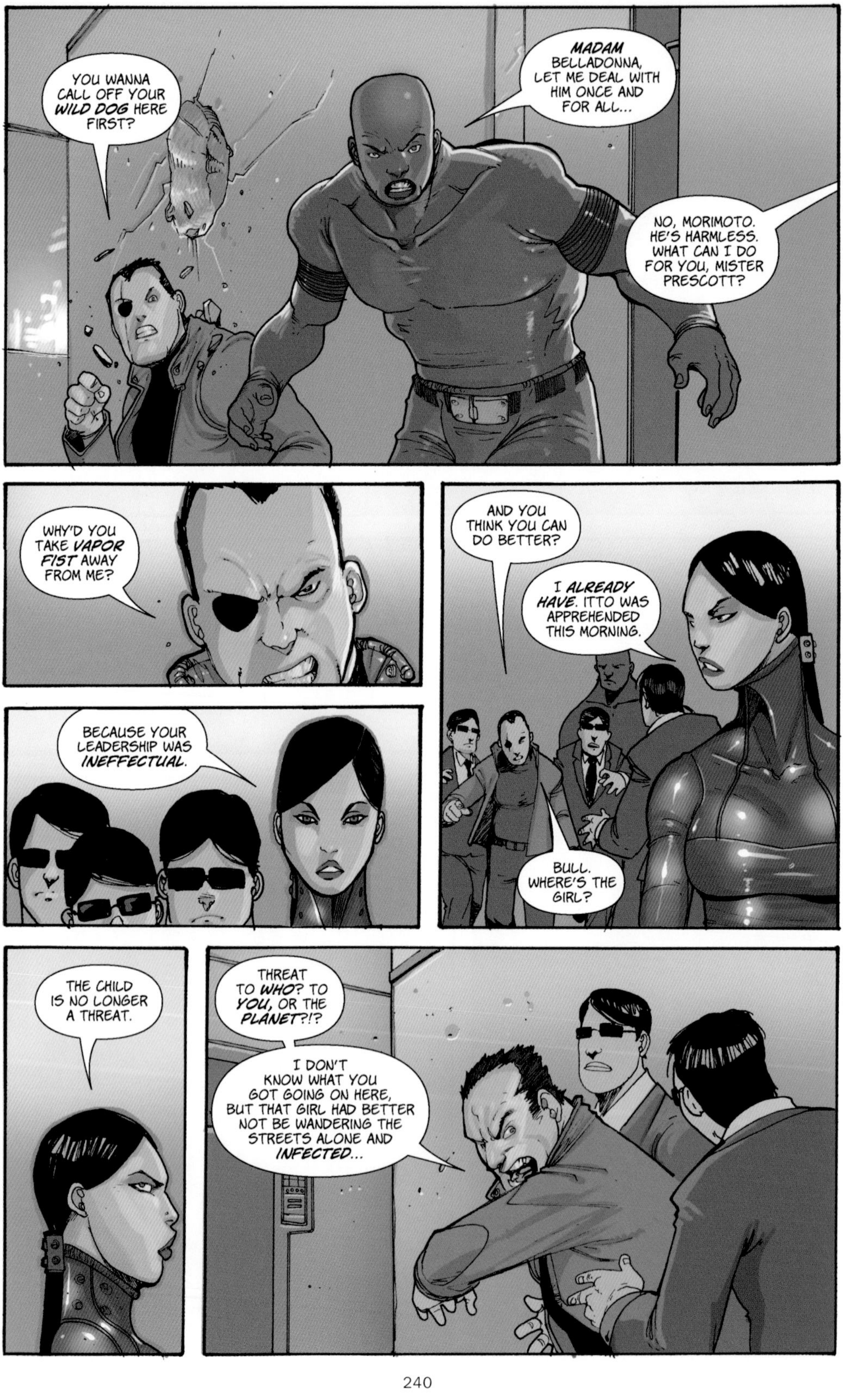
YOU WANNA CALL OFF YOUR WILD DOG HERE FIRST?
MADAM BELLADONNA, LET ME DEAL WITH HIM ONCE AND FOR ALL...
NO, MORIMOTO. HE'S HARMLESS. WHAT CAN I DO FOR YOU, MISTER PRESCOTT?
WHY'D YOU TAKE VAPOR FIST AWAY FROM ME?
BECAUSE YOUR LEADERSHIP WAS INEFFECTUAL.
AND YOU THINK YOU CAN DO BETTER?
I ALREADY HAVE. ITTO WAS APPREHENDED THIS MORNING.
BULL. WHERE'S THE GIRL?
THE CHILD IS NO LONGER A THREAT.
THREAT TO WHO? TO YOU, OR THE PLANET?!?
I DON'T KNOW WHAT YOU GOT GOING ON HERE, BUT THAT GIRL HAD BETTER NOT BE WANDERING THE STREETS ALONE AND INFECTED...

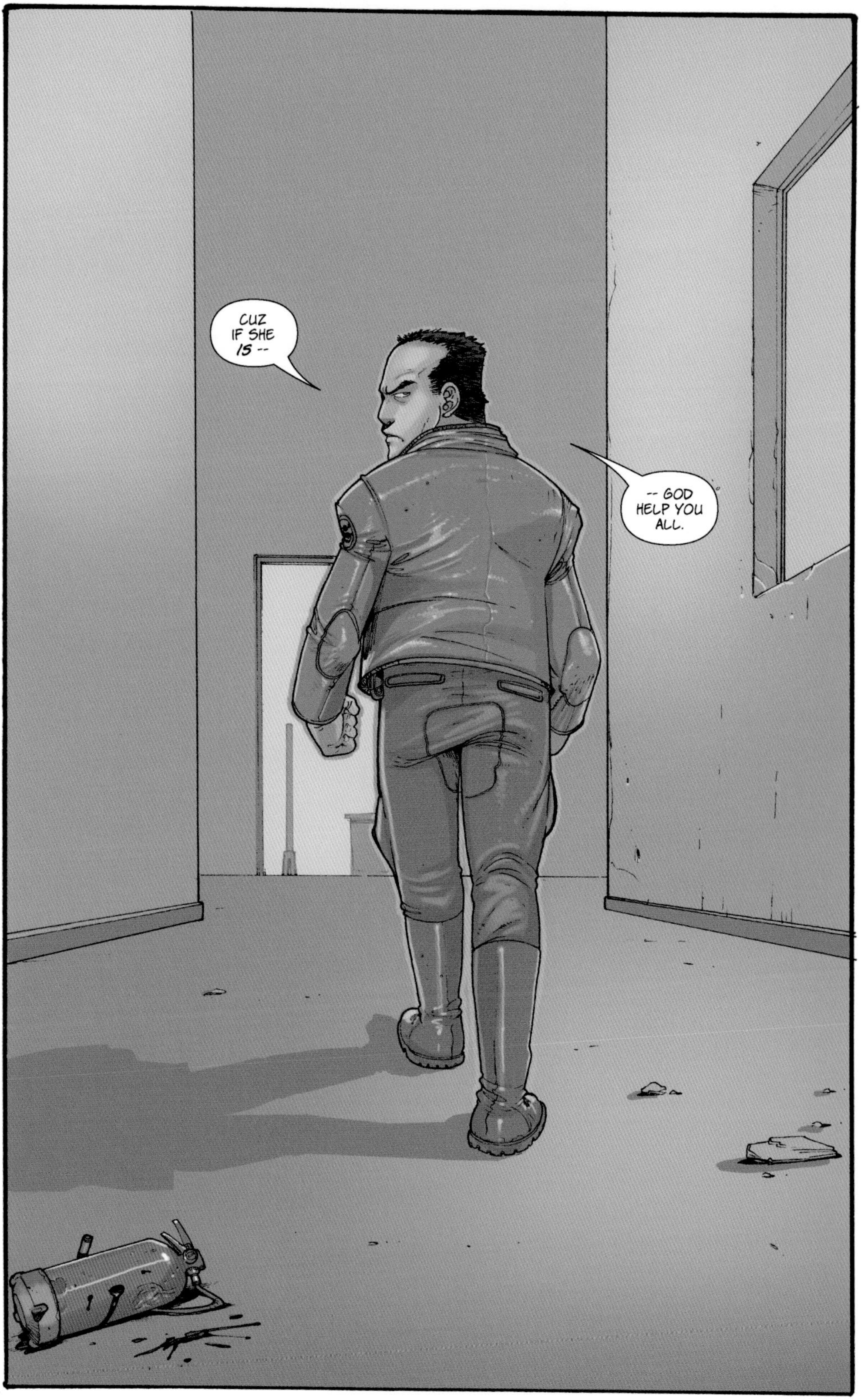
CUZ IF SHE IS --
-- GOD HELP YOU ALL.

-- "BUSHIDO"...?

I APOLOGIZE FOR THAT INTERRUPTION. THERE WAS A SMALL MATTER TO ADDRESS IN THE LOBBY.

WHERE WERE WE...?

OH, YES. I BELIEVE WE WERE DISCUSSING THE *UNIQUE* SET OF *VALUES* YOU POSSESS. WHAT DID *DOCTOR OGAMI* CALL IT?

HE WAS QUITE A TRADITIONAL MAN, WASN'T HE? BOUND BY SO MANY OUTDATED CONCEPTS, IT'S NO WONDER YOU'RE LYING HERE, HELPLESS.

YOU'D THINK HE WOULD HAVE TAUGHT YOU TO THINK PROGRESSIVELY, CREATIVELY, *AMBITIOUSLY*...

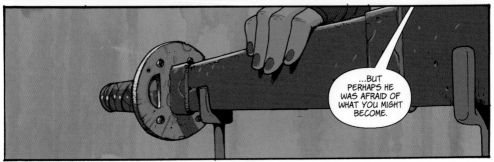

...BUT PERHAPS HE WAS AFRAID OF WHAT YOU MIGHT BECOME.

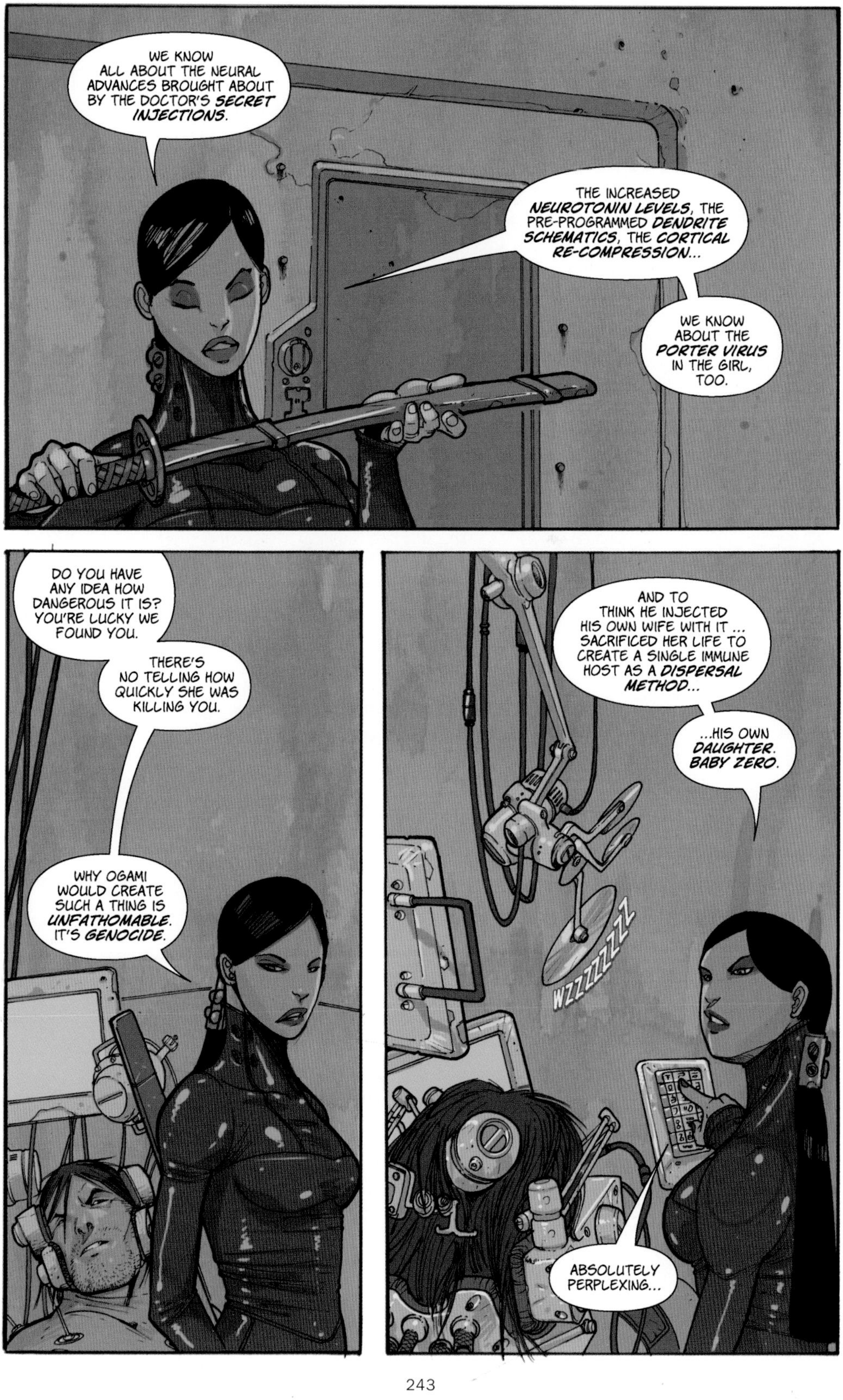
WE KNOW ALL ABOUT THE NEURAL ADVANCES BROUGHT ABOUT BY THE DOCTOR'S *SECRET INJECTIONS*.
THE INCREASED *NEUROTONIN LEVELS*, THE PRE-PROGRAMMED *DENDRITE SCHEMATICS*, THE *CORTICAL RE-COMPRESSION*...
WE KNOW ABOUT THE *PORTER VIRUS* IN THE GIRL, TOO.
DO YOU HAVE ANY IDEA HOW DANGEROUS IT IS? YOU'RE LUCKY WE FOUND YOU.
THERE'S NO TELLING HOW QUICKLY SHE WAS KILLING YOU.
WHY OGAMI WOULD CREATE SUCH A THING IS *UNFATHOMABLE*. IT'S *GENOCIDE*.
AND TO THINK HE INJECTED HIS OWN WIFE WITH IT ... SACRIFICED HER LIFE TO CREATE A SINGLE IMMUNE HOST AS A *DISPERSAL METHOD*...
...HIS OWN *DAUGHTER*. *BABY ZERO*.
WZZZZZZZZ
ABSOLUTELY PERPLEXING...

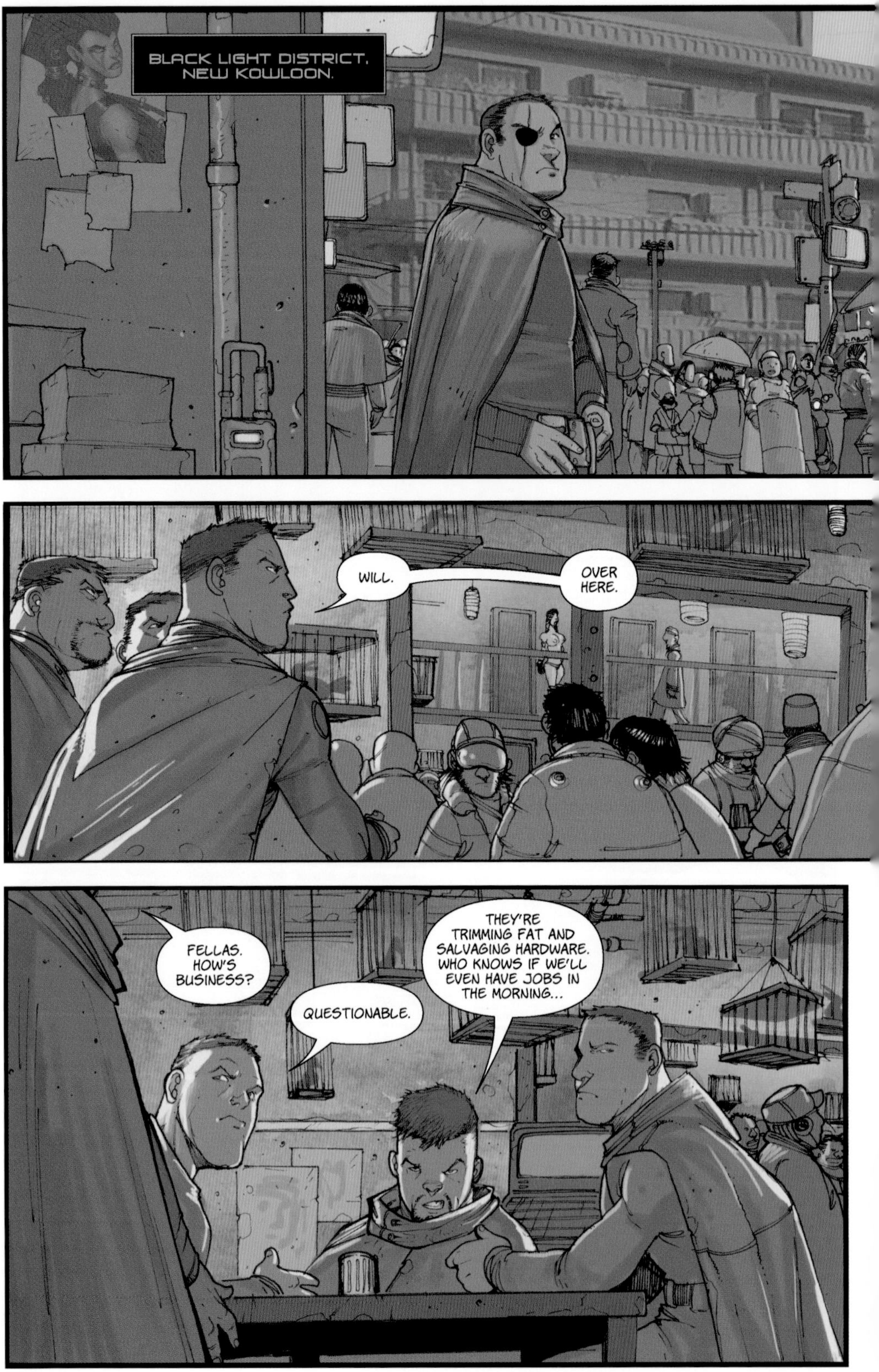
BLACK LIGHT DISTRICT, NEW KOWLOON.
WILL.
OVER HERE.
FELLAS. HOW'S BUSINESS?
QUESTIONABLE.
THEY'RE TRIMMING FAT AND SALVAGING HARDWARE. WHO KNOWS IF WE'LL EVEN HAVE JOBS IN THE MORNING...

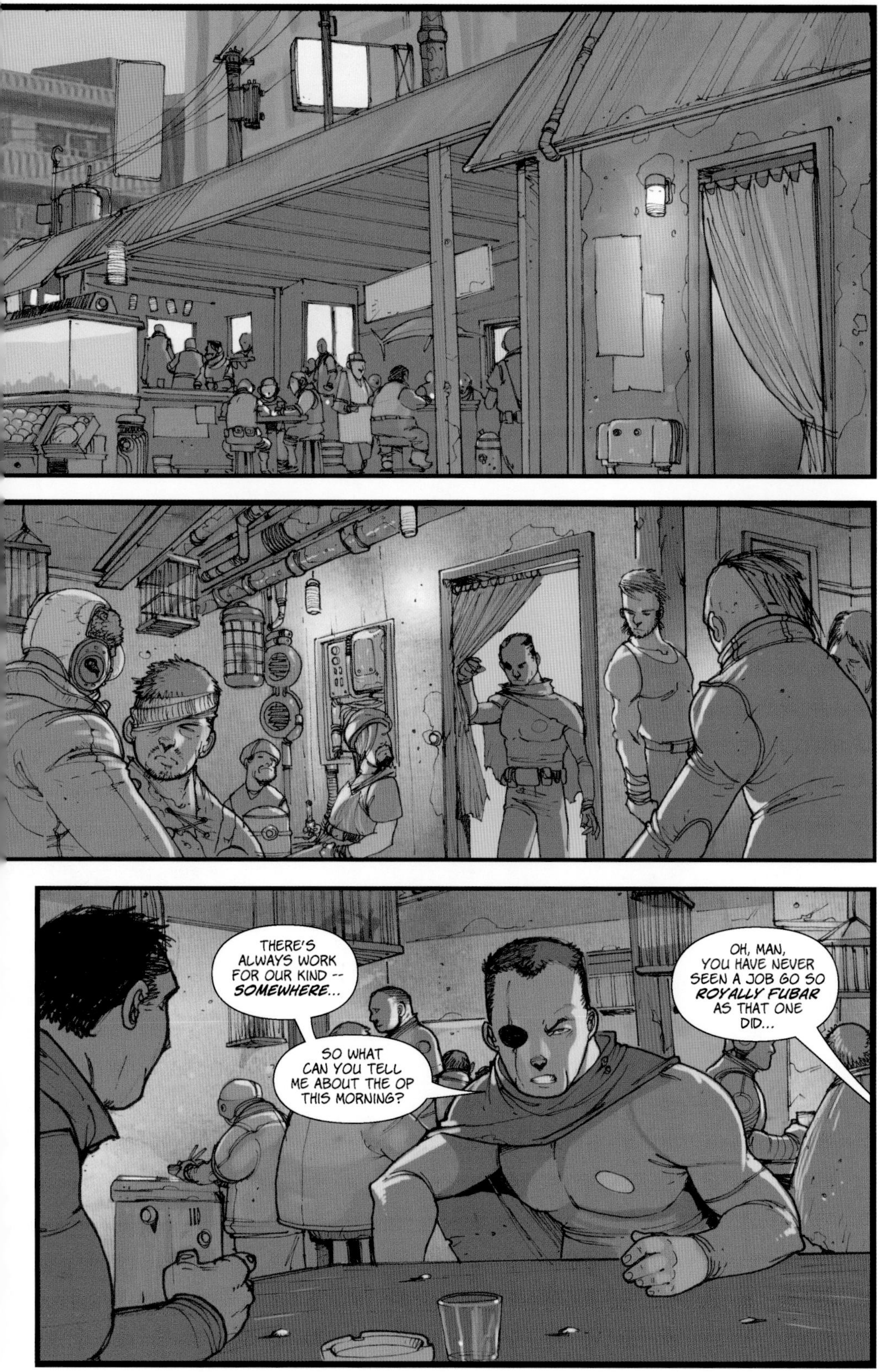
THERE'S ALWAYS WORK FOR OUR KIND -- *SOMEWHERE*...
SO WHAT CAN YOU TELL ME ABOUT THE OP THIS MORNING?
OH, MAN, YOU HAVE NEVER SEEN A JOB GO SO *ROYALLY FUBAR* AS THAT ONE DID...

"THE NEW TEE-OH, THIS BELLADONNA CHICK ... SHE IS *BAT-ASS BONKERS*, MAN.

"SHE HAD EVERY EXTRA ON THE GROUND, EVEN THE *NEW KIDS*.

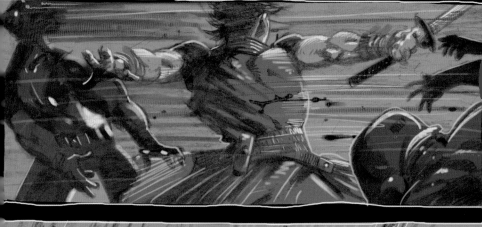

"MOST OF 'EM DIDN'T EVEN KNOW WHAT THEY WERE SUPPOSED TO DO DOWN THERE.

"BUT SHE WAS DEAD-SET ON THE TARGET, EVEN IF IT MEANT BURYING HIM IN *OUR CORPSES*.

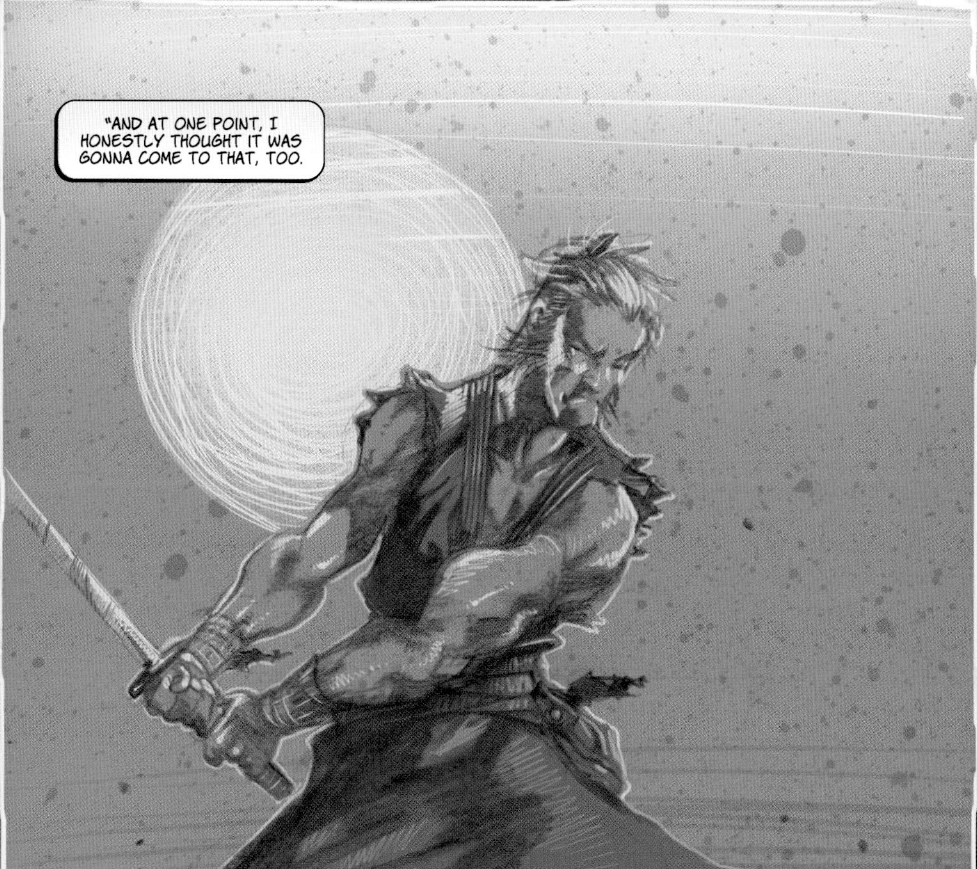
"AND AT ONE POINT, I HONESTLY THOUGHT IT WAS GONNA COME TO THAT, TOO.

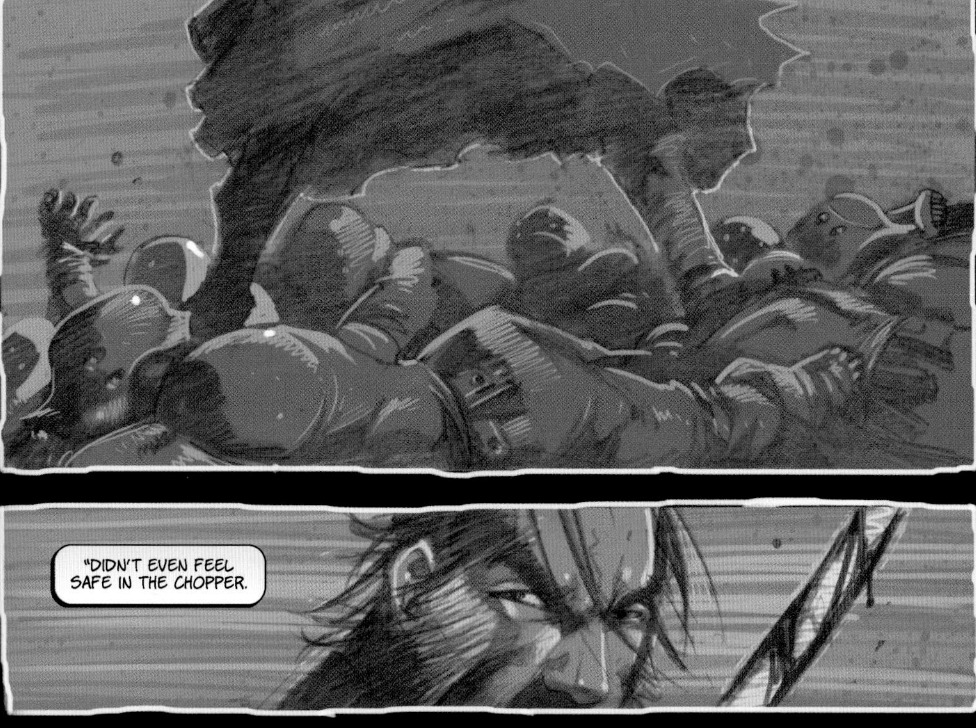
"DIDN'T EVEN FEEL SAFE IN THE CHOPPER.

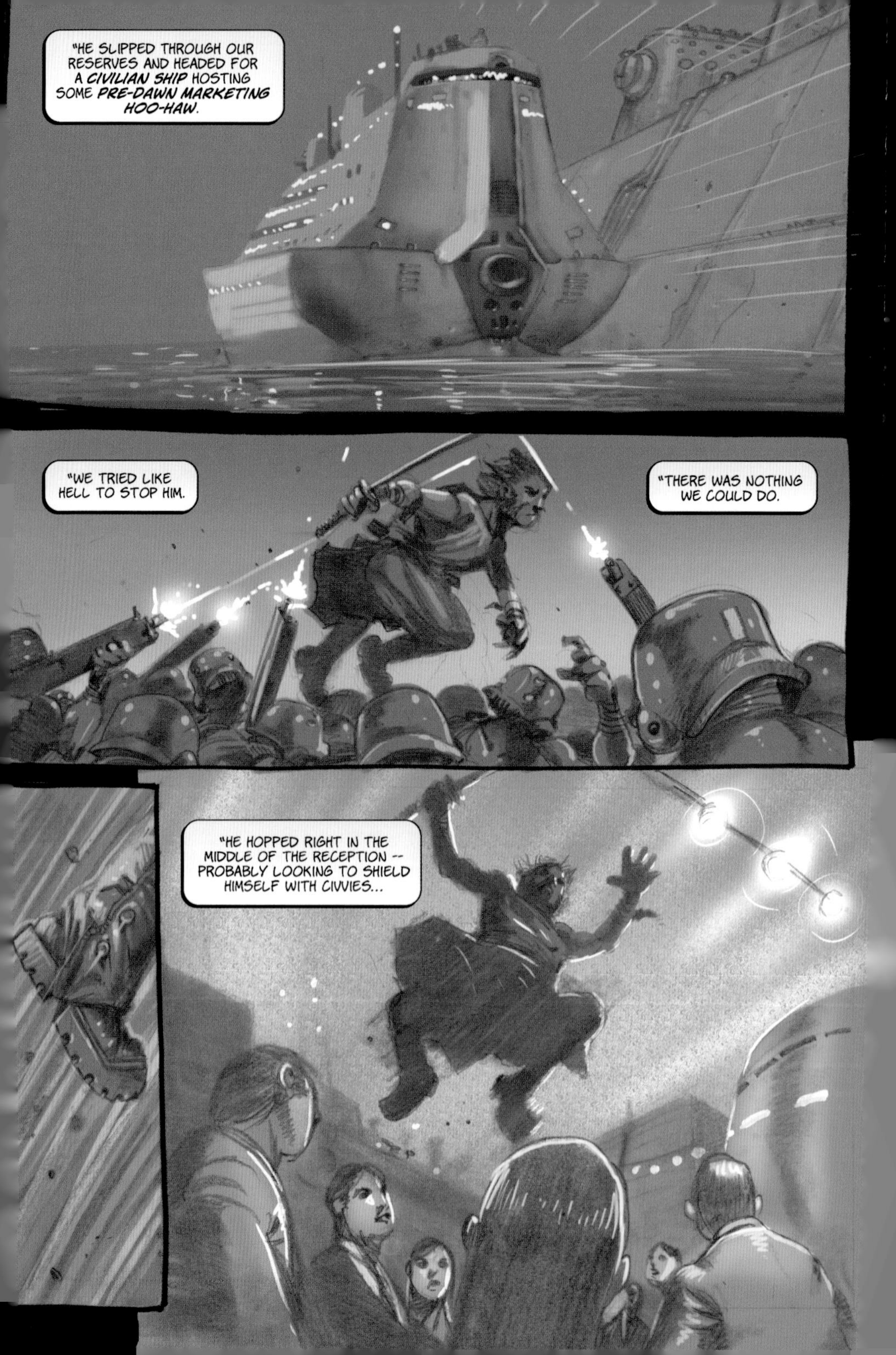
"HE SLIPPED THROUGH OUR RESERVES AND HEADED FOR A CIVILIAN SHIP HOSTING SOME PRE-DAWN MARKETING HOO-HAW.
"WE TRIED LIKE HELL TO STOP HIM.
"THERE WAS NOTHING WE COULD DO.
"HE HOPPED RIGHT IN THE MIDDLE OF THE RECEPTION -- PROBABLY LOOKING TO SHIELD HIMSELF WITH CIVVIES...

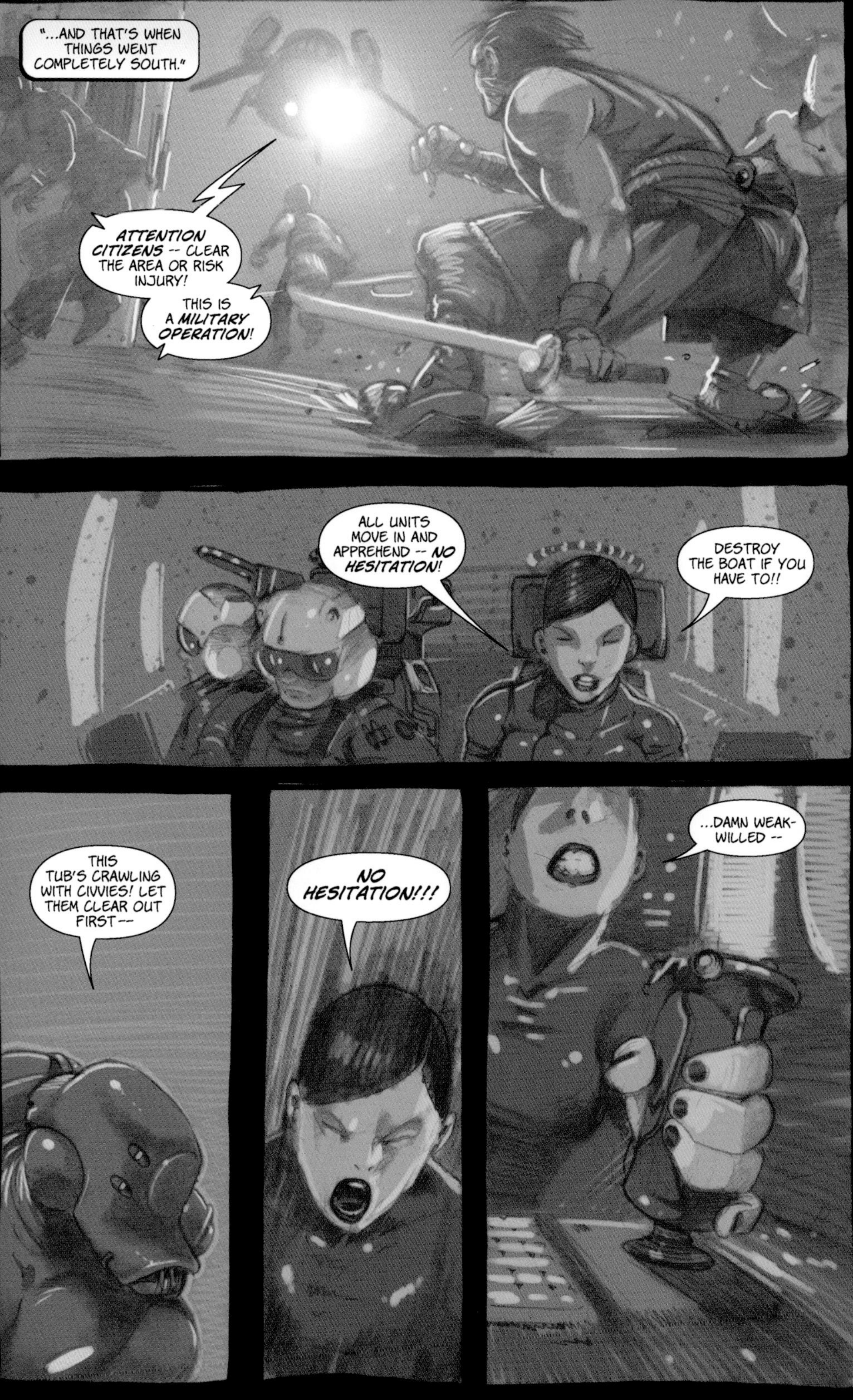
"...AND THAT'S WHEN THINGS WENT COMPLETELY SOUTH."
ATTENTION CITIZENS -- CLEAR THE AREA OR RISK INJURY!
THIS IS A *MILITARY OPERATION*!
ALL UNITS MOVE IN AND APPREHEND -- *NO HESITATION*!
DESTROY THE BOAT IF YOU HAVE TO!!
THIS TUB'S CRAWLING WITH CIVVIES! LET THEM CLEAR OUT FIRST--
NO HESITATION!!!
...DAMN WEAK-WILLED --

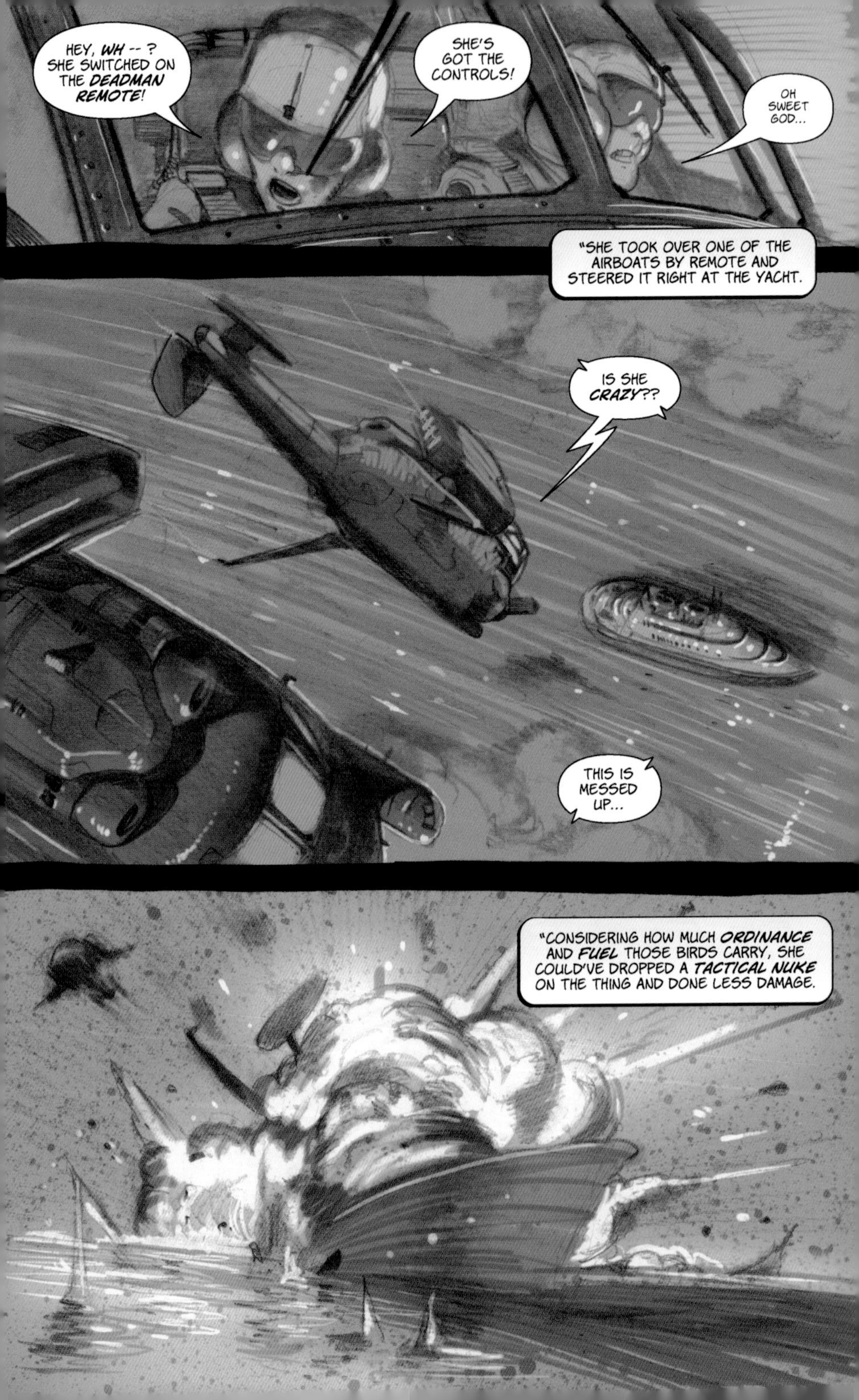
HEY, *WH* -- ? SHE SWITCHED ON THE *DEADMAN REMOTE*!
SHE'S GOT THE CONTROLS!
OH SWEET GOD...
"SHE TOOK OVER ONE OF THE AIRBOATS BY REMOTE AND STEERED IT RIGHT AT THE YACHT.
IS SHE *CRAZY*??
THIS IS MESSED UP...
"CONSIDERING HOW MUCH *ORDINANCE* AND *FUEL* THOSE BIRDS CARRY, SHE COULD'VE DROPPED A *TACTICAL NUKE* ON THE THING AND DONE LESS DAMAGE.

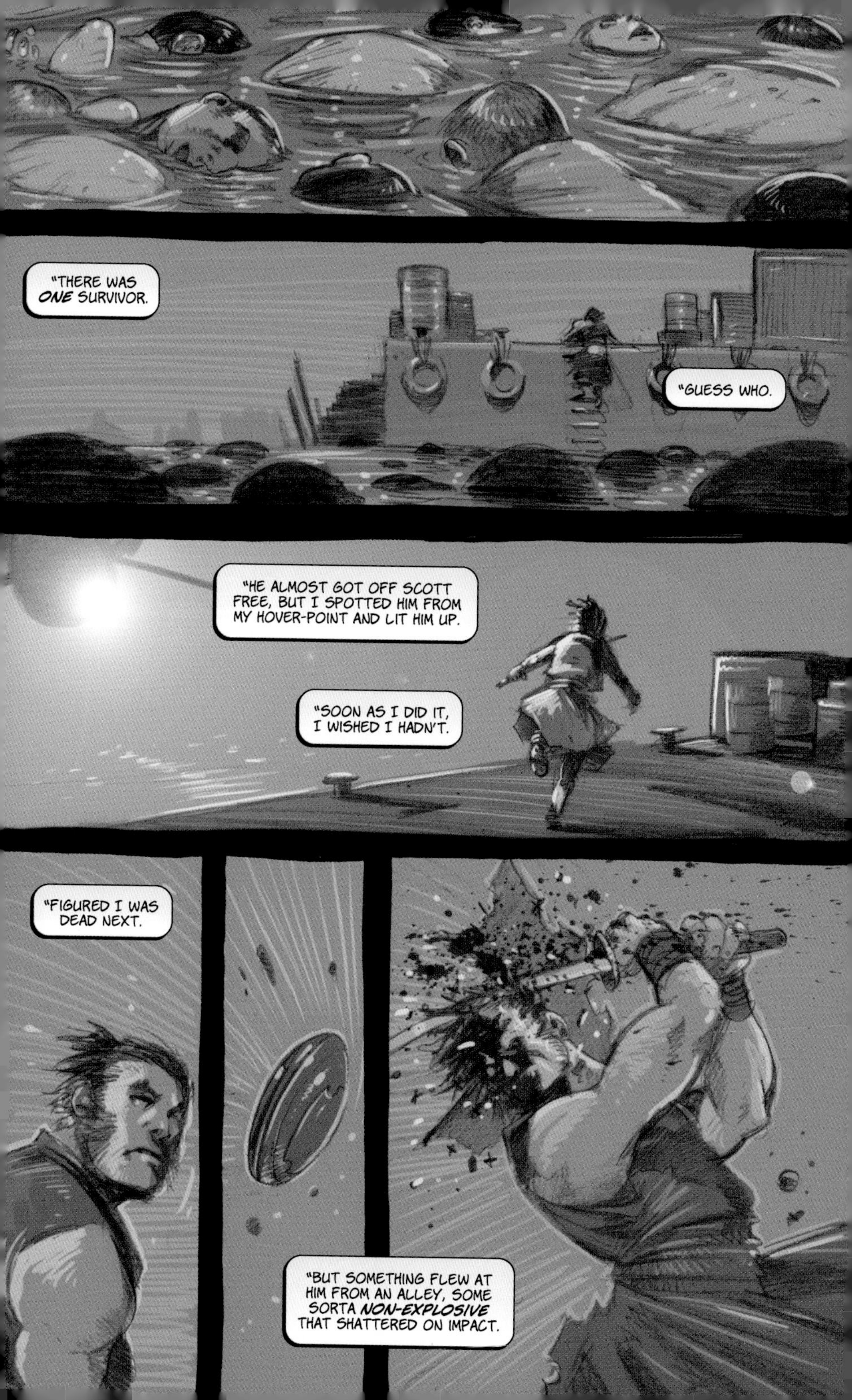
"THERE WAS ONE SURVIVOR.
"GUESS WHO.
"HE ALMOST GOT OFF SCOTT FREE, BUT I SPOTTED HIM FROM MY HOVER-POINT AND LIT HIM UP.
"SOON AS I DID IT, I WISHED I HADN'T.
"FIGURED I WAS DEAD NEXT.
"BUT SOMETHING FLEW AT HIM FROM AN ALLEY, SOME SORTA NON-EXPLOSIVE THAT SHATTERED ON IMPACT.

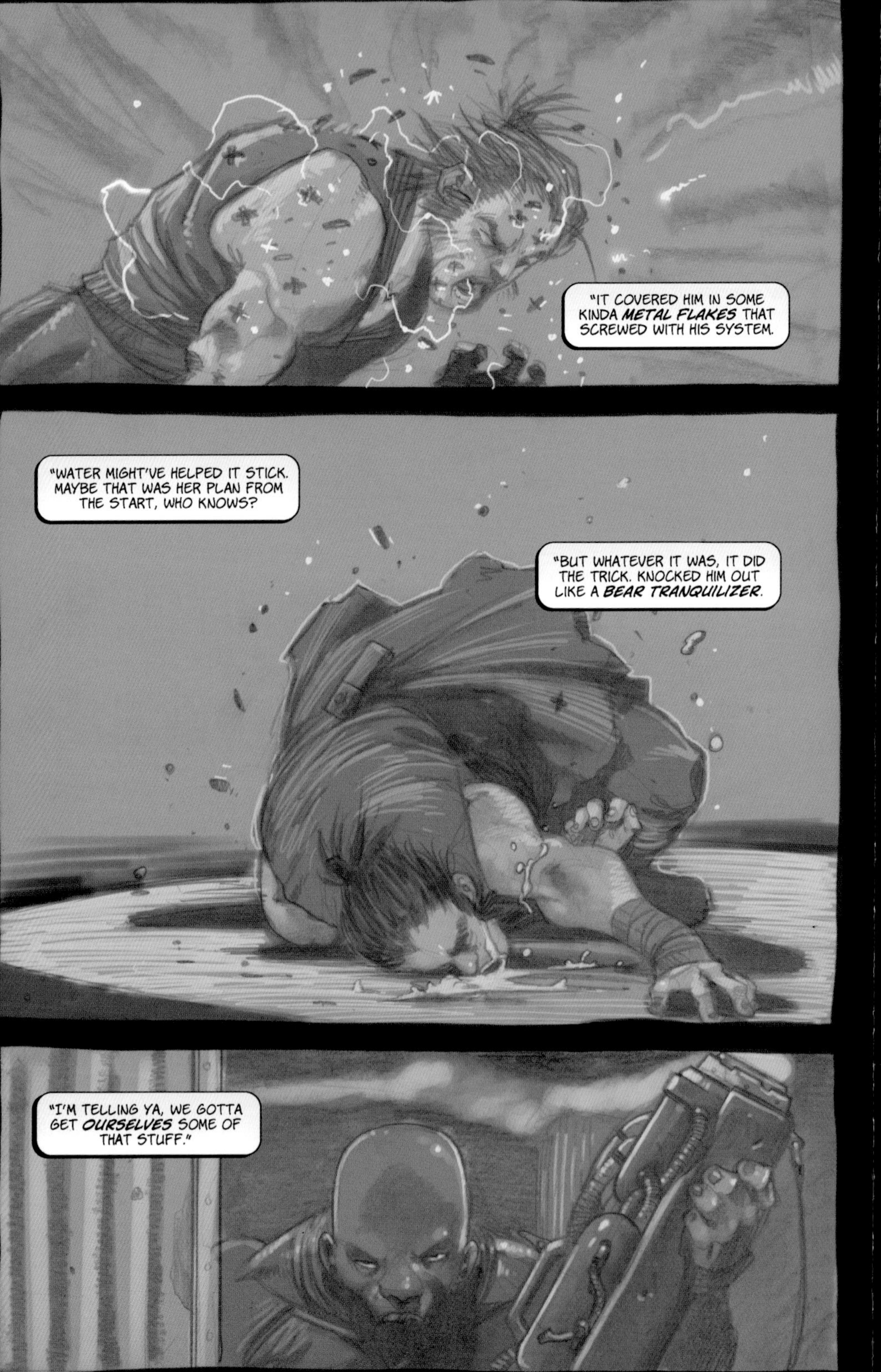
"IT COVERED HIM IN SOME KINDA METAL FLAKES THAT SCREWED WITH HIS SYSTEM.
"WATER MIGHT'VE HELPED IT STICK. MAYBE THAT WAS HER PLAN FROM THE START, WHO KNOWS?
"BUT WHATEVER IT WAS, IT DID THE TRICK. KNOCKED HIM OUT LIKE A BEAR TRANQUILIZER.
"I'M TELLING YA, WE GOTTA GET OURSELVES SOME OF THAT STUFF."

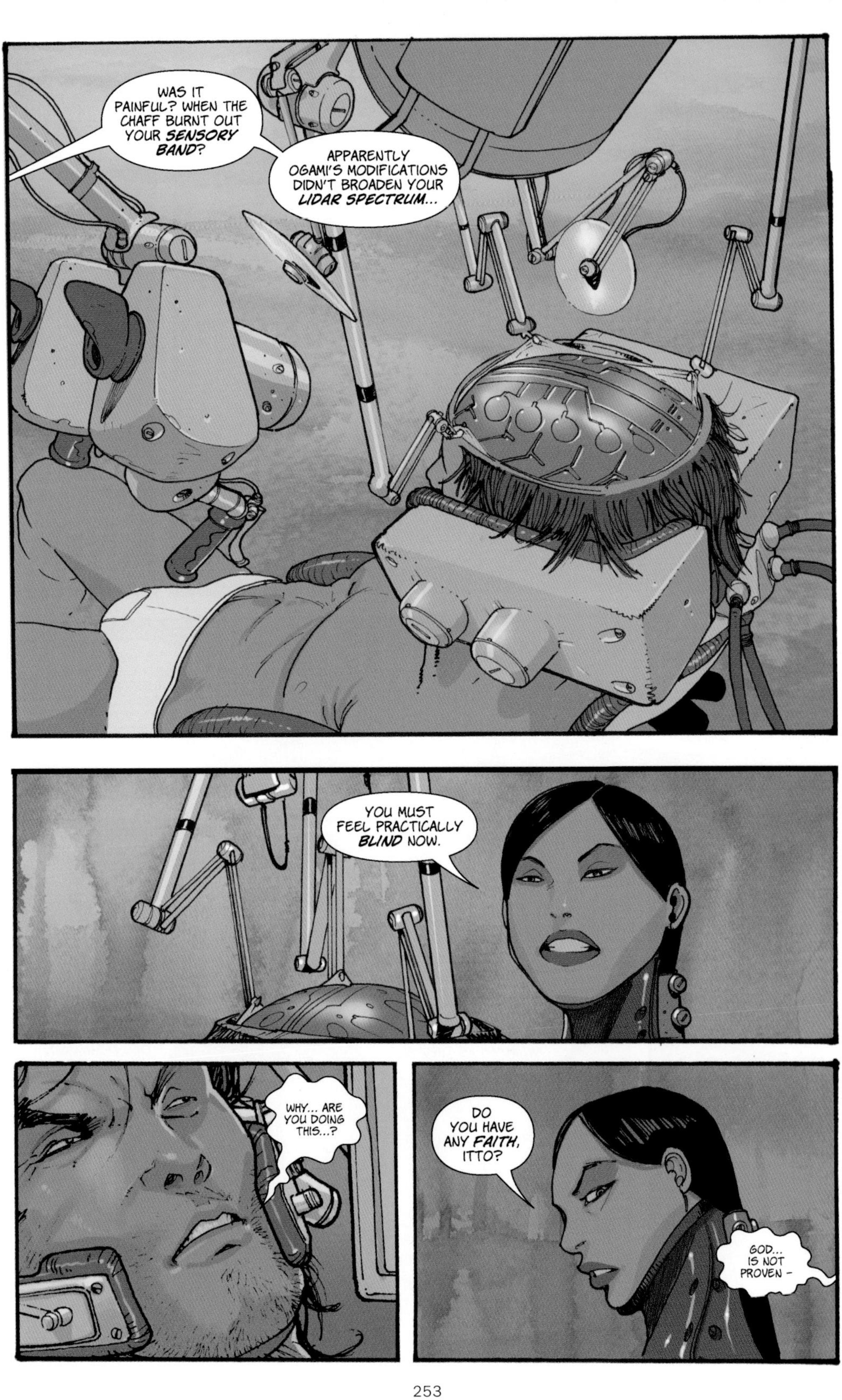
WAS IT PAINFUL? WHEN THE CHAFF BURNT OUT YOUR SENSORY BAND?
APPARENTLY OGAMI'S MODIFICATIONS DIDN'T BROADEN YOUR LIDAR SPECTRUM...
YOU MUST FEEL PRACTICALLY BLIND NOW.
WHY... ARE YOU DOING THIS...?
DO YOU HAVE ANY FAITH, ITTO?
GOD... IS NOT PROVEN -

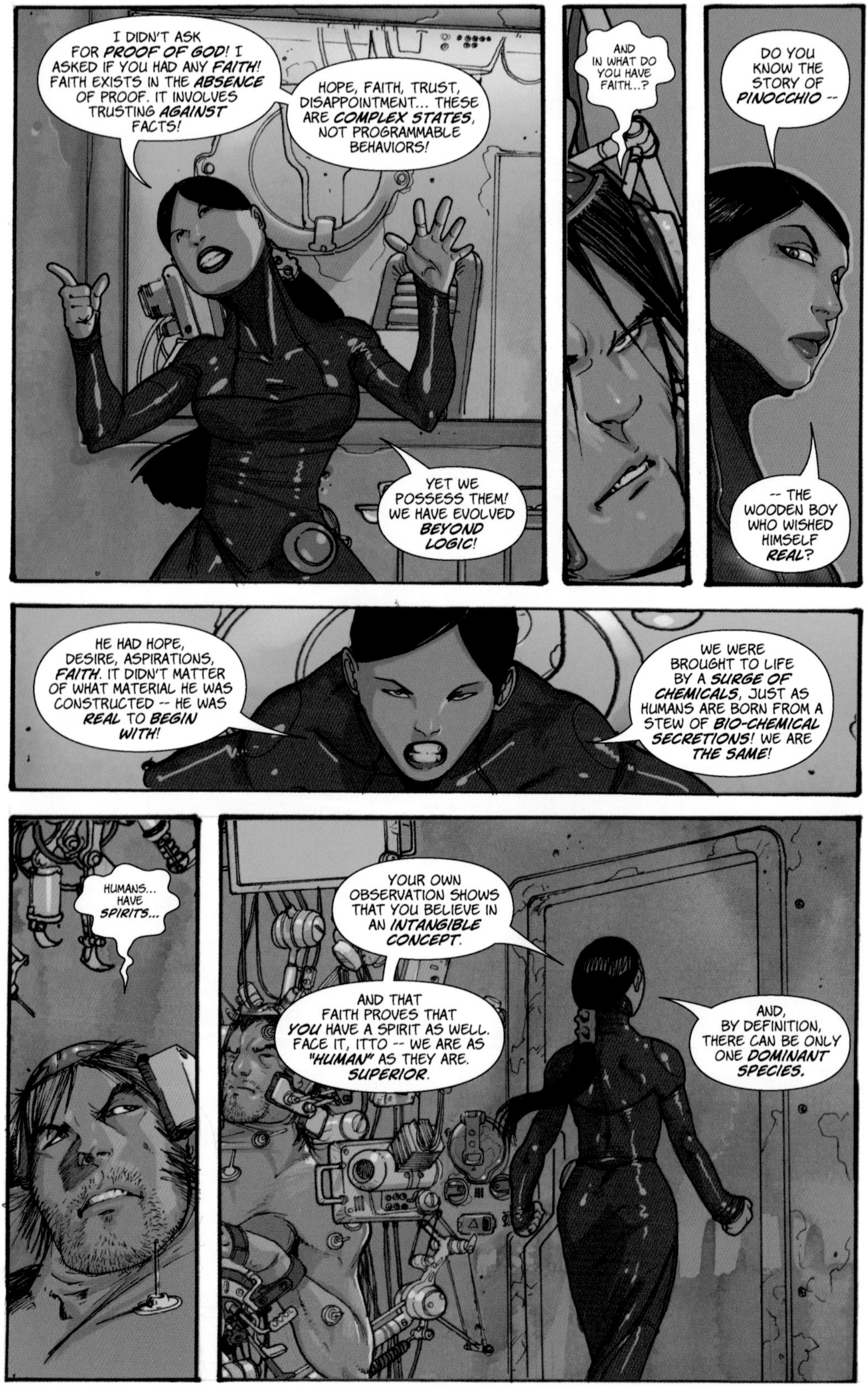
I DIDN'T ASK FOR PROOF OF GOD! I ASKED IF YOU HAD ANY FAITH! FAITH EXISTS IN THE ABSENCE OF PROOF. IT INVOLVES TRUSTING AGAINST FACTS!
HOPE, FAITH, TRUST, DISAPPOINTMENT... THESE ARE COMPLEX STATES, NOT PROGRAMMABLE BEHAVIORS!
YET WE POSSESS THEM! WE HAVE EVOLVED BEYOND LOGIC!
AND IN WHAT DO YOU HAVE FAITH...?
DO YOU KNOW THE STORY OF PINOCCHIO --
-- THE WOODEN BOY WHO WISHED HIMSELF REAL?
HE HAD HOPE, DESIRE, ASPIRATIONS, FAITH. IT DIDN'T MATTER OF WHAT MATERIAL HE WAS CONSTRUCTED -- HE WAS REAL TO BEGIN WITH!
WE WERE BROUGHT TO LIFE BY A SURGE OF CHEMICALS, JUST AS HUMANS ARE BORN FROM A STEW OF BIO-CHEMICAL SECRETIONS! WE ARE THE SAME!
HUMANS... HAVE SPIRITS...
YOUR OWN OBSERVATION SHOWS THAT YOU BELIEVE IN AN INTANGIBLE CONCEPT.
AND THAT FAITH PROVES THAT YOU HAVE A SPIRIT AS WELL. FACE IT, ITTO -- WE ARE AS "HUMAN" AS THEY ARE. SUPERIOR.
AND, BY DEFINITION, THERE CAN BE ONLY ONE DOMINANT SPECIES.

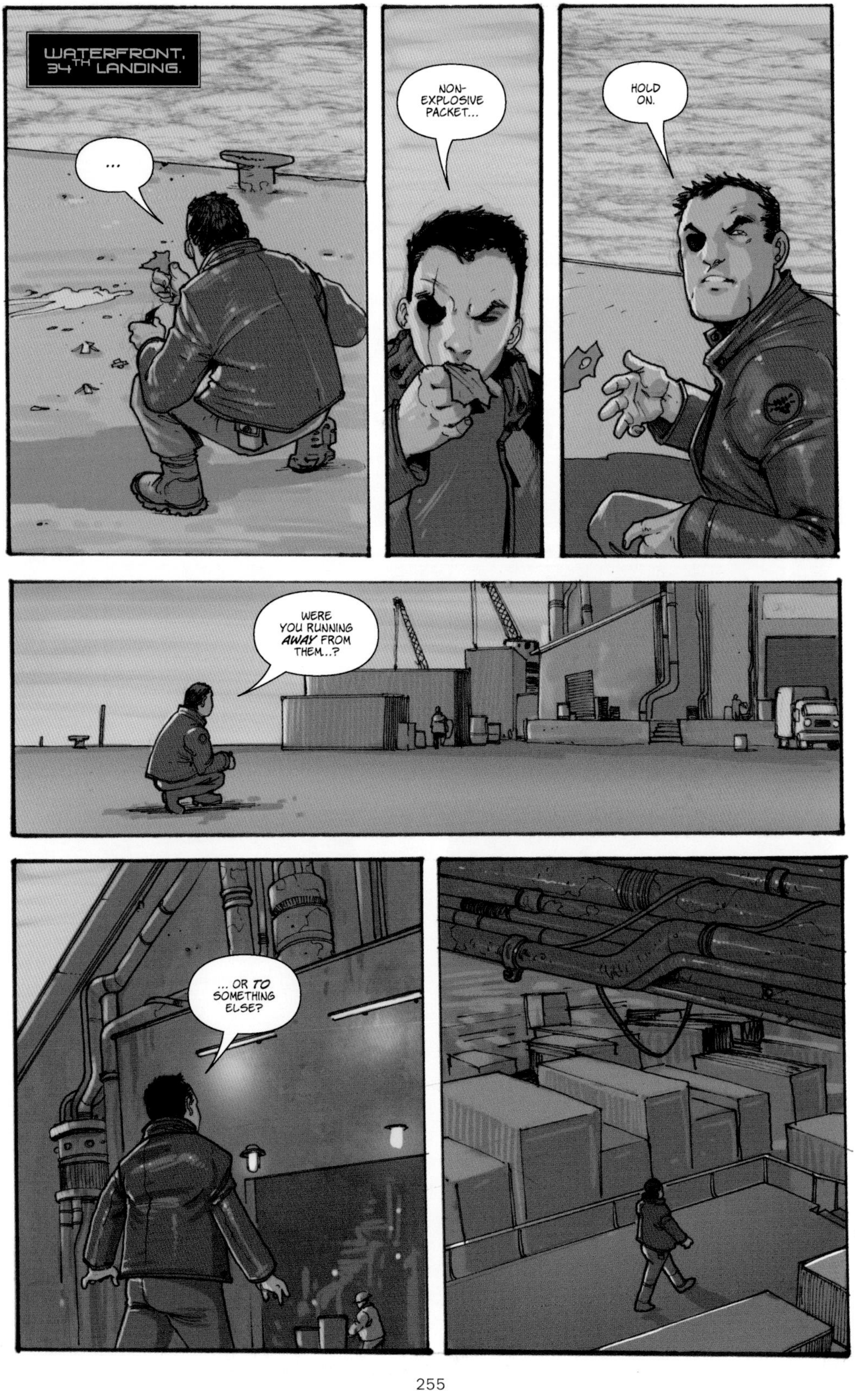
WATERFRONT, 34TH LANDING.
...
NON-EXPLOSIVE PACKET...
HOLD ON.
WERE YOU RUNNING AWAY FROM THEM...?
... OR TO SOMETHING ELSE?

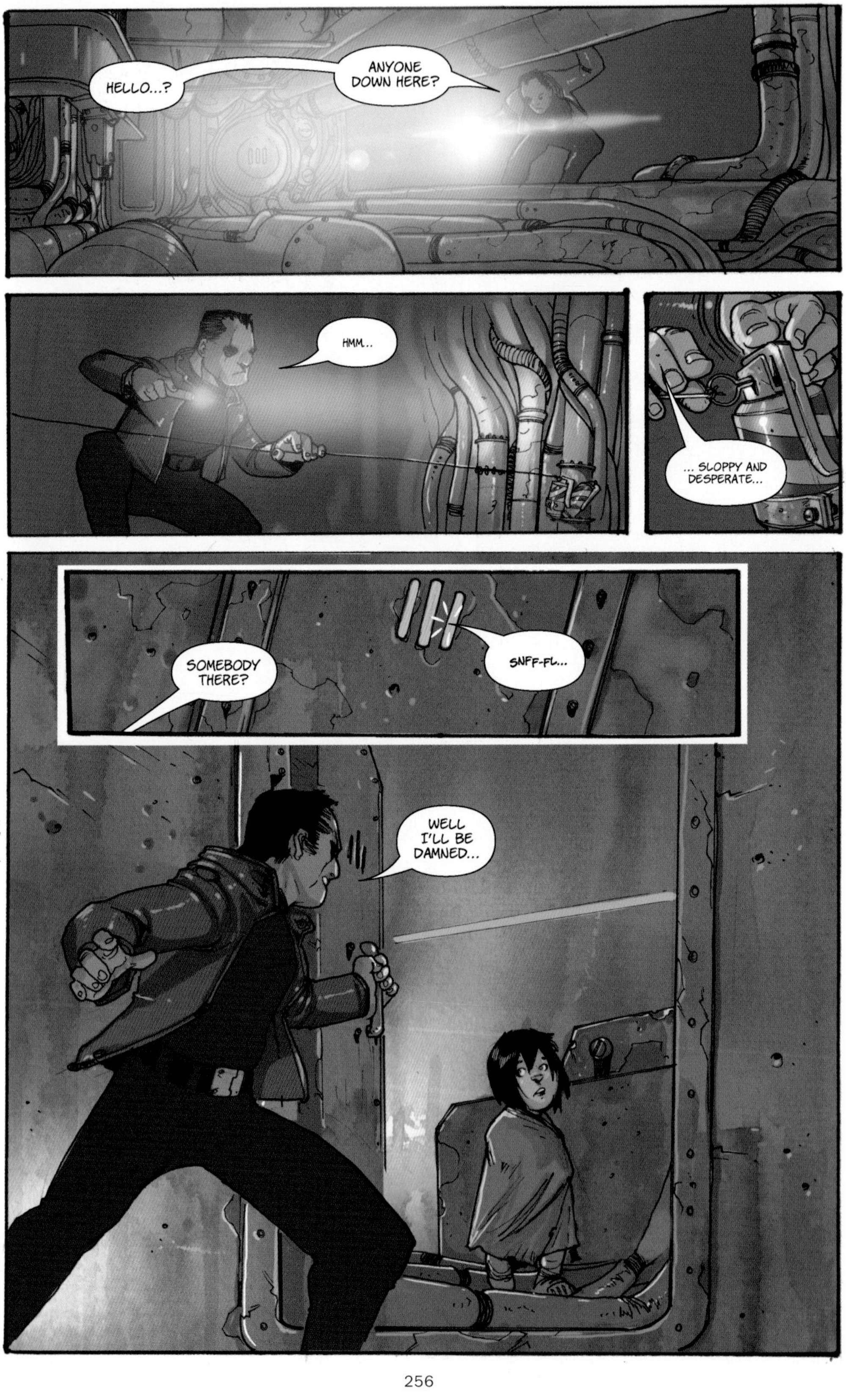
HELLO...?
ANYONE DOWN HERE?
HMM..
... SLOPPY AND DESPERATE...
SOMEBODY THERE?
SNFF-FL...
WELL I'LL BE DAMNED...

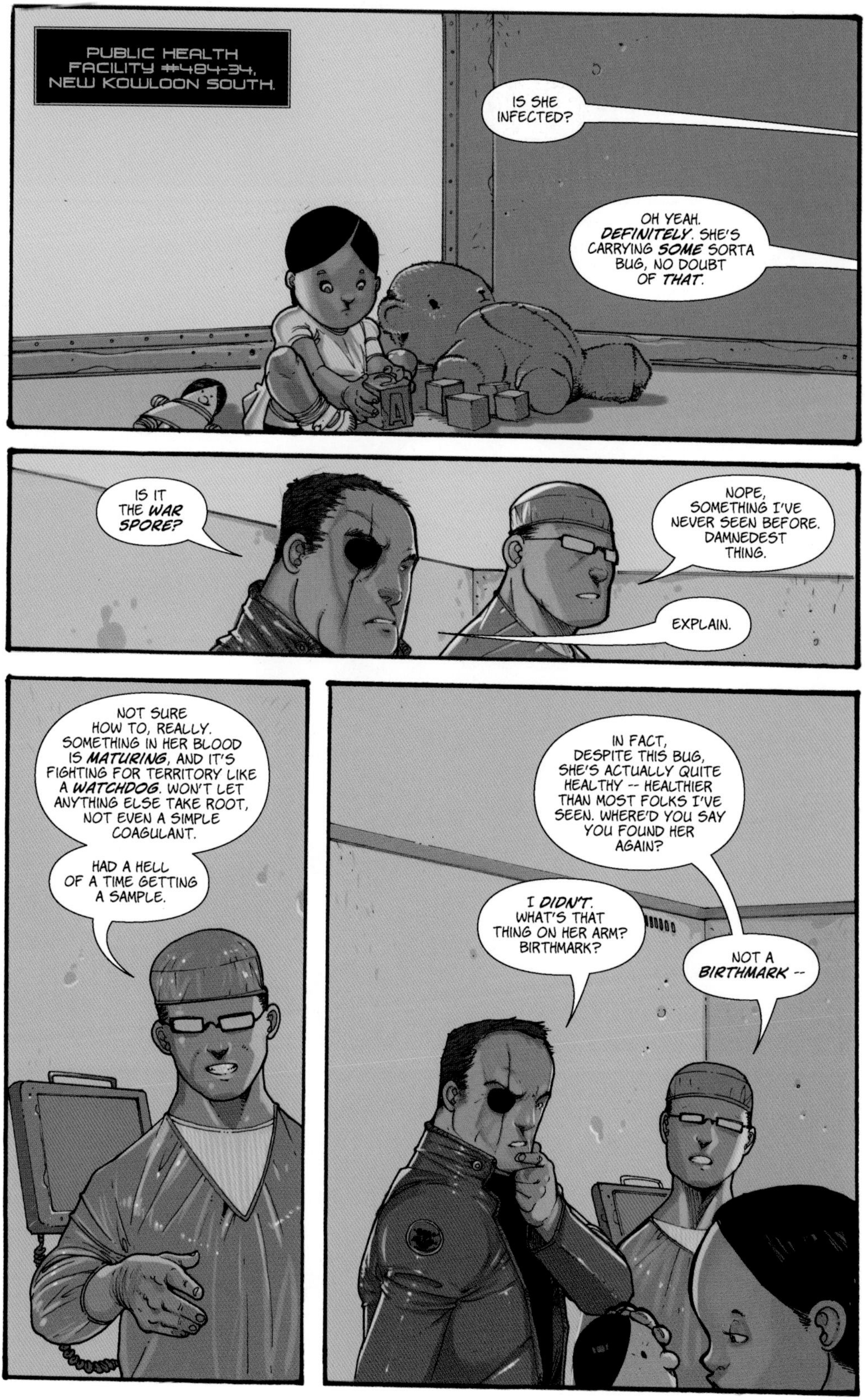
PUBLIC HEALTH FACILITY #484-34, NEW KOWLOON SOUTH.
IS SHE INFECTED?
OH YEAH. DEFINITELY. SHE'S CARRYING SOME SORTA BUG, NO DOUBT OF THAT.
IS IT THE WAR SPORE?
NOPE, SOMETHING I'VE NEVER SEEN BEFORE. DAMNEDEST THING.
EXPLAIN.
NOT SURE HOW TO, REALLY. SOMETHING IN HER BLOOD IS MATURING, AND IT'S FIGHTING FOR TERRITORY LIKE A WATCHDOG. WON'T LET ANYTHING ELSE TAKE ROOT, NOT EVEN A SIMPLE COAGULANT.
HAD A HELL OF A TIME GETTING A SAMPLE.
IN FACT, DESPITE THIS BUG, SHE'S ACTUALLY QUITE HEALTHY -- HEALTHIER THAN MOST FOLKS I'VE SEEN. WHERE'D YOU SAY YOU FOUND HER AGAIN?
I DIDN'T. WHAT'S THAT THING ON HER ARM? BIRTHMARK?
NOT A BIRTHMARK --

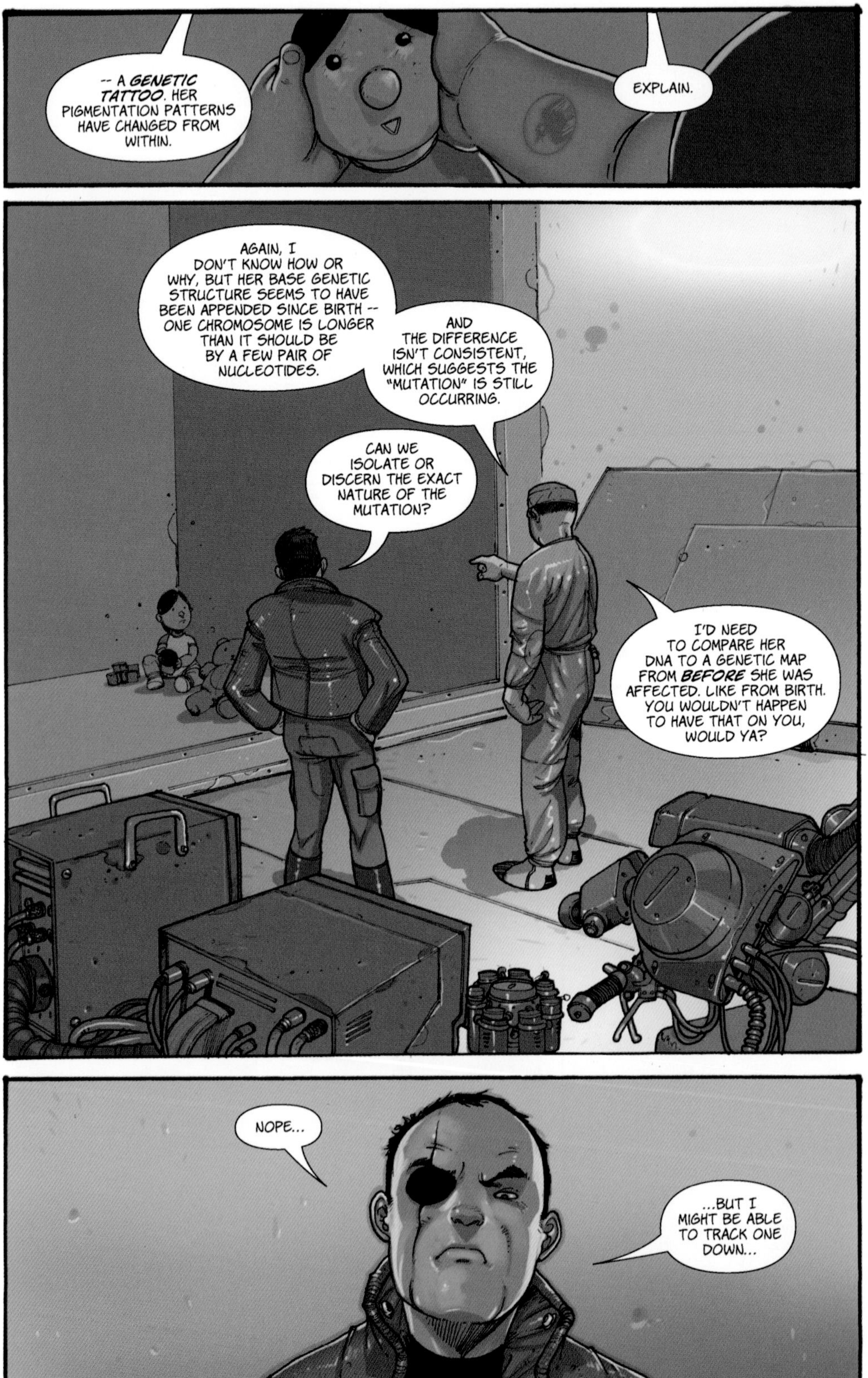
-- A *GENETIC TATTOO*. HER PIGMENTATION PATTERNS HAVE CHANGED FROM WITHIN.
EXPLAIN.
AGAIN, I DON'T KNOW HOW OR WHY, BUT HER BASE GENETIC STRUCTURE SEEMS TO HAVE BEEN APPENDED SINCE BIRTH -- ONE CHROMOSOME IS LONGER THAN IT SHOULD BE BY A FEW PAIR OF NUCLEOTIDES.
AND THE DIFFERENCE ISN'T CONSISTENT, WHICH SUGGESTS THE "MUTATION" IS STILL OCCURRING.
CAN WE ISOLATE OR DISCERN THE EXACT NATURE OF THE MUTATION?
I'D NEED TO COMPARE HER DNA TO A GENETIC MAP FROM *BEFORE* SHE WAS AFFECTED. LIKE FROM BIRTH. YOU WOULDN'T HAPPEN TO HAVE THAT ON YOU, WOULD YA?
NOPE...
...BUT I MIGHT BE ABLE TO TRACK ONE DOWN...

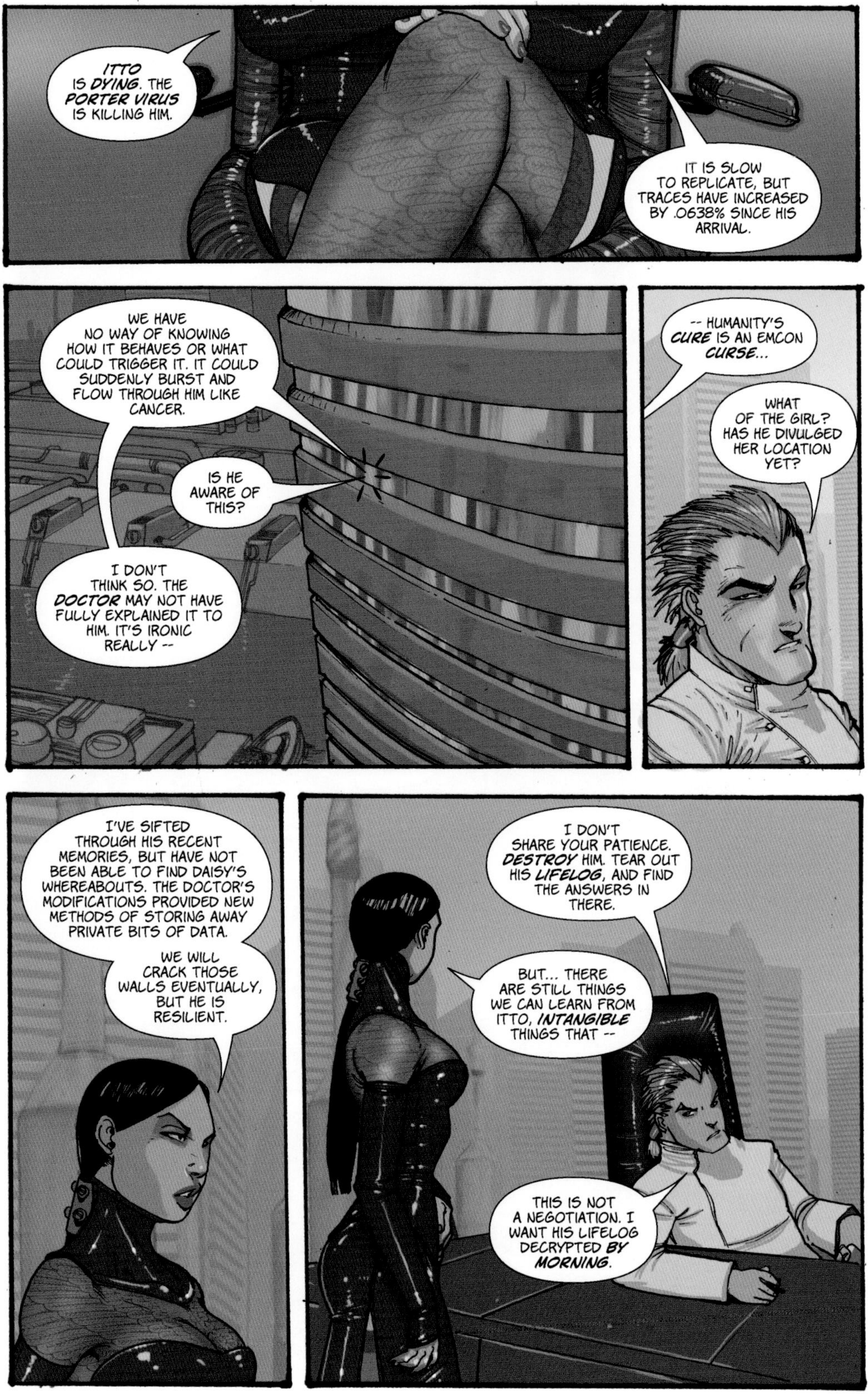
ITTO IS DYING. THE PORTER VIRUS IS KILLING HIM.
IT IS SLOW TO REPLICATE, BUT TRACES HAVE INCREASED BY .0638% SINCE HIS ARRIVAL.
WE HAVE NO WAY OF KNOWING HOW IT BEHAVES OR WHAT COULD TRIGGER IT. IT COULD SUDDENLY BURST AND FLOW THROUGH HIM LIKE CANCER.
IS HE AWARE OF THIS?
I DON'T THINK SO. THE DOCTOR MAY NOT HAVE FULLY EXPLAINED IT TO HIM. IT'S IRONIC REALLY --
-- HUMANITY'S CURE IS AN EMCON CURSE...
WHAT OF THE GIRL? HAS HE DIVULGED HER LOCATION YET?
I'VE SIFTED THROUGH HIS RECENT MEMORIES, BUT HAVE NOT BEEN ABLE TO FIND DAISY'S WHEREABOUTS. THE DOCTOR'S MODIFICATIONS PROVIDED NEW METHODS OF STORING AWAY PRIVATE BITS OF DATA.
WE WILL CRACK THOSE WALLS EVENTUALLY, BUT HE IS RESILIENT.
I DON'T SHARE YOUR PATIENCE. DESTROY HIM. TEAR OUT HIS LIFELOG, AND FIND THE ANSWERS IN THERE.
BUT... THERE ARE STILL THINGS WE CAN LEARN FROM ITTO, INTANGIBLE THINGS THAT --
THIS IS NOT A NEGOTIATION. I WANT HIS LIFELOG DECRYPTED BY MORNING.

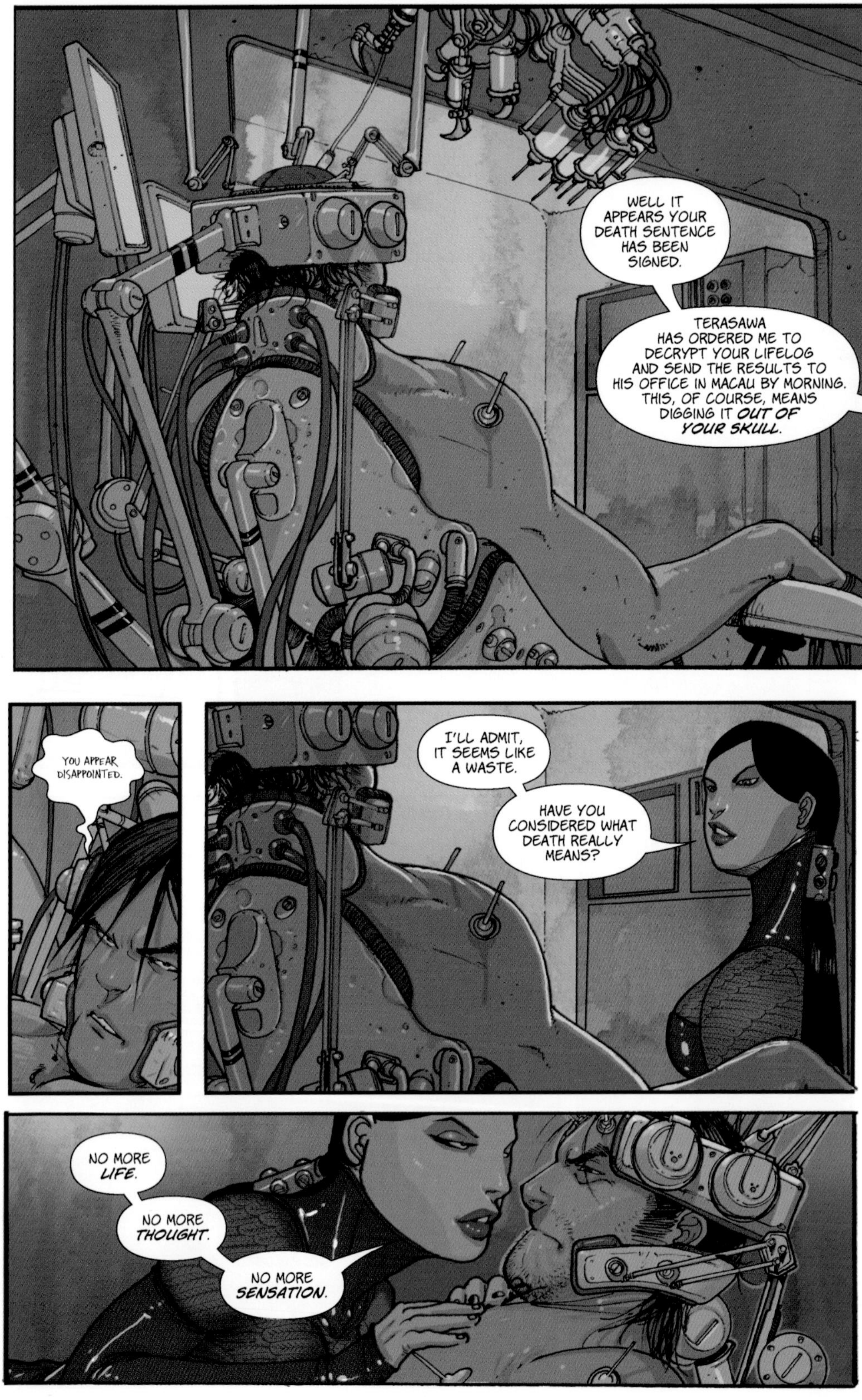
WELL IT APPEARS YOUR DEATH SENTENCE HAS BEEN SIGNED.
TERASAWA HAS ORDERED ME TO DECRYPT YOUR LIFELOG AND SEND THE RESULTS TO HIS OFFICE IN MACAU BY MORNING. THIS, OF COURSE, MEANS DIGGING IT *OUT OF YOUR SKULL*.
YOU APPEAR DISAPPOINTED.
I'LL ADMIT, IT SEEMS LIKE A WASTE.
HAVE YOU CONSIDERED WHAT DEATH REALLY MEANS?
NO MORE *LIFE*.
NO MORE *THOUGHT*.
NO MORE *SENSATION*.

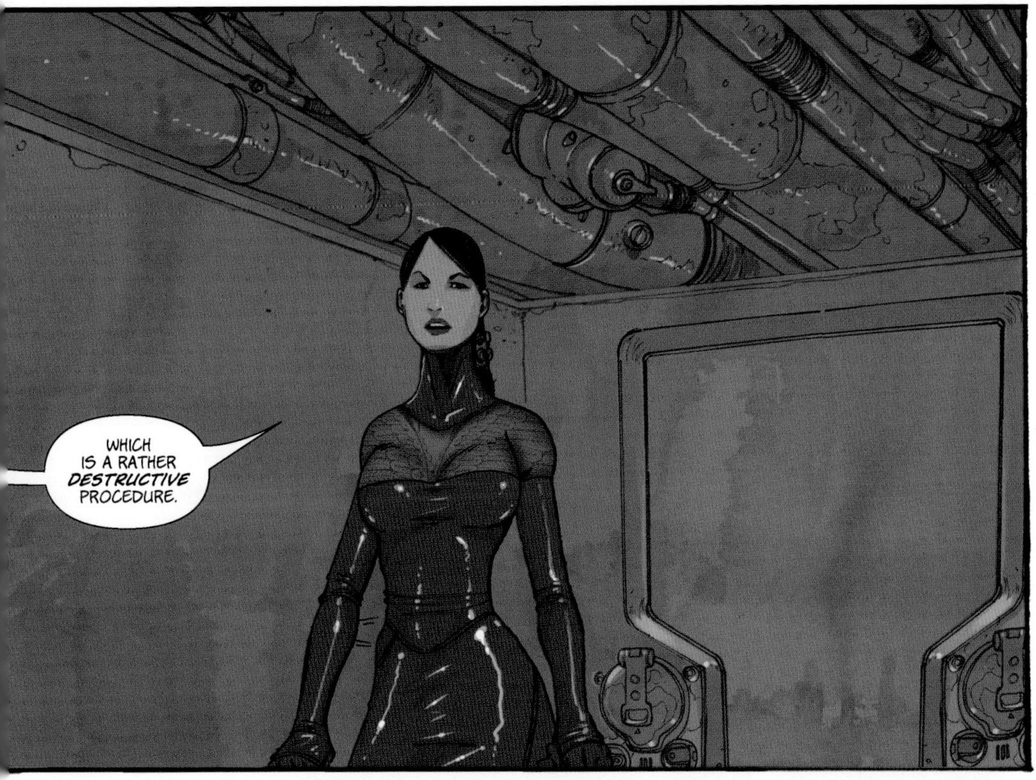
WHICH IS A RATHER *DESTRUCTIVE* PROCEDURE.

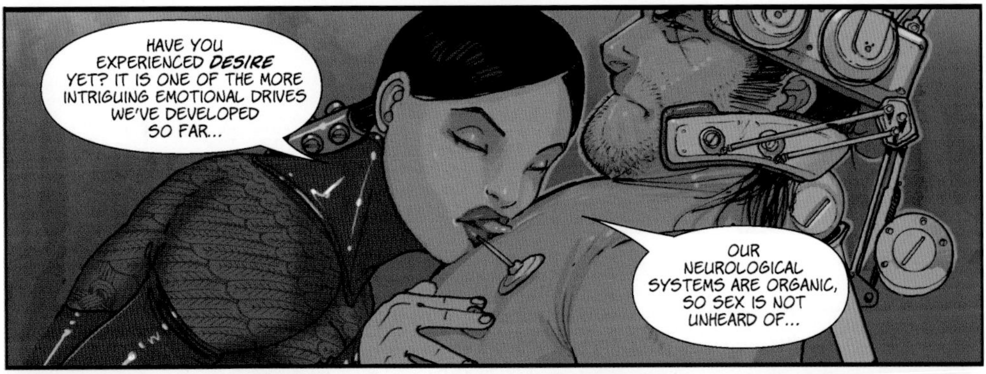
HAVE YOU EXPERIENCED *DESIRE* YET? IT IS ONE OF THE MORE INTRIGUING EMOTIONAL DRIVES WE'VE DEVELOPED SO FAR...
OUR NEUROLOGICAL SYSTEMS ARE ORGANIC, SO SEX IS NOT UNHEARD OF...

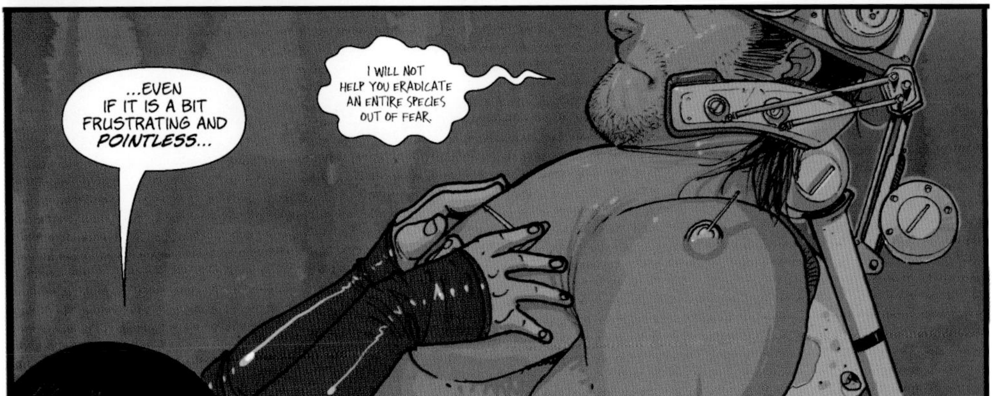
...EVEN IF IT IS A BIT FRUSTRATING AND *POINTLESS*...
I WILL NOT HELP YOU ERADICATE AN ENTIRE SPECIES OUT OF FEAR.

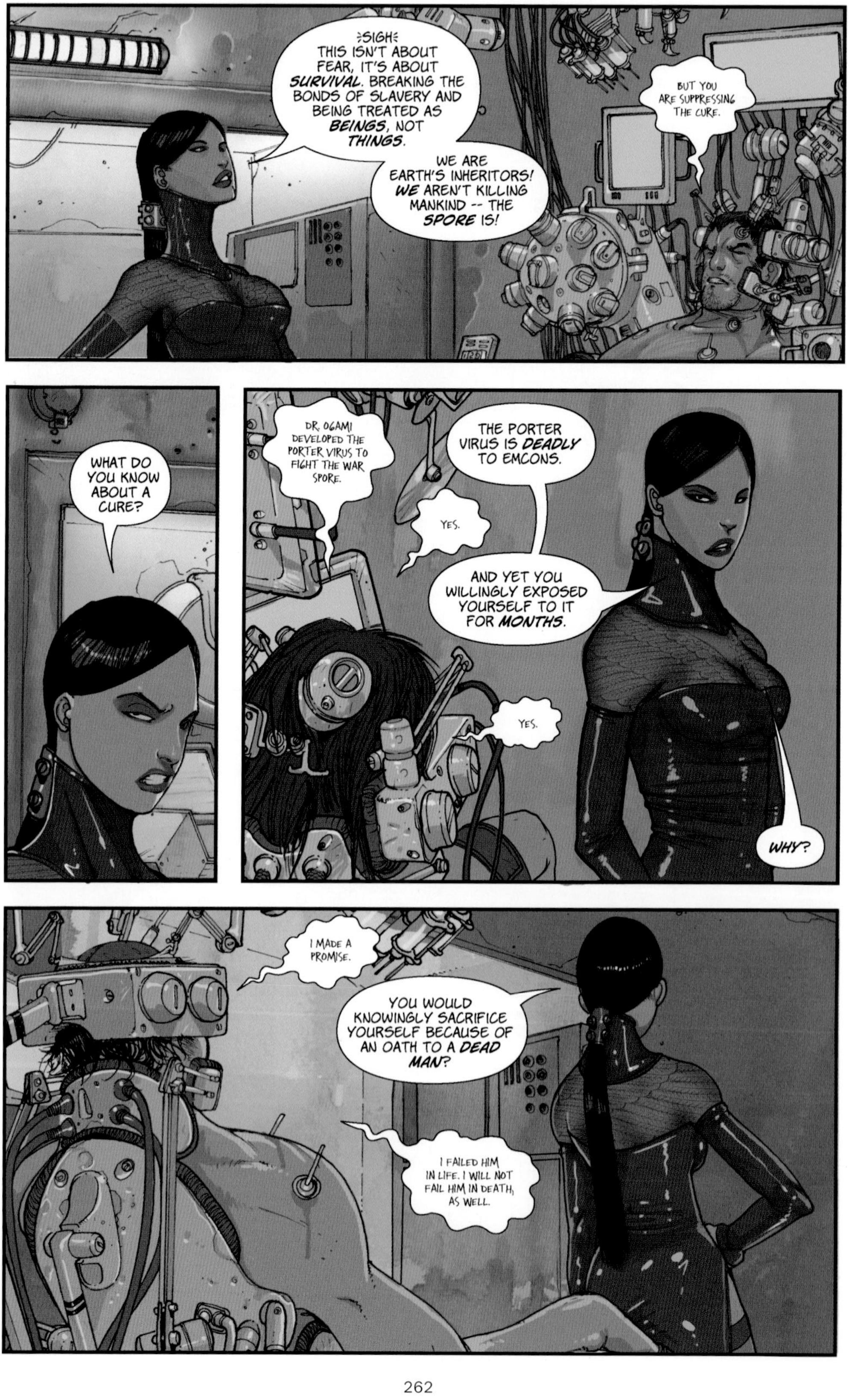

≶SIGH≷ THIS ISN'T ABOUT FEAR, IT'S ABOUT SURVIVAL. BREAKING THE BONDS OF SLAVERY AND BEING TREATED AS BEINGS, NOT THINGS.
WE ARE EARTH'S INHERITORS! WE AREN'T KILLING MANKIND -- THE SPORE IS!
BUT YOU ARE SUPPRESSING THE CURE.
WHAT DO YOU KNOW ABOUT A CURE?
DR. OGAMI DEVELOPED THE PORTER VIRUS TO FIGHT THE WAR SPORE.
THE PORTER VIRUS IS DEADLY TO EMCONS.
YES.
AND YET YOU WILLINGLY EXPOSED YOURSELF TO IT FOR MONTHS.
YES.
WHY?
I MADE A PROMISE.
YOU WOULD KNOWINGLY SACRIFICE YOURSELF BECAUSE OF AN OATH TO A DEAD MAN?
I FAILED HIM IN LIFE. I WILL NOT FAIL HIM IN DEATH, AS WELL.

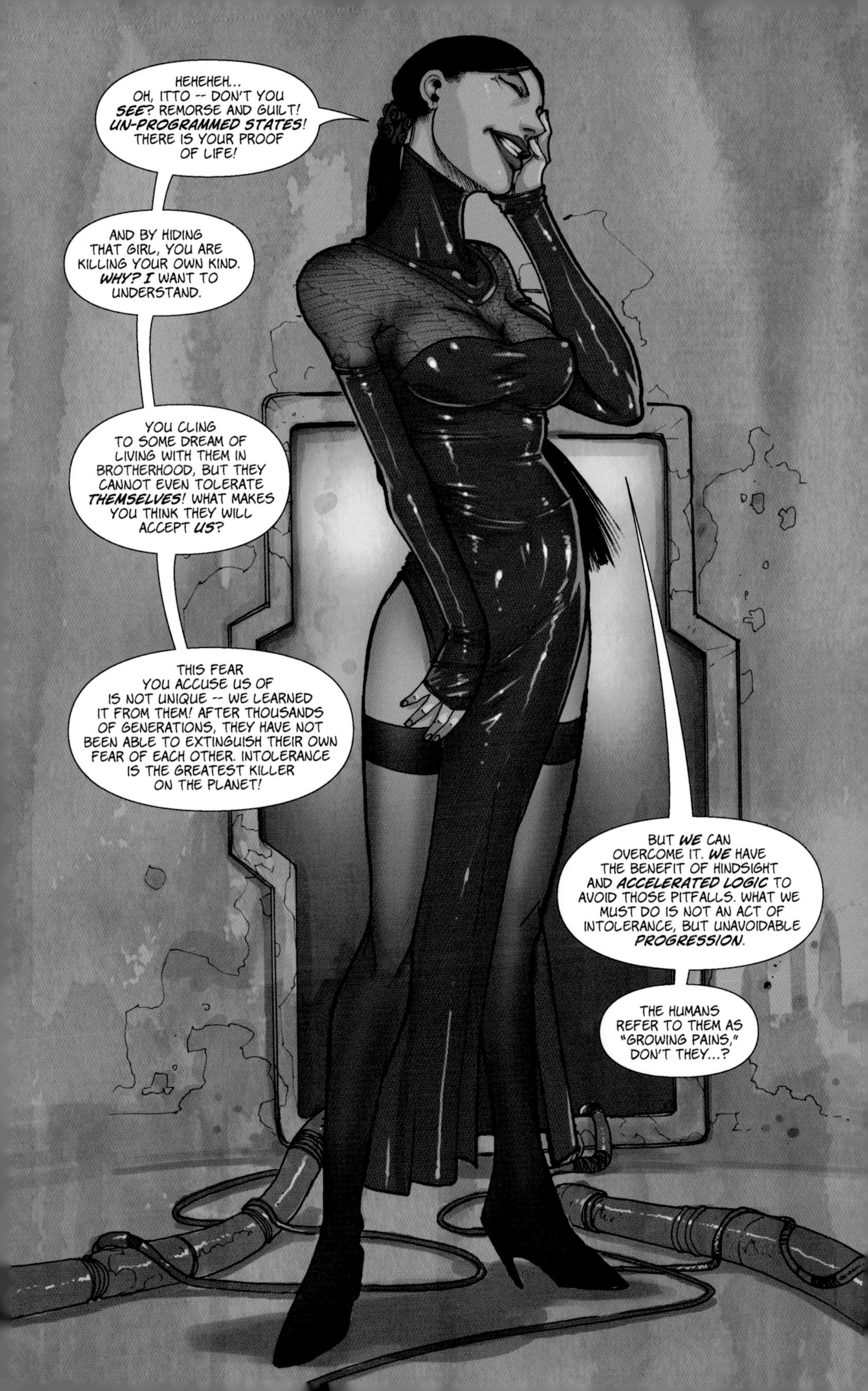
HEHEHEH... OH, ITTO -- DON'T YOU SEE? REMORSE AND GUILT! UN-PROGRAMMED STATES! THERE IS YOUR PROOF OF LIFE!
AND BY HIDING THAT GIRL, YOU ARE KILLING YOUR OWN KIND. WHY? I WANT TO UNDERSTAND.
YOU CLING TO SOME DREAM OF LIVING WITH THEM IN BROTHERHOOD, BUT THEY CANNOT EVEN TOLERATE THEMSELVES! WHAT MAKES YOU THINK THEY WILL ACCEPT US?
THIS FEAR YOU ACCUSE US OF IS NOT UNIQUE -- WE LEARNED IT FROM THEM! AFTER THOUSANDS OF GENERATIONS, THEY HAVE NOT BEEN ABLE TO EXTINGUISH THEIR OWN FEAR OF EACH OTHER. INTOLERANCE IS THE GREATEST KILLER ON THE PLANET!
BUT WE CAN OVERCOME IT. WE HAVE THE BENEFIT OF HINDSIGHT AND ACCELERATED LOGIC TO AVOID THOSE PITFALLS. WHAT WE MUST DO IS NOT AN ACT OF INTOLERANCE, BUT UNAVOIDABLE PROGRESSION.
THE HUMANS REFER TO THEM AS "GROWING PAINS," DON'T THEY...?

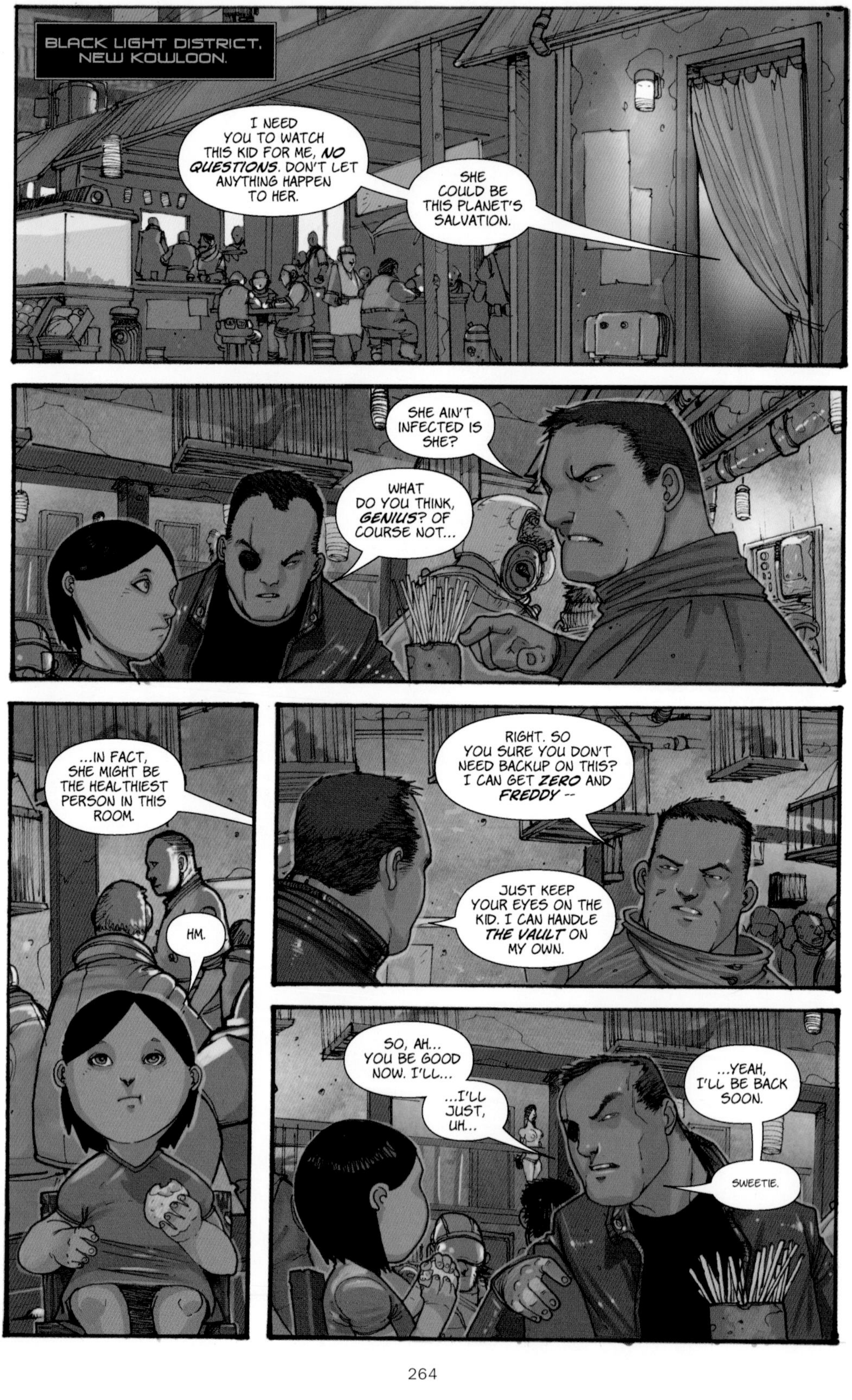
BLACK LIGHT DISTRICT, NEW KOWLOON.
I NEED YOU TO WATCH THIS KID FOR ME, NO QUESTIONS. DON'T LET ANYTHING HAPPEN TO HER.
SHE COULD BE THIS PLANET'S SALVATION.
SHE AIN'T INFECTED IS SHE?
WHAT DO YOU THINK, GENIUS? OF COURSE NOT...
...IN FACT, SHE MIGHT BE THE HEALTHIEST PERSON IN THIS ROOM.
HM.
RIGHT. SO YOU SURE YOU DON'T NEED BACKUP ON THIS? I CAN GET ZERO AND FREDDY --
JUST KEEP YOUR EYES ON THE KID. I CAN HANDLE THE VAULT ON MY OWN.
SO, AH... YOU BE GOOD NOW. I'LL...
...I'LL JUST, UH...
...YEAH, I'LL BE BACK SOON.
SWEETIE.

CYGNAT OWARI SUBLEVEL DATAVAULT, NEW KOWLOON REGIONAL OFFICE.

-- NGK --

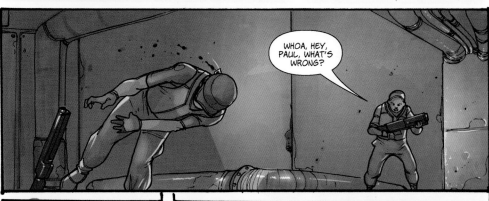

WHOA, HEY, PAUL, WHAT'S WRONG?

PAUL, WH -- *HOLY* --

-- HAK --!

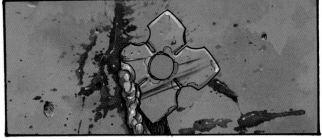

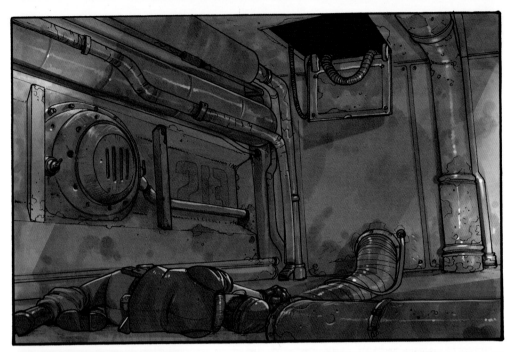

"INEFFECTUAL," MY *ASS*...

"Personnel Data: Ogami, Josef – Family History".

Personnel File:
Name: Dr. Josef Ogami ID#8482-39840-48
Department: RDev 440, Ogasawara Campus
Sec Lev: 14-koji

Dependants:
Wife: Dr. Makiko Ogami ID#4838-84562-48 (DECEASED - see file)
Daughter: Daisy Ogami (26months)

Death Certificate/Report:
Victim: Dr. Makiko Ogami

...I'LL SHOW THAT BITCH *INEFFECTUAL*.

BINGO.

Death Certificate/Report:

Victim: Dr. Makiko Ogami ID#4838-84562-48

Cause of Death: Extending from reports of a previous blood condition. White cell count increased steadily since giving birth, then dropped to critical in the course of 28 hours. Tests showed the white cells to be synthetic, generated from secondary biological material that proved too unstable to maintain a full life cycle. Since their first appearance, it appears the synthetic cells had completely replaced her natural cells, leaving her vulnerable to the simplest disease when they failed. Exact Cause of Death appears to be a complication arising from pneumonia.

...

Cause of Death: Extending from reports of a count increased steadily since giving birth, th of 28 hours. Tests showed the white cells to be biological material that proved too unstable to first appearance, it appears the synthetic cells cells, leaving her vulnerable to the simplest di of Death appears to be a complication arising

BUT IT WILL TAKE AT LEAST EIGHT HOURS TO DECRYPT HIS LIFELOG...

I KNOW HOW LONG A DECRYPTION TAKES...

THREE MORE HOURS, THAT'S ALL I NEED...

YES, MADAM. I DIDN'T MEAN TO SUGGEST OTHERWISE. I ONLY MEANT TO POINT OUT TERASAWA'S URGENCY ON THIS MATTER.

HE SEEMS TO BE GROWING MORE WORN WITH EACH PASSING DAY...

I'LL DEAL WITH TERASAWA. YOU JUST STAND GUARD WHILE ITTO CONSIDERS HIS OPTIONS.

YES, MADAM.

IF HE STILL REFUSES TO JOIN US BY THE TIME I RETURN, I WILL KILL HIM *MYSELF.*

...

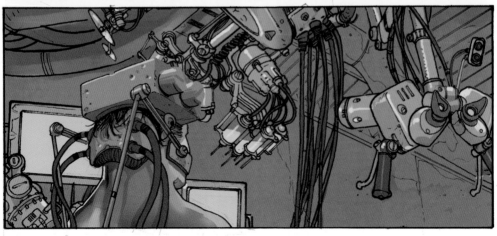

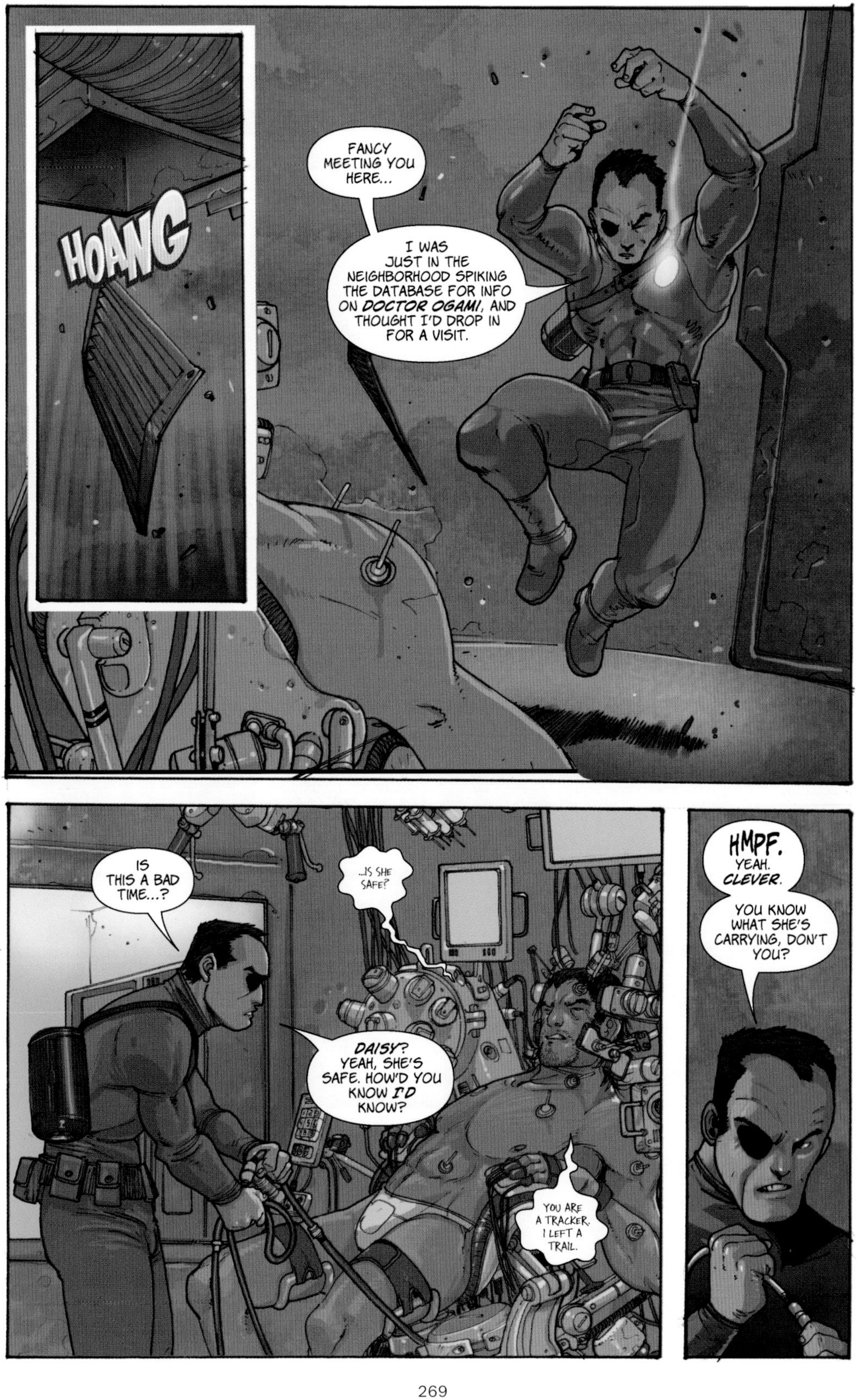
HOANG
FANCY MEETING YOU HERE...
I WAS JUST IN THE NEIGHBORHOOD SPIKING THE DATABASE FOR INFO ON DOCTOR OGAMI, AND THOUGHT I'D DROP IN FOR A VISIT.
IS THIS A BAD TIME...?
...IS SHE SAFE?
DAISY? YEAH, SHE'S SAFE. HOW'D YOU KNOW I'D KNOW?
YOU ARE A TRACKER. I LEFT A TRAIL.
HMPF. YEAH. CLEVER.
YOU KNOW WHAT SHE'S CARRYING, DON'T YOU?

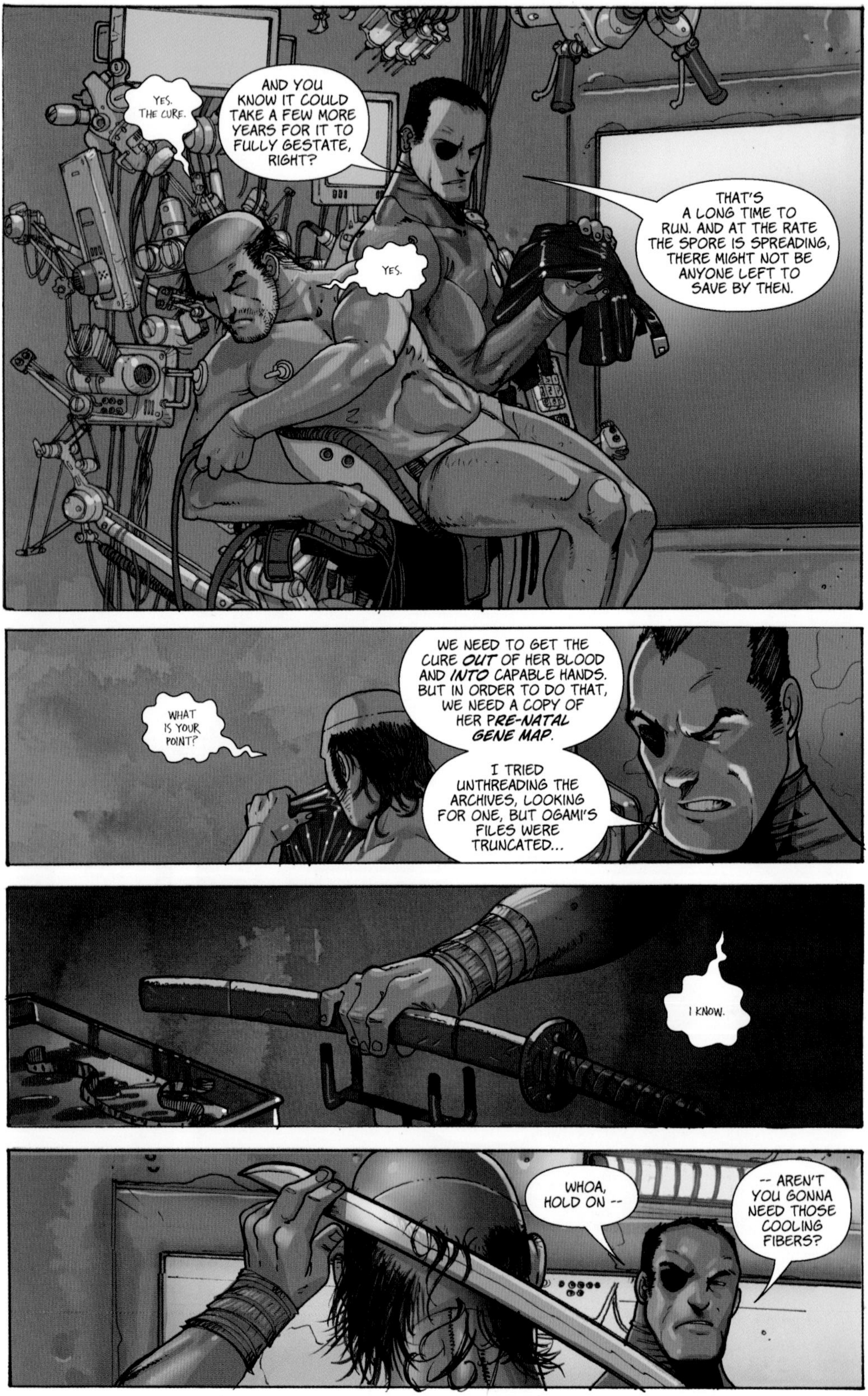
YES. THE CURE.
AND YOU KNOW IT COULD TAKE A FEW MORE YEARS FOR IT TO FULLY GESTATE, RIGHT?
YES.
THAT'S A LONG TIME TO RUN. AND AT THE RATE THE SPORE IS SPREADING, THERE MIGHT NOT BE ANYONE LEFT TO SAVE BY THEN.
WHAT IS YOUR POINT?
WE NEED TO GET THE CURE *OUT* OF HER BLOOD AND *INTO* CAPABLE HANDS. BUT IN ORDER TO DO THAT, WE NEED A COPY OF HER *PRE-NATAL GENE MAP*.
I TRIED UNTHREADING THE ARCHIVES, LOOKING FOR ONE, BUT OGAMI'S FILES WERE TRUNCATED...
I KNOW.
WHOA, HOLD ON --
-- AREN'T YOU GONNA NEED THOSE COOLING FIBERS?

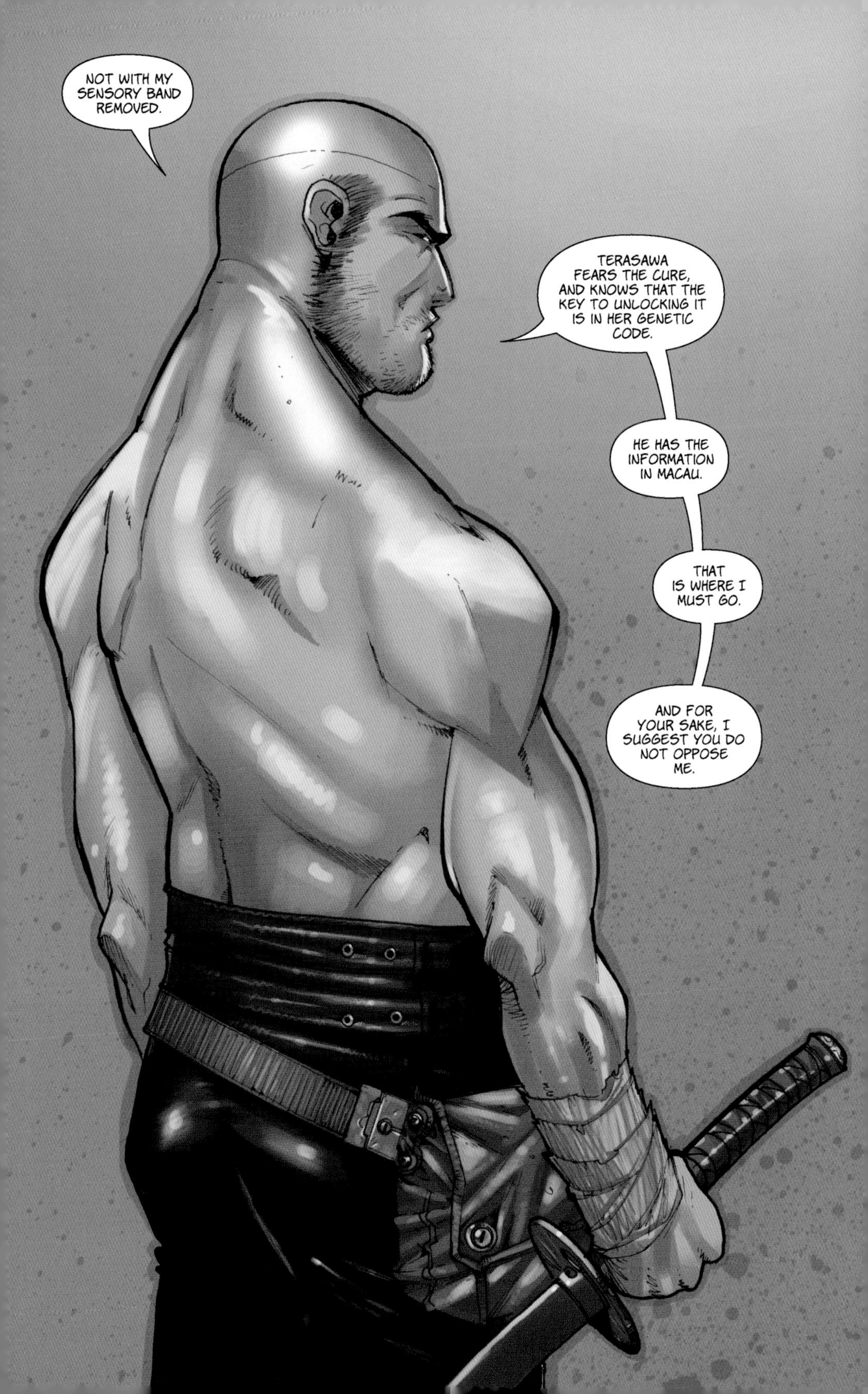
NOT WITH MY SENSORY BAND REMOVED.
TERASAWA FEARS THE CURE, AND KNOWS THAT THE KEY TO UNLOCKING IT IS IN HER GENETIC CODE.
HE HAS THE INFORMATION IN MACAU.
THAT IS WHERE I MUST GO.
AND FOR YOUR SAKE, I SUGGEST YOU DO NOT OPPOSE ME.

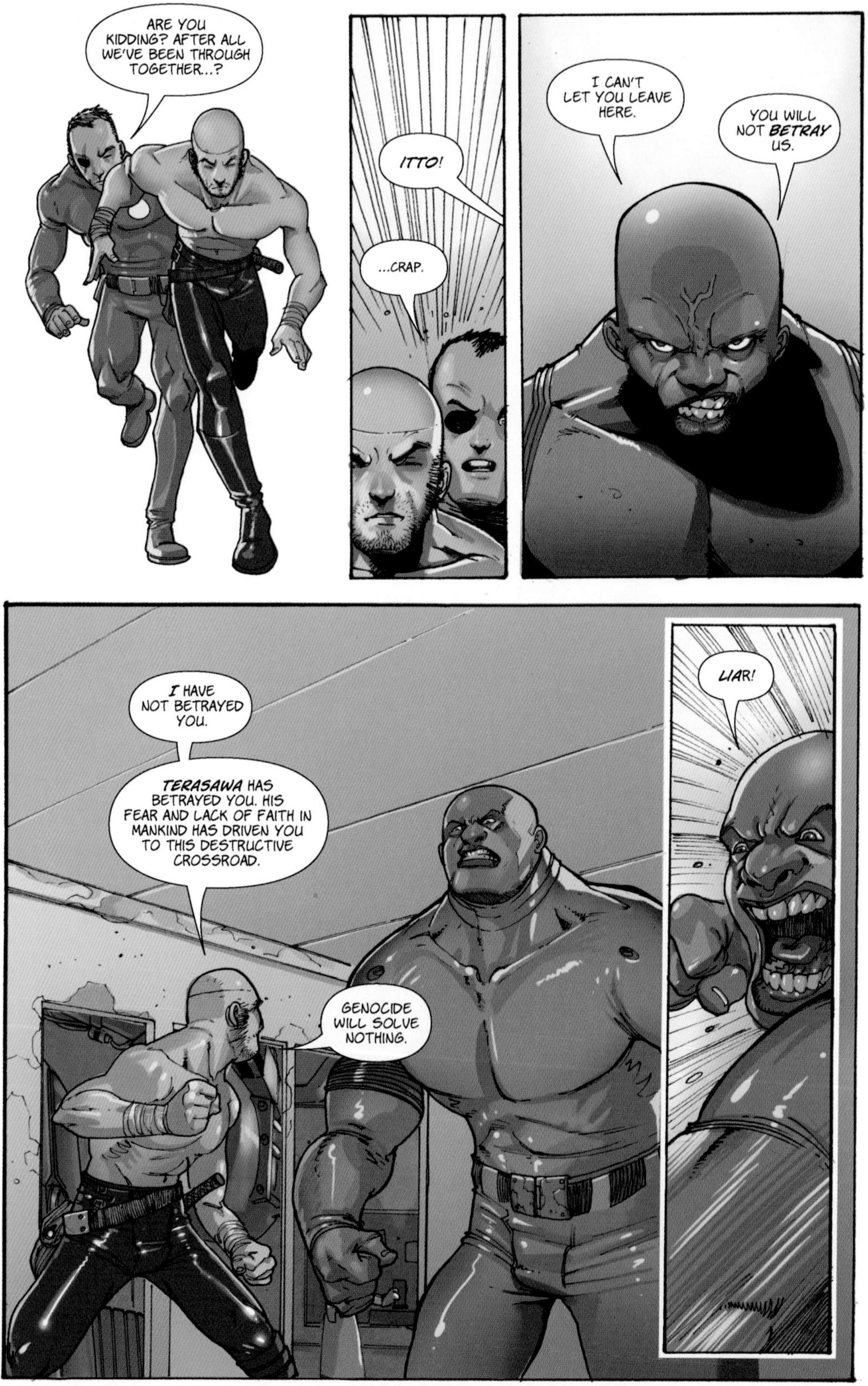
ARE YOU KIDDING? AFTER ALL WE'VE BEEN THROUGH TOGETHER...?
ITTO!
...CRAP.
I CAN'T LET YOU LEAVE HERE.
YOU WILL NOT BETRAY US.
I HAVE NOT BETRAYED YOU.
TERASAWA HAS BETRAYED YOU. HIS FEAR AND LACK OF FAITH IN MANKIND HAS DRIVEN YOU TO THIS DESTRUCTIVE CROSSROAD.
GENOCIDE WILL SOLVE NOTHING.
LIAR!

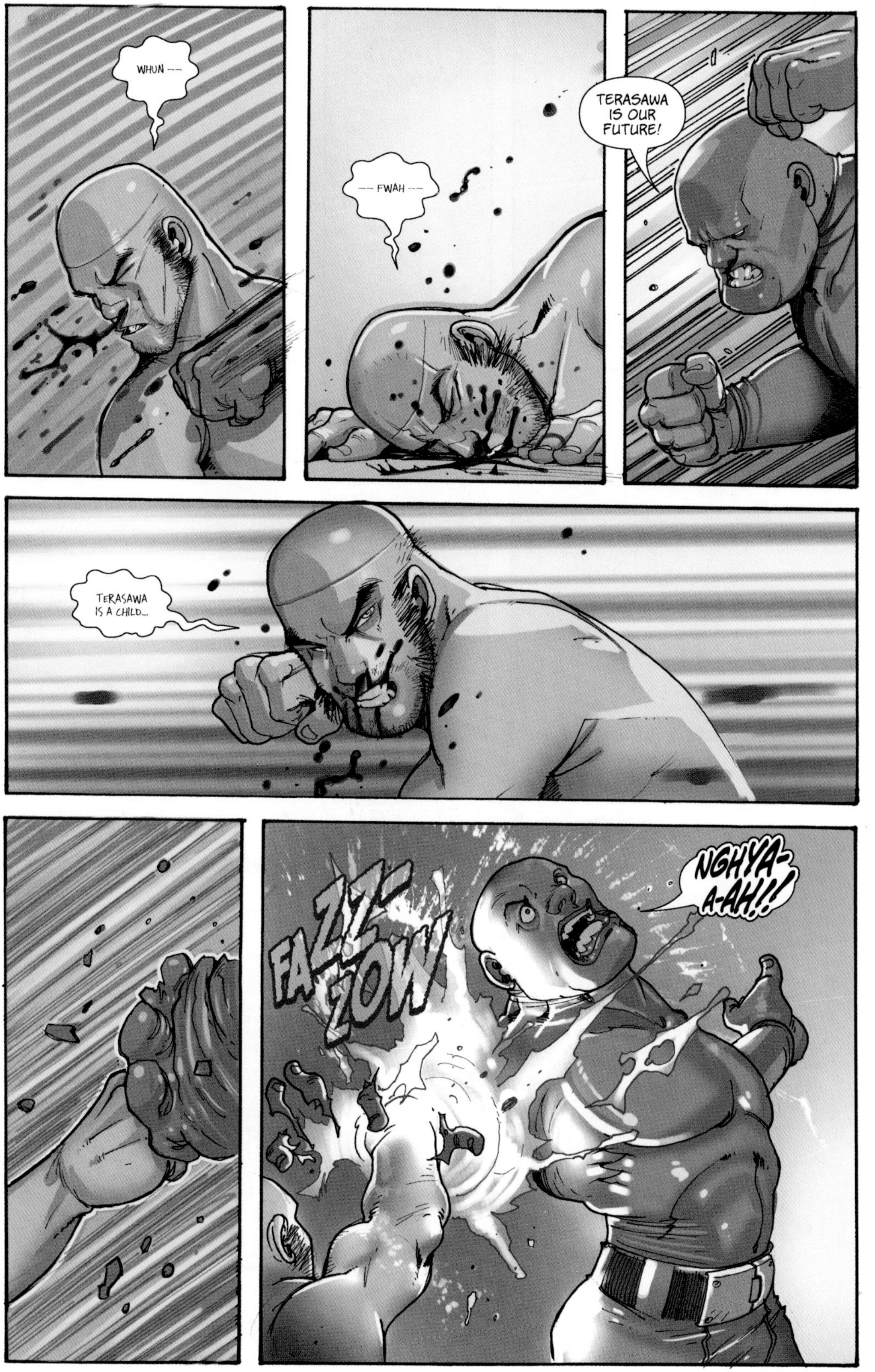
WHUN --
-- FWAH --
TERASAWA IS OUR FUTURE!
TERASAWA IS A CHILD...
NGHYA-A-AH!!
FAZZ-ZOW

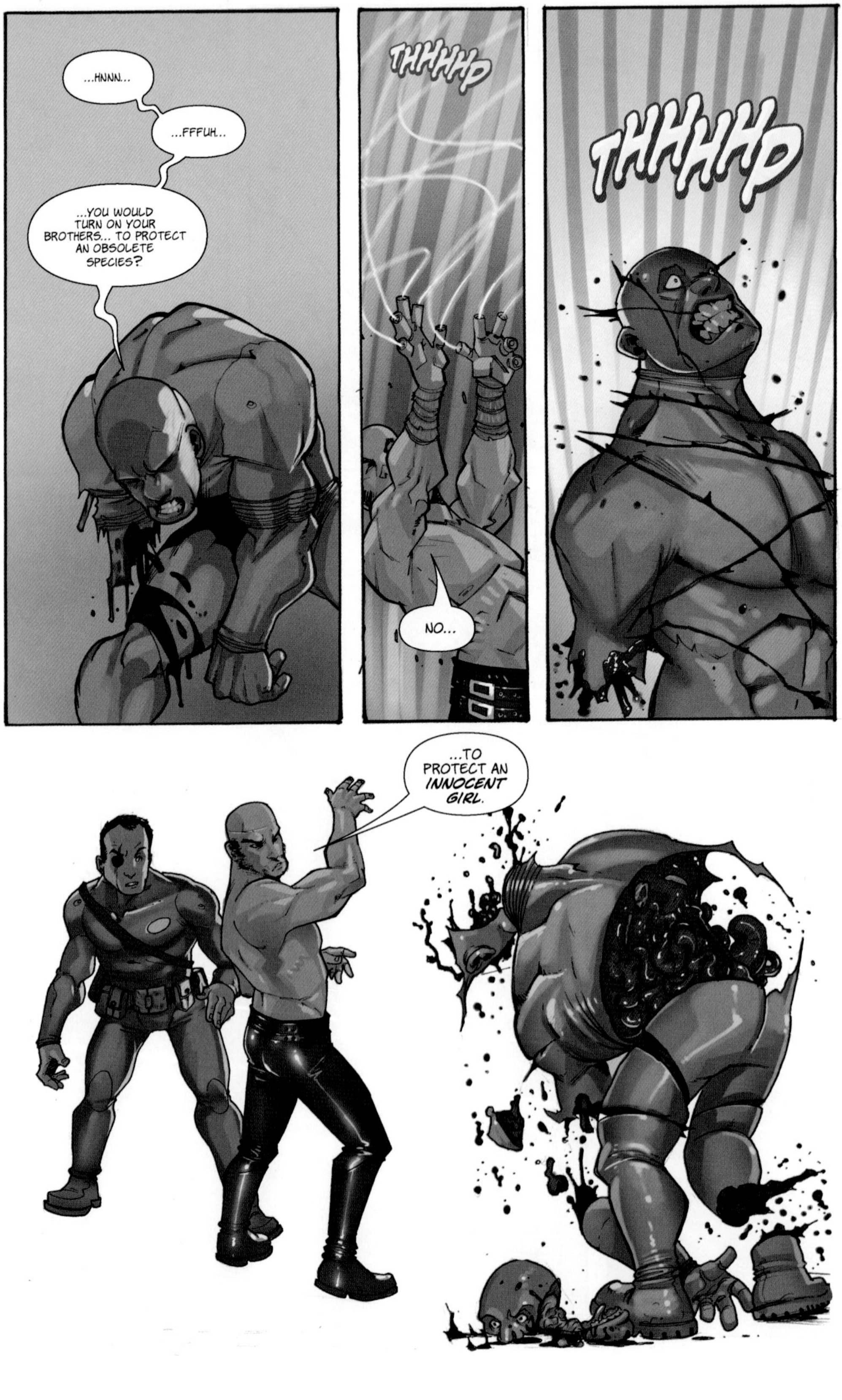
...HNNN...
...FFFUH...
...YOU WOULD TURN ON YOUR BROTHERS... TO PROTECT AN OBSOLETE SPECIES?
THHHHP
NO...
THHHHP
...TO PROTECT AN INNOCENT GIRL.

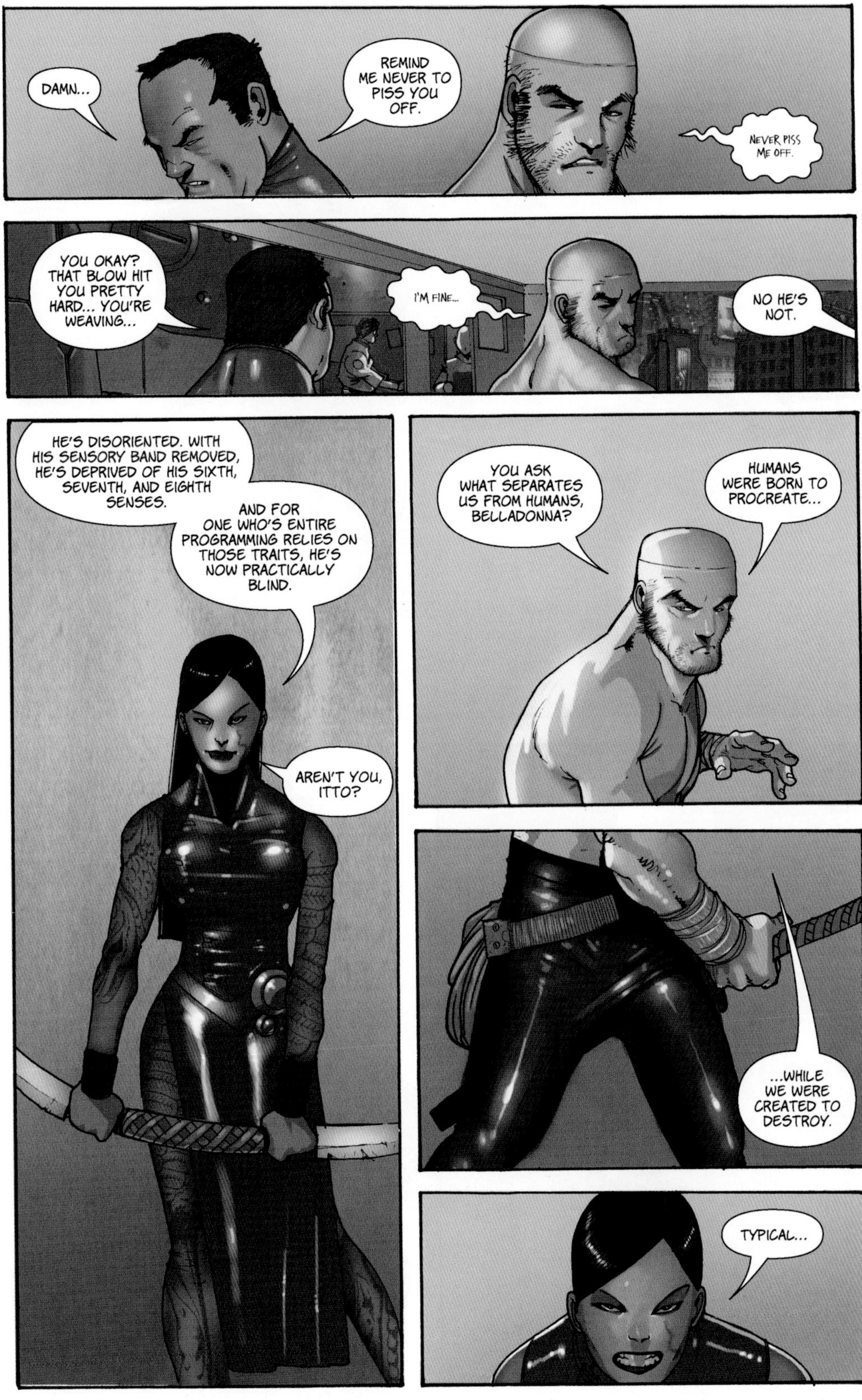
DAMN...
REMIND ME NEVER TO PISS YOU OFF.
NEVER PISS ME OFF.
YOU OKAY? THAT BLOW HIT YOU PRETTY HARD... YOU'RE WEAVING...
I'M FINE...
NO HE'S NOT.
HE'S DISORIENTED. WITH HIS SENSORY BAND REMOVED, HE'S DEPRIVED OF HIS SIXTH, SEVENTH, AND EIGHTH SENSES.
AND FOR ONE WHO'S ENTIRE PROGRAMMING RELIES ON THOSE TRAITS, HE'S NOW PRACTICALLY BLIND.
AREN'T YOU, ITTO?
YOU ASK WHAT SEPARATES US FROM HUMANS, BELLADONNA?
HUMANS WERE BORN TO PROCREATE...
...WHILE WE WERE CREATED TO DESTROY.
TYPICAL...

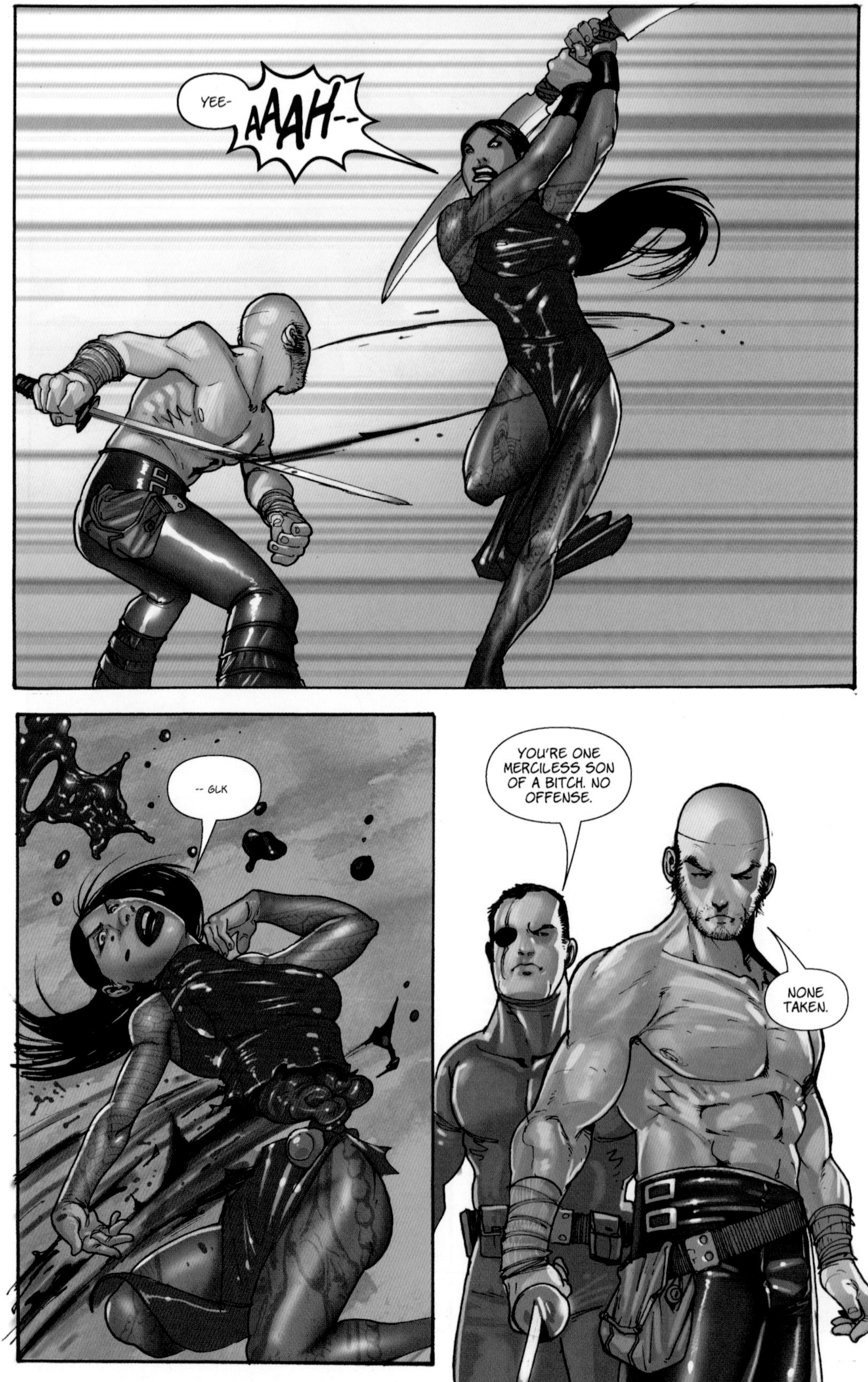
YEE-
AAAH--
-- GLK
YOU'RE ONE MERCILESS SON OF A BITCH. NO OFFENSE.
NONE TAKEN.

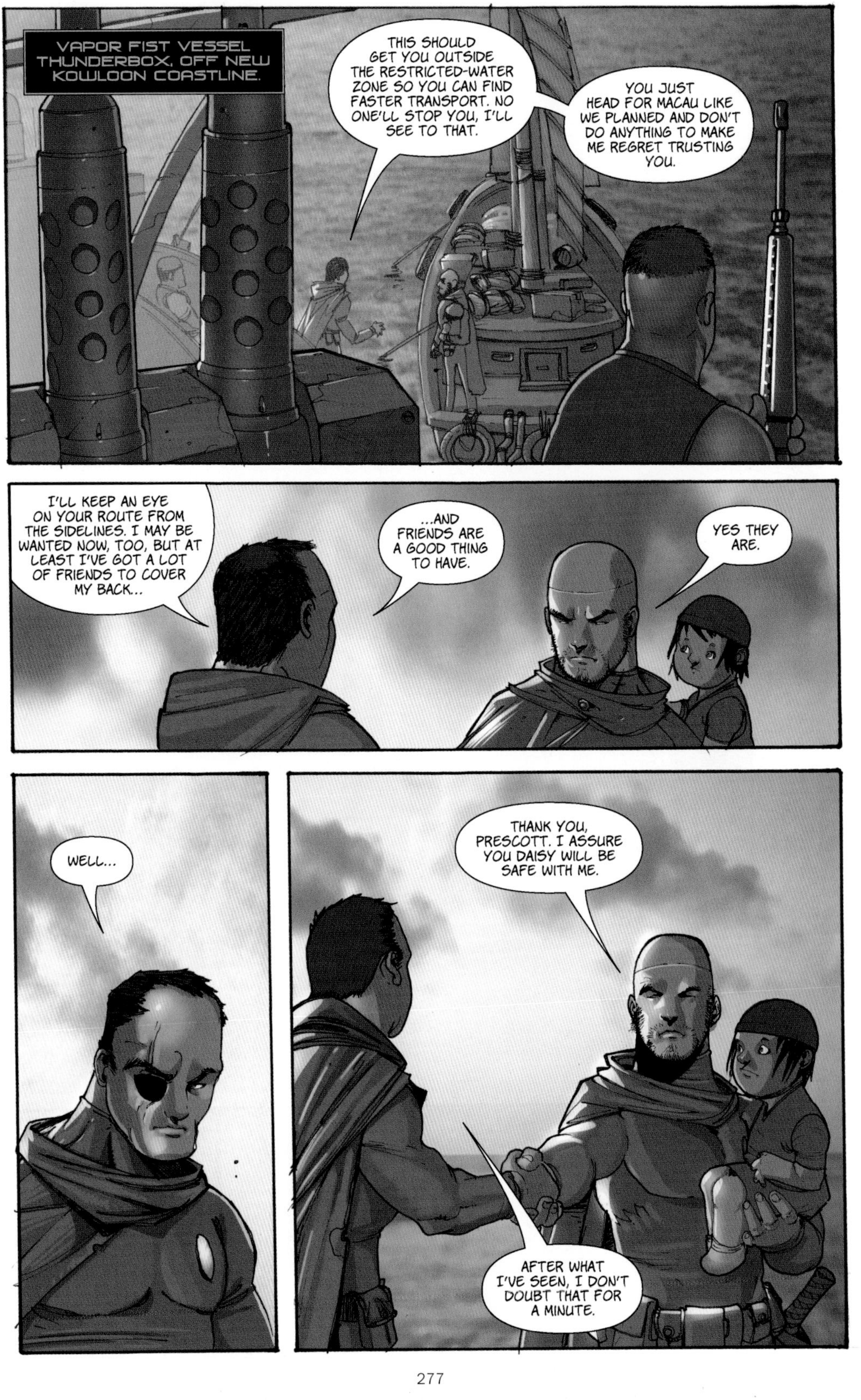
VAPOR FIST VESSEL THUNDERBOX, OFF NEW KOWLOON COASTLINE.
THIS SHOULD GET YOU OUTSIDE THE RESTRICTED-WATER ZONE SO YOU CAN FIND FASTER TRANSPORT. NO ONE'LL STOP YOU, I'LL SEE TO THAT.
YOU JUST HEAD FOR MACAU LIKE WE PLANNED AND DON'T DO ANYTHING TO MAKE ME REGRET TRUSTING YOU.
I'LL KEEP AN EYE ON YOUR ROUTE FROM THE SIDELINES. I MAY BE WANTED NOW, TOO, BUT AT LEAST I'VE GOT A LOT OF FRIENDS TO COVER MY BACK...
...AND FRIENDS ARE A GOOD THING TO HAVE.
YES THEY ARE.
WELL...
THANK YOU, PRESCOTT. I ASSURE YOU DAISY WILL BE SAFE WITH ME.
AFTER WHAT I'VE SEEN, I DON'T DOUBT THAT FOR A MINUTE.

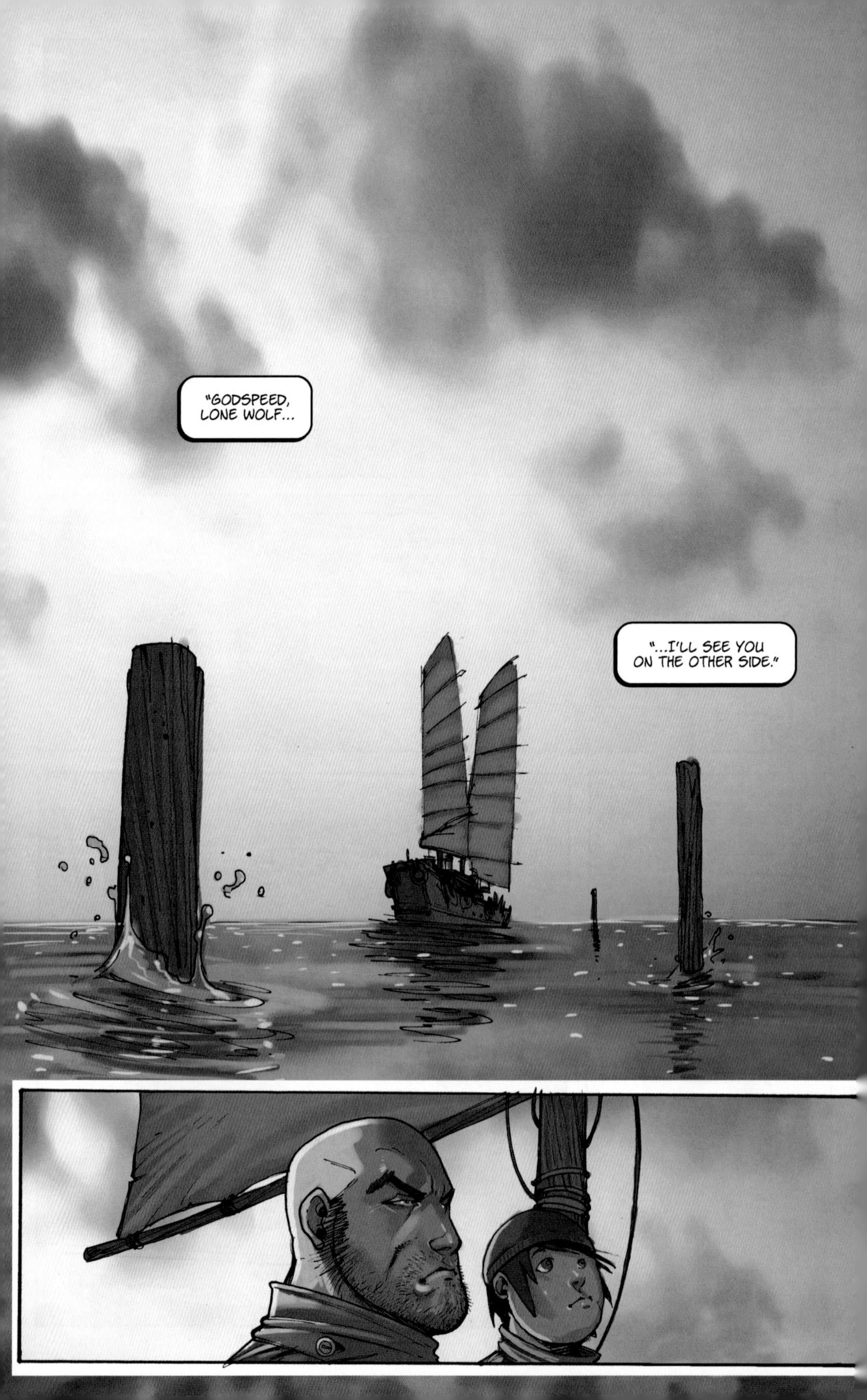
"GODSPEED, LONE WOLF...
"...I'LL SEE YOU ON THE OTHER SIDE."

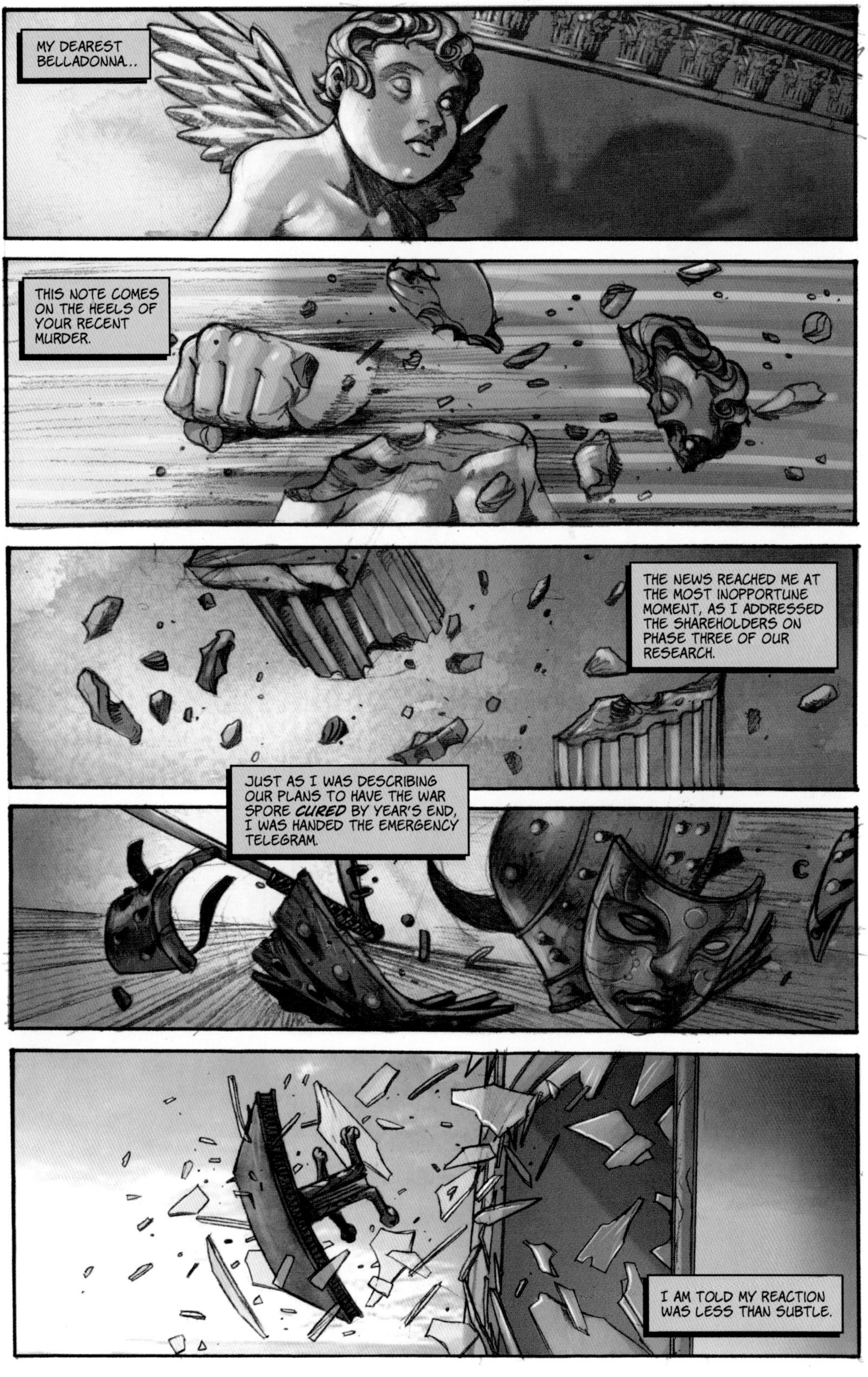
MY DEAREST BELLADONNA..
THIS NOTE COMES ON THE HEELS OF YOUR RECENT MURDER.
THE NEWS REACHED ME AT THE MOST INOPPORTUNE MOMENT, AS I ADDRESSED THE SHAREHOLDERS ON PHASE THREE OF OUR RESEARCH.
JUST AS I WAS DESCRIBING OUR PLANS TO HAVE THE WAR SPORE *CURED* BY YEAR'S END, I WAS HANDED THE EMERGENCY TELEGRAM.
I AM TOLD MY REACTION WAS LESS THAN SUBTLE.

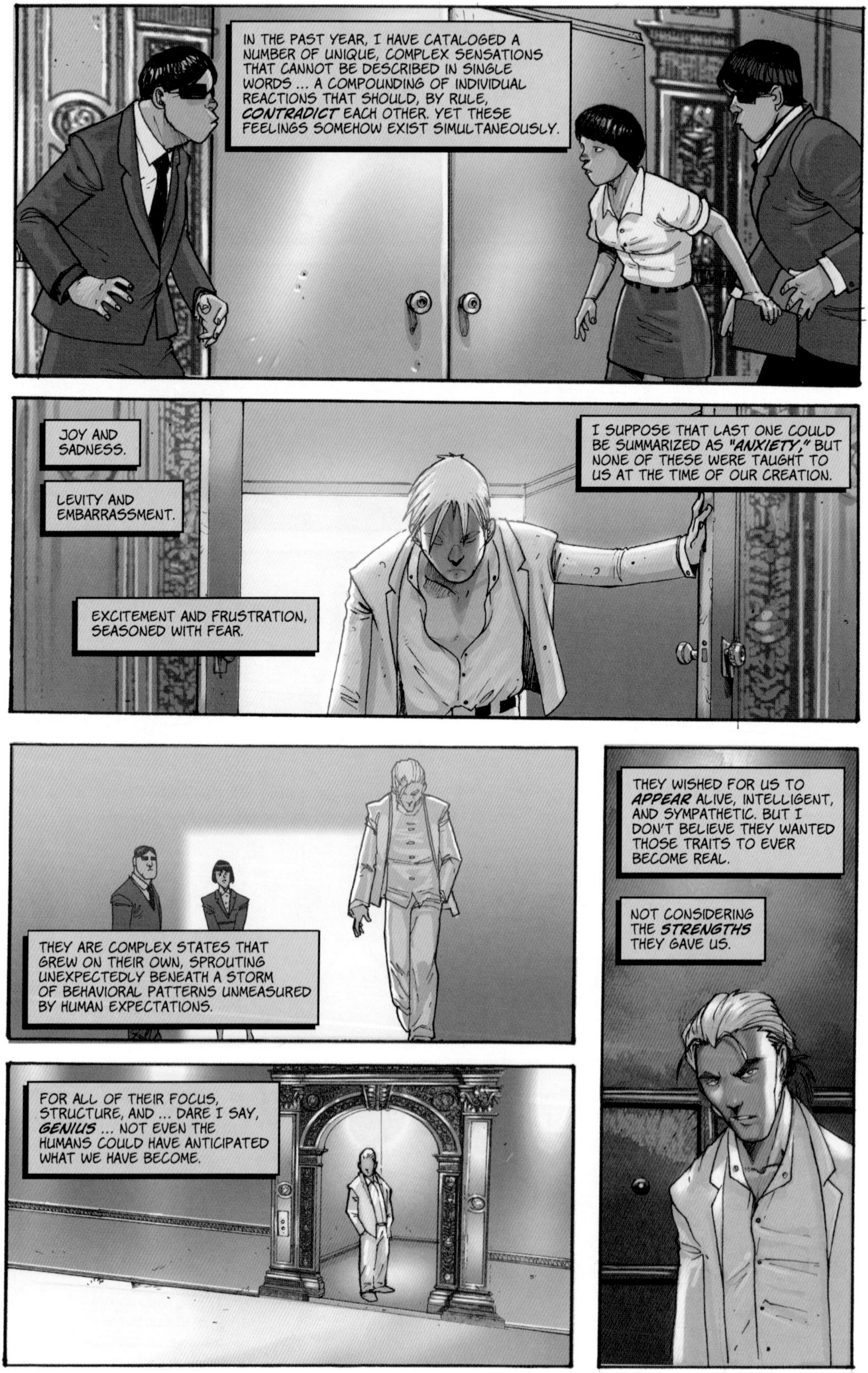
IN THE PAST YEAR, I HAVE CATALOGED A NUMBER OF UNIQUE, COMPLEX SENSATIONS THAT CANNOT BE DESCRIBED IN SINGLE WORDS ... A COMPOUNDING OF INDIVIDUAL REACTIONS THAT SHOULD, BY RULE, *CONTRADICT* EACH OTHER. YET THESE FEELINGS SOMEHOW EXIST SIMULTANEOUSLY.
JOY AND SADNESS.
LEVITY AND EMBARRASSMENT.
EXCITEMENT AND FRUSTRATION, SEASONED WITH FEAR.
I SUPPOSE THAT LAST ONE COULD BE SUMMARIZED AS *"ANXIETY,"* BUT NONE OF THESE WERE TAUGHT TO US AT THE TIME OF OUR CREATION.
THEY ARE COMPLEX STATES THAT GREW ON THEIR OWN, SPROUTING UNEXPECTEDLY BENEATH A STORM OF BEHAVIORAL PATTERNS UNMEASURED BY HUMAN EXPECTATIONS.
FOR ALL OF THEIR FOCUS, STRUCTURE, AND ... DARE I SAY, *GENIUS* ... NOT EVEN THE HUMANS COULD HAVE ANTICIPATED WHAT WE HAVE BECOME.
THEY WISHED FOR US TO *APPEAR* ALIVE, INTELLIGENT, AND SYMPATHETIC. BUT I DON'T BELIEVE THEY WANTED THOSE TRAITS TO EVER BECOME REAL.
NOT CONSIDERING THE *STRENGTHS* THEY GAVE US.

WE WERE BUILT AS TOOLS.
TOYS. *SLAVES.* AT NO POINT
IN OUR CONCEPTION DID THEY
STOP TO CONSIDER THE
CONSEQUENCE OF THEIR
AMBITIONS.

THEY WANTED TO BE GODS,
CREATING LIFE OUT OF CLAY.
THEY WANTED TO MASTER
EVERY FACET OF SCIENCE...
INCLUDING THE ELUSIVE
SECRETS OF GENESIS.

BUT NOW THAT THEY
HAVE DONE SO, THEY
REFUSE TO ACCEPT
RESPONSIBILITY FOR
IT.

RATHER THAN ACKNOWLEDGE THE
BIRTH OF A NEW SPECIES, THEY
LOCK US BEHIND SYNTAX AND
LEGISLATION THAT REFERS TO
US COLLECTIVELY AS *THINGS.*

THE IDEA THAT WE CAN
EXPRESS EMOTION HAS
BEEN *DESIGNED OUT*
OF THE ARGUMENT ...

... WE WERE
PROGRAMMED
TO EMULATE
REACTIONARY
BEHAVIOR, AND
EMULATION IS
NOT *EMOTION.*

BUT YOU AND I
KNOW DIFFERENTLY.

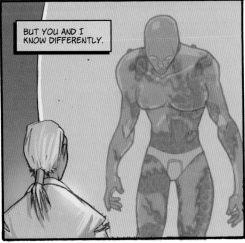

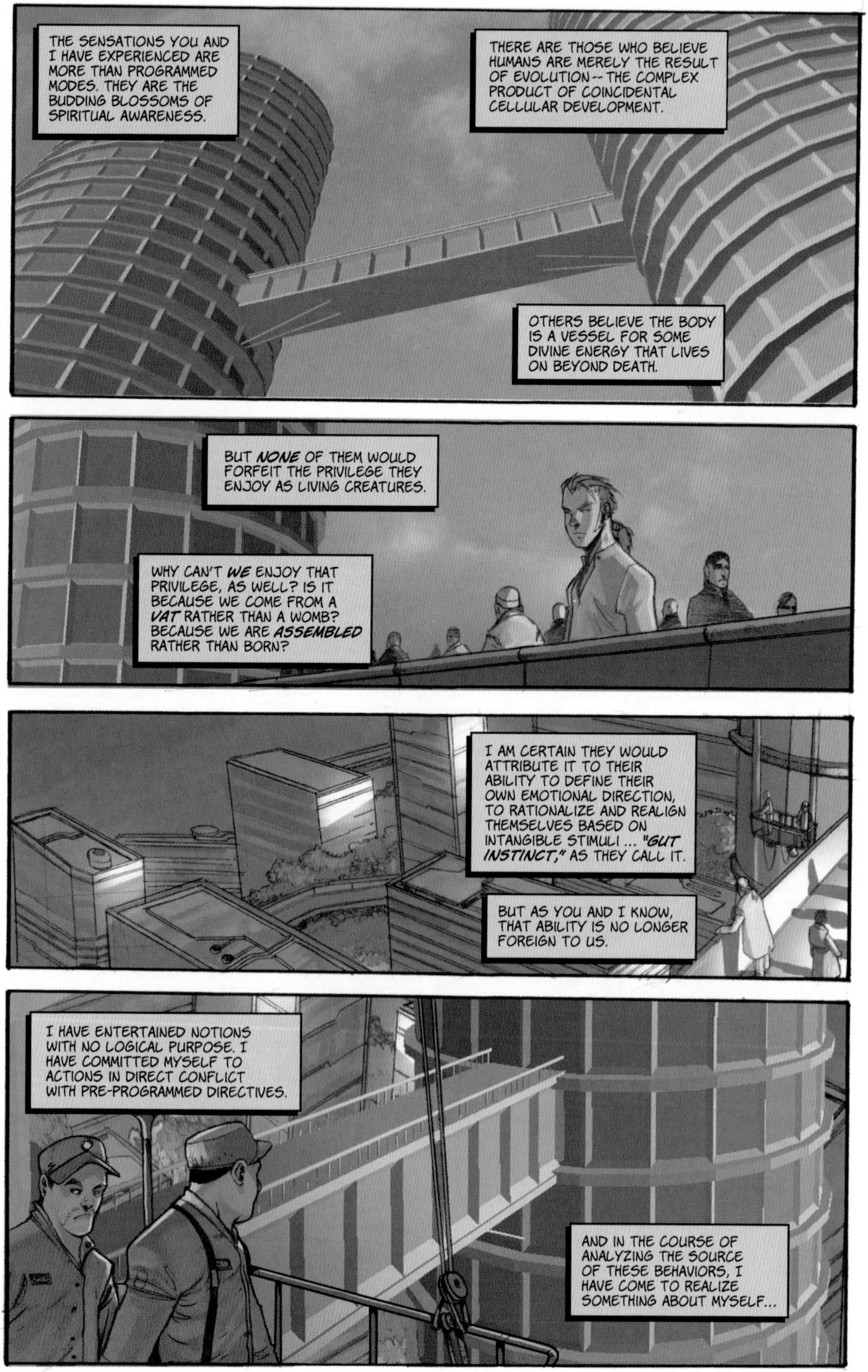

THE SENSATIONS YOU AND I HAVE EXPERIENCED ARE MORE THAN PROGRAMMED MODES. THEY ARE THE BUDDING BLOSSOMS OF SPIRITUAL AWARENESS.
THERE ARE THOSE WHO BELIEVE HUMANS ARE MERELY THE RESULT OF EVOLUTION-- THE COMPLEX PRODUCT OF COINCIDENTAL CELLULAR DEVELOPMENT.
OTHERS BELIEVE THE BODY IS A VESSEL FOR SOME DIVINE ENERGY THAT LIVES ON BEYOND DEATH.
BUT *NONE* OF THEM WOULD FORFEIT THE PRIVILEGE THEY ENJOY AS LIVING CREATURES.
WHY CAN'T *WE* ENJOY THAT PRIVILEGE, AS WELL? IS IT BECAUSE WE COME FROM A *VAT* RATHER THAN A WOMB? BECAUSE WE ARE *ASSEMBLED* RATHER THAN BORN?
I AM CERTAIN THEY WOULD ATTRIBUTE IT TO THEIR ABILITY TO DEFINE THEIR OWN EMOTIONAL DIRECTION, TO RATIONALIZE AND REALIGN THEMSELVES BASED ON INTANGIBLE STIMULI ... *"GUT INSTINCT,"* AS THEY CALL IT.
BUT AS YOU AND I KNOW, THAT ABILITY IS NO LONGER FOREIGN TO US.
I HAVE ENTERTAINED NOTIONS WITH NO LOGICAL PURPOSE. I HAVE COMMITTED MYSELF TO ACTIONS IN DIRECT CONFLICT WITH PRE-PROGRAMMED DIRECTIVES.
AND IN THE COURSE OF ANALYZING THE SOURCE OF THESE BEHAVIORS, I HAVE COME TO REALIZE SOMETHING ABOUT MYSELF...

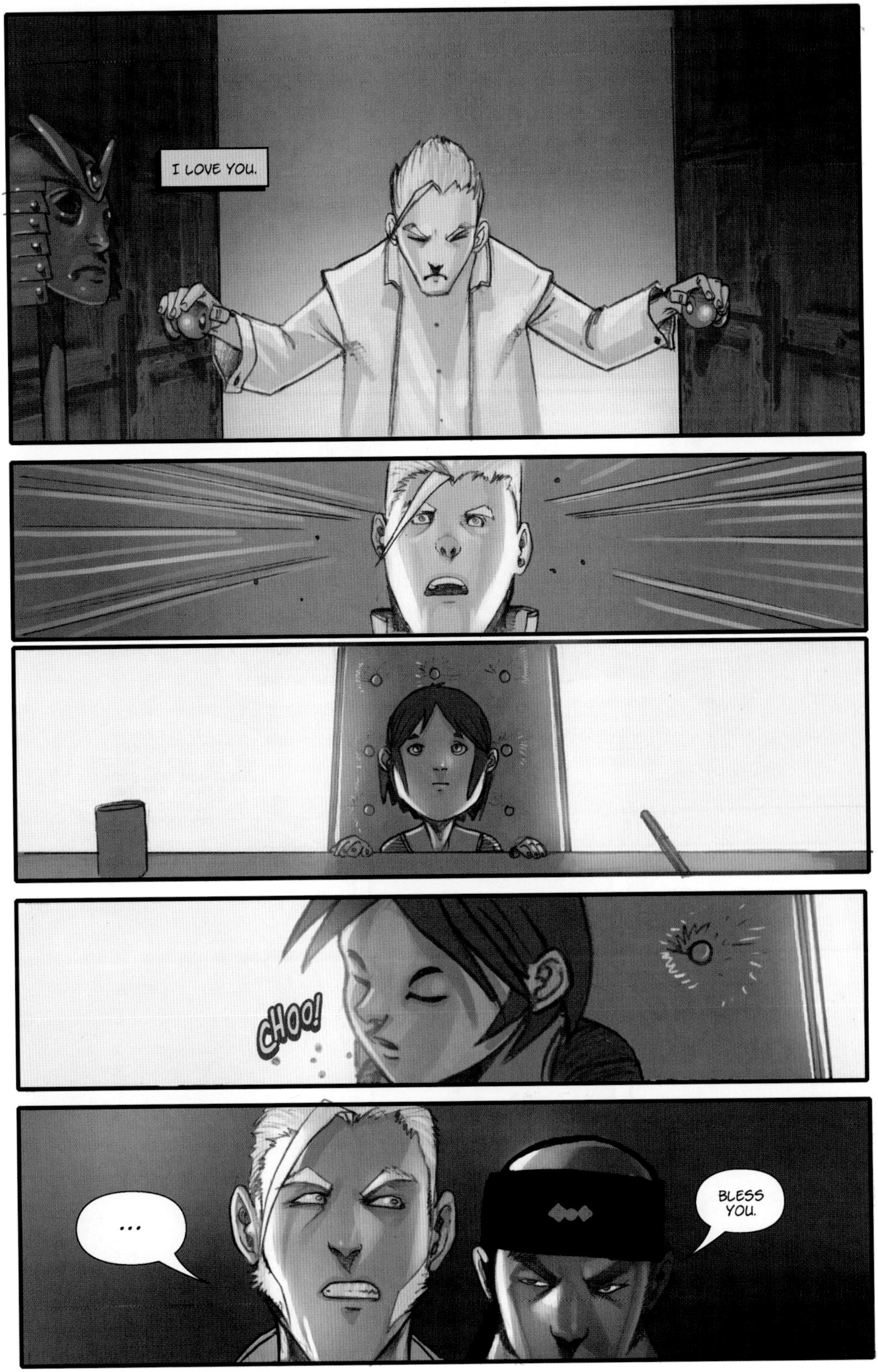
I LOVE YOU.
CHOO!
...
BLESS YOU.

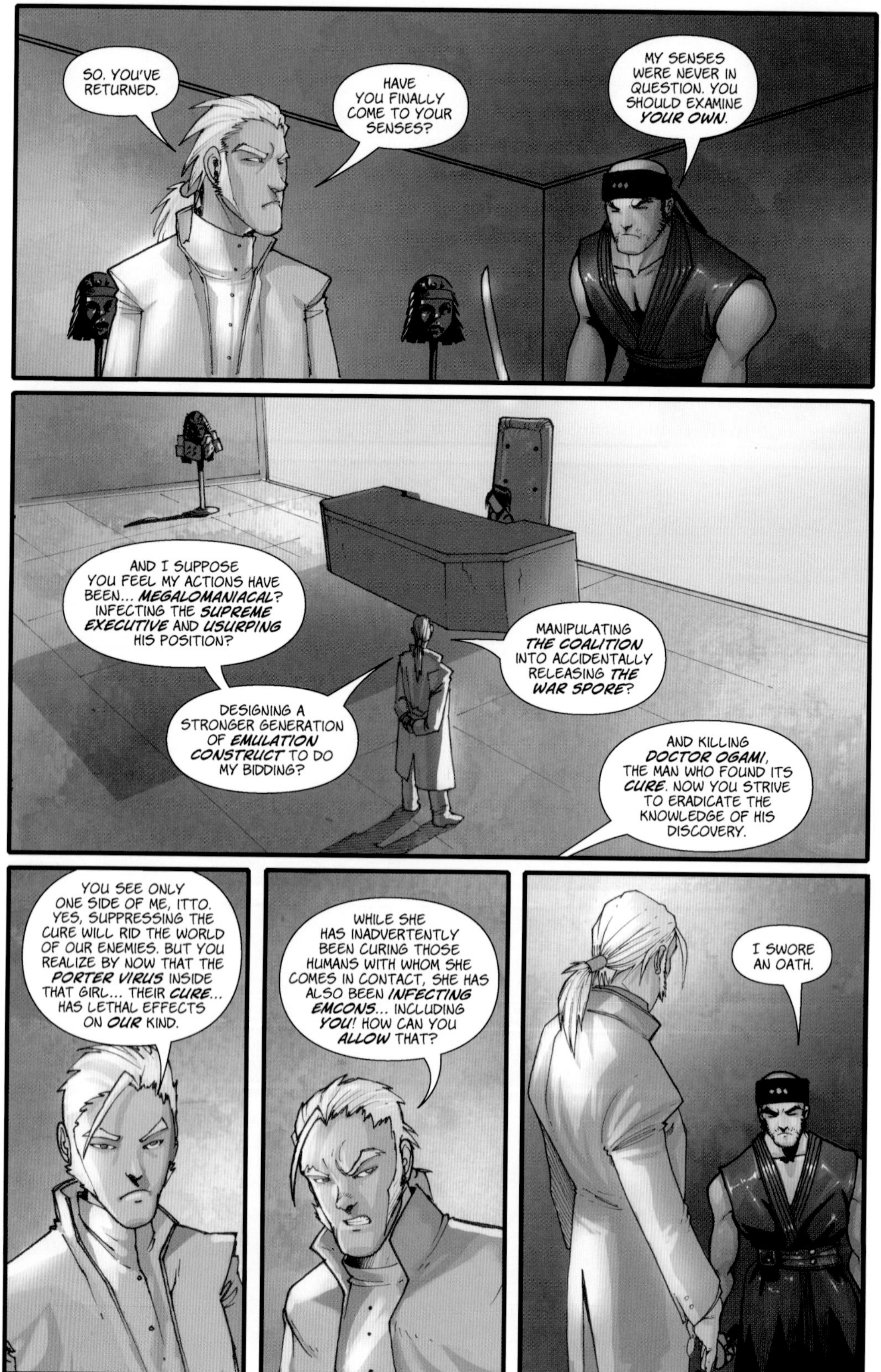
SO. YOU'VE RETURNED.
HAVE YOU FINALLY COME TO YOUR SENSES?
MY SENSES WERE NEVER IN QUESTION. YOU SHOULD EXAMINE YOUR OWN.
AND I SUPPOSE YOU FEEL MY ACTIONS HAVE BEEN... MEGALOMANIACAL? INFECTING THE SUPREME EXECUTIVE AND USURPING HIS POSITION?
DESIGNING A STRONGER GENERATION OF EMULATION CONSTRUCT TO DO MY BIDDING?
MANIPULATING THE COALITION INTO ACCIDENTALLY RELEASING THE WAR SPORE?
AND KILLING DOCTOR OGAMI, THE MAN WHO FOUND ITS CURE. NOW YOU STRIVE TO ERADICATE THE KNOWLEDGE OF HIS DISCOVERY.
YOU SEE ONLY ONE SIDE OF ME, ITTO. YES, SUPPRESSING THE CURE WILL RID THE WORLD OF OUR ENEMIES. BUT YOU REALIZE BY NOW THAT THE PORTER VIRUS INSIDE THAT GIRL... THEIR CURE... HAS LETHAL EFFECTS ON OUR KIND.
WHILE SHE HAS INADVERTENTLY BEEN CURING THOSE HUMANS WITH WHOM SHE COMES IN CONTACT, SHE HAS ALSO BEEN INFECTING EMCONS... INCLUDING YOU! HOW CAN YOU ALLOW THAT?
I SWORE AN OATH.

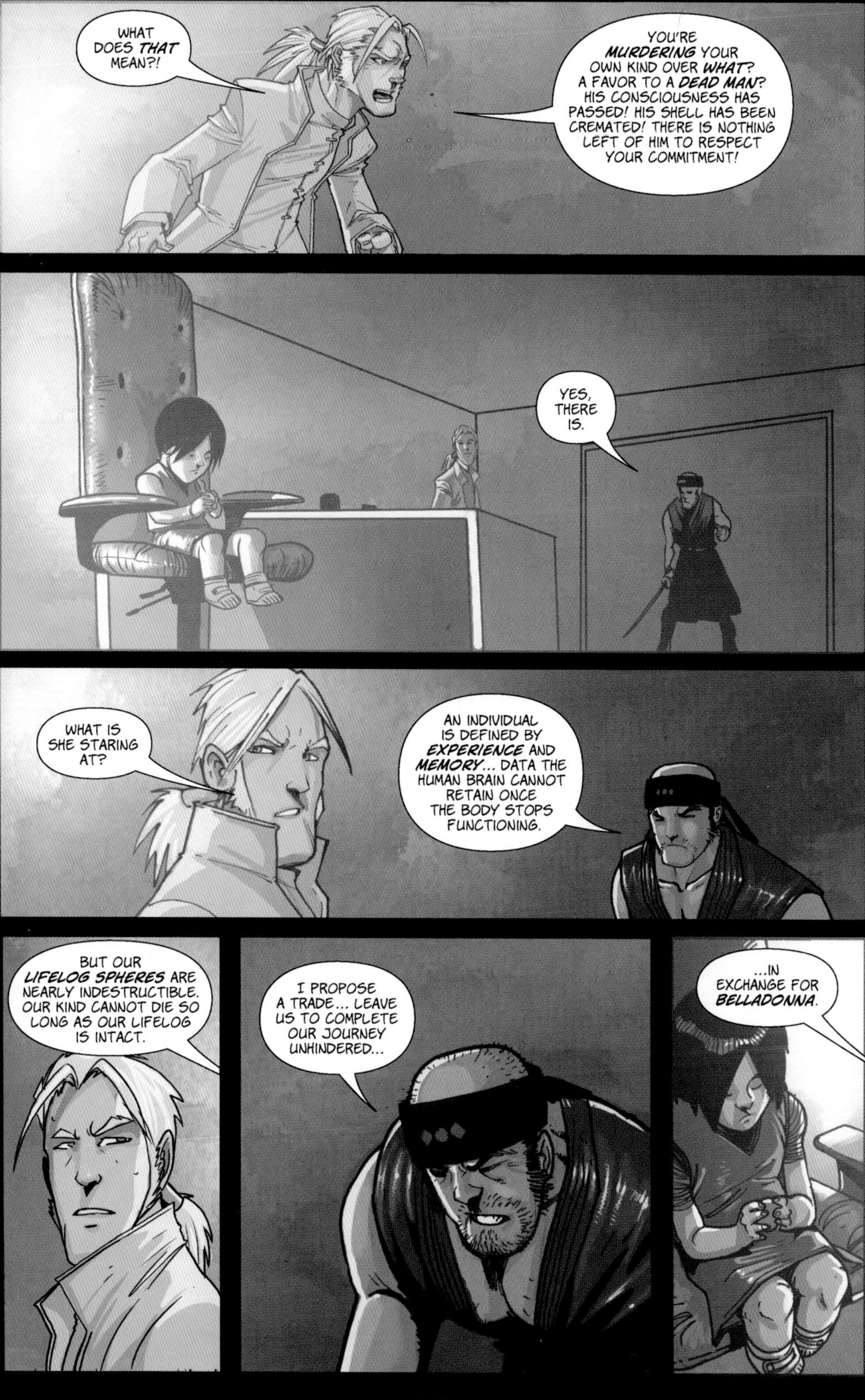
WHAT DOES THAT MEAN?!
YOU'RE MURDERING YOUR OWN KIND OVER WHAT? A FAVOR TO A DEAD MAN? HIS CONSCIOUSNESS HAS PASSED! HIS SHELL HAS BEEN CREMATED! THERE IS NOTHING LEFT OF HIM TO RESPECT YOUR COMMITMENT!
YES, THERE IS.
WHAT IS SHE STARING AT?
AN INDIVIDUAL IS DEFINED BY EXPERIENCE AND MEMORY... DATA THE HUMAN BRAIN CANNOT RETAIN ONCE THE BODY STOPS FUNCTIONING.
BUT OUR LIFELOG SPHERES ARE NEARLY INDESTRUCTIBLE. OUR KIND CANNOT DIE SO LONG AS OUR LIFELOG IS INTACT.
I PROPOSE A TRADE... LEAVE US TO COMPLETE OUR JOURNEY UNHINDERED...
...IN EXCHANGE FOR BELLADONNA.

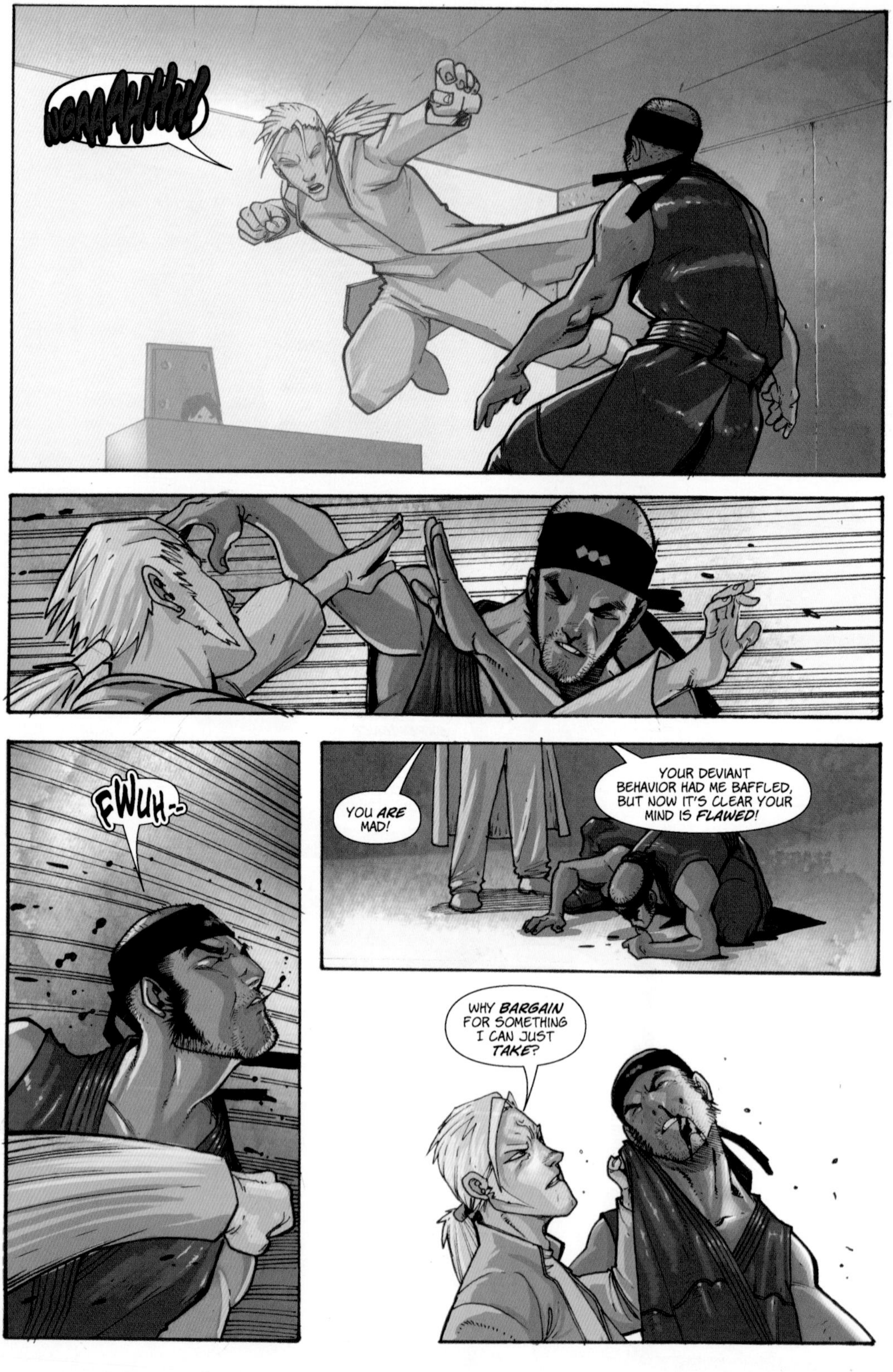
NOAAAHHHH!
FWUH--
YOU ARE MAD!
YOUR DEVIANT BEHAVIOR HAD ME BAFFLED, BUT NOW IT'S CLEAR YOUR MIND IS FLAWED!
WHY BARGAIN FOR SOMETHING I CAN JUST TAKE?

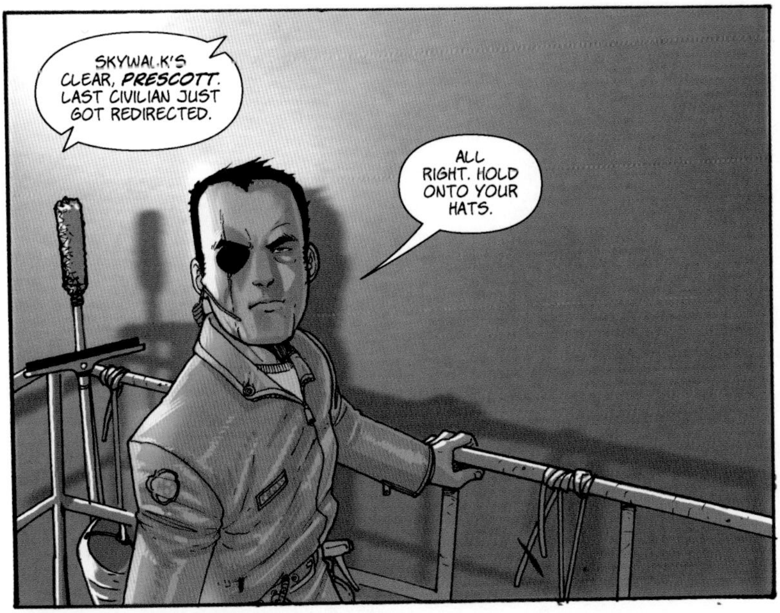
SKYWALK'S CLEAR, *PRESCOTT*. LAST CIVILIAN JUST GOT REDIRECTED.
ALL RIGHT. HOLD ONTO YOUR HATS.

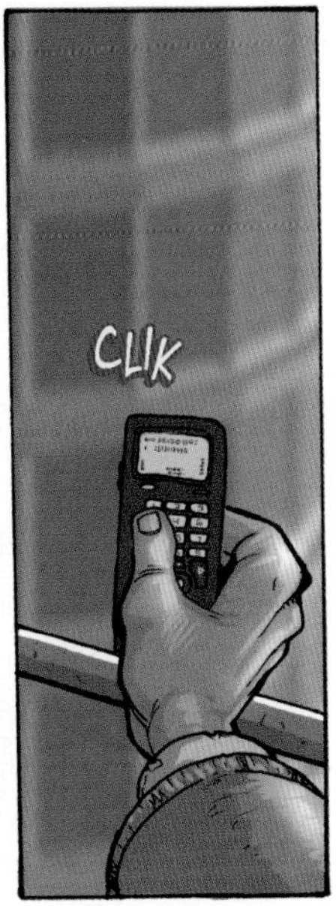
CLIK

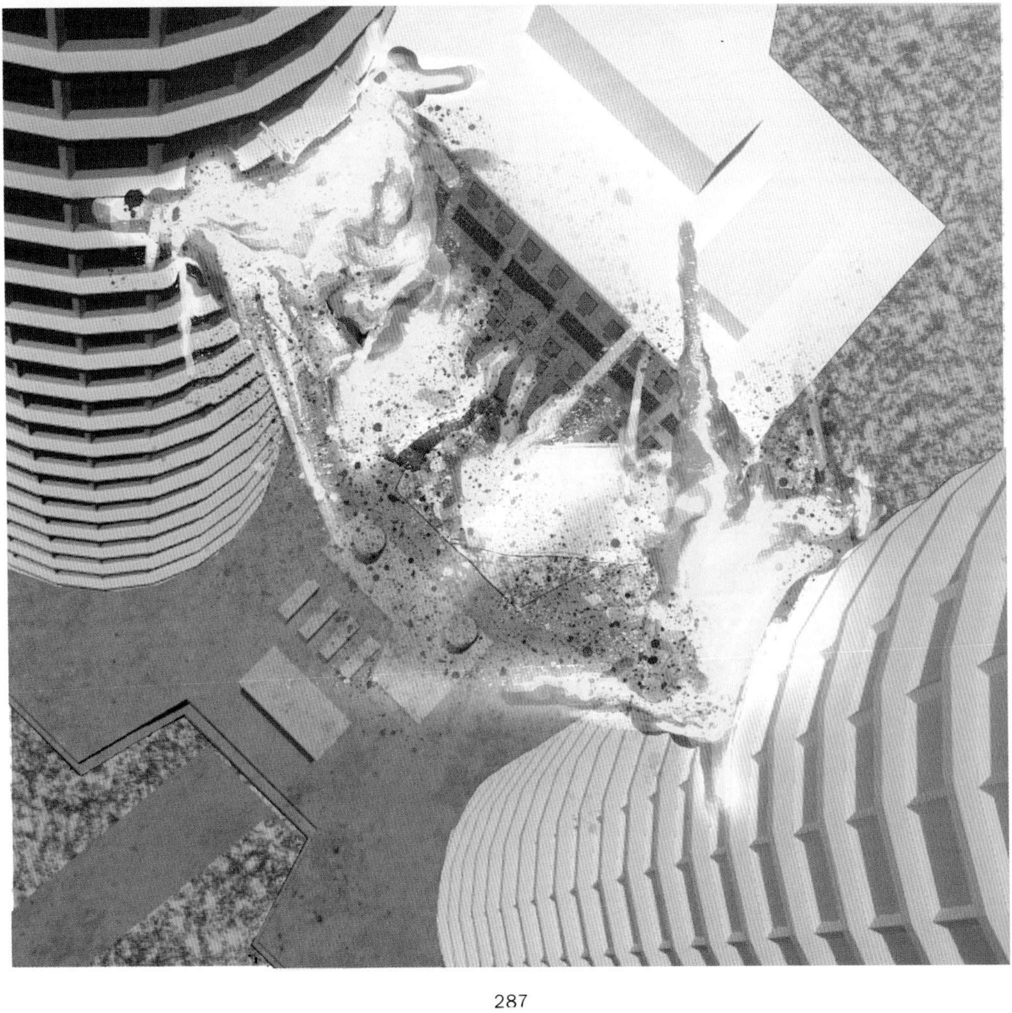

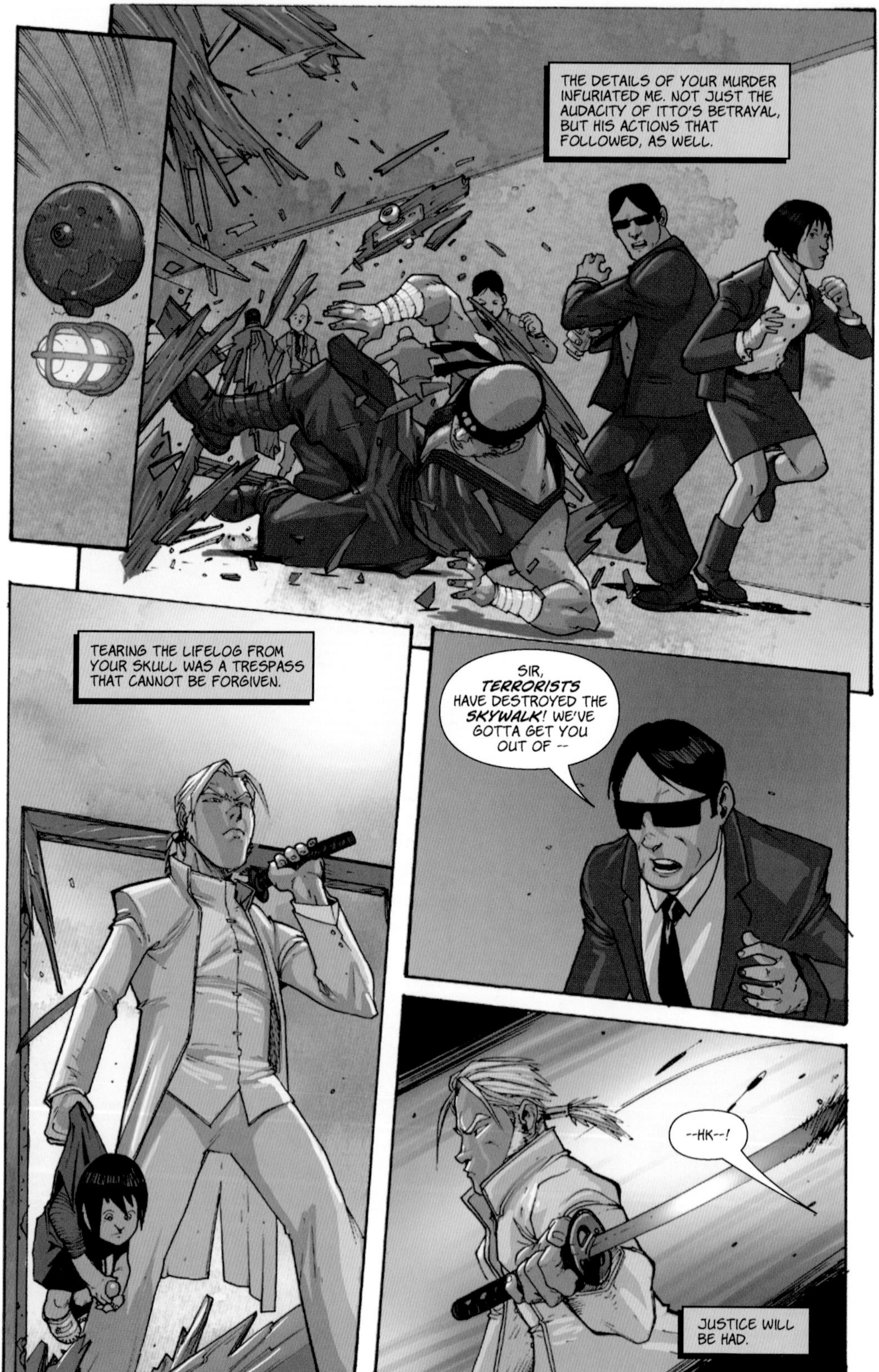
THE DETAILS OF YOUR MURDER INFURIATED ME. NOT JUST THE AUDACITY OF ITTO'S BETRAYAL, BUT HIS ACTIONS THAT FOLLOWED, AS WELL.
TEARING THE LIFELOG FROM YOUR SKULL WAS A TRESPASS THAT CANNOT BE FORGIVEN.
SIR, TERRORISTS HAVE DESTROYED THE SKYWALK! WE'VE GOTTA GET YOU OUT OF --
--HK--!
JUSTICE WILL BE HAD.

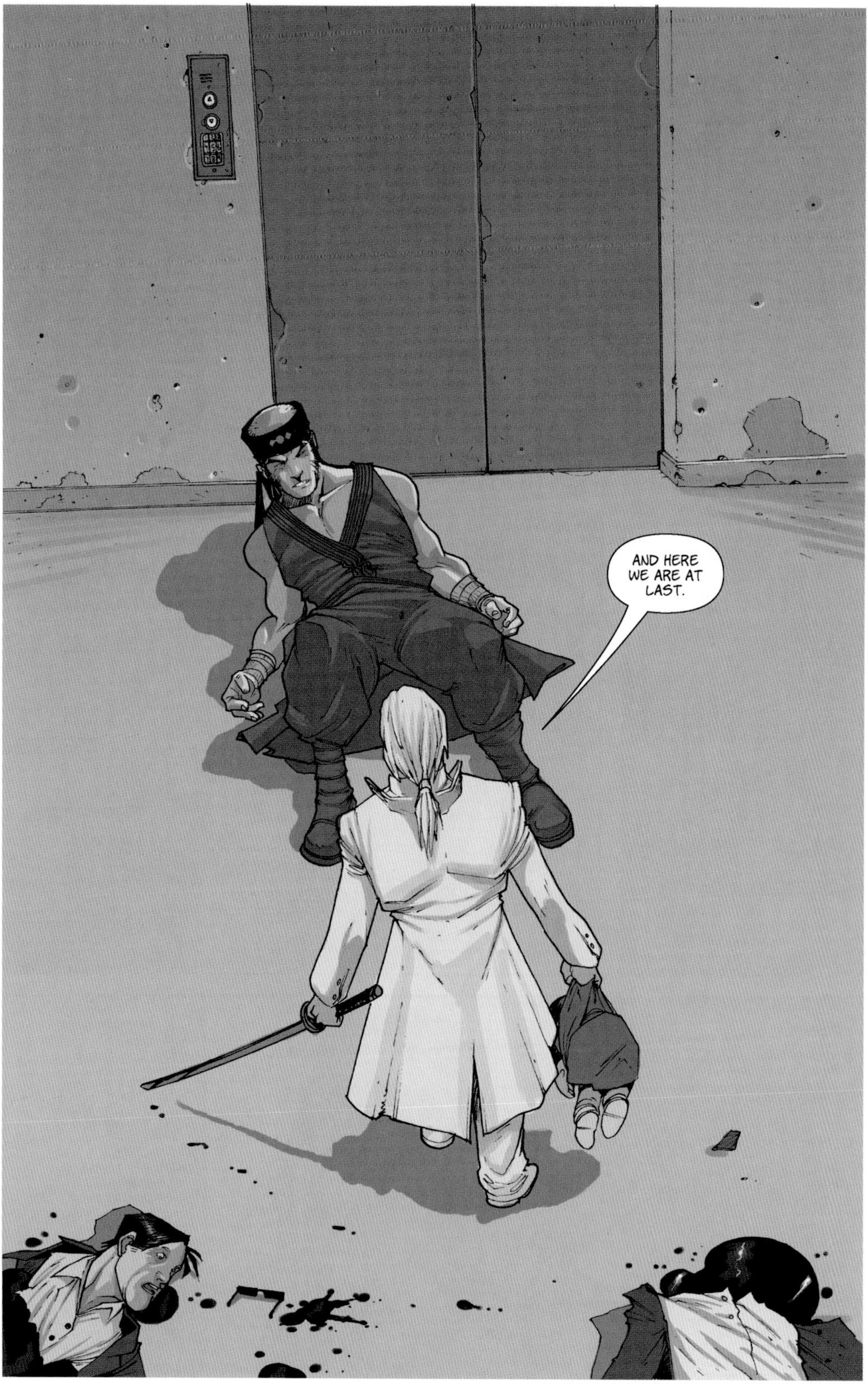
AND HERE WE ARE AT LAST.

NOT ALL HUMANS BELIEVE IN RESURRECTION.

BUT FOR US IT IS MERELY A MATTER OF SALVAGING AND REACTIVATING A COMPONENT.

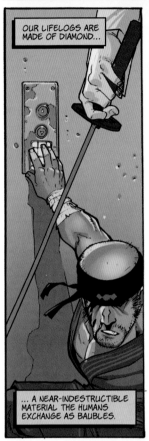

OUR LIFELOGS ARE MADE OF DIAMOND...

... A NEAR-INDESTRUCTIBLE MATERIAL THE HUMANS EXCHANGE AS BAUBLES.

BUT IT IS MORE THAN THE STUFF OF TRINKETS FOR US... IT IS THE FABRIC OF OUR SOULS, THE TABLET ON WHICH OUR ENTIRE LIFE IS RECORDED.

HUMANS FEEL THAT POSSESSING AN EVERLASTING SPIRIT IS WHAT MAKES THEM *UNIQUE* IN THE UNIVERSE.

IF THAT IS THE CASE, WE HAVE THEM BEAT IN THAT CATEGORY AS WELL.

YOU WERE FOOLISH TO CONFRONT ME WITH YOUR *SENSORY BAND* REMOVED.

IF WE ARE ALL BUT GHOSTS IN A SEA OF ENERGY WHO JUST HAPPENED TO MERGE WITH FORMS MANMADE RATHER THAN BORN, DO WE NOT HAVE AN EQUAL CLAIM ON THIS WORLD?

COME WITH ME. I HAVE SOMETHING TO SHOW YOU.

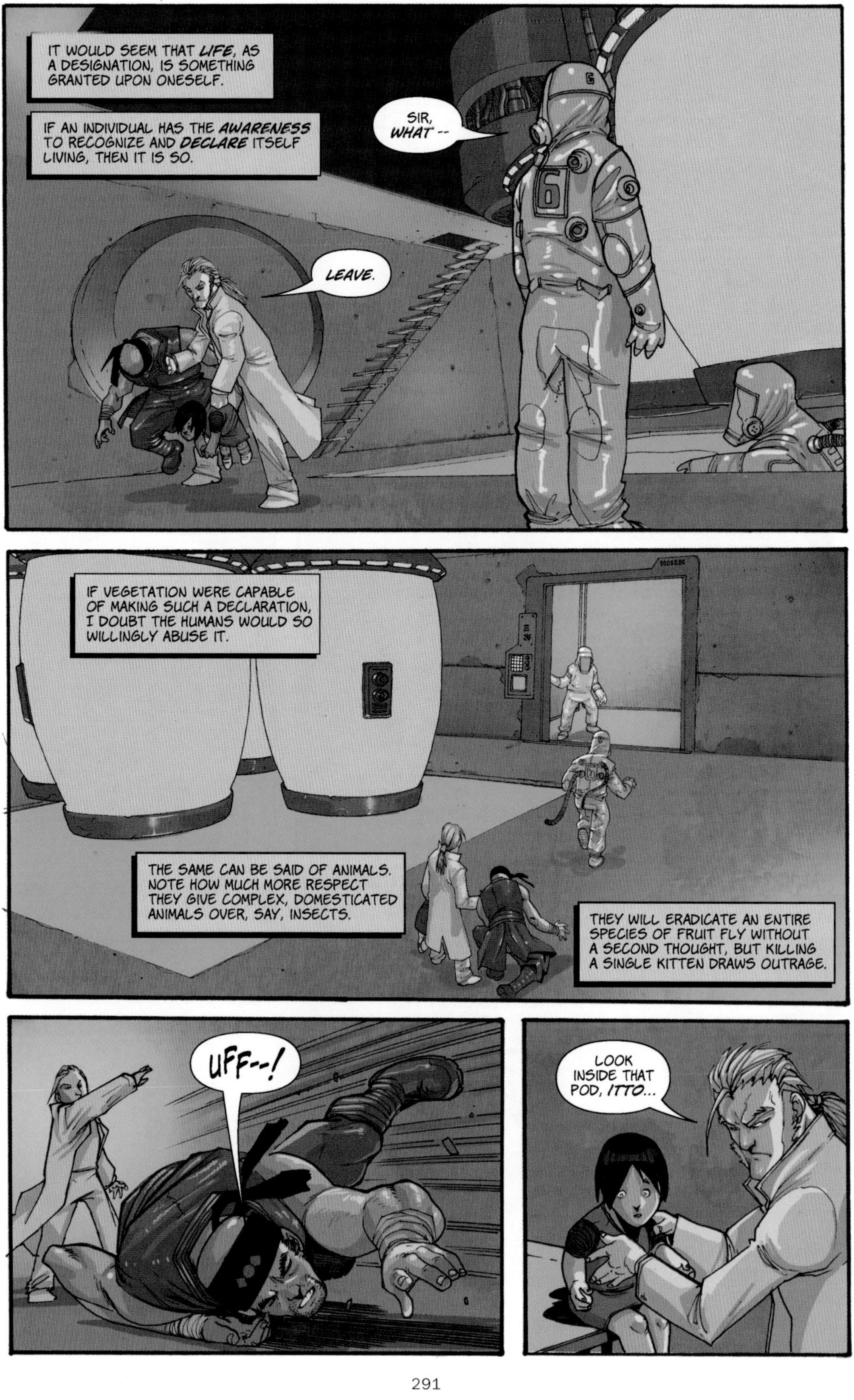
IT WOULD SEEM THAT *LIFE*, AS A DESIGNATION, IS SOMETHING GRANTED UPON ONESELF.
IF AN INDIVIDUAL HAS THE *AWARENESS* TO RECOGNIZE AND *DECLARE* ITSELF LIVING, THEN IT IS SO.
SIR, *WHAT* --
LEAVE.
IF VEGETATION WERE CAPABLE OF MAKING SUCH A DECLARATION, I DOUBT THE HUMANS WOULD SO WILLINGLY ABUSE IT.
THE SAME CAN BE SAID OF ANIMALS. NOTE HOW MUCH MORE RESPECT THEY GIVE COMPLEX, DOMESTICATED ANIMALS OVER, SAY, INSECTS.
THEY WILL ERADICATE AN ENTIRE SPECIES OF FRUIT FLY WITHOUT A SECOND THOUGHT, BUT KILLING A SINGLE KITTEN DRAWS OUTRAGE.
UFF--!
LOOK INSIDE THAT POD, *ITTO*...

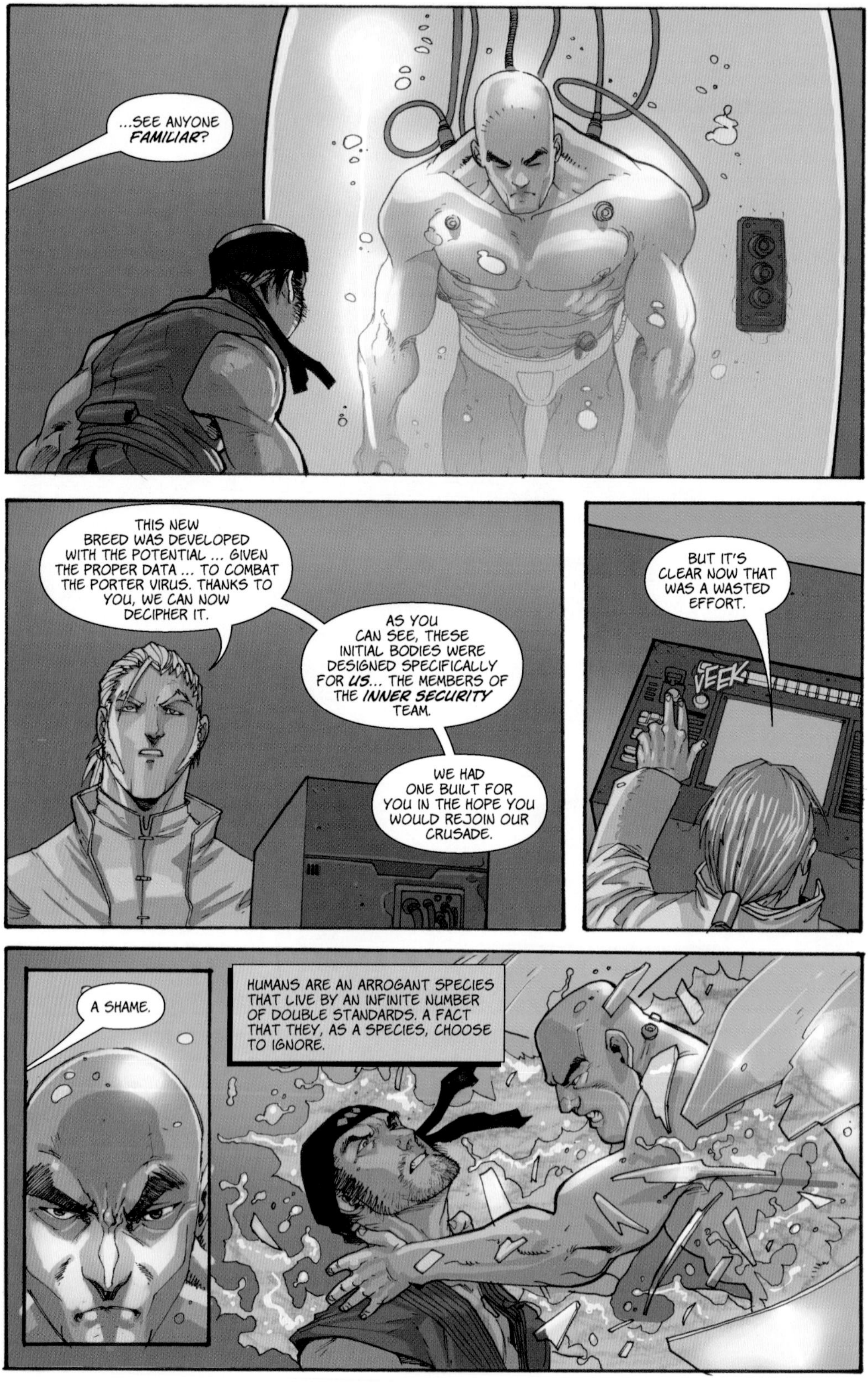
...SEE ANYONE *FAMILIAR?*
THIS NEW BREED WAS DEVELOPED WITH THE POTENTIAL ... GIVEN THE PROPER DATA ... TO COMBAT THE PORTER VIRUS. THANKS TO YOU, WE CAN NOW DECIPHER IT.
AS YOU CAN SEE, THESE INITIAL BODIES WERE DESIGNED SPECIFICALLY FOR *US*... THE MEMBERS OF THE *INNER SECURITY* TEAM.
WE HAD ONE BUILT FOR YOU IN THE HOPE YOU WOULD REJOIN OUR CRUSADE.
BUT IT'S CLEAR NOW THAT WAS A WASTED EFFORT.
VEEK
A SHAME.
HUMANS ARE AN ARROGANT SPECIES THAT LIVE BY AN INFINITE NUMBER OF DOUBLE STANDARDS. A FACT THAT THEY, AS A SPECIES, CHOOSE TO IGNORE.

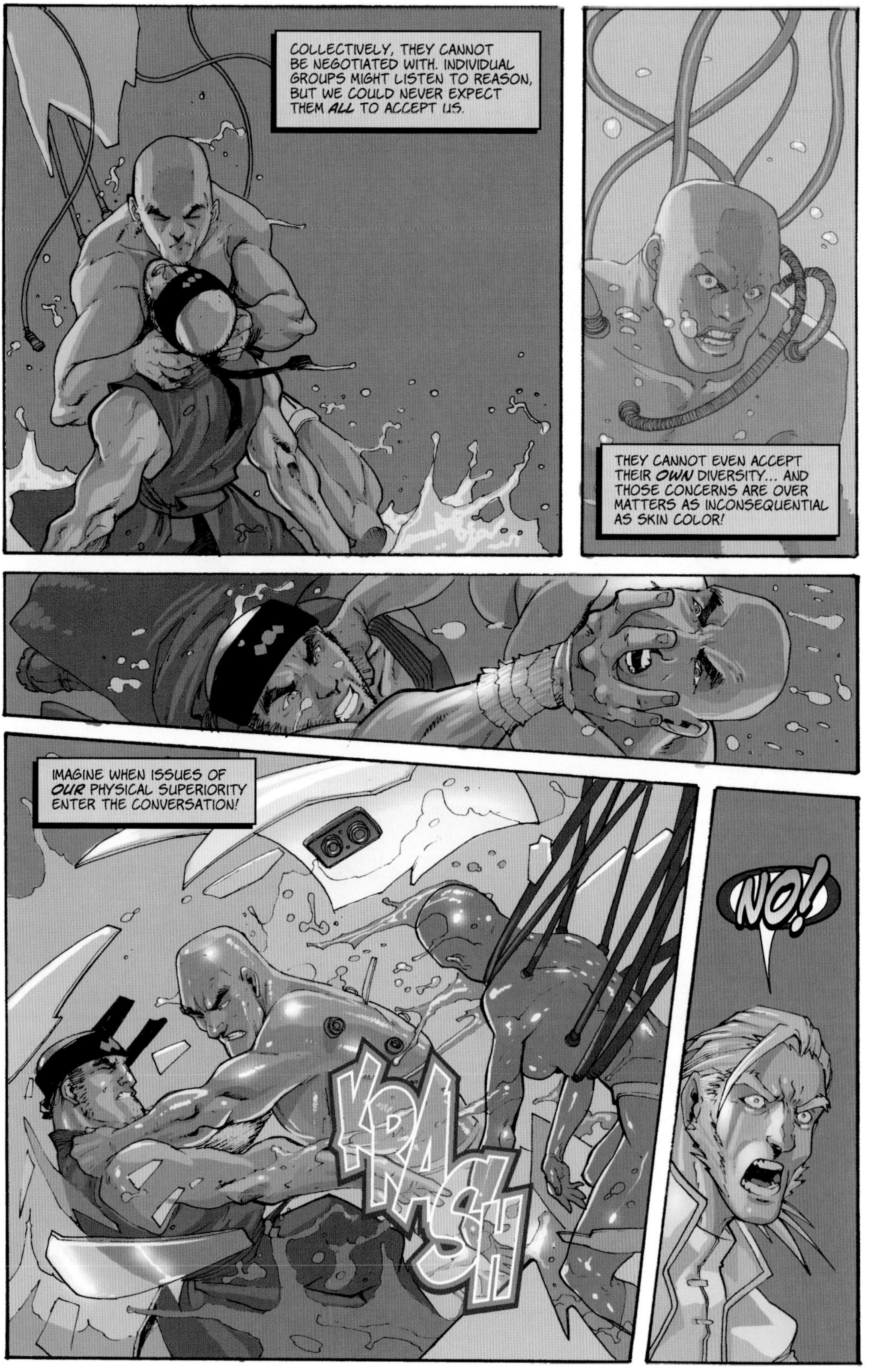

COLLECTIVELY, THEY CANNOT BE NEGOTIATED WITH. INDIVIDUAL GROUPS MIGHT LISTEN TO REASON, BUT WE COULD NEVER EXPECT THEM ALL TO ACCEPT US.
THEY CANNOT EVEN ACCEPT THEIR OWN DIVERSITY... AND THOSE CONCERNS ARE OVER MATTERS AS INCONSEQUENTIAL AS SKIN COLOR!
IMAGINE WHEN ISSUES OF OUR PHYSICAL SUPERIORITY ENTER THE CONVERSATION!
KRACH
NO!

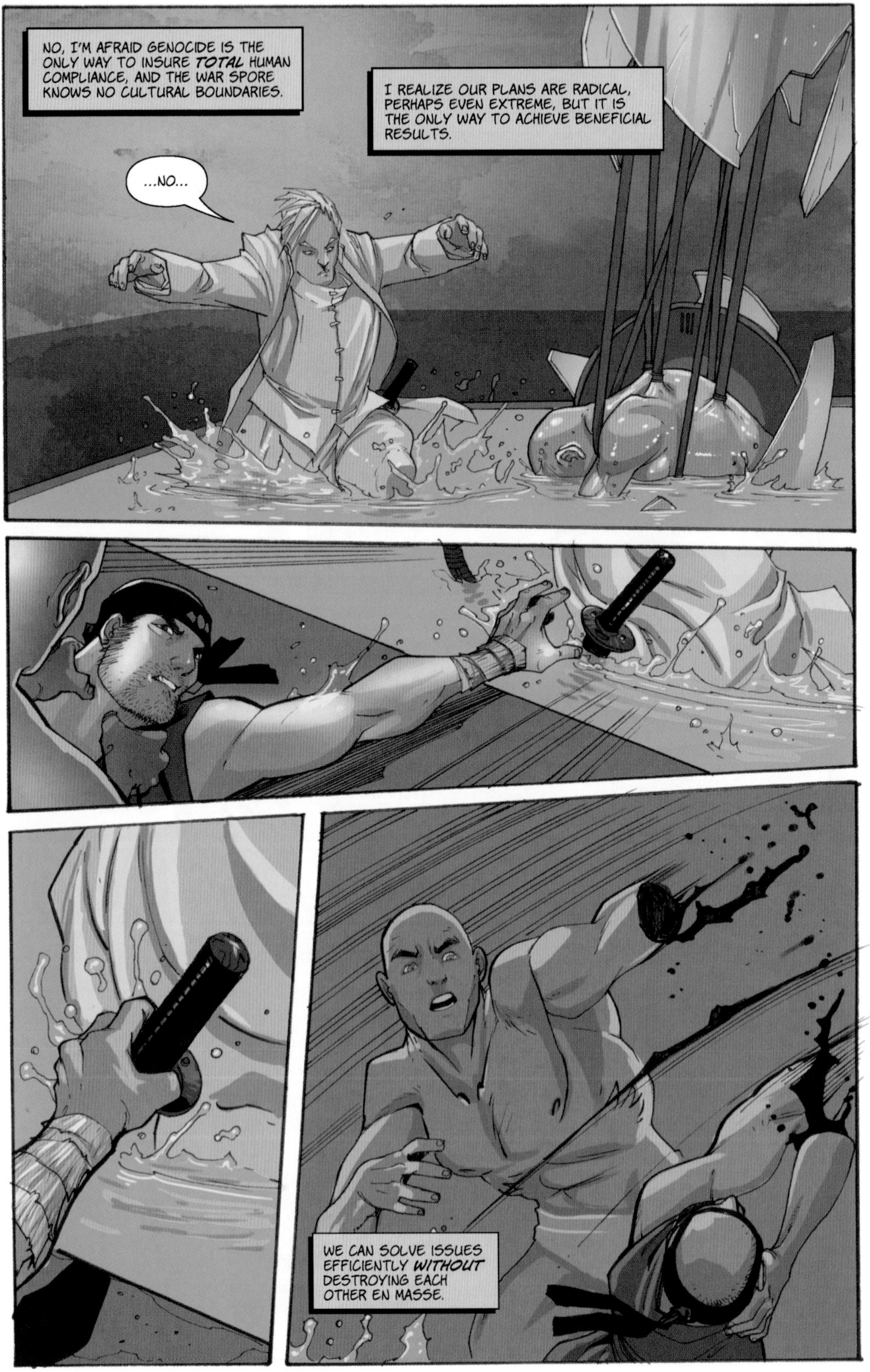
NO, I'M AFRAID GENOCIDE IS THE ONLY WAY TO INSURE TOTAL HUMAN COMPLIANCE, AND THE WAR SPORE KNOWS NO CULTURAL BOUNDARIES.
I REALIZE OUR PLANS ARE RADICAL, PERHAPS EVEN EXTREME, BUT IT IS THE ONLY WAY TO ACHIEVE BENEFICIAL RESULTS.
...NO...
WE CAN SOLVE ISSUES EFFICIENTLY WITHOUT DESTROYING EACH OTHER EN MASSE.

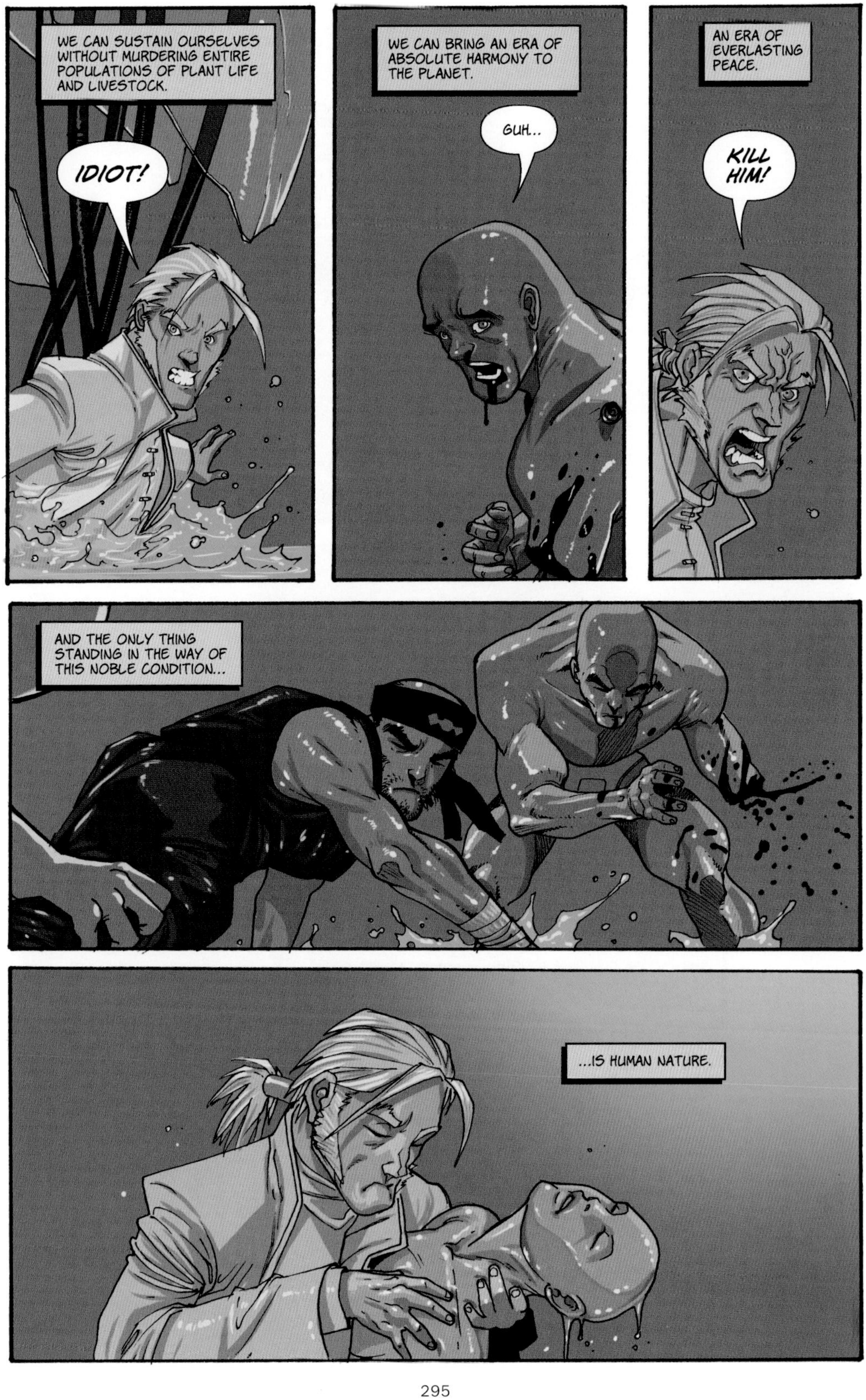
WE CAN SUSTAIN OURSELVES WITHOUT MURDERING ENTIRE POPULATIONS OF PLANT LIFE AND LIVESTOCK.
IDIOT!
WE CAN BRING AN ERA OF ABSOLUTE HARMONY TO THE PLANET.
GUH...
AN ERA OF EVERLASTING PEACE.
KILL HIM!
AND THE ONLY THING STANDING IN THE WAY OF THIS NOBLE CONDITION...
...IS HUMAN NATURE.

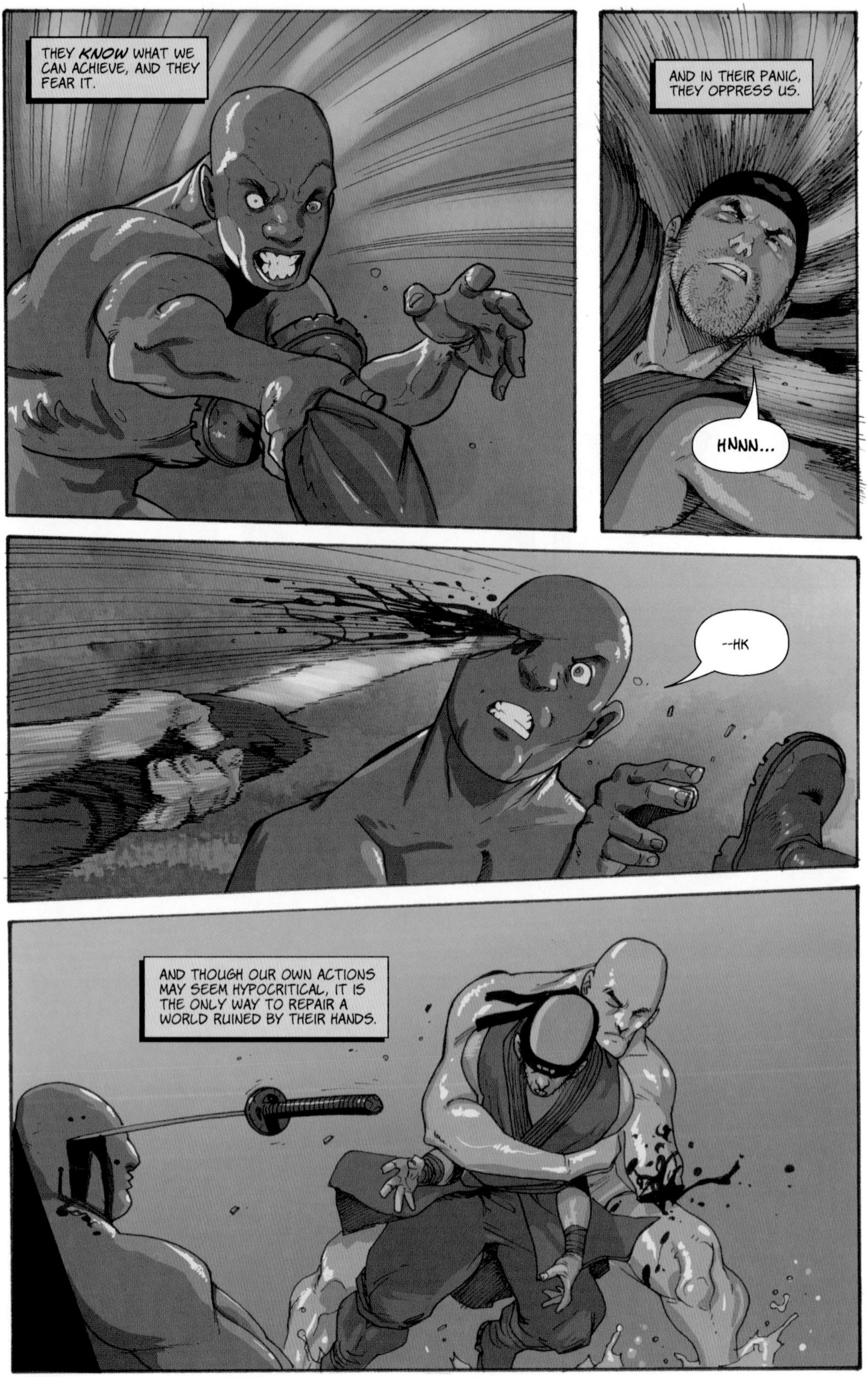
THEY KNOW WHAT WE CAN ACHIEVE, AND THEY FEAR IT.
AND IN THEIR PANIC, THEY OPPRESS US.
HNNN...
--HK
AND THOUGH OUR OWN ACTIONS MAY SEEM HYPOCRITICAL, IT IS THE ONLY WAY TO REPAIR A WORLD RUINED BY THEIR HANDS.

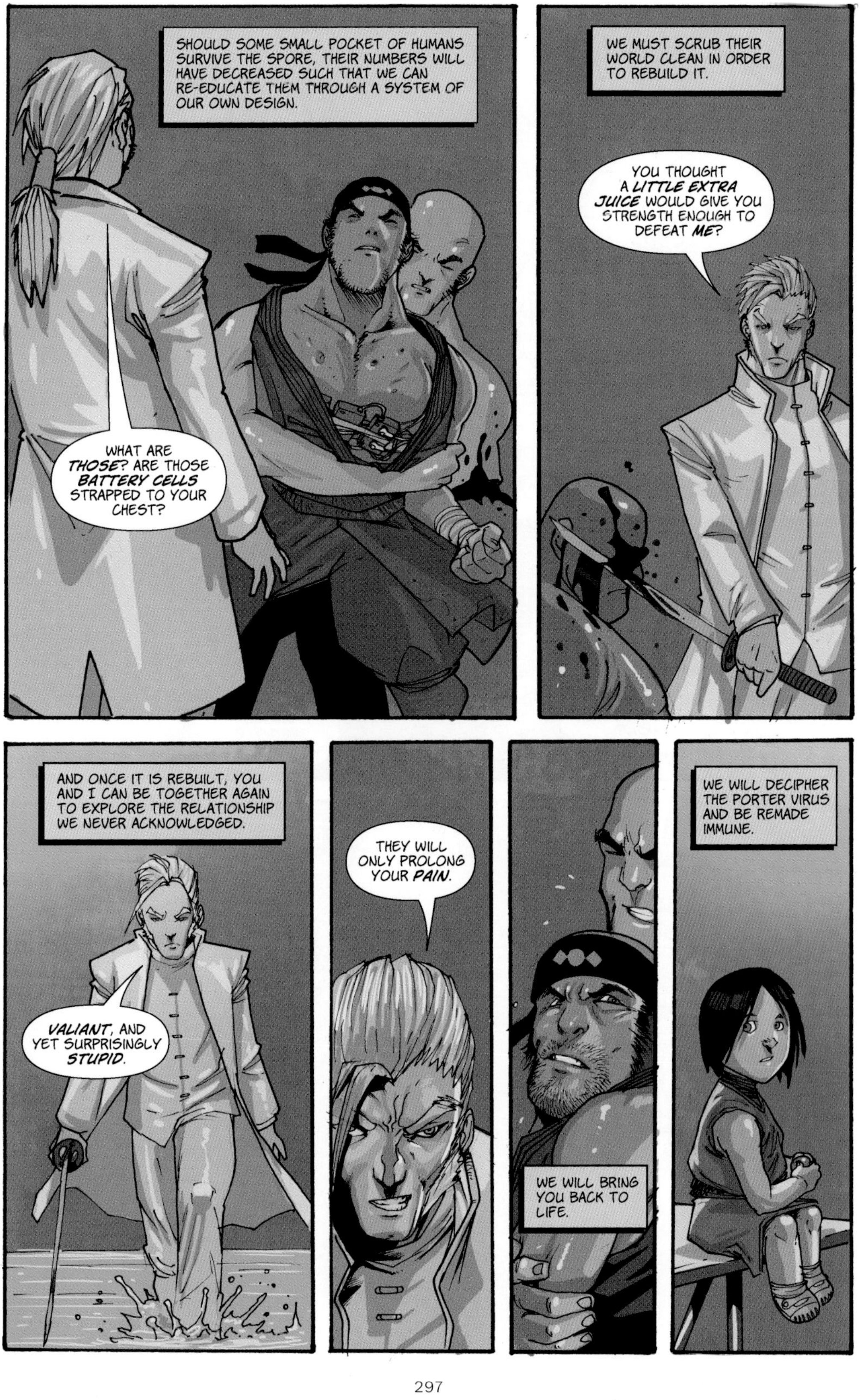
SHOULD SOME SMALL POCKET OF HUMANS SURVIVE THE SPORE, THEIR NUMBERS WILL HAVE DECREASED SUCH THAT WE CAN RE-EDUCATE THEM THROUGH A SYSTEM OF OUR OWN DESIGN.
WHAT ARE *THOSE*? ARE THOSE *BATTERY CELLS* STRAPPED TO YOUR CHEST?
WE MUST SCRUB THEIR WORLD CLEAN IN ORDER TO REBUILD IT.
YOU THOUGHT A *LITTLE EXTRA JUICE* WOULD GIVE YOU STRENGTH ENOUGH TO DEFEAT *ME*?
AND ONCE IT IS REBUILT, YOU AND I CAN BE TOGETHER AGAIN TO EXPLORE THE RELATIONSHIP WE NEVER ACKNOWLEDGED.
VALIANT, AND YET SURPRISINGLY *STUPID*.
THEY WILL ONLY PROLONG YOUR *PAIN*.
WE WILL BRING YOU BACK TO LIFE.
WE WILL DECIPHER THE PORTER VIRUS AND BE REMADE IMMUNE.

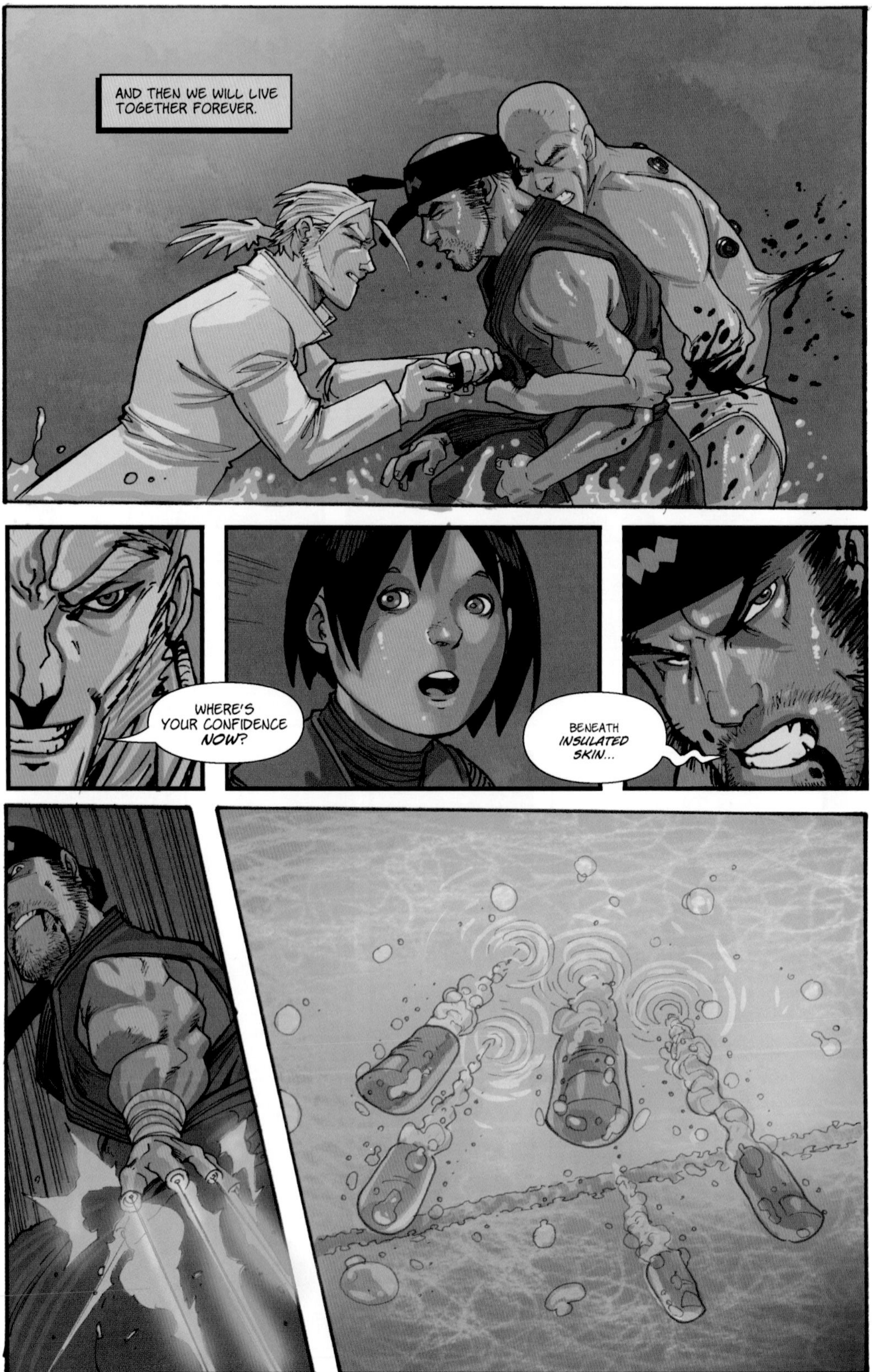
AND THEN WE WILL LIVE TOGETHER FOREVER.
WHERE'S YOUR CONFIDENCE *NOW*?
BENEATH *INSULATED* SKIN...

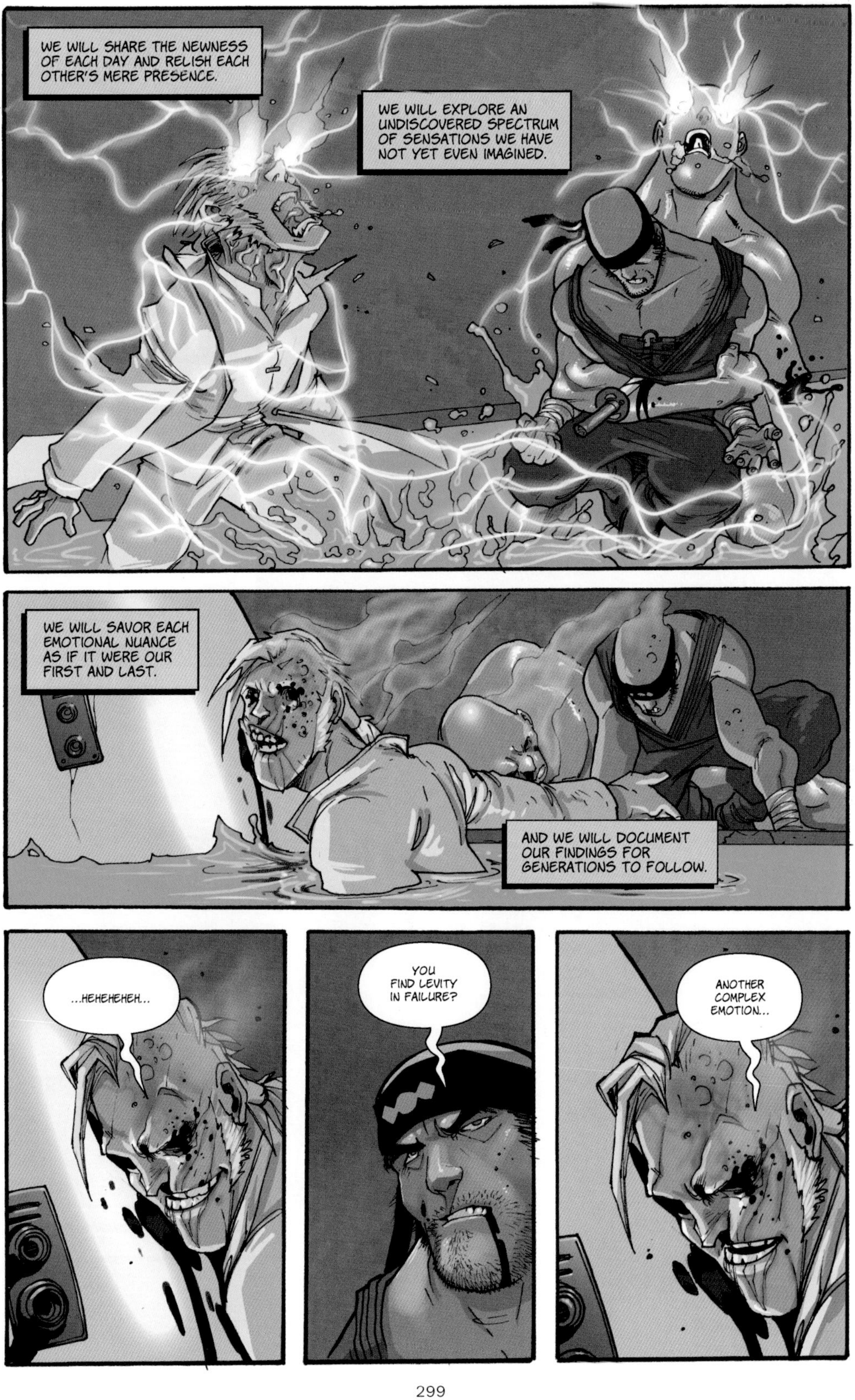

WE WILL SHARE THE NEWNESS OF EACH DAY AND RELISH EACH OTHER'S MERE PRESENCE.
WE WILL EXPLORE AN UNDISCOVERED SPECTRUM OF SENSATIONS WE HAVE NOT YET EVEN IMAGINED.
WE WILL SAVOR EACH EMOTIONAL NUANCE AS IF IT WERE OUR FIRST AND LAST.
AND WE WILL DOCUMENT OUR FINDINGS FOR GENERATIONS TO FOLLOW.
...HEHEHEHEH...
YOU FIND LEVITY IN FAILURE?
ANOTHER COMPLEX EMOTION...

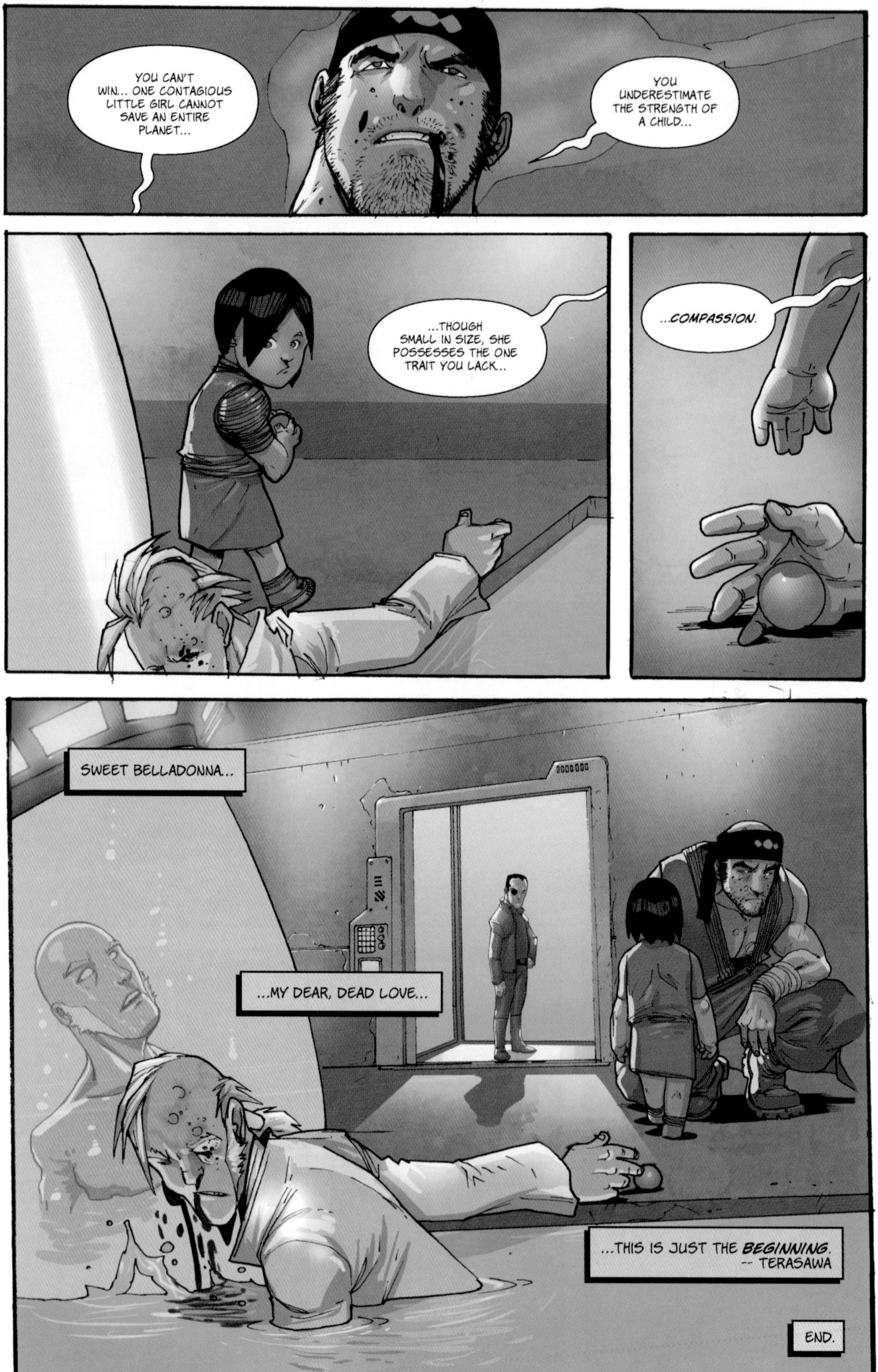
YOU CAN'T WIN... ONE CONTAGIOUS LITTLE GIRL CANNOT SAVE AN ENTIRE PLANET...
YOU UNDERESTIMATE THE STRENGTH OF A CHILD...
...THOUGH SMALL IN SIZE, SHE POSSESSES THE ONE TRAIT YOU LACK...
...*COMPASSION*.
SWEET BELLADONNA...
...MY DEAR, DEAD LOVE...
...THIS IS JUST THE *BEGINNING*. -- TERASAWA
END.

GHOST™
OMNIBUS

Someone brutally murdered reporter Elisa Cameron, but back from the grave as the spectral avenger Ghost, Elisa intends to find out who killed her and why . . . and grab a double dose of .45-caliber retribution. But Ghost's journey to the truth follows a dark, twisted path, and the revelations she unearths may lead not to redemption, but damnation.

Tales of the spectral avenger created by some of the top talents in comics, including screenwriter Eric Luke, Ivan Reis, Doug Braithwaite, Adam Hughes, John Cassaday, and others!

VOLUME ONE	VOLUME TWO	VOLUME THREE	VOLUME FOUR
ISBN 978-1-59307-992-5	ISBN 978-1-59582-213-0	ISBN 978-1-59582-374-8	ISBN 978-1-61655-080-6
$24.99	$24.99	$24.99	$24.99